# Communications
# in Computer and Information Science 393

Carlos Canal   Massimo Villari (Eds.)

# Advances in Service-Oriented and Cloud Computing

Workshops of ESOCC 2013
Málaga, Spain, September 11-13, 2013
Revised Selected Papers

 Springer

Volume Editors

Carlos Canal
Universidad de Málaga, Spain
E-mail: canal@lcc.uma.es

Massimo Villari
University of Messina, Italy
E-mail: mvillari@unime.it

ISSN 1865-0929                e-ISSN 1865-0937
ISBN 978-3-642-45363-2     e-ISBN 978-3-642-45364-9
DOI 10.1007/978-3-642-45364-9
Springer Heidelberg New York Dordrecht London

Library of Congress Control Number: 2013955300

CR Subject Classification (1998): D.2, H.3, H.2.8, C.2, K.6, J.1

*Typesetting:* Camera-ready by author, data conversion by Scientific Publishing Services, Chennai, India

Printed on acid-free paper

Springer is part of Springer Science+Business Media (www.springer.com)

# Preface

This volume contains the technical papers presented in the five high-quality workshops associated with ESOCC 2013 (European Conference on Service-Oriented and Cloud Computing, held in Malaga, September 11–13, 2013), focusing on specific topics in service-oriented and cloud computing-related domains: Cloud for IoT (CLIoT 2013), Cloud Storage Optimization (CLOUSO 2013), 12th International Workshop on Foundations of Coordination Languages and Self-Adaptative Systems (FOCLASA 2013), First Workshop on Mobile Cloud and Social Perspectives (MoCSoP 2013), and the Third International Workshop on Adaptive Services for the Future Internet (WAS4FI 2013).

There were a total of 51 submissions, from which 29 papers were accepted giving an acceptance rate of 56%. The review and selection process was performed rigorously, with each paper being reviewed by at least three Program Committee (PC) members. Here, a brief description of each workshop is given.

The CLIoT 2013 workshop aimed at discussing the limits and/or advantages of existing cloud solutions for IoT, and proposing original and innovative contributions for enhancing real-world resources over cloud environments. Smart connectivity with existing networks and context-aware computation is becoming indispensable for IoT. Cloud computing provides a very strategic virtual infrastructure that integrates monitoring devices, storage devices, analytics tools, visualization platforms, and client delivery. It supports enormous amounts of data generated for IoT purposes, which have to be stored, processed, and presented in a seamless, efficient, and easily interpretable form. The first part of this volume comprises all the technical papers of CLIoT 2013.

The CLOUSO 2013 workshop focused on research and development efforts in the domain of storage clouds, driven by the research outcomes in the framework of an EU-funded project, VISION Cloud. The workshop allowed the community to define the current state, identifying requirements and determining future goals, presenting architectures and services in the area of emerging storage cloud technologies. While the emergence of cloud environments has made feasible the delivery of Internet-scale services, current research efforts focus on key issues related to cloud storage, which are considered of major importance given the amount of data produced by various sources. The vast amounts of digital data being produced hold the key to creating such an advantage, but only if the data can be efficiently utilized. The second part of this volume comprises all the technical papers of CLOUSO 2013.

The goal of the FOCLASA 2013 workshop was to bring together researchers and practitioners in the fields of coordination languages and formal approaches to modelling and reasoning self-adaptive services, so as to share and identify common problems and to devise general solutions in the context of self-* systems. The organizers invited researchers and practitioners to submit novel works and experience reports on service coordination and self-adaptive behavior management in the areas of business process modeling, component-based and large-scale distributed systems, service-oriented and cloud computing, grid computing, and multi-agent and peer-to-peer system engineering. The organizers accepted relevant works on coordination and self-adaptive behavior in other areas, e.g., bio-inspired computing. The third part of this volume comprises all the technical papers of FOCLASA 2013.

The MoCSoP 2013 workshop focused on mobile cloud and social perspectives. In 2016 the network traffic generated from mobile devices is estimated to reach 50%. Such traffic is expected to be dedicated to cloud services consumption such as video streaming, email and instant messaging, or social media access. The interest in the development of cloud computing in the context of mobility is undeniable. However, the great interest in this type of services contrasts with the simplicity of their technological foundations. In most cases, their architectures consist in mobile apps interacting with cloud services, which, depending on their logic, interact with other clients. This was just the starting hypothesis of the MoCSoP workshop in which the organizers faced questions such as what kind of new services could be proposed? Are new communication protocols needed to manage them? How could the exposure of services in the mobile context be managed? What are the social perspectives of cloud computing in the mobile context? What is the impact on personal privacy in this context? Who owns the generated data? Several other questions come in mind, that provide a broad field for research in the coming years. MoCSoP tried to give an answer to these questions. The fourth part of this volume comprises all the technical papers of MoCSoP 2013.

The WAS4FI 2013 workshop focused on Future Internet (FI) technologies. The FI has emerged as a new initiative to pave a novel infrastructure linked to objects (things) of the real world to meet the changing global needs of business and society. It offers Internet users a standardized, secure, efficient, and trustable environment, which allows open and distributed access to global networks, services, and information. There is a need for both researchers and practitioners to develop platforms made up of adaptive FI applications. In this sense, the emergence and consolidation of service-oriented architectures (SOA), cloud computing, and wireless sensor networks (WSN) give benefits, such as flexibility, scalability, security, interoperability, and adaptability for building these applications. FI systems will need to sense and respond to a huge amount of signals sourced from different entities in real time. WAS4FI addresses different aspects of adaptive FI applications, emphasizing the importance of governing the convergence of contents, services, things, and networks to achieve building platforms for efficiency, scalability, security, and flexible adaptation. WAS4FI covered the foundations of these technologies as well as new emerging proposals. The fifth part of this volume comprises all the technical papers of WAS4FI 2013.

October 2013                                          Carlos Canal
                                                    Massimo Villari
                                                  Workshop Chairs
                                                     ESOCC 2013

# Organization

ESOCC 2013 was organized by the Department of Computer Science of the University of Málaga (Spain).

# Preface of CLIoT

The Internet of Things (IoT) seems to change the way we interact with the world around us. It aims to represent the physical world through uniquely identifiable and interconnected objects (things). Things have the capacity for sensing, processing, or actuating information about entities available from within the real world. Thus, information travels along heterogeneous systems, such as routers, databases, information systems, and the Internet, leading to the generation and movement of enormous amounts of data that have to be stored, processed, and presented in a seamless, efficient, and easily interpretable form. Both the IoT and cloud technologies address two important goals for distributed system: high scalability and high availability. All these features make cloud computing a promising choice for supporting IoT services. IoT can appear as a natural extension of cloud computing implementations, where the cloud allows one to access IoT-based resources and capabilities, to process and manage IoT environments, and to deliver on-demand utility IoT services such as sensing/actuation as a service.

CLIoT 2013 aimed at bringing together scientists, practitioners, and PhD students in order to discuss the limits and/or advantages of existing cloud solutions for IoT, and to propose original and innovative contributions for enhancing real-world resources over cloud environments.

Several contributions were presented and discussed during the workshop. Tomarchio et al. presented a middleware able to abstract sensors from their proprietary interfaces, offering their capabilities to third-party applications according to an as-a-service approach. Cirani et al. proposed a constrained version of the Session Initiation Protocol (SIP), named CoSIP, whose intent is to allow constrained devices to instantiate communication sessions in a lightweight and standard fashion. Fazio et al. discussed the design of a message-oriented middleware for cloud, called MOM4C, able to arrange customizable cloud facilities by means of a flexible federation-enabled communication system. Destefano et al. dealt with sensing and actuation as a service (SAaaS) architecture, introducing the module specifically conceived to deal with all the issues related to user-resource interfaces.

The workshop program included two invited presentations. In particular, Ian Thomas, Strategy Director at Fujitsu Enabling Software Technologies GmbH, gave a talk on cloud platforms for Web convergence. In addition, Antonio J. Iara, Assistant Professor at the University of Applied Sciences Western Switzerland (HES-SO), presented solutions, challenges, and opportunities of cloud computing for Smart Cities and the Internet of Things. Antonio is a vice-chair of the IEEE Communications Society Internet of Things Technical Committee, CTO and co-founder of the Smart Cities company viBrain Solutions.

Maria Fazio
Nik Bessis
Workshop Organizers
CLIoT 2013

# Organization

## Steering Committee

| | |
|---|---|
| Antonio J. Jara | University of Applied Sciences Western Switzerland (HES-SO), Switzerland |
| Orazio Tomarchio | University of Catania, Italy |
| Massimo Villari | University of Messina, Italy |

## Referees

| | | |
|---|---|---|
| Antonio Celesti | Natalia Kryvinska | Navonil Mustafee |
| Salvatore Distefano | Aimï£¡ Lay-Ekuakille | Chrysa Papagianni |
| Ciprian Dobre | Fei LI | Florin Pop |
| Pietro Ducange | Lu Liu | Stelios Sotiriadis |
| Luca Foschini | Giovanni Merlino | |

## Sponsoring Institutions

The event was co-sponsored by the IEEE ComSoc IoT Emerging Technical Committee.

# Preface of CLOUSO

The explosion of personal and organizational digital data is presently recognized as one of the most significant characteristics of the last few years. However, while the emergence of cloud environments has made feasible the delivery of Internet-scale services, current research efforts focus on key issues related to cloud storage, which are considered of major importance given the amount of data produced by various sources. The vast amounts of digital data being produced (a representative figure that highlights the huge amount of data being produced nowadays is the fraction of data on the Internet that is indexed by Google, which is only 0.004%) hold the key to creating such an advantage, but only if the data can be efficiently utilized. The latter poses the need for new, cloud-based and cloud-scalable technologies in order to overcome various limitations that affect the adoption of storage cloud services (86% of enterprises do not have specific plans in doing so). These limitations refer to: (1) the abstraction level of storage and the requirement to access content without dealing with details of the underlying infrastructure, (2) data mobility, (3) computational storage enabling computations to be performed close to storage, (4) service level agreements for data-intensive services, and (5) security and compliance considerations.

The aforementioned limitations were discussed, amongst others, during the Cloud Storage Optimization (CLOUSO) workshop that took place in conjunction with the European Conference on Service Oriented and Cloud Computing (ESOCC) in Malaga, Spain. The topics of interest for CLOUSO 2013 included but were not limited to:

- Data mobility and interoperability between cloud providers
- Scalability and elasticity in storage clouds
- Performance evaluation of storage cloud infrastructures
- Computational storage
- Energy-efficient data cloud design and management
- Data placement and scheduling
- Quality of service and service level agreements
- Data privacy and protection
- Data-intensive applications, characteristics, challenges
- Case studies of data-intensive computing in the clouds
- Future research challenges in storage clouds
- Test-beds and field trials
- Standardization and regulatory issues

The workshop focused on research and development efforts in the domain of storage clouds, driven by the research outcomes in the framework of an EU-funded project, namely, VISION Cloud [11]. In this context, an interesting approach for cloud storage performance and efficiency analysis ("peaCS - Performance and Efficiency Analysis for Cloud Storage") was presented during the workshop. The authors proposed a framework for the analysis, comparison, and optimization both of functional and non functional properties of storage services targeting the users' digital environment. With respect to multi-cloud environments and the corresponding security challenges for cloud storage, an approach was presented (*"Delegation for On-boarding Federation Across Storage Clouds"*) that proposes an architecture allowing the efficient migration of data between storage cloud providers. The approach enables users to delegate to the on-boarding layer a subset of his/her access rights on the source and destination clouds to enable on-boarding to occur in a safe and secure way. Focusing on availability, the authors presented quite novel work (*"Availability Assessment of a Vision Cloud Storage Cluster"*), in which they introduce a stochastic reward net model that allows quantification of the availability level in storage clouds from a user perspective. Besides availability, reliability and data mobility were also discussed during the workshop. The proposed approach (*"Data Reliability in Multi-Provider Cloud Storage Service with RRNS"*) enables customers to use concurrently different providers by guaranteeing at the same time redundancy and obfuscation. The basis of the presented work is the so-called *redundant residue number system (RRNS)* that allows files to be fragmented and stored in different providers. What is more, during the workshop, the application space was also addressed. More specifically, cross-layer management of dynamic IT service components was introduced through a work (*"Automated Provisioning of SaaS Applications over IaaS-based Cloud Systems"*) that placed emphasis on an infrastructure aimed to facilitate the composition of heterogeneous resources, such as single virtual machines (VMs), DB services and storage, and stand-alone services, by automating the provisioning of complex SaaS applications on top of OpenStack. Finally, open source topics were tackled (*"Open Source Issues with Cloud Storage Software"*), focusing on the contribution of different assets in cloud storage solutions and the corresponding licensing issues.

The approaches presented in these proceedings aim at providing insight into innovative research outcomes in the domain of cloud storage optimization. In the emerging era of the Future Internet the explosion of digital data highlights the need for cloud-based storage as the next-generation solution to address the data proliferation and the reliance on data. The latter is of major importance given that our society has become critically dependent on services to extract valuable information from the data and drive decision making by individuals, businesses, and government, across all aspects of life.

We would like to thank all Program Committee members for providing insightful review reports, the authors for submitting papers to the workshop, and the participants of the workshop in Málaga for productive discussions and useful comments.

Massimo Villari
Dimosthenis Kyriazis
CLOUSO 2013 Chairs

# Organization

## Program Committee

| | |
|---|---|
| Danilo Ardagna | Politecnico di Milano, Italy |
| Lorenzo Blasi | HP Technology Services |
| Ivona Brandic | Vienna University of Technology, Austria |
| Francesco D'andria | ATOS Spain |
| Patrizio Dazzi | ISTI-CNR, Italy |
| Kevin Doolin | Telecommunications Software & Systems Group |
| Anastasios Doulamis | Technical University of Crete, Greece |
| Luca Foschini | Università di Bologna, Italy |
| Alex Galis | University College London, UK |
| Emilio Javier Garcia Escobar | Telefonica I&D |
| Wolfgang Gentzsch | Executive HPC Consultant |
| Spyridon Gogouvitis | National Technical University of Athens, Greece |
| Burak Kantarci | University of Ottawa, Canada |
| Gabor Kecskemeti | University of Innsbruck, Austria |
| George Kousiouris | National Technical University of Athens, Greece |
| Andreas Menychtas | National Technical University of Athens, Greece |
| Dalit Naor | IBM Research Haifa, Israel |
| Antonios Niros | University of the Aegean, Greece |
| Suraj Pandey | IBM Research Melbourne, Australia |
| Dana Petcu | West University of Timisoara, Romania |
| Brian Pickering | University of Southampton, UK |
| Paolo Romano | INESC-ID |
| Rajiv Ranjan | CSIRO ICT Centre Canberra, Australia |
| Osama Sammodi | University of Duisburg-Essen, Germany |
| Aidan Shribman | SAP Israel |
| Domenico Talia | Università della Calabria, Italy |
| Jie Tao | Karlsruhe Institue of Technology, Germany |
| Johan Tordsson | Umea University, Sweden |
| Giovanni Toffetti | IBM Research - Haifa, Israel |
| Luis Vaquero | HP-UK |

# Preface of FOCLASA

The FOCLASA workshop provides a venue where researchers and practitioners meet, exchange ideas, identify common problems, and discuss fundamental issues related to coordination languages and self-adaptive systems. The special focus of this year's edition was the coordination and self-adaptive behavior in the Internet of services and cloud computing.

Modern software systems are distributed, concurrent, mobile, and often involve composition of heterogeneous components and stand-alone services. Service coordination and self-adaptation constitute the core characteristics of distributed and service-oriented systems. Coordination languages and formal approaches to modelling and reasoning about self-adaptive behavior help to simplify the development of complex distributed service-based systems, enable functional correctness proofs, and improve reusability and maintainability of such systems. The topics of interest for FOCLASA 2013 included but were not limited to:

- Theoretical models and frameworks for component and service coordination, service composition, service adaptation and concurrent system modeling
- Applications and usability studies for the aforementioned theoretical models, interaction and coordination challenges in various application domains
- Languages and specification protocols for component and service interaction, their semantics, expressiveness, validation and verification, type checking, static and dynamic analysis
- "Software as a service" models and dynamic software architectures, such as self-adaptive and self-organizing systems
- Tools and environments for the development of concurrent and customizable self-monitoring, self-adaptive and self-organizing applications
- Calculus, mathematical models and algorithms for Quality-of-Service (QoS) observation, storage, history-based analysis in self-adaptive systems (queuing models, load balancing, fault- tolerance analysis, machine learning systems)

This year, we received 15 submissions involving 38 authors from 18 different countries. Papers underwent a rigorous review process, and all papers received three review reports. After the review process, the international Program Committee (PC) of FOCLASA 2013 decided to select eight papers for presentation during the workshop and publication in the joint proceedings of the ESOCC 2013 workshops. These papers tackle different issues that are currently central to our community, namely, component and service composition, models and calculus for coordination in distributed systems, as well as implementation and tool support for existing coordination languages.

We would like to thank all Program Committee members and external reviewers for providing insightful review reports, the authors for submitting papers to the workshop, and the participants of the workshop in Málaga for productive discussions and useful comments.

Natallia Kokash
Javier Cámara Moreno
FOCLASA 2013 PC Chairs

# Organization

## Program Committee

| | |
|---|---|
| Carlos Cuesta | Rey Juan Carlos University, Spain |
| Holger Giese | University of Potsdam, Germany |
| Keijo Heljanko | Aalto University, Finland |
| Ludovic Henrio | INRIA Sophia Antipolis, France |
| Rogério de Lemos | University of Kent, UK |
| Antónia Lopes | University of Lisbon, Portugal |
| António Ravara | New University of Lisbon, Portugal |
| Liliana Pasquale | University of Limerick, Ireland |
| Pascal Poizat | Paris Ouest University and LIP6, France |
| José Proena | KU Leuven, Belgium |
| Bradley Schmerl | Carnegie Mellon University, USA |
| Marjan Sirjani | Reykjavik University, Iceland |
| Carolyn Talcott | SRI International, USA |
| Francesco Tiezzi | IMT Lucca Institute for Advanced Studies, Italy |
| Mirko Viroli | University of Bologna, Italy |
| Uwe Zdun | University of Vienna, Austria |
| Huibiao Zhu | East China Normal University, China |

## External Reviewers

| | |
|---|---|
| Ehsan Khamespanah | University of Tehran, Iran |
| Ali Jafari | Reykjavik University, Iceland |
| Stefano Mariani | Università di Bologna, Italy |
| Gregor Berg | University of Potsdam, Germany |
| Thomas Haitzer | University of Vienna, Austria |
| Qin Li | East China Normal University, China |
| Patrick Gaubatz | University of Vienna, Austria |
| Yongxin Zhao | East China Normal University, China |

## Steering Committee

| | |
|---|---|
| Farhad Arbab | CWI, The Netherlands |
| Antï£¡nio Brogi | University of Pisa, Italy |

| Carlos Canal | University of Malaga, Spain |
| Jean-Marie Jacquet | University of Namur, Belgium |
| Ernesto Pimentel | University of Malaga, Spain |
| Gwen Salan | Grenoble INP - Inria Grenoble - LIG, France |

## Publicity Chair

| José Antonio Martín Baena | University of Malaga, Spain |

# Preface of MoCSoP

In recent years cloud computing has emerged as one of the most active research topics. Many efforts have been invested in research to propose new technologies that provide IT solutions in different modalities, i.e., IaaS, PaaS or SaaS, always based on the utility-computing business model. The goal is to allow companies (both small and large) to purchase IT services from cloud vendors on a pay-as-you-go basis, rather than owning their own IT department and infrastructures. The main benefits reside in increased business agility, IT control, cost efficiency, and productivity, as well as a reduction in the number of management resources that are required. Thus, cloud computing has been recognized not only as a technological innovation but also as an IT market and business innovation. For that purpose techniques and technologies have been proposed for virtualization, balancing and efficient resource usage, easy and reliable remote services consumption, and avoiding services from being tied to the specification of particular cloud vendors.

While the general consensus establishes that the larger the company adopting the cloud alternative, the larger the benefits provided by this paradigm, real experiences of large companies massively adopting cloud computing are still needed. Companies manifest their intention and willingness to move to the cloud but they are still at the stage of studying its potential and actual benefits. This could cause doubts about the real potential of cloud computing. However, since millions of people already consume cloud services like Dropbox, Facebook, etc., one can argue that cloud computing is here to stay. Although these services are small and structurally simple, the magnitude of their success is reaffirmed by their figures. As an example, in 2011 Google billed 29.3 billion dollars, and in October 2012 Facebook reached its first billion users.

Such massive consumption of cloud services takes place in a context in which 25% of the global network traffic is generated from mobile devices. Smartphones and tablets are reaching, and even in some cases surpassing, the capabilities of laptops and desktop computers. In 2016 the network traffic generated from mobile devices is estimated to reach 50%. Such traffic is expected to be dedicated to cloud services consumption such as video streaming, email and instant messaging, or social media access. Thus, the interest in the development of cloud computing in the context of mobility is undeniable.

However, the great interest in this type of service contrasts with the simplicity of their technological foundations. In most cases, their architectures consist in a client (mobile app) interacting with a server (cloud service) which, depending on its logic, interacts with other clients. It seems as though there is still plenty of room for improvement in the technological richness of these architectures to offer services and applications that allow for more complex interactions with servers or even directly between clients. This is just the starting hypothesis of this workshop in which we would like to face questions such as what kind of new services could be proposed? Are new communication protocols needed to manage them? How could the exposure of services in the mobile context be managed? What are the social perspectives of cloud computing in the mobile context? What is the impact on personal privacy in this context? Who owns the generated data? Several other questions come in mind, which provide a broad field for research in the coming years.

Despite the interest aroused by these topics and the great growth prospects in this field, there are still very few conferences and workshops that focus specifically on cloud and mobility especially with respect to technical AND social aspects. We therefore believe that MoCSoP can help to attract a growing community to ESOCC that still does not have many specific conferences in which to meet. Eventually, this will lead ESOCC to strengthen its position in the field of cloud computing, service-oriented computing and mobility. The Workshop Organizing Committee greatly appreciates the contribution of the Program Committee members, without which rvIoCSop would not have been possible.

# Organization

## Organizing Committee

Muhammad Ali Babar
Marc Jansen
Tommi Mikkonen
Juan Manuel Murillo
Dana Petcu

## Program Committee

The Program Committee of the workshop was formed by

| | |
|---|---|
| Muhammad Ali Babar | IT University of Copenhagen |
| Timo Aaltonen | Tampere University of Technology |
| Lars Bollen | University of Twente |
| Carlos Canal | University of MǦlaga |
| Elisabetta Di Nitto | Politecnico Di Milano |
| Adam Giemza | University of Duisburg-Essen |
| Marc Jansen | University of Applied Sciences Ruhr West |
| Tomi Mnnist | University of Helsinki, Helsinki |
| Tommi Mikkonen | Tampere University of Technology |
| Juan M. Murillo | University of Extremadura |
| Dana Petcu | West University of Timisoara |
| Ivan Porres | Abo Akademi University |
| Ulf Schreier | Hochschule Furtwangen University |

# Preface of WAS4FI

As the proud Organizing Committee and chairs of the Third International Workshop on Adaptive Services for the Future Internet, we would like to take this opportunity to welcome you to the proceedings of WAS4FI 2013. We thank all participants for taking time out from their busy lives and work in their home countries to attend this workshop.

In this third edition, WAS4FI again aimed to bring together the community at ESOCC and addresses different aspects of adaptive Future Internet applications. In this workshop, we cover the foundations of the aforementioned technologies as well as new emerging proposals for their potential in Future Internet services. To promote collaboration, WAS4FI has a highly interactive format with short technical sessions complemented by discussions on adaptive services in the Future Internet applications. The broad scope of WAS4FI is reflected in the wide range of topics covered by the 15 submissions that we received. Of these, with the 24 members of the WAS4FI Program Committee from both academic and industrial research labs, we selected six research papers. These papers are grouped into two sessions, representing two key themes of Adaptive Services for the Future Internet

1. Security, Quality and Runtime Verification for Service Adaptation
2. Resources and Complex-Event Management forService Adaptation

We would like to thank all the people who contributed to make this workshop a reality, including the WAS4FI Program Committees, the ESOCC 2013 Workshop Chairs Massimo Villari and Carlos Canal and all the presenters, authors and participants.

Javier
Guadalupe
Juan
Howard
Winfried

# Organization

## Organizing Committee

| | |
|---|---|
| Javier Cubo | University of Málaga, Spain |
| Guadalupe Ortiz | University of Cádiz, Spain |
| Juan Boubeta-Puig | University of Cádiz, Spain |
| Howard Foster | City University London, UK |
| Winfried Lamersdorf | University of Hamburg, Germany |

## Program Committee

| | |
|---|---|
| Marco Aiello | University of Groningen, The Netherlands |
| Vasilios Andrikopoulos | University of Stuttgart, Germany |
| Antonio Brogi | University of Pisa, Italy |
| Anis Charfi | SAP Research CEC Darmstadt, Germany |
| Florian Daniel | University of Trento, Italy |
| Valeria de Castro | Universidad Rey Juan Carlos, Spain |
| Gregorio Díaz | Universidad de Castilla La Mancha, Spain |
| Schahram Dustdar | Vienna University of Technology, Austria |
| Nadia Gámez | University of Málaga, Spain |
| Laura González | Universidad de la República, Uruguay |
| Tiziana Margaria | University of Potsdam, Germany |
| E. Michael Maximilien | IBM Almaden Research, USA |
| Massimo Mecella | University of Rome La Sapienza, Italy |
| Andreas Metzger | University of Duisburg-Essen, Germany |
| Claus Pahl | Dublin City University, Ireland |
| Achille Peternier | University of Lugano, Switzerland |
| Franco Raimondi | Middlesex University, UK |
| Gustavo Rossi | Universidad Nacional de La Plata, Argentina |
| Romain Rouvoy | University of Lille 1, France |
| Antonio Ruiz-Cortés | University of Seville, Spain |
| Quanzheng Sheng | The University of Adelaide, Australia |
| Massimo Tivoli | University of L'Aquila, Italy |
| Willem-Jan van den Heuvel | Tilburg University, The Netherlands |
| Gianluigi Zavattaro | University of Bologna, Italy |

# Table of Contents

# FOCLASA Workshop Papers

# MoCSoP Workshop Papers

# WAS4FI Workshop Papers

# SNPS: An OSGi-Based Middleware for Wireless Sensor Networks

Giuseppe Di Modica, Francesco Pantano, and Orazio Tomarchio

Department of Electric, Electronic and Computer Engineering
University of Catania
Catania, Italy
`firstname.lastname@dieei.unict.it`

**Abstract.** We are witnessing a widespread deployment of sensors and sensor networks in any application domain. These sensors produce huge amounts of raw data that need to be structured, stored, analyzed, corre- lated and mined in a reliable and scalable way. Some application environ- ments also add real-time requirements which make things even harder to manage. The size of the produced data, and the high rate at which data are being produced, suggest that we need new solutions that combine tools for data management and services capable of promptly structur- ing, aggregating and mining data even just when they are produced. In this paper we propose a middleware, to be deployed on top of physical sensors and sensor networks, capable of abstracting sensors from their proprietary interfaces, and offering them to third party applications in an as-a-Service fashion for prompt and universal use. The middleware also offers tool to elaborate real-time measurements produced by sensors. A prototype of the middleware has been implemented.

## 1 Introduction

Nowadays, sensors are everywhere. You may find them in your smartphone, in your house, in your car, in streets, and so on. They measure various phenomena, and can be used for very different purposes: monitoring, surveillance, prediction, controlling. Their number is actually increasing day by day, as foreseen by the Internet of Things (IoT) vision [9]. A huge amount of data is generated each second but we are far from taking advantage of all this "potential" knowledge.

There are several reasons for that: heterogeneous sensor networks are usually disconnected among them, and often are still not connected to a globally acces- sible information network. Even in the case they are connected, we do not know how to search for those sensors which may be of help for our purpose. Moreover, when we find a potentially interesting sensor, often we are not able to get data from it due to its proprietary data interface or, if we succeed to get data, we need to correctly interpret its meaning. In addition, when developing an appli- cation that has to use a sensor network for monitoring a certain phenomena, the application programmer should only concentrate on application-level issues and ideally use the programming languages, tools and methodologies that he is accustomed to.

C. Canal and M. Villari (Eds.): ESOCC 2013, CCIS 393, pp. 1–12, 2013.

We believe that the service-oriented approach [7,13] provides adequate abstractions for application developers, and that it is a good approach to integrate heterogeneous sensors and different sensor network technologies with Cloud platforms through the Internet, by paving the way for new IoT applications.

In this paper we present an OSGi-based middleware, called *Sensor Node Plugin System (SNPS)*, where sensors are no longer low-level devices producing raw measurement data, but are seen as "services" able to be used and composed over the Internet in a simple and standardized way in order to build even complex and sophisticated applications.

The remainder of the paper is structured in the following way. Section 2 presents a review of the literature. In Section 3 the architecture of the proposed solution is introduced. In Section 4 we discuss and motivate the choice of the data model implemented in the middleware. Section 5 provides some details on the sensor composition process. We conclude our work in Section 6.

## 2    Related Work

The most notably effort in providing standard definition of Web service interfaces and data encodings to make sensors discoverable and accessible on the Web is the work done by the Open Geospatial Consortium (OGC) within the Sensor Web Enablement initiative [2,12]. The role of the SWE group is to develop common standards to determine sensors capabilities, to discover sensor systems, and to access sensors' observations. The principal services offered by SWE include:

- Sensor Model Language (SensorML): provides a high level description of sensors and observation processes using an XML schema methodology
- Sensor Observation Service (SOS): used to retrieve sensors data.
- Sensor Planning Service (SPS): used to determine if an observation request can be achieved, determine the status of an existing request, cancel a previous request, and obtain information about other OGC web services
- Web Processing Service (WPS): used to perform a calculation on sensor data.

A common misconception of the adoption of SWE standards is that they, instead of encapsulating sensor information on application level, were originally designed to operate directly on a hardware level. Of course, supporting interoperable access on the hardware level has some advantages and comes very close to the "plug and play" concept. Currently, some sensor systems such as weather stations and observation cameras already offer access to data resources through integrated web servers. However, besides contradicting the view of OGC SWE of uncoupling sensor information from sensor systems, the downside of this approach arise when dealing with a high number of specialized and heterogeneous sensor systems, and in resource-limited scenario (as typical WSNs) where communication and data transportation operations have to be highly optimized. Even a relatively powerful sensor gateway is not necessarily suitable as a web server  in many cases it may typically be networked via a low-bandwidth network and powered by a battery and so it has neither the energy or bandwidth resources required to provide a web service interface.

The need for an intermediate software layer (middleware) derives from the gap between the high-level requirements from pervasive computing applications and the complexity of the operations in the underlying WSNs. The complexity of the operations within a WSN is characterized by constrained resources, dynamic network topology, and low level embedded OS APIs, while the application requirements include high flexibility, re-usability, and reliability to cite a few. In general, WSN middleware helps the programmer develop applications in several ways: it provides appropriate system abstractions, reusable code services and data services. It helps the programmer in network infrastructure management and providing efficient resource services.

Some research efforts have been done on surveying the different aspects of middleware and programming paradigms for WSN. For example, [5] analyzed different middleware challenges and approaches for WSN, while [14] and [11] analyzed programming models for sensor networks.

As an example of different approaches, we cite here TinyDB [8], a query processing system based on SQL-like queries that are submitted by the user at a base station where the application intelligence resides. Enabling dynamic reconfiguration is one of the main motivations for component-based designs like the RUNES middleware [3]. Finally, operating systems for WSNs are typically simple, providing basic mechanisms to schedule concurrent tasks and access the hardware. In this respect, a representative example is TinyOS [15] and the accompanying nesC language.

Very recently, to provide high flexibility and for adding new and advanced functions to WSN middleware, the service-oriented approach has been applied to sensor environments [7,10]. The common idea of these approaches is that, in a sensor application, there are several common functionalities that are generally irrelevant to the main application. For example, most services will have to support service registries and discovery mechanisms and they will also need to provide some level of abstraction to hide the underlying environments and implementation details. Furthermore, all applications need to support some levels of reliability, performance, security, and QoS. All of these can be supported and made available through a common middleware platform instead of having to incorporate them into each and every service and application developed.

In this context, the OSGi technology [1] defines a standardized, component/service oriented, computing environment for networked services. Enabling a networked device with an OSGi framework adds the capability to manage the life cycle of the software components in the device from anywhere in the network without ever having to disrupt the operation of the device. In addition, the service oriented paradigm allows for a more smooth integration with Cloud platforms and for advanced discovery mechanisms also employing semantic technologies [4].

## 3   The SNPS Middleware

This section presents the proposal for a middleware devised to lay on the physical layer of wireless sensors, abstract away the sensors' specific features, and turn sensors into smart and composable services accessible through the Internet in an easy and standardized way. The middleware was designed to follow the basic principles of the IoT paradigm [9]. Sensors are not just sources of raw data, but are seen like smart objects capable of providing services like filtering, combining, manipulating and delivering information that can be readily consumed by any other entity over the Internet according to well-known and standardized techniques.

Primary goal of the middleware, which we called *Sensor Node Plug-in System (SNPS)*, is to bring any physical sensor (actuator) on an abstraction level that allows for easier and standardized management tasks (switch on/off, sampling), in a way that is independent of the proprietary sensor's specification. By the time a sensor is "plugged" into the middleware, it will constitute a resource/service capable of interacting with other resources (be them other sensors plugged into the middleware or third party services) in order to compose high-value services to be accessed in SOA-fashion. The middleware also offers a set of complimentary services and tools to support the management of the entire life cycle of sensors and to sustain the overall QoS provided by them.

Basically, the SNPS can be said to belong to the category of the service-oriented middlewares [13]. In fact, the provided functionality are exposed through a service-oriented interface which grants for universal access and high interoperability. Yet, all data and information gathered by sensors are stored in a database that is made publicly accessible and can be queried by third party applications. Further, the SNPS also support asynchronous communication by implementing the exchange of messages among entities (sensors, components, triggers, external services). All these features makes the middleware flexible to any application's need in any execution environment.

At design time it was decided not to implement the entire middleware from scratch. A scouting was carried out in order to identify the software framework that best supported, in a native way, all the characteristics of flexibility and modularity required by the project. Eventually, the OSGi framework[1] was chosen. The OSGi framework implements a component-oriented model, which natively supports the component's life cycle management, the distribution of components over remote locations, the seamless management of components' inter-dependencies, and the asynchronous communication paradigm.

The SNPS middleware was then organized into several components, and each component was later implemented as a software module (or "bundle") within the OSGi framework. Figure 1 depicts the architecture of the middleware and its main components.

The overall architecture can be broken down into three macro-blocks: Sensor Layer Integration, Core and related Components, Web Service Integration. In the following we provide a description of each macro-block.

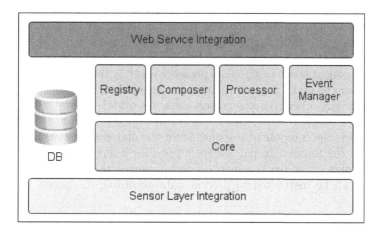

Fig. 1. SNPS architecture

## 3.1 Core and Related Components

The components we are about to discuss are charged the responsibility of providing most of the middleware's functionality. In Figure 2 the connections among the components are depicted.

*Core.* It is where the business logic of the Middleware resides. The Core acts as an orchestrator who coordinates the middleware's activities. Data and commands flowing forth and back from the web service layer to the sensor layer are dispatched by the Core to the appropriate component.

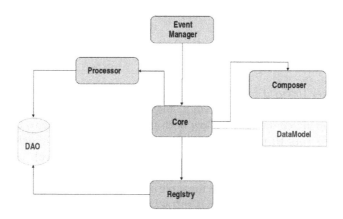

Fig. 2. Core and related Components

*Registry.* It is the component where all information about sensors, middleware's components and provided services are stored and indexed for search purpose. As for the sensors, data regarding the geographic position and the topology of the managed wireless sensor networks are stored in the Registry. Also, each working component needs to signal its presence and functionality to the Registry, which will have to make this information public and available so that it can be discovered by any other component/service in the middleware.

*Processor.* It is the component responsible for the manipulation of the data flow coming from the sensors. In particular, it provides a service to set and enforce a sampling plan on a single sensor or on an aggregate of sensors. Also, this component can be instructed to process data according to specific processing templates.

*Composer.* It represents the component which implements the sensors' composition service. Physical sensors can be "virtualized" and are given a uniform representation which allows for "aggregating" multiple virtualized sensors into one sensor that will eventually be exposed to applications. An insight and practical examples about this functionality are provided in Section 5.

*Event Manager.* It is one of the most important components of the middleware. It provides a publish/subscribe mechanism which can be exploited by every middleware's component to implement asynchronous communication. Components can either be producers (publishers) or consumers (subscribers) of every kind of information that is managed by the middleware. This way, data flows, alerts, commands are wrapped into "events" that are organized into topics and are dispatched to any entity which has expressed interest in them.

*DAO.* It represents the persistence layer of the middleware. It exposes APIs that allow service requests to be easily mapped onto storage or search calls to the database.

## 3.2   Sensor Layer Integration

The Sensor Layer Integration (SLI) represents the gateway connecting the middleware to the physical sensors. It implements a *bidirectional communication channel* (supporting commands to flow both from the middleware to the sensors and from the sensors to the middleware as well and a *data channel* (for data that are sampled by sensors and need to go up to the middleware).

The addressed scenario is that of wireless sensor networks implemented through so called Base Stations (BS) to which multiple sensors are "attached". A BS implements the logic for locally managing its attached sensors. Sensors can be wiredly or wirelessly attached to a BS, forming a network which is managed according to specific communication protocols, which are out of our scope. The SLI will then interact just with the BS, which will only expose its attached sensors hiding away the issues related to the networking.

The integration is realized by means of two symmetrical bundles, which are named respectively *Middleware Gateway bundle (iMdmBundle)* and *WSN Gateway Bundle (iWsnBundle)*. The former lives in the middleware's runtime context, and was thought to behave as a gateway for both commands and data coming from the BSs and directed to the middleware; the latter lives (runs) in the BS's runtime context, and forwards commands generated by the middleware to the BSs. Since the middleware and the BSs may be attached to different physical networks, the communication between the two bundles is implemented through a remote "OSGI Context", which is a specific OSGi's features allowing bundles living in different runtime contexts to communicate to each other's. In Figure 3 the two bundles and their respective runtime contexts are shown.

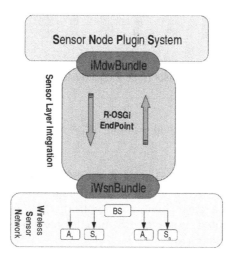

**Fig. 3.** OSGi bundles implementing the Sensor Layer Integration

The SLI was designed to work with any kind of BS, independently of the peculiarity of the sensors it manages, with the aim of abstracting and uniforming the access to sensors' functionality. Uniforming the management of the sensors' life cycle does not mean giving up the specific capabilities of sensors. Physical sensors will maintain the way they work and their peculiar features (in terms, for instance, of maximum sampling rate, sampling precision, etc.). But, in order for sensors (read base stations) to be pluggable into the middleware and be compliant to its management logic, a minimal set of requirements must be satisfied: the *iWsnBundle* to be deployed on the specific BS will have to interface to the local BS' logic and implement the functionality imposed by the SNPS middleware (switch on/off sensors, sample data, run sampling plan) by invoking the proprietary base station's API.

### 3.3    Web Service Integration

As depicted in Figure 4, the *OSGi bundle Wrapper* exports the functionality of the SNPS middleware to a Web Service context.

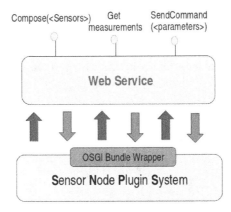

**Fig. 4.** Wrapping and exposing SPNS as a Web Service

SNPS services can be invoked from any OSGi compliant context. On the other hand, making the SNPS accessible as a plain Web Service will make its services profitable for a great number of applications in several domains. The functionality implemented by the SNPS' bundles have been packaged into the following categories of services:

- Search for sensors;
- Retrieve sensors capabilities and sensors data;
- Compose sensors;
- Send commands to sensors (enable/disable, set a sampling plan).

## 4    SNPS Data Model

The SNPS data model is one of the most interesting features of the middleware. Goals like integration, scalability, interoperability are the keys that drove the definition of the model at design time. The objective was then to devise a data model to structure both sensors' features (or capabilities) and data produced by sensors. The model had to be rich enough to satisfy the multiple needs of the middleware's business logic, but at the same time had to be light and flexible to serve the objectives of performance and scalability. We surveyed the literature in order to look for any proposal that might fit the middleware's requirement. Specification like SensorML and O&M [2] seam to be broadly accepted and widely employed in many international projects and initiatives. SensorML is an XML-based language which can be used to describe, in a relatively simple manner, sensors capabilities in terms of phenomena they are able to offer and other features of the specific observation they are able to implement. O&M is a specification for describing data produced by sensors, and is XML-based as well. XML-based languages are known to be hard to treat, and in many cases the burden for the management of XML-based data overcomes the advantage of using rigorous and well-structured languages. We therefore opted for a solution that calls on a reduced set of terms of the SensorML specification to describe the sensor capabilities, and makes use of a much lighter JSON[6] format to structure the data produced by sensors. An excerpt of what a description of sensor capabilities look like is depicted in Figure 5.

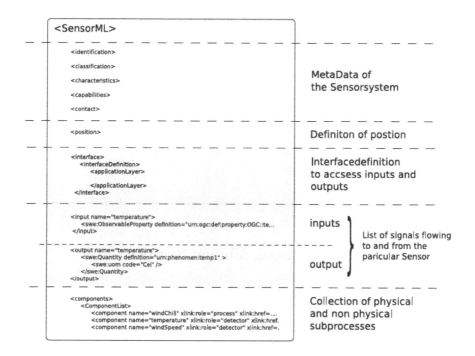

**Fig. 5.** Description of sensor capabilities in SensorML

This is the basic information that must be attached to any sensor before it is plugged into the middleware. Among others, it carries data regarding the phenomena being observed, the sampling capabilities, and the absolute geographic position. When the sensor wakes up, it sends this information to the middleware, which will register the sensor to the Registry bundle, and produce its *virtualized image*, i.e., a software alter-ego of the physical sensor which lives inside the middleware run-time. The virtual sensor has a direct connection with the physical sensor. Each interaction involving the virtual sensor will produce effects on the physical sensor too. It is important to point out that all virtual sensors are treated uniformly by the middleware's business logic.

Furthermore, SensorML is by its nature a process-oriented language. Starting from the atomic process, it is possible to build the so-called *process chain*. We exploited this feature to implement one of the main service provided by the SNPS, i.e., the sensors' composition service (see Section 5 for more details). This service, in fact, makes use of this feature to elaborate on measurements gathered by multiple sensors.

As regards the definition of the structure for sensor data, JSON was chosen because it ensures easier and lighter management tasks. The middleware is designed to handle (sample, transfer, store, retrieve) huge amounts of data, with the ambitious goal to also satisfy the requirements of real-time applications. XML-based structures are known to cause overhead in communication, storage and processing tasks, and therefore they do not absolutely fit our purpose. Another strong point of JSON is the ease of writing and analyzing data, which greatly facilitates the developer's task. A data sampled by a sensor will then be put in the following form:

```
Sensor_Measure:
{
    ''SensorId'':''value'',
    ''data'':''value'',
    ''type'':''value'',
    ''timestamp'':''value''
}
```

## 5   Building and Composing Virtual Sensors

Sensor Composition is the most important feature of the SNPS middleware. Simply said, it allows to get complex measurements starting from the samples of individual sensors. This composition service is provided by the Composer bundle (see Figure 1).

An important prerequisite of the composition is the sensor "virtualization", which is a procedure performed when a sensor is plugged into the SNPS middleware (see Section 3.2). Aggregates of sensors can be built starting from their software images (virtual sensors) that live inside the SNPS middleware. Therefore, in order to create a new composition (or aggregate) of sensors, the individual virtual sensors to be combined need to be first selected. Secondly, the operation that is to be applied to sensor's measurements must be specified. This is done by defining the so-called *Operator*, which is a function that defines the expected input and output formats of the operation being performed. The final composition is obtained by just applying the Operator to the earlier chosen virtual sensors. By that time, a new virtual sensor (the aggregate) is available in the system, and is exposed as a new sensor by the middleware.

Let us figure out a practical use case of sensor composition. Imagine that there are four temperature sensors available in four different rooms of an apartment. An application would like to know about the instant average temperature of the apartment. A new sensor can be built starting from the four temperature sensors applying the average operator, as depicted in Figure 6.

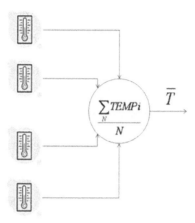

**Fig. 6.** Average operator

In this specific case, the input sensors are homogeneous. The middleware also provides for the composition of heterogeneous sensors (e.g., temperature, humidity, pressure, proximity), provided that the operator's I/O scheme is adequately designed to be compatible with the sensors' measurement types.

## 6  Conclusion

The size of data produced by sensors and sensor networks deployed worldwide is growing at a rate that current data analysis tools are not able to follow. Sources of data are multiplying on the Internet (think about smart devices equipped with photo/video cameras). There is a plethora of sensor devices producing information of any kind, at very high rates and according to proprietary specification. This complicates a lot the task of data analysis and manipulation. In this paper we have proposed a solution that aims to ease these tasks. What we have proposed is not just an early-stage idea but a concrete middleware that implements a mechanism to abstract sensors away from their proprietary interfaces and structure, and offers tool to aggregate and expose sensors and sensor data in the form of services to be accessed in SOA fashion. A prototype of the middleware has been implemented. In the future we are going to conduct extensive experiments to test the scalability and the performance of the middleware in distributed (even geographic) contexts.

**Acknowledgments.** This work has been partially funded by the Italian project "Sensori" (Industria 2015 - Bando Nuove Tecnologie per il Made in Italy) - Grant agreement n. 00029MI01/2011.

# References

1. OSGi Alliance: Open Service Gateway initiative, OSGi (2013),
   http://www.osgi.org/
2. Botts, M., Percivall, G., Reed, C., Davidson, J.: OGC Sensor Web Enablement: Overview and high level architecture. In: Nittel, S., Labrinidis, A., Stefanidis, A. (eds.) GSN 2006. LNCS, vol. 4540, pp. 175–190. Springer, Heidelberg (2008)
3. Costa, P., Coulson, G., Gold, R., Lad, M., Mascolo, C., Mottola, L., Picco, G.P., Sivaharan, T., Weerasinghe, N., Zachariadis, S.: The runes middleware for networked embedded systems and its application in a disaster management scenario. In: Fifth Annual IEEE International Conference on Pervasive Computing and Communications (PerCom 2007), pp. 69–78. IEEE Computer Society (2007)
4. Di Modica, G., Tomarchio, O., Vita, L.: A P2P based architecture for Semantic Web Service discovery. International Journal of Software Engineering and Knowledge Engineering 21(7), 1013–1035 (2011)
5. Hadim, S., Mohamed, N.: Middleware: Middleware challenges and approaches for wireless sensor networks. IEEE Distributed Systems Online 7(3), 1 (2006)
6. IEEE Network Working Group: JavaScript Object Notation, JSON (2006),
   http://www.ietf.org/rfc/rfc4627.txt?number=4627
7. Issarny, V., Georgantas, N., Hachem, S., Zarras, A., Vassiliadist, P., Autili, M., Gerosa, M.A., Hamida, A.B.: Service-oriented middleware for the Future Internet: state of the art and research directions. Journal of Internet Services and Applications 2(1), 23–45 (2011)
8. Madden, S.R., Franklin, M.J., Hellerstein, J.M., Hong, W.: Tinydb: an acquisitional query processing system for sensor networks. ACM Trans. Database Syst. 30(1), 122–173 (2005)
9. Miorandi, D., Sicari, S., Pellegrini, F.D., Chlamtac, I.: Internet of things: Vision, applications and research challenges. Ad Hoc Networks 10(7), 1497–1516 (2012)
10. Mohamed, N., Al-Jaroodi, J.: A survey on service-oriented middleware for wireless sensor networks. Service Oriented Computing and Applications 5(2), 71–85 (2011)
11. Mottola, L., Picco, G.P.: Programming wireless sensor networks: Fundamental concepts and state of the art. ACM Comput. Surv. 43(3), 19:1–19:51 (2011)
12. OGC: Sensor Web Enablement, SWE (2013),
    http://www.opengeospatial.org/ogc/markets-technologies/swe/
13. Papazoglou, M.P., van den Heuvel, W.J.: Service Oriented Architectures: approaches, technologies and research issues. VLDB Journal 16(3), 389–415 (2007)
14. Sugihara, R., Gupta, R.K.: Programming models for sensor networks: A survey. ACM Trans. Sen. Netw. 4(2), 8:1–8:29 (2008)
15. TinyOS community: TinyOS (2013), http://www.tinyos.net/

# CoSIP: A Constrained Session Initiation Protocol for the Internet of Things

Simone Cirani, Marco Picone, and Luca Veltri

Department of Information Engineering
University of Parma
Viale G.P. Usberti, 181/A
43124 Parma, Italy
{simone.cirani,marco.picone,luca.veltri}@unipr.it

**Abstract.** The Internet of Things (IoT) refers to the interconnection of billions of constrained devices, denoted as "smart objects" (SO), in an Internet-like structure. SOs typically feature limited capabilities in terms of computation and memory and operate in constrained environments, such low-power lossy networks. As IP has been foreseen as the standard for smart-object communication, an effort to bring IP connectivity to SOs and define suitable communication protocols (i.e. CoAP) is being carried out within standardization organisms, such as IETF. In this paper, we propose a constrained version of the Session Initiation Protocol (SIP), named "CoSIP", whose intent is to allow constrained devices to instantiate communication sessions in a lightweight and standard fashion. Session instantiation can include a negotiation phase of some parameters which will be used for all subsequent communication. CoSIP can be adopted in several application scenarios, such as service discovery and publish/subscribe applications, which are detailed. An evaluation of the proposed protocol is also presented, based on a Java implementation of CoSIP, to show the benefits that its adoption can bring about, in terms of compression rate with the existing SIP protocol and message overhead compared with the use of CoAP.

**Keywords:** Internet of Things, service discovery, communication protocols, constrained applications, SIP, CoAP.

## 1 Introduction

The Internet of Things (IoT) refers to the interconnection of billions of constrained devices, denoted as "smart objects" (SO), in an Internet-like structure. Smart objects have limited capabilities, in terms of computational power and memory (e.g., 8-bit microcontrollers with small amounts of ROM and RAM), and might be battery-powered devices, thus raising the need to adopt particularly energy efficient technologies. Smart objects typically operate in constrained networks which often have high packet error rates and a throughput of tens of kbit/s. In order to interconnect smart objects, it is required to use standard and interoperable communication mechanisms. The use of IP has been foreseen

C. Canal and M. Villari (Eds.): ESOCC 2013, CCIS 393, pp. 13–24, 2013.
© Springer-Verlag Berlin Heidelberg 2013

as the standard for interoperability for smart objects by standardization organisms, such as the IETF and the IPSO Alliance. As billions of smart objects are expected to come to life and IPv4 addresses have eventually reached depletion, IPv6 has been identified as a candidate for smart-object communication. Within the IETF, several working groups have been set in order to address the issues related to smart-object communication. The IETF 6LoWPAN Working Group is defining encapsulation and other adaptation mechanisms to allow IPv6 packets to be sent to and received from over Low power Wireless Personal Area Networks, such as those based on IEEE 802.15.4. For the application layer, the IETF CoRE Working Group is currently defining a Constrained Application Protocol (CoAP) [1], to be used as a generic web protocol for RESTful constrained environments, targeting Machine-to-Machine (M2M) applications, and that can be seen as a compressed version of HTTPCoAP includes the following features: request/response interaction model between application endpoints, built-in discovery of services and resources and key concepts of the Web such as URIs and Internet media types.

As CoAP is designed to be used by constrained nodes, such as duty-cycled devices, in constrained environments, CoAP uses UDP as a lightweight transport. Besides a request/response communication paradigm, CoAP also supports a publish/subscribe paradigm, by letting CoAP clients to "observe" resources. When observing resources, the CoAP server, following client's subscription, sends multiple responses to the client. There are many other applications in both constrained and non-constrained environments that feature non-request/response communication model. Some of these applications require the creation and management of a session. A session is an exchange of data between an association of participants. The Session Initiation Protocol (SIP) [2] is an Internet application-layer control protocol which aims at enabling the endpoints of the communication to create, modify, and terminate multimedia sessions, such as VoIP calls, multimedia conferences, or any point-to-multipoint data distribution communications. Once a multimedia session has been established, the media are transmitted typically by using other application-layer protocols, such as RTP and RTCP, or as raw UDP data, directly between the endpoints, in a peer-to-peer fashion. SIP is a text protocol, similar to HTTP, which can run on top of several transport protocols, such as UDP (default), TCP, or SCTP, or on top of secure transport protocol such as TLS and DTLS. Session parameters are exchanged as SIP message payloads; a standard protocol used for this purpose is the Session Description Protocol.The SIP protocol also supports intermediate network elements which are used to allow endpoint registration and session establishment, such as SIP Proxy servers and Registrar servers. SIP also defines the concepts of transaction, dialog, and call as groups of related messages, at different abstraction layers. As asserted before, also in constrained environments, establishing a session is a likely event to occur, as communication between nodes might go beyond simple request/response pairs, as accomplished by using CoAP. Although in principle CoAP encapsulation could be used also for carrying data in non-request/response fashion, for example by using CoAP POST request in non-confirmable mode, it could be much more efficient to instantiate a session between constrained nodes first, while negotiating some parameters for subsequent communication, and then perform a more lightweight communication by using the session parameters already negotiated, rather then having to carry on the burden of CoAP headers, which in most cases would end up being equal in any request/response. Such session initiation could be still performed through the standard SIP protocol, also in constrained environments. Moreover, SIP and its extensions, such as event notification [3], already include mechanisms that are being defined for CoAP, such as observing resources [4], which allows for a subscribe/notify communication paradigm, and resource directory [5], which can be used for resource discovery. For this reason, SIP appears to be a suitable alternative to many mechanisms defined in CoAP and related proposals that might be used to address these issues. The main drawback of using standard SIP protocol in constrained environments is the large size of text-based SIP messages (compared to other binary protocols such CoAP), and the processing load required for parsing such messages.

For this reason, in this paper, we propose a constrained version of the Session Initiation Protocol, named "CoSIP", whose intent is to allow constrained devices to instantiate communication sessions in a lightweight and standard fashion and can be adopted in M2M application scenarios. Session instantiation can include a negotiation phase of some parameters which will be used for all subsequent communication. CoSIP is a binary protocol which maps to SIP, similarly to CoAP and HTTP. CoSIP can be adopted in several application scenarios, such as service discovery and publish/subscribe applications.

The rest of this paper is organized as follows. In Section 2, an overview of related works is presented. In Section 3, the CoSIP protocol is detailed together with its architecture and preliminary implementation. Use cases for CoSIP-based applications in Internet of Things scenarios are presented in Section 4 and a performance evaluation of the proposed protocol is shown in Section 5. Finally, in Section 6 we draw our conclusions.

## 2    Related Work

Smart objects typically are required to operate using low-power and low-rate communication means, featuring unstable (lossy) links, such as IEEE 802.15.4, usually termed Low-power Wireless Personal Area Networks (LoWPANs) or Low-power and Lossy Networks (LLNs). The Internet Engineering Task Force (IETF) has setup several working groups in order to address many issues related to bringing IP connectivity to LoWPAN smart objects. In particular, the 6LoWPAN (IPv6 over Low power WPAN) WG was chartered to work on defining mechanisms that optimize the adoption of IPv6 in LoWPANs and the ROLL (Routing Over Low power and Lossy networks) WG was chartered to develop optimal IPv6 routing in LLNs. Finally, the CoRE (Constrained RESTful Environments) WG has been chartered to provide a framework for RESTful applications in constrained IP networks. The CoRE WG is working on the definition of a standard application-level protocol, named CoAP, which can be used to let constrained devices communicate with any node, either on the same network or on the Internet, and provides a mapping to HTTP REST APIs. CoAP is intended to provide, among others, Create-Read-Update-Delete (CRUD) primitives for resources of constrained devices and publish/subscribe communication capabilities. While the work on CoAP is already at an advanced stage, the CoRE WG is also investigating mechanisms for discovery and configuration, but the work on these issues is still at an early stage and therefore open to proposals. The "observer" CoAP extension [4] allows to let CoAP clients observe resources (subscribe/notify mechanism) and be notified when the state of the observed resource changes. This approach requires the introduction of a new CoAP *Observe* option to be used in GET requests in order to let the client register its interest in the resource. The server will then send "unsolicited" responses back to the client echoing the token specified by the client in the GET request and reporting an Observe option with a sequence number used for reordering purposes. As we will describe later, we envision that the instantiation of a session could significantly reduce the amount of transmitted bytes, since, after the session has been established, only the payloads could be sent to the observer, thus eliminating the overhead due to the inclusion of the CoAP headers in each notification message.

As for service discovery, the CoRE WG has defined a mechanism, denoted as *Resource Directory* (RD) [5], to be adopted in M2M applications. The use of a RD is necessary because of the impracticality of a direct resource discovery, due to the presence of duty-cycled nodes and unstable links in LLNs. The registration of a resource in the RD is performed by sending a POST request to the RD, while the discovery can be accomplished by issuing a GET request to the RD targeting the .well-known/core URI. This discovery mechanism is totally self-contained in CoAP as it uses only CoAP messages. The adoption of the CoSIP protocol provides an alternative mechanism to register resources on a RD, which may be also called CoSIP Registrar Server. The advantage of using a CoSIP based registration mechanism is that it might be possible to register resources other than those reachable through CoAP, thus providing a scalable and generic mechanism for service discovery in constrained applications with a higher degree of expressiveness, such as setting an expiration time for the registration.

## 3  CoSIP

As described in Section 1, in both constrained and non-constrained environments there are many applications that may require or simply may obtain advantages by negotiating end-to-end data sessions. In this case the communication model consists in a first phase in which one endpoint requests the establishment of a data communication and, optionally, both endpoints negotiate some communication parameters (transfer protocols, data formats, endpoint IP addresses and ports, encryption algorithms and keying materials, and other application specific parameters) of the subsequent data sessions. This may be useful for both client-server or peer-to-peer applications, regardless the data sessions evolve or not according to a request/response model. The main advantage is that all such parameters, including possible resource addressing, may be exchanged in advance, while no such control information is required during data transfer. The longer the data sessions, the more the advantage is evident respect to a per-message control information. Also in case of data sessions that may vary formats or other parameters during time, such adaptation may be supported by performing session renegotiation. A standard way to achieve all this onto an IP-based network may be by using the Session Initiation Protocol [2]. In fact SIP has been defined as standard protocol for initiating, modifying and tearing down any type of end-to-end multimedia sessions. SIP is independent from the protocol used for data transfer and from the protocol used for negotiating the data transfer (such negotiation protocol can be encapsulated transparently within the SIP exchange). In order to simplify the implementation, SIP reuses the same message format and protocol fields of HTTP. However, differently from HTTP, SIP works by default onto UDP, by directly implementing all mechanisms for a reliable transaction-based message transfer. This is an advantage in duty-cycled constrained environment where some problems may arise when trying to use connection-oriented transports, such as TCP. However, SIP may also run onto other transport protocols such as TCP, SCTP, TLS or DTLS. Unfortunately SIP derives from HTTP the text-based protocol syntax that, even if it simplifies the implementation and debugging, results in larger message sizes and bigger processing costs (and source code size / RAM footprint) required for message parsing. Note that the SIP standard defines also a mechanism for reducing the overall size of SIP messages; this is achieved by using a compact form of some common header field names. However, although it allows a partial reduction of the message size, it may still result in big messages, especially if compared to other binary formats, for example those defined for CoAP. For this reason we tried to define and implement a new message format for SIP in order to take advantages of the functionalities already defined and supported by SIP and by a new binary and very compact message encoding. We naturally called such new protocol CoSIP, that stands for Constrained Session Initiation Protocol, or, simply, Constrained SIP. Due to the protocol similarities between SIP and HTTP, in order to maximize the reuse of protocol definitions and source code implementations, we decide to base CoSIP onto the same message format that has been defined for CoAP, thanks to the role that CoAP plays respect to HTTP. However, it is important to note that, while CoAP required to define new message exchanges, mainly due to the fact that CoAP need to operated in constrained and unreliable networked scenario over UDP transport protocol, while HTTP works over TCP, CoSIP may completely reuse all SIP message exchanges and transactions already defined by the SIP standard, since SIP already works over unreliable transport protocols (e.g. UDP).

SIP is structured as a layered protocol, where at the top there is the concept of dialog, that is a peer-to-peer relationship between two SIP nodes that persists for some time and facilitates sequencing of different request-response exchanges (transactions). In CoAP there is no concept equivalent to SIP dialogs, and, if needed, it has to be explicitly implemented at application level. Under the dialog there is the transaction layer, that is the message exchange that comprises a client request, the following optional server provisional responses and the server final response. The concept of transaction is also present in CoAP where requests and responses are bound and matched through a token present as message header field. Under the transaction there is the messaging layer where messages are effectively formatted and sent through an underlying non-SIP transport protocol (such as UDP or TCP). Instead of completely re-designing a session initiation protocol for constrained environments, we propose to reuse the SIP layered architecture of SIP, by simply re-defining the messaging layer with a constrained-oriented binary encoding. For such a purpose, we propose to reuse the same CoAP message syntax [1]. Figure 1(a) shows the CoSIP message format derived by CoAP. A CoSIP message starts with the 2-bit Version field (1), followed by the 2-bit Type field (1 = Non-confirmable), the 4-bit CoAP TKL field (set to 0), the 8-bit Code field that encode request methods (for request messages) and response codes (for response messages), the 16-bit CoAP Message ID field, followed by zero or more Option fields. In case a CoSIP message body is present, as in CoAP it is appended after Options field, prefixed by an 1-byte marker (0xFF) that separates CoSIP header and payload. Options are encoded as in CoAP in Type-Length-Value (TLV) format and encode all CoSIP header fields (From, Via, Call-ID, etc.) included in the CoSIP message. For each header field a different option number has been set. In order to increase the SIP-to-CoSIP compression ratio, alternatively of encoding the header field value as an opaque byte string, a per SIP header field encoding rule has been also defined.

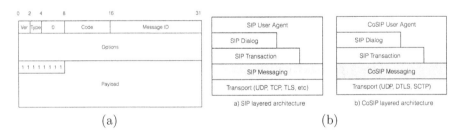

(a)                                    (b)

**Fig. 1.** CoSIP Protocol: (a) CoSIP message format; (b) Comparison of the layered architectures of SIP (a) and CoSIP (b)

Since CoSIP re-uses the transaction layer of SIP, no CoAP optional Token field is needed [1] and the TKL (Token Length) field can be permanently set to 0. Moreover, since CoSIP already has reliable message transmission (within the transaction layer), no Confirmable (0), Acknowledgement (2) nor Reset (3) message types are needed, and the only type of message that must be supported is Non-confirmable (1).

The comparison of the layered architecture of CoSIP and SIP is shown in Figure 1(b). One problem in reusing the current CoAP message format [1] is that in CoAP the 8-bit Code field is used to encode all possible request methods and response codes. In particular, for response messages the 8-bit Code field is divided by CoAP into two sub-fields "class" (3 bits) and "details" (5 bits); the upper three bits ("class") encodes the CoAP response classes 2xx (Success), 4xx (Client Error), and 5 (Server Error), while the remaining 5 bits ("details") encode the sub-type of the response within a given class type. For example a 403 "Forbidden" response is encoded as 4 ("class") and 03 ("details"). Unfortunately, this method limits the number of possible response codes that can be used (for example, using only 5 bits for "details" does not allow the direct encoding of response codes such as 480 "Temporarily Unavailable" or 488 "Not Acceptable Here"). In CoSIP, we overcome this problem by encoding within the Code field only the response class (2xx, 4xx, etc.) and by adding an explicit Option field that encodes the response sub-type. Moreover, in order to support all SIP/CoSIP response codes we also added the classes 1xx (Provisional) and 3xx (Redirect) used in SIP.

## 4    IoT Application Scenarios

In this section, we will describe the most significant for IoT applications, intended to provide an overview of the capabilities and typical usage of the CoSIP protocol. In all the scenarios, we consider a network element, denoted as "IoT Gateway", which includes also a HTTP/CoAP proxy, which can be used by nodes residing outside the constrained network to access CoAP services.

### 4.1    CoAP Service Discovery

CoSIP allows smart objects to register the services they provide to populate a CoSIP Registrar Server, which serves as a Resource Directory. The terms "Registrar Server" and "Resource Directory" are here interchangeable. Figure 2 shows a complete service registration and discovery scenario enabled by CoSIP. We consider a smart object that includes a CoAP server, which provides one or more RESTful services, and a CoSIP agent, which is used to interact with the CoSIP Registrar Server. The smart object issues a REGISTER request (denoted with the letter "a" in the figure) which includes registration parameters, such as the Address of Record (AoR) of the CoAP service and the actual URL that can be used to access the resource (Contact Address). Note that, while the original SIP specification states that the To header MUST report a SIP or SIPS URI, CoSIP allows to specify any scheme URI in the To header, e.g. a CoAP URI. Upon receiving the registration request, the Registrar Server stores the AoR-to-Contact Address mapping in a Location Database and then sends a 200 OK response. When a REST client, either CoAP or HTTP, is willing to discover the services, it can issue a GET request targeting the .well-known/core URI, which is used as a default entry point to retrieve the resources hosted by the Resource Directory, as defined in [6]. The GET request is sent to the HTTP/CoAP proxy, which returns a 200 OK (in case of HTTP) or a 2.05 Content (in case of CoAP) response containing the list of services in the payload.

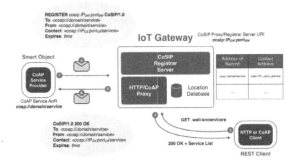

**Fig. 2.** CoAP Service Discovery

## 4.2   Session Establishment

A session is established when two endpoints need to exchange data. CoSIP allows the establishment of session in a standard way without binding the session establishment method to a specific session protocol. For instance, CoSIP can be used to negotiate and instantiate a RTP session between constrained nodes. Once a session has been established, the data exchange between the endpoints occurs (logically) in a peer-to-peer fashion. Figure 3 shows how CoSIP can be used to establish a session between two endpoints. Let's assume an IoT Agent (IoT-A$_1$) identified by the CoSIP URI *cosip:user1@domain*, which includes at least a CoSIP agent, has registered its contact address to an IoT Gateway in the same way as described in the previous subsection (steps 1 and 2). If another IoT-A$_2$ *cosip:user2@domain* wants to establish a session with IoT-A$_1$, it will send a proper INVITE request to the IoT Gateway, which will act as a CoSIP Proxy relaying the request to IoT-A$_1$ (steps 3 and 4). IoT-A$_1$ will then send a 200 OK response to IoT-A$_2$ (steps 5 and 6), which will finalize the session creation by sending an ACK message to IoT-A$_2$ (steps 7 and 8). At this point the session has been setup and data flow between IoT-A$_1$ and IoT-A$_2$ can occur directly. The session establishment process can be used to negotiate some communication parameters, for instance by encapsulating Session Description Protocol (SDP) or equivalent in the message payload.

## 4.3   Subscribe/Notify Applications

IoT scenarios typically involve smart objects which might be battery-powered devices. It is crucial to adopt energy-efficient paradigms, e.g. OS tasks, application processing, and communication. In order to minimize the power consumed, duty-cycled smart objects are adopted. Sleepy nodes, especially those operating in LLNs, aren't guaranteed to be reached, therefore it is more appropriate for smart objects to use a Subscribe/Notify, also denoted as Publish/Subscribe (Pub/Sub), approach to send notifications regarding the state of their resources, rather than receive and serve incoming requests. Such a behavior can be achieved

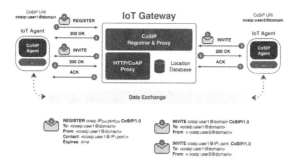

**Fig. 3.** CoSIP Session Establishment

by leveraging on the inherent capabilities of SIP, and therefore of CoSIP, as sketched in Figure 4. The depicted scenarios considers several Pub/Sub interactions: notifications can be sent either by a Notifier IoT Agent (IoT-$A_N$) or by an IoT Gateway, and subscribers can be either Subscriber IoT Agents (IoT-$A_S$), IoT Gateways, or generic Remote Subscribers. Let's assume that all the notifiers have previously registered with their CoSIP Registrar Server (this step is also denoted as the Publishing phase in a typical Pub/Sub scenario). The standard subscription/notification procedure is the following: i) the subscriber sends a SUBSCRIBE request to the notifier, also specifying the service events it is interested in; ii) the notifier stores the subscriber's and event information and sends a 200 OK response to the subscriber; iii) whenever the notifier's state changes, it sends a NOTIFY request to the subscriber; iv) the subscriber sends a 200 OK response back to the notifier.

Figure 4 reports all the use cases when a Pub/Sub might be used. An IoT-$A_S$ can subscribe to the service of an IoT-$A_N$ in the same network, in case it is willing to perform some task, such as data/service aggregation. The IoT Gateway can subscribe to the IoT-$A_N$'s in order to collect sensed data, e.g. to store them in the cloud, without the need to periodically poll for data. Finally, the IoT Gateway itself might be a notifier for remote subscribers, which are interested in notifications for specific services provided by the gateway, which may or may not be the same of existing IoT-$A_N$ nodes managed by the gateway. The adoption of CoSIP in IoT scenarios allows to easily set up efficient Pub/Sub-based applications in a standard way, thus allowing for seamless integration and interaction with the Internet.

## 5  Protocol Evaluation

In order to evaluate the performance of CoSIP, an implementation of the protocol has been developed together with some test applications. In this work, we have decided to focus on network performance as a metric by measuring the amount of network traffic generated by the test applications. The CoSIP protocol has been implemented in Java language, due to its simplicity, cross-platform support, and the availability of already developed SIP and CoAP libraries [7,8]. The

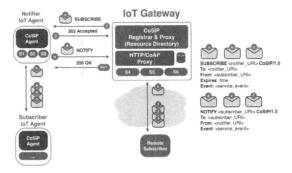

**Fig. 4.** Subscribe/Notify applications with CoSIP

source code of the CoSIP implementation is freely available at [9]. The performance results show that many advantages can be achieved by using CoSIP, both in constrained and non-constrained applications. The first evaluation compares CoSIP and SIP in terms of bytes transmitted for the signalling part related to the instantiation and termination of a session. Each CoSIP request and response message is separately compared with its SIP counterpart. The results are illustrated in Figure 5(a). Table 1 shows the compression ratio for each CoSIP/SIP message pair. Regarding the session as a whole, CoSIP yields an overall compression ratio of slightly more than 0.55.

**Table 1.** Comparison between CoSIP and SIP signalling (bytes per message) for session instantiation and establishment

| Message type | CoSIP (bytes) | SIP (bytes) | compression ratio |
|:---:|:---:|:---:|:---:|
| INVITE | 311 | 579 | 0.537 |
| 100 Trying | 141 | 279 | 0.505 |
| 180 Ringing | 173 | 372 | 0.465 |
| 200 OK | 293 | 508 | 0.577 |
| ACK | 216 | 363 | 0.595 |
| BYE | 183 | 309 | 0.592 |
| 200 OK | 162 | 274 | 0.591 |

Another evaluation has been made to show the advantage of using session in constrained applications. Figure 5(b) shows the amount of network traffic (in bytes) generated by two constrained applications: the first application uses CoSIP to establish a session and then performs the data exchange by sending the payloads over UDP; the second is a standard CoAP-based application where the communication occurs between a CoAP client and a CoAP server, using confirmed CoAP POST requests. In both cases data is sent at the same rate of one data message every 2 seconds. The figure shows that the lightweight CoSIP session is instantiated in a very short period of time and after the session has been established few bytes are exchanged between the endpoints. On the other hand the CoAP-based application has no overhead at the beginning due to the instantiation of the session but, soon after, the amount of traffic generated by this application exceeds that of the CoSIP-based application, since in the CoAP-based scenario data is exchanged within CoAP messages resulting in an unnecessary CoAP overhead. Note that in the depicted scenario the CoSIP signaling used for session initiation includes all SIP header fields normally used in standard non-constrained SIP application, that is no reduction in term of header fields has been performed. Instead for the CoAP application we considered only mandatory CoAP header fields resulting in the best-case scenario for CoAP in term of CoAP overhead (minimum overhead). This means that in other CoAP applications the slope of the line could become even steeper, thus reducing the time when the break-even point with CoSIP is reached.

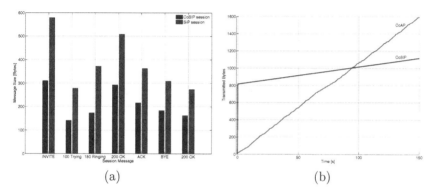

(a)    (b)

**Fig. 5.** Evaluation of the CoSIP Protocol: (a) transmitted bytes for CoSIP and SIP session (signalling only); (b) transmitted bytes in a CoSIP Session vs. CoAP confirmed POST requests and responses

# 6    Conclusions

In this paper, we have introduced a low-power protocol, named "CoSIP", for establishing sessions between two or more endpoints targeting constrained environments. Many applications, both in constrained and non-constrained scenarios, do benefit from establishing a session between the participants in order to minimize the communication overhead and to negotiate some parameters related to the data exchange that will occur. The CoSIP protocol is a constrained version of the SIP protocol intended to minimize the amount of network traffic, and therefore energy consumption, targeted for IoT scenarios. A similar effort in trying to minimize the amount of data in IoT and M2M applications is being carried on in standardization organizations, such as the IETF CoRE Working Group, which is currently defining a protocol (CoAP) to be used as a generic web protocol for RESTful constrained environments and maps to HTTP. Similarly, in this work we have proposed to apply the same approach to define a protocol for session instantiation, negotiation, and termination. We have described some interesting IoT scenarios that might benefit from using such a protocol, namely service discovery, session establishment, and services based on a subscribe/notify paradigm. A Java-language implementation of CoSIP has been developed and tested to evaluate the performance of the newly proposed protocol, by measuring the amount of transmitted bytes compared to other solutions based on SIP and CoAP respectively. The results show that applications that use CoSIP can outperform other SIP- and CoAP-based applications in terms of generated network traffic: SIP signalling can be compressed of nearly 50% and long-running applications based on CoAP require less bytes to be transmitted since CoAP options do not need to be sent along in each transmitted message, thus reducing the need for packet fragmentation (in 6LoWPAN networks) and the energy consumption of the nodes involved in the data exchange.

**Acknowledgments.** The work of Simone Cirani and Luca Veltri is funded by the European Community's Seventh Framework Programme, area "Internet-connected Objects", under Grant no. 288879, CALIPSO project - Connect All IP-based Smart Objects. The work reflects only the authors views; the European Community is not liable for any use that may be made of the information contained herein.

# References

1. Shelby, Z., Hartke, K., Bormann, C.: Constrained Application Protocol (CoAP). IETF Internet-Draft draft-ietf-core-coap (May 2013),
   http://tools.ietf.org/id/draft-ietf-core-coap
2. Rosenberg, J., Schulzrinne, H., Camarillo, G., Johnston, A., Peterson, J., Sparks, R., Handley, M., Schooler, E.: SIP: Session Initiation Protocol. RFC 3261 (Proposed Standard) (June 2002); Updated by RFCs 3265, 3853, 4320, 4916, 5393, 5621, 5626, 5630, 5922, 5954, 6026, 6141, 6665, 6878 (June 2002)
3. Roach, A.B.: Session Initiation Protocol (SIP)-Specific Event Notification. RFC 3265 (Proposed Standard) (June 2002); Obsoleted by RFC 6665, updated by RFCs 5367, 5727, 6446
4. Hartke, K.: Observing Resources in CoAP. IETF Internet-Draft draft-ietf-core-observe (February 2013), http://tools.ietf.org/id/draft-ietf-core-observe
5. Shelby, Z., Krco, S., Bormann, C.: CoRE Resource Directory. IETF Internet-Draft draft-ietf-core-resource-directory (June 2013),
   http://tools.ietf.org/id/draft-ietf-core-resource-directory
6. Shelby, Z.: Constrained RESTful Environments (CoRE) Link Format. RFC 6690 (Proposed Standard) (August 2012)
7. mjSIP project, http://mjsip.org/
8. mjCoAP project, http://mjcoap.org/
9. CoSIP project, http://cosip.org/download/

# Design of a Message-Oriented Middleware
# for Cooperating Clouds

Maria Fazio, Antonio Celesti, and Massimo Villari

DICIEAMA, University of Messina,
Contrada Di Dio, 98166 Sant'Agata - Messina
{mfazio,acelesti,mvillari}@unime.it
http://mdslab.unime.it

**Abstract.** Nowadays, Cloud services are not always able to promptly deal with the new emerging customers' requirements. A possible solution to such a problem consists in developing a piece of middleware able to combine available services in order to address different scenarios. In this paper, we present a Message Oriented Middleware for Cloud (MOM4C) able to arrange customizable Cloud facilities by means of a flexible federation-enabled communication system. From the customer's the point of view, Cloud facilities are composed as well as a planetary system model, in which the central star is the communication system and planets are utilities (e.g., storage, computation, security, sensing, data analytics, etc). More specifically, we describe the key features of the proposed architecture and its applicability in different scenarios.

**Keywords:** message oriented middleware, cloud computing, federation, service provisioning, planetary system model.

## 1 Introduction

The Cloud technology has reached an amazing level of complexity embracing many application fields. In spite of the number of services and virtualization tools that are rising on the market, often, many Cloud providers do not easily find the right Cloud solutions that properly suit their business requirements. For this reason, Cloud operators are looking for alternative approaches for the development of next generation versatile mash-up applications. Such a need leads to the necessary development of Cloud architectures aimed at integrating different types of technologies and hardware/software solutions.

In order to better describe such next generation Cloud services, in the rest of the paper we will refer to "utility" and "Cloud facilities". We define "Cloud utility" a specific Cloud service (e.g., storage, network, computation, security, sensing, data analytics, etc), instead, we define "Cloud Facilities" a mash-up Cloud service composed using one or more Cloud utilities.

A possible approach for the achievement of such next generation Cloud services consists in considering a management "middleware" able to set up Cloud facilities aggregating several available Cloud utilities across one or more enterprises in a federated environment. In simple words, the aim of the middleware

C. Canal and M. Villari (Eds.): ESOCC 2013, CCIS 393, pp. 25–36, 2013.

is to acts as a liaison among utilities in order to support the deployment of advanced, flexible, and differentiated Cloud facilities [1]. In such a versatile scenario, enterprises become, at the same time, Cloud customers and providers.

In this paper, we present a Message-Oriented Middleware For Cloud (MOM4C), a distributed system that aims to fulfill the requirements of the aforementioned next generation Cloud services. MOM4C provides flexibility, efficiency, and elasticity for the setup of Cloud facility to Cloud providers, seamlessly integrating the utilities belonging to different heterogeneous environments. It allows to expand existing Cloud systems and to integrate several virtual and physical resources. Its ability of collecting heterogeneous utilities and abstracting their functionalities to high level services, is strategic. In fact, it is useful to support the development of advanced applications for Internet of Things (IoT) environments.

MOM4C has been designed according to the Message-Oriented model. This model has already been used for the designing of Cloud middleware such as IBM WebSphere MQ (MQSeries), TIBCO Rendezvous, and RabbitMQ. In comparison with them, MOM4C has very innovative features, that make the Cloud service provisioning efficient, scalable and versatile. MOM4C enables the development of distributed services over an asynchronous instant-messaging architecture, which can be used for both intra- and inter-domain communications.

MOM4C allows to compose Cloud facilities according to client requirements. Making a simile, the MOM4C works as a planetary system, where the central star includes the "core", i.e., all the basic communication functionalities of the middleware and the planets are the Cloud utilities that can be used. Such a service provisioning model guarantees high scalability and customization of the required service. In addition, besides the basic communication functionalities, the core, includes security mechanisms for guaranteeing secure data exchange.

The rest of the paper is organized as follows. Section 2 describes related works. Motivations are discussed in Section 3. An overview of MOM4C service provisioning strategy is provided in Section 4. In Section 5, we present the MOM4C architecture also discussing our designing choices. Section 6, concludes the paper.

## 2   Related Works

Some works in literature deal with the need of Cloud middleware, addressing specific issues and exploiting different technologies. To support application execution in the Cloud, in [2], authors present CloudScale. It is a piece of middleware for building Cloud applications like regular Java programs and easily deploy them into IaaS Clouds. It implements a declarative deployment model, in which application developers specify the scaling requirements and policies of their applications using the Aspect-Oriented Programming (AOP) model. A different approach is proposed in [3], which presents a low latency fault tolerance middleware to support distributed applications deployment within a Cloud environment. It is based on the leader/follower replication approach for maintaining strong replica consistency of the replica states. If a fault occurs, the reconfiguration/recovery mechanisms implemented in the middleware ensure that a backup replica obtains all the information it needs to reproduce the actions of the application. The middleware presented in [4] has been designed aiming mission assurance for critical Cloud applications across hybrid Clouds. It is centered on policy-based event monitoring and dynamic reactions to guarantee the accomplishment of "end-to-end" and "cross-layered" security, dependability and timeliness. In [5], the authors present a piece of middleware for enabling media-centered cooperation among home networks. It allows users to join their home equipments through a Cloud, providing a new content distribution model that simplifies the discovery, classification, and access to commercial contents within a home networks. Mathias and Baude [6] focus their work on the integration of different types of computational environments. In fact, they propose a lightweight component-based middleware intended to simplify the transition from clusters, to Grids and Clouds and/or a mixture of them. The key points of this middleware are a modular infrastructure, that can adapt its behavior to the running environment, and application connectivity requirements. The problem of integrating multi-tenancy into the Cloud is addressed in [7]. The authors propose a Cloud architecture for achieving multi-tenancy at the SOA level by virtualizing the middleware servers running the SOA artifacts and allowing a single instance to be securely shared between tenants or different customers. The key idea of the work is that the combination between virtualization, elasticity and multi-tenancy makes it possible an optimal usage of data center resources (i.e., CPU, memory, and network). A piece of middleware designed for monitoring Cloud resources is proposed in [8]. The presented architecture is based on a scalable data-centric publish/subscribe paradigm to disseminate data in multi-tenant Cloud scenarios. Furthermore, it allows to customize both granularity and frequency of received monitored data according to specific service and tenant requirements. The work proposed in [9] aims to support mobile applications with processing power and storage space, moving resource-intensive activities into the Cloud. It abstracts the API of multiple Cloud vendors, thus providing a unique JSON-based interface that responds according to the REST-based Cloud services. The current framework considers the APIs from Amazon EC2, S3, Google and some open source Cloud projects like Eucalyptus. In [10], the authors present a piece of middleware to support fast system implementation and ICT cost reduction by making use of private Clouds. The system includes application servers that run a Java Runtime Environment (JRE) and additional modules for service management and information integration, designed according to a Service Oriented Architecture (SOA). As highlighted by this state of the art analysis, our effort arises from the evident need of a piece of middleware for versatile evolving Cloud scenarios. Differently from the aforementioned solutions, MOM4C abstracts the type of offered services, providing a framework able to integrate both the current and future Cloud solutions, offering to the clients the possibility to customize their Cloud facilities.

## 3   Motivation

Analyzing the trend of the Cloud computing market, we can highlight, on the one hand, a growing number of providers that are investing in Cloud-based services and infrastructures and, on the other hand, the interest of companies in long-term, customizable and complex business solutions, which must be easy to be set up, reliable and accessible through the Internet. MOM4C has been design to bridge this gap, integrating Cloud facilities, infrastructures and resources into one efficient, scalable, reactive and secure wide system. Its deployment can be strategic for many different stakeholder, as shown in Figure 1. MOM4C enables

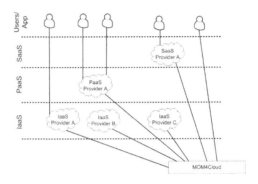

**Fig. 1.** Reference scenario

third-party enterprises and developers to implement Cloud facilities in an easy way, integrating different CLoud utilities according to a mash-up development model. Specifically, end-users (i.e., consumers and/or enterprises) can quickly push for basic CLoud utilities and advanced Cloud facilities. MOM4C enables Cloud providers to abstract the service level. Typically, Cloud providers can deliver three main service levels, i.e., Infrastructure as a Service (IaaS), Platform as a Service (PaaS), and Software as a Service (SaaS). According to such a classification, MOM4C allows to develop Cloud facilities in form of IaaS, PaaS, and SaaS instances. It is important to notice that also Cloud utilities themselves can be hardware/software functionality delivered in form of IaaS, PaaS, and SaaS.

IaaS Providers deliver computers and devices (i.e., physical and/or virtual) and other resources. Typically, a Virtual Infrastructure Manager (VIM) manages one or more hypervisors each one running several Virtual Machines (VMs) as guests. A VIM allows to manage a large numbers of VMs (e.g., preparing disk images, setting up networking, starting, suspending, stopping VM, etc) and to scale services up/down according to customers' requirements. An example is represented by a provider that offers on-demand VMs to end-users. PaaS providers deliver a computing platform, typically including operating system, programming language execution environment, database, and web server. Software developers can implement and run their software solutions on a cloud platform without the cost and complexity of buying and managing the underlying hardware and software layers. The underlying computer and storage resources scale automatically to match application demand. An example is represented by a provider that offers a platform that collects data coming from one or more sensor networks and that offer Application Program Interfaces (APIs) for data processing, hence enabling developers to implement intelligent sensing applications. SaaS providers, typically deliver on-demand pieces of software via Web 2.0 that are usually priced on a pay-per-use basis. Providers install and operate application software in the cloud and cloud users access the software from cloud clients, generally web browsers. An example is represented by a provider that offers via Web 2.0 interface an office automation software suite such as Google Drive to manage documents.

All the providers and clients exploiting MOM4C will be organized in a federated system. In a federation, each entity is independent and can not be conditioned by a "central government" in its activities. The components of a federation are in some sense "sovereign" with a certain degree of autonomy from the "central government": this is why a federation can be intended more than a mere loose alliance of independent entities. Moreover, the treatment of all the data and information transfered through MOM4C is performed according to secure policies able to assure: data confidentiality, data integrity, data authenticity, non-repudiation of the sender, non-repudiation of the receiver.

# 4    Service Provisioning: A Planetary System Model

Due to its native ability in integrating heterogeneous infrastructures and systems, MOM4C can potentially offer a wide plethora of utilities, which can combined each other in order to provide complex, customizable and differentiated services.

## 4.1    Design Overview

A monolithic design of the proposed system is inconceivable, since it implies an heavy management effort for all the available components, low scalability and useless service availability for clients. On the contrary, to guarantee the maximum flexibility, we have conceived MOM4C as a very modular architecture, in which every client can compose a Cloud utility according to his requirements. From the client point of view, we can schematize MOM4C as well as a planetary system, as shown in Figure 2. The planetary system is composed by one or more planets that orbit around a central star. According to our abstraction, Planets identify available utilities. For example, planets can be: i) VIM IaaS, for on-demand VM provisioning; ii) Sensing PaaS, collecting data by different sensing environments; iii) Distributed Processing PaaS, providing high computational power; iv) Big Data Storage, providing distribute storage for huge amount of

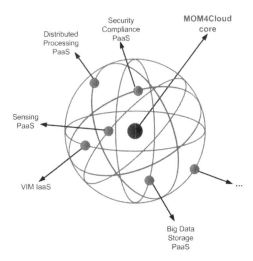

**Fig. 2.** Planetary system model for service provisioning through MOM4C

data, and so on. The core of MOM4C is the star of the planetary system. It provides all the basic functionalities necessary for the life of planets. Specifically, it includes a scalable messaging and presence system, security mechanisms for data integrity, confidentiality and non-repudiation, federation management and other specific communication features for the management and integration of heterogeneous utilities.

All the possible combinations of planets specialize the behavior of the planetary system. According to our similitude, a specific planetary system configuration, including target planets defines the Cloud facility. In fact, according to our definition, the Cloud facility has to be customizable from clients in order to suit specific public and/or business scenarios. This concept will be better explained in Section 4.2. In the following, we will show the benefits of the proposed planetary system with reference to different Cloud facilities.

### 4.2   Cloud Utility Combinations with MOM4C: The Cloud Facility

Thanks to its modularity, MOM4C allows to instantiate different types of composed services. As well as a planetary system is composed by a star with several planets that turn around it along their orbits, in MOM4C, a Cloud facility is built around a distributed management system or core (i.e., the central star) and several Cloud utilities (i.e., planets). In order to better explain the planetary system model at the basis of the MOM4C design, let us consider four different Cloud utilities: i) *VIM*, which allows to dynamically orchestrate VMs regardless of the underlying hypervisor (e.g., Xen, KVM, VMware, Virtual Box, Virtual PC, etc), ii) *Sensing*, which allows to collect, filter, and expose through web services data coming from several sensing environments and devices, iii) *Trusted computing*, for building a chain of trust among several hardware and software components, iv) *Big data storage*, which allows to store and retrieval huge amount of data in a distributed fashion.

The *VIM utility* allows to aggregate heterogeneous computing infrastructures, providing suitable interfaces at the high-level management layer for enabling the integration of high-level features, such as public Cloud interfaces, contextualization, security [11][12] and dynamic resources provisioning [13].

The *Sensing utility* allows to virtualize different types of sensing infrastructures, adding new capabilities in data abstraction. It gathers sensing information from a peripheral decision-maker, called Virtual Pervasive Element (VPE), able to interact with smart sensing devices or sensing environments [14]. The Sensing PaaS utility is compliant with the Sensor Web Enablement (SWE) standard defined by the Open Geospatial Consortium, which allows to make all types of sensors, transducers and sensor data repositories discoverable, accessible and usable via the Web.

The *Trusted Computing utility* allows interact with the Trusted Platform Module (TPM) on the physical host [15] by means of a software agent. The TPM is a hardware micro-controller that allows to combine hardware and software components by building a chains of trust. In addition by means of the remote and deep attestation protocols, the utility is able to verify the configuration of physical hosts and VMs.

The *Big Data Storage utility* allows to perform an efficient retrieval of big data adopting, for example the map/reduce paradigm and the Hadoop system. The hadoop system includes three main nodes: master, backup, and worker. The master node takes the input, divides it into smaller sub-problems, and distributes them to worker nodes. The worker node processes the smaller problem, and passes the answer back to the master node that produces the output. The backup node is a passive master node.

In the following, we briefly describe three different planetary systems, i.e., Cloud facilities, originated by some possible combinations of the aforementioned utilities and we discuss their applicability in different scenarios.

- **Antares**: it is composed of Sensing PaaS and the Big Data Storage utilities, in order to collect informations on the environments, which are stored into the Cloud. This Cloud facility offers a scalable tool that can be very useful in Smart Cities. Cities of the future will need to collect data from a lot of heterogeneous *urban sensors*, such as smart water, electric meters, GPS devices, building sensors, weather sensors and so on [16], in order to monitor available services and citizens requirements. However, the heavy penetration of sensing devices will cause the explosion of the amount of data to be stored and managed.
- **Omicron**: it is composed of VIM, Big Data Storage and Trusted Computing utilities. The Cloud facility offers a scalable and elastic virtual infrastructure able to verify the integrity of both physical hosts and VMs, tracking all the activities of the system components. Such a mash-up service is very useful for the compliance management of distributed systems deployed on a virtual infrastructure through the VIM utility. It can identify problems

and regulate configuration and software changes, thanks the abilities of the Trusted Computing utility, which allows to track "who has done what", and the Big Data Storage utility, which allows to manage log information and output files.

- **Vega**; it is composed of VIM and Trusted Computing utilities. Such a Cloud facility offers a secure dynamic Content Delivery Network (CDN) for web server mirroring. In fact, the VIM utility allows to elastically deploy distribute server mirrors all over the world into VMs (a similar scenario is discussed in [17]) and the Trusted Computing utility guarantees that different mirrors are consistent from the point of view of the security. For example, let us consider the web site of a press agency, which has to manage news regarding a sudden event, such as a big sport event. The site has to extend the service by increasing the number of mirrors, in order to meet the peak of client requests. At the same time, it has to guarantee that the VMs on which web server mirrors are deployed have not been corrupted with false news.

It is important to notice that logically, different planetary systems, i.e, Cloud facilities can coexist on the same physical system.

## 5  MOM4C Architecture

We have designed MOM4C according to the message-oriented paradigm, in order to provide an efficient communication framework among distributed components into the Cloud system. From the message-oriented paradigm, MOM4C inherits a primary benefit, that is loosing coupling between participants in a system due their asynchronous interaction. It results in a highly cohesive, decoupled system deployment. It also decouples the performance of the subsystems from each other. Subsystems can be independently scaled, with little or no disruption of performance into the other subsystems. With reference to the management of unpredictable activity overloads in a subsystem, the message-oriented model allows to accept a message when it is ready, rather than being forced to accept it. MOM4C adds important features, that are strategic for business in Cloud. Its major benefits includes:

- **Modularity**: the middleware can be quickly extended in terms of available utilities and it can be easily customized in order to suits a specific Cloud scenario.
- **Polymorphism**: each distributed entity in the system can play different roles according to the system requirements. Different rules includes both the core management tasks and the utility-related tasks.
- **Security**: an indispensable requirement for the large-scale adoption Cloud computing is security, especially in business scenarios. Security has to be natively addressed at any level of communication (intra-module, inter-module, and inter-domain), providing guarantees in terms of data confidentiality and data integrity

– **Federation**: it is a strategic approach to promote collaboration among co-operating Cloud providers.

### 5.1 Two-Layer Architecture

As depicted in Figure 3, MOM4C is based on a distributed architecture, organized in two layers, that are the Cluster Layer (CL) and the Execution Layer (EL). The Cluster Layer includes an overlay network of decentralized Cluster

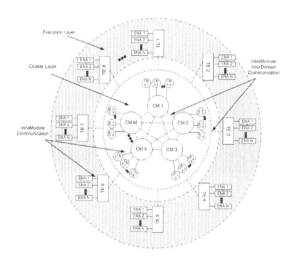

**Fig. 3.** MOM4C basic scheme

Manager (CM) nodes. Each CM is responsible for the working activities of the Task Executor (TE) nodes belonging to the cluster. The EL is composed of TEs, which are intended to perform operative tasks. TEs can be trained to perform a specific task. It means that they do not instantiate all the services and utilities available in MOM4C, but they download code, initialize and configure services, launch software agents whenever they receives instructions from the CM. An appropriate utility module configuration into TEs allows to specialize MOM4C services. According to the specific code in execution at TEs, we have different characterizations of the EL.

To perform different types of tasks (e.g., VM execution and sensing data gathering), we set up specialized ELs, which independently works according to the CL specifications. Such an organization of roles and activities carries out high modularity to the MOM4C system. Building around the Cluster Layer many TE layers at the same time characterizes the MOM4C behavior. Thus, an ad-hoc layers configuration is designed to support a specific scenario. With reference to the planetary system model discussed in Section 4, the star includes all the functionalities of the Cluster Layer, which sustains the whole system. Any orbit represents a specific Execution Layer and the planet is the utility offered by TEs belonging to the related Execution Layer.

Another important feature of MOM4C is the polymorphic nature of nodes. At different times, each physical node can serve as CM or TE. However, only a node in a cluster is elected as CM and actively works for managing the whole cluster. Some other node are elected as "passive CMs", which are redundant CMs that can quickly replace the active CM if it fails. This approach improves the fault tolerance of the CL. The size of the cluster depends on the system workload and it can dynamically change according to the specific elasticity requirements of the system. About TEs, they can belong to one or more ELs, hence they work at different Cloud utilities. Such a concept is better explained in Figure 4. For

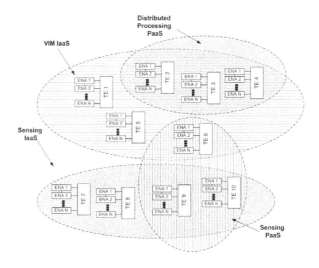

**Fig. 4.** Hybrid Executor Node Layer composition

example, TE 1, 2, 3, 4, 5, 6 are hypervisor servers working to provide a VIM IaaS. At the same time, TE 2, TE 3, and TE 4 work also to provide a Distributed Processing PaaS, since software agents running on TEs are independent active processes. Following the example in Figure 4, TE 7, 8, 9, and 10 work as embedded devices for Sensing IaaS provisioning, whereas TE 6, 9, and 10 works for a Sensing PaaS, for example collecting sensing data from TE 9 and 10 and providing services through the AJAX Web APIs of Web application deployed in TE 6.

## 5.2   Communication System

MOM4C supports three types of communications:

- **IntraModule Communication**: itcharacterizes information exchange inside each node of the architecture, both CMs and TEs. It guarantees a seamless way for allowing their internal software modules to communicate each other.

- **InterModule Communication**: it governs communications between CMs and TEs and viceversa.
- **InterDomain Communication**: is specific for communications among CMs belonging to different administrative domains, hence enabling InterCloud or Cloud federation scenarios.

In order to ensure as much as possible the middleware modularity, the tasks running on each node are mapped on different processes within the Operating System, which communicate each other by means of an Inter Process Communication (IPC) or InterModule communication. According to the message-oriented design of MOM4C, InterModule communications are based on an Instant Messaging and Presence (IMP) protocol. A presence system allows participants to subscribe to each other and to be notified about changes in their state. On the other hand, Instant messaging is defined as the exchange of content between a set of participants in near real time. InterDomain communications among different administrative domains are managed considering the federation agreements among the domains. Federation allows Cloud providers to "lend" and "borrow" resources. Thus, a CM of a domain is able to control one or more TEs belonging to other domains.

## 6  Conclusion

In this paper, we have presented MOM4C. The middleware offers a very scalable solution for integrating several utilities in a federated environment. The key feature of MOM4C is the high customization of Cloud utilities. In particular, service provisioning can be modeled as a planetary system, in which the central star is the core communication system and the planets are the Cloud utilities that orbits around the star. Combining different planets, it is possible to carry out different planetary systems, i.e., Cloud facilities. We presented the MOM4C architecture, in which distributed nodes are organized into a cluster-based structure, in order to separate the core communication system from specific utilities. Finally, several service composition use cases have been analyzed.

## References

1. Ranabahu, A., Maximilien, M.: A Best Practice Model for Cloud Middleware Systems. In: Best Practices in Cloud Computing: Designing for the Cloud (2009)
2. Leitner, P., Satzger, B., Hummer, W., Inzinger, C., Dustdar, S.: Cloudscale: a novel middleware for building transparently scaling cloud applications. In: SAC 2012, pp. 434–440 (2012)
3. Wenbing, Z., Melliar-Smith, P., Moser, L.: Fault Tolerance Middleware for Cloud Computing. In: IEEE 3rd CLOUD 2010, pp. 67–74 (July 2010)
4. Campbell, R., Montanari, M., Farivar, R.: A middleware for assured clouds. Journal of Internet Services and Applications 3(1), 87–94 (2012)

5. Diaz-Sanchez, D., Almenarez, F., Marin, A., Proserpio, D., Arias Cabarcos, P.: Media Cloud: an open cloud computing middleware for content management. IEEE Transactions on Consumer Electronics 57(2), 970–978 (2011)
6. Manias, E., Baude, F.: A component-based middleware for hybrid grid/cloud computing platforms. Concurrency and Computation: Practice and Experience 24(13), 1461–1477 (2012)
7. Azeez, A., Perera, S., Gamage, D., Linton, R., Siriwardana, P., Leelaratne, D., Weerawarana, S., Fremantle, P.: Multi-tenant SOA Middleware for Cloud Computing. In: IEEE CLOUD 2010, pp. 458–465 (2010)
8. Povedano-Molina, J., Lopez-Vega, J.M., Lopez-Soler, J.M., Corradi, A., Foschini, L.: Dargos: A highly adaptable and scalable monitoring architecture for multi-tenant clouds. Future Generation Computer Systems (May 2013)
9. Flores, H., Srirama, S.N.: Dynamic Re-configuration of Mobile Cloud Middleware based on Traffic. In: IEEE MASS 2012, October 8-1 (2012)
10. Nagakura, H., Sakurai, A.: Middleware for creating private clouds. Fujitsu Scientific & Technical Journal (FSTJ) 47(3), 263–269 (2011)
11. Celesti, A., Fazio, M., Villari, M., Puliafito, A.: Se clever: A secure message oriented middleware for cloud federation. In: IEEE Symposium on Computers and Communications (ISCC 2013), ISCC 2012 (2013)
12. Juels, A., Oprea, A.: New approaches to security and availability for cloud data. Communication of the ACM 56(2), 64–73 (2013)
13. Celesti, A., Tusa, F., Villari, M., Puliafito, A.: Integration of clever clouds with third party software systems through a rest web service interface. In: IEEE Symposium on Computers and Communications (ISCC 2012), pp. 827–832 (2012)
14. Fazio, M., Paone, M., Puliafito, A., Villari, M.: Huge amount of heterogeneous sensed data needs the cloud. In: SSD 2012 (2012)
15. Celesti, A., Fazio, M., Villari, M., Puliafito, A., Mulfari, D.: Remote and deep attestations to mitigate threats in cloud mash-up services. In: World Congress on Computer and Information Technologies (WCCIT 2013), Sousse, Tunisia (2013)
16. Naphade, M., Banavar, G., Harrison, C., Paraszczak, J., Morris, R.: Smarter cities and their innovation challenges. Computer 44(6), 32–39 (2011)
17. Celesti, A., Fazio, M., Villari, M., Puliafito, A.: Virtual machine provisioning through satellite communications in federated cloud environments. Future Generation Computer Systems 28(1), 85–93 (2012)

# The Core Approach of SAaaS in Action: The Planning Agent

Lionel Cremer[1], Salvatore Distefano[2], Giovanni Merlino[3,4], and Antonio Puliafito[3]

[1] Haute Ecole de la Province de Liege, 4020, Belgium
lionel_cremer@hotmail.com
[2] Dip. di Elettronica, Informazione e Bioingegneria, Politecnico di Milano, 20133 Milano, Italy
salvatore.distefano@polimi.it
[3] Dip. di Ingegneria, Università di Messina, 98166 Messina, Italy
{gmerlino,apuliafito}@unime.it
[4] Dip. di Ingegneria (DIEEI), Università di Catania, 95125 Catania, Italy
giovanni.merlino@dieei.unict.it

**Abstract.** The main goal of the sensing and actuation as a service (SAaaS) approach is to enrol and aggregate sensing resources from heterogeneous sensor networks and smart devices, providing them as a service in a Cloud-wise fashion. SAaaS aims at providing handles on sensing and actuation resources, abstracted and virtualized on top of physical ones, shared by contributors to the SAaaS. This requires adequate mechanisms for letting SAaaS end users interact with the contributing nodes hosting the provided resources. In this paper we focus on such problem, introducing the module of our SAaaS architecture specifically conceived to deal with all the issues related to user-resource interfaces: the Planning Agent (PA). The modular architecture of the PA and its main interactions with SAaaS stakeholders and framework components are described. The development of the PA on the Android platform is detailed, thus implementing a preliminary version of the SAaaS framework, targeted at mobiles: SAaaS4mobile.

**Keywords:** Cloud, sensors and actuators, sensing abstraction and virtualisation, OGC Sensor Web Enablement.

## 1 Introduction and Motivations

In the current worldwide ICT scenario, a constantly growing number of devices (mobile devices, sensors, RFID tags, etc.) join the Internet foreshadowing a world of (more or less) smart devices or "things" in the Internet of Things (IoT) perspective. It is therefore necessary to think about possible ways and solutions to face an all-encompassing challenge, where such ecosystem of geographically distributed sensors and actuators may be discovered, selected according to the functionalities they provide, interacted with, and may even cooperate for pursuing a specific goal.

Taking this need into consideration and following current trends for models and approaches, such as service oriented and Cloud computing-based ones, in previous work [1,2] we presented an innovative framework for dealing with a geographic-wide sensing environment involving mobile devices and sensor networks. The sensing and actuation

C. Canal and M. Villari (Eds.): ESOCC 2013, CCIS 393, pp. 37–46, 2013.

as a service (SAaaS) approach aims at collecting sensors and actuators shared by both mobile device owners and sensor network administrators into a unique sensing infrastructure, thus providing sensing resources to users on demand, as a service, adopting a Cloud-oriented provisioning model.

The novelty of this approach is to consider a sensor or an actuator as resources that can be abstracted and virtualized, as virtual machines in an IaaS-fashion, and then provided to end users that can operate directly on the sensing resources, thus implementing a *sensing Cloud*. Existing models for sensing Clouds mainly feature a *data-driven* approach, collecting sensed data on provider-side databases, then exposing searching and filtering facilities to the end user, much like a Software as a Service (SaaS). This does not allow end users to directly operate or handle sensing and actuation resources. This is a severe limitation when e.g. certain configuration parameters for resources are to be set, or in case some data preprocessing is required before sending.

In order to pursue a *device-driven* approach it is necessary to provide the end user with adequate interfaces to sensing resources. In the SAaaS architecture, the core module devoted to this task is the *Planning Agent* (PA), a component of the SAaaS *Hypervisor*. The PA is in charge of directly interfacing with the contributing node on behalf of the end user, implementing facilities for handling and configuring the instances of sensing resources, as provided to the customers. In this paper we focus on the PA, proposing an overall modular architecture and discussing its implementation on Android-powered smart devices. We named this specific implementation *SAaaS4mobile*. More specifically, we describe how to create a scheme for planning and configuring the sensors on smart devices through the SAaaS4mobile PA interface, dealing with hardware and interoperability issues. To this purpose we based the SAaaS4mobile PA implementation on the Open Geospatial Consortium (OGC) Sensor Web Enablement (SWE) [3] standards.

The paper is organized as follows. Background concepts and an overview of the state of the art are provided in Section 2, while a brief description of the SAaaS Hypervisor is given in Section 3. Then, the modular architecture of the PA is described in Section 4, and the SAaaS4mobile PA implementation on Android smart devices is described in Section 5. Some conclusive remarks and future work discussed in Section 6 close the paper.

## 2   Background and Related Work

### 2.1   SAaaS

The main aim of SAaaS [1] is to adapt the IaaS paradigm to sensing platforms, bringing to a Cloud of sensors, where sensing and actuation resources may be discovered, aggregated, and provided as a service, according to a Cloud provisioning model.

The inclusion of sensors and actuators in geographic networks as Cloud-provisioned resources brings new opportunities with regards to contextualization and geo-awareness. By also considering mobiles, possibly joining and leaving at any time, the result can be a highly dynamic environment. The issue of node churn can only be addressed through volunteer contribution paradigms [4,1]. Furthermore, the SAaaS has to manage contributions coming from sensor networks, mobiles or any other "smart" device equipped with sensors and actuators, to ensure interoperability in a Cloud environment. It must

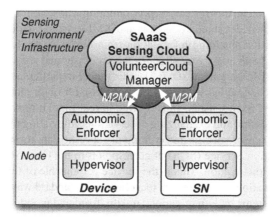

**Fig. 1.** SAaaS reference architecture

also be able to provide the mechanisms necessary for self-management, configuration and adaptation of nodes, without forgetting to provide the functions and interfaces for the activation and management of voluntarily shared resources.

The SAaaS reference architecture [1] comprises three modules, Hypervisor, Autonomic Enforcer and VolunteerCloud Manager, shown in Fig. 1. The *Hypervisor* allows to manage, abstract, virtualise and customise sensing and actuation resources that could be provided by enrolling either mobile device or SN *nodes*. Among key features are: abstraction of devices and capabilities, virtualization of abstracted resources, communications and networking, customization, isolation, semantic labeling, and thing-enabled services. All these features are presented in the next section. At a higher level with respect to the Hypervisor, the *Autonomic Enforcer* and the *VolunteerCloud Manager* deal with issues related to the interaction among nodes. The former is responsible of the enforcement of local and global Cloud policies, subscription management, cooperation on overlay instantiation. The VolunteerCloud Manager is in charge of exposing the Cloud of sensors via Web service interfaces, indexing of resources, monitoring Quality of Service (QoS) metrics and adherence to Service Level Agreements (SLAs) [5,6,7].

## 2.2   OGC: Sensor Web Enablement

The OGC provides a large number of specifications, among which we can find the Sensor Web Enablement (SWE) family of standards. Designed for the management of sensor data on the web, ia unique and revolutionary framework of open standards for exploiting Web-connected sensors and sensor systems of all types is the focus of the specifications. SWE standards aim at making all types of Web sensors, instruments, and imaging devices accessible and controllable on the Web. The SWE framework is composed of seven standards, four of them have been approved as official standards by the OGC members.

- SensorML: it is a language based on XML schema to describe the sensor systems. It encodes a lot of features for sensors, such as discovery, geolocation processing observations, mechanisms for sensor programming, subscriptions to sensor alerts. In particular, it provides standard models and XML schemas to describe processes, and instructions for obtaining information from observations. SensorML enables discovery, access and query execution for the processes and sensors it models.

– Observations & Measurements (O & M): this model in particular is featured in the SOS specification, coupled with an XML encoding for observations and measurements originating from sensors, and archived in real-time. It provides standardized methods for accessing and exchanging observations, alleviating the need to support a wide range of sensor-specific and community specific data formats.

– Sensor Observation Service (SOS): it corresponds to the Observation Agent specified in the previous section. This is the service responsible of the transmission of measured observations, from sensors to a client, in a standard way that is consistent for all sensor systems including remote, in-situ, fixed and mobile sensors. It allows the customer to control the measurement retrieval process. This is the intermediary between a client and an observation or near real-time sensor repository.

– Sensor Planning Service (SPS): it corresponds to the Planning Agent, whose design and implementation this paper focuses on.

## 2.3 State of the Art

Research about the design and implementation issues of a unified interface to sensors belonging to different administrative domains is not available, but some investigations amenable to the main topics under consideration have been made. A few of these deal with implementations of the SWE Sensor Observation Service on mobiles. The Mobile phone Sensor Network concept demonstrator proposed in [8] enables mobiles to collect observations from Bluetooth-enabled sensing devices, to be then uploaded to a central database via an SOS, directly integrated on the mobile, to convert the observations into Sensor Web Protocol-enabled ones.

In the same vein, the platform running on mobile devices proposed in [9] implements the same type of measurements conversion, afterwards injecting the measurements into a sensor service. The aim is to use the processing capabilities of latest generation of mobile devices for converting low-level sensor protocols into higher-level Sensor Web Enablement ones for data. Then the storage of these measurements into the Sensor Web is carried out using the transactional interface of an SOS.

The opposite approach is proposed in [10], including mechanisms to discover sensor data, retrieve the data using the SOS as sensor metadata protocol endpoint, and expose the data using a mapping application. Along the same lines, the project described in [11] features a generic mobile client for SOS to visualize any SOS-provided data in a map or tabular view.

The Human Sensor Web [12] aims to integrate two kinds of human-provided observations, by leveraging the SWE standard framework. Those two kinds of observations are human-sensed ones (such as textual descriptions) on one hand, and information gathered from sensors carried (i.e. worn) by people. From these works we can argue that using the SWE standards on a mobile phone to gather or to insert sensor observations is a first step towards a full SWE implementation on mobiles, a starting point for the present work.

SWE turns out to be also one of the privileged solutions to enable interoperability between all kinds of devices, as exemplified in [13] where the authors describe how SWE enables developers to leverage mechanisms for a high level of interoperability in the domain of sensor networks.

A technical treatment for SWE is available in [3] comprising many standard models. The *Sensor Model Language* enables the description of sensor systems and processes associated with sensor observations. The encoding of sensor observations and measurements is described in the *Observations & Measurements* standard, where also standard web service interfaces are specified. The *Sensor Observations Service* (SOS) enables the collection of observations and system information, while the *Sensor Planning Service* (SPS) enables the planning of observations. The *Sensor Alert Service* (SAS) enables the publication of, and subscription to, alerts, as produced by sensors, while *Web Notification Service* is in charge of delivering messages and alerts from SAS and SPS, in an asynchronous manner. A service-oriented sensor Web architecture, leveraging the SWE standards, is presented in [14].

## 3   Overview of the Hypervisor

An SAaaS Hypervisor [2] can be viewed as the foundational component of our device-driven approach to infrastructure-focused Clouds of sensors: it manages the resources related to sensing and actuation, introducing layers of abstraction and mechanisms for virtualization, operating at the level of a single SAaaS node, defined either as an entire sensor network, as long as under exclusive tenancy, or a set of sensors, as built-in to a standalone device. As a single node can be as dispersed as "smart dust", as in typical WSN scenarios, in order to provide mechanisms of direct interaction with, and manipulation of, sensing resources the Hypervisor is split among a centralized (nodal) device, possibly embedding one or more sensors, and the *motes*, i.e. small-footprint

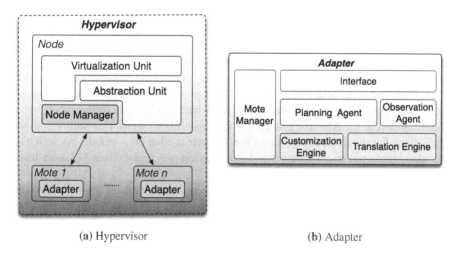

(a) Hypervisor                    (b) Adapter

**Fig. 2.** The SAaaS Hypervisor and Adapter modular architecture

edge devices in a SN, bearing built-in sensors or even driving standalone (albeit wired to) ones. This kind of two-level separation of concerns and assignment of operations descends also from the need for certain duties to be (self-)managed through autonomic approaches, typical of distributed entities.

A high-level, modular view of the Hypervisor architecture comprises four main building blocks: Adapter, Node Manager, Abstraction Unit and Virtualization Unit as shown in Fig. 2a.

As depicted in Fig. 2b, the lowest component of the Hypervisor, the *Adapter*, plays several distinct roles: on one hand, exposing a standards-compliant customer-friendly *Interface* to on-board resources. The *Observation Agent* requests, retrieves and eventually pre-processes measurements. As we are going to describe in the following sections, in terms of both behaviour and implementation details, the *Planning Agent* pushes requests for actions (*tasks*) to the device, for preparing the resource to carry out a variety of duties (reservation of functionalities, tuning of parameters, scheduling of observations). These commands allow management of operating parameters such as duty cycle, sampling frequency, etc. The jargon we are using talking about observation and planning operations traces back to our aim to be compliant with the SWE standards [3]. These two agents rely on the presence of a platform-specific driver, the *Translation Engine*, responsible for converting the high-level directives in native commands. The Hypervisor is also in charge of processing requests for reconfiguration of the device, using the *Customization Engine*, an interpreter able to execute on the sensing device the code needed to tailor the sensing activities to customer-mandated requirements. Finally, an autonomic approach is adopted delegating some management tasks of the Adapter to the *Mote Manager* running mote-side, performing specific operations such as power-driven self-optimization in collaboration with the Node Manager.

Above the Adapter, there is the *Node Manager*. It works only at the node level and is in charge of sensing resources operations and implementing policies.

The upper level contains the *Abstraction Unit*. It replicates planning and observation facilities modeled after those featured in the Adapter but on a node-wide scale, combining the pool of resources of the whole SN or smartphone.

Along this short descriptions, summarizing the Abstraction Unit, coupled with those about the Node Manager and the Adapter with its submodules, we referred to motes and nodes, per our definitions, thus sticking to WSN-like topologies. In this sense, when depicting the diagrams, we intentionally left out any standalone-centered device model, as in that case our architecture degenerates to a simpler one, where the node is the smart device itself, thus featuring an Abstraction Unit which fills the role of the upper layers of the Adapter (e.g. the Agents), just leaving the Customization and Translation Engines in their place for the reduced version of the Adapter needed on a mobile. As well, the Node Manager is not needed on a standalone device, where the Mote Manager itself makes up for the combination of the two modules.

At last, at the top of the layered model of the Hypervisor we have the *Virtualization Unit*, whose main task is slicing, i.e. generating possible partitioning schemes for the cluster of resources exposed by the Abstraction Unit. These partitioning schemes can be subsequently ranked according to a number of criteria including sensor provenance, proximity, QoS, security and so on.

## 4    Planning Agent

The SAaaS PA works side-by-side with the Observation Agent, complementing its features. Unlike the latter, engaged in providing upper layers with XML-encoded measurements (*observations*), sampled while driving the sensing resources, the former is mainly devoted to the tuning of sampling parameters according to user-defined preferences, still to be interfaced with by means of extensible standards-compliant encoding of requests for *tasks*, and corresponding responses. Other than tuning, tasks for scheduling of observations can be consumed by the PA: it may be following a predefined schedule, or upon the occurrence of a particular event, or simply a request from a client. The main aim of this effort is exposing all underlying knobs to make them available for customers to operate on transparently.

In order to meet the aforementioned requirements, an architecture comprising the six modules shown in Fig. 3 has been designed: a Request Dispatcher, a Sensors Prober, a Task Explorer, a Task Manager, an Observation Access Provider and an Interface. The

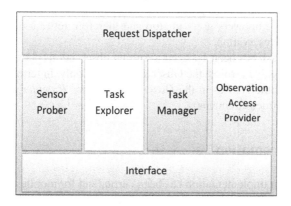

**Fig. 3.** SAaaS Planning Agent architecture

*Request Dispatcher* has to identify and demultiplex a request to the modules underneath. The lowest *Interface* has to interact with low-level services, i.e. the Customization Engine, the Translation Engine and the Mote Manager.

The *Sensor Prober* is in charge of enumerating all the sensors and actuators within a sensors platform, however rich and complex, by low-level platform-specific system probing. These sensors are then identified according to their types, supported observation facilities and sampling specs, overall (nominal) features and manufacturing details (brand, model, etc.).

The *Task Explorer* is responsible for enumeration of available tasks, to be provided by probing sensors as listed by the aforementioned Prober. In terms of tasks, those related to parameter tuning for sensing resources differ logically, according to sensor type and technology, so it is possible to e.g. plan retrieval of temperature samples from a thermometer, once a certain threshold has been exceeded, change the relative position and the focal length of a camera, or simply schedule reading of sensor observations at fixed intervals, etc. Moreover, in order to assess feasibility of a certain task, among the ones enumerated for selection, the sensor has to be queried and provide (runtime) confirmation, or else denial, of availability for servicing (or reservation thereof). It's then up to the querying party to decide what to do after feasibility assessment for the task under consideration.

The *Task Manager* controls tasks' lifecycle, since feasibility assessment through reservation/submission stages, then following up, and acting upon, running task progress.

If required, a user may reserve a task for a period of time, during which he/she gets exclusive access to the underlying resource, as no other user can submit or reserve it. The task will then be executed as soon as the user confirms for the real processing stages to commence. The *Reservation Manager* is responsible for both reservation of tasks, and its confirmation. The *Feasibility Controller* has to check if a task is feasible, as detailed above. The feasibility of a task depends on the availability of any resource essential for task servicing, e.g. if not still allocated due to a previous request.

Then, the *Task Updater* is in charge of updating configuration parameters of a task, if some modifications have to be pushed after tasks enter into processing stages. Lastly, the *Task Canceller* empowers users to stop and therefore retire a task, when already submitted or under reservation.

Finally, once a task has been serviced, resulting observations get stored. Any observation will be accessible through the Observation Agent only. In terms of observations, the sole duty up to the PA lies in the *Observation Access Provider* ability to provide endpoints to access measurements.

## 5   The Implementation

The Planning Agent implementation has been carried out for mobiles equipped by Android OS 4.0, using the NDK developer libraries and API provided by the Android community [15]. It is based on the SWE Sensor Planning Service (SPS) 2.0 standard [16]. It enables the interaction among user clients and sensor and actuator services using XML schemas to submit requests and to allow the service to reply. Modeling behavior by following the SPS standard, the functionalities of the Sensor Prober, Task Explorer, Task Manager and Observation Access Provider modules described in Section 4 have been developed.

The Sensor Prober has to retrieve information regarding: i) the contributor, if available (the extent of such information disclosure is totally up to the contributor); ii) the node sensors and their descriptions, also including the measured phenomenon and corresponding metrics; and iii) the geographic area (range) inside which observations are significant. This feature is implemented by the SPS *GetCapabilities* primitive. A *GetCapabilities* request is composed of four sections. The first one is *ServiceIdentification* containing the contributing node metadata, i.e. generic info on the type of the node, brand, model and similar. Then the *ServiceProvider* section provides information on the contributor, if available and public. The third section is the *OperationsMetadata* one, with metadata about the operations specified by the service and implemented by the node. The last is the Content section, it contains metadata about the sensors provided by the Planning Agent and the communication mechanisms supported (XML, SOAP, etc.).

The Task Explorer retrieves the list of tasks that can be performed on a sensor through specific SPS *DescribeTasking* requests. A description of the available configuration operations for the sensor is thus obtained and provided to the Task Manager. The request just contains a *Procedure* element to enquiry a sensor in the list about the tasks that can be performed. The tasks are identified by the name, the description, and the capabilities' configuration information.

The Task Manager implements a set of SPS requests. The *Submit* one allows the user to launch the execution of a configured task. Eventually, before submitting a job request, it is possible to enquire about its feasibility through the *GetFeasibility* primitive. The reply can be "Feasible" or "Not Feasible" and, optionally, it may contain a list of alternative sets of tasking parameters that might help during revision of the request. The user can also reserve the resources required to perform a specific task and then launch the task through the *Reserve* and *Confirm* requests. In a *Reserve* request a time limit has to be specified. At expiration time, all the reserved resources are to be released if the task has not been confirmed. It is possible to check the progress of a task by sending a *Status* request. A task can be in one out of six different states: "In Execution" if the service is executing it, "Completed" if it was completed as planned, "Reserved" if it has been reserved, "Failed" if execution fails, "Expired" when the task reservation expires and "Cancelled" if the task was cancelled. The client can eventually update or cancel a task, with *Update* and *Cancel* requests respectively.

Finally, the PA Observation Access Provider aims at providing the client with mechanisms, if needed, and endpoints to access the observations and measurements obtained during execution. It implements processing of SPS *DescribeTaskingResult* requests to interact with a certain sensor or task.

# 6   Conclusions

In this paper, we presented the Planning Agent, a core element of the nodal (contributor-side) modules for a SAaaS-based system.

This Agent provides essential features for offering infrastructure Clouds of sensors and actuators, like setting parameters on the device itself, or a virtualised instance thereof, as long as customers get to access handles on contributed devices. The architecture of the Planning Agent is specified, identifying some specific modules also considering the interactions between the end-user and the contributing node. Afterwards we delved in deeper details about the interactions and commands, looking at those in light of our prototype implementation into Android-powered smart devices.

Future efforts in relation to this work will possibly expand at a lower-level, e.g. platform specific abstractions. Amid ongoing research developments, we believe we'll also have the chance to explore compelling use cases and application scenarios, including further evaluations on performance, while also trying to validate a SAaaS approach to sensing resource provisioning according to Cloud paradigms by verifying remarkable advantages and exclusive functionalities.

**Acknowledgement.** This work is partially funded by PhD programme under grant PON R&C 2007/2013 "Smart Cities", by Simone project under grant POR FESR Sicilia 2007/2013 n. 179 and by the Cost-Action IC1303 "Algorithms, Architectures and Platforms for Enhanced Living Environments (AAPELE)".

# References

1. Distefano, S., Merlino, G., Puliafito, A.: Sensing and actuation as a service: A new development for clouds. In: Proceedings of the 2012 IEEE 11th International Symposium on Network Computing and Applications. NCA 2012, pp. 272–275. IEEE Computer Society, Washington, DC (2012)
2. Distefano, S., Merlino, G., Puliafito, A., Vecchio, A.: A hypervisor for infrastructure-enabled sensing clouds. In: IEEE International Conference on Communications, Budapest, Hungary, June 9-13 (2013)
3. Reed, C., Botts, M., Davidson, J., Percivall, G.: Ogc(r) sensor web enablement: overview and high level achhitecture. In: 2007 IEEE Autotestcon, pp. 372–380 (September 2007)
4. Cunsolo, V.D., Distefano, S., Puliafito, A., Scarpa, M.: Cloud@home: Bridging the gap between volunteer and cloud computing. In: Huang, D.-S., Jo, K.-H., Lee, H.-H., Kang, H.-J., Bevilacqua, V. (eds.) ICIC 2009. LNCS, vol. 5754, pp. 423–432. Springer, Heidelberg (2009)
5. Bruneo, D., Distefano, S., Longo, F., Puliafito, A., Scarpa, M.: Reliability assessment of wireless sensor nodes with non-linear battery discharge. In: Wireless Days (WD). IFIP, pp. 1–5. IEEE Press (2010)
6. Bruneo, D., Distefano, S., Longo, F., Puliafito, A., Scarpa, M.: Evaluating wireless sensor node longevity through markovian techniques. Computer Networks 56(2), 521–532 (2012)
7. Distefano, S.: Evaluating reliability of wsn with sleep/wake-up interfering nodes. International Journal of Systems Science 44(10), 1793–1806 (2013)
8. Clarke, J., Lethbridge, J., Liu, R., Terhorst, A.: Integrating mobile telephone based sensor networks into the sensor web. In: 2009 IEEE Sensors, pp. 1010–1014 (2009)
9. Jamsa, J., Luimula, M., Schulte, J., Stasch, C., Jirka, S., Schoning, J.: A mobile data collection framework for the sensor web. In: Ubiquitous Positioning Indoor Navigation and Location Based Service (UPINLBS), pp. 1–8 (2010)
10. Foerster, T., Nüst, D., Bröring, A., Jirka, S.: Discovering the sensor web through mobile applications. In: Gartner, G., Ortag, F. (eds.) Advances in Location-Based Services. Lecture Notes in Geoinformation and Cartography, pp. 211–224. Springer, Heidelberg (2012)
11. Tamayo, A., Viciano, P., Granell, C., Huerta, J.: Sensor observation service client for android mobile phones. In: Workshop on Sensor Web Enablement 2011 (SWE 2011), Banff, Alberta, Canada (October 2011)
12. The Human Sensor Web Consortium: The human sensor web project (2011), http://www.unhabitat.org/content.asp?typeid=19&catid=635&cid=7662
13. Sarakis, L., Zahariadis, T., Leligou, H.C., Dohler, M.: A framework for service provisioning in virtual sensor networks. EURASIP Journal on Wireless Communications and Networking 2012(1), 135 (2012)
14. Chu, X., Buyya, R.: Service oriented sensor web. In: Mahalik, N. (ed.) Sensor Networks and Configuration, pp. 51–74. Springer, Heidelberg (2007)
15. Google Inc.: Android ndk, http://developer.android.com/tools/sdk/ndk/index.html
16. Open Geospatial Consortium: OGC(R) Sensor Planning Service Implementation Standard. OGC. 2.0 edn. (2011)

# peaCS-Performance and Efficiency Analysis for Cloud Storage

Josef Spillner, Maximilian Quellmalz, Martin Friedrich, and Alexander Schill

Technische Universität Dresden,
Faculty of Computer Science,
{josef.spillner,alexander.schill}@tu-dresden.de,
{maximilian.quellmalz,martin.friedrich}@mailbox.tu-dresden.de

**Abstract.** Those who need to store larger amounts of data either for burst periods or for convenient synchronisation between devices are currently looking at new ways of how to integrate cloud storage services into the data processing applications. The benefits (on-demand access and pricing, elasticity) and the drawbacks (reduced control, increased dependencies on providers) need to be well balanced. Recently, a new class of applications called cloud storage controllers or integrators appeared with a high potential to become a standard feature of operating systems and network gateways. They seamlessly integrate single and bundled storage services into the users' digital environment. However, it is not clear which controllers are better than others. Some are open source, some commercial, some perform better than others, but some of the others provide more data pre-processing and routing features. We solve this problem by introducing peaCS as a test framework to analyse, compare and optimise the functional and non-functional properties of such client-side storage service integration solutions.

## 1 Motivation

Access to the cloud is shifting from an ad-hoc style to planned and systematic integration. Often, either a hardware appliance (e.g. for cryptographic key management) or a software gateway (e.g. for enforcing a policy of not using compute clouds during expensive periods) is used to manage the controlled access. For cloud storage services in particular, differently named service-independent client-side storage controllers, integrators, gateways, "cloud filesystems" or access applications are becoming more popular [26]. The popularity causes an increasing number of prototypes to become available and thus ensures healthy competition [20,10]. On the downside, it becomes more difficult to evaluate and assess the best solution for this task. Especially non-functional properties such as performance or efficiency, while becoming more commonplace as standard metrics in service descriptions [16], are hard to determine in an objective, reproducible and portable manner for client-side integration tools beyond arbitrary test series [9]. The difficulty aggravates when considering coordinated distributed storage integration across multiple independent services in which the individual service metrics shall be encapsulated as much as possible [21].

C. Canal and M. Villari (Eds.): ESOCC 2013, CCIS 393, pp. 47–58, 2013.

This trend motivates us to present a test framework to systematically determine these metrics. Fig. 1 positions the testing methodology as a special case of Service Bundle Integration Testing (SBIT) in which a number of independent reference services, real or simulated, are used in combination during the test execution. SBIT is distinct from Service Testing (ST) [7,13] which focuses more on invocation and protocols and less on the eventual effect on the client. It is also unlike most Service Integration Testing (SIT) methods which focus on a single service interface with one or multiple applications during one test run [3]. SBIT is applicable to all XaaS service classes, including Cloud Storage on the IaaS and PaaS levels for which the combination technique is data splitting, multiplexing and dispersion.

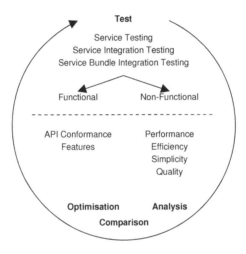

**Fig. 1.** General overview about Service Bundle Integration Testing

The next section gives an overview about testable cloud storage controllers and storage service integrators. Then, the *peaCS* test framework is introduced and explained with multiple experiments in which we analyse, compare and optimise storage controllers. In the fourth section, its functionality is compared to related work, before concluding the paper in the fifth section.

## 2   Overview about Multiplexing Cloud Storage Controllers and Libraries

The client-side integration of single and multiple cloud storage services happens on multiple layers. The lowest layer encompasses the algorithmic treatment and pre-processing of data, which includes coding, dispersion, replication, de-duplication and encryption. A middle layer offers an interface to applications, e.g. through a service interface or a virtual file system, to let data in to and out of the lowest layer. Higher layers offer storage service selection, attachment and configuration as well as user and permission management. Such multi-layer integration systems for cloud storage services are usually called storage controllers or integrators. We will first present a number of file system-based cloud-of-clouds $(1 : n)$ prototypes which appear to be the least common denominator among all types and are typically a superset of all service-specific $(1 : 1)$ unification interfaces like DeltaCloud or jClouds. Afterwards, we extend the presentation to promising libraries for data treatment which may influence future storage controllers and hence motivate the need for systematic testing and comparison.

## 2.1   Controllers, Integrators, Gateways and Filesystems

NubiSave [21] is an Optimal Cloud Storage Controller which takes storage service properties into account to achieve an optimal data distribution through replication and dispersion. It offers a FUSE file system interface and hence is a valid candidate for file-based testing on all operating systems supported by FUSE, such as Linux, BSD and Mac OS X. A strong characteristic of NubiSave concerning testing is the hot-plugging of storage service providers by means of writing configuration files into a special directory. ChironFS[1] is a RAIFS controller, essentially functioning like a RAID controller on a file system level. Compared to NubiSave, it only replicates files and doesn't allow for more fine-grained configuration. The dispersing Secure Cloud Storage Integrator for Enterprises (SecC-SIE) [18] focuses on Intranet integration and offers a CIFS interface to network clients. Most operating systems can natively import CIFS drives as local directories. In a similar way, the Least Authority File System (Tahoe-LAFS) operates as a gateway with HTTP(S) and (S)FTP interfaces which can be mapped to a local directory [27]. Hence, SecCSIE and Tahoe-LAFS are also valid candidates for file system-based testing. One design difference between them is that SecCSIE integrates arbitrary storage services whereas the Tahoe-LAFS gateway assumes Tahoe-LAFS storage backends. This difference is well hidden behind a unifying file system interface. RACS, a Redundant Array of Cloud Storage proxy [1], exposes an S3 bucket interface for which FUSE file system translators exist. FUSE pass-through adapters typically add an overhead of about 8-15% in the worst case so it remains feasible to test RACS. The Iris cloud file system, in contrast, already offers a remote file system natively [22]. More FUSE modules exist for individual online and cloud storage services, e.g. CloudFusion[2] for DropBox and SugarSync, S3QL for Amazon S3, Google Storage and OpenStack Swift, FuseDav for WebDAV and CurlFtpFs for FTP. In general, single-service integration offers less parametrisation space compared to multi-service integration, but otherwise the former is a subset of the latter and hence the same test methods are applicable.

Additional storage integration tools exist without an appropriate data management interface which can be accessed automatically as part of a SIT or SBIT

---

[1] ChironFS: http://www.furquim.org/chironfs/index.en.html
[2] CloudFusion: https://github.com/joe42/CloudFusion

test execution. Trust Store [12], for instance, requires the drag and drop interaction with a GUI to initiate the storage and retrieval of files. Such tools are out of scope for peaCS and require GUI testing frameworks like Sikuli. Similarly, Dependable Sky [4] only offers a library interface, the commercial product Trusted Safe a Windows plugin interface and another unnamed platform [17] a web interface which all require additional test agents with user interface interaction intelligence. For Cloud Shredder [25], the interface is not specified. A survey on distributed cloud storage integration compares the security characteristics which are hard to measure and hard to assess in an automated way [20]. Characteristics determined in such a manual process complement the expected results of automated test frameworks. Therefore, our work aims at a subset of storage controllers (those with a file system interface) and a subset of metrics (which can be measured or calculated).

## 2.2   Data Pre-processing Libraries

The transformation and distribution of files and file parts is often captured in specific libraries which are used by some of the systems presented in the previous paragraph. A well-known dispersion and secret sharing library is Jerasure in version 1.2 and 2.0 [14]. It performs erasure coding with optional encryption of the resulting file fragments. Each fragment is then distributed to a storage service by the surrounding controller. Erasure codes and implementations thereof are still subject to research, for instance, to adapt them to efficient SIMD processor instructions and hard-wired cryptographic routines or to speed up the recovery process with regenerating codes. Therefore, a test framework is useful to track the progress of integration systems over time even when only internal parts like a pre-processing library change.

Alternative dispersion libraries with comparable functionality are JigDFS, Schifra, dsNet, Crypto++, IDA-Java, the Tahoe-LAFS library ZFec, JSharing, CORE and StorageCORE. Varying run-time characteristics result from design and implementation differences between them, last but not least due to different programming languages – C/C++, Java, Python, Haskell and VHDL for the mentioned libraries. Further pre-processing, which includes compression, encryption, de-duplication, steganography and versioning, is realised either by FUSE modules or by additional libraries. For some algorithms, like AONT-RS secret sharing or Chinese remainders splitting, no publicly available implementations exist. An overview about algorithms and emerging techniques for networked distributed storage systems is given in [8].

It is important to understand that the performance and efficiency of distributed storage depends not only on the algorithms and implementations, but also heavily on configurable parameters such as redundancy, degree of parallelism, distribution scheduling, streaming support and file system buffers. For cloud storage service bundles, service selection preferences influence the results further. For arbitrary combinations of these parameters, a test framework must support multi-dimensional result sets. The most common parameters are $k$ and

$m$, referring to the number of significant and redundant storage targets, and $w$ as the coding word size.

# 3    The peaCS Test Framework

We introduce the test framework *peaCS*, which stands for Performance and Efficiency Analysis for Cloud Storage, in order to allow for systematic testing, analysis and comparison of file-based cloud storage controllers and integrators. The strength of peaCS is the coordinated, controlled and repeatable test of variegated storage service combinations by instrumenting a target controller as the subject of testing.

## 3.1    peaCS Architecture

Driven by the desired features, the design of peaCS mandates flexibility concerning the definition of test executions, extensibility of test cases and reproducibility of test results. The resulting test suite architecture is shown in Fig. 2. The main application of peaCS is implemented as a shell script. It can be extended by plugins (realised as include scripts) which perform the controller configuration and subsequently the actual test runs. The behaviour of peaCS is driven by both a configuration file and overriding command-line switches and interactive commands. Test results can be compared against previously measured and determined gold standards. All output, including temporary scratch files, informative logs, numerical results and visualisations derived from them are stored in appropriately versioned locations. On the implementation level, Git, Gnuplot and various measurement tools like Iozone are used in this workflow.

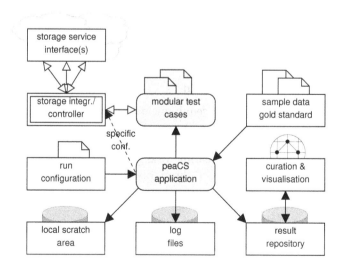

**Fig. 2.** Architecture of peaCS for coordinated storage integration testing

Within peaCS, variability is achieved by combining server-side parameters such as storage service selection and configuration with client-side parameters such as weights, redundancy and scheduling methods. Storage services and datasets can be simulated through mass-generated local directories and files, but can also be picked up from an existing configuration. Remote storage services can be integrated semi-automatically by supplying a file with a list of accounts, typically consisting of user names and passwords or access keys.

The variability is captured in the modular run configuration. Each step of the test sequence can be switched on and off. Adapter scripts translate each portable configuration directive into a controller-specific one. Listing 1.1 conveys the structure of the peaCS configuration file with portions of the key-value parameter pairs.

**Listing 1.1.** Configuration file sections of peacs.conf

```
[global]
mntpoint = /media/cloud
syslog = /var/log/peacs.log
[samplefiles]
[sampledirectories]
[samplewebdavs]
[redundancytest]
startbyredundancy = 1
[iozonetest]
[availabilitytest]
strategy = AllUseInParallel
[directorytest]
[plot]
```

The goal of peaCS is to determine the performance and the resource utilisation efficiency of storage integration combinations. Additionally, deterministic functional and calculable tests are offered to build regression detection series. These metrics will be discussed in the following three paragraphs before completing the prototype presentation with an example of a test run.

### 3.2  Performance Determination

In times of increasing big data requirements [5], high performance for data storage, retrieval, search and general processing becomes paramount. Storage controllers should not cause performance penalties through compute-intensive dispersion, encryption or de-duplication tasks, and yet offer these powerful mechanisms with high quality. In peaCS, throughput and performance are measured through Iozone.

### 3.3  Efficiency Determination

Efficiency and high utilisation of minimal resources are two largely overlapping primary goals in utility and cloud computing. This applies both to energy efficiency [2] and to hardware resource allocation scheduling [11] in addition to efficient time utilisation through high performance. Computational resource consumption, i.e. processor, main memory, disk and network adapter, is measured through Smem, Iozone and further tools in peaCS.

### 3.4  Functional Testing and Calculations

Functional tests verify the capabilities of the file system interface by invoking all possible functions on it. These functions encompass directory, file and metadata management. As an example, maximum file name lengths and directory nesting limits can be found out this way. Calculations are performed to determine availability values for certain storage service combinations and other repeatable per-configuration results. Higher-level calculations combine measured and calculated values. For example, peaCS can determine the efficiency of required storage capacity per redundancy level.

### 3.5  Test Run Examples

peaCS allows for multi-dimensional combinatorial variations which result in diagrams with an additional dimension for the calculated or measured target metric, for instance, per-thread performance or RAM utilisation efficiency. The following test results were achieved with the NubiSave cloud storage controller.

Fig. 3 gives an example of a two-dimensional variation. It has been created by 1000 repeated availability calculation calls for each of the two main file part distribution strategies. The results are independent of the hardware and must be reproducible on any machine. In contrast, measured metrics differ depending on the experimentation system and must at least be normalised before a comparison.

Fig. 4 represents a different visualisation of the availability calculation. peaCS generates multiple table and plotting instruction files by default. This increases the chance to spot anomalies and interesting artefacts.

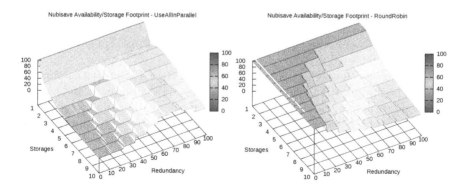

**Fig. 3.** Comparison of the ratio of file availability and storage requirements, depending on both redundancy and number of storage targets, for both parallel (left) and round-robin (right) scheduling

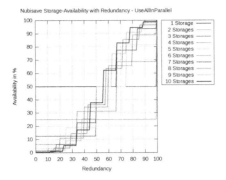

**Fig. 4.** Alternative visualisation of the parallel availability calculation results

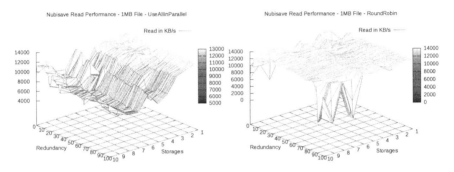

**Fig. 5.** Comparison of the read performance for both parallel (left) and round-robin (right) scheduling

Fig. 5 is an example of a measured result. For both strategies, the read performance for a 1 MB file is determined. Given that the experiment used only one hard disk (notebook HDD) to simulate up to 10 storage providers, it comes at no surprise that the performance suffers when the file needs to be assembled from independently read file parts (fragments) under the UseAllInParallel strategy, compared to a single large read with nearly constant performance under the RoundRobin strategy.

Fig. 6 contrasts the performance in Fig. 5 with the CPU utilisation for read requests. The optimisation goal is to minimise the CPU utilisation and to maximise the performance. However, the optimum resides within the corner of only one storage service with no redundancy, which is not a desired configuration for practical use due to the lack of safety against unavailability and security against confidentiality.

After performing the measurements, the results of peaCS can be analysed and compared between implementations and parametrisations to derive optimisation targets. Fig. 7 shows an example of a comparison between the ChironFS replication file system and NubiSave with two strategies at 100% redundancy. For all three configurations, a video file of 87 MB was copied 100 times to the integration

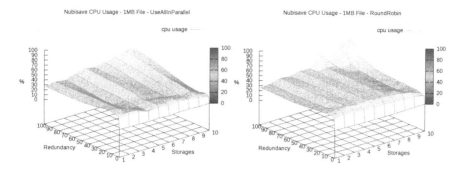

**Fig. 6.** Comparison of the CPU utilisation for both parallel (left) and round-robin (right) scheduling

folder which replicated the file to a number of simulated cloud storage folders, each of which was located on the same disk. The experiments were conducted on a notebook with Intel Core i7 M620 CPU (4 cores) and a 320 GB Hitachi SATA II disk (5400 RPM, 8 MB cache) running Debian 7.0 for AMD64. The results clearly show an overall optimisation potential for NubiSave, which can be attributed due to its implementation being Java while ChironFS is written in C++, and a particular optimisation potential for the case of 5 or more storages, depending on the number of cores.

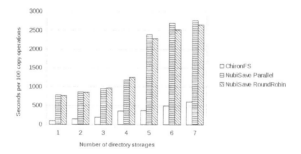

**Fig. 7.** Comparison between ChironFS and NubiSave $n$-fold replication performance for $1 \leq n \leq 7$

## 4   Related Research

Those who define analysis and comparison frameworks should not forget to analyse and compare the framework itself. There are already both experimental and simulation approaches to compare cloud services and file systems, but thus far none to evaluate complementary client-side integration solutions with filesystem or alternative interfaces.

CloudSim [6] uses simulation supports the modelling of distributed cloud environments and simulated experiments inside them. Although it is extensible, it currently does not cover the integration of services on the client. C-Meter [24], a tool developed from its Grenchmark ancestry, lets the user define artificial workloads which are then executed in the cloud. It is not suitable for storage service bundle integration testing due to its focus on compute clouds. Central storage and filesystem performance comparison, on the other hand, is a well established activity, both for native [23] and for user-space filesystems [15]. Coordinated measurements of multiple file systems for distributed cloud storage service integration are however not covered by these approaches and require the flexible selection and configuration approach taken in peaCS. Some researchers have proposed proof-of-retrievability (PoR) techniques for cloud storage services [19]. These are currently not covered by peaCS but may be added as probes in the future so that the tool will gain usefulness for security-related non-functional properties.

Industrial practice considers cloud storage service testing and certification a necessity[3]. However, as opposed to related industrial domains such as high-performance computing with its omnipresent Linpack benchmark, there is no standard benchmark tool available for storage services and their integration yet. Our intention is that tools like peaCS contribute to the development of a standard way of assessing the client-side combination of cloud storage services.

## 5   Conclusion

The increasing availability of unified filesystem-based access to dedicated cloud storage providers or mixed local and cloud storage areas calls for a systematic testing tool. We have motivated the need for such a tool for both users (comparison) and developers (regression testing), gathered use cases through an analysis of integration interfaces, and designed the peaCS framework accordingly. Clearly, peaCS is work in progress and warrants large-scale experiments with deduced comparative results. We intend to perform this work in the near future through a grant which is publicly described at a Lab website[4]. Its success depends on the availability of storage integration interfaces to the research community.

**Acknowledgements.** This work has received funding under project number 080949277 by means of the European Regional Development Fund (ERDF), the European Social Fund (ESF) and the German Free State of Saxony.

## References

1. Abu-Libdeh, H., Princehouse, L., Weatherspoon, H.: RACS: A Case for Cloud Storage Diversity. In: 1st ACM Symposium on Cloud Computing (SoCC), Indianapolis, Indiana, USA, pp. 229–240 (June 2010)

---

[3] Industrial storage service testing: `http://www.nasuni.com/blog/15-testing_the_cloud_storage_providers_part_1-api`

[4] NubiSave Lab: `http://lab.nubisave.org/`

2. Beloglazov, A., Buyya, R.: Energy Efficient Resource Management in Virtualized Cloud Data Centers. In: Proceedings of the 2010 10th IEEE/ACM International Conference on Cluster, Cloud and Grid Computing (CCGrid), Melbourne, Australia, pp. 826–831 (May 2010)
3. Bertolino, A., Polini, A.: SOA Test Governance: Enabling Service Integration Testing across Organization and Technology Borders. In: International Conference on Software Testing, Verification and Validation Workshops (ICSTW), Denver, Colorado, USA, pp. 277–286 (April 2009)
4. Bessani, A., Correia, M., Quaresma, B., André, F., Sousa, P.: DEPSKY: Dependable and Secure Storage in a Cloud-of-Clouds. In: Proceedings of EuroSys, Salzburg, Austria (2011)
5. Boyd, D., Crawford, K.: Six Provocations for Big Data. In: Decade, A. (ed.) A Decade in Internet Time: Symposium on the Dynamics of the Internet and Society, Oxford Internet Institute (September 2011)
6. Calheiros, R.N., Ranjan, R., Rose, C.A.F.D., Buyya, R.: CloudSim: A Novel Framework for Modeling and Simulation of Cloud Computing Infrastructures and Services. Tech. Rep. GRIDS-TR-2009-1, Grid Computing and Distributed Systems Laboratory, The University of Melbourne, Australia (March 2009)
7. Canfora, G., Penta, M.D.: Testing Services and Service-Centric Systems: Challenges and Opportunities. IT Professional 8(2), 10–17 (2006)
8. Datta, A., Oggier, F.: An Overview of Codes Tailor-made for Better Repairability in Networked Distributed Storage Systems. ACM SIGACT News Distributed Computing Column (March 2013)
9. Khan, O., Burns, R., Plank, J., Pierce, W., Huang, C.: Rethinking Erasure Codes for Cloud File Systems: Minimizing I/O for Recovery and Degraded Reads. In: 10th USENIX Conference on File and Storage Technologies (FAST), San Jose, California, USA (February 2012)
10. Livenson, I., Laure, E.: Towards Transparent Integration of Heterogeneous Cloud Storage Platforms. In: Proceedings of the Fourth International Workshop on Data-Intensive Distributed Computing (DIDC), San Jose, California, USA, pp. 27–34 (June 2011)
11. Meng, X., Isci, C., Kephart, J., Zhang, L., Bouillet, E., Pendarakis, D.: Efficient Resource Provisioning in Compute Clouds via VM Multiplexing. In: Proceedings of the 7th IEEE/ACM International Conference on Autonomic Computing (ICAC), Washington, DC, USA, pp. 11–20 (June 2010)
12. Nepal, S., Friedrich, C., Henry, L., Chen, S.: A Secure Storage Service in the Hybrid Cloud. In: Fourth IEEE/ACM International Conference on Utility and Cloud Computing (UCC), Melbourne, Australia, pp. 334–335 (December 2011)
13. Noikajana, S., Suwannasart, T.: An Improved Test Case Generation Method for Web Service Testing from WSDL-S and OCL with Pair-Wise Testing Technique. In: 33rd Annual IEEE International Computer Software and Applications Conference (COMPSAC), Seattle, Washington, USA, pp. 115–123 (July 2009)
14. Plank, J.S., Simmerman, S., Schuman, C.D.: Jerasure: A Library in C/C++ Facilitating Erasure Coding for Storage Applications. Tech. Rep. UT-CS-08-627, University of Tennessee, Knoxville, Tennessee, USA (August 2008)
15. Rajgarhia, A., Gehani, A.: Performance and Extension of User Space File Systems, Sierre, Switzerland (March 2010)
16. Reiff-Marganiec, S., Yu, H.Q., Tilly, M.: Service Selection Based on Non-functional Properties. In: Di Nitto, E., Ripeanu, M. (eds.) ICSOC 2007. LNCS, vol. 4907, pp. 128–138. Springer, Heidelberg (2009)

17. Schnjakin, M., Meinel, C.: Plattform zur Bereitstellung sicherer und hochverfüg-barer Speicherressourcen in der Cloud. In: Sicher in die Digitale Welt von Morgen – 12. Dt. IT-Sicherheitskongress des BSI. SecuMedia Verlag, Bonn (May 2011)
18. Seiger, R., Groß, S., Schill, A.: SecCSIE: A Secure Cloud Storage Integrator for Enterprises. In: 13th IEEE Conference on Commerce and Enterprise Computing, Workshop on Clouds for Enterprises, Luxembourg, pp. 252–255 (September 2011)
19. Shacham, H., Waters, B.: Compact Proofs of Retrievability. In: Pieprzyk, J. (ed.) ASIACRYPT 2008. LNCS, vol. 5350, pp. 90–107. Springer, Heidelberg (2008)
20. Slamanig, D., Hanser, C.: On cloud storage and the cloud of clouds approach. In: The 7th International Conference for Internet Technology and Secured Transactions (ICITST), London, United Kingdom, pp. 649–655 (December 2012)
21. Spillner, J., Müller, J., Schill, A.: Creating Optimal Cloud Storage Systems. Future Generation Computer Systems 29(4), 1062–1072 (June 2013), doi:http://dx.doi.org/10.1016/j.future.2012.06.004
22. Stefanov, E., van Dijk, M., Oprea, A., Juels, A.: Iris: A Scalable Cloud File System with Efficient Integrity Checks. In: 28th Annual Computer Security Applications Conference (ACSAC), Orlando, Florida, pp. 1–33 (December 2012)
23. Vanninen, M., Wang, J.Z.: On Benchmarking Popular File Systems. Clemson University Study (2009)
24. Yigitbasi, N., Iosup, A., Epema, D., Ostermann, S.: C-Meter: A Framework for Performance Analysis of Computing Clouds. In: 9th IEEE/ACM International Symposium on Cluster Computing and the Grid (CCGRID), Shanghai, China, pp. 472–477 (May 2009)
25. Zhang, N., Jing, J., Liu, P.: Removing the Laptop On-Road Data Disclosure Threat in the Cloud Computing Era. In: Proceedings of the 6th International Conference on Frontier of Computer Science and Technology (FCST). IEEE Digital Library (November 2011)
26. Zhao, G., Rong, C., Li, J., Zhang, F., Tang, Y.: Trusted Data Sharing over Untrusted Cloud Storage Providers. In: IEEE Second International Conference on Cloud Computing Technology and Science (CloudCom), Indianapolis, Indiana, USA, pp. 97–103 (December 2010)
27. Zooko, W.B., Hopwood, D., Secor, P., Deppierraz, F., McDonald, P., Marti, F., Tooley, M., Carstensen, K.: Tahoe-LAFS: The Least Authority File System. Open source project (2013), http://tahoe-lafs.org/

# Delegation for On-boarding Federation Across Storage Clouds

Elliot K. Kolodner[1], Alexandra Shulman-Peleg[1], Gil Vernik[1],
Ciro Formisano[2], and Massimo Villari[3]

[1] IBM Haifa Research Lab, Israel
[2] Engineering Ingegneria Informatica SPA, Italy
[3] Dept. of DICIEMA, University of Messina, Italy
`ciro.formisano@eng.it`, {`kolodner,shulmana,gilv`}`@il.ibm.com`,
`mvillari@unime.it` `http://www.visioncloud.eu`

**Abstract.** On-boarding federation allows an enterprise to efficiently migrate its data from one storage cloud provider to another (e.g., for business or legal reasons), while providing continuous access and a unified view over the data during the migration. On-boarding is provided through a federation layer on the new destination cloud providing delegation for accessing object on the old source cloud. In this paper we describe a delegation architecture for on-boarding where the user delegates to the on-boarding layer a subset of his/her access rights on the source and destination clouds to enable on-boarding to occur in a safe and secure way, such that the on-boarding layer has the least privilege required to carry out its work. The added value of this work is in evaluating all security implications of a delegation necessary to be taken into account during the on-boarding phase. We also show how this delegation architecture can be implemented using Security Assertion Markup Language.

**Keywords:** Storage Cloud, Federation, Delegation, SAML.

## 1 Introduction

Existing storage clouds do not provide true data mobility and do not provide adequate mechanisms for allowing efficient migration of their data across providers. Indeed in their work "Above the Clouds" Armbrust et al. [1] cite "data lock-in" as being one of the top ten obstacles for growth in Cloud Computing. In a recent paper Vernik et al. [2] present an architecture for on-boarding federation to deal with this problem. On-boarding federation allows an enterprise to efficiently migrate its data from one storage cloud provider to another (e.g., for business or legal reasons), while providing continuous access and a unified view over the data over the course of the migration. On-boarding is provided through a federation layer on the new destination cloud by setting up a relationship between its containers and the containers on the old source cloud. Once the relationship is set up, the on-boarding layer is responsible to carry out the

C. Canal and M. Villari (Eds.): ESOCC 2013, CCIS 393, pp. 59–70, 2013.

migration on behalf of the user, reading objects from the old source cloud and writing objects to the new destination cloud. This layer acts on behalf of the user and requires authorization from the user to act in his/her name with the old and new providers.

In this paper we present a detailed delegation architecture for on-boarding. In particular, when a user sets up an on-boarding relationship between a container in the new and old clouds, the user also delegates a subset of his/her access rights to the federation layer of the new cloud. This subset should include the minimum rights needed for the federation layer to on-board objects of the old container. We also show how to implement the delegation architecture using SAML.

We are currently in the process of implementing the delegation mechanism in the context of VISION Cloud [3], an EU-funded project where we are developing advanced features for cloud object stores, such as on-boarding, and use case scenarios to demonstrate the features.

The paper is organized as follows. Section 2 highlights related work on the subject of delegation. Section 3 provides background on VISION Cloud and Section 4 its approach to on-boarding federation. The main principles on Access Control and Delegation are described in Section 5, whereas Section 6 introduces two possible techniques for Delegation. Our delegation architecture and implementation using SAML is reported in Section 7. We conclude in Section 8.

## 2 Related Work

In this section we describe existing works falling into the area of *Federation of Access control* looking at *SAML for identity federation* and *Delegation technologies*.

### 2.1 Access Control in a Federation

Usually federation consists of the establishment of a trust context between parties with the purpose of benefiting of business advantages. Several pending issues concerning security and privacy still have to be addressed and it is not clear what cloud federation actually means and what the involved issues are (see [4]). Indeed, the cloud has not kept pace with the enormous volume of user identities that network administrators must manage and secure. The concept of *Identity Fabric* described in *Architecting a Cloud-Scale Identity Fabric* (see [5]), is a possible solution. The authors in [6] produced several works on the ti They range from: *Federated Identity*, to *Delegation Of Authority*, and *Levels Of Assurance*, *Attributes*, *Access Rights*, till *Authorization*. In this work, the authors described all APIs they introduced, and applied them to a real cloud middleware, the Eucalyptus S3 Service.

**SAML for Identity Federation.** Service federation over the Internet is currently a well established approach: it is supported by a mechanism for trusting identities across different domains, which is identity federation. The latest trend to federate identities over the Internet is represented by the Identity Provider/Service Provider (IdP/SP) model [7], supported by digital certificates used in Security Assertion Markup Language (SAML) [8] profiles and Shibboleth [9,10].

Although these are becoming the most popular technologies, they are designed for static environments requiring, for example, a priori policy agreements: this is a limitation in cloud environment, which is dynamic and heterogeneous and requires particular security and policy arrangements.

Interoperability in federated heterogeneous cloud environments is addressed in [11], in which the authors propose a trust model where the trust is delegated between trustworthy parties which satisfy certain constrains. Pearson at al. [12] also introduce a privacy manager in order to care for data compliance according to the laws of different jurisdictions.

Huang et al. present relevant work [13] about an Identity Federation Broker for service clouds. They addressed federation in the context of SaaS services in which SAML represents the basic protocol.

The works presented above justify the adoption of SAML in our solution, but they consider it in a different aspect which is not suitable for our aims. Here, in addition to presenting standard SAML flows, we discuss a slightly modified version allowing to simplify the on-boarding federation.

**Delegation Technologies.** Grid systems have widely used credentials and delegations leveraging the PKI technology: right now, a recent trend for managing credential and delegations in federated cloud scenarios appears to make use of X.509 certificates. An example is given in OpenStack with Keystone in PKI configuration (see [14]).

In the direction of managing identity and authorization for Community Clouds using PKI is discussed in [15]. The authors introduce an *identity broker* to bind the Web Single Sign-on to a key-based system. In particular they implemented a solution (*libabac* package) using the Attribute-based Access Control (ABAC) and the role-based trust management (RT): RT/ABAC. The *libabac* uses X.509 as a transport. RT/ABAC credentials are X.509 attribute certificates. The RT/ABAC may handle the processing of delegation chains.

A recent and detailed work on delegation is described in the paper entitled: *OAuth and ABE based Authorization in Semi-Trusted Cloud computing, [16]*. Here the authors enhanced the OAuth capabilities using the encryption in attribute-based access control system exploiting metadata. They introduced a complex model in which authentication, authorization, delegation, access trees, new tokens, time slots, user certificates are investigated.

# 3   Vision Cloud at a Glance

The VISION Cloud architecture is designed to support tens of geographically dispersed data centers where each DC may contain tens of clusters each with hundreds of storage-rich compute nodes. An object consists of data and metadata where the data can be of arbitrary size and type, and the metadata can include arbitrary key value pairs, typically describing the content of the object. Object data cannot be updated, but an entire new version of an object can be created.

In contrast, new metadata can be appended to an object and updated over time. Data objects are grouped in containers, and each data object has a unique name within a container. Containers provide context and are used for purposes of data management, isolation, and placement (i.e., containers are the minimal units of placement and can not be split across clusters.) Metadata can also be associated with containers.

The account model includes tenants and users. A tenant subscribes to cloud storage services and usually represents a company or an organization. A tenant may have many users. A user is the entity that actually uses storage services, and may refer to a person or to an application. A user belongs to one and only one tenant, although a person might own a user account in more than one tenant. Users, who are created by tenant administrators, have unique identifiers within a tenant and possess credentials allowing them to authenticate themselves to the cloud. A user may create containers and data objects in them.

## 4   On-boarding

Vernik et al. [2] introduce the concept of on-boarding federation for storage clouds to prevent the vendor lock-in. A federation layer on the new destination cloud imports data from an old source cloud without requiring any special function from the old cloud. Applications and users access their data through the new cloud immediately after the on-boarding setup, without waiting for the migration process to complete. Migrating data via on-boarding federation directly between the clouds leads to a significant savings in time and cost.

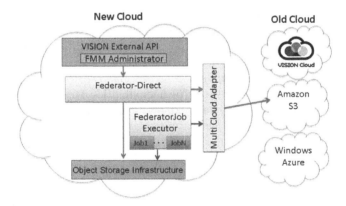

**Fig. 1.** On-boarding Architecture

Figure 1 illustrates the on-boarding architecture presented by Vernik et al. The architecture specifies three primary flows: (1) on-boarding set-up, (2) direct access, and (3) background on-boarding.

*On-boarding Set-up.* An on-boarding relationship between a container in the old cloud and a container in the new cloud is set up through the FMM (Federation and Monitoring Administrator Module). This relationship and the parameters describing it is persisted through the metadata of the container on the new cloud.

*Direct Access.* Once the relationship is set-up, all client's applications may start immediately to access the objects of the old container through the new cloud. When a client accesses an object on the new cloud that has not yet been on-boarded, the Federator-Direct module gets the object from the old cloud, puts it in the new cloud and returns it to the client. Access to the old cloud is mediated through the Multi-cloud Adapter component, which translates the access request to the proper format for the specific cloud. The authorization to access the old cloud on the user's behalf is granted by using delegation mechanisms (described in Section 7).

*Background On-boarding.* The FederatorJobExecutor creates background jobs on the the new cloud that fetch objects from the container in the old cloud and copy them to the container in the new cloud. These jobs run when the resource utilization (e.g., CPU and network) in the new cloud is low so that they do not interfere with the normal operation of the cloud. These jobs also need authorization from the user to access the old cloud and depending on the architecture may also need authorization the write the objects on the new cloud.

## 5 Identity and Access Management Systems for Access Control

Tenants and users for accessing their data objects stored in the cloud need to be authenticated and authorized by the **Identity and Access Management systems (IAM)** of cloud providers through their web portals. There are two typologies of configuration with at least three total identity management architectures that are relevant for federation:

- **One IAM**, that could be *shared* or *external*.
- **Two IAMs**, defining two administrative domains.

For the on-boarding procedure described in Section 4 in both cases delegation is needed, but in the second, more complex case, also the issues caused by inter-domain accesses must be addressed.

Before to discuss how to solve the problem, we analyze the concept of delegation (see Sec. 5.1) taking into account a comparison of current solutions aimed at web environments (see Sec. 6).

## 5.1   Concept of Delegation

The Delegation is the possibility for an user (U1) to delegate a subset of his/her access privileges to another user or process (U2). U1 is called *delegator* while U2 is the *delegate*. Both users keep their own identities, but U2 obtains a document signed by U1 and stating that U2 is authorized to act on behalf of U1 for a reduced set of operations. This means that U2 doesn't obtain the identity of U1: he/she doesn't impersonate U1, but is explicitly authorized to perform several actions on behalf of U1. Let's consider, as an example, the use case of a human context, in which a person going to a public office needs to get a certificate on behalf of another person. For specific certificates this operation is possible as long as the *delegate* shows his/her own personal *ID card* and the delegation document (called a Power of Attorney) signed by the *delegator* and a copy of the delegator *ID Card*. In computer science the context is identical, in particular:

- The *delegator* gives to the *delegate* an electronic document digitally signed, containing the details of the delegation (permitted operations, possibility to have more level of delegation etc).
- The *delegate* provides his/her credentials and the document mentioned above, to formalize delegation and granting the rights for accessing the resource.

## 5.2   Difference between Web Single Sign On (SSO) and Web Delegation

Identity Federation avoids the necessity to have multiple accounts to access different administrative domains. SSO is a way in which it is possible to log in once and access several services: when these services refer to different IMSs for AuthN and AuthZ, SSO is built on an Identity Federation. We begin this section describing the Identity Federation/SSO system, in order to clarify its difference with Web Delegation. Figure 2 shows all parts composing a typical SSO system. The picture shows a *Relying Party* (*RP*), an *IAM* (Identity Provider or OpenID

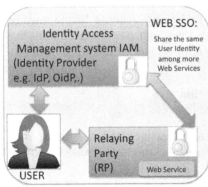

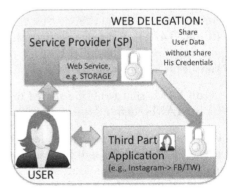

**Fig. 2.** An example of Web Singe Sign On procedure

**Fig. 3.** An example of Web Delegation procedure

Provider - *IdP*, *OIdP*), and the *end-user*. End-user has an identity registered on IAM and needs to access a certain web resource on RP:

1. he is redirected to IAM for the authentication (the authentication **must** be performed on the home domain)
2. if the authentication has succeeded, he/she is redirected to RP for obtaining the requested resource

Several implementations of Identity Federation/SSO are based on SAML protocol [8] or OpenID protocol [17]; CAS protocol [18] is an example of simple SSO not associated with Identity Federation.

The Web Delegation procedure is conceptually different: it is the mechanism employed, for example, when client applications want to use the functionalities provided by Social Networks (such as Facebook or GooglePlus) on behalf of end users. The *end-user* who decides to exploit these applications using these functionalities, at first authorizes the client applications to use the functionalities on his/her behalf, then the applications will continue to work without any user supervision. In particular the user obtains a *special* token granting temporary limited access and allowing partial operations on behalf of the user. Figure 3 depicts all parts composing a typical Web Delegation system. In the Figure the SP can be assimilated to the Social Network, whereas the Third Part Application is equivalent to client applications (i.e. Instagram).

To summarize:

– In the Web SSO it is necessary to *Share the same User Identity* among more Web Services.
– In the Web Delegation it is necessary to *Share User Data* (or web resources) without share his/her credentials.

Web delegation has been widely used in multiple applications implemented by with well know protocols like OAuth [16]. However, when considering the setups with delegation across two clouds these protocols are insufficient since they assume an existence of an IAM server shared between the clouds. Another way to setup the Delegation is using a modified version of SAML protocol. We remark that SAML was born for solving the SSO issues, but with several new specifications is able to deal with delegation needs (SAML 2.0 Condition to Delegate [19]). The next section introduces OAuth and SAML2DEL solutions, highlighting pro and cons of each one.

## 6   A Brief Presentation of OAuth 2.0 and SAML2Del

In this section we discuss the main difference existing between SAML delegation mechanism against the OAuth 2.0. The early has been introduced by OASIS consortium following the standardization of XML docs (i.e. SAML[8], XACML [20]), where OAuth 2.0, specializes the existing features of OAuth 1.0.

OAuth 2.0 Authorization Framework, defined by the IETF standard standard board, is described in the RFC 6749 (for further details see the reference [21]).

According to Figure 4, we can see the following actors: *Client*, *Resource Owner*, and *Authorization Server*. **Resource Server** is the application that needs accessing protected resources on the user behalf. **Resource Owner** is the user owning the protected resources that the client needs to be accessed. **Authorization Server** is the server releasing access tokens to the client after the user has been authenticated and has granted access to his resources. **Resource Server** is the server managing the user protected resources. All steps characterizing the protocol are shown using the $A - F$ letters.

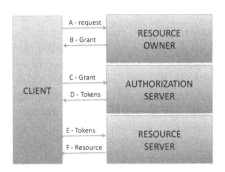  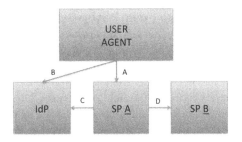

**Fig. 4.** OAuth2.0 Abstract Protocol Flow    **Fig. 5.** SAML2DEL Abstract Protocol Flow

## 6.1  SAML2Del

SAML 2.0 Condition to Delegate (SAML2Del) is described in [19]. The specification shows how to use of SAML 2.0 protocol in the case of delegation. In particular SAML2DEL describes different delegation-like scenarios, that are **Proxying, Impersonation** and **Forwarding**, and defines the **Delegation**, which *goes beyond the forwarding scenario by adding information to the assertion that explicitly identifies all the parties through which a transaction flows*. Figure 5 depicts how the delegation works in SAML. The User Agent (the Client for OAuth 2.0 model) gains the access on Service Provider $\underline{A}$ (SP $\underline{A}$), using his credentials stored in the Identity Provider (IdP). The SP $\underline{A}$ also obtains a SAML Assertion (using its credentials against IdP) hence it can access the resource on SP $\underline{B}$. The SAML Assertion of SP $\underline{A}$ is different respect to the User Agent version; it is modified. In the Figure, all steps characterizing the protocol are shown using the $A - D$ letters.

## 6.2  Comparison of SAML2Del Versus OAuth 2.0

An interesting work is reported in "OAuth 2.0 Threat Model and Security Considerations"[22] that shows what are the main threats that OAuth 2.0 can suffer. The main reason of the weakness of OAuth 2.0 is due to its evolution from OAuth 1.0 along with the adoption of incremental improvements that have exposed the system to possible flaws (i.e., ($a_1$) the effects of attackers in the communication among the parties, ($b_1$) Obtaining Client Secrets, ($c_1$) Eavesdropping Access Tokens, etc.). In reality the OAuth 2.0 protocol provides a greater degree of flexibility respect to OAuth 1.0, especially in how it can be applied and the use cases that it can address, as it was argued in [22].

SAML is a much more mature framework conceived for many security purposes, in which the exchange of XML "assertion" guarantees a high degree of security, if we consider the possibility offered by SAML to sign all communications (i.e. this avoids the threat in ($a_1$) case), with certificates and XML (see the XML Signature and XML Encryption Native Support of SAML 2.0 [23]). In the next sections we analyze the utilization of SAML for delegation, describing our adoption. In this direction is also moving the working draft of IETF in which *SAML 2.0 Profile is used for OAuth 2.0 Client Authentication and Authorization Grants* [24].

# 7   Delegation Solution for On-boarding in VISION Cloud

In this section we describe the delegation solution that we have designed for on-boarding federation as described in Section 4. We first describe the flow for the SAML-based delegation mechanism that we have chosen, and then show how we apply it for on-boarding.

We chose to implement delegation using SAML2Del (described in Section 6). The delegation document is a signed SAML assertion containing the details of the delegation, held in a specific field called Condition. To describe the delegation flow, we consider the simple case of a single IAM system and two users, U1 and U2. Both users must be registered on the IAM and their credentials must be known to the IAM. A user could also be a process or an infrastructure can also be registered as a trusted user, (e.g., through a certificate that is stored in the trust-store of the IAM).

The flow is as follows: (1) U1 logs into the IAM using her credentials and asks to generate a signed delegation assertion stating that U2 is authorized to perform, for example, GET operations on behalf of U1 for 1 day. (2) U1 provides the assertion to U2. (3) U2 logs into the IAM using her credentials, provides the assertion and is authorized to perform GET operations for the entire day.

Figure 6 shows the on-boarding delegation flow. It shows two VISION Clouds, that is the New Cloud and the Old Cloud. Each has its own IAM incorporating an Identity Provider (IdP) and a Service Provider (SP). The New Cloud also includes a Federator component, representing both the Federator-Direct and the Background-Federator (see Section 4).

The Federator has an identity on both clouds. In particular, let $F@OLD_{IAM}$, denote the federator identity (F) in the IAM of the Old Cloud ($OLD_{IAM}$) and let $F@NEW_{IAM}$ denote its identity (F) in the IAM of the New Cloud ($NEW_{IAM}$). The user (U) that requests the on-boarding also has an identity on each cloud, in particular, $U@OLD_{IAM}$ (in the Old Cloud) and $U@NEW_{IAM}$ (on the New Cloud). All the identities must be registered on their own IAM, asso-

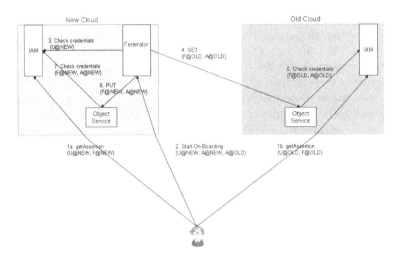

**Fig. 6.** Delegation Flow for On-boarding in VISION Cloud

ciated with suitable credentials (e.g. username/password) where the credentials of $F@OLD_{IAM}$ and $F@NEW_{IAM}$ should be securely stored.

The delegation flow is modeled using two delegations, in particular: (1) $U@OLD_{IAM}$ delegates $F@OLD_{IAM}$ to GET her objects from her container on Old Cloud; and (2) $U@NEW_{IAM}$ delegates $F@NEW_{IAM}$ to PUT objects on her container in New Cloud.

Now we can describe the delegation flow for on-boarding.

1. The user performs the login in both clouds obtaining delegation assertion for both.
   - The user gets the delegation assertion $(A@NEW_{IAM})$, providing $U@NEW_{IAM}$ username/password and $F@NEW_{IAM}$ userid
   - The user gets the delegation assertion $(A@OLD_{IAM})$, providing $U@OLD_{IAM}$ username/password and $F@OLD_{IAM}$ userid
2. The user starts the federation process. Since the Federator is part of New Cloud, the parameters needed are the following: (1) $U@NEW_{IAM}$ username/password for being authorized to access as the Federator; (2) $A@NEW_{IAM}$: the assertion ID delegating $F@NEW_{IAM}$ to ask for PUT operations on behalf of $U@NEW_{IAM}$; (3) $A@OLD_{IAM}$: the assertion ID delegating $F@OLD_{IAM}$ to ask for GET operations on behalf of $U@OLD_{IAM}$.
3. The Federator validates with IAM the credentials of $U@NEW_{IAM}$ (who starts the process).
4. The Federator performs a GET operation to the Old Cloud using $F@OLD_{IAM}$ credentials as delegate of $U@OLD_{IAM}$.
5. The Object Service checks the credentials and the delegation with the IAM of the Old Cloud.
6. The Federator PUTs the retrieved object to the New Cloud using $F@NEW_{IAM}$ credentials as Delegate of $U@NEW_{IAM}$.

7. The Object Service checks the credentials and the delegation with the IAM of the New Cloud.

For the integration of the system in VISION Cloud a generic SAML enabled IdP has to be deployed and integrated with the IAM of the tenant. The IdP is compliant with SAML 2.0 condition to delegate standard, in particular Shibboleth IdP is integrated with a plug in. The generic case of web browser login can be used also in this case and it is integrated with the specific use case to be taken into account. The interface between the User and the Federator is not an issue, from the point of view of Delegation, but it is important that username/password and delegation assertion ids can be passed as parameters. The Federator has to ask for GET and PUT operations using the parameters described previously.

## 8    Conclusions and Future Work

The added value of this paper is in considering all security implications in using the delegation technique for the on-boarding procedure. We also show how this delegation architecture can be implemented using SAML 2.0 Condition to Delegate extension. We are currently implementing the solution as part of our work on VISION cloud: in the future we will evaluate the impact of it on the whole architecture, analyzing its complexity and performance.

**Acknowledgments.** The research leading to the results presented in this paper has received funding from the European Union's Seventh Framework Programme (FP7 2007-2013) Project VISION-Cloud under grant agreement number 217019.

## References

1. Armbrust, M., Fox, A., Griffith, R., Joseph, A.D., Katz, R.H., Konwinski, A., Lee, G., Patterson, D.A., Rabkin, A., Zaharia, M.: Above the Clouds: A Berkeley View of Cloud Computing. Technical Report UCB/EECS-2009-28, EECS Department, University of California, Berkeley (February 2009)
2. Vernik, G., Shulman-Peleg, A., Dippl, S., Formisano, C., Jaeger, M., Kolodner, E., Villari, M.: Data on-boarding in federated storage clouds. In: IEEE CLOUD 2013 IEEE 6th International Conference on Cloud Computing, Santa Clara Marriott, CA, USA (Center of Silicon Valley), June 27-July 2 (2013)
3. Kolodner, E.K., Tal, S., Kyriazis, D., Naor, D., Allalouf, M., Bonelli, L., Brand, P., Eckert, A., Elmroth, E., Gogouvitis, S.V., Harnik, D., Hernández, F., Jaeger, M.C., Lakew, E.B., Lopez, J.M., Lorenz, M., Messina, A., Shulman-Peleg, A., Talyansky, R., Voulodimos, A., Wolfsthal, Y.: A cloud environment for data-intensive storage services. In: CloudCom, pp. 357–366 (2011)
4. Leavitt, N.: Is cloud computing really ready for prime time? Computer, 15–20 (January 2009)
5. Olden, E.: Architecting a cloud-scale identity fabric. Computer 44(3), 52–59 (2011)
6. Chadwick, D.W., Casenove, M.: Security apis for my private cloud - granting access to anyone, from anywhere at any time. In: Proceedings of the 2011 IEEE Third International Conference on Cloud Computing Technology and Science, CLOUD-COM 2011, pp. 792–798. IEEE Computer Society, Washington, DC (2011)

7. Liberty: An alliance project (2013), `http://projectliberty.org`
8. SAML-OASIS: V2.0 technical (January 2013),
   `http://www.oasis-open.org/specs/index.php`
9. Shibboleth: System standards (January 2012),
   `http://shibboleth.internet2.edu/`
10. Villari, M., Tusa, F., Celesti, A., Puliafito, A.: How to federate vision clouds through saml/shibboleth authentication. In: De Paoli, F., Pimentel, E., Zavattaro, G. (eds.) ESOCC 2012. LNCS, vol. 7592, pp. 259–274. Springer, Heidelberg (2012)
11. Li, W., Ping, L.: Trust model to enhance security and interoperability of cloud environment. In: Jaatun, M.G., Zhao, G., Rong, C. (eds.) Cloud Computing. LNCS, vol. 5931, pp. 69–79. Springer, Heidelberg (2009)
12. Pearson, S., Shen, Y., Mowbray, M.: A privacy manager for cloud computing. In: Jaatun, M.G., Zhao, G., Rong, C. (eds.) Cloud Computing. LNCS, vol. 5931, pp. 90–106. Springer, Heidelberg (2009)
13. Huang, H.Y., Wang, B., Liu, X.X., Xu, J.M.: Identity federation broker for service cloud. In: 2010 International Conference on Service Sciences (ICSS), pp. 115–120 (May 2010)
14. KEYSTONE: Welcome to keystone, the openstack identity service (2013), `http://docs.openstack.org/developer/keystone`
15. Chase, J., Jaipuria, P.: Managing identity and authorization for community clouds. Technical report, Department of Computer Science, Duke University, Technical Report CS-2012-08 (2012)
16. Tassanaviboon, A., Gong, G.: Oauth and abe based authorization in semi-trusted cloud computing: aauth. In: Proceedings of the Second International Workshop on Data Intensive Computing in the Clouds, DataCloud-SC 2011, pp. 41–50. ACM, New York (2011)
17. Recordon, D., Reed, D.: Openid 2.0: a platform for user-centric identity management. In: Proceedings of the Second ACM Workshop on Digital Identity Management, pp. 11–16. ACM, New York (2006)
18. CAS: Central authentication service (June 2013), `http://www.jasig.org/cas`
19. SAML-DEL: V2.0 condition for delegation (2013), `http://docs.oasis-open.org/security/saml/saml/Post2.0/sstc-saml-delegation-cs-01.pdf`
20. XACML: Cross-enterprise security and privacy authorization (xspa) profile of xacmlv2.0 for healthcare version 1.0, `http://www.oasis-open.org/committees/document.php?document_id=34164&wg_abbrev=xacml`
21. Hardt, D.: The OAuth 2.0 Authorization Framework. RFC 6749 (Proposed Standard) (October 2012)
22. Lodderstedt, T., McGloin, M., Hunt, P.: OAuth 2.0 Threat Model and Security Considerations. RFC 6819 (Informational) (January 2013)
23. SAML-ENHANC: 2.0 enhancements (2007),
    `http://saml.xml.org/saml-2-0-enhancements`
24. SAML-OAUTH: Saml 2.0 profile for oauth 2.0 client authentication and authorization grants", note=" (2013),
    `http://datatracker.ietf.org/doc/draft-ietf-oauth-saml2-bearer`

# Availability Assessment of a Vision Cloud Storage Cluster*

Dario Bruneo[1], Francesco Longo[1], David Hadas[2], and Hillel Kolodner[2]

[1] Dipartimento di Ingegneria DICIEAMA,
Università degli Studi di Messina
Messina, Italy
{dbruneo,flongo}@unime.it
[2] IBM Research Labs Haifa
Haifa, Israel
{kolodner,davidh}@il.ibm.com

**Abstract.** VISION Cloud is a European Commission funded project, whose aim is to design and propose a new architecture for a scalable and flexible cloud environment. The VISION Cloud reference architecture considers a single cloud as composed by multiple distributed data centers each of which can be composed by a great number of storage clusters. On top of the storage rich nodes forming each cluster, a distributed file system is built. In this paper, we provide an stochastic reward net model for a storage cluster in the context of the storage cloud environment proposed by the VISION Cloud project. The proposed model represents a first step in the direction of obtaining a quantification of the availability level reached through the use of the VISION Cloud proposed architecture from a user perspective.

## 1 Introduction

Cloud computing allows to dramatically reduce the cost of service provisioning by providing IT assets as commodities and on-demand usage patterns. Resource provisioning is efficiently adapted to the dynamic user demands through virtualization of hardware, rapid service provisioning, scalability, elasticity, accounting granularity and cost allocation models. However, the rich digital environment we are experiencing nowadays poses new requirements and challenges mainly related to the explosion of personal and organizational digital data. In fact, in the emerging era of the Future Internet and the Internet of Things, the explosion of raw data and the dependence on data services will surely be amplified due to the strong proliferation of data-intensive services and the digital convergence of telecommunications, media, and ICT.

In the last years, several research trends have been investigated in the Cloud computing area, system performance and dependability [1,2], energy consumption [3], workload characterization [4] are only few examples. VISION Cloud [5]

---

* The research leading to these results has received funding from the European Communitys Seventh Framework Programme (FP7/2007-2013) under grant agreement number 257019.

C. Canal and M. Villari (Eds.): ESOCC 2013, CCIS 393, pp. 71–82, 2013.

is a European Commission Seventh Framework Programme (FP7/2006-2013) funded project, whose aim is to design and propose a new architecture for a scalable and flexible cloud environment addressing the challenge of providing data-intensive storage cloud services through raising the abstraction level of storage, enabling data mobility across providers, allowing computational and content-centric access to storage and deploying new data-oriented mechanisms for QoS and security guarantees. In such a context, QoS guarantees are not only related to performance aspects but also, even more strictly, to reliability, availability, and fault tolerance and resiliency characteristics of the provided services.

The VISION Cloud reference architecture considers a single cloud as composed by multiple distributed data centers interconnected through dedicated networks. Each data center can be composed by a large number of storage clusters each of which involves several storage rich nodes. VISION Cloud considers nodes belonging to the same cluster as a single storage resource able to store data objects and provide computational power on top of it in a transparent way. This is obtained by the use of a distributed file system installed on top of the storage cluster. In the proposed implementation of the architecture, General Parallel File System for Shared Nothing Clusters (GPFS-SNC) [6] is exploited. High level of availability and resiliency to faults are achieved by replicating data objects among different storage cluster.

Aim of this paper is to provide an analytic model for a storage cluster in the context of the storage cloud environment proposed by the VISION Cloud project. The model is based on stochastic reward nets (SRNs) [7], an extension of generalized stochastic Petri nets, that are useful in capturing the key concepts of large-scale distributed systems [8,9]. From such a model, information about the reached availability level varying the system parameters can be obtained. Parameters include structural parameters and timing parameters. Structural parameters are related to the number of nodes in the cluster, number of disks in each node, cluster file system metadata replication level, and similar information. Timing parameters involve information about the time necessary to specific events (e.g., disk or node failure) to occur or specific operations (e.g., disk or node repair, cluster file system metadata recovery) to be performed.

The proposed model represents a first step in the direction of obtaining a quantification of the availability level reached through the use of the VISION Cloud proposed architecture from a user perspective. Several works in the literature deal with performance analysis of storage Cloud infrastructure [10] while few effort has been put in the context of availability analysis [11]. In this context, the majority of the work mainly consider replica placement policies [12,13] without taking into consideration real case studies as done in our work. In fact, our model could be exploited by a VISION Cloud administrator in order to opportunely build the infrastructure accordingly to the desired availability level both from the hardware (e.g., computation, storage, network resources) and the software (e.g., replication schema, cluster file system configuration) points of view. Moreover, it could represent an useful instrument for a modeled assisted SLAs management.

The paper is organized as follows. Section 2 provides an overview about the VISION Cloud reference architecture and illustrates how GPFS-SNC is exploited within the proposed storage cloud environment. Section 3 formally describes the considered scenario while Section 4 illustrates how such a scenario is modeled through the use of SRNs. Section 5 provides some numerical results. Finally, Section 6 concludes the paper with some final remarks on the proposed approach and on possible future work.

# 2    The VISION Cloud Storage Environment

In this section, we provide an overview of the storage cloud environment proposed by the VISION Cloud project [5] focusing on the implemented physical infrastructure and on the data model. We also provide details about GPFS-SNC [6] and about how it is exploited in the VISION Cloud architecture.

## 2.1    The Proposed Storage Cloud Environment

Goal of the VISION Cloud project is to provide efficient support for data-intensive applications. Moreover, a content-centric view of storage services is provided. Five main areas of innovation drive the VISION Cloud platform design and implementation [14]: i) content is managed through data objects that can be associated with a rich metadata model, ii) data lock-in is avoided by allowing migration of data across administrative domains, iii) computations are moved close to data through the use of storlets in order to avoid costly data transfers, iv) efficient retrieval of objects is allowed based on object content, properties, and relationships, and v) a high QoS level is guaranteed together with security and compliance with international regulations.

The storage cloud environment proposed by the VISION Cloud project is built on top of an infrastructure consisting of multiple data centers, potentially distributed worldwide. Each data center can be composed of one or more storage clusters containing physical resources providing computational, storage, and networking capabilities. The data centers need to be connected by dedicated high speed networks.

Each storage cluster is composed of several storage rich nodes that can be build from commodity hardware and connected by commodity network devices. In fact, as common for cloud infrastructures, the storage cloud is built from low cost components and the desired reliability level is assured through the software layer. The software stack also builds advanced functionalities on top of this foundation. An example of initial hardware configuration could be 4 or 8 multiprocessor nodes with 12 to 16 GB of RAM each. Each node could have 12 to 24 high capacity direct attached disks (e.g., 2TB SATA drives). The architecture, design, and implementation of the VISION Cloud architecture supports a system with hundreds of storage clusters, where each storage cluster can have several hundred nodes and the storage clusters are spread out over dozens of data centers.

The VISION Cloud data model is based on the concept of data object. A data object contains data of arbitrary type and size. It has a unique identifier that allows users to access it through the whole cloud. An object is written as a whole and cannot be partially updated even if it can be partially read. An object may be overwritten, in which case the whole content of the object is replaced. Versioning is supported. Data objects are contained in containers and each data object resides within the context of a single container. Containers provide easy data management, isolation, and placement policies. Object are associated with a rich metadata model that allows system and user metadata to be associated to containers or to single objects. User metadata is set by the user and is transparent to cloud storage system. System metadata has concrete meaning to the cloud storage system.

The VISION Cloud data model extends traditional storage cloud models to include computation on the data objects, which is performed within the cloud storage environment through storlets. Storlets are software agents that are triggered according to specific events.

Objects may be replicated across multiple clusters and data centers. The degree of replication and placement restriction policies are defined and associated with the object container. VISION Cloud employs a symmetric replication mechanism, where any operation on an object can be handled at any of its replicas. A storlet, when triggered, is executed once, usually at the site where the triggering condition first occurred.

## 2.2   GPFS-SNC as Underlying Distributed File System

In the storage cloud environment proposed by the VISION Cloud project, the simpler and lower level storage unit is the storage cluster. On top of the storage resources provided by each cluster (i.e., the direct attached disks), a distributed file system is built. This allows each node to access the data objects stored in the cluster and to provide computational power on top of it by serving user requests and allowing the execution of storlets. In the current implementation of the VISION Cloud stack, General Parallel File System for Shared Nothing Clusters (GPFS-SNC) is exploited in order to build such a distributed file system.

General Parallel File System (GPFS) [15] is a parallel file system for computer clusters providing the services of a general-purpose POSIX file system running on a single machine. GPFS supports fully parallel access to both file data and file system data structures (file system metadata). Moreover, administrative actions (e.g., adding or removing of disks) are also performed in parallel without affecting access to data. GPFS achieves its scalability through its shared-disk architecture where all nodes in the cluster have equal access to all disks. Files are striped across all disks in the file system providing load balancing and high throughput. Large files are divided into equal sized blocks which are placed on different disks in a round-robin fashion. GPFS uses distributed locking to synchronize access to shared disks ensuring file system consistency while still allowing the necessary parallelism. As an alternative or a supplement to RAID, GPFS supports replication, storing two or more copies of each data or file system metadata block on different disks. Replication can be enabled separately for data and file system metadata.

The GPFS-SNC file system [6] builds on the existing GPFS distributed file system extending it to a shared-nothing cluster architecture. Such scenario is the one being used in the current implementation of VISION Cloud. In shared-nothing cluster architecture, every node has local disks behaving as primary server for them. If a node tries to access data and such a data is not present on a local disk, a request is sent to the its primary server to transfer it.

As formally described in Section 3, VISION Cloud exploit GPFS-SNC functionalities as follows. Files corresponding to VISION Cloud objects are neither stripped nor replicated on a single cluster, i.e., each object is stored as a whole in a single disk. Additional object replicas are created in other VISION Cloud clusters in order to guarantee the desired level of availability. Typically a $(1+1, 1+1)$ schema is used for objects replication, i.e., each object is replicated in two data centers at two storage clusters in each data center. However, other replication schema can be used. GPFS-SNC file system metadata are replicated with a certain level of redundancy in order to guarantee that the file system structure is preserved in the presence of faults and that it is possible to determine which object has been lost and needs to be recovered.

## 3   Problem Formulation

In the following, we formally describe the scenario we take into consideration in the present work. Let us consider a VISION Cloud cluster composed by $N$ nodes. Each node is associated with $D$ directed attached storage (DAS) disks where both the distributed file system metadata and data (VISION Cloud objects) are stored. Note that, in the following we will consider only the distributed file system metadata (simply *metadata* from now on) while we will completely neglect system and user metadata associated to VISION Cloud objects being them treatable as object files from the cluster file system point of view. Disks and nodes can fail. Let us suppose that the time to fail of a single disk (node) is exponentially distributed with rate $\lambda_{df}$ ($\lambda_{nf}$). Disks (nodes) are repaired in an exponentially distributed time with rate $\mu_{dr}$ ($\mu_{nr}$).

Disk and node failures are supposed to be destructive. In other words, when a disk fails the metadata and data stored in it are lost. Similarly, in order to maintain the distributed file system consistency, when a node fails metadata and data stored in all its attached disks are considered lost. VISION Cloud objects are stored in the cluster without any striping or data replication, i.e., each object is fully contained in a single disk as a single file. On the other hand, metadata is scattered on the cluster disks and metadata records for each file are replicated on different nodes. Let us assume the level of metadata replication for each file to be $R$. When a disk fails the metadata that was present on it is replicated in a working disk in order to restore the correct level of replication. The process of metadata replication recovery takes an exponentially distributed amount of time with rate $\mu_{mr}$ to be performed.

VISION Cloud objects are replicated in other clusters. In the case of failure, the VISION Cloud Resiliency Manager (RM) is responsible for returning the storage Cloud to the proper level of resiliency. In fact, if a disk fails, a scan of the distributed file system metadata allows the RM to determine which objects were lost. Then, the RM contacts the other clusters in the Cloud (clusters in the same data center are usually queried first, since they are the closest) in order to recover the data from a replica and restore the objects into the cluster.

Let us consider a single VISION Cloud object $X$ stored in the cluster. Objects are distributed over the cluster disks in a uniform manner so that if a disk fails the probability that object $X$ becomes unavailable (if it was still available at the failure time) is $1/x$ where $x$ is the number of disks actually working with $0 < x \leq N \cdot D$. On the other hand, if a node fails the probability that object $X$ becomes unavailable depends on the number of working disks that were attached to the failed node. In a first approximation, we assume that, given a VISION Cloud replication schema, at least one of the clusters in which object $X$ was stored is always available for data recovery. Moreover, let us assume that, in order to recover an entire disk full of data, an exponentially distributed time is necessary with rate $\mu_{fd}$. Among other factors, such a time can depend on the network bandwidth that is present between the consider cluster and the cluster from which the objects will be recovered.

Of course, given that the RM performs the data recovery as soon as possible after a disk failure, free space on other available disks is necessary in order to restore the lost objects in the cluster. Let us assume that the recovery can be performed only if there are at least $K$ working disks in the local cluster. $K$ can be computed considering the average disk capacity, the average object dimension, and the average number of objects in a cluster. For example, if $c$ is the average fraction of occupied space in a disk then $K = \lceil N \cdot D \cdot c \rceil$. The time that is necessary to recover a single disk is also affected by the parameter $c$. In fact, the time needed to recover a single disk (characterized by an average fraction of occupied space $c$) is considered as exponentially distributed with rate $\mu_{obr} = \mu_{fd}/c$.

Disk failures can affect the availability of a generic VISION Cloud object $X$ even if it is not stored in the disk that fails. In fact, the distributed file system correctly works only until at least one metadata replica for each file is present on a working disk. If all the metadata replica for a single generic file are lost, the cluster file system is unmounted thus making object $X$ unavailable. We suppose that when the cluster file system is unmounted no disk failures can occur and no objects recovery can be performed. The file system will be mounted again only when a sufficient number of disks are available again (we suppose such a sufficient number to be $K$). Moreover, all the objects that were originally present on the cluster need to be recovered. This is assumed to take an exponentially distributed time with rate $\mu_{gr}$ that can be computed as a function of $\mu_{fd}$. In particular, if $N \cdot D$ disks are present in the cluster with an average fraction of occupied space $c$, then $\mu_{gr} = \mu_{fd}/(c \cdot K) = \mu_{fd}/(c \cdot \lceil N \cdot D \cdot c \rceil)$.

## 4   The Model

Figure 1 shows the SRN model for the Vision Cloud cluster described above. Three layers have been identified: physical layer (concerning node and disk failures and repairs), distributed file system layer (modeling the cluster file system metadata), and Vision Cloud layer (associated to object availability).

Places $P_d$ and $P_{df}$ represent working and failed disks, respectively. Place $P_d$ initially contains $N \cdot D$ tokens while place $P_{df}$ is initially empty. Each token represents a single disk. Transitions $T_{df}$ and $T_{dr}$ represent disk failure and repair events moving tokens between places $P_d$ and $P_{df}$. Rates of these transitions are considered to be dependent on the number of tokens in places $P_d$ and $P_{df}$, respectively, so that the overall disk failure rate is equal to $\lambda_{df}$ multiplied by the number of available disks while the overall repair rate is given by $\mu_{dr}$ multiplied by the number of failed disks. These marking dependent firing rates are represented by the # symbol near the corresponding arc.

Transitions $T_{nf}$ and $T_{nr}$ represent node failure and repair events. The failure of a single node is modeled as the contemporaneous failure of more than one disk by letting transition $T_{nf}$ to move more than one token from place $P_d$ to place $P_{df}$. This is obtained by associating to the arcs connecting transition $T_{nf}$ to places $P_d$ and $P_{df}$ a multiplicity that depends on the actual status of the net through function $[m_1]$. In particular, the number of disks that contemporaneously fail when a node fails is assumed to be dependent on the actual number of failed

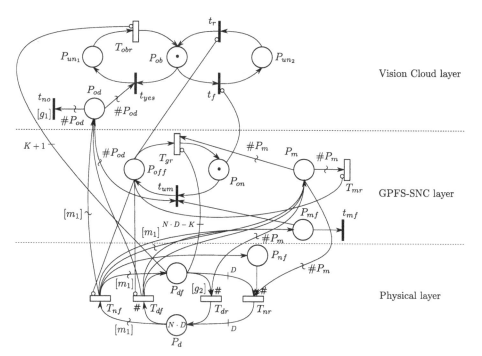

**Fig. 1.** SRN model for a Vision Cloud cluster

nodes and disks: if $nf$ nodes and $df$ disks are failed, then we assume that the average number of disks that fail when a node fails is given by $(N \cdot D - df)/(N - nf)$. Considering that transition $T_{nf}$ also puts a token in place $P_{nf}$ at each node failure event (i.e., tokens in place $P_{nf}$ model the number of failed nodes), we have:

$$[m_1] = \#P_d/(N - \#P_{nf})^1.$$

The rate of transition $T_{nf}$ also depends on the actual status of the net and, in particular, it is equal to $\lambda_{nf}$ multiplied by the number of working nodes, i.e., $\lambda_{nf} \cdot (N - \#P_{nf})$. The repair of a single node is modeled as the contemporaneous repair of $D$ disks. For such a reason, each firing of transition $T_{nr}$ moves $D$ tokens from place $P_{df}$ to place $P_d$. Also, one token is removed from place $P_{nf}$ in order to model a single node being repaired. The rate of transition $T_{nr}$ depends on the number of tokens in place $P_{nf}$ so that the overall node repair rate is equal to $\lambda_{nr}$ multiplied by the number of failed nodes.

Finally, transition $T_{dr}$ is associated with guard function $[g_2]$ that allows single disks to be repaired only if there is a sufficient number of working nodes:

$$[g_2] = \begin{cases} 1, & \text{if } \#P_{df} > D \cdot \#P_{nf} \\ 0, & \text{otherwise} \end{cases}$$

In this way, if all the failed disks correspond to failed nodes, transition $T_{dr}$ is disabled.

Place $P_m$ represents failed metadata replicas that need to be restored. It initially contains zero tokens. As soon as a disk fails (transition $T_{df}$ fires) or a node fails (transition $T_{nf}$ fires), a number of tokens equal to the number of failed disks is moved in place $P_m$ representing the corresponding metadata replicas being lost. Transition $T_{mr}$ represents the time necessary for the failed metadata replicas to be restored on the cluster. It is associated with a rate equal to $\mu_{mr}$ and, as soon as it fires, it flushes the content of place $P_m$ modeling all the metadata replicas being restored. This is implemented by associating to the arc connecting transition $T_{mr}$ to place $P_m$ a multiplicity equal to the number of tokens in such a place.

As soon as a certain number of disks fail (either transition $T_{df}$ or transition $T_{nf}$ fires), a token is also put in place $P_{mf}$ enabling the conflicting immediate transitions $t_{mf}$ and $t_{um}$. Transition $t_{mf}$ models the probability for the cluster file system to continue to work properly after the newly occurred failure conditioned to the fact that it was correctly working when the failure occurred. Such a probability depends on the actual number of working nodes and metadata replicas present in the cluster so it can be computed as a function of the current number of tokens in places $P_d$ and $P_m$. As soon as transition $t_{mf}$ fires, it removes the token from place $P_{mf}$ leaving everything else unmodified. On the other hand, transition $t_{um}$ models the probability for the cluster file system to be unmounted after the newly occurred failure conditioned to the fact that it was

---

[1] The notation $\#P$ indicates the number of tokens in place $P$.

correctly working when the failure occurred. Also in this case, such a probability depends on the actual number of working nodes and metadata replicas present in the cluster and it can be computed as a function of the current number of tokens in places $P_d$ and $P_m$. Given that transitions $t_{mf}$ and $t_{um}$ are conflicting and no other transition is contemporaneously enabled the sum of their associated probabilities needs to be equal to one. As soon as transition $t_{mf}$ fires, a token is moved from place $P_{on}$ to place $P_{off}$. Moreover, the token in place $P_{mf}$ is removed.

Place $P_{on}$ represents a working distributed file system while place $P_{off}$ represents a faulty file system. When the cluster file system is down, no new metadata replica can be created (inhibitor arc from place $P_{off}$ to transition $T_{mr}$) and no disks or nodes can fail (inhibitor arcs from place $P_{off}$ to transitions $T_{df}$ and $T_{nf}$).

Transition $T_{gr}$ represents the time necessary to repair the distributed file system after a crash due to metadata destruction, to recover all the objects from the replicas in other Vision Cloud clusters, and to create the metadata replicas. It is associated with a rate equal to $\mu_{gr}$. Such recovery operation can be performed only after the repair of at least $K$ disks (inhibitor arc from place $P_{df}$ to transition $T_{gr}$ with multiplicity $N \cdot D - K$). As soon as transition $T_{gr}$ fires, a token is put back to place $P_{on}$ (the cluster file system is up again) and all the tokens in place $P_m$ are flushed modeling the recovery of all the failed metadata replicas. This is implemented by associating to the arc connecting transition $T_{gr}$ to place $P_m$ a multiplicity equal to the number of tokens in such a place.

A token in place $P_{ob}$ represents the object being available. As soon as a failure occurs, a number of tokens equal to the number of failed disks is moved in place $P_{od}$ by transitions $T_{df}$ or $T_{nf}$. Such tokens enable the conflict between transitions $t_{yes}$ and $t_{no}$ representing the object being contained in the disks that failed or not, respectively. The probabilities associated to transitions $t_{yes}$ and $t_{no}$ ($p_{yes}$ and $p_{no}$, respectively) depend on the system status and are given by the following functions:

$$p_{yes} = 1/(\#P_d + \#P_{od})$$

$$p_{no} = \begin{cases} 1, & \text{if } \#P_d = 0 \text{ AND } \#P_{un_1} = 1 \\ 1 - 1/(\#P_d + \#P_{od}), & \text{otherwise} \end{cases}$$

Transition $t_{no}$ is also associated with a guard function ($[g_1]$) that prevents it to fire if the last disk failed:

$$[g_1] = \begin{cases} 0, & \text{if } \#P_d = 0 \text{ AND } \#P_{ob} = 1 \\ 1, & \text{otherwise} \end{cases}$$

If transition $t_{no}$ fires, the object was not contained in the disks that failed and it is still available. If transitions $t_{yes}$ fires, the object was contained in one of the disks that failed and the token in place $P_{ob}$ is moved in place $P_{un_1}$ modeling the object being unavailable. Transition $T_{obr}$ represents the time necessary to recover the object from another Vision Cloud cluster where a replica of that object is present. It is associated with a rate equal to $\mu_{obr}$. The recovery operation can be performed only when at least $K$ disks are available (inhibitor arc from place $P_{df}$ to transition $T_{obr}$). The token in place $P_{ob}$ can also be moved in place $P_{un_2}$ when the cluster file system is unmounted for a metadata destruction (transition $t_f$). A soon as the cluster file system is repaired, transition $t_r$ fires and the object becomes available again.

## 5  Results

The SRN model reported in Fig. 1 can be analytically solved by using ad-hoc tools (e.g., the SPNP tool [16]) thus allowing us to investigate the influence of system parameters on the desired performance indexes. Several powerful measures can be obtained. One interesting index is the availability $A_{ob}$ of a generic object $X$. It can be obtained by computing the probability for place $P_{ob}$ to contain one token:

$$A_{ob} = pr[\#P_{ob} = 1]. \tag{1}$$

In this section, we present some preliminary results focusing on the object availability and taking into account only disk failures (i.e., considering fully reliable nodes). The relaxation of such an assumption, as well as the investigation of other performance indexes will be covered in future works.

System parameters have been set as follows. The number of nodes $N$ has been fixed to 80 and the number of disks per node $D$ has been fixed to 12, also considering the average fraction of occupied space in a disk $c$ equal to 0.5. The disk mean time to failure (MTTF) $1/\lambda_{df}$ has been considered equal to 2 *years* while the mean time to repair (MTTR) $1/\mu_{dr}$ has been set to 48 $h$. Finally, the mean time to recover a metadata replica $1/\mu_{mr}$ has been set to 20 $m$. The mean time to recovery an entire disk from a remote cluster has been computed by assuming the disk dimension equal to 500 $GB$ and considering an Internet-like connectivity (20 $Mb/sec$ bandwidth). Starting from the above reported assumptions, the values of the mean time to recover a disk $1/\mu_{obr}$ and the mean time to recover an entire cluster file-system $1/\mu_{gr}$ have been computed, as described in Section 3.

Our aim is to investigate the influence of the metadata replication level $R$ on the object availability, as reported in Table 1. It can be observed that the parameter $R$ plays an important role on the setting of the infrastructure. In fact, when $R$ changes from 3 to 5, we obtain a percentage gain, with respect to $A_{ob}$, of about 4%.

**Table 1.** Object availability $A_{ob}$ varying $R$

| R | $A_{ob}$ |
|---|----------|
| 3 | 0.9548245227 |
| 4 | 0.9983792830 |
| 5 | 0.9983795900 |

# 6   Conclusions

In the context of the VISION Cloud project reference architecture, we provided an SRN model for a storage cluster able to provide information about the reached availability level. The model can be exploited as a tool for an assisted SLA management and a guided dimensioning of the VISION infrastructure.

Future work will focus on extending the obtained results to the case of node failures and relaxing the simplifying hypothesis that we took into consideration in the present work. Moreover, an high level methodology for the management of VISION Cloud storage infrastructures based on our model will be set up providing a powerful tool for both business and administrator choices.

# References

1. Bruneo, D., Distefano, S., Longo, F., Puliafito, A., Scarpa, M.: Workload-based software rejuvenation in cloud systems. IEEE Transactions on Computers 62(6), 1072–1085 (2013)
2. Ostermann, S., Iosup, A., Yigitbasi, N., Prodan, R., Fahringer, T., Epema, D.: A Performance Analysis of EC2 Cloud Computing Services for Scientific Computing. In: Avresky, D.R., Diaz, M., Bode, A., Ciciani, B., Dekel, E. (eds.) Cloud Computing. LNICST, vol. 34, pp. 115–131. Springer, Heidelberg (2010)
3. Bruneo, D., Fazio, M., Longo, F., Puliafito, A.: Smart data centers for green clouds. In: 2013 IEEE 18th International Symposium on Computer and Communications (ISCC), pp. 1–8 (2013)
4. Khan, A., Yan, X., Tao, S., Anerousis, N.: Workload characterization and prediction in the cloud: A multiple time series approach. In: 2012 IEEE Network Operations and Management Symposium (NOMS), pp. 1287–1294 (2012)
5. VISION Cloud Project, funded by the European Commission Seventh Framework Programme (FP7/2006-2013) under grant agreement n. 257019, http://www.visioncloud.eu/
6. Jain, R., Sarkar, P., Subhraveti, D.: Gpfs-snc: An enterprise cluster file system for big data. IBM Journal of Research and Development 57(3/4), 5:1–5:10 (2013)
7. Ciardo, G., Blakemore, A., Chimento, P.F., Muppala, J.K., Trivedi, K.S.: Automated generation and analysis of Markov reward models using stochastic reward nets. IMA Volumes in Mathematics and its Applications: Linear Algebra, Markov Chains, and Queueing Models 48, 145–191 (1993)
8. Bruneo, D., Scarpa, M., Puliafito, A.: Performance evaluation of glite grids through gspns. IEEE Transactions on Parallel and Distributed Systems 21(11), 1611–1625 (2010)
9. Bruneo, D.: A stochastic model to investigate data center performance and qos in iaas cloud computing systems. IEEE Transactions on Parallel and Distributed Systems PP, 1–10 (2013)
10. Krishnamurthy, S., Sanders, W., Cukier, M.: Performance evaluation of a probabilistic replica selection algorithm. In: Proceedings of the Seventh International Workshop on Object-Oriented Real-Time Dependable Systems (WORDS 2002), pp. 119–127 (2002)
11. Venkatesan, V., Iliadis, I., Hu, X.-Y., Haas, R., Fragouli, C.: Effect of replica placement on the reliability of large-scale data storage systems. In: 2010 IEEE International Symposium on Modeling, Analysis Simulation of Computer and Telecommunication Systems (MASCOTS), pp. 79–88 (2010)

12. Krishnamurthy, S., Sanders, W., Cukier, M.: A dynamic replica selection algorithm for tolerating timing faults. In: International Conference on Dependable Systems and Networks, DSN 2001, pp. 107–116 (2001)
13. Venkatesan, V., Iliadis, I., Fragouli, C., Urbanke, R.: Reliability of clustered vs. declustered replica placement in data storage systems. In: 2011 IEEE 19th International Symposium on Modeling, Analysis Simulation of Computer and Telecommunication Systems (MASCOTS), pp. 307–317 (2011)
14. Kolodner, E., Tal, S., Kyriazis, D., Naor, D., Allalouf, M., Bonelli, L., Brand, P., Eckert, A., Elmroth, E., Gogouvitis, S., Harnik, D., Hernandez, F., Jaeger, M., Lakew, E., Lopez, J., Lorenz, M., Messina, A., Shulman-Peleg, A., Talyansky, R., Voulodimos, A., Wolfsthal, Y.: A cloud environment for data-intensive storage services. In: 2011 IEEE Third International Conference on Cloud Computing Technology and Science (CloudCom), pp. 357–366 (2011)
15. Schmuck, F., Haskin, R.: Gpfs: A shared-disk file system for large computing clusters. In: Proceedings of the 2002 Conference on File and Storage Technologies (FAST), pp. 231–244 (2002)
16. Hirel, C., Tuffin, B., Trivedi, K.S.: SPNP: Stochastic Petri Nets. Version 6.0. In: Haverkort, B.R., Bohnenkamp, H.C., Smith, C.U. (eds.) TOOLS 2000. LNCS, vol. 1786, pp. 354–357. Springer, Heidelberg (2000)

# Data Reliability in Multi-provider Cloud Storage Service with RRNS

Massimo Villari, Antonio Celesti, Francesco Tusa, and Antonio Puliafito

DICIEMA, University of Messina,
C.Da Di Dio 1, 98166, Messina, Italy
{mvillari,acelesti,ftusa,apuliafito}@unime.it
http://mdslab.unime.it

**Abstract.** Nowadays, more and more Cloud storage providers are appearing on the market. Nevertheless, data availability and confidentiality represent critical issues considering Cloud computing. This paper discusses an approach that on one hand enables customers to use at the same time different Cloud storage providers, and that on the other hand guarantees both data redundancy and obfuscation. According to our approach, files are fragmented and stored in different Cloud storage providers by means of the Redundant Residue Number System (RRNS). Besides providing us data redundancy, RRNS allows us to preserve the data confidentiality by means of an obfuscation-base strategy spreading metadata over different cloud providers. In addition, our approach allows a customer to retrieve his/her files even if a cloud storage provider is not available anymore. Experiments highlight the factors that have to be considered to configure the system according to the customer's requirements.

**Keywords:** Cloud Computing, Storage, Big Data, Reliability, Confidentiality.

## 1 Introduction

Cloud computing allows to leverage new business opportunity by means of emerging technologies enabling service integration over the web. [1]. Thanks to Cloud computing, services in different application fields are possible [2] considering Infrastructure as a Service (IaaS) [3] [4], Platform as a Service (PaaS) [5], and Software as a Service (SaaS) [6] [7]. Considering the storage service in the Cloud, it is becoming more than a way for synchronizing and maintain data for long time. In fact, it represents a good opportunity for customers and providers to make new services, hence new business. The emerging business in this field is motivated by the increasingly number of providers working in such a context (e.g., Dropbox, Google Drive, Copy, Amazon S3, SkyDrive, etc). To remark the high ferment in this context, recently another commercial service has appeared in the IT market, i.e., Storage Made Easy (SME) [8]. SME provides a hybrid Cloud storage system that federates over 35 public clouds and that offers a front-end able to simplify the access to many operators. Nevertheless, SME

C. Canal and M. Villari (Eds.): ESOCC 2013, CCIS 393, pp. 83–93, 2013.

does not introduce any additional data reliability services, in fact files as stored as whole. The drawback of this model is represented by the threat in misusing personal data. This threat is sadly true, in fact cloud operators can see the files stored in their servers. In addition, the NSA PRISM [9] program (US surveillance program) has recently claimed a direct access to Cloud storage providers' servers including Google, Apple and Facebook and so on [10]. They motivated their intrusion with national security and safety purposes.

In this paper, we aim to address a scenario such as the one described in Figure 1 in which files of customers can be spread over different Cloud storage providers. In our view for adopting clouds is necessary to guarantee a strong level of security and privacy [11,12]. Differently from SME, our work aims to achieve two additional objectives: on one hand it aims to solve the problem of data confidentiality by means of an obfuscation strategy, and on the other hand it aims to enable data availability even if a cloud storage provider is not available anymore by means of a data redundancy strategy. A provider cannot be available for different reasons, e.g., for hardware failure, for disappearing from the IT market, or due to an expired contract with the customer.

An interesting feature of our approach is that no operator can have full access to the stored files. This is possible by splitting each file in several residue-segments by means of the RRNS and sending them to different Cloud storage providers. Each file is described by means of XML metadata files tracking where the different residue-segments are stored. Even such a metadata files are spread over different Cloud storage providers. Only the user is aware of number of pieces of file and their distribution, using the XML metadata file. The end-user is in charge to gather all data and she/he is the only responsible for reconstructing XML metadata, residue-segments distribution and involved providers.

The remainder of the paper is organized as follows: Section 2 describes related works, highlighting the lack of a resilient and confidential multi-provider Cloud

**Fig. 1.** multi-provider Cloud storage service distributed over the Internet

storage service. Section 3 briefly describe the RRNS on which our approach is based. Our approach for a reliable and confidential multi-provider Cloud storage service according to the RRNS is described in Section 4. Experiments are described in Section 5. Conclusion and lights to the future are summarized in Section 6.

## 2   Related Work

Data distribution [13] along with Data Migration [14] are topics quite relevant in the context of Cloud storage. The needs to send big data over the Internet is important as well as the possibility to overcome data lock-in issues. Many works are available in licterature regarding data reliability in datacenters and in Cloud Infrastructure as a Service (IaaS).

In [15], the authors describe a technique for optimizing the file partition considering a Network Storage Environment. They present a strategy to efficiently distribute files inside a cluster taking into account concepts of reliability, availability and serviceability. In particular they deal with the possibility to partition files into blocks to be spread among different storage servers. A file partitiong approach for Cloud computing is described in [16] in which a smart procedure is used to optimize the placement of each data block according to its size. In [17], the authors faced the issue existing when a laptop is lost or stolen. The system guarantees that data cannot be accessed, but after an a priori vulnerability time window configuration. The authors make XOR operations using splitting and merging of files that haveto be protected. The procedure is hard to be applicable to other scenarios because it requires to customize kernel-base of the involved servers.

In [18], a data restore is performed using regenerating codes. In such a work, both redundancy and check controls are used for guaranteeing the possibility to repair data during the transfer over an unreliable network. A work starting from our same assumption about the storing pieces of file inside VMs is discussed in [19] in which an enhanced distributed Cloud storage is described. Nevertheless, the adopted protocol is rather complex and hard to be adapted our scenario.

## 3   Redundant Residue Number System

The Redundant Residue Number System (RRNS) bases its fundamentals on the Residue Number System (RNS). For the sake of completeness, hereby we are going to describe the RNS before, followed by the description of the RRNS.

If you consider $p$ prime, pairwise and positive integers $m_1, m_2, \cdots, m_p$ called *modulus* such as $M = \prod_{i=1}^{p} m_i$ and $m_i > m_{i-1}$ for each $i \in [2, p]$. Given $W \geq 0$, we can define $w_i = W \mod m_i$ the residue of $W$ modulo $m_i$. The $p$-tuple $(w_1, w_2, \cdots, w_p)$ is named the *Residue Representation* of $W$ with the given modulus and each tuple element $w_i$ is known as the $i^{th}$ residue digit of the representation. For every $p$-tuple $(w_1, w_2, \cdots, w_p)$, the corresponding $W$ can be reconstructed by means of the Chinese Remainder Theorem:

$$W = \left( \sum_{i=1}^{p} w_i \frac{M}{m_i} b_i \right) \mod M \tag{1}$$

where $b_i$, $i \in [1, p]$ is such that $\left( b_i \dfrac{M}{m_i} \right) \mod m_i = 1$ (i.e. the multiplicative inverse of $\dfrac{M}{m_i}$ modulo $m_i$). We call *Residue Number System (RNS)*, with residue modulus $m_1, m_2, \cdots, m_p$, the number system representing integers in $[0, M)$ through the $p$-tuple $(w_1, w_2, \cdots, w_p)$. Considering $p + r$ modulus $m_1, \cdots, m_p, m_{p+1}, \cdots, m_{p+r}$ we have:

$$M = \prod_{i=1}^{p} m_i \tag{2}$$

and

$$M_R = \prod_{i=p+1}^{r} m_i \tag{3}$$

without loss of generality $m_i > m_{i-1}$ for each $i \in [2, p + r]$. We define *Redundant Residue Number System (RRNS)* of modulus $m_1, \cdots, m_{p+r}$, range M and redundancy $M_R$, the number system representing integers in $[0, M)$ by means of the $(p + r)$-tuple of their residue modulus $m_1, \cdots, m_{p+r}$. Although the above mentioned *RRNS* can provide representations to all integers in the range $[0, M \cdot M_R)$, the legitimate range of representation is limited to $[0, M)$, and the corresponding $(p + r)$-tuples are called *legitimate*. Integers in $[M, M \cdot M_R)$ together with the corresponding $(p + r)$-tuples are instead called *illegitimate*. Let now consider an *RRNS* whose range is $M$ and redundancy $M_R$, where $(m_1, m_2, \cdots, m_p, m_{p+1}, \cdots, m_{p+r})$ is the $(p + r)$-tuple of modulus and $(w_1, w_2, \cdots, w_p, w_{p+1}, \cdots, w_{p+r})$ is the legitimate representation on an $W$ integer in $[0, M)$. If an event making unavailable $d$ arbitrary digits in the representation occurs, we have two new sets of elements $\{w'_1, w'_2, \cdots, w'_{p+r-d}\} \subseteq \{w_1, \cdots, w_{p+r}\}$ with the corresponding modulus $\{m'_1, m'_2, \cdots, m'_{p+r-d}\} \subseteq \{m_1, \cdots, m_{p+r}\}$. This status is also known as *erasures* of multiplicity $d$. If the condition $d \leq r$ in true, the *RNS* of modulus $\{m'_1, m'_2, \cdots, m'_{p+r-d}\}$ has range:

$$M' = \prod_{i=1}^{p+r-d} m'_i \leq M \tag{4}$$

since $W < M$, $(w_1, w_2, \cdots, w_p, w_{p+1}, \cdots, w_{p+r})$ is the unique representation of $W$ in the latter *RNS*. Integer $W$ can be reconstructed from the $p + r - d$-tuple $(w'_1, w'_2, \cdots, w'_p, w'_{p+1}, \cdots, w'_{p+r-d})$ by means of the Chinese Remainder Theorem (as in the case of equation 1):

$$W = \left( \sum_{i=1}^{p+r-d} w'_i \frac{M'}{m'_i} b'_i \right) \mod M' \tag{5}$$

where $b_i$ is such that $\left( b_i' \dfrac{M'}{m_i'} \right)$ mod $m_i' = 1$ and $i \in [1, p + r - d]$. As a consequence, the above mentioned *RRNS* can tolerate erasures up to multiplicity $r$. It can be proved (see [20] for further details) that the same *RRNS* is able to detect any error up the multiplicity $r$ and it allows to correct any error up the multiplicity $\lfloor \frac{r}{2} \rfloor$.

## 4   Data Availability and Confidentiality in a Multi-provider Cloud Storage Providers

In this Section, considering the assumptions made on the RRNS and the cloud users' requirements regarding the storage discussed in the introduction, we are going to describe our approach aimed at improving the user experience while interacting with Cloud storage services: we remark the two key-points on which our solution is based, consist in guaranteeing data availability (resiliency) and increasing data confidentiality through the *obfuscation technique*. In order to pursue these goals, we implemented a software application able to receive as input one or more files belonging to a given user with some particular constraints, and to accomplish the upload of those files on the Cloud according to the specified constraints. The process makes use of a particular algorithm based on the RRNS to spread pieces of file across different cloud storage providers, allowing the owner only to be aware of its logical distribution and thus of its potential reconstruction. Thanks to the RRNS properties already discussed in Section 3, each time the encoding process is applied to a file, depending on the user requirements (i.e. the constraints given as input to the software application), data is vertically split (as depicted in Figure 2) on different segments according to a given degree of redundancy. These residue-segments will then be copied and stored on (possibly) different Cloud storage providers through the traditional APIs they make available to users. At the end of the encoding/upload process,

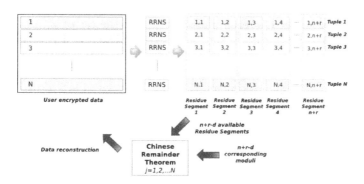

**Fig. 2.** Representation of the RRNS encoding and decoding performed on a set of user data: the upper side part shows the encoding procedure, while the underside one depicts the decoding process

a single cloud holding the whole file will not exist and this will lead to some direct consequences: even though there's no encryption on data, a self-contained file will not exist on any storage provider, leading to an increased confidentiality degree (this type of data access restriction is also know as *Data obfuscation*); thanks to the redundancy introduced by the RRNS, in case either of temporary unavailability of one (or more, according to condition 5) XML wrappers or the unlikely event of data loss from a provider, the user file might still be reconstructed from the owner.

The introduced redundancy obviously increases the resulting amount of data to be stored and transferred, but this drawback could sometimes be minimized under particular network conditions. In the case where one of the storage provider is heavily overwhelmed from users' requests, having data spread among different storage providers might be faster than waiting for the transmission of a monolithic block from the overloaded one: different data segments might be downloaded in parallel from the storage providers on the client, allowing a more efficient bandwidth occupation from the client point of view. After having introduced the general concepts regarding our idea and the related software application, in the following we are going to discuss the details of its implementation, analysing both the way by means of data is encoded before the upload process, and how the logical meta-data catalogue is created to let the owner rebuild his/her file(s) after all the needed XML wrappers are downloaded from the Cloud during the decoding process. First of all, we need to describe the steps allowing a generic file given in input to our software application, to be "expanded" into a set of residue-fragments: for the sake of simplicity, we can assume a file as a logic set of records and we will apply the RRNS encoding over the whole set of data, considering each record at a time as an integer value.

Figure 2 depicts how this task is logically carried out: the top part of the picture represents the RRNS encoding procedure, while the underside one presents schematically the RRNS decoding. Considering the encoding phase, the left part of the picture shows the encrypted user data, whose structure was considered as a sequence of $N$ records. In terms of RRNS encoding, each record will be assumed as an integer value (the $P$ value introduced in Section 3) and the RRNS encoding will be applied to each record obtaining the set of *residue-segments* represented in the right part of the same Figure. The set of $n + r$-tuples obtained as output will then be grouped following the approach still reported in figure: all the $i^{th}$ digits from the whole set of N tuples will be included within a corresponding $i^{th}$ residue-segment. The aforementioned set of tasks, will be carried out according to the redundancy degree selected by the user, who will provide his/her constraints into a separate file given as input to the software application named *init*. The same file will contain also information about the cloud storage providers involved in the data upload: more specifically, as soon as the RRNS has been carried out on the whole dataset, each residue-segment will then be BASE-64 encoded and attached within a different XML wrapper. Each XML wrapper, in turn, will then be uploaded to one of the cloud service providers specified by the user. In order to track the location where each fragment was uploaded, for each user file going through the encoding process, a meta-data catalogue has to be created: moreover, this catalogue will have to be accessible from the data owner only, who will be able to rebuild the original file through the information stored within during the decoding. Depending on the number of available providers and the number of XML chunks resulting from the encoding, one or more provider may be in charge of storing many pieces of data belonging to a given user's file. At the end of the encoding process, the java software application will produce as output both the set of XML chunks associated to the source file (with the requested resiliency degree) and the meta-data catalogue, represented by an XML file named *map*. This latter will be similar to the one reported below:

```
<OWNER>ownerInfo</OWNER>
<BIGFILE>noBig</BIGFILE>
<STUFFING>1</STUFFING>
<FILE>
    [...]
    <CHUNK num="11">Path/to/the/StorageProviderX/
        94090e1381a1700fb8c34a0069bc6533.xml</CHUNK>
    <CHUNK num="5">Path/to/the/StorageProviderY/
        eaf2bcdcb47cd1eba2a4392857e66b33.xml</CHUNK>
    [...]
</FILE>
```

The first element of the file, *owner* merely contains the owner information. The next two ones, are used by the java software application during the encoding/decoding operations and their description is out of the scope of this Section. The *FILE* element contains a variable number of *CHUNK* elements: while the attribute *num* refers to the chunk sequence number, its content represents a combination of the path on the client machine associated to a given cloud storage provider, and the name of the XML file containing the residue-segment. Information stored within the above XML document will allow to build up the original file during the decoding process. It is straightforward foreseeing that the *map* meta-data catalogue represents a key-point of the whole process: its accidental lost or unavailability may likely lead to the inability of building up the user data previously uploaded on the Cloud. For this reason, the software application in charge of carrying out the encoding/decoding process, has been designed to store the catalogue on the Cloud together with the chunks. Uploading such a sensitive information on a third-party storage, may be controversial in terms of data confidentiality: for this reason, during the process, the map is split on two different components (i.e. two different files, *servicelist* and *trusted*, each uploaded to a different provider to hide (to malicious service providers) the actual mapping between chunks and their physical location on the Cloud.

## 5   Performance Evaluation

In order to evaluate our system, we conducted several experiments considering a real testbed composed of a client interacting with three different commercial

Cloud storage providers, i.e., Google Drive, Dropbox, and Copy. In our experiments, we splitted a file in different residue-segments and we stored them balancing the workload among the three Cloud storage providers, so that we evaluated the time needed for sending out the residue-segments to the three providers. The local testbed was arranged at DICIEAMA GRID Laboratory of the University of Messina. The system was developed considering the Java programming language deployed in a blade with the following hardware configuration CPU Dual-Core AMD Opteron(tm) Processor 2218 HE, RAM 6GB, OS: ubuntu server 12.04.2 LTS 64 BIT. In order to understand the behavior of the system in a real scenario, we considered files with different sizes and with different redundancy factors. More specifically, we considered sizes of 10KB, 100KB, 1MB, 10MB: we fixed p=5 and r=1, r=4 and r=7. According to the formula of the RRNS 5, we split each file respectively in 6, 9, and 12 residue-segments and we stored them balancing the workload in Cloud storage providers, so that in each one we stored respectively 2, 3, and 4 pieces of file. Each experiment was repeated 30 times in order to consider mean values and confidence intervals at 95%.

Figure 3 shows the time required to send the different residue-segments. We grouped the histograms according to the file size. For each group, we considered the time required for sending the residue-segments in parallel to Google Drive, Copy, and Dropbox. More specifically for r=1, 4, and 7 we respectively sent 2, 3, and 4 residue-segments to each cloud storage provider. For files of 10KB and 100KB we experienced very similar transfer times with Google Drive resulting as the slowest. For files of 10KB with r=1 the transfer time to Copy and Dropbox respectively takes about 523 msec and 543 msec. With Google Drive, the transfer instead takes about 4603 msec. We observed a similar trend considering r=4 and r=7 as well. We had a similar trend also for files of 100KB. As the file size grew over 1MB, the results began to change. Google Drive was the slowest provider again, but we observed that the transfer times increased considering different redundancy factors. Analyzing the result, we distinguished different behaviors between Copy and Dropbox: the former was the most efficient, instead the latter began to degrade in performance. For files of 10MB, we observed an interesting behavior: Google Drive began to became more efficient instead in Copy and Dropbox we experienced performance degradation. In fact, with r=7 the transfer time took 11223 msec, 12461 msec, and 19015 msec respectively with Google Drive, Copy and Dropbox. This results analysis means that for small file sizes (¡100KB) Copy and Dropbox are more efficient than Google DRIVE, instead with big file (¿10MB) Drive is more efficient than Copy and Dropbox. In particular, Copy has a trend slightly worse than Google Drive, instead Dropbox results absolutely the worst.

The graph of Figure 4 analyzes the transfer time of a file with size=10MB and r=7. More specifically, we considered four possible configurations. In configuration a) we stored 4 residue-segments per provider, instead in configurations b), c), and d) we stored all the 12 residue-segments respectively in Google Drive,

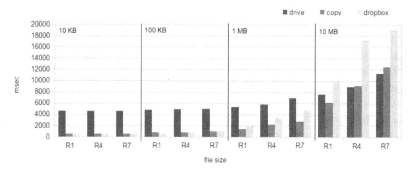

**Fig. 3.** Graphical representation of timing related to the upload process to the three different providers, while data size and redundancy change

Copy, and Dropbox. Considering configurations b) and c), Google Drive and Copy have similar transfer time (respectively 22465 msec and 25841 msec), even though the first result is slightly more efficient. Instead Considering configuration d), Dropbox is absolutely the worst in term data storing with 120138 msec. Analyzing configuration a), since groups of 4 residue-segments are sent in parallel to the three providers, the time required for data transfer is determined by the slowest one, i.e., Dropbox in this case, that requires 19015 msec for storing 4 pieces of file (this is the time reported on the graph for case a). Although Dropbox is the slowest one, thanks to residue-segments balancing, we managed to get a slight improvement in performance compared to the 22465 msec required by Google Drive. From our experiments, we can definitely conclude that for emerging multi-provider cloud storage systems, a critical issue is represented by the choice of providers. According to the customer requirements different factors have to be taken into account for example the expected QoS, the type of file that have to be distributed in term of size and the degree of required fault-tolerance.

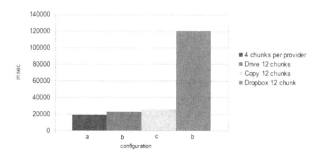

**Fig. 4.** Performance Comparison of the upload process considering parallel transfer vs single storage provider transfer

# 6    Conclusion and Future Work

In this paper, we discuss the data reliability and confidentiality problems considering a multi-provider Cloud storage service. By means of the RRNS, our approach consists in splitting a file in p+r pieces sending them to different providers. The advantage of such an approach is twofold: on one hand each single provider cannot access the whole file, and on the other hand if a provider is not available, files can be retrieved considering p pieces of files stored in other providers. Experiments have highlighted the factors affecting the configuration of such a system. In future works, we aim to better investigate such an approach also considering different data encryptin techniques.

# References

1. Celesti, A., Tusa, F., Villari, M., Puliafito, A.: How the dataweb can support cloud federation: Service representation and secure data exchange. In: Second Symposium on Network Cloud Computing and Applications (NCCA 2012), pp. 73–79 (2012)
2. Fazio, M., Celesti, A., Villari, M.: Design of a message-oriented middleware for cooperating clouds. In: Canal, C., Villari, M. (eds.) ESOCC 2013. CCIS, vol. 393, pp. 25–36. Springer, Heidelberg (2013)
3. Celesti, A., Tusa, F., Villari, M., Puliafito, A.: Integration of clever clouds with third party software systems through a rest web service interface. In: IEEE Symposium on Computers and Communications (ISCC 2012), pp. 827–832 (2012)
4. Celesti, A., Puliafito, A., Tusa, F., Villari, M.: Energy sustainability in cooperating clouds. In: Proceedings of the 3rd International Conference on Cloud Computing and Services Science (CLOSER 2013), pp. 83–89 (2013)
5. Celesti, A., Peditto, N., Verboso, F., Villari, M., Puliafito, A.: Draco paas: a distributed resilient adaptable cloud oriented platform. In: 27th IEEE International Parallel & Distributed Processing Symposium (IPDPS 2014), pp. 1490–1497 (2013)
6. Celesti, A., Fazio, M., Villari, M., Puliafito, A.: Virtual machine provisioning through satellite communications in federated cloud environments. Future Generation Computer Systems 28(1), 85–93 (2012)
7. Mulfari, D., Celesti, A., Villari, M., Puliafito, A.: How cloud computing can support on-demand assistive services. In: International Cross-Disciplinary Conference on Web Accessibility (W4A 2013) (2013)
8. SME: Storage made easy (2013), http://storagemadeeasy.com
9. NSA-PRISM: surveillance program (2013), http://en.wikipedia.org/wiki/PRISM_(surveillance_program)
10. NSA: Prism program taps in to user data of apple, google and others (June 2013), http://www.guardian.co.uk/world/2013/jun/06/us-tech-giants-nsa-data
11. Celesti, A., Tusa, F., Villari, M., Puliafito, A.: Se clever: A secure message oriented middleware for cloud federation. In: IEEE Symposium on Computers and Communications (ISCC 2013) (2013)
12. Vernik, G., Shulman-Peleg, A., Dippl, S., Formisano, C., Jaeger, M., Kolodner, E., Villari, M.: Data on-boarding in federated storage clouds. In: IEEE CLOUD 2013 IEEE 6th International Conference on Cloud Computing, Santa Clara Marriott, CA, USA, June 27-July 2. Center of Silicon Valley (2013)

13. Zhang, Y., Liu, W., Song, J.: A novel solution of distributed file storage for cloud service. In: 2012 IEEE 36th Annual Computer Software and Applications Conference Workshops (COMPSACW), pp. 26–31 (2012)
14. Nahar, P., Joshi, A., Saupp, A.: Data migration using active cloud engine. In: 2012 IEEE International Conference on Cloud Computing in Emerging Markets (CCEM), pp. 1–4 (2012)
15. Hai-Jia, W., Peng, L., Wei-wei, C.: The optimization theory of file partition in network storage environment. In: 2010 9th International Conference on Grid and Cooperative Computing (GCC), pp. 30–33 (2010)
16. Fan, K., Zhao, L., Shen, X., Li, H., Yang, Y.: Smart-blocking file storage method in cloud computing. In: 2012 1st IEEE International Conference on Communications in China (ICCC), pp. 57–62 (2012)
17. Zhang, N., Jing, J., Liu, P.: Cloud shredder: Removing the laptop on-road data disclosure threat in the cloud computing era. In: 2011 IEEE 10th International Conference on Trust, Security and Privacy in Computing and Communications (TrustCom), pp. 1592–1599 (2011)
18. Shum, K., Hu, Y.: Functional-repair-by-transfer regenerating codes. In: 2012 IEEE International Symposium on Information Theory Proceedings (ISIT), pp. 1192–1196 (2012)
19. Srivastava, S., Gupta, V., Yadav, R., Kant, K.: Enhanced distributed storage on the cloud. In: 2012 Third International Conference on Computer and Communication Technology (ICCCT), pp. 321–325 (2012)
20. Szabo, N.S., Tanaka, R.I.: Residue Arithmetic and its Applications to Computer Technology. Mc Graw-Hill, New York (1967)

# Automated Provisioning of SaaS Applications over IaaS-Based Cloud Systems

Paolo Bellavista[1], Antonio Corradi[1],
Luca Foschini[1], and Alessandro Pernafini[2]

[1] Dipartimento di Informatica – Scienza e Ingegneria (DISI), Bologna, Italy
{paolo.bellavista,antonio.corradi,luca.foschini}@unibo.it
[2] Centro Interdipartimentale di Ricerca Industriale ICT (CIRI ICT), Bologna, Italy
alessandro.pernafini@unibo.it

**Abstract.** Software as a Service (SaaS) applications fully exploit the potential of elastic Cloud computing Infrastructure as a Service (IaaS) platforms by enabling new highly dynamic Cloud provisioning scenarios where application providers could decide to change the placement of IT service components at runtime, such as moving computational resources close to storage so to improve SaaS responsiveness. These highly dynamic scenarios require automating the whole SaaS provisioning cycle spanning from resource management to dynamic IT service components placement, and from software deployment to enable needed component re-activation and rebinding operations. However, notwithstanding the core importance of these functions to truly enable the deployment of complex SaaS over IaaS environments, at the current stage only partial and ad-hoc solutions are available. This paper presents a support infrastructure aimed to facilitate the composition of heterogeneous resources, such as single Virtual Machines (VMs), DB services and storage, and stand-alone services, by automating the provisioning of complex SaaS applications over the widely diffused real-world open-source OpenStack IaaS.

**Keywords:** Cloud computing, Service orchestration, OpenStack, Juju, BPEL.

## 1    Introduction

Novel Cloud computing infrastructures consisting of worldwide fully interconnected data centers offering their computational resources as IaaS on a pay-per-use basis are opening brand new challenges and opportunities to develop novel SaaS-based applications. These novel Cloud systems are typically characterized by both agile and continuous developments and deployments as well as ever-changing service loads, and call for highly novel automatic solutions able to dynamically and continuously supervise and facilitate the whole application management lifecycle.

Focusing on SaaS-over-IaaS solutions, enabling the management and especially the provisioning of complex SaaS applications over highly dynamic and large-scale Cloud environments is still a difficult task that requires to solve several open management issues spanning from virtualization issues, such as Virtual Machine

C. Canal and M. Villari (Eds.): ESOCC 2013, CCIS 393, pp. 94–105, 2013.
© Springer-Verlag Berlin Heidelberg 2013

(VM), storage, and network virtualization, to large-scale Cloud monitoring, from optimal resource placement computation to standardization and interoperability of the different deployment frameworks and Application Programming Interfaces (APIs) adopted by various Cloud providers, and so forth.

Among all these challenging issues, the purpose of this paper is to present an architecture that offers a support for the orchestration of all the steps needed to publish a SaaS application within a Cloud IaaS. A *SaaS application* inside a Cloud environment can be viewed as a collection of opportunely configured *service components* deployed into a set of dynamically created IaaS resources. In modern datacenters, there is a high availability of computational, storage, and network resources, but it is still missing a mechanism to automatically orchestrate all the involved entities to allocate resources, to deploy and configure various software components, and to manage their interactions in order to provide the requested application. Indeed, before application providers can provide an application, they need to manually perform a set of operations (i.e., request new VMs, install and configure software) that, especially for large-scale deployments, could be really time consuming thus reducing the advantages of having flexible compute infrastructures.

In this context, we claim the necessity of new fully-integrated automated SaaS provisioning facilities that start from the management of virtual resources, pass through the installation, configuration and management of software components, and end with the coordination of these components. That would be highly beneficial both for SaaS application providers, to ease the realization of new SaaS applications through the composition of existing single service components in a mash-up like fashion, and for IaaS Cloud providers, by taking over all the error-prone and timely-consuming deployment and configuration operations at the IaaS level.

To address all these open issues, this paper proposes a novel automated SaaS-over-IaaS provisioning support that adopts three main original guidelines. First, it provides to both IaaS Cloud providers and to SaaS application providers a tool that transparently takes over the execution of software deployments and updates with almost no need for human intervention. Second, it proposes a general automated application provision support that integrates with state-of-the-art technologies, such as the highly interoperable OpenStack IaaS and the standard Business Process Execution Language (BPEL), to ease the definition of all main deployment, configuration, and monitoring steps. Third, our prototype has been implemented as an open-source tool based on the open-source OpenStack Cloud platform and is made available to the Cloud community.

The remainder of this paper is organized as follows. In Section 2, we give an overview of related work in the literature. In Section 3, we introduce needed background material about all main involved standards, technologies, and support tools; in Section 4, we present our framework and outline its main components. Finally, in Section 5, we provide some implementation details about our presented architecture. Conclusions and directions of future work end the paper.

## 2    Related Works

The on-demand provisioning of services and resources in distributed architectures has been deeply investigated in recent years. For the sake of space limitations, we will focus on two research directions only: we start with works that provide solutions for the deployment and lifecycle management of software components; then we move towards solutions that, closer to our proposal, enable automated provisioning of applications by integrating software lifecycle as part of the wider Cloud IaaS management operations.

Focusing on the first research direction, the design, deployment, and management of software components can be challenging in systems distributed on a large scale, and several different systems provide solutions to automate these processes. [1] presents a system management framework that, given a model of configuration and lifecycle, automatically builds a distributed system. Similarly, [2] introduces a model-based solution to automatically configure system specifications and provide this system on-demand to the user. Finally, in [3], authors presented a solution to face change management issues; this solution aims to automate all the steps required to handle software or hardware changes to existing IT infrastructures, with the goal of an high degree of parallelism. All these solutions provide the automation of the deployment and management of software components, so relieving administrator of the burden of manually configure distributed systems; however, they only focus on the deployment of software components and do not consider virtual infrastructure management, that instead assumes a central role in Cloud environments.

Along the second research directions, some seminal works have started to analyze the automated provisioning of applications in Cloud systems. [4] describes a multi layer architecture that enables the automated provisioning and management of cloud services; with this solution users can select a service from a catalog of service templates, then the service can be configured by the user and deployed automatically. [5] presents a solution for on-demand resource provisioning based on BPEL [6]. This solution extends BPEL implementations with the possibility to schedule workflow steps to VMs having a low load and the possibility to add new VMs on-demand in peak-loud situations. Both solutions focus on one of the most challenging aspects of Cloud computing, i.e. the capability to request and use computational resources in a small lapse of time, resulting in a fast performance increment and in a decrease of management costs. However, these works do not consider VMs monitoring and reconfiguration issues: every virtual resource is, in fact, allocated before software deployment and there is no mechanism to move VMs among different physical nodes in order to face peak-load situations.

In our previous works, to which we refer interested readers for additional details, we have proposed advanced monitoring features to dynamically and efficiently adapt and use all available virtual and physical resources in the Cloud system [7-8]. The present paper completes that support and, starting from virtual resources management and service components orchestration functions, enables automate Cloud application provisioning facilities within large-scale Cloud data centers.

## 3    Background

This section introduces some background knowledge to provide a better understanding of the area. Section 3.1 presents Cloud IaaS environments and provides needed details about the standard-de-facto OpenStack IaaS [9]. Section 3.2 presents Juju, a scripting-based tool to ease the deployment of service components [10]. Finally, Section 3.3 gives some needed background material about the BPEL standard that we use to orchestrate the whole application provisioning process through the definition of proper workflows [6].

Before starting, let us introduce some terminology about the three main types of actors in Cloud systems: *Application users, Application providers*, and *Cloud providers*. Application users are the final clients that require access to particular online SaaS application and use its resources. Application providers build and expose SaaS applications, typically composed by several service components, to the end users, and tend to externalize the execution of their own services to avoid the deployment of costly private IT infrastructure. Finally, Cloud providers supply application providers with resources on a pay-per-use fashion, in order to let them execute their applications over their IaaS-based environment. In this paper, we will focus mainly on the application providers and on how they interact with Cloud providers to enable, declare, and monitor the provisioning of complex applications consisting of multiple service components.

### 3.1    OpenStack

OpenStack is an open-source project for building and managing private and public Cloud infrastructures [9], proposed and promoted by NASA and Rackspace in 2010. OpenStack belongs to the category of Infrastructure as a Service (IaaS) systems, whose goal is to provide resources, such as virtual machines, virtual storage blocks, etc., on-demand from large pools installed in datacenters. OpenStack is based on a very flexible architecture supporting a very large set of hardware devices and hypervisors (i.e. Hyper-V, KVM, ESX, etc.) and even small businesses are allowed to deploy their own private Cloud because of the open-source nature of this solution. However, OpenStack still lacks a monitoring and dynamic reconfiguration mechanism to favor a dynamic deployment of applications on a large scale, thus requiring a manual management to tailor specific scenarios and deployments.

OpenStack manages computation, storage and networking resources on the Cloud in order to provide dynamic allocation of VMs [9]. OpenStack is based on five main services: the first one, called Nova, to manage both computational and networking resources; the second one, named Glance, to manage and provide VMs images; the third one, Neutron to manage network resources, and, finally, Swift and Cinder to manage storage resources. To better understand our work, we provide a more detailed description of Nova service.

*Nova* manages the creation and the configuration of VMs, starting from images stored in *Glance* catalog. Nova does not implement any virtualization software, rather it defines some standard interfaces to control the underlying virtualization mechanisms. Nova is composed by various main components that interact with each other in order to manage the entire lifecycle of a VM: *nova-compute* launches and configures VMs within a certain physical host, by communicating with the underlying hypervisor; *nova-network* manages all the aspects related to network management, making it possible to create virtual networks that allow communications between different instances of VMs; finally, *nova-scheduler* determines on which node a VM should be booted. All the requests made to Nova components are sent through RESTful APIs to *nova-api* that acts as a front-end to export all OpenStack IaaS functionalities, such as VM creation and termination, through Web Services. To maintain compatibility towards multiple vendors and to facilitate the migration toward different Cloud providers, OpenStack also supports Amazon EC2 APIs to deploy applications written for Amazon Web Services with a minimal porting effort [11].

## 3.2    Juju

Juju is a tool for the deployment and the orchestration of services that grants the same ease of use we can see in some widely used packet management systems such as Advanced Packaging Tool (APT) or Red Hat Package Manager (RPM) [10].

Juju focuses on the management and deployment of various service units and components needed to provide a single application, by taking over the configuration and installation of required software on the VMs where these service components will be deployed. Juju allows independent service components to communicate through a simple configuration protocol. End-users can deploy these service components inside the Cloud, in a similar way they can install a set of packets with a single command. As a result, it is possible to obtain an environment consisting of multiple machines whose service components cooperate to provide the requested application.

Juju is independent from the underlying Cloud Infrastructure Layer and supports several Cloud providers such as OpenStack, Amazon Web Services, HP Cloud, Rackspace, etc. Thus, it is possible to migrate a service component between different Clouds with minimal re-deploy effort.

A service component represents an application or a group of applications integrated as a single component inside a Juju environment that can be used by other components in order to build an higher level application. In this paper we consider a use case where we publish WordPress, an open-source platform to create, manage, and create dynamic Web site [12], by configuring and orchestrating two distinct service components: a service component exposing the MySQL database needed by WordPress, and another service component running the WordPress engine. A service component instance is called Service Unit and it is possible to add more of these

Service Units to the environment in order to scale the whole system, thus reducing the load on each VM.

Three main concepts are at the basis of services publication: *charms*, *hooks* and *relations*.

A *charm* encapsulates the logic required to publish and manage a service component inside a Juju environment. A charm provides the definition of a service component, including its metadata, its dependences on other service components, the software packets we need to install in a VM, along with the logic needed to manage the service component. Through the definition of a charm, it is possible to define the functionalities exposed by the service component and, if we are dealing with a composed service, all the sub-services required.

*Hooks* are executable files used by Juju to notify a service component about changes related to its lifecycle or about other events happened inside the environment. When a hook is executed, it can modify the underlying VM (i.e. it could install new software packets) or it can change relations between two or more service components.

Finally, *relations* allow the communication between different service components. Relations are defined inside a charm to declare the interfaces needed/exposed by a service component, that are offered/used by another service component. Low level communications between service components are based on TCP sockets.

The *environment* is a fundamental concept at the basis of Juju: it can be seen as a container where service components can be published; environments are managed through a configuration file where it is possible to define some configuration parameters such as used Cloud provider, IP address of the Cloud provider, authentication credentials, etc.

It is possible to execute an environment through the bootstrap operation exposed by Juju's API. The bootstrap operation initialize the system, instantiating a VM that will act as the controller node of the environment. Zookeeper and Provisioning Agent are two of the main software components executed on controller node. Zookeeper can be viewed as a file systems that stores all the information about the environment, while Provisioning Agent interacts with the underlying Cloud provider in order to instantiate and terminate VMs where service components are going to be deployed.

### 3.3   BPEL

BPEL is the de facto standard to define business processes and business interaction protocols [6]. The BPEL language, based on XML, allows to express the orchestration of multiple Web Services by defining business interactions modeled after a sequence of message exchanges between involved entities. A BPEL document contains the control logic required to coordinate all the Web Services involved in a workflow.

BPEL provides many language constructs and mechanisms to define a sequence of activities like *invoke*, *receive* and *reply*, parallel and sequential execution, transactional execution of a group of activities, and exception handling. A *partnerLink* is an important construct defined by BPEL to represent an external service that is invoked by a process or that invokes the process itself.

A BPEL engine elaborates a BPEL document, by defining an orchestration logic, and consequently executes all the activities according to the order defined by the logic. Typically, a BPEL engine exposes the business process through a Web Service interface that can be either accessed by Web Service clients or used in other business processes. One of the main advantages of BPEL is that the several activities of a business process can be executed simultaneously, instead of imposing a sequential execution.

## 4     Architecture

This section presents our architecture proposal to face all the main service orchestration challenges described in the previous sections: the proposed architecture provides the support to orchestrate all the steps involved in the publication of an application inside a Cloud platform, starting from the instantiation of required VMs to the deployment of required software components, together with the definition of their relationships. First, we briefly introduce this architecture and then we give a more in deep description of its components.

The proposed architecture is easily extensible, due to its multi-layer nature; it allows to arbitrarily manage the software components that form an application, and to use several Cloud providers. Starting from requests asking for application provisioning sent from application providers, it is possible to automatically satisfy their requests by monitoring all the steps involved in the application publication and notifying application providers about the progress of their request.

The proposed architecture (see Fig. 1) consists of a *Cloud Infrastructure Layer* and a *Service Orchestrator Layer* that, in its turn, we logically divided in two sub-layers: an *Abstraction Layer* and an *Orchestration Layer*.

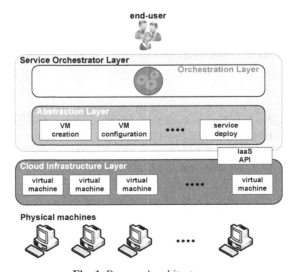

**Fig. 1.** Proposed architecture

The Cloud Infrastructure Layer represents the virtual resources provided by the Cloud infrastructure through the IaaS API: it contains VMs instances and defines the APIs required to create, configure and destroy VMs used by upper layers; it also offers a connection mechanism in order to grant access to VMs. In our implementation, we choose to use OpenStack as Cloud Infrastructure Layer, as it is a widely adopted open-source solution; at the same time, thanks to the highly flexible nature of our architecture, it is possible to use any other Cloud provider.

The Orchestration Layer and the Abstraction Layer compose together the Service Orchestrator Layer. It is the composition of these two layers that makes it possible to create an orchestration support. Once the user has sent a request, this layer will coordinate and execute all the activities to satisfy that request, by opportunely configuring and communicating with the VMs provided by the Cloud Infrastructure Layer.

Abstraction Layer's goal is hiding the complexity of the underlying Cloud Infrastructure Layer by providing a high level interface to the Orchestration Layer which encapsulates the functionalities offered by the Cloud Infrastructure Layer. This abstraction mechanism obtains a highly flexible architecture working with several Cloud providers. The functionalities exposed by this layer are useful to manage the entire VM lifecycle, in addition to the services offered by that VM. This makes it possible to create a VM with a chosen operating system and install on it all the software components required to build a service. Moreover, it is also possible to add relationships between different services in order to allow them to cooperate. Let us introduce an example to better understand the functionalities. If we want to build a service exposing a dynamic web site, we need to instantiate and deploy two sub-services: a web server and a database to store all objects and data required by the web server. To deploy this scenario, the Abstraction Layer will create two VMs (one for the web server and the other one for the database), install all the required software packages, and configure and start the two services. However, in order to publish a working web server, these services need to communicate to each other. This can be done by defining a relationship between the two services and specifying the functionalities exposed by each service along with the required functionalities. It is essential that the Abstraction Layer could access the VMs where the two services are deployed in order to monitor and, possibly, reconfigure the services; this is achieved by establishing SSH tunnels to VMs.

The Orchestration Layer represents the orchestration engine inside our architecture. When an application provider submits a request to this layer, it coordinates and orchestrates all the steps required to automatically provide the application provider with the requested application. Every request received by the Orchestration Layer contains a description of the required application, that can be seen as a model defining the service components that compose the application, along with the description of their relationships to determine how they must mutually interact. Typically, many activities are involved in exposing an application, so this layer needs to manage transitions between these activities, by taking into account the dependencies between service components as shown in Fig. 2-a. These dependencies represent the synchronization points between operation sequences executed inside a workflow.

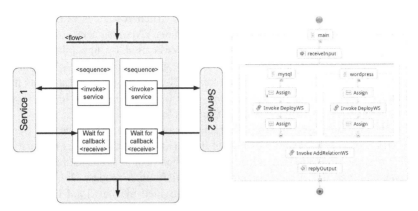

**Fig. 2. a)** Typical Orchestration Layer workflow and **b)** BPEL workflow

Going back to our previous example, it is impossible to publish a web server before the database is ready, because it would lack the required support to manage data. When the database is ready and the web server has been deployed, we can specify the relationship between these two software components. The Service Orchestrator Layer deploys those service components in parallel, monitoring the involved steps; that allows to simultaneously deploy several service components. In our solution, we implement this layer by using a BPEL engine.

# 5     Implementation Details

This section provides some implementation insights about our solution, based on both proprietary and ad-hoc software. Our presentation will follow a bottom-up approach, starting from the physical layer up to the Orchestration Layer. For the Cloud Infrastructure Layer, we have chosen OpenStack due to its highly flexible and open-source nature; in particular, we used the latest Grizzly release. Atop OpenStack, we use Juju to implement our Abstraction Layer: functionalities exposed by Juju encapsulate APIs provided by OpenStack, so we opportunely configured Juju environment in order to work with OpenStack, hiding these configuration details to the end user. Other open-source service management tools, such as Puppet [13] or Chef [14], could be used to implement the Abstraction Layer; we chose to use Juju because it is a very recent solution, continuously evolving with the introduction of new useful features. The Orchestration Layer, using Juju charms, enables the composition of complex applications and offers monitoring facilities through the monitoring events forwarded by Zookeeper. The Orchestration layer represents the engine of our support towards services orchestration: this layer makes it possible to coordinate the publication of SaaS applications, defining reusable and modular workflows.

In our case study, we deploy a complete WordPress platform composed by two service components: a MySQL database and a WordPress engine running on a web server. In order to deploy a working WordPress platform, we need, at first, to deploy the database service component and the WordPress engine, and then to add a relation between them to let them cooperate. We mapped all these steps into the BPEL workflow shown in Fig. 2-b.

The BPEL process, defined as an XML document, contains all the references to the external Web Services employed in the workflow; this can be done by populating the `<partnerLinks>` section. In our case study, we inserted references to DeployWS and AddRelationWS, to let the BPEL engine invoke them. These two Web Services represents respectively the Web Service used to deploy a service component, and the Web Service used to add a relation between two already deployed service components. The BPEL engine will also fill the request sent to DeployWS with the name of the service component that need to be deployed. BPEL constructs allow to execute the deployment of MySQL and WordPress service components (namely, two different instances of the DeployWS, see Fig. 2-b) in parallel on different VMs, and, through the definition of synchronization points, it is possible to orchestrate them. In particular, we use BPEL `<flow>` construct to achieve parallelism. A `<flow>` terminates its execution only when all activities included inside this tag have completed: in our case study, the completion of `<flow>` activity will occur only after both WordPress and MySQL have been deployed. Only at this time, we can invoke AddRelationWS to add a relation between these two service components.

We encapsulated the functionalities exposed by Juju, to deploy and monitor a service component inside the Web Services published on Apache Axis2. The name of the service component that needs to be published is specified inside the request sent to the Web Service.

DeployWS is realized by two Java classes: Executor, that invokes `juju deploy` command in order to deploy the service component, and DataMonitor, that manages ZooKeeper events in order to monitor the progress of the request. The following shows an excerpt of the WSDL file relative to DeployWS (see Fig. 3).

```
<wsdl:message name="deployWSRequest">
      <wsdl:part name="parameters" element="ns:deployWS"/>
   </wsdl:message>
   <wsdl:message name="deployWSResponse">
      <wsdl:part name="parameters" ele-
ment="ns:deployWSResponse"/>
   </wsdl:message>
   <wsdl:portType name="DeployWSPortType">
      <wsdl:operation name="deployWS">
         <wsdl:input message="ns:deployWSRequest"
wsaw:Action="urn:deployWS"/>
         <wsdl:output message="ns:deployWSResponse"
wsaw:Action="urn:deployWSResponse"/>
      </wsdl:operation>
   </wsdl:portType>
```

**Fig. 3.** DeployWS WSDL code

AddRelationWS invokes `juju add-relation` command and communicates the result of this operation to the BPEL Engine.

In order to publish WordPress and MySQL services, we need to write the corresponding charm to be memorized inside the bootstrap node and sent, during the creation of a VM, to the node were that service component will be deployed. When deploying a MySQL service component, the hook 'install' will be executed to download and configure MySQL related packets, and finally to start the service component. In the same way, all these steps will be repeated when deploying a WordPress service. After deploying MySQL and WordPress service components, we add a relation between these service components, by executing the respective relation-joined hooks. The relation-joined script relative to WordPress will write, in the WordPress configuration file, a reference to the host where MySQL database is running, together with the credentials to access the database. The following is an excerpt of the WordPress relation-joined hook used in our tests, as shown in Fig. 4.

```
database=`relation-get database`
user=`relation-get user`
password=`relation-get password`
host=`relation-get private-address`
juju-log "Writing wordpress config file $config_file_path"
# Write the wordpress config
cat > $config_info_path <<EOF
<?php
define('DB_NAME', '$database');
define('DB_USER', '$user');
define('DB_PASSWORD', '$password');
define('DB_HOST', '$host');
define('SECRET_KEY', '$secret_key');
define('WP_CACHE', true);
```

**Fig. 4.** Juju hook script

## 6    Conclusion and Future Works

In this paper, we presented a management support to automate the provisioning of complex SaaS applications over Cloud based infrastructures. Due to BPEL-based orchestration, our solution can achieve high expressivity in the definition of the application provisioning logic, including not only deployment issues, but also advanced monitoring of service component status; moreover, it enables concurrent execution of parallelizable service component deployment steps, thus significantly reducing the time needed to activate complex SaaS applications in large-scale Cloud environments. Moreover, the use of BPEL and workflow processes enables a higher degree of flexibility and reusability of our framework; indeed, already existing provisioning workflows can be reused to provide new SaaS applications.

Encouraged by these results, we are considering several future directions: on the one hand, we are currently integrating our new application provisioning facilities with our IaaS runtime monitoring and management support; on the other hand, we are developing an automatic application live-migration support to move the whole application, including all needed service components and relations, from local private Cloud IaaS to public ones, by dynamically re-binding all needed virtual resources therein; finally, we are implementing a mechanism to define multi-tenant network infrastructures and to provide isolation for multi-tenant SaaS applications deployed atop them.

**Acknowledgment.** This research was partly funded by CIRI, technology transfer center for ICT, of the University of Bologna; we also thank CINECA for its support.

# References

1. Goldsack, P., et al.: The SmartFrog configuration management framework. ACM SIGOPS Operating Systems Review 43(1), 16–25 (2009)
2. Singhal, S., Arlitt, M., Beyer, D., Graupner, S., Machiraju, V., Pruyne, J., Rolia, J., et al.: Quartermaster — A Resource Utility System. In: 9th IFIPIEEE International Symposium on Integrated Network Management, pp. 265–278. IEEE Press (2005)
3. Keller, A., Hellerstein, J.L.L., Wolf, J.L.L., Wu, K.-L.L., Krishnan, V.: The CHAMPS system: change management with planning and scheduling. In: 2004 IEEE/IFIP Network Operations and Management Symposium, pp. 395–408. IEEE Press (2004)
4. Kirschnick, J., Alcaraz Calero, J.M., Edwards, N.: Toward an architecture for the automated provisioning of cloud services. IEEE Communications Magazine 48(12), 124–131 (2010)
5. Dornemann, T., Juhnke, E., Freisleben, B.: On-Demand Resource Provisioning for BPEL Workflows Using Amazon's Elastic Compute Cloud. In: 9th IEEE/ACM International Symposium on Cluster Computing and the Grid, pp. 140–147. IEEE Press (2009)
6. Andrews, T., Curbera, F., Dholakia, H., Goland, Y., Klein, J., Leymann, F., Liu, K., Roller, D., Smith, D., Thatte, S., Trickovic, I., Weerawarana, S.: Business Process Execution Language for Web Services Version 1.1. 1.1 Edition. Microsoft, IBM, Siebel, BEA, and SAP (2003)
7. Povedano-Molina, J., et al.: DARGOS: A highly adaptable and scalable monitoring architecture for multi-tenant clouds. Future Generation Computer Systems. Elsevier (2013)
8. Foschini, L., Tortonesi, M.: Adaptive and Business-driven Service Placement in Federated Cloud Computing Environments. In: IFIP/IEEE International Workshop on Business-driven IT Management 2013, pp. 1245–1251. IEEE Computer Society Press (2013)
9. OpenStack Cloud Software, http://www.openstack.org/ (retrieved June 2013)
10. Juju homepage, https://juju.ubuntu.com (retrieved June 2013)
11. Amazon Elastic, Compute Cloud, http://aws.amazon.com/ec2/ (retrieved June 2013)
12. Wordpress, http://wordpress.org/ (retrieved July 2013)
13. Puppet, http://puppetlabs.com/ (retrieved July 2013)
14. Chef, http://www.opscode.com/chef/ (retrieved July 2013)

# Open Source Issues with Cloud Storage Software

Michael C. Jaeger

Siemens AG, Corporate Technology
Otto-Hahn-Ring 6, D-80200 Munich, Germany
michael.c.jaeger@siemens.com

**Abstract.** A brief look at the available cloud storage software projects reveals that many of them are built as open source efforts. Compared with other server technology, such as application servers, relational databases or messaging systems, this high degree of open source project development represents a special characteristic of cloud storage software. Therefore, when working with this technology also basic issues with open source projects are relevant and should be understood when choosing or evaluating such projects. The issues cover for example the consequence of the licensing for the desired use or the quality of the open source project.

## 1 Introduction

Cloud storage represents a broad term, the meaning of the term cloud storage can target NoSQL database software as well as storage solutions provided in a cloud-computing manner. The understanding about NoSQL databases is that referring database servers or services follow a different approach than the traditional table-model provided by relational database servers. This approach represents an adaptation to distributed systems and cloud computing environments. One basic view formulates that NoSQL databases do not provide the ACID (Atomicity, Consistency, Isolation, Durability) characteristics of the traditional (relational) database servers; instead they are characterized by the so-named BASE acronym which stands for *Basic Availability, Soft state, Eventual consistency* [1]. This characteristic suits the cloud computing paradigm of a distributed environment leveraging horizontal scalability.

Cloud storage as cloud computing service applies the traditional characteristics of cloud computing to storage, which are a) virtually unlimited resources, b) no upfront commitment and c) pay per use [2]. Depending on the definition or view point a couple of other characteristics are also relevant, for example, one software offering runs in a mode supporting multiple tenants serving different customers at once.

Today, a large number of solutions are available for development projects. For software solutions that can be locally installed or extended for own purposes, a large number of open source projects are currently available. In the area of distributed systems and server software this represents an exception, because most software areas provide mixed offerings, proprietary and open source projects, for example:

C. Canal and M. Villari (Eds.): ESOCC 2013, CCIS 393, pp. 106–113, 2013.

- Java application servers, are both available as open source and proprietary software. Both types of licensing are also very popular. For example, besides the open source project Glassfish, Oracle offers a proprietary version, named Weblogic.
- Relational database software: While there are well-known examples for open source relational database servers, such as MySQL, MariaDB or PostgeSQL, also proprietary database serves are very popular. Examples are the Oracle RDBMS or Microsoft SQL Server.
- Messaging systems or middleware show also popularity in both areas, open source and proprietary. For example, considering the Java world: While open source implementations of the JEE spec exist, also software companies have released messaging software since years, such as products from Tibco in this area.

This situation is different for cloud storage as available software project or distribution. Referring to so-named NoSQL databases we can see the majority being open source projects or non-proprietary software. Even cases exist in which software is developed following an open source approach, but the main contributors are employed or affiliated at a single company (e.g. Neo4j backed by a company named Neo Technology). In another similar case, a company which has developed this project as part of their software or services, has released this software as open source (e.g. Cassandra was originally developed by Face-book [3]). Having a close look at the page nosql-database.org, reveals that many of the offered solutions are in fact open source projects.

An overview about how much of them are open source is given in the Table 1 in the Appendix. The table lists the open source software projects from the three first categories of nosql-databases.org, column-based databases, document databases and key-value stores as an example. Some companies actually develop one of the open source databases while releasing the software using an open source license and require a commercial license for some enterprise use cases (e.g. RavenDB). From the listing at nosql-databases.org table, projects were omitted where no license information was found on the Web (investing a reasonable amount of efforts) or the license situation could not been determined. Also, commercial products have been omitted. A full list can be found on nosql-databases.org.

Having such a large list of projects available, the question arises, how to choose such projects. One major criterion is the actual functionality, of course. Functional and non-functional requirements can represent the main input to choose either one or another software. However, when it comes to commonality use, for example basic use of a relational database in a software project, relevant differences between major (open source) database servers can become irrelevant: Unless for example, one does not require special XML query methods or similar features of one particular database server, choosing between the major open source relational database servers can turn out in a very ambivalent decision. From an open source point of view, it is not. For example, the license of the MySQL server, which is the GNU GPL, can represent a conflict for some commercial use cases of software that builds upon the MySQL server. Then, in the MySQL case, the acquisition of an enterprise license could be considered. In summary, the remainder of the paper will introduce two basic issues with open source software here: the licensing issues in Section 2 and the software product quality issues in Section 3.

## 2    License Issues

The license is among the most important open source issues to consider. It is important to evaluate the license of a project planned for use or integration against own plans. Among other things, own plans can refer to whether software is considered for distribution or for in-house operations. The distinction is relevant, because from a legal point of view, the two cases ask for different rights. The right for distribution is often separately covered from the right for use. For usage, popular points are:

- Is the software allowed for commercial use? Some licenses forbid commercial use, which includes also in-house usage. By some point of view, a license which forbids commercial use does not implement the open source spirit because it limits the freedom of use of the software.
- Also, some licenses express some a statement like "Do not do something bad with it". Theoretically this can also exclude commercial use, because it might be difficult to prove that the own case of commercial use does not represent something bad. A case where such consideration applies is the Code Project Open License (CPOL), for example, which is used by the RaptorDB. This license states that improper use of this software is forbidden (cf. paragraph 5f of the CPOL 1.02), therefore the licensee must evaluate if the own planned use is to be considered 'improper".
- Is the license for usage valid? Admitted this sounds special on the first hand, but it might be that some condition of the usage contradicts against some license statement and then, the license may loose its validity. Without a valid license, the use of the software may not be allowed (most likely case). This situation can occur, for example, with patent clauses in licenses. A popular license condition expresses that the usage right invalidates, if the licensee rises a patent infringement claim against the licensor. Given that major IT companies in the smart phone sector are or have been in patent law suits against each other, while some of them release open source software, such case appears possible and is thus relevant for commercial use.

The mentioned points apply for using the software, for example in order to provide an internal system capturing travel expenses in a company. If the software is subject for distribution, different terms are relevant. Example, redistribution covers the case of selling a software product which contains or integrates the open source NoSQL database. Or for example, also selling an appliance where such software is installed can represent a case of redistribution. While complete consequences for all licenses in all cases cannot be given, some points to check are:

- Does the license require the delivery of own source code to the user? From the products listed in Table 1 some of them are licenses using different versions of the GNU General Public License (GPL) where such conditions may apply. Choosing this software requires evaluation for compatibility with own business interests.
- Does the license asks you for documenting that the software is included and is that documentation is actually in place? For many open source project developers, it is important to have presented at least the "credits". Therefore it must be ensured that appropriate copyright or authorship statements are given. The challenge for this task lies in how to generate such information with an evolving software project. In the ideal case, the development tooling keeps track of involved open source projects and referring "credit" information.
- Does the license asks you for delivering the open source software in complete or some defined form and is the delivery of the own software combined with the open source software compliant to this? Again, as with the previous point, this challenge is of organizational nature, because it requires to keep track of involved open source projects and their complete distributions.

While these points seem obvious, it must be noted that the number of individual licenses is in the hundreds. As a consequence, each individual license must be read and understood in order to have an understanding of what rights are allowed for usage and distribution. As a general rule, these issues should be clarified before the software is actually chosen. If the software is already in the software project and it turns out that the license is incompatible with own plans for distribution, migration to a different database server can become cumbersome and difficult.

This issue is especially important with NoSQL-databases: Because unlike with relational databases, a standard interface or commonly used query language may exist. But those do not share the popularity of SQL or JDBC. Therefore, choosing a particular NoSQL solution likely results in the use of specific interfaces.

## 3   Open Source Project Quality

Most open source projects work very open in terms of project communication and work. In the usual case, project mailing lists, documentation, common source repository and issue tracking are public. Therefore, some characteristics of the project can be easily looked at in order to get an idea about the quality of project work. Also, looking at the project's Web facilities may help for getting an idea of the software. Furthermore, such evaluation of the project allows for determining if the software has reached some kind of end-of-life status. End of life means here that the main developers have abandoned or closed the project. While an end-of-life project can have resulted in good software, this information is still relevant: In this phase no community support for bug fixes or closing security holes can be expected. Besides the end of life, there are some more common characteristics that are relevant to check (cf. [4]):

- How does the issue tracker look like? Does the project work on tickets, or is the majority of tickets open since long time ago? Kuru and Tao, for example have published a general analysis about the duration of open tickets in open source projects [5].
- How many developers commit actually source code to the repository? Is it just only one main developer? Then, maybe this project is fragile in terms of that it could be abandoned, if the life of that single developer changes.
- What are the threads of the mailing list? What are the main issues the project talks about? Having a brief look at the mailing list archive can quickly reveal issues or common problems with the software project.
- How does the commit history look like? Did the project commit larger pieces a long time ago and since the past year not much activity is apparent? Is the project maybe in stabilization phase? Some software may not get further large changes after it has been established and the desired it works. So stabilization phase cannot be considered a bad sign.

Most of the mentioned metrics can be looked at in the `ohloh.net` Web site. This Web site provides analysis and data repositories of thousands of open source projects. Users can access commit statistics, the number of active developers and so on. For a first look of an open source project it represents a relevant source of statistical information. The Figure 1 provides an example view of such comparison on ohloh.net with example projects from the documents database section. The example are "MongoDB", "RethinkDB" and "ThruDB". For a first look, MongoDb and RethinkDB appear in the same area w.r.t. project activity and software project size. This comparison reveals also that ThruDB represents a smaller project in comparison to the previous two.

Since the source code is available, also the code could be downloaded and analyzed using some code analysis tools [6]. Some of them might be available as open source as well. Other tools exist that are proprietary. The results gained from such analyses are similar to the points mentioned above: In all cases, natural explanations for surprising numbers / scores / ranks can exist. Therefore, the experience of an expert cannot be replaced by tools and statistics, of course.

Another, rather subjective information for the estimation of the project quality represents the origin of the project. For example, CassandraDB was initially developed by Facebook employees. Obviously, Facebook did not decide to make a business out of selling software licenses and decided rather to release their own written software in an open source project.

The advantage is clear: if the development community grows larger than the involved group of Facebook developers, the software will grow quicker and become richer in functionality as the group of own developers could have done. The advantage for the software project is that in the case of CassandraDB, obviously a large use case (use at Facebook) exists which represents an indicator that the project will be kept maintained in future.

# 4   Conclusions

For cloud storage we can distinguish two major forms: One is the actually hosted version of cloud storage involving a cloud-like business model for this hosting. And another is the form of a cloud storage software for own deployment or use in software development projects. For the latter, it was pointed out that a major number of projects are in fact open source projects. Therefore, considering basic open source issues is required for choosing the right software – besides the function and non-functional requirements.

The brief overview about open source issues shows that open source software does not come for "free".[1] Rather, it is "open" and requires the understanding of basic issues in order to be able to leverage its full advantages.

# References

1. Tudorica, B.G., Bucur, C.: A comparison between several NoSQL databases with comments and notes. In: 2011 10th Roedunet International Conference (RoEduNet), June 23-25, pp. 1–5 (2011)
2. Armbrust, M., Fox, A., Griffith, R., Joseph, A.D., Katz, R., Konwinski, A., Lee, G., Patterson, D., Rabkin, A., Stoica, I., Zaharia, M.: A view of cloud computing. Commun. ACM 53(4), 50–58 (2010)
3. Lakshman, A., Prashant, M.: Cassandra: a decentralized structured storage system. ACM SIGOPS Operating Systems Review 44(2), 35–40 (2010)
4. Ruffin, C., Christof, E.: Using open source software in product development: A primer. IEEE Software 21(1), 82–86 (2004)
5. Koru, A.G., Tian, J.: Defect handling in medium and large open source projects. IEEE Software 21(4), 54–61 (2004)
6. Stamelos, I., Angelis, L., Oikonomou, A., Bleris, G.L.: Code quality analysis in open source software development. Information Systems Journal 12(1), 43–60 (2002)
7. Stallmann, R.: The Free Software Definition, Free Software Foundation (2013), http://www.gnu.org/philosophy/free-sw.html

---

[1] R. Stallmann expressed this view as follows: "Free software is a matter of liberty, not price. To understand the concept, you should think of free as in free speech, not as in free beer." [7]

# Appendix

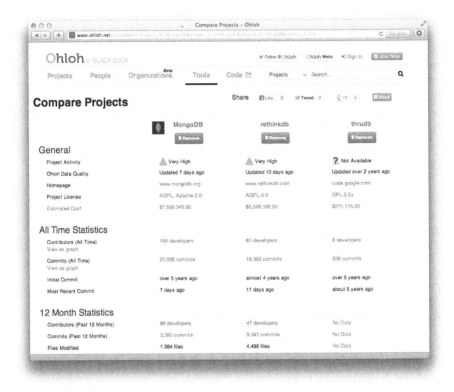

**Fig. 1.** Example for Comparison of Open Source Projects on ohloh.net

**Table 1.** Selection of Open Source Projects Listed on nosql-databases.org. Lines of code and number of contributors according to `http://www.ohloh.net/`, retrieved in June 2013. The number of contributors covers the past 12 months. Please note that data from this Web site is licensed under the "CC BY 3.0" license, available at `https://creativecommons.org/licenses/by/3.0/`.

| Project / Software | License | Lines of Code | Contributors |
|---|---|---|---|
| Wide Column Store / Column Families | | | |
| HBase (based on Hadoop) | Apache License 2.0 | 577,000 | 23 |
| Cassandra | Apache License 2.0 | 191,000 | 20 |
| Hypertable | GNU GPL v2 | 410,000 | 17 |
| Accumulo | Apache License 2.0 | 148,000 | 15 |
| Cloudata | Apache License 2.0 | 156,000 | currently n.a. |
| HPCC | Apache License 2.0 | 1.520,000 | 23 |
| Stratosphere | Apache License 2.0 | n.a. | n.a. |
| OpenNeptune | Apache License 2.0 | 70,000 | currently n.a. |
| Document Store | | | |
| MongoDB | GNU AGPL v3.0 | 513,000 | 87 |
| Elasticsearch | Apache License 2.0 | 276,000 | 53 |
| CouchDB | Apache License 2.0 | 135,000 | 44 |
| RethinkDB | Driver: Apache License 2.0 | 614,000 | 49 |
| RavenDB | GNU AGPL 3.0+ | 1,070,000 | 80 |
| ThruDB | BSD License | 21,400 | currently n.a. |
| Terrastore | Apache License 2.0 | 23,900 | currently n.a. |
| RaptorDB | Code Project Open License | 14,300 | currently n.a. |
| JasDB | MIT X11 License | n.a. | n.a. |
| SisoDB | MIT License | n.a. | n.a. |
| djondb | GNU GPL | n.a. | n.a. |
| EJDB (Embedded JSON database) | LGPL License | 197,000 | 8 |
| DensoDB | GNU AGPL 3.0+ | 197,000 | 8 |
| Key Value / Tuple Store | | | |
| Riak | Apache License 2.0 | 105,000 | 53 |
| Redis | BSD License | 100,000 | 43 |
| LevelDB | BSD License | 39,200 | 4 |
| Berkeley DB | GNU AGPL 3.0 | n.a. | n.a. |
| BangDB | BSD License | n.a. | n.a. |
| Chordless | GNU GPL v2 | n.a. | n.a. |
| Scalaris | Apache License 2.0 | 140,000 | 9 |
| Tokyo Cabinet / Tyrant | GNU LGPL | n.a. | n.a. |
| Scalien | GNU AGPL 3.0 | 21,900 | n.a. |
| Voldemort | Apache License 2.0 | 160,000 | 18 |
| Dynomite | BSD License | n.a. | n.a. |
| KAI | Apache License 2.0 | 47,000 | currently n.a. |
| MemcacheDB | BSD License | 13,900 | n.a. |
| Tarantool/Box | BSD License | 235,000 | 12 |
| Maxtable | GNU GPL v3 | n.a. | n.a. |
| Pincaster | MIT License | 58,500 | 2 |
| nessDB | GNU GPL | n.a. | n.a. |
| Mnesia | Open Source Erlang Licence | n.a. | n.a. |
| LightCloud | BSD License | n.a. | n.a. |
| Hibari | Apache License 2.0 | n.a. | n.a. |
| OpenLDAP | OpenLDAP Public License | 558,000 | 21 |
| Genomu | Apache License 2.0 | n.a. | n.a. |
| BinaryRage Titan | Apache License 2.0 | n.a. | n.a. |
| Elliptics | GNU GPLv2+ | 28,700 | 19 |

# A Calculus of Computational Fields

Mirko Viroli[1], Ferruccio Damiani[2], and Jacob Beal[3]

[1] University of Bologna, Italy
mirko.viroli@unibo.it
[2] University of Torino, Italy
ferruccio.damiani@unito.it
[3] Raytheon BBN Technologies, USA
jakebeal@bbn.com

**Abstract.** A number of recent works have investigated the notion of "computational fields" as a means of coordinating systems in distributed, dense and mobile environments such as pervasive computing, sensor networks, and robot swarms. We introduce a minimal core calculus meant to capture the key ingredients of languages that make use of computational fields: functional composition of fields, functions over fields, evolution of fields over time, construction of fields of values from neighbours, and restriction of a field computation to a sub-region of the network. This calculus can act as a core for actual implementation of coordination languages and models, as well as pave the way towards formal analysis of properties concerning expressiveness, self-stabilisation, topology independence, and relationships with the continuous space-time semantics of spatial computations.

## 1 Introduction

In a world ever more densely saturated with computing devices, it is increasingly important to have effective tools for developing coordination strategies that can govern collections of these devices. The goals of such systems are typically best expressed in terms of operations and behaviours over aggregates of devices, e.g., "send a tornado warning to all phones in the forecast area,", or "activate all displays in the route towards the nearest group of friends of mine." Effective models and programming languages are needed to allow the construction of distributed systems at the natural level of aggregates of devices, contrasting with the classical individual-device view that often obfuscates the system design.

Recently, approaches based on models of computation over continuous space and time have been introduced, which promise to deliver aggregate programming capabilities for the broad class of *spatial computers*: networks of devices embedded in space, such that the difficulty of moving information between devices is strongly correlated with the physical distance between devices. Examples of spatial computers include sensor networks, robot swarms, mobile ad-hoc networks, reconfigurable computing, emerging pervasive computing scenarios, and colonies of engineered biological cells.

A large number of formal models, programming languages, and infrastructures have been created with the aim of supporting computation over space-time, surveyed in [5]. Several of these are directly related to the field of coordination models and languages,

C. Canal and M. Villari (Eds.): ESOCC 2013, CCIS 393, pp. 114–128, 2013.
© Springer-Verlag Berlin Heidelberg 2013

such as the pioneer model of TOTA [11], the (bio)chemical tuple-space model [17], the $\sigma\tau$-Linda model [19], and the pervasive ecosystems model in [13]. Their recurrent core idea is that through a process of diffusion, recombination, and composition, information injected in one device (or a few devices) can produce global, dynamically evolving *computational fields*—functions mapping each device to a structured value. Such fields are aggregate-level distributed data structures which, due to the ongoing feedback loops that produce and maintain them, are generally robust to changes in the underlying topology (e.g., due to faults, mobility, or openness) and to unexpected interactions with the external environment. They are thus useful for implementing and composing self-organising coordination patterns to adaptively regulate the behaviour of complex distributed systems [11,17,18].

A sound engineering methodology for space-time coordination systems will require more than just specification, but the ability to predict to a good extent the behaviour of computational fields from the underlying local interaction rules—a problem currently solved only for particular cases [4]. This paper contributes to that goal by introducing a core calculus meant to precisely capture a set of key ingredients of programming languages supporting the creation of computational fields: composition of fields, functions over fields, evolution of fields over time, construction of fields of values from neighbours, and restriction of a field computation to a sub-region of the network.

The proposed calculus is largely inspired by Proto [3,12], the archetypal spatial computing language (and is in fact a fragment of it). As with Proto, it is based on the idea of expressing aggregate system behaviour by a functional composition of operators that manipulate (evolve, combine, restrict) continuous fields. Critically, these specifications can be also interpreted as local rules on individual devices, which are iteratively executed in asynchronous "computation rounds", comprising reception of messages from neighbours, computing the local value of fields, and spreading messages to neighbours. The operational semantics of the proposed calculus precisely models single device computation, which is ultimately responsible for the whole network execution. The distinguished interaction model of this approach, which is first formalised into a calculus in this paper, is based on representing state and message content in an unified way as an annotated evaluation tree. Field construction, propagation, and restriction are then supported by local evaluation "against" the evaluation trees received from neighbours.

The calculus thus developed formalises key constructs of existing coordination languages or models targeting spatial computing. As such, we believe it paves the way towards formal analysis of key properties applicable to various coordination systems, concerning soundness, expressiveness, self-stabilisation, topology independence, and relationships with the continuous space-time semantics of spatial computations.

The remainder of the paper is organized as follows. Section 2 describes the proposed linguistic constructs and their application to system coordination. Section 3 illustrates how single devices interpret the proposed constructs locally. Section 4 presents the formal calculus. Section 5 discusses the soundness property of the calculus. Section 6 concludes by discussing related works and outlining possible directions for future works.

| | |
|---|---|
| e ::= x $\mid$ l $\mid$ (o ē) $\mid$ (f ē) $\mid$ (rep x w e) $\mid$ (nbr e) $\mid$ (if e e e) | expression |
| w ::= x $\mid$ l | variable or value |
| F ::= (def f(x̄) e) | function |
| P ::= F̄ e | program |

**Fig. 1.** Surface syntax

## 2   Computational Fields

Generalising the common notion of scalar and vector field in physics, a computational field is a map from every computational device in a space to an arbitrary computational object. Examples of fields used in distributed situated systems include temperature in a building as perceived by a sensor network (a scalar field), the best routes to get to a location (a vector field), the area near an object of interest (a boolean indicator field), or the people allowed access to computational resources in particular areas (a set-valued field). With careful choice of operators for manipulating fields, the aggregate and local views of a program can be kept coherent and each element of the aggregate-level program can be implemented by simple, automatically generated local interaction rules [2]. Following this idea, in this section we present a core language to express such operators. This language is identified based on the strengths and commonalities across many different approaches to spatial computing reviewed in [5] (though we do not rule out the possibility that others may be identified), and drawing on the Proto [3,12] implementations of these mechanisms.

We describe the selected mechanisms directly showing the syntax of the proposed calculus, reported in Figure 1. We take the global, aggregate-level viewpoint, considering the main syntactic element e as being a field expression, or simply a field. As a standard syntactic notation in calculi for object-oriented and functional languages [10], we use the overbar notation to denote metavariables over lists, e.g., we let ē range over lists of expressions, written $e_1 e_2 \ldots e_n$.

A basic expression can be a literal value l (also called local value), such as a floating point number, a boolean, or a tuple—note most of the ideas of computational fields are agnostic to the structure of such values. According to the global viewpoint, a literal field expression l actually represents the constant function mapping l to all nodes. A basic expression can also be a variable x, which can be the formal parameter of a function or a store of information to support stateful computations (see rep construct below).

Such basic expressions (values and variables) can be composed by the following 5 constructs. The first one is *functional composition*, a natural means of manipulating fields as they are functions themselves: (o $e_1 e_2 \ldots e_n$) is the field obtained by composing together all the fields $e_1$, $e_2$, ..., $e_n$ by an operator o. Operators are built-in, and include standard mathematical ones (e.g. addition, sine): they are applied in a pointwise manner to all devices. For instance, if $e_t$ is a field of Fahrenheit temperatures, then the corresponding field of Celsius temperatures is naturally written (* (/ 5 9) (- $e_t$ 32)). Execution of built-in operators is context-dependent, i.e., it can be affected by the current state of the external world. So, 0-ary operator self gives a field that maps each device to its identifier, dt maps each device to the time elapsed since its previous computation round, and finally `nbr-range` maps each device to a table associating estimated distances to each neighbour (such a table being a field itself).

The second construct is *function (definition and) call*, which we use as abstraction tool and to support recursion: $(f\ e_1\ e_2\ ...\ e_n)$ is the field obtained as result of applying user-defined function `f` to the fields $e_1, e_2, ...\ e_n$. Such functions are declared with syntax $(def\ f(\bar{x})\ e)$. For instance, after definition `(def convert (x) (* (/ 5 9) (- x 32)))`, expression $(convert\ e_t)$ denotes the same field of Celsius temperatures as above. Note that function definitions, along with the top-level expression, form a program P.

The third construct is *time evolution*, used to keep track of a changing state over time: `(rep x w e)` is initially the field `w` (a local value or a variable) that is stored in the new variable `x`, and at each step in time is updated to a new field as computed by `e`, based on the prior value of `x`. For instance, `(rep x 0 (+ x 1))` is the (evolving) field counting in each device how many rounds that device has computed. Similarly, `(rep x 0 (+ x (dt)))` is the field of time passing.

The fourth construct is *neighbourhood field construction*, the mechanism by which information moves between devices: `(nbr e)` maps each device to the field of its neighbours' local value of field `e`; hence, it is a field of neighbourhood fields like the output of `nbr-range` above. As an example, let `min-hood` be the operator taking a neighbourhood field and returning its minimum value, then $(min\text{-}hood\ (nbr\ e_t))$ is the field mapping each device to the minimum temperature perceived in its neighbourhood.

The last construct is *domain restriction*, a sort of distributed branch: $(if\ e_0\ e_1\ e_2)$ is the field obtained by superimposing field $e_1$ computed everywhere $e_0$ is true and $e_2$ everywhere $e_0$ is false. As an example $(if\ e_{fah}\ e_t\ (convert\ e_t))$ is the field of temperatures provided in Fahrenheit (resp. Celsius) where the field $e_{fah}$ is true (resp. false). Restriction is the most subtle of the five mechanisms, because it has the effect of preventing the unexpected spreading of computation to devices outside of the required domain, even within arbitrarily nested function calls, as will be clarified in the following.

We now present some examples to illustrate how these five key mechanisms can be combined to implement useful spatial patterns.

```
(def gossip-min (source) (rep d source (min-hood (nbr d))))

(def distance-to (source)
   (rep d infinity (mux source 0 (min-hood (+ (nbr d) (nbr-range))))))

(def distance-obs-to (source obstacle)
      (if (not obstacle) (distance-to source) infinity))
```

We first exemplify how constructs `rep` and `nbr` can be nested to create a long-distance computation, to achieve network-wide propagation processes. Function `gossip-min` takes a `source` field and produces a new field mapping each device to the minimum value that `source` initially takes. The `rep` construct initially sets the output variable `d` at `source`, and it iteratively updates the value at each device with the minimum one available in d's neighbours. Hence, `gossip-min` describes a process of gossiping values until the minimum one converges throughout the network.

Similarly, function `distance-to` takes as its input a `source` field holding boolean values, and returns a new scalar field that maps each device to the estimated distance to the nearest device where `source` is true. This works by first setting d to infinity, then updating it as follows: sources are of course at distance 0, while all other devices use the triangle inequality, finding the minimum sum of a neighbour's estimated distance d and the distance to that neighbour. Operator `mux`, used to combine the two, is a purely functional multiplexer, which uses the first input to choose whether to return the second or third. The field returned by `distance-to` is often also referred to as a *gradient* [11,4,17], and is a key building block for many computations in mobile ad-hoc networks, such as finding routes to points of interest. There are many similar variants with different purposes, most of which automatically repair themselves when either the sources or network structure change.

The last definition exemplifies the use of construct `if`. It creates two different spatial domains: one where the obstacle is present (field `obstacle` holds positive boolean value) and one where is not. In the former an infinity constant field is computed; in the latter we spread the `distance-to` field. As a result, distance estimation as provided by `distance-to` automatically takes into account the need of circumventing obstacle areas, since information does not cross the two domains due to the semantics of `nbr` as explained in next section.

A number of coordination mechanisms can be constructed on the basis of these examples, like the gradient-based patterns discussed in [17,13,19], which find applications in many areas, including crowd steering in pervasive computing.

## 3   From Global to Local

The description of field constructs so far has focused on what we can call the *global viewpoint*, in which the computation is considered as occurring on the overall computational fields distributed in the network. For the calculus to be actually executed, however, each device has to perform a specific set of actions at particular times, including interaction with neighbours and local computations. The result of these local actions then produces the overall evolution of computational fields. We call this description of the language in term of individual devices the *local viewpoint*, and it is this view that we shall use for the operational semantics. Let us now begin with an informal presentation of the peculiar aspects of that operational semantics, to aid in understanding the full formalisation presented in Section 4.

Following the approach considered in Proto [12] and many other distributed programming languages, devices undergo computation in rounds. In each round, a device sleeps for some limited time, wakes up, gathers information about messages received while sleeping, performs its actual field evaluation, and finally emits a message to all neighbours with information about the outcome of computation, before going back to sleep.

Taking the local viewpoint, we may model a field computation by modeling the evaluation of a single device at a single round, assuming the scheduling of such rounds across the network be fair and non-synchronous—either fully asynchronous or partially synchronous, meaning that devices cannot execute infinitely quickly. Assuming that the main bottleneck in the system is communication rather than computation (which is frequently the case in wireless communication networks), this model can be readily achieved by any collection of devices with internal clocks that schedule execution of rounds at regular intervals. So long as the relative drift between clocks is not extreme, execution on such a system will be fair and partially synchronous.

To support the combination of field constructs, we design our operational semantics as follows. First, our functional style of composition, definition and calls, fits well with a small-step evaluation semantics, in which we start from the initial expression to evaluate and reduce it to a normal form representing the outcome of computation, including the local value of the resulting field and the information to be spread to neighbours. In order to keep track of the state of variables introduced by rep constructs, and values at nbr constructs to be exchanged with neighbours, we take our computational state to be the dynamically produced evaluation tree. During a round of computation, such a tree is incrementally decorated with partial results expressed as *annotations* of the form "$\cdot v$" or *superscripts* "$^{s}$". These decorations track the local outcome of evaluation and determine which subexpression will be next evaluated.

To illustrate our management of evaluation order and computational rounds, as well as the rep construct, let us begin by considering expression (rep x 0 (+ x 1)) (cf. Section 2). As this tree is evaluated according to the operational semantics, it goes through a sequence of four transitions. We show these informally by in each step underlining the next portion of the tree to be rewritten, by coloring the changes introduced by each rewrite red (they will appear grey in a non-color print of the paper), and by labelling the transitions with the (nested) rules of the operational semantics causing the transition. The rules may be ignored for now, and be considered later to understand the formal calculus in Section 4. The first computation round goes as follows:

$$(\text{rep x 0 (+ } \underline{x}\ 1)) \xrightarrow{\text{[REP,CONG,VAR]}} (\text{rep x 0 (+ x}\cdot 0\ \underline{1})) \xrightarrow{\text{[REP,CONG,VAL]}}$$

$$(\text{rep x 0 } \underline{(\text{+ x}\cdot 0\ 1\cdot 1)}) \xrightarrow{\text{[REP,CONG,OP]}} (\text{rep x 0 (+ x}\cdot 0\ 1\cdot 1)\cdot 1)$$

$$\xrightarrow{\text{[REP]}} (\text{rep}^1 \text{ x 0 (+ x}\cdot 0\ 1\cdot 1)\cdot 1)\cdot 1$$

Annotations are computed depth-first in the expression tree until eventually reaching the outer expression: we first annotate variable x with its current (initial) value 0, then simply identically annotate value 1, then perform built-in operation + causing annotation of its sub-tree with 1, and finally execute the rep construct, which records the result value as a superscript to rep and as an annotation of the whole expression.

Once the evaluation is complete, with the result value in the outer-most annotation, the whole evaluation tree will be shipped as a message to neighbours, in order to align nbr statements and share values between neighbours, as described later. Pragmatically, of course, any implementation might massively compress the tree, sending only enough information for nbr statements to be aligned.

The subsequent round begins after an initialisation that erases all non-superscript decorations. This second round leads to evaluation tree $(\text{rep}^2 \text{ x 0 (+ x}\cdot 1\ 1\cdot 1)\cdot 2)\cdot 2$, third one to $(\text{rep}^3 \text{ x 0 (+ x}\cdot 2\ 1\cdot 1)\cdot 3)\cdot 3$, and so on.

The main purpose of managing evaluation trees in this way is to support information exchange through the nbr construct. Consider the expression (min-hood (nbr (t))) (cf. Section 2), where t is a 0-ary built-in operator that returns the temperature perceived in each device. If a device $\sigma$ perceives a temperature of 7 degrees Celsius, and executes its first computation round before its neighbours, then the result of computation should clearly be 7. This is implemented by the following sequence of transitions:

$$(\text{min-hood } (\text{nbr } \underline{(t)})) \xrightarrow{[\text{CONG,CONG,OP}]} (\text{min-hood } (\text{nbr } \underline{(t)\cdot 7})) \xrightarrow{[\text{CONG,NBR}]}$$

$$(\text{min-hood } \underline{(\text{nbr } (t)\cdot 7)\cdot(\sigma \mapsto 7)}) \xrightarrow{[\text{OP}]} (\text{min-hood } (\text{nbr } (t)\cdot 7)\cdot(\sigma \mapsto 7))\cdot 7$$

We first enter the subexpression with the 0-ary operator t which yields 7. We then evaluate nbr to the field of neighbour values, associating only $\sigma$ to 7, written $(\sigma \mapsto 7)$. Finally, we evaluate unary operator min-hood, which extracts the smallest element of the input field, which in this case is 7.

Construct nbr retrieves values from neighbours using the *tree environment* of the device $\sigma$, which models its store of recent messages received from neighbours. The tree environment is a mapping $\Theta = (\sigma_1 \mapsto e_1, \ldots, \sigma_n \mapsto e_n)$ created at each round, from neighbours $(\sigma_i)$ to their last-received evaluation tree $(e_i)$, which we call the *neighbour tree* of $\sigma_i$. The evaluation of (nbr e), where e is evaluated to local value l, takes values from the tree environment to produce a field $(\sigma \mapsto l, \sigma_1 \mapsto l_1, \ldots, \sigma_n \mapsto l_n)$, mapping $\sigma$ to l and each neighbour $\sigma_i$ to the corresponding local value $l_i$ from $\sigma_i$.

In the example above we assumed that none of the neighbours of $\sigma$ had already completed a round of computation, and that therefore $\Theta$ was empty and accordingly (nbr (t)) gave simply $(\sigma \mapsto 7)$. If we instead assume that the first round of computation on the device $\sigma$ takes place when the neighbours $\sigma_1$ and $\sigma_2$ have completed exactly one round of computation, perceiving temperatures of 4 and 9 degrees respectively, then the tree environment of $\sigma$ would be $(\sigma_1 \mapsto e_1, \sigma_2 \mapsto e_2)$, where $e_1 = (\text{min-hood } (\text{nbr } (t)\cdot 4)\cdot(\sigma \mapsto 4))\cdot 4$ and $e_2 = (\text{min-hood } (\text{nbr } (t)\cdot 9)\cdot(\sigma \mapsto 9))\cdot 9$. The computation goes similarly, the only difference is that the evaluation of (nbr (t)·7) now produces the field $\phi = (\sigma \mapsto 7, \sigma_1 \mapsto 4, \sigma_2 \mapsto 9)$ and the final outcome of the computation round on $\sigma$ is the tree (min-hood (nbr (t)·7)·$\phi$)·4.

More specifically, the extraction of values from neighbours is achieved by computing the local evaluation tree "against" the set of its neighbour trees: when evaluation enters a subtree, in the tree environment $\Theta$ we correspondingly enter the corresponding subtree on all of its neighbour trees, which are structurally compatible by construction since each node executes the same program. This process on neighbour trees is called *alignment*. So, in the example above, sub-tree (nbr (t)·7) is recursively evaluated against the neighbour sub-trees $(\sigma_1 \mapsto (\text{nbr } (t)\cdot 4) \cdot (\sigma_1 \mapsto 4), \sigma_2 \mapsto (\text{nbr } (t)\cdot 9) \cdot (\sigma_2 \mapsto 9))$, in which the neighbour values are immediately available as the outermost annotation of the argument of nbr.

One reason for using this structural alignment mechanism is to seamlessly handle the cases where nbr subtrees could be nested at a deep level of the evaluation tree because of (possibly recursive) function calls. Assume definition (def f (x) (min-hood (nbr x))), and the main expression (f (t)) whose expected behaviour is then equivalent to our prior example $(\texttt{min-hood}\ (\texttt{nbr}\ (\texttt{t})))$. This expression would be handled by the following sequence of transitions:

$$(\texttt{f}\ \underline{(\texttt{t})}) \xrightarrow{\text{[CONG,OP]}} (\texttt{f}\ (\texttt{t})\cdot 7) \xrightarrow{\text{[FUN,CONG,CONG,VAR]}} (\texttt{f}^{(\texttt{min-hood}\ \underline{(\texttt{nbr}\ \texttt{x}\cdot 7)})}\ (\texttt{t})\cdot 7) \xrightarrow{\text{[FUN,CONG,NBR]}}$$

$$(\texttt{f}^{\underline{(\texttt{min-hood}\ (\texttt{nbr}\ \texttt{x}\cdot 7)\cdot\phi)}}\ (\texttt{t})\cdot 7) \xrightarrow{\text{[FUN,OP]}} (\texttt{f}^{(\texttt{min-hood}\ (\texttt{nbr}\ \texttt{x}\cdot 7)\cdot\phi)}\ (\texttt{t})\cdot 7)\cdot 4$$

After the function arguments are all evaluated, the second transition creates a superscript to function $\texttt{f}$, holding the evaluation tree corresponding to its body. This gets evaluated as usual, and its resulting annotation 4 is transferred to become the annotation of the function call. So, note that the evaluation tree is a dynamically expanding data structure because of such function superscripts being generated and navigated at each call, with alignment automatically handling $\texttt{nbr}$ construct, even for arbitrary recursive call structures. Note that this mechanism also prevents terminating recursive calls from implying infinite evaluation trees, since only those calls that are actually made are annotated.

This management of memory trees also easily accommodates the semantics of restriction. An $\texttt{if}$ sub-expression is evaluated by first evaluating its condition, then evaluating the selected branch, and finally erasing all decorations on the non-taken branch, including superscripts. In this way, neighbour trees corresponding to devices that took a different branch will be automatically discarded at alignment time, since entering the same subexpression is impossible because of a bad match. For example, consider expression $(\texttt{if}\ (\texttt{b})\ (\texttt{f}\ (\texttt{t}))\ 0)$, where operator b returns a boolean field that is true at $\sigma$ and $\sigma_2$, and false at $\sigma_1$. Assuming again that first round of $\sigma$ happens after first round of $\sigma_1$ and $\sigma_2$, we have:

$$(\texttt{if}\ \underline{(\texttt{b})}\ (\texttt{f}\ (\texttt{t}))\ 0) \xrightarrow{\text{[CONG,OP]}} (\texttt{if}\ (\texttt{b})\cdot\texttt{true}\ (\texttt{f}\ (\texttt{t}))\ 0) \to^*$$

$$(\texttt{if}\ (\texttt{b})\cdot\texttt{true}\ (\texttt{f}^{(\texttt{min-hood}\ (\texttt{nbr}\ \texttt{x}\cdot 7)\cdot(\sigma\mapsto 7,\sigma_2\mapsto 9))}\ (\texttt{t})\cdot 7)\cdot 7\ 0) \xrightarrow{\text{[THEN]}}$$

$$(\texttt{if}\ (\texttt{b})\cdot\texttt{true}\ (\texttt{f}^{(\texttt{min-hood}\ (\texttt{nbr}\ \texttt{x}\cdot 7)\cdot(\sigma\mapsto 7,\sigma_2\mapsto 9))}\ (\texttt{t})\cdot 7)\cdot 7\ |0|)\cdot 7$$

The reason why the $\texttt{rep}$ sub-expression now yields field $(\sigma \mapsto 7, \sigma_2 \mapsto 9)$ is that the neighbour tree of $\sigma_1$ cannot be aligned, for it has $(\texttt{b})$ annotated with $\texttt{false}$, which does not match. Hence, $\texttt{nbr}$ will retrieve values only from the *aligned nodes* that followed the same branch, avoiding interference from nodes residing in different regions of the partition made by restriction. The erasure of the non-taken branch by operator $|.|$ (0 trivially erases to 0 in this case) is used to completely reinitialise computation there, since the node no longer belongs to the domain in which the non-taken branch should be evaluated.

## 4    The Computational Field Calculus

The computational field calculus formalisation is set forth in Figure 2 and described here in turn after a few preliminaries. We let $\sigma$ range over device unique identifiers and $\phi$ over field values (mapping set of devices to local values). Given any meta-variable $y$ we let $\mathring{y}$ range over an element $y$ or the *null decoration* (which in the calculus is $\circ$ when it has to be expressed, and blank otherwise). The calculus is agnostic to the syntax of local values: we only assume they include at least device identifiers and value 0. We let metavariables $f$ and $t$ range over boolean-interpreted values, orderly 0 and any other value.

**Runtime Expression Syntax:**

| | | |
|---|---|---|
| $e$ | $::= a\cdot\mathring{v}$ | runtime expression (rte) |
| $a$ | $::= \mathtt{x} \mid v \mid (\mathtt{nbr}\, e) \mid (\mathtt{if}\, e\, e\, e) \mid (\mathtt{rep^s}\, \mathtt{x}\, \mathtt{w}\, e) \mid (\mathtt{f^s}\, \overline{e}) \mid (\mathtt{o}\, \overline{e})$ | auxiliary rte |
| $v$ | $::= \mathtt{l} \mid \phi$ | runtime value |
| $s$ | $::= \mathring{a}$ | superscript |
| $\mathtt{w}$ | $::= \mathtt{x} \mid \mathtt{l}$ | variable or local value |
| $\phi$ | $::= \overline{\sigma} \mapsto \overline{\mathtt{l}}$ | field value |
| $\Theta$ | $::= \overline{\sigma} \mapsto \overline{e}$ | tree environment |
| $\Gamma$ | $::= \overline{\mathtt{x}} := \overline{v}$ | variable environment |

**Congruence Contexts:**

$$\mathbb{C} ::= (\mathtt{nbr}\, []) \mid (\mathtt{f^s}\, \overline{e}\, []\, \overline{e}) \mid (\mathtt{o}\, \overline{e}\, []\, \overline{e}) \mid (\mathtt{if}\, []\, e\, e) \mid (\mathtt{if}\, a{\cdot}t\, []\, e) \mid (\mathtt{if}\, a{\cdot}f e\, [])$$

**Alignment contexts:**

$$\mathbb{A} ::= \mathbb{C} \mid (\mathtt{rep^s}\, \mathtt{x}\, \mathtt{w}\, []) \mid (\mathtt{f}^{[]}\, \overline{a\cdot v})$$

**Auxiliary functions:**

$$\pi_{\mathbb{A}}(\Theta, \Theta') = \pi_{\mathbb{A}}(\Theta), \pi_{\mathbb{A}}(\Theta')$$
$$\pi_{\mathbb{A}}(\sigma \mapsto (\mathbb{A}'[e])\cdot v) = \sigma \mapsto e \qquad \text{if } \mathbb{A}' :: \mathbb{A}$$
$$\pi_{\mathbb{A}}(\sigma \mapsto e) = \bullet \qquad \text{otherwise}$$

$$s \rhd a = a$$
$$s \rhd \mathtt{o} = s$$

$$(\mathtt{nbr}\, []) :: (\mathtt{nbr}\, [])$$
$$(\mathtt{f^{s'}}\, e'_1...e'_{i-1}\, []\, e'_{i+1}...e'_n) :: (\mathtt{f^s}\, e_1...e_{i-1}\, []\, e_{i+1}...e_n)$$
$$(\mathtt{o}\, e'_1...e'_{i-1}\, []\, e'_{i+1}...e'_n) :: (\mathtt{o}\, e_1...e_{i-1}\, []\, e_{i+1}...e_n)$$
$$(\mathtt{if}\, []\, e'_1\, e'_2)) :: (\mathtt{if}\, []\, e_1\, e_2))$$
$$(\mathtt{if}\, a'{\cdot}t\, []\, e') :: (\mathtt{if}\, a{\cdot}t\, []\, e)$$
$$(\mathtt{if}\, a'{\cdot}f e\, []) :: (\mathtt{if}\, a{\cdot}f e\, [])$$
$$(\mathtt{rep^{s'}}\, \mathtt{x}\, \mathtt{w}\, []) :: (\mathtt{rep^s}\, \mathtt{x}\, \mathtt{w}\, [])$$
$$(\mathtt{f}^{[]}\, e'_1...e'_n) :: (\mathtt{f}^{[]}\, e_1...e_n)$$

**Reduction Rules:**

[THEN]
$$\Theta; \Gamma \vdash (\mathtt{if}\, a{\cdot}t\, a'{\cdot}\mathtt{l}\, e) \to (\mathtt{if}\, a{\cdot}t\, a'{\cdot}\mathtt{l}\, |e|)\cdot\mathtt{l}$$

[VAL]
$$\Theta; \Gamma \vdash v \to v\cdot v$$

[ELSE]
$$\Theta; \Gamma \vdash (\mathtt{if}\, a{\cdot}f e\, a'{\cdot}\mathtt{l}) \to (\mathtt{if}\, a{\cdot}f\, |e|\, a'{\cdot}\mathtt{l})\cdot\mathtt{l}$$

[VAR]
$$\Theta; \Gamma \vdash \mathtt{x} \to \mathtt{x}\cdot\Gamma(\mathtt{x})|_{dom(\Theta), \varepsilon(\mathtt{self})}$$

[CONG] $\dfrac{\pi_{\mathbb{C}}(\Theta); \Gamma \vdash a \to e}{\Theta; \Gamma \vdash \mathbb{C}[a] \to \mathbb{C}[e]}$

[NBR]
$$\dfrac{\pi_{(\mathtt{nbr}\, [])}(\Theta) = \overline{\sigma} \mapsto \overline{a}\cdot\overline{\mathtt{l}} \quad \phi = (\overline{\sigma} \mapsto \overline{\mathtt{l}}, \varepsilon(\mathtt{self}) \mapsto \mathtt{l})}{\Theta; \Gamma \vdash (\mathtt{nbr}\, a\cdot\mathtt{l}) \to (\mathtt{nbr}\, a\cdot\mathtt{l})\cdot\phi}$$

[REP] $\dfrac{\pi_{(\mathtt{rep^i}\, \mathtt{x}\, \mathtt{w}\, [])}(\Theta); \Gamma, (\mathtt{x} := (\Gamma(\mathtt{w}) \rhd \mathring{\mathtt{l}})) \vdash a \to a'\cdot\mathring{v}}{\Theta; \Gamma \vdash (\mathtt{rep^i}\, \mathtt{x}\, \mathtt{w}\, a) \to (\mathtt{rep}^{\mathtt{l}\rhd\mathring{v}}\, \mathtt{x}\, \mathtt{w}\, a'\cdot\mathring{v})\cdot\mathring{v}}$

[OP]
$$\Theta; \Gamma \vdash (\mathtt{o}\, \overline{a\cdot v}) \to (\mathtt{o}\, \overline{a\cdot v})\cdot\varepsilon(\mathtt{o}, \overline{v})$$

[FUN] $\dfrac{\pi_{(\mathtt{f^s}\, \overline{a\cdot v})}(\Theta); (args(\mathtt{f}) := \overline{v}) \vdash (body(\mathtt{f}) \rhd s) \to a\cdot\mathring{v}}{\Theta; \Gamma \vdash (\mathtt{f^s}\, \overline{a\cdot v}) \to (\mathtt{f^a}\, \overline{a\cdot v})\cdot\mathring{v}}$

**Fig. 2.** Device Semantics

**Runtime Expression Syntax.** A runtime expression is the evaluation tree created out of a surface expression. It is similar to expressions in the surface syntax (cf. Figure 1) with the following differences (see Figure 2): *(i)* a (runtime) value $v$ is either a local value $\mathtt{l}$ or a field value $\phi$; *(ii)* a run-time expression $e$ can be coupled (at any level of depth) with optional *annotation* $\mathring{v}$ representing the transient side-effect of a computation; *(iii)* constructs rep and function calls can have a *superscript* (s) representing the durable side-effect of a computation. Note that, syntactically, surface syntax expressions can (and will) be used to denote runtime expressions with null decorations in all annotations and superscripts.

The erasure operator $|\cdot|$ turns a runtime expression $e$ (or an auxiliary rte $a$) to the surface expression $|e|$ (resp. $|a|$) obtained by dropping all annotations and superscripts. The erasure of an expression $e$ (or $a$) is defined if and only if for every auxiliary rte $a'$ occurring in $e$ (resp. $a$): $(i)$ $a' = (\mathtt{nbr}\, a''\cdot v)$ implies that the runtime value $v$ is a local value, and $(ii)$ $a' = (\mathtt{f}^{a''}\, \overline{e})$ implies that $|a''|$ is the body of the the function $\mathtt{f}$.

Note that fields are actually mappings, for which we introduce some syntactic conventions and operators. A field value $\phi$ can either be written as $\sigma_1 \mapsto \mathtt{1}_1, \ldots, \sigma_n \mapsto \mathtt{1}_n$ or be shortened by notation $\overline{\sigma} \mapsto \overline{\mathtt{1}}$. The domain of $\phi$, which is the set $\{\sigma_1, \ldots, \sigma_n\}$, is denoted by $\mathbf{dom}(\phi)$. The value $\mathtt{1}_i$ associated to a given device $\sigma_i$ by field $\phi$ is retrieved by notation $\phi(\sigma_i)$. Since a field can be seen as a list, we use the notation $\bullet$ for the empty field, and comma as list concatenation operator: e.g. $\phi, \phi'$ is the field having both the mappings of $\phi$ and $\phi'$. We shall sometime restrict the domain of a field $\phi$ to a given set of devices $\overline{\sigma}$, which we denote as $\phi|_{\overline{\sigma}}$. When restriction is applied to local values it works as the identity function. A tree environment, $\Theta$, maps devices to runtime expressions (namely, it keeps neighbour trees), and a variable environment, $\Gamma$, maps variables to runtime values. Since tree environments and variable environments are also mappings, all the above conventions and operators will be used for them as well.

To take into account special constants, mathematical operations, usual abstract data types operations, and context-dependent operators, we introduce a special function $\varepsilon$. This is such that $\varepsilon(\mathtt{o}, \overline{v})$ computes the result of applying built-in operator $\mathtt{o}$ to values $\overline{v}$. In particular, we assume constant $\mathtt{self}$ gets evaluated to the current device identifier. In order not to escape the domain restricted by operator $\mathtt{if}$, as discussed in Sections 2 and 3, for each primitive operator $\mathtt{o}$ we assume that: $(i)$ $\varepsilon(\mathtt{o}, v_1, \cdots, v_n)$ is defined (i.e., its evaluation does not get stuck) only if all the field values in $v_1, \ldots, v_n$ have the same domain; and $(ii)$ if $\varepsilon(\mathtt{o}, v_1, \cdots, v_n)$ returns a field value $\phi$ and there is at least one field value $v_i$ in $v_1, \ldots, v_n$, then $\mathbf{dom}(\phi) = \mathbf{dom}(v_i)$.

**Congruence Contexts and Alignment Contexts.** The operational semantics uses *congruence contexts*, ranged over by $\mathbb{C}$, to impose an order of evaluation of subexpressions in an orthogonal way with respect to the actual semantic rules; and it uses *alignment contexts*, ranged over by $\mathbb{A}$, to properly navigate into evaluation trees. In particular, note that $\mathbb{C}$ is a subcase of $\mathbb{A}$ (see Figure 2).

A context $\mathbb{A}$ is an auxiliary runtime expression with a *hole* $[]$. As usual, we write $\mathbb{A}[e]$ to denote runtime expression obtained by filling the hole of $\mathbb{A}$ with the runtime expression $e$. If a given runtime expression $e$ matches $\mathbb{C}[e']$, then $e'$ is the next subexpression of $e$ where evaluation will occur, positioned in $e$ as described by the position of $[]$ in $\mathbb{C}$. The way the syntax of congruence contexts $\mathbb{C}$ is structured constraints the operational semantics to evaluate the first argument of $\mathtt{if}$ and then, depending on its outcome, the second or third, and to non-deterministically evaluate arguments in function and operation calls. For instance, the runtime expression $(\ast\ 1 \cdot 1\ (+\ 2 \cdot 2\ 3))$ matches $\mathbb{C}'[e']$ only by $\mathbb{C}' = (\ast\ 1 \cdot 1\ [])$ and $e' = (+\ 2 \cdot 2\ 3)$: this means that $e'$ contains the next subexpression to evaluate. The expression $e'$, in turn, matches $\mathbb{C}''[e'']$ only by $\mathbb{C}'' = (+\ 2 \cdot 2\ [])$ and $e'' = 3$. Therefore 3 is the next subexpression to evaluate (becoming $3 \cdot 3$).

**Auxiliary Functions.** The projection operator $\pi$ implements the mechanism for synchronising navigation of an evaluation tree with those of neighbour trees. Namely, $\pi_{\mathbb{A}}(\Theta)$ takes a tree environment $\Theta$ and extracts a new tree environment obtained by discarding the trees that do not match the alignment context $\mathbb{A}$ (according to the *alignment context matching relation* "::") and extracting the corresponding subtree matching the hole in the remaining ones. As an example, given $\Theta_0 = (\ \sigma_1 \mapsto (\texttt{if}\ \textit{at}\ e_1\ e_2)\cdot v_1,\ \sigma_2 \mapsto (\texttt{if}\ a'f e_3\ e_4)\cdot v_2\ )$ and $\mathbb{A} = (\texttt{if}\ a't\ [\ ]\ e'_2)$, we have $\pi_{\mathbb{A}}(\Theta_0) = (\sigma_1 \mapsto e_1)$. In fact, the evaluation tree for $\sigma_2$ is discarded since it does not match $\mathbb{A}$ due to the label of first argument being $f$, while the evaluation tree for $\sigma_1$ matches and extracts $e_1$.

The replacement operator $\triangleright$ is introduced that retains the right-hand side if this is not empty, otherwise it takes the left-hand side. It is useful to handily update null decorations.

**Reduction Rules.** Following [10], we formulate the reduction relation by means of reduction rules (which may be applied at any point in an expression) and congruence rules (which express the fact that if $e \to e'$ then $(\texttt{o}\ e_1 \ldots e_{i-1}\ e\ e_{i+1} \ldots e_n) \to (\texttt{o}\ e_1 \ldots e_{i-1}\ e'\ e_{i+1} \ldots e_n)$, and so on). The reduction relation is of the form $\boxed{\Theta; \Gamma \vdash e \to e'}$, to be read "expression $e$ reduces to expression $e'$ in one step", where $\Theta$ is the current tree environment and $\Gamma$ is the current store of variables (which is built incrementally in each reduction step by the congruence rules [REP] and [FUN] when evaluation enters the third argument of a rep-expressions or the body of a function, respectively).

The reduction relation models the execution of a single computation round, computed as $\Theta; \bullet \vdash a \to^* a' \cdot v$ where: $\Theta$ is the set of evaluation trees produced by neighbours at their prior computation round; the variable environment is empty (the main expression must not contain free variables); and $a$ is the runtime expression resulting from the computation of previous round with all the annotations (not superscripts) erased—at very first round $a$ is simply the top-level surface expression. During computation steps the run-time expression will be decorated with annotations, until one appears at top level in the final runtime expression $a' \cdot v$, where $v$ represents the local value of the computational field currently computed. Also some superscripts will be present at the end of the round, for they represent the side-effect of computation on the evaluation tree that should be transferred to next round. In particular, as already mentioned: *(i)* the final runtime expression $a' \cdot v$ will be shipped to neighbours replacing there the one previously sent (and being dropped only when the current device exists the neighbourhood); *(ii)* the runtime expression obtained from $a' \cdot v$ by dropping all annotations (not superscripts), denoted by $init(a' \cdot v)$, will be used as starting point for the next round computation.

We now describe each reduction rule in turn. Computation rules have a common pattern: they compute a result value $v$, which appears as top-level annotation—in the following we shall say that $v$ is the "local result". Rule [VAL] simply identically annotates a value. Rule [VAR] looks at the value $\Gamma(x)$ associated to x by the variable environment, and (in case it is a field) restricts it to the set of currently aligned neighbours $\overline{\sigma}$ (plus the local device $\varepsilon(\texttt{self})$). Rule [NBR] is the one actually exploiting $\Theta$: let 1 be the value locally computed, we extract the corresponding values $\overline{1}$ from aligned neighbours $\overline{\sigma}$, and use as local result the corresponding field $\overline{\sigma} \mapsto \overline{1}$ (adding the local slot $\texttt{self} \mapsto 1$). Rule [OP] computes the result of applying operator o to values $\overline{v}$ (done by function $\varepsilon$, which gives semantics to operators), to be used as local result. Rules [THEN] and [ELSE] handle condition branching: rule [THEN] (resp. [ELSE]) uses the label of second (resp. third) argument as local result in case of positive (resp. negative) condition, and erases the other branch (which may contain superscripts generated in the previous round).

Rule [CONG] can be understood as a compact representation for six different congruence rules, corresponding to the 6 cases for the context $\mathbb{C}$. While navigating the evaluation tree inside context $\mathbb{C}$ to identify the next evaluation site $a$ (which should be non-annotated), this rule contemporarily enters the same context into all slots of the tree environment $\Theta$, guaranteeing that the expression to evaluate is kept synchronised with the corresponding trees in $\Theta$. Note that rule [CONG] does not describe the congruence rules for rep-expressions and function applications. In fact, the metavariable $\mathbb{C}$ does not range over contexts of the form $(\text{rep}^{\hat{\imath}}\ \text{x}\ \text{w}\ [])$ and $(\text{f}^{[]}\ \bar{a} \cdot \bar{v})$. The rational for this choice is that the corresponding rules, [REP] and [FUN], need to update the variable environment $\Gamma$ by adding to $\Gamma$ the rep-bound variable x or by completely replacing $\Gamma$ with the environment for the function formal parameters $args(\text{f})$, respectively. Moreover, [REP] and [FUN] are not pure congruence rules: each of them encodes a congruence rule possibly followed by a computation rule. Note that this encoding exploits the notation $\mathring{y}$ and the auxiliary function $\triangleright$ defined above.

Rule [REP] handles evolution of a field. When the superscript $\mathring{\imath}$ is null, the evaluation of the body of rep-expression is carried on in an environment that assigns to the rep-bound variable x the value of the variable or local value w—with abuse of notation we indicate it as $\Gamma(\text{w})$: when w is a local value $\text{l}$ we assume $\Gamma(\text{l}) = \text{l}$. When the superscript $\mathring{\imath}$ is a local value $\text{l}$, the evaluation of the body of rep-expression is carried on in an environment that assigns to the rep-bound variable x the value $\text{l}$. If the reduction step performed (in the premise of the rule) on the body of the rep-expression produces an evaluated runtime expression (i.e., if the annotation $\mathring{v}$ is not null), then the local result is propagated to the rep-expression (which becomes evaluated).

When the actual parameters of a function call are evaluated, rule [FUN] performs a reduction step on the function body in an environment consisting of the proper association of formal parameters $args(\text{f})$ to values $\bar{v}$: the (possibly null) resulting annotation $\mathring{v}$ is transferred as local result. If the superscript s is null, replacement operator $\triangleright$ guarantees the function body is used instead.

# 5   Properties

A key property to pave the way towards advanced forms of behavioural analysis is the following soundness. We say that the operational semantics of the field calculus is *sound* to mean that the execution of a *well-formed* surface program satisfies the following two properties:

**P1.** The reduction does not get stuck.
**P2.** The domain of every field value arising during the reduction consists of the identifiers of the aligned neighbours and of the identifier of the self device.

While the former follows from the standard type soundness argument, the latter is needed to guarantee a proper handling of restriction. Of course, it is key to find a definition of well-formedness for expressions that filters out those expressions which would eventually lead to either P1 or P2 failing to hold, without restring the expressive power of the language.

Let us illustrate how well-formedness should work with some counter-examples, all connected to the novel issues of field values rather than just the more typical elements shared with many other calculi. Any program containing a non-well-formed function or expression is non-well-formed. An example of a non-well-formed function is (def wrong-distance-to (x) (distance-to (nbr x))), using the function distance-to defined in Section 2. In this example, the field value $\phi$, which is produced by (nbr x) and passed into distance-to, conflicts with its use as the first input to mux, which requires a local value for $\varepsilon$. Rule [OP] thus cannot be applied, and the evaluation cannot be completed.

Another example is the function (def wrong-f-two (x) (min-hood (min-hood (nbr (nbr x))))), which tries to find the minimum value of x within two hops. This fails to evaluate because Rule [NBR] requires its input to be a local value, and thus cannot be applied to the outer nbr. This prevents the need to communicate a field value whose size scales linearly with the number of neighbours, which might be extremely burdensome. A well-formed alternative that produces the same computational result as wrong-f-two is intended to is (def right-f-two (x) (min-hood (nbr (min-hood (nbr x))))). This takes advantage of the commutative property of minimisation to break the minimisation into two stages, thus avoiding the communication explosion of the not well-formed formulation.

A final example is the function (def wrong-nbr-if (x y z) (min-hood (- (if (sense 1) (nbr x) (nbr y)) (nbr z))). This will fail to evaluate on Rules [THEN] and [ELSE], since they require local values for the test and returned values. This prevents conflicts between field domains, as in this case, where the field produced by (nbr z) would contain all neighbours, while the field produced by the if expression would contain only a subset, leaving the fields mismatched in domain at the subtraction. A correct alternative is (def right-nbr-if (x y z) (min-hood (- (nbr (if (sense 1) x y)) (nbr z))), which conducts the test locally, ensuring that the domains of the two fields match.

We argue that these sorts of well-formedness problems are detectable as type errors through static analysis, without having to evaluate the program in a full context. We are currently working at a formalisation of the notion of well-formed surface program by means of a simple type system designed to support the formal statement for properties P1 and P2.

# 6    Conclusion, Related and Future Work

A number of works present notions of computational fields; a thorough review may be found in [5]. Regarding the most similar: the Hood sensor network abstraction [20] and Butera's "paintable computing" hardware model [7] implement computational fields using only the local view, and thus do not ensure well-formed domains. The $\sigma\tau$-Linda model [19] proposes an extension of Linda with few constructs for spreading tuples to form fields, and adopting a notion of computation rounds very similar to the one we formalised. More generally, while all of the key ingredients for programming computational fields are supported in a number of different languages (see [5]), at present only Proto supports all five that we found critical to include in the calculus.

A number of other formal calculi have also been developed for parallel computations in structured environments, like $3\pi$-calculus [8], Ambient calculus [9], and P-systems [14]: they all describe parallel computation over variously abstracted notions of space; differently from our calculus they do not focus on raising the level of abstraction beyond local interaction rules and up to aggregate-level descriptions.

A core operational semantics for discrete execution of Proto programs was developed in [15]. Although closely related to the present one, it was a preliminary attempt extremely limited in the types of computations it could represent, since it did not tackle the fully general problem of combining restriction, evolution, and recursive function calls (i.e. dynamically expanding evaluation trees), which we have addressed through the idea of aligning annotated evaluation trees. Based on [15], in [16] a full formalisation of discrete Proto was provided. This resulted in a rather large semantics aimed at a faithful representation of every construct in Proto and of their execution by the platform—e.g., including an intricate technique for optimising message size. The resulting model is then too complicated to readily use in proving language properties. In contrast, the operational semantics of the calculus presented in this paper is general enough to cover all of Proto and many other spatial languages [5], and is compact enough to be suitable as a basis for tackling interesting properties.

In particular, we believe that equipping the calculus with a sound static type system can bootstrap investigations on other important properties. For example, the work in [6] develops a precise model of spatial computing covering the same key mechanisms considered in this paper, but for fields over *continuous space-time* rather than discrete device executions. In future works, we mean to prove that there is a broad class of cases where our model converges to the continuous one in the limit, as the density of devices increases and the length of time steps decreases. This would allow characterisation of those programs that have a predictable conformation to the aggregate-level behavior independently on the topology (density) and on the timing of devices. Another interesting thread concerns finding a characterisation of expressiveness of spatial computing languages [1], with clear implications in the design of new mechanisms.

This calculus should thus serve as an important step toward identifying an engineering methodology for developing spatial computing and coordination systems able to make use of complex yet predictably well-behaved self-organising mechanisms, both in today's and in emergent distributed computing scenarios.

**Acknowledgements.** We thank the anonymous FOCLASA referees for comments and suggestions for improving the presentation.

# References

1. Beal, J.: A basis set of operators for space-time computations. In: Spatial Computing Workshop (2010), http://www.spatial-computing.org/scw10/
2. Beal, J.: Engineered self-organization approaches to adaptive design. In: Roy, R., Shehab, E., Hockley, C., Khan, S. (eds.) 1st International Conference on Through-life Engineering Services, pp. 35–42. Cranfield University Press (November 2012)

3. Beal, J., Bachrach, J.: Infrastructure for engineered emergence in sensor/actuator networks. IEEE Intelligent Systems 21, 10–19 (2006)
4. Beal, J., Bachrach, J., Vickery, D., Tobenkin, M.: Fast self-healing gradients. In: Proceedings of ACM SAC 2008, pp. 1969–1975. ACM (2008)
5. Beal, J., Dulman, S., Usbeck, K., Viroli, M., Correll, N.: Organizing the aggregate: Languages for spatial computing. In: Mernik, M. (ed.) Formal and Practical Aspects of Domain-Specific Languages: Recent Developments, ch. 16, pp. 436–501. IGI Global (2013), A longer version available at: http://arxiv.org/abs/1202.5509
6. Beal, J., Usbeck, K., Benyo, B.: On the evaluation of space-time functions. The Computer Journal (2012), Online first, available through doi:10.1093/comjnl/bxs099
7. Butera, W.: Programming a Paintable Computer. PhD thesis, MIT, Cambridge, MA, USA (2002)
8. Cardelli, L., Gardner, P.: Processes in space. In: Ferreira, F., Löwe, B., Mayordomo, E., Mendes Gomes, L. (eds.) CiE 2010. LNCS, vol. 6158, pp. 78–87. Springer, Heidelberg (2010)
9. Cardelli, L., Gordon, A.D.: Mobile ambients. Theoretical Computer Science 240(1), 177–213 (2000)
10. Igarashi, A., Pierce, B.C., Wadler, P.: Featherweight Java: A minimal core calculus for Java and GJ. ACM Transactions on Programming Languages and Systems 23(3) (2001)
11. Mamei, M., Zambonelli, F.: Programming pervasive and mobile computing applications: The tota approach. ACM Trans. on Software Engineering Methodologies 18(4), 1–56 (2009)
12. MIT Proto, http://proto.bbn.com (retrieved January 1, 2012)
13. Montagna, S., Viroli, M., Fernandez-Marquez, J.L., Di Marzo Serugendo, G., Zambonelli, F.: Injecting self-organisation into pervasive service ecosystems. Mobile Networks and Applications 18(3), 398–412 (2013)
14. Paun, G.: Computing with membranes. Journal of Computer and System Sciences 61(1), 108–143 (2000)
15. Viroli, M., Beal, J., Casadei, M.: Core operational semantics of Proto. In: Proceedings of ACM SAC 2011, pp. 1325–1332. ACM (March 2011)
16. Viroli, M., Beal, J., Usbeck, K.: Operational semantics of proto. Science of Computer Programming 78(6), 633–656 (2013)
17. Viroli, M., Casadei, M., Montagna, S., Zambonelli, F.: Spatial coordination of pervasive services through chemical-inspired tuple spaces. ACM Transactions on Autonomous and Adaptive Systems 14, 14:1–14:24 (2011)
18. Viroli, M., Casadei, M., Omicini, A.: A framework for modelling and implementing self-organising coordination. In: Proceedings of ACM SAC 2009, vol. III, pp. 1353–1360, March 8-12. ACM (2009)
19. Viroli, M., Pianini, D., Beal, J.: Linda in space-time: an adaptive coordination model for mobile ad-hoc environments. In: Sirjani, M. (ed.) COORDINATION 2012. LNCS, vol. 7274, pp. 212–229. Springer, Heidelberg (2012)
20. Whitehouse, K., Sharp, C., Brewer, E., Culler, D.: Hood: a neighborhood abstraction for sensor networks. In: Proceedings of the 2nd International Conference on Mobile Systems, Applications, and Services. ACM Press (2004)

# Trace- and Failure-Based Semantics for Bounded Responsiveness

Walter Vogler[1], Christian Stahl[2], and Richard Müller[2,3]

[1] Institut für Informatik, Universität Augsburg, Germany
vogler@informatik.uni-augsburg.de
[2] Department of Mathematics and Computer Science,
Technische Universiteit Eindhoven, The Netherlands
c.stahl@tue.nl
[3] Institut für Informatik, Humboldt-Universität zu Berlin, Germany
richard.mueller@informatik.hu-berlin.de

**Abstract.** We study open systems modeled as Petri nets with an interface for asynchronous communication with other open systems. As a minimal requirement for successful communication, we investigate *bounded responsiveness*, which guarantees that an open system and its environment always have the possibility to communicate, while the number of pending messages never exceeds a previously known bound. Bounded responsiveness *accordance* describes when one open system can be safely replaced by another open system. We present a trace-based characterization for accordance. As this relation turns out not to be compositional (i.e., it is no precongruence), we characterize the *coarsest compositional relation* (i.e., the coarsest precongruence) that is contained in this relation, using a variation of should testing, and show *decidability*.

## 1 Introduction

Today's software systems are complex distributed systems that are composed of less complex *open systems*. In this paper, we focus on open systems that have a well-defined interface and communicate with each other via *asynchronous message passing*. Service-oriented systems like Web-service applications [15] and systems based on wireless network technologies like wireless sensor networks [2], medical systems, transportation systems, or online gaming are examples of such distributed systems. During system evolution, often one open system is replaced by another one—for example, when new features have been implemented or bugs have been fixed. This requires a *refinement* notion, which should respect *compositionality*.

In this paper, we model an open system as a Petri net with finitely many states. As a *minimal requirement* for successful communication, *bounded responsiveness* demands that an open system and its environment (called a *controller*) always have the possibility to communicate, while their composition is finite-state and in particular the number of pending messages never exceeds a previously known bound. The bound on the message channels thereby ensures that

C. Canal and M. Villari (Eds.): ESOCC 2013, CCIS 393, pp. 129–143, 2013.
© Springer-Verlag Berlin Heidelberg 2013

the composition is again finite state. An open system is in bounded responsiveness *accordance* with another one, if it can replace the latter without affecting this property. Responsiveness has gained interest because, in addition to deadlock freedom, it also ensures the possibility to communicate, which is crucial in the setting of interacting open systems. Rather ad-hoc variants of bounded responsiveness have been introduced in [21,11], mainly motivated by algorithmic considerations for deciding the respective accordance, but without characterizing the latter semantically or studying compositionality.

Usually, controller-based preorders like ours are precongruences and, thus, a compositional refinement notion on open systems; but for bounded responsiveness accordance this was an open question.

In [20], we considered *unbounded* responsiveness, where an open system and its environment should always have the possibility to communicate. This variant of accordance is not a precongruence, and we characterized its coarsest precongruence, using a failure-based semantics close to should testing [17]. In this paper, we study bounded responsiveness for two reasons. First, in unpublished work, we showed undecidability for the precongruence for unbounded responsiveness. Second, in practice, distributed systems operate on a middleware with buffers that are of bounded size. The actual buffer size can be the result of a static analysis of the underlying middleware or of the communication behavior of an open system, or simply be chosen sufficiently large.

Our contribution is fourfold. First, we give a *trace-based characterization for bounded responsiveness accordance*, thereby adapting and combining results from the unbounded variant in [20] and work on traces that cannot be used reliably by any controller [12]. Due to the latter traces, accordant systems may violate language inclusion. Second, as accordance turns out not to be a precongruence, we characterize—along the lines of our previous results [20]—the *coarsest precongruence* which is contained in the accordance relation. Such a characterization is vital, because the definition of a coarsest precongruence considers arbitrary parallel environments and is, therefore, hard to check in concrete cases. Third, based on our characterization, we prove the coarsest precongruence to be *decidable* by reducing it to the setting of should testing [17]. Fourth, we sketch a practically attractive, but more involved approach where also reachability of a final marking counts as successful communication.

Like in our previous works [18,20], we contribute to a general theory on open systems and consider an asynchronous unqueued communication scheme. Although we present only the theory, open systems specified in industrial languages such as WS-BPEL or BPMN can be translated into our formal model and then be analyzed [10].

After some background in Sect. 2, Sect. 3 introduces $b$-bounded responsiveness, characterizes the respective accordance relation semantically, presents a characterization of the coarsest precongruence which is contained in this relation, and proves its decidability. Section 4 sketches bounded responsiveness in the presence of final states. We close with a discussion of related work and a conclusion in Sect. 5.

## 2    Preliminaries

This section provides the basic notions, such as Petri nets, open nets for modeling open systems, and environments for describing the semantics of open nets.

### 2.1    Petri Nets

For two sets $A$ and $B$, let $A \uplus B$ denote the disjoint union; writing $A \uplus B$ implies that $A$ and $B$ are implicitly assumed to be disjoint.

We use Place/Transition Petri nets extended by either transition labels or—later—specific interface places.

**Definition 1 ((labeled) net).** A *net* $N = (P, T, F, m_N, \Omega)$ consists of finite disjoint sets $P$ of *places* and $T$ of *transitions*, a *flow relation* $F \subseteq (P \times T) \uplus (T \times P)$, an *initial marking* $m_N$, where a marking $m : P \to \mathbb{N}$ is a *multiset* over the set $P$, and a set $\Omega$ of final markings.

A *labeled net* $N = (P, T, F, m_N, \Omega, I, O, l)$ is a net $(P, T, F, m_N, \Omega)$ together with an *alphabet* $\Sigma = I \uplus O$ of *input actions* $I$ and *output actions* $O$ and a *labeling function* $l : T \to \Sigma \uplus \{\tau\}$, where $\tau$ represents an invisible, internal action. We only consider labeled nets in which, for every transition $t$, the label $l(t)$ of $t$ is either $\tau$ or $t$ itself.

Graphically, a circle represents a place, a box represents a transition, and the directed arcs between places and transitions represent the flow relation. A marking is a distribution of tokens over the places. Graphically, a black dot represents a token.

Let $x \in P \uplus T$ be a node of a net $N$. As usual, ${}^\bullet x = \{y \mid (y, x) \in F\}$ denotes the *preset* of $x$ and $x^\bullet = \{y \mid (x, y) \in F\}$ the *postset* of $x$. We interpret presets and postsets as multisets when used in operations also involving multisets.

A transition $t \in T$ is *enabled* at a marking $m$, denoted by $m \xrightarrow{t}$ , if for all $p \in {}^\bullet t$, $m(p) > 0$. If $t$ is enabled at $m$, it can *fire*, denoted by $m \xrightarrow{t} m'$, thereby changing the marking $m$ to a marking $m' = m - {}^\bullet t + t^\bullet$. A sequence of transition firings $m_1 \xrightarrow{t_1} \ldots \xrightarrow{t_{k-1}} m_k$ is a *run* of $N$ if $m_i \xrightarrow{t_i} m_{i+1}$ for all $0 < i < k$. A marking $m'$ is *reachable from* a marking $m$ if there exists a (possibly empty) run $m_1 \xrightarrow{t_1} \ldots \xrightarrow{t_{k-1}} m_k$ with $m = m_1$ and $m' = m_k$; for $v = t_1 \ldots t_{k-1}$, we also write $m_1 \xrightarrow{v} m_k$. A marking $m'$ is *reachable* if it is reachable from the initial marking. The set $M_N$ represents the set of all reachable markings of $N$.

In the case of labeled nets, we lift runs to traces: If $m_1 \xrightarrow{v} m_k$ and $w$ is obtained from $v$ by replacing each transition with its label and removing all $\tau$-labels, we write $m_1 \xRightarrow{w} m_k$ (or sometimes just $m_1 \xRightarrow{w}$) and refer to $w$ as a *trace*. The *language* $L(N)$ of a labeled net $N$ is the set of all traces of $N$ starting from $m_N$. Marking $m$ *weakly enables* some $a \in \Sigma$ if $m \xRightarrow{a}$. The *reachability graph* $RG(N)$ of $N$ has the reachable markings $M_N$ as its nodes and an $l(t)$-labeled edge from $m$ to $m'$ whenever $m \xrightarrow{t} m'$ in $N$.

Let $\Sigma$ be an alphabet. With $v \sqsubseteq w$ we denote that $v$ is a *prefix* of $w$, and $\varepsilon$ denotes the empty word. For a set of traces $U \in \mathcal{P}(\Sigma^*)$, $\downarrow U = \{u \in \Sigma^* \mid \exists v \in$

$U : u \sqsubseteq v\}$ is the *prefix closure* of $U$ and $v^{-1}U = \{u \in \Sigma^* \mid vu \in U\}$ is the *remainder* of $v$ in $U$.

A marking $m$ of a net $N$ is *b-bounded* for a bound $b \in \mathbb{N}$, if $m(p) \leq b$ for all $p \in P$. The net $N$ is *b-bounded* if every reachable marking is $b$-bounded; it is *bounded* if it is $b$-bounded for some $b \in \mathbb{N}$. Throughout the paper, $b$ denotes a bound—a positive natural number.

## 2.2 Open Nets and Environments

An open system consists of a control structure describing its behavior and of an interface to interact with other open systems. We model the behavior of an open system as an *open net* [19,9]. In the model, we abstract from data and identify each message with the label of its message channel. An open net extends a net by an interface consisting of two disjoint sets of input and output places; these correspond to asynchronous input and output channels. We consider only open nets that have either at least one input and one output place or no input and output places; open nets with just input or just output places cannot really take part in a responsive communication.

**Definition 2 (open net).** An *open net* $N$ is a tuple $(P, T, F, m_N, I, O, \Omega)$ such that $(P \uplus I \uplus O, T, F, m_N, \Omega)$ is a net; the initial and all final markings leave all places in $I \uplus O$ empty; the set $I$ of *input places* satisfies for all $p \in I$, ${}^\bullet p = \emptyset$; the set $O$ of *output places* satisfies for all $p \in O$, $p^\bullet = \emptyset$; finally, $I = \emptyset$ if and only if $O = \emptyset$. If $I = O = \emptyset$, then $N$ is a *closed net*. Two open nets are *interface-equivalent* if they have the same sets of input and output places.

Graphically, we represent an open net like a net with a dashed frame around it. An interface place $p$ is positioned on the frame; an additional arrow indicates whether $p$ is an input or an output place.

For the composition of open nets, we assume that their ingredients are pairwise disjoint and that the interfaces intentionally overlap. We require that all communication is *bilateral* and *directed*; that is, every shared place $p$ has only one open net that sends into $p$ and one open net that receives from $p$. In addition, we require that either all interface places are shared or there is at least one input and one output place which are not shared. We refer to open nets that fulfill these conditions as *composable*. We compose two composable open nets by merging shared interface places and turning these places into internal places. Below, for example, $m_1 + m_2$ is the marking that coincides with $m_i$ on the places of $N_i$, $i \in \{1, 2\}$.

**Definition 3 (open net composition).** Two open nets $N_1$ and $N_2$ are *composable* if $(P_1 \uplus T_1 \uplus I_1 \uplus O_1) \cap (P_2 \uplus T_2 \uplus I_2 \uplus O_2) = (I_1 \cap O_2) \uplus (I_2 \cap O_1)$, and $I = (I_1 \uplus I_2) \setminus (O_1 \uplus O_2)$ and $O = (O_1 \uplus O_2) \setminus (I_1 \uplus I_2)$ are both either empty or nonempty. The *composition* of two composable open nets $N_1$ and $N_2$ is the open net $N_1 \oplus N_2 = (P, T, F, m_N, I, O, \Omega)$, where $P = P_1 \uplus P_2 \uplus (I_1 \cap O_2) \uplus (I_2 \cap O_1)$, $T = T_1 \uplus T_2$, $F = F_1 \uplus F_2$, $m_N = m_{N_1} + m_{N_2}$, and $\Omega = \{m_1 + m_2 \mid m_1 \in \Omega_1, m_2 \in \Omega_2\}$.

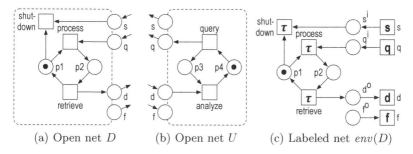

(a) Open net $D$          (b) Open net $U$          (c) Labeled net $env(D)$

**Fig. 1.** The open nets $D$ and $U$, and the environment $env(D)$ of $D$

To give an open net $N$ a *trace-based semantics*, we consider its environment $env(N)$, which we define similarly to Vogler [19]. The net $env(N)$ can be constructed from $N$ by adding to each interface place $p \in I$ ($p \in O$) a $p$-labeled transition $p$ in $env(N)$ and renaming the place $p$ to $p^i$ ($p^o$). The net $env(N)$ is just a tool to define our characterizations and prove our results. But intuitively, one can understand the construction as translating the asynchronous interface of $N$ into a buffered synchronous interface (with potentially unbounded buffers) described by the transition labels of $env(N)$.

**Definition 4 (open net environment).** The *environment of an open net $N$* is the labeled net $env(N) = (P \uplus P^I \uplus P^O, T \uplus I \uplus O, F', m_N, \Omega, I, O, l')$, where

- $P^I = \{p^i \mid p \in I\}$,  $P^O = \{p^o \mid p \in O\}$,
- $F' = \quad ((P \uplus T) \times (T \uplus P)) \cap F$
  $\quad \uplus \{(p^i, t) \mid p \in I, t \in T, (p, t) \in F\} \uplus \{(t, p^o) \mid p \in O, t \in T, (t, p) \in F\}$
  $\quad \uplus \{(p^o, p) \mid p \in O\} \uplus \{(p, p^i) \mid p \in I\}$, and
- $l'(t) = \tau$ if $t \in T$, and $l'(t) = t$ if $t \in I \uplus O$.

**Convention:** Throughout the paper, each trace set for labeled nets is implicitly extended to any open net $N$ via $env(N)$—for example, $L(N) = L(env(N))$.

*Example 1.* Figure 1 illustrates our running example. It shows two open systems, each modeled as an open net. The open net $D$ models a database server. After processing a received query (input place $q$), it responds with the retrieved data (output place $d$). A user may shut down $D$ by sending a shutdown message (input place $s$). $D$ has the (unused) capability to forward messages (output place $f$). The open net $U$ models a user of the database. It repeatedly queries the database and analyzes the returned data. $U$ never sends a shutdown message and ignores any forwarded message from $D$. Clearly, $D$ and $U$ are composable, and their composition (not shown in Fig. 1) can be obtained by merging equally labeled interface places. Finally, Fig. 1c shows the environment of $D$.

## 3  Bounded Responsiveness

Two open nets are bounded responsive if at least one net can repeatedly talk while respecting the message bound. *This property depends on $N_1$ and $N_2$ in combination*: In the composition, $N_1$ ($N_2$) will usually not reach all markings it could reach in other compositions; for the definition, it suffices that just one component can enable an output.

**Definition 5 ($b$-responsiveness).** Let $N_1$ and $N_2$ be composable open nets. A marking $m$ of $N_1 \oplus N_2$ is *responsive* if we can reach from $m$ a marking that enables a transition $t$ with $t^\bullet \cap (O_1 \uplus O_2) \neq \emptyset$; $m$ is *$b$-responsive* if it is $b$-bounded and responsive. Open nets $N_1$ and $N_2$ are *responsive* (*$b$-responsive*) if their composition $N_1 \oplus N_2$ is a closed net and every reachable marking in $N_1 \oplus N_2$ is responsive ($b$-responsive).

A natural criterion for "good" behavior is deadlock freedom; that is, each reachable marking of $N_1 \oplus N_2$ enables some transition. This can be fulfilled by one of the components internal transitions without effects to the outside. But this is presumably not satisfactory, and responsiveness is the natural improved requirement. Observe that, so far, final markings are ignored.

*Example 2.* The open nets $D$ and $U$ are $b$-responsive and thus responsive: $D \oplus U$ has only one infinite run whose transition sequence is ($query, process, retrieve, analyze$)$^\omega$. Suppose we remove the place $p_4$ from $U$ to obtain an open net, say $U'$. Then, $D$ and $U'$ are responsive, but not $b$-responsive as the places $q$ and $p_3$ are unbounded in $D \oplus U'$.

In contrast to responsiveness [20], $b$-responsiveness guarantees that *each* net always can send a message (possibly after some messages from the other net). This property, as formulated in Prop. 6, can be directly verified by a model checker.

**Proposition 6.** *Let open nets $N_1$ and $N_2$ be $b$-responsive. Then, from any reachable marking $m$ of $N_1 \oplus N_2$, markings $m_1$ and $m_2$ are reachable such that $m_1 \xrightarrow{t_1}$ and $m_2 \xrightarrow{t_2}$ with $t_1^\bullet \cap O_1 \neq \emptyset$ and $t_2^\bullet \cap O_2 \neq \emptyset$.*

We define the notion of a *br-controller* of an open net $N$ as an open net $C$ such that $N$ and $C$ are $b$-responsive. If the *br*-controllers of an open net are a superset of the *br*-controllers of another open net, then the first open net is a refinement of the second; intuitively, it makes more users happy due to $b$-responsive interaction than the latter. We refer to the resulting refinement relation as *br-accordance*, which yields an equivalence similar to safe $P$-deadlock equivalence in [19]. For modular reasoning, a refinement relation should be a precongruence for composition. Because *br*-accordance shall turn out not to be one, we will make it stricter (smaller) as far as needed to obtain such a precongruence, and we already introduce a notation for this coarsest precongruence.

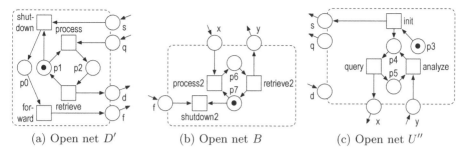

(a) Open net $D'$          (b) Open net $B$          (c) Open net $U''$

**Fig. 2.** Example showing that $br$-accordance is a not precongruence for $\oplus$

**Definition 7** ($br$-**controller,** $br$-**accordance**)**.** An open net $C$ is a $br$-*controller* of an open net $N$ if $N$ and $C$ are $b$-responsive. For interface-equivalent open nets *Impl* and *Spec*, *Impl* $br$-*accords with Spec*, denoted by *Impl* $\sqsubseteq_{br,acc}$ *Spec*, if for all open nets $C$: $C$ is a $br$-controller of *Spec* implies $C$ is a $br$-controller of *Impl*. We denote the coarsest precongruence contained in $\sqsubseteq_{br,acc}$ by $\sqsubseteq^c_{br,acc}$.

While every open net has at least one responsive controller (i.e., in the setting of [20]), this is not the case for $b$-responsiveness: Consider an open net that performs a self loop and in every cycle puts a token onto an output place, thereby violating any bound.

*Example 3.* In the example, $D$ is a $br$-controller of $U$ but not of $U'$ (i.e., $U$ without $p_4$). Figure 2a depicts a modified database server $D'$. It has the same functionality as $D$ but forwards a received shutdown message to the output place $f$. No $br$-controller of $D$ sends a message $s$, as otherwise $D$ could fire *shutdown* and then could not produce any output, contradicting Prop. 6. Thus, $D'$ $br$-accords with $D$ although language inclusion does not hold. For instance, $sf$ is a trace of $env(D')$ but not of $env(D)$. However, $sf$ cannot be used reliably by any $br$-controller of $D'$. We therefore refer to $sf$ as an *uncoverable trace*. That standard language inclusion can be too strict has been observed for a stronger termination criterion than responsiveness in [12]. Uncoverable traces shall be a crucial ingredient for our trace-based semantics. Extending the example with the open nets $B$ and $U''$ in Fig. 2, we can show that $br$-accordance is not compositional: $U''$ is a $br$-controller of $D \oplus B$ but not of $D' \oplus B$. Whereas the transition *shutdown2* of $B$ can be fired in $D' \oplus B$ (blocking $br$-responsiveness), it cannot be fired in $D \oplus B$.

Definition 7 refers to all possible $br$-controllers and, thus, $br$-accordance is an *external* concept. To characterize it *internally*, we first give a trace-based semantics for $b$-responsiveness. Then, we characterize the coarsest precongruence that is contained in the $br$-accordance relation and, finally, prove its decidability.

### 3.1   A Trace-Based Semantics for Bounded Responsiveness

A natural candidate for a trace-based semantics for $b$-responsiveness of an open net $N$ considers three sets of traces of its environment $env(N)$: (1) A *stop-trace* records a trace of $env(N)$ that ends in a marking weakly enabling actions of $I$ only, such that $N$ does not produce an output unless some input is provided. These traces were also used in the semantics for unbounded responsiveness in [20]. (2) A bound violation is a marking that is not $b$-bounded, and we investigate the traces leading to such a bound violation, called *strict $bound_b$-violators*. They have been introduced in the $b$-bounded *stop dead*-semantics in [18]. A bound violation is regarded as catastrophic because it cannot be corrected. Thus, the behavior after a bound violation does not matter, and we will hide all possible differences by treating all strict $bound_b$-violators and their continuations in the same way. Technically, we achieve the hiding by including all continuations of strict $bound_b$-violators in a set $bound_b$, the set of *$bound_b$-violators*. For the same reason, $bound_b$ is added to the stop-traces and to the third component of our semantics, the language of $N$. This technique is called *flooding* in [7].

However, to encode the covering nature of $br$-accordance in the trace-based semantics, we have to *replace* the set $bound_b$ with a larger set that captures all *$br$-uncoverable* traces; that is, traces $w$ that cannot be executed by (the environment of) any $br$-controller of $N$, regardless whether $w$ can be executed in $env(N)$ or not.

**Definition 8 (coverable $b$-bounded *stop*-semantics).** A marking $m$ of a labeled net $N$ is a *stop except for inputs* if there is no $o \in O$ such that $m \xrightarrow{o}$. Let $stop(N) = \{w \in (I \uplus O)^* \mid m_N \xrightarrow{w} m$ and $m$ is a stop except for inputs$\}$. A word $w$ is a *strict $bound_b$-violator* of $N$ if there exists a marking $m$ with $m_N \xrightarrow{w} m$ that is not $b$-bounded; each continuation of a strict $bound_b$-violator of $N$ is a *$bound_b$-violator* of $N$. Let $bound_b(N) = \{w \in (I \uplus O)^* \mid w$ is a $bound_b$-violator of $N\}$, $stop_b(N) = stop(N) \cup bound_b(N)$, and $L_b(N) = L(N) \cup bound_b(N)$.

A word $w$ is a *$br$-uncoverable trace* of an open net $N$ if there does not exist a $br$-controller $C$ of $N$ with $w \in L_b(C)$. The *coverable $b$-bounded stop-semantics* of $N$ is defined by the three sets of traces

- $uncov_{br}(N) = \{w \in (I \uplus O)^* \mid w$ is an $br$-uncoverable trace of $N\}$,
- $uL_{br}(N) = L(N) \cup uncov_{br}(N)$, and
- $ustop_{br}(N) = stop(N) \cup uncov_{br}(N)$.

Note that $bound_b(N) \nsubseteq L(N)$ because $bound_b(N)$ also contains all continuations of strict $bound_b$-violators. Moreover, $bound_b(N) \subseteq uncov_{br}(N)$ and the set $uncov_{br}(N)$ is closed under continuation.

*Example 4.* Consider again the open net $D$. For example, we have $\{\epsilon, qd\} \subseteq stop(D)$ and $\{ss, qq, qqf\} \subseteq bound_1(D)$. More precisely, $ss$ and $qq$ are strict $bound_1$-violators whereas $qqf$ is a continuation of $qq$ and, clearly, $qqf \notin L(D)$. Furthermore, $s$ is an example of an $br$-uncoverable trace of $D$, see Ex. 3.

We show that $br$-accordance coincides with component-wise inclusion of the coverable $b$-bounded *stop*-semantics. Interestingly, the "only-if" part also holds if we replace $br$-uncoverable traces in each component of the semantics with the $bound_b$-violators.

**Theorem 9 (trace characterization of $br$-accordance).** *For any interface-equivalent open nets Impl and Spec, we have* $Impl \sqsubseteq_{br,acc} Spec$ *iff* $uncov_{br}(Impl) \subseteq uncov_{br}(Spec) \wedge uL_{br}(Impl) \subseteq uL_{br}(Spec) \wedge ustop_{br}(Impl) \subseteq ustop_{br}(Spec).$

*Example 5.* In the example, $D' \sqsubseteq_{br,acc} D$. Although $sf \in L(D') \setminus L(D)$, this difference is hidden due to flooding: $sf \in uL_{br}(D') \subseteq uL_{br}(D)$.

Despite the external definition of the trace set $uncov_{br}$, we can compute the coverable $b$-bounded *stop*-semantics of an open net $N$ by using the notion of a most permissive controller [21], which is a controller that can visit all the markings that can be visited using any controller. For space reasons, we do not show the construction.

## 3.2  Deriving the Coarsest Precongruence for Bounded Responsiveness

As for the unbounded variant of responsiveness in [20], we shall characterize the coarsest precongruence $\sqsubseteq^c_{br,acc}$ in terms of Vogler's $\mathcal{F}^+$-semantics [19], a variant of failure semantics [4]. The latter consists of pairs $(w, X)$, where $w$ is a trace and $X$ is a subset of the alphabet—a *refusal set*; the more informative $\mathcal{F}^+$-semantics considers pairs $(w, X)$, where $X$ is a *set of traces* that can be refused; such a pair is a *tree failure*. The traces in $X$ are linked to a certain marking $m$ that is reached by executing $w$. Different markings $m$ can be reached by $w$ because of nondeterminism, possibly giving rise to different sets $X$. To cope with the restriction to $b$-boundedness, our novel semantics consists of the $bound_b$-violations and the $\mathcal{F}^+$-semantics extended with all tree failures $(w, X)$, where $w$ is a trace in $bound_b$ and $X$ is any set of words.

**Definition 10 ($b$-bounded $\mathcal{F}^+$-semantics).** *The $b$-bounded $\mathcal{F}^+$-semantics of a labeled net $N$ consists of (1) $bound_b(N)$ and (2) $\mathcal{F}^+_b(N) = \mathcal{F}^+(N) \cup B\mathcal{F}^+_b(N)$, where* $\mathcal{F}^+(N) = \{(w, X) \in \Sigma^* \times \mathcal{P}(\Sigma^+) \mid \exists m \in M_N : m_N \overset{w}{\Longrightarrow} m \wedge \nexists w' \in X : m \overset{w'}{\Longrightarrow}\}$ *and* $B\mathcal{F}^+_b(N) = \{(w, X) \mid w \in bound_b(N) \wedge X \in \mathcal{P}((I \uplus O)^+)\}.$

For the present setting, the tree failures used in the $b$-bounded $\mathcal{F}^+$-semantics give too much information about the moment of choice in an open net. This information can be removed by closing up under an ordering over tree failures. It is a pleasant discovery that this modification—developed for the $\mathcal{F}^+$-semantics in [17]—also works smoothly in combination with $bound_b$. It yields the following refinement relation.

**Definition 11 ($\mathcal{F}^+_b$-refinement).** *For two labeled nets Impl and Spec, Impl* $\mathcal{F}^+_b$*-refines Spec, denoted by $Impl \sqsubseteq_{\mathcal{F}^+_b} Spec$, if*

1. $bound_b(Impl) \subseteq bound_b(Spec)$ *and*
2. $\forall (w, X) \in \mathcal{F}^+_b(Impl) : \exists x \in \{\varepsilon\} \cup \downarrow X : (wx, x^{-1}X) \in \mathcal{F}^+_b(Spec).$

For two interface-equivalent open nets *Impl* and *Spec*, we define $Impl \sqsubseteq_{\mathcal{F}^+_b} Spec$, if $env(Impl) \sqsubseteq_{\mathcal{F}^+_b} env(Spec)$.

The $\mathcal{F}_b^+$-refinement relation is a precongruence for the composition operator $\oplus$. The proof uses the precongruence result for $\mathcal{F}^+$-refinement (i.e., should testing [17]) on labeled nets. Even more, $\mathcal{F}_b^+$-refinement is the coarsest precongruence contained in $br$-accordance.

**Theorem 12 (coarsest precongruence).** *For any interface-equivalent open nets Impl and Spec, we have* $Impl \sqsubseteq_{br,acc}^c Spec$ *iff* $Impl \sqsubseteq_{\mathcal{F}_b^+} Spec$.

*Example 6.* For our example, we have $(sf, \emptyset) \in \mathcal{F}_b^+(D')$ but $(sf, \emptyset) \notin \mathcal{F}_b^+(D)$; thus, $D'$ does not $\mathcal{F}_b^+$-refine $D$. Whereas $br$-accordance does not distinguish open nets due to some common uncoverable trace (e.g., $sf$ in $D$ and $D'$), this can happen with the $b$-bounded $\mathcal{F}^+$-semantics. This is necessary, because the example proving that $br$-accordance is not a precongruence for $\oplus$ (see Fig. 2) illustrates that such uncoverable traces may destroy compositionality.

### 3.3 Decidability of $\mathcal{F}_b^+$-Refinement

We show that checking $\mathcal{F}_b^+$-refinement is decidable. Checking $\mathcal{F}_b^+$-refinement entails checking both items of Def. 11. The first item of Def. 11 is decidable because we can represent each of the languages $bound_b(Spec)$ and $bound_b(Impl)$ as a finite automaton with the following construction: For a labeled net $N$, transform the reachability graph $RG(N)$ by adding a new vertex $U$ with a self-loop for each action $a \in I \uplus O$, and replacing each arc $m \xrightarrow{a} m'$ by $m \xrightarrow{a} U$ whenever $m$ is $b$-bounded while $m'$ is not; finally, restrict the graph to the vertices reachable from $m_N$ and consider only $U$ as final state.

*Example 7.* Figure 3a sketches the automaton that represents $bound_1(D)$. Parts of the automaton in Fig. 3a that can only be reached with an $s$-transition are not shown. For example, we have $\{qq, qqqq, qqf\} \subseteq bound_1(D)$. The marking $[p_1, q^i, q^i]$ is not 1-bounded; therefore, the transition $[p_1, q^i] \xrightarrow{q} [p_1, q^i, q^i]$ in $RG(env(D))$ was replaced with $[p_1, q^i] \xrightarrow{q} U$. The traces $qq$ and $qqqq$ are strict $bound_1$-violators, as they lead from the initial state $[p_1]$ to the final state $U$ while visiting state $U$ only once (for trace $qqqq$ with three $\tau$-transitions in-between). The traces $qqqq$ and $qqf$ visit $U$ more than once.

To decide the second item of Def. 11, we use the decidability of $\mathcal{F}^+$-refinement for finite-state systems proven by Rensink and Vogler [17, Thm. 61]. Essentially, we construct for each labeled net $N$ a finite automaton (or rather a labeled transition system, because we do not consider final states) that has $\mathcal{F}_b^+(N)$ as its $\mathcal{F}^+$-semantics. The previous automaton does not work, because each bound violator reaches $U$ and then no trace can be refused. Thus, we replace $U$ by two copies $U_1$ and $U_2$, remove the self-loops of $U_2$, and add arcs $U_1 \xrightarrow{a} U_2$ for each $a \in I \uplus O$. The resulting $U_{12}(N)$ almost does the job but still, after some $w \notin bound_b(N)$, it might be impossible to refuse some traces due to the self-loops at $U_1$. We get the following:

**Lemma 13.** *For a labeled net $N$, $\mathcal{F}^+(U_{12}(N)) \subseteq \mathcal{F}_b^+(N)$ and $(w, X) \in \mathcal{F}_b^+(N) \setminus \mathcal{F}^+(U_{12}(N))$ implies $\exists u \in \downarrow X \setminus X$ such that $wu \in bound_b(N)$.*

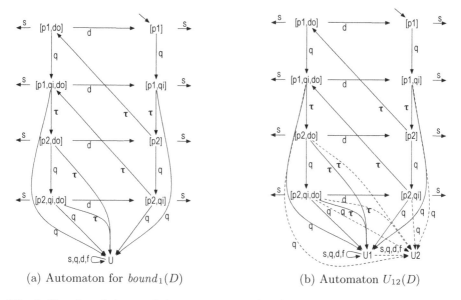

(a) Automaton for $bound_1(D)$                    (b) Automaton $U_{12}(D)$

**Fig. 3.** Sketches of the two finite automata used in the proof of Thm. 15. A transition involving $s$ is indicated by an arrow without sink.

*Example 8.* Figure 3b shows a part of the automaton $U_{12}(D)$. For example, we have $(qqqq, \{f\}) \in \mathcal{F}_b^+(D) \cap \mathcal{F}^+(U_{12}(D))$, because the trace $qqqq$ may lead to the state $U_2$ and then refuse $f$. Further, we have $(q, \{qqf\}) \in \mathcal{F}_b^+(D) \setminus \mathcal{F}^+(U_{12}(D))$—observe $f$ can never fire in $env(D)$, while any state reached by $q$ in $U_{12}(D)$ can reach $U_1$ with $qq$ and then add $f$. There is $q \in \downarrow \{qqf\} \setminus \{qqf\}$ and the trace $qq$ is a $bound_1$-violator of $D$.

Deciding $\mathcal{F}_b^+$-refinement for two labeled nets can be reduced to checking $\mathcal{F}^+$-refinement for their $U_{12}$-automata, from which we conclude decidability (also for interface-equivalent open nets).

**Lemma 14.** *Let Impl and Spec be labeled nets having the same alphabet and satisfying $bound_b(Impl) \subseteq bound_b(Spec)$; then $Impl \sqsubseteq_{\mathcal{F}_b^+} Spec$ iff $U_{12}(Impl) \sqsubseteq_{\mathcal{F}^+} U_{12}(Spec)$.*

**Theorem 15.** *Checking $\sqsubseteq_{\mathcal{F}_b^+}$ is decidable for labeled and for open nets.*

## 4    Final Bounded Responsiveness

In this section, we extend our considerations to final markings. We refer to the resulting variant as *bf-responsiveness*. Two open nets are *bf-responsive* if and only if they are *f-responsive* and their composition is *b-bounded*. Semantically, each net has always the chance to send a message or the composition can terminate, and proper termination can certainly signal a successful communication.

**Definition 16** (*bf-responsiveness*). Let $N_1$ and $N_2$ be composable open nets. A marking $m$ of $N_1 \oplus N_2$ is *bf-responsive* if $m$ is $b$-bounded and either responsive or we can reach a final marking of $N_1 \oplus N_2$ from $m$. Open nets $N_1$ and $N_2$ are *bf*-responsive if their composition $N_1 \oplus N_2$ is a closed net and every reachable marking in $N_1 \oplus N_2$ is *bf*-responsive.

We redefine the notion of a controller and of accordance for this variant of responsiveness. Using the open nets in Fig. 2 with the empty set of final markings (see Ex. 3), we can show that also this variant of accordance is not a precongruence; thus, we also introduce its coarsest precongruence.

**Definition 17** (*bfr-controller*, *bfr-accordance*). An open net $C$ is a *bfr-controller* of an open net $N$ if $N$ and $C$ are *bf*-responsive. For interface-equivalent open nets *Impl* and *Spec*, *Impl bfr-accords with Spec*, denoted by *Impl* $\sqsubseteq_{bfr,acc}$ *Spec*, if for all open nets $C$ holds: $C$ is a *bfr*-controller of *Spec* implies $C$ is a *bfr*-controller of *Impl*. We denote the coarsest precongruence contained in $\sqsubseteq_{bfr,acc}$ by $\sqsubseteq^c_{bfr,acc}$.

We give a trace-based semantics for *bf*-responsiveness of an open net $N$. Like the coverable $b$-bounded *stop*-semantics, it also consists of the uncoverable traces, the language, and the stop-traces. The presence of final markings requires to add a fourth set of traces, *dead-traces*, to distinguish between stop-traces leading to a final or a nonfinal marking. Furthermore, we need to slightly adopt the notion of an uncoverable trace to the present setting.

**Definition 18** (**coverable $b$-bounded** *stopdead*-**semantics**). A marking $m$ of a labeled net $N$ is *dead except for inputs* if $m$ is a stop except for inputs and there exists no final marking $m'$ of $N$ with $m \xRightarrow{\varepsilon} m'$. Let $dead(N) = \{w \in (I \uplus O)^* \mid m_N \xRightarrow{w} m$ and $m$ is dead except for inputs$\}$.

A word $w \in (I \uplus O)^*$ is a *bfr-uncoverable trace* of an open net $N$ if there does not exist a *bfr*-controller $C$ of $N$ with $w \in L_b(C)$. The *coverable $b$-bounded stopdead-semantics* of $N$ is defined by the sets of traces

- $uncov_{bfr}(N) = \{w \in (I \uplus O)^* \mid w$ is a *bfr*-uncoverable trace of $N\}$,
- $uL_{bfr}(N) = L(N) \cup uncov_{bfr}(N)$,
- $ustop_{bfr}(N) = stop(N) \cup uncov_{bfr}(N)$, and
- $udead_{bfr}(N) = dead(N) \cup uncov_{br}(N)$.

*Example 9.* Suppose $\Omega_D = \{[p_1]\}$. Then we have $\{\varepsilon, s, qd\} \subseteq stop(D)$ but only $s \in dead(D)$ because of the final marking.

We show that *bfr*-accordance coincides with component-wise inclusion of the coverable $b$-bounded *stopdead*-semantics.

**Theorem 19** (**trace characterization of** *bfr*-**accordance**). *For any interface-equivalent open nets Impl and Spec, we have Impl $\sqsubseteq_{bfr,acc}$ Spec iff* $uncov_{bfr}(Impl) \subseteq uncov_{bfr}(Spec)$, $uL_{bfr}(Impl) \subseteq uL_{bfr}(Spec)$, $ustop_{bfr}(Impl) \subseteq ustop_{bfr}(Spec)$, *and* $udead_{bfr}(Impl) \subseteq udead_{bfr}(Spec)$.

To derive the coarsest precongruence contained in *bfr*-accordance, we integrate the bound-violations into the $\mathcal{F}_{fin}^+$-semantics of [20]. The $\mathcal{F}_{fin}^+$-semantics was defined for the unbounded variant of *bf*-responsiveness. It consists of triples $(w, X, Y)$ where $(w, X)$ is a tree failure and $Y$ a set of traces that cannot lead to a final marking. Whereas $X$ is used to identify stop-traces, $Y$ ensures that we can identify dead-traces.

**Definition 20 (b-bounded $\mathcal{F}_{fin}^+$-semantics).** The *b-bounded $\mathcal{F}_{fin}^+$-semantics* of a labeled net $N$ consists of (1) $bound_b(N)$ and (2) $\mathcal{F}_{b,fin}^+(N) = \mathcal{F}_{fin}^+(N) \cup finbound_b(N)$, where $\mathcal{F}_{fin}^+(N) = \{(w, X, Y) \in \Sigma^* \times \mathcal{P}(\Sigma^+) \times \mathcal{P}(\Sigma^*) \mid \exists m \in M_N : m_N \stackrel{w}{\Longrightarrow} m \wedge \forall x \in X : m \stackrel{x}{\not\Longrightarrow} \wedge \forall y \in Y : \forall m' : m \stackrel{y}{\Longrightarrow} m'$ implies $m' \notin \Omega_N\}$ and $finbound_b(N) = bound_b(N) \times \mathcal{P}(\Sigma^+) \times \mathcal{P}(\Sigma^*)$.

The $\mathcal{F}_{b,fin}^+$-refinement relation is similarly defined as $\mathcal{F}_b^+$-refinement in Def. 11 by closing up under an ordering over the elements in $\mathcal{F}_{b,fin}^+$, thereby removing the too detailed information about the moment of choice in an open net.

**Definition 21 ($\mathcal{F}_{b,fin}^+$-refinement).** For two labeled nets *Impl* and *Spec*, *Impl* $\mathcal{F}_{b,fin}^+$-*refines Spec*, denoted by *Impl* $\sqsubseteq_{\mathcal{F}_{b,fin}^+}$ *Spec*, if

1. $bound_b(Impl) \subseteq bound_b(Spec)$ and
2. $\forall(w, X, Y) \in \mathcal{F}_{b,fin}^+(Impl) : \exists x \in \{\varepsilon\} \cup \downarrow X \cup \downarrow Y : (wx, x^{-1}X, x^{-1}Y) \in \mathcal{F}_{b,fin}^+(Spec)$.

For two interface-equivalent open nets *Impl* and *Spec*, we define *Impl* $\sqsubseteq_{\mathcal{F}_{b,fin}^+}$ *Spec*, if $env(Impl) \sqsubseteq_{\mathcal{F}_{b,fin}^+} env(Spec)$.

$\mathcal{F}_{b,fin}^+$-refinement is the coarsest precongruence which contained in the *bfr*-accordance relation.

**Theorem 22 (coarsest precongruence).** *For any interface-equivalent open nets Impl and Spec, we have Impl $\sqsubseteq_{bfr,acc}^c$ Spec iff Impl $\sqsubseteq_{\mathcal{F}_{b,fin}^+}$ Spec.*

Also $\sqsubseteq_{\mathcal{F}_{b,fin}^+}$ is decidable. The rather complicated proof generalizes the construction of Rensink and Vogler [17, Theorem 61] for deciding $\mathcal{F}^+$-refinement of two finite LTS to decide $\mathcal{F}_{fin}^+$-refinement (i.e., Def. 21(2) for $\mathcal{F}_{fin}^+$). Then, we reduce deciding $\mathcal{F}_{b,fin}^+$-refinement of two labeled nets to checking $\mathcal{F}_{fin}^+$-refinement of (a variant of) their $U_{12}$-automata.

**Theorem 23.** *Checking $\sqsubseteq_{\mathcal{F}_{b,fin}^+}$ is decidable for labeled and for open nets.*

# 5   Conclusion

We studied an accordance preorder describing whether an open system can safely be replaced by another open system, thereby guaranteeing bounded responsiveness of the overall system. The latter guarantees deadlock freedom and the permanent possibility to mutually communicate while maintaining a previously known message bound. We presented a trace-based characterization of accordance using a set comprising the stop-traces, the language, and a set of uncoverable traces collecting catastrophic traces that cannot be used reliably. We showed that the accordance preorder is not a precongruence, characterized the coarsest precongruence contained in the respective preorder, and proved decidability. This precongruence is the should testing preorder [17] extended by information about bound violations.

We also sketched bounded responsiveness in the presence of final states. The extensions follow the same line as for bounded responsiveness without final states. In the presence of final states, we need to distinguish successful and unsuccessful complete traces resulting in an additional component in the trace-based and failure-based semantics. We characterized the preorder, the coarsest precongruence contained in this preorder, and proved decidability. This precongruence is the should testing preorder extended by information about traces that do not lead to a final marking and bound violations.

Compared to our previous work on deadlock freedom in [18], finer trace sets are required to characterize the preorders based on responsiveness. While traces are adequate for the precongruence dealing with deadlock freedom [18], they do not suffice to characterize the coarsest precongruence for responsiveness, and we had to use some kind of failures instead.

The idea of responsiveness for finite state open systems with final states has been coined by Wolf in [21]. Together with the less restrictive variant in [11], it defines responsiveness for single open nets and considers only such responsive nets; this guarantees a weak form of our responsiveness. More generally, we deal with open nets that are responsive in some open net compositions but not in others. Müller [14] presents an asymmetrical definition from the point of view of one individual open system in a composition. Our notion of responsiveness leads to precongruences, where the related equivalence is similar to P-deadlock equivalence in [19]. Responsiveness in [5] is stricter than our notion because it additionally requires that no messages in any channel is ignored forever.

In other work, the term responsiveness refers to different properties: Reed et al. [16] aim at excluding certain deadlocks, whereas responsiveness in our setting refers to the ability to communicate. The works [1,8,6] consider with the $\pi$-calculus a more expressive model than open nets but in the setting of synchronous communication, whereas we consider asynchronous communication. Moreover, responsiveness in [1,6] and lock-freedom in [8] guarantees that communication over a certain channel is eventually possible. In contrast, our notion of responsiveness requires that communication over some channel is always possible. The three approaches mainly differ from each other in their type systems.

It is future work to study the relation of our semantics and the compact representation of all controllers in [11]. Another issue is *weak termination* [12,3,13] as a minimal requirement: Reaching a final state should always be possible. This criterion is very close to the idea of should testing, but it is not clear how to characterize the respective accordance [12,3,13] (which is a precongruence itself).

In contrast, we characterized precongruences related to responsiveness with semantical ideas that also worked for should testing.

# References

1. Acciai, L., Boreale, M.: Responsiveness in process calculi. Theor. Comp. Sci. 409(1), 59–93 (2008)
2. Akyildiz, I., Su, W., Sankarasubramaniam, Y., Cayirci, E.: Wireless sensor networks: a survey. Computer Networks 38(4), 393–422 (2002)
3. Bravetti, M., Zavattaro, G.: A foundational theory of contracts for multi-party service composition. Fundam. Inform. 89(4), 451–478 (2008)
4. Brookes, S.D., Hoare, C.A.R., Roscoe, A.W.: A theory of communicating sequential processes. J. ACM 31(3), 560–599 (1984)
5. Desai, A., Gupta, V., Jackson, E., Qadeer, S., Rajamani, S.K., Zufferey, D.: P: safe asynchronous event-driven programming. In: PLDI 2013, pp. 321–332. ACM (2013)
6. Gamboni, M., Ravara, A.: Responsive choice in mobile processes. In: Wirsing, M., Hofmann, M., Rauschmayer, A. (eds.) TGC 2010, LNCS, vol. 6084, pp. 135–152. Springer, Heidelberg (2010)
7. van Glabbeek, R.J.: The coarsest precongruences respecting safety and liveness properties. In: Calude, C.S., Sassone, V. (eds.) TCS 2010. IFIP AICT, vol. 323, pp. 32–52. Springer, Heidelberg (2010)
8. Kobayashi, N.: A type system for lock-free processes. Information and Computation 177(2), 122–159 (2002)
9. Lohmann, N., Massuthe, P., Wolf, K.: Operating guidelines for finite-state services. In: Kleijn, J., Yakovlev, A. (eds.) ICATPN 2007. LNCS, vol. 4546, pp. 321–341. Springer, Heidelberg (2007)
10. Lohmann, N., Verbeek, E., Dijkman, R.: Petri net transformations for business processes – A survey. In: Jensen, K., van der Aalst, W.M.P. (eds.) Transactions on Petri Nets and Other Models of Concurrency II. LNCS, vol. 5460, pp. 46–63. Springer, Heidelberg (2009)
11. Lohmann, N., Wolf, K.: Compact representations and efficient algorithms for operating guidelines. Fundam. Inform. 107, 1–19 (2011)
12. Malik, R., Streader, D., Reeves, S.: Conflicts and fair testing. Journal of Foundations of Computer Science 17(4), 797–813 (2006)
13. Mooij, A.J., Stahl, C., Voorhoeve, M.: Relating fair testing and accordance for service replaceability. J. Log. Algebr. Program. 79(3-5), 233–244 (2010)
14. Müller, R.: On the notion of deadlocks in open nets. In: AWPN 2010. CEUR WS Proc., vol. 643, pp. 130–135 (2010)
15. Papazoglou, M.P.: Web Services: Principles and Technology. Pearson (2007)
16. Reed, J.N., Roscoe, A.W., Sinclair, J.E.: Responsiveness and stable revivals. Formal Asp. Comput. 19(3), 303–319 (2007)
17. Rensink, A., Vogler, W.: Fair testing. Inf. Comput. 205(2), 125–198 (2007)
18. Stahl, C., Vogler, W.: A trace-based service semantics guaranteeing deadlock freedom. Acta Inf. 49(2), 69–103 (2012)
19. Vogler, W.: Modular Construction and Partial Order Semantics of Petri Nets. LNCS, vol. 625. Springer, Heidelberg (1992)
20. Vogler, W., Stahl, C., Müller, R.: A trace-based semantics for responsiveness. In: ACSD 2012, pp. 42–51. IEEE (2012)
21. Wolf, K.: Does my service have partners? In: Jensen, K., van der Aalst, W.M.P. (eds.) ToPNoC II. LNCS, vol. 5460, pp. 152–171. Springer, Heidelberg (2009)

# On the Introduction of Time
# in Distributed Blackboard Rules

Jean-Marie Jacquet[1], Isabelle Linden[2], and Mihail-Octavian Staicu[1]

[1] Faculty of Computer Science,
University of Namur, Belgium
{jean-marie.jacquet,mihail.staicu}@unamur.be
[2] Business Administration Department,
University of Namur, Belgium
isabelle.linden@unamur.be

**Abstract.** In the realm of coordination languages, reactivity by means of blackboard rules has been used in order to increase the dynamic behavior of data-spaces by enriching them with programmable capabilities. In real-life scenarios time constraints come as a natural requirement. In this paper we introduce this temporal aspect in the definition of distributed blackboard rules in several ways in order to accommodate requirements which impose observing sets of events that occur at given time points as well as within given time frames. Moreover, this allows to define contexts as ordered sequences of events and to change their significance according to the amount of time in which they are satisfied.

**Keywords:** coordination languages, blackboard rules, time.

## 1 Introduction

The passive stance of data in coordination languages has been rendered dynamic with the introduction of *reactivity*. The road paved by GAMMA [1] and later by the *chemical abstract machine* [2] gave rise to other models which exploited the possibility of surveilling events occurring on the data-space. In models such as MARS [5], TuCSoN [25], ReSpecT [8,9] and LIME [22,26] the reactive paradigm is defined, in very generic lines, by the action to be taken once a given event occurs on the data-space. By extending the detection of single events to the detection of sets of events and/or sets of information it is possible to achieve *context-awareness*. This concept first appeared in conjunction with the mobility of hosts [27] and was related to sensing changes in their physical location. Recent pieces of work [10] stress out that context-awareness must provide the desired information to the interested user in a proper way and at the required time and location.

Our proposition of context definition is based on the declarative blackboard rules presented in [17], where this concept is modeled in terms of information being present on (by means of *in* primitives) or absent from (by means of *nin* primitives) the blackboard (*i.e.* data-space). The general declarative representation is $LHS \longrightarrow RHS$ and means that as long as the condition expressed in the

C. Canal and M. Villari (Eds.): ESOCC 2013, CCIS 393, pp. 144–158, 2013.

*left hand side*(LHS) is verified, the *right hand side*(RHS) is made true. In this paper, we enrich the language by adding time specifications to both *in* and *nin* primitives. In the LHS this translates to new functionalities such as *scheduling* (a rule becomes active only when the required information is available at the right time) and *ordering* (using time it is possible to monitor whether pieces of information became available in a desired sequence). In the RHS, adding time allows for the statements to be made true with given *delays*. Omitting it, results in having the default behaviour, that is as soon as the rule becomes active.

A key application of such concepts may be found in the modern trend of *smart cities*. The recent work of Chourabi *et al.* [7] emphasizes that the challenges of a *smart city* may be seen from different points of view: *"management and organization, technology, governance, policy context, people and communities, economy, built infrastructure, and natural environment."* Let us see how we can address some of these issues from the perspective of coordination languages and timed context-awareness. The purpose is not to conduct an exhaustive study, but to present some pointers of applicability.

In terms of *traffic management*, we can imagine that the main highway leading to the center of the city has, by default, two lanes in each direction but that these lanes can be dynamically re-allocated if needed, either for entering or exiting. For example, in the case where incoming heavy traffic is detected in the morning between 6AM and 10AM it would be desirable to have three of the four lanes for the traffic flowing towards the city. This translates in a simple rule of the form:

$$in(\text{inHeavyTraffic}, [06:10]) \longrightarrow in(\text{enter1}), in(\text{enter2}), in(\text{enter3}), in(\text{exit4})$$

In symmetry, in the afternoon between 4PM and 8PM there is normally heavy traffic going out of the city. In that case, it is desirable to allocate three lanes for exiting the city however only in the case where no concert or sport event are announced in the evening. As such, the rule modelling this behavior would be:

$$in(\text{outHeavyTraffic}, [16:20]), nin(\text{concert}, [20:24]), nin(\text{sportEvent}, [20:24])$$
$$\longrightarrow in(\text{enter1}), in(\text{exit2}), in(\text{exit3}), in(\text{exit4}).$$

From the *environmental* perspective, it is common in large cities to have small weather stations that monitor the quality of air, especially in the city center. It may be desired, in situations in which pollution levels rise above predefined limits between 10AM and 4PM and there is no wind, to divert traffic away from the city center. Once the levels drop to acceptable limits, the traffic may be restored to its normal flow.

This amounts to using the following two rules:

$$in(\text{qualityAlarm}, [10:16]), nin(\text{wind}) \longrightarrow in(\text{blockCirculation})$$
$$nin(\text{qualityAlarm}, [10:16]) \longrightarrow in(\text{allowCirculation})$$
(1)

In covering *social and cultural aspects*, we can model a customizable information flow subscription service. Each subscription may be defined by a reaction rule. If a user desires to receive on Saturday all the announcements published on the subject of *"theater"* from Monday to Friday, it would suffice to use the rule $in(\text{eventManager}, \text{theatre}, [1 : 5]) \longrightarrow in(\text{userID}, \text{theatre}, 6)$, where *event-Manager* represents the blackboard of the system handling the subscriptions and *userID* the blackboard of the user. The subscription is handled with the dedicated primitives presented in [17]: $tellr(b, r)$ for outputting a rule $r$ to a blackboard $b$, $getr(b, r)$ for removing it, $askr(b, r)$ for querying its presence and $naskr(b, r)$ for querying its absence. In this light, making the aforementioned subscription amounts to executing the following rule:

$tellr(eventManager,$

$"in(\text{eventManager}, \text{theatre}, [1 : 5]) \longrightarrow in(\text{userID}, \text{theatre}, 6)")$

With these applications in mind, the main contribution of this paper lies in studying different ways of formally introducing time in rules. We explore the discrete and continuous perspectives, as well as absolute (for single activations) and relative (for repeated activations) approaches. This purpose is extended by a short description of a proposed implementation of the chosen solution that would fit real-life scenarios. We will present as well the limitations that need to be imposed in order to provide a feasible prototype for distributed blackboards.

The remainder of this paper is organized as follows. Section 2 evinces the interest of introducing time in blackboard rules. Section 3 presents the blackboard rules in a discrete time context, while Section 4 presents the continuous time approach. We continue with some general lines on our current implementation in Section 5. A study on related work is conducted in Section 6. Finally, section 7 draws our conclusions and shows some perspectives for future work.

## 2     Timing Context-Awareness

The interest of introducing the temporal aspect in coordination languages, beginning with TSpaces [32] and JavaSpaces [11], was advocated by the need to model real-life coordination applications. It may not be desirable to keep processes waiting indefinitely for pieces of information that may never become available. Or, pieces of information should be present on the data-space only for given amounts of time. This translates to adding a temporal parameter to the primitives that interact with the blackboard, respectively to the tuples. On these lines, studies have been conducted on the relative-time approach [18] as well as on the absolute-time one [15] by exploring the expressiveness of delays in primitive execution and limited lifetime for tuples on the blackboard. Such features may also be extended to the reactive mechanisms which provide the dynamic and programmable features to the blackboards.

In our proposal we add the temporal dimension to the blackboard rules refined in [17] by complementing their building blocks, the *in* and *nin* primitives, with dedicated time parameters:

$in(a_1, u_1, t_1), in(a_2, u_2, t_2), in(a_3, u_2, t_4),$

$in(a_4, u_3, t_3), in(a_5, u_4, t_2), nin(b, u_4, t_5)$

$$\longrightarrow \quad in(c, u_5, t_5), nin(d, u_6, t_6) \qquad (2)$$

with the intuitive meaning that as long as some pieces of information $u_1, u_2, u_3$ are present on the respective blackboards $a_1$ to $a_5$, at the respective time points $t_1$ to $t_4$ and some information $u_4$ is not present on blackboard $b$ on time $t_5$, then we can assume that some information $u_5$ will become available on blackboard $c$ on time $t_5$ and some information $u_6$, if present, will no longer be available on blackboard $d$ on time $t_6$. A graphical representation of the context is given in Fig. 1(a), where for each position $(t_i, u_i)$, with $1 \leq i \leq 4$, 1 denotes the presence of a tuple, 0 denotes the absence and $\perp$ denotes that no check should be performed. By exploring different semantic variations and refinements it may be possible to model use scenarios in discrete or continuous time, expressed in either absolute or relative fashion. For example, from a discrete perspective, we may define a blackboard rule that detects the successful execution of a workflow. Since a workflow is comprised of an ordered list of activities, by outputting a tuple to signal the end of each activity we can detect their correct completion and in the right order. Other scenarios may require having multiple instances of the same tuple at one given time point. For example, such a context would amount to the writing in Equation 3 and the graphical representation in Fig. 1(b).

$$in(a_1, u_1, t_3), in(a_2, u_2, t_2), in(a_2, u_2, t_2),$$
$$in(a_2, u_2, t_2), in(a_5, u_4, t_1), in(a_6, u_4, t_1), nin(b, u_4, t_4)$$
$$\longrightarrow \quad in(c, u_5, t_5), nin(d, u_6, t_6) \qquad (3)$$

In the declarative reading of the rule it is not imposed to have an ordering in the primitives over the timestamps, but they are represented in such a way for the ease of reading. By corroborating Equation 2 with the results obtained in [17], we have the following generic representation of a timed blackboard rule:

$$in(b_1, u_1, t_1), \ldots, in(b_1, u_1, t_n), \ldots, in(b_n, u_n, t_1), \ldots, in(b_n, u_n, t_n)$$
$$nin(b_{n+1}, u_{n+1}, t_{n+1}), \ldots, nin(b_{n+1}, u_{n+1}, t_m),$$
$$\ldots, nin(b_m, u_m, t_{n+1}), \ldots, nin(b_m, u_m, t_m) \longrightarrow$$
$$in(b_{m+1}, u_{m+1}, t_{m+1}), \cdots, in(b_p, u_p, t_p),$$
$$nin(b_{p+1}, u_{p+1}, t_{p+1}), \cdots, nin(b_q, u_q, t_q) \qquad (4)$$

Such a rule becomes active when the context defined in the LHS is verified. Following the intuition, from the graphical representation in Fig. 1(a), the activation condition may be modelled in the form of a matrix:

$$AM_{n \times m} = \begin{cases} am_{i,j} = 1, & 1 \leq i, j \leq n \text{ and } \exists\, in(b_i, u_i, t_j) \in LHS \\ am_{i,j} = 0, & n+1 \leq i, j \leq m \text{ and } \exists\, nin(b_i, u_i, t_j) \in LHS \\ am_{i,j} = \perp, & 1 \leq i, j \leq m \text{ in the remaining positions} \end{cases} \qquad (5)$$

In the cases with multiple instances and with respect to Fig. 1(b), in the *activation matrix* depicted in Equation 5, the $am_{i,j}$ elements corresponding to the *in* primitives are equal to the number of instances of tuples $u_i$ that must be present on $b_i$ at time $t_i$.

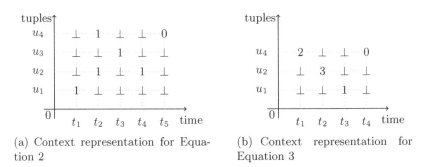

(a) Context representation for Equation 2

(b) Context representation for Equation 3

**Fig. 1.** Context representation

The actions defined in the RHS of the rule may be taken only after the rule has been activated. Formally, this translates into the following integrity constraint: $min(t_{m+1}, \ldots, t_q) \geq max(t_1, \ldots, t_m)$. Furthermore, two scenarios arise. If, on the one hand, immediate actions are demanded, the primitives in the RHS do not need to be timed. Their execution is triggered by the rule's activation. If, on the other hand, delays are desired, time should be specified in agreement with the aforementioned constraint.

The time constructs in Equation 4 should be adapted in such a way to accommodate the representation of either discrete or continuous time, in a relative or absolute fashion, as will be detailed in the following sections 3 and 4.

Such rules are introduced in a Linda-like language developed at the University of Namur, called Bach. Introduced in [16], the Bach coordination language is built upon the principle of a *blackboard* (the equivalent of Linda's *tuple space*) represented by a shared memory space through which *agents* can communicate. The interaction with the blackboard is ensured by the use of four timed primitives: *tell* for outputting information on the blackboard, *ask* for querying the presence of information, *get* for retrieving information and *nask* for querying the absence of information. In order to express more complex actions, the four primitives can be linked by three composition operators to form more complex *agents*, namely: ";" for sequential composition, "||" for parallel composition and " + " for nondeterministic choice. The blackboard is complemented with a set of rules responsible for the detection of desired contexts. Whenever the agents modify the content of the blackboard through the *tell* and *get* primitives, the tuple making the object of the execution is compared to the tuples specified in the LHS of the rules associated with the blackboard in question. This allows each rule to keep track whether its LHS may be expressed from the current content of the blackboard. Reversly, when a rule becomes active it must make true all the actions described by its RHS. This translates the *in* primitives to *tell* ones and the *nin* to *get* ones. Furthermore, these new agents may be destined for the local blackboard or remote ones, according to the specifications.

The time extensions of the language have been introduced with respect to [14] and follows the classical *two-phase functioning* approach to real-time systems illustrated, among others, by Lustre [6], Esterel [3] and Statecharts [12]. In a first phase, all the atomic actions of the statements are executed. They are assumed to take no time. Furthermore, composition operators induce no extra cost to the execution. In a second phase, when no actions can be reduced or when all components encounter a special timed action, time progresses by one unit.

## 3    Discrete Time Points

We now turn to the introduction of time in blackboard rules. The approach, called discrete, is useful in scenarios where it is important to specify precise time points in which the tuples defining the context are present on or absent from the blackboard. In Equation 4, the temporal parameter $t_k$ $(1 \leq k \leq q)$ of each primitive may be expressed either as an absolute timestamp or as a number depicting the units of time relatively to the current time point.

Surveying the moment when a rule reaches its activation condition is achieved in an incremental fashion by using the events which alter the content of the blackboard. The effect of *tell* and successful *get* primitives as well as expired tuples being removed are the events that change the contents of the blackboard. This new snapshot of the blackboard, together with the time points of occurring events, allow to keep track on how the rule is impacted by the changes. In addition to the *activation matrix* introduced in Equation 5, each rule must be associated with a *blackboard counter matrix* in which the evolution of the blackboard will be reflected. The initial structure of the *blackboard counter matrix* is the following:

$$CM_{n \times m} = \begin{cases} cm_{i,j} = 0, & if\, 1 \leq i,j \leq n \text{ and } \exists\, in(b_i, u_i, t_j) \in LHS \\ cm_{i,j} = 0, & if\, n+1 \leq i,j \leq m \text{ and } \exists\, nin(b_i, u_i, t_j) \in LHS \\ cm_{i,j} = \bot, & if\, 1 \leq i,j \leq m \text{ in the remaining positions} \end{cases}$$
(6)

Whenever a *tell* primitive puts a tuple $u_i$ on blackboard $b_i$ at the right moment $t_i$, the corresponding element of the matrix, $cm_{i,i}$ is incremented $(1 \leq i \leq m)$. Symmetrically, successful *get* primitives and expired tuples removed from the blackboard will decrement the counter. We define the maximum value for the time points given in the LHS of the rule as $t_{max} = max(t_1, \ldots, t_m)$. Once $t_{max}$ is reached, the rule can be evaluated for possible activation by verifying the requirements:

$$\begin{cases} cm_{i,j} \geq am_{i,j} & if\, 1 \leq i,j \leq n, \\ cm_{i,j} = 0 & if\, n+1 \leq i,j \leq m. \end{cases}$$

In terms of time representation, absolute or relative values may be used. For absolute values we refer to a standard date-time point and it would be fair to say that the underlying system provides the functionalities to obtain it. The downside, however, is that absolute time points occur only once, thus the rule

$$AM = \begin{pmatrix} 1 & \dots & 1 & 0 & \dots & 0 \\ t_{1,1} & \dots & t_{n,1} & t_{n+1,1} & \dots & t_{m,1} \\ t_{1,2} & \dots & t_{n,2} & t_{n+1,2} & \dots & t_{m,2} \end{pmatrix} \qquad CM = \begin{pmatrix} bc_1 & \dots & bc_n & bc_{n+1} & \dots & bc_m \\ fi_1 & \dots & fi_n & fi_{n+1} & \dots & fi_m \\ li_1 & \dots & li_n & li_{n+1} & \dots & li_m \end{pmatrix}$$

(a) Activation matrix    (b) Blackboard counter matrix

**Fig. 2.** Absolute time approach

can be triggered at most once. For usage scenarios where repetitive actions are required, a relative representation might be more desirable. This is achieved by specifying the temporal offsets between the moments when the desired tuples should be present or absent from the blackboard.

## 4    Continuous Time Intervals

The discrete time approach seems to be very rigid and gives rise to questions like: how can we be sure that the system will capture the event at the right time with pin-point accuracy? Can we a-priori predict with precision when pieces of information become available? In real life scenarios, depending on the application domain, some degree of flexibility should be provided. To accommodate for such requirements we make two propositions, in an absolute and relative time fashion.

### 4.1    Absolute Time Approach

For these types of rules we define the time intervals in the form of absolute time windows, having the general representation given in Equation 7. The activation follows the intuition: for each $in$ primitive, at least one instance of tuple $u_i$ must be present on the respective blackboard within the $[t_{i,1}, t_{i,2}]$ time interval ($1 \leq i \leq n$), while for the $nin$ primitives no instances of tuples $u_j$ must be present on the respective blackboard in the $[t_{j,1}, t_{j,2}]$ time interval ($n + 1 \leq j \leq m$).

$$\begin{aligned} in(b, u_1, [t_{1,1} : t_{1,2}]), & \dots, in(b, u_n, [t_{n,1} : t_{n,2}]), \\ nin(b, u_{n+1}, [t_{n+1,1} : t_{n+1,2}]), & \dots, nin(b, u_m, [t_{m,1} : t_{m,2}]) \longrightarrow \\ & in(b_{m+1}, u_{m+1}, t_{m+1}), \cdots, in(b_p, u_p, t_p), \\ & nin(b_{p+1}, u_{p+1}, t_{p+1}), \cdots, nin(b_q, u_q, t_q) \quad (7) \end{aligned}$$

Formally, the *activation matrix* for such a rule is represented in Fig. 2(a). It is comprised of three lines: the first one contains the number of instances required for each tuple, the second one contains the lower bound of each time interval and the third one is composed of the upper bound of each time interval.

Keeping track on how the blackboard activity affects such a rule is achieved with a *blackboard counter matrix* of the form depicted in Fig. 2(b), where, for every $1 \leq k \leq m$, $bc_k$ is the blackboard counter corresponding to the tuple $u_k$, $fi_k$ represents the timestamp of the first tuple $u_k$ present on the blackboard after the adding of the rule and $li_k$ represents the timestamp of the last tuple $u_k$ added on the blackboard after the adding of the rule.

$$AM = \begin{pmatrix} 1 & \dots & 1 & 0 & \dots & 0 \\ d_1 & \dots & d_n & d_{n+1} & \dots & d_m \end{pmatrix}$$
(a) Activation matrix

$$CM = \begin{pmatrix} bc_1 & \dots & bc_n & bc_{n+1} & \dots & bc_m \\ fi_1 & \dots & fi_n & fi_{n+1} & \dots & fi_m \\ li_1 & \dots & li_n & li_{n+1} & \dots & li_m \end{pmatrix}$$
(b) Blackboard counter matrix

**Fig. 3.** Relative time approach

The activation of the rule is achieved when all of the following conditions are met:

$$\begin{cases} cm_{1,i} \geq am_{1,i}, & if \ 1 \leq i \leq n, \\ cm_{1,j} = 0 & , n+1 \leq j \leq m, \\ cm_{2,k} \geq am_{2,k}, & if \ 1 \leq k \leq m, \\ cm_{3,l} \leq am_{3,l}, & if \ \leq l \leq m. \end{cases}$$

Furthermore, the activation can occur only in a fixed time frame $[t_{min}, t_{max}]$, where:

$$t_{min} = min(t_{1,1}, t_{1,2}, \dots, t_{n,1}, t_{n,2}, t_{n+1,1}, t_{n+1,2}, \dots, t_{m,1}, t_{m,2})$$
$$t_{max} = max(t_{1,1}, t_{1,2}, \dots, t_{n,1}, t_{n,2}, t_{n+1,1}, t_{n+1,2}, \dots, t_{m,1}, t_{m,2})$$

### 4.2  Relative Time Approach

For these types of rules we define the time intervals in the form of relative durations, having the general representation given in Equation 8. The activation follows the intuition: for each $in$ primitive, at least one instance of tuple $u_i$ must be added to the blackboard within a $d_i$ time frame for every $1 \leq i \leq n$, while for the $nin$ primitives no instances of tuples $u_j$ must be present on the blackboard within a $d_j$ time frame, for every $n+1 \leq j \leq m$. The semantic is that the relative durations imply that there exists a time point within that given time frame in which the information must be detected as present or absent.

$$in(b, u_1, d_1), \dots, in(b, u_n, d_n), nin(b, u_{n+1}, d_{n+1}), \dots, nin(b, u_m, d_m)$$
$$\longrightarrow in(b_{m+1}, u_{m+1}), \cdots, in(b_p, u_p), nin(b_{p+1}, u_{p+1}), \cdots, nin(b_q, u_q) \quad (8)$$

Formally, the *activation matrix* for such a rule is represented in Fig. 3(a). It is comprised of two lines: the first one contains the number of instances required for each tuple and the second represents the minimum duration in which a tuple must be present respectively absent from the blackboard.

Keeping track on how the blackboard activity affects such a rule is achieved with a *blackboard counter matrix* of the form depicted in Fig. 3(b), where, for every $1 \leq k \leq m$, $bc_k$ is the blackboard counter corresponding to the tuple $u_k$, $fi_k$ represents the timestamp of the first tuple $u_k$ present on the blackboard after the adding of the rule and $li_k$ represents the timestamp of the last tuple $u_k$ added on the blackboard after the adding of the rule.

The activation of the rule is achieved when all of the following conditions are met:

$$\begin{cases} cm_{1,i} \geq am_{1,i}, & for\ 1 \leq i \leq n, \\ cm_{1,j} = 0, & for\ n+1 \leq j \leq m, \\ cm_{3,k} - cm_{2,k} \geq am_{2,k}, & for\ 1 \leq k \leq m. \end{cases}$$

As opposed to the absolute timed rules, the relative timed ones may wait indefinitely for their activation and are not bound to a fixed interval.

# 5   Implementation

Following the ideas presented in Section 4, the continuous time approach presents several practical advantages over the discrete one. First of all, expecting events to happen at very precise moments in time is rather hard to predict. Second of all, single time points may be considered as a particular case of time interval in which the lower bound is identical to the upper bound. Consequently, for our current implementation, we have chosen the variant of absolute continuous time. Furthermore, the relative time may be easily translated into absolute one by adding a proper time offset.

## 5.1   General Principles

As a language designed for distributed systems, Bach has been implemented in a client-server fashion, but only in terms of the architecture. Each device acts independently and is responsible for establishing connections with neighboring devices and no devices are designated as central managers. No hypothesis is made on a-priori knowledge of the network architecture. The server-side and the client-side represent just a separation of concepts and tasks.

The server-side component is responsible for handling the communication, the blackboard and its operations, a rule space for containing the reaction rules associated with the blackboard, a request space for the agents that need to be processed and a solved request space for storing the results of the agents execution. The client-side handles the parsing of string representations of agents, dispatches requests to a local or remote blackboard depending on needs and receives the replies. Parsing an agent returns a tree-like structure with the nodes consisting of the composition operators that link the primitives, which are stored in the leaves. The processing of the tree begins at the root node with the recursive creation of sub-agents until the leaves are reached, moment at which requests are formed towards the server.

## 5.2   Implementation Techniques

The activation condition of a rule represents a context defined on multiple black-boards. However, a full implementation of that general rule would involve a costly mechanism and heavy network loading in order to check whether the condition becomes active or not. In this hypothesis, in accordance with the results in [17], the wise choice is to restrict the context definition to only one blackboard. We do not restrict in any way the actions to be taken upon the rule's activation since they translate into remote calls to local or distant blackboards.

In order to handle the timing aspects, we enrich the tuples with an additional attribute in which to store the timestamp of their arrival on the blackboard. The blackboard rules are implemented as a structure comprised of two ordered arrays, one for the LHS and one for the RHS, to store the sets of *in* and *nin* primitives.

In order to define the activation condition of a rule, it is not mandatory to have a context composed solely of different tuples. Depending on the needs, several instances of the same tuple may be required. This would translate by placing a sequence of $in(b, u)$ primitives in the condition. In order to avoid writing repeatedly one *in* primitive for each needed instance of the tuple $u$ we provide a syntactic shortcut allowing to add an index to specify the total number of instances. Subsequently, $in_c(b, u)$ states that a total of $c$ instances of tuple $u$ are required on blackboard $b$. Testing the absence of a tuple amounts to having 0 instances on the blackboard. By complementing Equation 7 with this notation we obtain the following:

$$in_{c_1}(b, u_1, [t_{1,1} : t_{1,2}]), \ldots, in_{c_n}(b, u_n, [t_{n,1} : t_{n,2}]),$$
$$nin(b, u_{n+1}, [t_{n+1,1} : t_{n+1,2}]), \ldots, nin(b, u_m, [t_{m,1} : t_{m,2}]) \longrightarrow$$
$$in(b_{m+1}, u_{m+1}, t_{m+1}), \cdots, in(b_p, u_p, t_p),$$
$$nin(b_{p+1}, u_{p+1}, t_{p+1}), \cdots, nin(b_q, u_q, t_q) \quad (9)$$

Consequently, to accommodate this syntactic shortcut, the activation matrix depicted in Fig. 2(a) becomes:

$$AM = \begin{pmatrix} c_1 & \ldots & c_n & 0 & \ldots & 0 \\ t_{1,1} & \ldots & t_{n,1} & t_{n+1,1} & \ldots & t_{m,1} \\ t_{1,2} & \ldots & t_{n,2} & t_{n+1,2} & \ldots & t_{m,2} \end{pmatrix} \quad (10)$$

At the same time, each rule must keep track of the changes occurring on the blackboard. With the execution of *tell* or *get* primitives, tuples are respectively added or removed. By supervising the tuples that transit the blackboard it is possible to determine the moment when the context is met for the rule to become active. To this purpose, we reduce the *blackboard matrix* represented in Fig. 2(b) to a vector having the form:

$$CM = \begin{pmatrix} dict_1 & \ldots & dict_n & dict_{n+1} & \ldots & dict_m \end{pmatrix}$$

The elements $dict_i (1 \leq i \leq m)$ are dictionary-like objects, in which the entries have a *key* represented by the tuple identifier of the instance that concerns the respective *in* or *nin* primitive and a *value* represented by the instance timestamp of its adding to the blackboard:

$$dict_i = \{< instance_1, timestamp_1 >, \ldots, < instance_{last}, timestamp_{last} >\}$$

Due to the time constraints, only a selection of these tuples may participate to the activation of the rule. The total number, denoted $bc_i$, is obtained in a SQL-like fashion: select and count all the instances $instance_i$ where their timestamp $timestamp_i$ is present in the interval $[t_{i,1}, t_{i,2}]$.

The total number of times a rule's context may be expressed using the content of the blackboard represents the maximum triggering counter for the respective rule and is given by the combinatorial formula:

$$\prod_{k=1}^{n} \binom{bc_{t_k}}{c_k}$$

As advocated in the beginning of the section, the continuous time implementation is flexible and generic enough to accommodate the discrete time approach described in Section 3. Indeed, by abuse of notation, a time point $t_i$ is equivalent to the time interval $[t_{i,1}, t_{i,2}]$ iff $t_{i,1} = t_{i,2}$. As such, the activation matrix in 10 will have its third line identical to the second.

## 6   Related Work

Let us now offer a bird's eye-view over existing lines of research related to the idea of reactivity and timed extensions and see how they are placed with respect to our proposal.

### 6.1   Chemical Models

The road of reactivity was paved by the GAMMA model [1] which introduced the idea of transforming multi-sets of data by means of mechanisms inspired by chemistry. Accordingly, the multi-set is metaphorically seen as a chemical solution on top of which different reaction rules are defined. The multi-set evolves as long as the reaction condition is met, after which a stable point is reached.

*Timed-Gamma* [21] addresses the time issue from a performance-related perspective, in particular the computation time. To this aim, the rules are enriched with *timing specifications* denoting either finite or infinite durations. The proposed timed-computation is decomposed as a three stage process: scheduling, computation and commitment.

As an extension of GAMMA, the *chemical abstract machine* [2] added the notions of *membranes* and *airlocks*. Membranes act as containers for sub-solutions, thus enforcing local reactions. Airlocks enable the communication between these enclosed sub-solutions and their containing environment.

More recent developments of the chemical metaphor are those related to biochemical tuple spaces [29], service competition or service composition [30] and pervasive ecosystems [31]. Such propositions are similar to our current one from the point of view of declarative transformations. However, these eco-laws rely on an underlying framework covering the global space of neighbor devices. In our approach, rules are stored on the blackboards themselves, and connect them without other middleware.

Compared to these pieces of work, our proposal keeps the same idea of reactivity. However, it refines it by enhancing the patterns of the rules in distinguishing the presence or absence of information on both sides at given points in time or within given time frames and by providing an efficient implementation. We provide no counterpart for probabilistic reasonings, but consider this as orthogonal to our work. As a result, ideas from [29, 30] can be introduced directly in our work. Such ideas will be the subject of future work.

## 6.2    Reactive Models

In another line of research, the articles [4, 13] explore models relying on the idea of reactive tuple spaces. Among others, they are used for the coordination of mobile agents. This has also been treated in a series of work, such as: MARS [5], TuCSoN [25], ReSpecT [8, 9], LIME [22, 26].

More concretely, the MARS model proposes reactions in the form of a four components set consisting of: the reaction type, the tuple wild-card to be matched, the type of operation on the tuple space that should be monitored, the agent's identity. This mechanism is very flexible and is able to express a wide range of scenarios: the most general situation occurs when only the reaction type is specified and is rendered more precise by adding values to the other components.

In TuCSoN, the approach is to define programmable logic tuple centers which consist of a tuple space enhanced by the notion of *behavior specification*. Such specifications are defined with the ReSpecT language, which implements the reactions in the form of two special types of tuples. The first represents an association between a communication primitive and a logical event, allowing for groups of primitives to be connected to one identical logical event or for one primitive to generate several events. The second is an association between the logical events and the actual reaction body, which consists of either state primitives, term predicates or primitives of the tuple space. The timed extension, introduced in [24], is twofold: dedicated predicates are introduced to access the tuple-center or event time and reactions may be scheduled before/after given times or within intervals. The paper [23] augments the language with the introduction of a *guard*, that may enforce additional requirements for an event, such as its source, destination or trigger time.

The multiple blackboard approach for ReSpecT has been explored in [19] by studying its interactions with LOGOP, introduced in [28] and later refined in [20]. LOGOP presents itself as an extension of LINDA for the management of multiple tuple space environments. The execution of primitives in such a hypothesis is supported by the introduction of composed tuple spaces in their definition. A dedicated logOp tuple center uses the ReSpecT language to react to LOGOP primitives and form requests for each tuple center forming the composition. It also receives the replies and forms the final answer.

Offering a different perspective from the previous models, LIME associates reactions to the context of the tuple space rather than the set of primitives executed on it. Reactions are triggered by matching tuples on the tuple space with given patterns, thus defining specific contexts.

To sum up, the main characteristics of related work are fourfold: *(i)* the reaction condition is expressed only in terms of data being present on the blackboard, *(ii)* some reactions are triggered on the execution of primitives, *(iii)* the reaction rules mostly concern a single blackboard, *(iv)* the timing of the rules is done in a schedule like fashion.

In our approach we provide a finer control over the reaction conditions, which can be defined in terms of data presence (by means of the *in* primitive) and data absence (by means of the *nin* primitive). This allows the specification of more precise and strict contexts, not possible in other pieces of work. In addition, our rule mechanism is designed to be used also in multi-blackboard systems. In terms of temporal aspects, our focus is not on specifying when a rule should be activated but on providing a time axis for the context in which a rule becomes active.

### 6.3   Final Remarks

In summary, as may be appreciated by the reader, our work presents significant differences with respect to related work. In addition to the chemical models, our approach allows the definition of more complex contexts consisting not only of information that needs to be present, but also of information that needs to be absent. In the terms of the chemical metaphor, our proposition offers the possibility to model the idea of an *inhibitor*, a substance capable of stopping or retarding a chemical reaction. By means of the *nin* primitive it is possible to express reactions which occur in the absence of given inhibitors.

With respect to the reactive models, in which the main focus is put on reacting to the execution of atomic primitives, our declarative approach, offers advantages in terms of flexibility and expressiveness for expressing context-awareness.

## 7   Conclusions

In this paper, we propose a solution for coordination by means of declarative timed rules. The focus is oriented on introducing time in the process of context detection. We have shown how one set of pieces of information may be interpreted differently depending on when the pieces become available. We find this perspective to be different from that or related pieces of work in which the accent is put on rule scheduling. Certainly, the idea of rules and reactivity is not a novelty to coordination models. However, we have introduced new variants based on a declarative reading which we have shown to be expressive, yet being efficiently implementable. Taking an incremental approach on the computation bypasses the need for a transactional mechanism, since keeping track of how the blackboard content is reflected on the rule's activation condition there is no need to reevaluate it after each primitive execution.

For future work we aim at introducing dedicated mechanisms to specify the triggering counter for a rule. This would overwrite the default behavior and give the user more flexibility in modelling his needs. By exploiting the rules mechanism we also aim to obtain capabilities for complex event processing.

# References

1. Banâtre, J.-P., Coutant, A., Métayer, D.L.: A Parallel Machine for Multiset Transformation and its Programming Style. Future Generation Computer Systems 4(2), 133–144 (1988)
2. Berry, G., Boudol, G.: The Chemical Abstract Machine. In: Proceedings of the 17th ACM SIGPLAN-SIGACT Symposium on Principles of Programming Languages, POPL 1990, pp. 81–94. ACM, New York (1990)
3. Berry, G., Gonthier, G.: The ESTEREL Synchronous Programming Language: Design, Semantics, Implementation. SCP 19(2), 87–152 (1992)
4. Bosschere, K.D., Jacquet, J.-M.: $\mu^2 Log$: Towards Remote Coordination. In: Hankin, C., Ciancarini, P. (eds.) COORDINATION 1996. LNCS, vol. 1061, pp. 142–159. Springer, Heidelberg (1996)
5. Cabri, G., Leonardi, L., Zambonelli, F.: Reactive Tuple Spaces for Mobile Agent Coordination. In: Rothermel, K., Hohl, F. (eds.) MA 1998. LNCS, vol. 1477, pp. 237–248. Springer, Heidelberg (1998)
6. Caspi, P., Pilaud, D., Halbwachs, N., Plaice, J.: LUSTRE: A Declarative Language for Real-time Programming. In: Proceedings of the 14th ACM SIGACT-SIGPLAN Symposium on Principles of Programming Languages, POPL 1987, pp. 178–188. ACM, New York (1987)
7. Chourabi, H., Nam, T., Walker, S., Gil-Garcia, J., Mellouli, S., Nahon, K., Pardo, T., Scholl, H.: Understanding Smart Cities: An Integrative Framework. In: Proceedings of the 2012 45th Hawaii International Conference on System Sciences, HICSS 2012, pp. 2289–2297. IEEE Computer Society, Washington, DC (2012)
8. Denti, E., Natali, A., Omicini, A.: On the Expressive Power of a Language for Programming Coordination Media. In: Proceedings of the 1998 ACM Symposium on Applied Computing, SAC 1998, pp. 169–177. ACM, New York (1998)
9. Denti, E., Omicini, A.: Designing Multi-agent Systems around an Extensible Communication Abstraction. In: Meyer, J.-J.C., Schobbens, P.-Y. (eds.) ModelAge-WS 1997. LNCS (LNAI), vol. 1760, pp. 90–102. Springer, Heidelberg (2000)
10. Fischer, G.: Context-Aware Systems: The 'Right' Information, at the 'Right' Time, in the 'Right' Place, in the 'Right' Way, to the 'Right' Person. In: Proceedings of the International Working Conference on Advanced Visual Interfaces, AVI 2012, pp. 287–294. ACM, New York (2012)
11. Freeman, E., Arnold, K., Hupfer, S.: JavaSpaces Principles, Patterns, and Practice, 1st edn. Addison-Wesley Longman Ltd., Essex (1999)
12. Harel, D.: Statecharts: A Visual Formalism for Complex Systems. SCP 8(3), 231–274 (1987)
13. Jacquet, J.-M., Bosschere, K.D.: Blackboard Relations in the $\mu Log$ Coordination Language. New Generation Computing (19), 23–56 (2001)
14. Jacquet, J.-M., De Bosschere, K., Brogi, A.: On Timed Coordination Languages. In: Porto, A., Roman, G.-C. (eds.) COORDINATION 2000. LNCS, vol. 1906, pp. 81–98. Springer, Heidelberg (2000)
15. Jacquet, J.-M., Linden, I.: On the Expressiveness of Absolute-Time Coordination Languages. In: De Nicola, R., Ferrari, G.-L., Meredith, G. (eds.) COORDINATION 2004. LNCS, vol. 2949, pp. 232–247. Springer, Heidelberg (2004)
16. Jacquet, J.-M., Linden, I.: Coordinating Context-aware Applications in Mobile Ad Hoc Networks. In: Proceedings of the First ERCIM Workshop on eMobility (2007)

17. Jacquet, J.-M., Linden, I., Staicu, M.-O.: Blackboard Rules for Coordinating Context-aware Applications in Mobile Ad Hoc Networks. In: Proceedings 11th International Workshop on Foundations of Coordination Languages and Self Adaptation. EPTCS, vol. 91, pp. 63–78. Open Publishing Association (2012)
18. Linden, I., Jacquet, J.-M., Bosschere, K.D., Brogi, A.: On the Expressiveness of Relative-Timed Coordination Models. ENTCS 97, 125–153 (2004)
19. Menezes, R., Omicini, A., Viroli, M.: Have ReSpecT for LOGOP. In: De Paoli, F., Manzoni, S., Poggi, A. (eds.) AI*IA/TABOO Joint Workshop "Dagli Oggetti Agli Agenti: Dall'informazione Alla Conoscenza". Pitagora Editrice Bologna (2002)
20. Menezes, R., Omicini, A., Viroli, M.: On the Semantics of Coordination Models for Distributed Systems: The LOGOP Case Study. ENTCS 97, 97–124 (2004)
21. Mousavi, M., Basten, A., Reniers, M., Chaudron, M.: Timed-Gamma and its coordination language. Nordic Journal of Computing (2013)
22. Murphy, A.L., Picco, G.P., Roman, G.-C.: LIME: A Coordination Model and Middleware Supporting Mobility of Hosts and Agents. ACM Trans. Softw. Eng. Methodol. 15(3), 279–328 (2006)
23. Omicini, A.: Formal ReSpecT in the A&A perspective. ENTCS 175(2), 97–117 (2007)
24. Omicini, A., Ricci, A., Viroli, M.: Time-Aware Coordination in ReSpecT. In: Jacquet, J.-M., Picco, G.P. (eds.) COORDINATION 2005. LNCS, vol. 3454, pp. 268–282. Springer, Heidelberg (2005)
25. Omicini, A., Zambonelli, F.: Tuple Centres for the Coordination of Internet Agents. In: 1999 ACM Symposium on Applied Computing, SAC 1999, San Antonio, TX, USA, pp. 183–190. ACM (1999)
26. Picco, G.P., Murphy, A.L., Roman, G.-C.: LIME: Linda Meets Mobility. In: Proceedings of the 21st International Conference on Software Engineering, ICSE 1999, pp. 368–377. ACM, New York (1999)
27. Schilit, B., Theimer, M.: Disseminating Active Map Information to Mobile Hosts. IEEE Network 8, 22–32 (1994)
28. Snyder, J., Menezes, R.: Using Logical Operators as an Extended Coordination Mechanism in Linda. In: Arbab, F., Talcott, C. (eds.) COORDINATION 2002. LNCS, vol. 2315, pp. 317–331. Springer, Heidelberg (2002)
29. Viroli, M., Casadei, M.: Biochemical Tuple Spaces for Self-organising Coordination. In: Field, J., Vasconcelos, V.T. (eds.) COORDINATION 2009. LNCS, vol. 5521, pp. 143–162. Springer, Heidelberg (2009)
30. Viroli, M., Casadei, M.: Chemical-inspired Self-composition of Competing Services. In: Proceedings of the 2010 ACM Symposium on Applied Computing, SAC 2010, pp. 2029–2036. ACM, New York (2010)
31. Viroli, M., Pianini, D., Montagna, S., Stevenson, G.: Pervasive Ecosystems: a Coordination Model Based on Semantic Chemistry. In: Proceedings of the 2012 ACM Symposium on Applied Computing, SAC 2012, pp. 295–302. ACM, New York (2012)
32. Wyckoff, P., McLaughry, S.W., Lehman, T., Ford, D.: T spaces. IBM Syst. J. 37(3), 454–474 (1998)

# Data Abstraction in Coordination Constraints[*]

José Proença[1,2] and Dave Clarke[2]

[1] HASLab / INESC TEC, Universidade do Minho, Portugal
[2] iMinds-DistriNet, Dep. Computer Science, KU Leuven, Belgium
{jose.proenca,dave.clarke}@cs.kuleuven.be

**Abstract.** This paper studies complex coordination mechanisms based on constraint satisfaction. In particular, it focuses on data-sensitive connectors from the Reo coordination language. These connectors restrict how and where data can flow between loosely-coupled components taking into account the data being exchanged. Existing engines for Reo provide a very limited support for data-sensitive connectors, even though data constraints are captured by the original semantic models for Reo.

When executing data-sensitive connectors, coordination constraints are not exhaustively solved at compile time but at runtime on a per-need basis, powered by an existing SMT (satisfiability modulo theories) solver. To deal with a wider range of data types and operations, we abstract data and reduce the original constraint satisfaction problem to a SAT problem, based on a variation of predicate abstraction. We show soundness and completeness of the abstraction mechanism for well-defined constraints, and validate our approach by evaluating the performance of a prototype implementation with different test cases, with and without abstraction.

## 1 Introduction

Coordination languages describe how data can be exchanged among components, focusing on the glue code and abstracting away the computations performed by components. An ongoing trend for these languages over the last years leans towards more expressive coordination models, aiming at more compact and manageable representations of complex behaviour than basic models such as Linda.

This paper focuses on coordination models whose glue code is given by connectors, expressed as logical constraints. Using constraints to describe how data flows in a connector has been investigated, for example, for the BIP [3,4] and the Reo [1,7,15] coordination languages. Constraints have also been used to describe desirable properties of process algebras, such as Bruni's et al.'s compensable processes [5]. In order to keep the problem of producing and executing connectors tractable, only properties that bear no computation are captured by the constraints. These are then analysed using off-the-shelf constraint solvers.

Engines for BIP and Reo have incorporated various properties into their coordination constraints, such as history of the connector, some notions of priority, and simple data restrictions. These coordination-related properties are encoded

---

[*] This research is supported by the FCT grant SFRH/BPD/91908/2012.

C. Canal and M. Villari (Eds.): ESOCC 2013, CCIS 393, pp. 159–173, 2013.

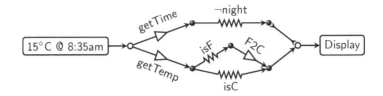

**Fig. 1.** Filtering communication between a sensor and a display based on data

as boolean formulas or as formulas over a decidable theory, which can be analysed by a given off-the-shelf constraint solver. An implementation of BIP [4] relies on BDD libraries for constraint solving, and some Reo implementations rely on SAT solvers [7] and on Computer Algebra Systems [6]. Using constraint solvers to execute connectors brings more flexibility than compiling them into state machines that list all coordination patterns, since it supports larger connectors, and changes to the system have a low impact on performance.

This paper exploits the usage of constraints to describe coordination patterns that use complex (and possibly undecidable) data predicates. This is achieved by decoupling the evaluation of complex data predicates from the constraint solving problem. We propose a method that encodes formulas over data structures into a boolean formula, by incorporating in the final formula the results of operations over data that influence coordination. We show that this method is sound and complete with respect to a class of constraints that covers all Reo connectors over data that we encountered in the literature. An earlier version of this work with the detailed proofs can be found in a companion technical report [16]. Our technique has been recently exploited to introduce interaction between the solver and external components during constraint solving [15]. More generally, our approach falls within the implicit programming paradigm [14], wherein constraints specify the computation and SAT and SMT solvers perform the computation. Our contribution to this field is the use of constraint satisfaction to implement coordination patterns. More specifically, this paper deals with the problem of increasing the complexity of data used to coordinate components.

We use the Reo coordination language as the source of coordination constraints, based on our previous work [7]. Reo is a synchronous graph-based visual language wherein complex connectors are built out of simpler primitive connectors. Each primitive connector imposes restrictions on how and where data can flow, and the behaviour of a composite connector is given by the composition of the constraints of all primitives involved. A connector evolves on a per-round basis, and in each round data flows atomically through some of the ports of this connector, based on its combined constraints. After each round the state of the connector may change, resulting in new constraints.

The Reo connector depicted in Fig. 1 has a data producer and a data consumer that displays a given temperature value. The data producer tries to publish a temperature value of 15°C, measured at 8:35am. This producer is connected to two *transformer* channels, depicted with a triangle, that extract the time and the temperature attributes from the data. These values are then filtered by *filter* channels, depicted with zig-zag lines, that allow data to flow if the associated predicate holds for the data flowing. For example, isF checks if the temperature is measured in Fahrenheit degrees. The result from the ¬night filter acts as a barrier to the temperature value, allowing data to flow to the display only if it is daytime. The connector evolves atomically, in the sense that data only flows from the producer to the consumer if it is daytime, if the temperature is in Fahrenheit or in Celsius, and if the display accepts data. If the predicates ¬night and isC hold but the display cannot receive data, then the producer is not allowed to publish the value. This reflects the role of data-constraints for coordination, where the mere attempt to send data influences dataflow.

Summarizing, we model and execute synchronous connectors where arbitrary data operations can influence dataflow—even when these cannot be handled by SMT solvers—, by using a SAT solver after a pre-analysis of the coordination constraints. These data operations can be described, for example, using Java methods. We show that our approach is sound and complete, and we compare the overhead cost of decoupling the data analysis against more traditional approaches where the data constraints are directly solved by an SMT solver. Our small benchmark shows that using data values and operations that can be encoded into complex integer calculations can be more efficiently handled using our methodology. However, when they can be encoded with simple integer expressions the performance of using the SMT solver directly is sometimes similar or better than our approach, depending on the number of new boolean variables introduced during the encoding into a boolean formula.

The rest of this paper is organised as follows. Section 2 motivates our approach. Section 3 presents a constraint-based semantics for Reo. Section 4 describes predicate abstraction. Section 5 evaluates the performance of abstracting over data. Section 6 discusses related work and Section 7 concludes our paper.

## 2   Motivation

When viewing coordination as constraints, the decision of what and where data can flow is made using constraint solving techniques. More precisely, a connector imposes a set of constraints, which evolve during the lifetime of the connector, whose solutions describe the dataflow through the connector. Finding these solutions is an NP problem, wich can be solved using off-the-shelf SAT and SMT solvers. By doing this the expressivity of coordination constraints becomes tighly coupled with the expressivity of the constraint solver. For example, if a connector wants to filter all time references based on a predicate night, the constraint solver needs to represent constraints over time references. This paper proposes an approach that allows operations over data values to be performed outside the underlying constraint solver, allowing functions and predicates to be defined in a more conventional programming language such as Java.

The main challenge when implementing an engine that executes connectors such as the one in Fig. 1 is to decide which data should flow in each of the ports, taking into account operations over arbitrary data types, including temperature values and time references. We consider two main approaches to this challenge:

**SMT.** The time references and temperature values are represented as integers that are used by an off-the-shelf SMT solver to find a solution. This encoding into integers can be done, for example, by representing the time in minutes and combining it with the value of the temperature using simple arithmetic operations. This restricts the expressivity of the constraints to the language of the SMT solver.

**SAT.** The data constraints are reduced to a simpler constraint over boolean variables using an abstraction technique, and solved using an off-the-shelf SAT solver. The actual values flowing through the ports are calculated based on solutions from the SAT solver. In our example a possible boolean solution could say that only the predicates ¬night and isC hold, and that there is flow in all three ports. Based on this solution we can infer that the value 8:35am flows on the port connected to the display.

Not all solutions to an abstract constraints are guaranteed to produce a solution to the original constraints. Therefore we focus on a subset of constraints that provide this guarantee. For example, we consider the connector from Fig. 1 to be ill-defined without the data producer, since a solution for the abstract constraints would not clearly map to a solution in the original formula.

## 3   Coordination as Constraints

Connectors are viewed as a set of constraints representing valid coordination patterns, following our previous work [7]. Each port has a boolean variable $x \in \mathcal{X}$ indicating presence of dataflow and a data variable $\widehat{x} \in \widehat{\mathcal{X}}$ indicating what data flows. Coordination evolves in rounds: in each round the coordinated components contribute to the constraints of the connector, a solution for these constraints is found, and both the connector and components are updated accordingly.

### 3.1   Guarded Commands

When compared with the original formulation of coordination constraints for Reo [7], we use an (asymmetric) attribution operator for data variables instead of equality, and we allow attributions to be only in positive positions (they can never be negated). The resulting data causality is exploited in our abstraction technique and in the definition of well-defined connectors, but it is does not modify the semantics of connectors. The requirement of having assignments in positive positions facilitates the analysis of connectors, while reflecting the concept of connectors as structures where data flows through. Formulas are represented by Dijkstra's guarded commands [8].

$$\psi ::= \phi \to s \mid \psi_1 \, \psi_2 \mid \top \qquad \qquad \text{(formulas)}$$

$$\phi ::= x \ (\in \mathcal{X}) \mid P(\widehat{x}) \mid \phi_1 \wedge \phi_2 \mid \neg\phi \qquad \text{(guards)}$$

$$s ::= \phi \mid s_1 \wedge s_2 \mid \widehat{x} := d \ (\in \mathbb{D}) \mid \widehat{x} := \widehat{y} \mid \widehat{x} := f(\widehat{y}) \qquad \text{(statements)}$$

**Table 1.** Channel Encodings

| Channel | Representation | Constraints | Channel | Representation | Constraints |
|---|---|---|---|---|---|
| Sync | $a \longrightarrow b$ | $a \leftrightarrow b$ <br> $b \to \widehat{b} := \widehat{a}$ | LossySync | $a \dashrightarrow b$ | $b \to a$ <br> $b \to \widehat{b} := \widehat{a}$ |
| SyncDrain | $a \blacktriangleright\!\!-\!\!\blacktriangleleft b$ | $a \leftrightarrow b$ | FIFO-E | $a \multimap\!\square\!\to b$ | $\neg b$ |
| SyncSpout | $a \longleftrightarrow b$ | $a \leftrightarrow b$ | FIFO-F(d) | $a \multimap\!\boxed{d}\!\to b$ | $\neg a$ <br> $b \to \widehat{b} := d$ |
| Merger | $\substack{a \\ b} \!\!>\!\!\longrightarrow c$ | $c \leftrightarrow (a \lor b)$ <br> $\neg(a \land b)$ <br> $a \to \widehat{c} := \widehat{a}$ <br> $b \to \widehat{c} := \widehat{b}$ | Replicator | $a \longrightarrow\!\!<\substack{b \\ c}$ | $a \leftrightarrow b$ <br> $a \leftrightarrow c$ <br> $a \to \begin{array}{l}\widehat{b} := \widehat{a} \land \\ \widehat{c} := \widehat{a}\end{array}$ |
| Filter(P) | $a \xrightarrow{P}\!\!\!w\!\!\!\to b$ | $b \leftrightarrow (a \land P(\widehat{a}))$ <br> $b \to \widehat{b} := \widehat{a}$ | Transf(f) | $a \xrightarrow{f}\!\!\triangleright b$ | $a \leftrightarrow b$ <br> $b \to \widehat{b} := f(\widehat{a})$ |
| Writer(d) | $\boxed{W(d)}\!\to a$ | $a \to \widehat{a} := d$ | Reader | $\boxed{R}\!\leftarrow a$ | $\top$ |

*Synchronous variables* $x \in \mathcal{X}$ range over booleans and *data variables* in $\widehat{\mathcal{X}} = \{\widehat{x} \mid x \in \mathcal{X}\}$ range over a global data set $\mathbb{D}$. Each synchronous variable corresponds to exactly one port of a Reo connector. $\top$ is *true*, $P \in \mathbb{P}$ is a unary predicate over data variables, and $f \in \mathbb{F}$ is a unary total function. A guarded command $\phi \to s$ is interpreted as $\neg\phi \lor s$, $\psi \, \psi'$ as $\psi \land \psi'$, and $\widehat{x} := \widehat{y}$ as $\widehat{x} = \widehat{y}$. The other logical connectives for guards can be encoded as usual.

**Definition 1 (solution).** *A solution to a formula* $\psi$ *defined over ends* $\mathcal{X}$ *is a mapping* $\sigma$ *from* $\mathcal{X}$ *to* $\{\top, \bot\}$*, and from* $\widehat{\mathcal{X}}$ *to data values* $\mathbb{D}$*, such that* $\sigma$ *satisfies* $\psi$*, regarded as a boolean expression, according to the satisfaction relation* $\sigma \models \psi$ *defined below. Each predicate symbol* $P$ *and function symbol* $f$ *have an associated interpretation, denoted by* $\mathcal{I}(P)$ *and* $\mathcal{I}(f)$*, such that* $\mathcal{I}(P) \subseteq \mathbb{D}$ *and* $\mathcal{I}(f) \subseteq \mathbb{D}^2$.

$$\sigma \models \top \quad\quad always$$
$$\sigma \models \widehat{x} := d \quad iff\ \sigma(\widehat{x}) = d$$
$$\sigma \models \widehat{x} := \widehat{y} \quad iff\ \sigma(\widehat{x}) = \sigma(\widehat{y})$$
$$\sigma \models \widehat{x} := f(\widehat{y}) \quad iff\ (\sigma(\widehat{y}), \sigma(\widehat{x})) \in \mathcal{I}(f)$$

$$\sigma \models x \quad\quad iff\ \sigma(x) = \top$$
$$\sigma \models \neg\psi \quad\quad iff\ \sigma \not\models \psi$$
$$\sigma \models \psi_1 \land \psi_2 \quad iff\ \sigma \models \psi_1\ and\ \sigma \models \psi_2$$
$$\sigma \models P(\widehat{x}) \quad iff\ \sigma(\widehat{x}) \in \mathcal{I}(P)$$

### 3.2   Reo as Constraints

Table 1 presents the formulas of some of the most common Reo primitives [7]. It includes a writer that produces a data value $d$ and reader that receives any data value, which are used to abstract away the behaviour of more complex components. We write $\psi_c$ to denote the current formula imposed by a connector $c$. Composition of a connector is simply given by the conjunction of their formulas.

The formula $\psi_{ni}$ below constrains the connector on the left of Fig. 2, a simplified version of the connector in Fig. 1.

$$x \to \widehat{x} := 8\text{:}35\text{am} \quad x \leftrightarrow y \quad y \to \widehat{y} := \mathsf{DST}(\widehat{x}) \quad (y \wedge \neg\mathsf{night}(\widehat{y})) \leftrightarrow z \quad z \to \widehat{z} := \widehat{y}$$

A possible solution for $\psi_{ni}$ is $\{x, y, z \mapsto \top; \widehat{x} \mapsto 8\text{:}35\text{am}; \widehat{y}, \widehat{z} \mapsto 9\text{:}35\text{am}\}$, assuming DST adds one hour, and that $\neg\mathsf{night}(9\text{:}35\text{am})$ holds. This solution states that $x, y, z$ have dataflow, 8:35am flows through $x$, and 9:35am flows throw $y$ and $z$.

### 3.3   Well-Defined Formulas

A well-defined formula is a formula to which our predicate abstraction can be applied. More precisely, a well-defined formula must have solutions that produce only *well-defined routes*, where each route is a set of data assignments derived from a given solution. Well-definedness of a route reflects (1) the absence of loops, (2) the absence of multiple assignments to a single variable, and (3) the existence of a data value at the end of each tree of assignments. For example, the following two formulas are ill-defined: $(a \wedge b) \to \widehat{a} := \widehat{b} \quad a \to \widehat{a} := 5$ and $a \to (\widehat{a} := \widehat{b} \wedge \widehat{b} := \widehat{a})$. The first assigns $\widehat{a}$ to $\widehat{b}$ and to 5 when $a \wedge b$ holds, which could be fixed by replacing the second guard by $a \wedge \neg b$. The second assigns $\widehat{a}$ and $\widehat{b}$ to each other, creating a loop of data assignments. Both formulas have routes that violate condition (3), which could be fixed by extending them with the guarded command $\top \to \widehat{b} := 7$.

**Definition 2 (route).** *A route $r$ of a formula $\psi$ is a set of assignments associated to a solution $\sigma \models \psi$, given by $\mathsf{route}_\sigma(\psi)$ defined below.*

$$\mathsf{route}_\sigma(\phi \to s) = \begin{cases} \mathsf{route}_\sigma(s) & \text{if } \sigma^*(g) \\ \emptyset & \text{otherwise} \end{cases}$$

$$\mathsf{route}_\sigma(\psi_1 \ \psi_2) = \mathsf{route}_\sigma(\psi_1) \cup \mathsf{route}_\sigma(\psi_2)$$
$$\mathsf{route}_\sigma(\phi) = \emptyset$$
$$\mathsf{route}_\sigma(\widehat{x} := d) = \{\widehat{x} \mapsto d\}$$
$$\mathsf{route}_\sigma(\widehat{x} := \widehat{y}) = \{\widehat{x} \mapsto \widehat{y}\}$$
$$\mathsf{route}_\sigma(\widehat{x} := f(\widehat{y})) = \{\widehat{x} \mapsto \widehat{y}\}$$
$$\mathsf{route}_\sigma(s_1 \wedge s_2) = \mathsf{route}_\sigma(s_1) \cup \mathsf{route}_\sigma(s_2)$$

*where:*
$$\sigma^*(x) = \sigma(x)$$
$$\sigma^*(\neg\phi) = \neg(\sigma^*(\phi))$$
$$\sigma^*(\phi_1 \wedge \phi_2) = \sigma^*(\phi_1) \wedge \sigma^*(\phi_2)$$
$$\sigma^*(P(\widehat{x})) = \sigma(\widehat{x}) \in \mathcal{I}(P)$$

**Notation.**   $\mathsf{routes}(\psi)$ represents the set of all $\mathsf{route}_\sigma(\psi)$ for any $\sigma$, and $\mathsf{route}_\top(\psi)$ the set of all assignments in $\psi$. Then for every $r \in \mathsf{routes}(\psi)$, $r \subseteq \mathsf{route}_\top(\psi)$.

**Definition 3 (well-definedness).** *A route $r$ is* well-defined *if the conditions below hold. A formula $\psi$ is* well-defined *if all its routes are well-defined.*

1. *The transitive closure of $r$ is not reflexive (no loops).*
2. *Each variable $\widehat{x}$ is assigned at most once in $r$ (single assignment).*
3. *If $(\widehat{x} \mapsto t) \in r$, then $t \in \mathbb{D}$ or exists $t'$ such that $(t \mapsto t') \in r$ (data source).*

Given a well-defined route it is always possible to calculate the data values flowing on this route. This is intuitively done by copying data starting from the data values, and using the functions extracted from guarded commands with guards that evaluate to true. In the formula $\psi_{ni}$ defined in Section 3.2, and using the solution $\sigma$ presented there, $\mathsf{route}_\sigma(\psi_{ni})$ returns $\{\widehat{z} \mapsto \widehat{y}; \widehat{y} \mapsto \widehat{x}; \widehat{x} \mapsto$ 8:35am$\}$. This route can be used to retreive back the values of $\widehat{y}$ and $\widehat{z}$, knowing that $\widehat{y} := \mathsf{DST}(\widehat{x})$, which can be inferred from $\psi_{ni}$ and $\sigma$.

In practice, connectors with well-defined formulas need to explicitly mention what data values can be sent by producers; data cannot "created" during constraint solving. Two concerns emerge from this formulation of well-definedness. First, it seems unnatural to build a route from a given solution $\sigma$, and to use this route later to discover what values should flow through the route, since this is already given by $\sigma$. Second, checking well-definedness (as it is) requires iterating over all solutions. Our first observation is that $\mathsf{route}_\sigma(\cdot)$ does not use the values flowing on the ports: only the synchronisation variables and the validity of the predicates. The abstraction technique described later will provide exactly this information. Regarding the cost of verifying well-definedness, we chose to test sufficient (yet not necessary) conditions for being well-defined. We dedicate the next subsection to this. Furthermore, our data abstraction technique (cf. Section 4) will not produce invalid behaviour from ill-defined connectors; in the worse case it may fail to find the next step.

### 3.4   Verifying Well-Definedness

We provide a simple procedure to guarantee well-definedness, which does not cover all well-defined formulas. We address each of the three conditions in Definition 3 separately, and informally discuss the correctness of our procedure.

**Loop Free.** Instead of searching for loops in routes from $\mathsf{routes}(\psi)$, we do so in $\mathsf{route}_\top(\psi)$. Since every route is a subset of $\mathsf{route}_\top(\psi)$, these will also be loop free. An example of a loop-free formula that will be wrongly identifed as having loops is $a \to \widehat{b} := \widehat{c}$   $\neg a \to \widehat{c} := \widehat{b}$, since the mutual data dependency between $\widehat{b}$ and $\widehat{c}$ is guarded by a variable $a$ that guarantees that the loop never occurs.

When considering formulas from traditional Reo primitive connectors, the direction of dataflow is fixed. It is still possible to create Reo connectors that yield wrongly identifed loops, but we find these to be complex and unnatural.

**Single Assignment.** We guarantee each variable to be uniquely assigned by construction. More precisely, we provide a condition that guarantees that the composition (conjunction) of two formulas preserves the single-assignment property. Intuitively two formulas are *pluggable* if they assign different variables.

**Definition 4 (read and write variables, pluggable).** *We say $\widehat{x}$ is a* read *variable in $\psi$ if either $(\widehat{y} := \widehat{x}) \in \mathsf{route}_\top(\psi)$ or $(\widehat{y} := f(\widehat{x})) \in \mathsf{route}_\top(\psi)$, and is a* write *variable in $\psi$ if $(\widehat{x} := t) \in \mathsf{route}_\top(\psi)$, for some $f$, $\widehat{y}$, and $t$. Write $?\psi$ and $!\psi$ to denote all read and write variables of $\psi$, respectively. Two formulas $\psi_1$ and $\psi_2$ are* pluggable *if:*

$$!\psi_1 \cap !\psi_2 = \emptyset.$$

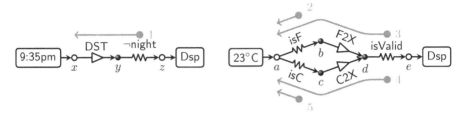

**Fig. 2.** Calculating dependencies of predicates; DST updates the time according to the daylight saving time, and F2X and C2X create a structure X that it verified by isValid

By composing only pluggable formulas the effort of verifying the single-assignment property is restricted to only smaller formulas of primitive connectors. All formulas from Table 1 obey the single-assignment property.

**Data Source.** We guarantee routes of a formula to always end up in a data value also by construction, by requiring (1) formulas to be pluggable and (2) each primitive formula $\psi_p$ to use only data variables with dataflow. More precisely, every solution $\sigma \models \psi_p$ must obey $\hat{x} \in \mathsf{var}(\mathsf{route}_\sigma(\psi_p)) \Rightarrow \sigma(x)$, where $\mathsf{var}(\cdot)$ returns the variables present in a route. Finally, we also require (3) all read variables to be write variables in the global formula $\psi$, that is, $\hat{x} \in ?\psi \Rightarrow \hat{x} \in !\psi$.

All formulas in Table 1 obey requirement (2): in all solutions of these formulas if a variable $\hat{x}$ is written or read then $x$ is set to true. Dropping the guard $b$ in the formula of the Sync channel, for example, would break this property, since $\hat{b}$ could be read even when $b$ is false. The third requirement is violated every time the SyncSpout is connected to a channel via a shared port $x$, since $\hat{x}$ will be a read variable but not a write variable. This can be solved without violating other requirements simply by using a variation of the SyncSpout channel that always outputs a constant value. In fact, we do not know any system modelled in Reo that uses the data value produced by the SyncSpout channel.

## 4   Data Abstraction

This section describes how to encode formulas over data into boolean formulas. This is done in two phases: (1) the dependencies for each predicate are calculated by tracing back the provenience of data, and (2) new boolean variables replace the existing data variables, used to dictate which predicates hold.

Fig. 2 illustrates the dependency analysis for predicates. From trace 3, for example, we deduce that isValid depends on the evaluation of isValid(F2X(23°C)). By evaluating the traces 1 to 5 the data values are no longer needed when searching for valid solutions. This section will describe how to transform formulas— such as the one in Section 3.2—into formulas over booleans—such as the one below. The expression within square brackets is replaced by its evaluation. Observe that $z$ does not have any data variable, since it does not affect any predicate.

$$x \to \hat{x}_{\mathsf{ni.dst}} := [\mathsf{night}(\mathsf{DST}(8{:}35\mathsf{am}))]   x \leftrightarrow y   y \to \hat{y}_{\mathsf{ni}} := \hat{x}_{\mathsf{ni.dst}}   (y \wedge \neg \hat{y}_{\mathsf{ni}}) \leftrightarrow z$$

## 4.1   Precomputed Domain Invariants

Write $P.f_1.f_2 \ldots f_n$ to denote a predicate $P \in \mathbb{P}$ with an associated sequence of functions that have to be evaluated before the predicate. Define:

$$(P.f_1.\cdots .f_n) \circ f = \begin{cases} \text{Error} & \text{if } f \in \{f_1, \ldots, f_n\} \\ P.f_1.\cdots .f_n.f & \text{otherwise} \end{cases}$$

and write $\{P_1, \ldots, P_n\} \bar{\circ} f$ to denote $\{P_1 \circ f, \ldots, P_n \circ f\} \setminus \{\text{Error}\}$. Note that every function in a connector is considered unique.

For each port $x \in \mathcal{X}$ in a formula $\psi$ we define its *domain invariant* $\mathcal{D}_x$ as the set of predicates and functions that can be reachable, intuitively captured by the 5 traces in Fig. 2. More precisely, each $\mathcal{D}_x$ is the smallest set of predicates such that $\rho(\psi)$ holds, where $\rho(\cdot)$ is defined as:

$$\rho(P(\widehat{x})) = \mathcal{D}_x \supseteq \{P\} \qquad \rho(\phi \to s) = \rho(\phi) \wedge \rho(s) \qquad \rho(\psi_1\ \psi_2) = \rho(\psi_1) \wedge \rho(\psi_2)$$
$$\rho(\widehat{x} := \widehat{y}) = \mathcal{D}_y \supseteq \mathcal{D}_x \qquad \rho(\phi_1 \wedge \phi_2) = \rho(\phi_1) \wedge \rho(\phi_2) \qquad \rho(\neg\psi) = \rho(\psi)$$
$$\rho(\widehat{x} := f(\widehat{y})) = \mathcal{D}_y \supseteq (\mathcal{D}_x \bar{\circ} f) \qquad \rho(s_1 \wedge s_2) = \rho(s_1) \wedge \rho(s_2) \qquad \rho(\_) = true.$$

Domain invariants are always finite sets because the definition of $\bar{\circ}$ prevents the application of the same function twice. Well-definedness does not prevent this duplication because it relies on $\text{routes}(\cdot)$, while $\rho(\cdot)$ relies on all assignments.

The formula $\psi_{ni}$ for the left connector of Fig. 2, presented in Section 3.2, yields the following domain invariants.

$$\mathcal{D}_x = \{\text{ni.dst}\} \qquad\qquad \mathcal{D}_y = \{\text{ni}\} \qquad\qquad \mathcal{D}_z = \emptyset$$

We write ni and dst as shorthands for night and DST, respectively. These domain invariants are indeed the smallest solution for the constraints given by $\rho(\psi_{ni})$, namely $\mathcal{D}_x \supseteq (\mathcal{D}_y \bar{\circ} \text{dst})$ and $\mathcal{D}_y \supseteq \{\text{ni}\}$. Applying the same reasoning for the connector on the right of Fig. 2 we can conclude that $\mathcal{D}_a = \{\text{isF}, \text{F2X.isValid}, \text{C2X.}$ isValid, isC$\}$. The remaining domain invariants can be calculated in a similar way.

## 4.2   Predicate Abstraction

This subsection formalises the encoding from a formula $\psi$ into a new boolean formula, such as the one exemplified right before Section 4.1.

Let $[P.f_1.\cdots .f_n(d)] = P(f_1(\ldots (f_n(d))))$, where $n \geq 0$ and $d \in \mathbb{D}$.[1] The function $[\cdot]$, defined below, receives a formula $\psi$ over arbitrary data types in $\mathbb{D}$ and returns a new formula over booleans, i.e., data variables in $[\psi]$ range over booleans. This transformation is a variant of *predicate abstraction* [9].

$$[\phi \to s] = [\phi] \to [s] \qquad [x] = x \qquad [P(\widehat{x})] = \widehat{x}_P \qquad [\neg\psi] = \neg[\psi]$$
$$[\psi_1\ \psi_2] = [\psi_1]\ [\psi_2] \qquad [\widehat{x} := d] = \bigwedge_{P \in \mathcal{D}_x} \widehat{x}_P := [P(d)]$$
$$[\phi_1 \wedge \phi_2] = [\phi_1] \wedge [\phi_2] \qquad [\widehat{x} := \widehat{y}] = \bigwedge_{P \in (\mathcal{D}_x \cap \mathcal{D}_y)} \widehat{x}_P := \widehat{y}_P$$
$$[s_1 \wedge s_2] = [s_1] \wedge [s_2] \qquad [\widehat{x} := f(\widehat{y})] = \bigwedge_{P \in \mathcal{D}_x, (P \circ f) \in \mathcal{D}_y} \widehat{x}_P := \widehat{y}_{P \circ f}$$

---

[1] More precisely, $[P.f_1.\cdots .f_n(d)]$ iff $(n = 0) \wedge (d \in \mathcal{I}(P))$ **or** $\exists_{d_1,\ldots,d_n \in \mathbb{D}} \cdot (d_1 \in \mathcal{I}(P)) \wedge (\forall_{i \in \{1,\ldots,n\}} \cdot (d_{i+1}, d_i) \in \mathcal{I}(f_i))$, where $d_{n+1} = d$.

Predicates and functions are computed during the encoding of data assignments $\widehat{x} := d$. Each of these assignments originates a new variable $\widehat{x}_P$ for every $P \in \mathcal{D}_x$ given by the domain invariants, explained before, such that $\widehat{x}_P \leftrightarrow P(\widehat{x})$. Hence the number of new variables depends on the size of the domain invariants. Ports with an empty domain invariant will not have variables in the abstract formula, and ports that can affect $n$ predicates will have at least $n$ new variables.

### 4.3  Soundness and Completeness

Our main claim is that every solution for a well-defined formula $\psi$ can be found by finding a solution for its predicate abstraction $[\psi]$. This requires the abstraction function $[\cdot]$ to be *sound* and *complete*. Soundness means that every solution $\sigma$ of $\psi$ must also be a solution of $[\psi]$, after mapping each data assignment to the assignments of the new data variables as follows.

$$
\begin{aligned}
[\sigma] \ = \ & \{\widehat{x}_P \mapsto [P(\sigma(\widehat{x}))] \mid \widehat{x} \in \mathsf{dom}(\sigma) \cap \widehat{\mathcal{X}}, P \in \mathcal{D}_x\} \\
\cup \ & \{x \ \mapsto \sigma(x) \qquad \mid x \in \mathsf{dom}(\sigma) \cap \mathcal{X}\}
\end{aligned}
$$

Completeness means that every solution of $[\psi]$ must be the abstraction of at least one solution in $\psi$. Both proofs of soundness and completeness rely on the definition of $\rho(\cdot)$ and $[\cdot]$, and completness requires formulas to be well-defined.

**Theorem 1 (Soundness).**  $\sigma \models \psi \ \Rightarrow \ [\sigma] \models [\psi]$.

*Proof.* Start by fixing the domain invariant of every port. The proof follows by induction on the structure of formulas, applied to guards, statements, and to guarded commands. Soundness of the conjunction of guarded commands follows directly from the soundness of guarded commands and the definition of $\models$.  □

**Theorem 2 (Completeness).**
  $\psi$ *is well-defined* **and** $\sigma' \models [\psi] \ \Rightarrow \ \exists_\sigma \cdot (\sigma \models \psi) \wedge (\sigma' = [\sigma])$.

*Proof.* We build a solution $\sigma$ for $\psi$ based on $\sigma'$, knowing that $\psi$ is well defined.

1. Start with the smallest $\sigma$ such that $\forall x \in (\mathsf{dom}(\sigma') \cap \mathcal{X}) \cdot \sigma(x) = \sigma'(x)$.
2. Assume (so far) that, for every $\widehat{x}_P \in \mathsf{dom}(\sigma')$, $\sigma'(\widehat{x}_P) = \top \Rightarrow \sigma(\widehat{x}) \in \mathcal{I}(P)$. Calculate $r = \mathsf{route}_{\sigma'}(\psi)$ using the assumption above to resolve $\sigma^*(P(\widehat{x}))$.
3. The route $r$ is well-defined (based on the assumption mentioned above), hence it is possible to calculate the data flowing in every port along these routes. Starting from each data value in $r$, apply the assignments and functions induced by $r$ to calculate these data values.

Observe that not all $x$ and $\widehat{x}$ need to have a value assigned by $\sigma$. Extending $\sigma$ with assignments of variables not in $\sigma$ will not modify $\sigma \models \psi$, since the validity of the route is enough to guarantee satisfaction.

The assumption introduced in (2) can be shown based on the the construction of $\sigma$ and on the routes induced by $\sigma'$ on both $\psi$ and its abstraction.  □

# 5   Evaluation

We validate our approach by applying predicate abstraction to five connectors with varying sizes. All but the last connector use integers as the data domain, allowing us to compare the performance of our techniques against the direct usage of an SMT solver. The goal of this evaluation is to understand the overhead of pre-computing the operations over data before invoking a SAT solver, possibly introducing a larger number of variables. The last connector uses a Java data structure instead of integers, showing that the performance is not compromised when dealing with other data domains, and to emphasise that our abstraction technique supports more expressive data-sensitive connectors.

Our prototype implementation uses the Z3 SMT solver[2] to solve expressions with booleans and integers. Z3 is a high-performance theorem prover with an incorporated SMT solver being developed by Microsoft. In our experiments we use only integer arithmetic, although Z3 supports many other theories.

We evaluate our test cases using the following solver configurations.

**Z3**   Z3 is used to solve the original data constraints.

**[Z3]**   The original constraints are encoded into boolean constraints using predicate abstraction, and solved with Z3; and a solution for the original constraint is produced.

Our prototype implementation is developed using the Scala language,[3] which produces Java binary classes, can import Java libraries, and supports functional programming. The source code and our benchmarks can be found online.[4] To integrate Z3 with Scala we use the Scala^Z3 libraries developed at EPFL [13].

## 5.1   Test Cases

Our approach is evaluated using five test cases: the temperature connector from our motivating example, a set of transactional functions in sequence and in parallel, and two variants of an approval system.

**Temperature.**   This connector (Fig. 3) is based on our motivating example from Section 1. The data value is regarded as an integer, the transformer channels perform simple arithmetic operations, and the predicates use simple inequalities.

**Transactional functions**   We define a transactional function to be a tuple $\langle \mathsf{pre}, \mathsf{f}, \mathsf{f}^{-1}, \mathsf{post} \rangle$, where $\mathsf{f}$ is the main function, $\mathsf{f}^{-1}$ is a compensation that must be applied to undo $\mathsf{f}$, and $\mathsf{pre}$ and $\mathsf{post}$ are pre- and post-conditions of $\mathsf{f}$. The test cases consist of the sequential and parallel composition of transactional functions (Fig. 4). Data enters the connector via the *in* port and exits either via *out* if both conditions hold, or via *stopped* otherwise. The *stop* port propagates the stopping signal in the sequential composition. Predicates and functions use again simple arithmetic operations and inequalities, and are setup so that all transactions succeed except the last transaction in the sequence.

---

[2] http://research.microsoft.com/projects/z3
[3] http://www.scala-lang.org
[4] http://is.gd/reopp

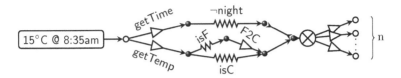

**Fig. 3.** Temperature connector connected to $n$ outputs

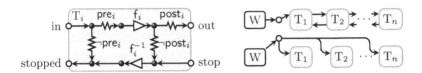

**Fig. 4.** Connectors with transactional functions

**Approval System.** The approval system (Fig. 5) captures the merging from several applicants, each publishing their classification. Each applicant provides a tuple of 5 integers, consisting of a unique identifier and 4 classifications from 0 to 20. The predicates isApproved and isDenied check if these ratings are within a certain thresholds, encoded in two variants: (1) as expressions that require arithmetic operations to convert back and forward tuples (based on conversions to and from base 21), and (2) as Java methods over tuples of elements.

## 5.2   Results and Discussion

The constraints for our test cases are solved using a 8-core 2.4 GHz Intel Xeon desktop with 16 GB RAM running Ubuntu Linux. Each measurement was performed 10 times, and the average was used (Fig. 6). The time covers the building of formulas, the solving of constraints, and the calculation of the dataflow, performed at runtime. In the first and last two graphs a log-log scale is used.

Z3 uses SAT solving to iteratively search for solutions to more complex theories, in our case the theory of integers. Our abstraction also reduces a more complex problem to a SAT problem. Probably due to internal optimisations in Z3, and the usage of more efficient memory operations, its performance is in some cases similar or better than predicate abstraction.

The transactional functions running in parallel exhibit the best results for predicate abstraction compared to Z3. This is partially justified by the small

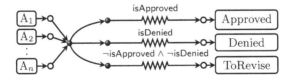

**Fig. 5.** Approval $n$-ary connector

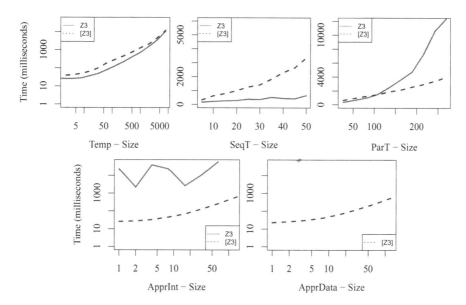

**Fig. 6.** Performance evaluation of our five parameterised test case connectors

number of variables added during predicate abstraction, and because pre-compilation of the predicates is not more expensive since all predicates need to be evaluated also for Z3. Conversely, the number of variables in the sequence of transactional functions is very high, reducing the performance of [Z3]. The unexpected variations of time for Z3 in the approval system are probably a consequence of the complexity of its predicates and of the high valued integers involved.[5] This complexity has little impact when using predicate abstraction, which performs faster and more consistently. Furthermore abstraction allows the usage of Java data structures and operations, allowing a reimplementation of the approval system in a more structured way and without loss of performance.

Summarising, we conjecture that scenarios with complex data functions and predicates benefit from our predicate abstraction mechanism, scenarios with a large number of simple functions and predicates and no complex calculations benefit from using SMT solvers, and in scenarios with a smaller number of data operations the difference of performance is small. Using predicate abstraction can also be beneficial in scenarios with a large number of predicates and functions, provided the encoding does not produce a large number of variables, as in ParT.

## 6    Related Work

A recent attempt to coordinate Erlang actors uses special actors with associated Reo connectors [11]. That work illustrates the need to support data constraints, since there was no automatic tool to generate coordination code from

---

[5] A number of runs for Z3 timed out after 5 min and were left out of this benchmark.

Reo connectors. From the verification perspective, model checking techniques for Reo connectors exist based on mCRL2 and on its representation of data structures [12]. Regarding implementations of Reo, Changizi et. al [6] extended the automata-based compilation approach with filters and transformers. These are handled by a SAT/SMT solver, though the choice of filters and transformers is limited to those expressible in the language of the solver. Their process of building an automaton searches for all solutions for all states. Our work is more flexible by considering only one state and solution at a time during execution, and it supports formulas with data operations outside the underlying solver. Jongmans et al.[10] orchestrated web services based on Reo, and integrated external functionality by generating Java code corresponding to the automata-with-data-constraints model of Reo. The resulting code has an exponential number of formulas, without data transformations, that are checked sequentially. Our approach improved on these implementations by exploiting the flexibility of constraints, not limited by the expressivity of the underlying constraint solver, and by identifying a suitable set of connectors for our abstraction techniques.

Predicate abstraction is a technique used to reduce complex problems to simpler ones while preserving some relevant properties [9]. This technique is commonly used for model checking [2], where concrete states of a system are mapped to a smaller set of abstract states based on a set of predicates. New predicates can be added to expand the set of abstract states, in a process called *abstraction refinement*. Our variation of predicate abstraction modifies an original system by replacing operations over data by boolean variables that reflect properties over this data. Instead of refining the abstraction until a solution is found (also experimented outside this paper), we identify systems that do not require abstraction refinement.

Our work falls within the implicit programming paradigm. Köksal et al. proposed to integrate the power of SAT/SMT solvers non-intrusively into sequential, imperative programs [14]. In contrast, our approach targets coordination languages, and addresses the expressivity of data-sensitive synchronous systems.

## 7    Conclusions

This paper explores an execution model for data-sensitive connectors based on predicate abstraction. We exploit the fact that the vast majority of connectors includes concrete data values to precompute the predicates used by the connector before solving the data constraints. A simple analysis of the constraints yields which predicates should be computed for each variable, and the original predicates are abstracted to boolean variables holding the precomputed results. Our approach is shown to be sound and complete for well-defined connectors. As a result, one can specify and run the coordination layer between components using high-level constraints that inspect and manipulate data offered by producers.

This abstraction technique has been exploited to investigate new interaction mechanisms between the solver and external components during constraint solving, by using functions and predicates that perform interaction [15]. An interesting direction for future work is to encode generic data constraints into formulas over simple theories, instead of boolean formulas, making a tradeoff between relying on more powerful solvers and avoiding the potential increase of variables.

# References

1. Baier, C., Sirjani, M., Arbab, F., Rutten, J.J.M.M.: Modeling component connectors in Reo by constraint automata. Science of Computer Programming 61(2), 75–113 (2006)
2. Ball, T., Podelski, A., Rajamani, S.K.: Relative completeness of abstraction refinement for software model checking. In: Katoen, J.-P., Stevens, P. (eds.) TACAS 2002. LNCS, vol. 2280, pp. 158–172. Springer, Heidelberg (2002)
3. Bliudze, S., Sifakis, J.: Synthesizing Glue Operators from Glue Constraints for the Construction of Component-Based Systems. In: Apel, S., Jackson, E. (eds.) SC 2011. LNCS, vol. 6708, pp. 51–67. Springer, Heidelberg (2011)
4. Bozga, M., Jaber, M., Maris, N., Sifakis, J.: Modeling dynamic architectures using dy-bip. In: Gschwind, T., De Paoli, F., Gruhn, V., Book, M. (eds.) SC 2012. LNCS, vol. 7306, pp. 1–16. Springer, Heidelberg (2012)
5. Bruni, R., Ferreira, C., Kauer, A.K.: First-order dynamic logic for compensable processes. In: Sirjani [17], pp. 104–121
6. Changizi, B., Kokash, N.: Arbab. A constraint-based method to compute semantics of channel-based coordination models. In: International Conference on Software Engineering Advances (2012)
7. Clarke, D., Proença, J., Lazovik, A., Arbab, F.: Channel-based coordination via constraint satisfaction. Science of Computer Programming 76 (2011)
8. Dijkstra, E.W.: Guarded commands, nondeterminacy and formal derivation of programs. Commun. ACM 18(8), 453–457 (1975)
9. Graf, S., Saïdi, H.: Construction of abstract state graphs with PVS. In: Grumberg, O. (ed.) CAV 1997. LNCS, vol. 1254, pp. 72–83. Springer, Heidelberg (1997)
10. Jongmans, S.-S.T.Q., Santini, F., Sargolzaei, M., Arbab, F., Afsarmanesh, H.: Automatic code generation for the orchestration of web services with Reo. In: De Paoli, F., Pimentel, E., Zavattaro, G. (eds.) ESOCC 2012. LNCS, vol. 7592, pp. 1–16. Springer, Heidelberg (2012)
11. Khosravi, R., Sabouri, H.: Using coordinated actors to model families of distributed systems. In: Sirjani [17], pp. 74–88
12. Kokash, N., Krause, C., de Vink, E.P.: Reo + mCRL2: A framework for model-checking dataflow in service compositions. Formal Aspects of Computing 24(2), 187–216 (2012)
13. Köksal, A.S., Kuncak, V., Suter, P.: Scala to the power of Z3: Integrating SMT and programming. In: Bjørner, N., Sofronie-Stokkermans, V. (eds.) CADE 2011. LNCS, vol. 6803, pp. 400–406. Springer, Heidelberg (2011)
14. Köksal, A.S., Kuncak, V., Suter, P.: Constraints as control. SIGPLAN Not. 47(1), 151–164 (2012)
15. Proença, J., Clarke, D.: Interactive interaction constraints. In: De Nicola, R., Julien, C. (eds.) COORDINATION 2013. LNCS, vol. 7890, pp. 211–225. Springer, Heidelberg (2013)
16. Proença, J., Clarke, D.: Solving data-sensitive coordination constraints. CW Reports CW637, Department of Computer Science, KU Leuven (February 2013)
17. Sirjani, M. (ed.): COORDINATION 2012. LNCS, vol. 7274. Springer, Heidelberg (2012)

# Global Consensus through
# Local Synchronization

Sung-Shik T.Q. Jongmans and Farhad Arbab

Centrum Wiskunde and Informatica, Amsterdam, Netherlands
{jongmans,farhad}@cwi.nl

**Abstract.** Coordination languages have emerged for the specification and implementation of interaction protocols among concurrent entities. Currently, we are developing a code generator for one such a language, based on the formalism of constraint automata (CA). As part of the compilation process, our tool computes the CA-specific synchronous product of a number of CA, each of which models a constituent of the protocol to generate code for. This ensures that implementations of those CA at run-time reach a consensus about their global behavior in every step. However, using the existing product operator on CA can be practically problematic. In this paper, we provide a solution by defining a new, local product operator on CA that avoids those problems. We then identify a sufficiently large class of CA for which using our new product instead of the existing one is semantics-preserving.

## 1 Introduction

*Context.* Coordination languages have emerged for the specification and implementation of interaction protocols among concurrent entities (services, threads, etc.). This class of languages includes Reo [1,2], a graphical dataflow language for compositional construction of *connectors*: communication media through which entities can interact with each other. Figure 1 shows example connectors in their usual graphical syntax. Briefly, connectors consist of one or more *channels*, through which data items flow, and a number of *nodes*, on which channel ends coincide. Through connector *composition* (the act of gluing connectors together on their common nodes), users can construct arbitrarily complex connectors.

To implement and use connectors in real applications, one must derive implementations from their graphical specification [3,4,5,6,7,8,9], as precompiled executable code or using a run-time interpretation engine. Roughly two implementation approaches currently exist. In the *distributed approach*, one implements the behavior of each of the $k$ constituents of a connector and runs these $k$ implementations concurrently as a distributed system; in the *centralized approach*, one computes the behavior of a connector as a whole, implements this behavior, and runs this implementation sequentially as a centralized system.

Currently, we are developing a Reo-to-Java code generator using the centralized approach based on the formalism of *constraint automata* (CA) [10]. On input of a graphical connector specification (as an XML file), our tool automatically

C. Canal and M. Villari (Eds.): ESOCC 2013, CCIS 393, pp. 174–188, 2013.
© Springer-Verlag Berlin Heidelberg 2013

**Fig. 1.** Four example connectors. Open circles represent *boundary nodes*, on which entities perform I/O-operations; filled circles represent nodes for internal routing. Every connector in this figure consists of two *primitives* (i.e., minimal subconnectors); the pairs of primitives in the first, third, and fourth connector have one common node.

generates code in four steps. *First*, it extracts from the specification a list of the channels constituting the specified connector. *Second*, it consults a database to find for every channel in the list a "small" CA that formally describes the behavior of that particular channel. *Third*, it computes the product of the CA in the constructed collection to obtain one "big" CA describing the behavior of the whole connector. *Fourth*, it feeds a data structure representing that big CA to a template. Essentially, this template is an incomplete Java class with "holes" that need be "filled" (with information from the data structure). The class generated in this way implements Java's `Runnable` interface. This means that a Java virtual machine can execute the implemented `run` method (declared in `Runnable` and generated by our tool), which simulates the big CA computed in the third step, sequentially in a separate thread (details appear elsewhere [4]).

*Problem.* Computing one big CA (the third step of the centralized approach) and afterward translating it to sequential code (the fourth step) can be problematic: at run-time, the generated implementation may unnecessarily restrict parallelism among independent transitions.[1] The problem is implementing such a big CA using exactly one thread: single-threaded programs cannot execute multiple independent transitions simultaneously, but instead, they force those transitions to execute one after the other (see Section 2 for details). Consequently, although formally sound, the generated implementation may run overly sequentially (e.g., if the first transition to execute takes a long time to complete, while other transitions could have fired manifold during that time).

One approach to this problem is to *not* compute one big CA but generate code directly for each of the small CA instead, essentially moving from the centralized approach to the distributed approach: the implementations of the small CA compute the product operators between them at run-time instead of at compile-time. Although this approach solves the stated problem—independent transitions can execute simultaneously—the necessary distributed algorithms for run-time product computation may inflict a substantial amount of overhead.

---

[1] Independent transitions cannot disable each other by firing.

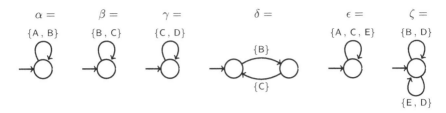

**Fig. 2.** Port automata, denoted by $\alpha$, $\beta$, $\gamma$, $\delta$, $\epsilon$, and $\zeta$, describing the behavior of the primitives constituting the example connectors in Figure 1: $\alpha$ and $\beta$ model the primitives in the first connector, $\alpha$ and $\gamma$ the primitives in the second, $\alpha$ and $\delta$ the primitives in the third, and $\epsilon$ and $\zeta$ the primitives in the fourth.

*Contribution.* This paper provides a better solution to the stated problem by offering a middle ground between centralized and distributed approaches, wherein some subsets of the constituent automata are statically composed to comprise a distributed system of locally centralized automata. Typically, each locally centralized automaton interacts/synchronizes with few other such automata for its transitions, while it represents the composition of a subset of the constitutent automata that interact/synchronize with each other relatively heavily.

Taking the purely distributed approach as our starting point, we define a new product operator whose computation at run-time requires only relatively simple distributed algorithms—CA need to communicate only locally (i.e., with "neighbors") instead of globally (i.e., with everybody)—while allowing independent transitions to execute simultaneously. We then characterize a class of product automata where substituting the existing product operator with our new product operator is semantics-preserving. This class includes product automata whose constituents communicate only *asynchronously* with each other, and so, the optimization technique based on the identification of synchronous and asynchronous regions of connectors can be combined with our results [8].

Although inspired by Reo, we can express our main results in a purely automata-theoretic setting. We therefore skip an introduction to Reo; interested readers may consult [1,2].

## 2   Preliminaries: Port Automata

Many formalisms exist for mathematically defining the semantics of connectors [11]; our code generator, for instance, relies on constraint automata (CA). In this paper, however, we adopt a simplification of CA, called *port automata* (PA) [12]. We prefer PA, because they allow us to focus on the core of our problem (synchronization of communication) without getting distracted by those details of CA (the data exchanged in communication) irrelevant to our present purpose. The results in this paper straightforwardly carry over from PA to CA.

A PA consists of a finite set of states and transitions between them, each of which has a set of *ports* as label. A transition represents an execution step of a

connector, from one internal configuration to the next, where synchronous interaction occurs on the ports labeling that transition. Let PORT and STATE denote
global sets of ports and states (see [13, Appendix A] for formal definitions).

**Definition 1 (Universe of port automata).** *The universe of* PA, *denoted by*
$\mathbb{P}\text{A}$ *and typically ranged over by* $\alpha$, $\beta$, *or* $\gamma$, *is the largest set of tuples* $(Q, \mathcal{P}, \longrightarrow, \imath)$ *where:[2]*

| | |
|---|---|
| – $Q \subseteq \text{STATE}$; | *(states)* |
| – $\mathcal{P} \subseteq \text{PORT}$; | *(ports)* |
| – $\longrightarrow \subseteq Q \times \wp(\mathcal{P}) \times Q$; | *(transitions)* |
| – and $\imath \in Q$. | *(initial state)* |

Figure 2 shows example PA. For instance, the $\{\text{A}, \text{B}\}$-transition of $\alpha$ describes
the only (infinitely repeated) execution step of the horizontal primitive, say Prim,
of the first connector in Figure 1. In that execution step, Prim has synchronous
interaction on nodes A (a write of data $d$ by the environment) and B (the flow
of a copy of $d$ from the horizontal to the vertical primitive). Similarly, the $\{\text{A}, \text{C}, \text{E}\}$-transition of $\epsilon$ means that the left-hand primitive of the fourth connector
in Figure 1 has synchronous interaction on nodes A (a write of data $d$ by the
environment), C (a take of a copy of $d$ by the environment), and E (the flow of
another copy of $d$ from the left-hand to the right-hand primitive).

If $\alpha$ denotes a PA, let $\text{State}(\alpha)$, $\text{Port}(\alpha)$, and $\text{init}(\alpha)$ denote its states, ports,
and initial state (see [13, Appendix A] for formal definitions).

We adopt strong bisimilarity on PA as behavioral equivalence [12]: if $\alpha$ and $\beta$
are bisimilar, denoted by $\alpha \approx \beta$, $\alpha$ can "simulate" every transition of $\beta$ in every
state and vice versa (see [13, Appendix A] for a formal definition).

Individual PA describe the behavior of individual connectors; the application
of the existing product operator to such PA models connector composition [12].
We define this operator in two steps.[3] First, we introduce a relation that defines
when a transition of one PA, say Alice, and a transition of another PA, say Bob,
represent execution steps in which Alice and Bob *weakly agree* on their behavior.
In that case, Alice and Bob agree on which of their common ports to fire while
allowing each other to simultaneously fire other ports. In the following definition,
we represent a transition of Alice as a pair of port-sets: one for all Alice's ports
$(\mathcal{P}_\alpha)$ and one that labels a particular transition of hers $(P_\alpha)$. Likewise for Bob.

**Definition 2 (Weak agreement relation).** *The weak agreement relation, de-
noted by* $\Diamond$, *is the relation on* $\wp(\text{PORT})^2 \times \wp(\text{PORT})^2$ *defined as:*

$$(\mathcal{P}_\alpha, P_\alpha) \Diamond (\mathcal{P}_\beta, P_\beta) \quad \textbf{iff} \quad \begin{bmatrix} P_\alpha \subseteq \mathcal{P}_\alpha \text{ and } P_\beta \subseteq \mathcal{P}_\beta \\ \text{and } \mathcal{P}_\alpha \cap P_\beta = \mathcal{P}_\beta \cap P_\alpha \end{bmatrix}$$

Next, we define the existing product operator on PA in terms of $\Diamond$.

---

[2] Let $\wp(\_)$ denote the power set operator.
[3] This simplifies relating this product operator to the product operator of Section 3.

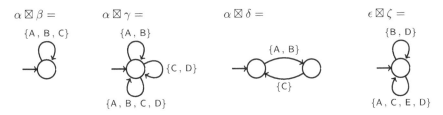

**Fig. 3.** Port automata describing the behavior of the example connectors in Figure 1, constructed using $\boxtimes$ ($\alpha$, $\beta$, $\gamma$, $\delta$, $\epsilon$, and $\zeta$ denote the PA in Figure 2).

**Definition 3 (Product operator).** *The product operator, denoted by* $\_\boxtimes\_$*, is the operator on* $\mathbb{P}\mathrm{A} \times \mathbb{P}\mathrm{A}$ *defined by the following equation:*

$$\alpha \boxtimes \beta = (\mathsf{State}(\alpha) \times \mathsf{State}(\beta),\, \mathsf{Port}(\alpha) \cup \mathsf{Port}(\beta),\, \longrightarrow,\, (\mathsf{init}(\alpha),\, \mathsf{init}(\beta)))$$

*where* $\longrightarrow$ *denotes the smallest relation induced by:*

$$\frac{q_\alpha \xrightarrow{P_\alpha}_\alpha q'_\alpha \text{ and } q_\beta \xrightarrow{P_\beta}_\beta q'_\beta \text{ and } (\mathsf{Port}(\alpha),\, P_\alpha)\, \Diamond\, (\mathsf{Port}(\beta),\, P_\beta)}{(q_\alpha,\, q_\beta) \xrightarrow{P_\alpha \cup P_\beta} (q'_\alpha,\, q'_\beta)} \text{ (WKAGR)}$$

$$\frac{q_\alpha \xrightarrow{P_\alpha}_\alpha q'_\alpha \text{ and } q_\beta \in Q_\beta \text{ and } P_\alpha \cap \mathsf{Port}(\beta) = \emptyset}{(q_\alpha,\, q_\beta) \xrightarrow{P_\alpha} (q'_\alpha,\, q_\beta)} \text{ (INDEPA)} \qquad \frac{q_\beta \xrightarrow{P_\beta}_\beta q'_\beta \text{ and } q_\alpha \in Q_\alpha \text{ and } P_\beta \cap \mathsf{Port}(\alpha) = \emptyset}{(q_\alpha,\, q_\beta) \xrightarrow{P_\beta} (q_\alpha,\, q'_\beta)} \text{ (INDEPB)}$$

The previous definition reformulates the product of PA in [12], which is a simplification of the product of CA in [10]. Figure 3 shows examples of the application of $\boxtimes$. The {A, B, C, D}-transition in the second PA results from applying rule WKAGR to disjoint sets of ports. This models that two independent transitions *coincidentally* can happen simultaneously (true concurrency). The following lemma states that bisimilarity is a congruence. See [12, Theorem 1] for a proof.

**Lemma 1.** $\left[\alpha \approx \beta \text{ and } \gamma \approx \delta\right]$ *implies* $\alpha \boxtimes \gamma \approx \beta \boxtimes \delta$

Furthermore, $\boxtimes$ is associative and commutative.

Interestingly, $\boxtimes$ *"transitively" propagates synchrony* over successive applications. We explain what this means with an example. Suppose Alice knows about ports {A, B} and has one transition in which she fires exactly those ports. Similarly, suppose Bob knows about ports {B, C} and has one transition in which he fires exactly those ports. Because these two transitions satisfy $\Diamond$, the product of Alice and Bob has one transition labeled by {A, B, C}. This means that Alice and Bob always synchronize on their common port B: Alice can perform her transition (i.e., is *willing* to fire B) only if Bob can perform his (i.e., is *ready* to fire B) and vice versa. Now, suppose Carol knows about ports {C, D} and has one transition in which she fires exactly those ports. By the same reasoning as before, the product of [the product of Alice and Bob]$^4$ and Carol has one transition labeled by {A, B, C, D}. Thus, in the product of Alice, Bob, and Carol, Alice "transitively" synchronizes with Carol, through Bob.$^5$

The problem addressed in this paper is that code generators using the centralized approach produce connector implementations that may unnecessarily restrict parallelism. To illustrate this problem, suppose Dave knows about ports {E, F} and has one transition in which he fires exactly those ports. The product of Alice, Bob, Carol, and Dave computed by a tool using the centralized approach has three transitions: one labeled by {A, B, C, D} (Alice, Bob, Carol make a transition), another labeled by {E, F} (Dave makes a transition), and yet another labeled by {A, B, C, D, E, F} (Alice, Bob, Carol and Dave coincidentally make a transition at the same time by true concurrency). At run-time, in every iteration of its main loop, the thread simulating this big automaton nondeterministically picks one of those transitions, checks it for enabledness (in which case all ports are ready to fire), and if so, executes it. By this scheme, as soon as the automaton thread has selected the transition labeled by {A, B, C, D}, the transition labeled by {E, F} has to wait for the next iteration, even if it is enabled already in the current iteration. In other words, Dave cannot execute at its own pace despite being independent of Alice, Bob, and Carol.

Although the centralized approach may unnecessarily restrict parallelism, it guarantees high *throughput* compared to the alternative, distributed approach of generating code for Alice, Bob, Carol, and Dave individually. The problem with the distributed approach is the communication necessary for computing ⊠ at run-time. To see this, suppose that we indeed have separate threads simulating the automata of Alice, Bob, Carol, and Dave. Now, if Alice at some point becomes willing to execute her {A, B} transition, she must ask Bob if he is ready to execute his {B, C} transition. Before he can answer Alice's question, however, Bob in turn must ask Carol if she is ready to execute her {C, D} transition. All this communication negatively affects throughput: it takes much longer for Alice, Bob, and Carol to agree on synchronously executing their individual transitions than for one big automaton to make and carry out such a decision by itself. Nevertheless, the distributed approach enhances parallelism: Dave can execute his transition *while* Alice, Bob, and Carol communicate to come to an agreement.

## 3    A New Local Product Operator

The approaches of the previous section force one to choose between two desirable properties: high throughput between *inter*dependent port automata (PA), at the cost of parallelism, and maximal parallelism between *ind*ependent ones, at the cost of throughput. We need to find a middle ground between the purely centralized and fully distributed approaches that has both these desirable qualities.

---

$^4$ Square brackets for readability.
$^5$ This property of ⊠ models an important feature of Reo: compositional construction of globally synchronous protocol steps out of locally synchronous parts.

Working toward such an approach, we start from the purely distributed approach of computing $\boxtimes$ at run-time through global, transitive communication between automaton threads (e.g., Alice talks to Bob, who in turn talks to Carol, etc.). The idea is to bound this transitivity: generally, when some Alice asks some Bob if he is ready to fire a transition involving common ports, Bob *should* immediately answer *without engaging others*. By doing so, Alice and Bob achieve a higher throughput, while independent others can still execute at their own pace.

In the proposed approach, automaton threads no longer compute $\boxtimes$: instead, they compute a new product operator whose run-time computation requires only local communication. Problematically, however, computing that new product operator instead of $\boxtimes$ can be unsound or incomplete, sometimes to the extent of deadlock. Which of those two happens depends on *how* Bob immediately answers Alice in cases where he actually should have consulted Carol (and possibly others). If Bob replies being ready, the firing of Alice's ports (including her ports common with Bob) incorrectly introduces asynchrony between Bob's two ports. However, if Bob always replies *not* being ready, he and Alice never interact on their common ports. In the rest of this section, we formalize the new product operator and make a first effort at studying under which circumstances substituting $\boxtimes$ with the new product operator is semantics-preserving.

First, we introduce a relation that defines when transitions of Alice and Bob represent execution steps in which they *strongly agree* on their behavior (cf. Definition 2 of $\Diamond$). In that case, they agree on which of their common ports to fire (possibly none), and either Alice forbids Bob to simultaneously fire any other port or vice versa. Afterward, we define our new product operator on PA.

**Definition 4 (Strong agreement relation).** *The strong agreement relation, denoted by* $\blacklozenge$, *is the relation on* $\wp(\mathbb{P}\text{ORT})^2 \times \wp(\mathbb{P}\text{ORT})^2$ *defined as:*

$$(\mathcal{P}_\alpha\,,\,P_\alpha) \blacklozenge (\mathcal{P}_\beta\,,\,P_\beta) \ \textbf{iff} \ \begin{bmatrix} P_\alpha \subseteq \mathcal{P}_\alpha \ \text{and} \ P_\beta \subseteq \mathcal{P}_\beta \ \text{and} \\ \begin{bmatrix} P_\alpha = \mathcal{P}_\alpha \cap P_\beta \ \text{or} \ P_\beta = \mathcal{P}_\beta \cap P_\alpha \\ \text{or} \ \mathcal{P}_\alpha \cap P_\beta = \emptyset = \mathcal{P}_\beta \cap P_\alpha \end{bmatrix} \end{bmatrix}$$

**Definition 5 (Local product operator, l-product).** *The local product operator, l-product, denoted by* $\_ \boxdot \_$, *is the operator on* $\mathbb{P}\text{A} \times \mathbb{P}\text{A}$ *defined by the following equation:*

$$\alpha \boxdot \beta = (\mathsf{State}(\alpha) \times \mathsf{State}(\beta)\,,\, \mathsf{Port}(\alpha) \cup \mathsf{Port}(\beta)\,,\, \longrightarrow\,,\, (\mathsf{init}(\alpha)\,,\, \mathsf{init}(\beta)))$$

*where* $\longrightarrow$ *denotes the smallest relation induced by* INDEPA, INDEPB, *and:*

$$\frac{q_\alpha \xrightarrow{P_\alpha}_\alpha q'_\alpha \ \text{and} \ q_\beta \xrightarrow{P_\beta}_\beta q'_\beta \ \text{and} \ (\mathsf{Port}(\alpha)\,,\, P_\alpha) \blacklozenge (\mathsf{Port}(\beta)\,,\, P_\beta)}{(q_\alpha\,,\, q_\beta) \xrightarrow{P_\alpha \cup P_\beta} (q'_\alpha\,,\, q'_\beta)} \ (\text{STAGR})$$

Figure 4 shows examples of the application of $\boxdot$. The following lemma states that bisimilarity is a congruence. See [13, Appendix D] for a proof.

**Lemma 2.** $[\alpha \approx \beta \ \text{and} \ \gamma \approx \delta]$ *implies* $\alpha \boxdot \gamma \approx \beta \boxdot \delta$

$\alpha \boxdot \beta = \qquad\qquad \alpha \boxdot \gamma = \qquad\qquad\qquad \alpha \boxdot \delta = \qquad\qquad\qquad\qquad \epsilon \boxdot \zeta =$

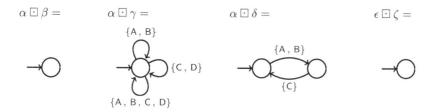

**Fig. 4.** Port automata constructed using $\boxdot$ ($\alpha$, $\beta$, $\gamma$, $\delta$, $\epsilon$, and $\zeta$ denote the PA in Figure 2).

Furthermore, $\boxdot$ is commutative but generally *not* associative. This makes using $\boxdot$ for modeling purposes nontrivial. We address this issue in Section 5. To minimize numbers of parentheses in our notation, we assume right-associativity for $\boxdot$. For instance, we write $\alpha \boxdot \beta \boxdot \gamma \boxdot \delta$ for $\alpha \boxdot (\beta \boxdot (\gamma \boxdot \delta))$.

As informally explained earlier, substituting $\boxtimes$ with $\boxdot$ is not always semantics-preserving. It is, for instance, for the two l-products in the middle of Figure 4 (cf. the two products in the middle of Figure 3) but not for the l-products on the sides. To determine when substituting $\boxtimes$ with $\boxdot$ is semantics-preserving, we first define when Alice is a *subautomaton* of Bob. In that case, Bob has at least every transition that Alice has.

**Definition 6 (Subautomaton relation).** *The subautomaton relation, denoted by $\sqsubseteq$, is the relation on $\mathbb{PA} \times \mathbb{PA}$ defined as:*

$$(Q, \mathcal{P}, \longrightarrow_\alpha, \imath) \sqsubseteq (Q, \mathcal{P}, \longrightarrow_\beta, \imath) \text{ iff } \longrightarrow_\alpha \subseteq \longrightarrow_\beta$$

The following proposition follows directly from the previous definition. In the rest of this section, we investigate under which circumstances its premise holds.

**Proposition 1.** $[\alpha \sqsubseteq \beta \text{ and } \beta \sqsubseteq \alpha]$ implies $\alpha = \beta$

Before showing that the l-product of Alice and Bob is a subautomaton of their product, the next lemma states that strong agreement implies weak agreement: if Alice fires exactly those common ports that Bob fires or vice versa, Alice and Bob agree on their common ports. See [13, Appendix D] for a proof.

**Lemma 3.** $(\mathcal{P}_\alpha, P_\alpha) \blacklozenge (\mathcal{P}_\beta, P_\beta)$ implies $(\mathcal{P}_\alpha, P_\alpha) \lozenge (\mathcal{P}_\beta, P_\beta)$

The next lemma states that the l-product of Alice and Bob is a subautomaton of their product: the product of Alice and Bob can do *at least* the same as their l-product. See [13, Appendix D] for a proof (which uses Lemma 3).

**Lemma 4.** $\alpha \boxdot \beta \sqsubseteq \alpha \boxtimes \beta$

The product of Alice and Bob is not necessarily a subautomaton of their l-product: if Alice and Bob agree on which of their common ports to fire, this does not necessarily mean that they fire no other ports. To characterize the cases in which they do, we define *conditional strong agreement* as a relation "in between" of ♦ and ◊ (and lifted from transitions to PA): Alice and Bob conditionally strongly agree iff, for each of their transitions, their weak agreement on which of their common ports to fire implies their strong agreement.

**Definition 7 (Conditional strong agreement relation).** *The conditional strong agreement relation, denoted by* ♦, *is the relation on* $\mathbb{P}\mathrm{A} \times \mathbb{P}\mathrm{A}$ *defined as:*

$$
\begin{array}{c}
(Q_\alpha, \mathcal{P}_\alpha, \longrightarrow_\alpha, \imath_\alpha) \\
\blacklozenge\,(Q_\beta, \mathcal{P}_\beta, \longrightarrow_\beta, \imath_\beta)
\end{array}
\text{ iff }
\left[
\begin{array}{c}
\left[
\begin{array}{l}
\left[
\begin{array}{l}
q_\alpha \xrightarrow{P_\alpha}_\alpha q'_\alpha \text{ and } q_\beta \xrightarrow{P_\beta}_\beta q'_\beta \text{ and} \\
(\mathsf{Port}(\alpha),\, P_\alpha) \lozenge (\mathsf{Port}(\beta),\, P_\beta)
\end{array}
\right] \\
\textbf{implies } (\mathsf{Port}(\alpha),\, P_\alpha) \blacklozenge (\mathsf{Port}(\beta),\, P_\beta)
\end{array}
\right] \\
\textbf{for all } q_\alpha,\, q_\beta,\, q'_\alpha,\, q'_\beta,\, P_\alpha,\, P_\beta
\end{array}
\right]
$$

The next lemma states that if Alice and Bob conditionally strongly agree, their product is a subautomaton of their l-product (cf. Lemma 4). See [13, Appendix D] for a proof.

**Lemma 5.** $\alpha \blacklozenge \beta$ **implies** $\alpha \boxtimes \beta \sqsubseteq \alpha \boxdot \beta$

We end this section with the following theorem: if Alice and Bob conditionally strongly agree, substituting $\boxtimes$ with $\boxdot$ is semantics-preserving (in fact, not just under bisimilarity but even under structural equality). See [13, Appendix D] for a proof (which uses Proposition 1 and Lemmas 4, 5).

**Theorem 1.** $\alpha \blacklozenge \beta$ **implies** $\alpha \boxdot \beta = \alpha \boxtimes \beta$

## 4   Substituting $\boxtimes$ with $\boxdot$, a Cheaper Characterization

To test if Alice and Bob conditionally strongly agree, one must pairwise compare their transitions. This can be computationally expensive (i.e., $\mathcal{O}(n_1 n_2)$, where $n_1$ and $n_2$ denote the numbers of transitions), and it makes the ♦-based characterization, although (conjectured to be) complete, hard to apply in practice. In this section, we therefore study a cheaper characterization of (a subset of) conditionally strongly agreeing port automata (PA) without restricting the applicability of $\boxdot$ for our present purpose.

In Section 2, we explained reduction of parallelism in terms of independent PA. Therefore, substituting $\boxtimes$ with $\boxdot$ should be semantics-preserving at least when applied to such PA. We start by formally defining when Alice and Bob are independent: in that case, they have no common ports.

**Definition 8 (Independence relation).** *The independence relation, denoted by* $\asymp$, *is the relation on* $\mathbb{P}\mathrm{A} \times \mathbb{P}\mathrm{A}$ *defined as:*

$$
\alpha \asymp \beta \text{ iff } \mathsf{Port}(\alpha) \cap \mathsf{Port}(\beta) = \emptyset
$$

The next lemma states that if Alice and Bob are independent, they conditionally strongly agree (because their independence means that Alice and Bob have no common ports). See [13, Appendix D] for a proof.

**Lemma 6.** $\alpha \asymp \beta$ implies $\alpha \,\diamondsuit\, \beta$

Lemma 6 and Theorem 1 imply that substituting $\boxtimes$ with $\boxdot$ is semantics-preserving, if their operands satisfy the independence relation. Moreover, checking $\asymp$ costs less than checking whether PA conditionally strongly agree: $\mathcal{O}(1)$ versus $\mathcal{O}(n_1 n_2)$. The next lemma states another important property, namely that $\boxdot$ preserves independence: if Alice is independent of Bob and Carol individually, she is independent of Bob and Carol together. See [13, Appendix D] for a proof.

**Lemma 7.** $\big[\alpha \asymp \beta$ and $\alpha \asymp \gamma\big]$ implies $\alpha \asymp \beta \boxdot \gamma$

Although checking PA for independence is cheap, the result implied by Lemma 6 and Theorem 1 in its present form has limited practical value: total independence is a condition rarely satisified by the PA encountered in code generation of a composite system. To get a more useful similar result, we now introduce the notion of *slavery* and afterward combine it with independence. We start by formally defining when Bob is a slave of Alice: in that case, every transition of Bob that involves *some* ports common with Alice, involves *only* ports common with Alice. In other words, if common ports are involved, Alice completely dictates what Bob does. Our notion of slavery does not prevent Bob from freely executing transitions involving only ports that Alice does not know about.

**Definition 9 (Slave relation).** *The slave relation, denoted by $\mapsto$, is the relation on $\mathbb{P}\mathrm{A} \times \mathbb{P}\mathrm{A}$ defined as:*

$$
\begin{array}{c}(Q_\beta,\, \mathcal{P}_\beta,\, \longrightarrow_\beta,\, \imath_\beta) \\ \mapsto \alpha\end{array} \textbf{ iff } \left[\begin{bmatrix} q_\beta \xrightarrow{P_\beta} q'_\beta \text{ and} \\ P_\beta \cap \mathsf{Port}(\alpha) \neq \emptyset \end{bmatrix} \text{ implies } P_\beta \subseteq \mathsf{Port}(\alpha)\right] \\ \textbf{for all } q_\beta,\, q'_\beta,\, P_\beta
$$

The next lemma states that if Bob is a slave of Alice, they conditionally strongly agree (i.e., Alice forces her will upon Bob). See [13, Appendix D] for a proof.

**Lemma 8.** $\beta \mapsto \alpha$ implies $\beta \,\diamondsuit\, \alpha$

Lemma 8 and Theorem 1 imply that substituting $\boxtimes$ with $\boxdot$ is semantics-preserving, if their operands satisfy the slave relation. Moreover, checking $\mapsto$ costs less than checking whether PA conditionally strongly agree: $\mathcal{O}(n_1)$ versus $\mathcal{O}(n_1 n_2)$. The next lemma states another important property, namely that $\boxdot$ preserves slavery: if Bob is a slave of Alice, he is a slave of Alice and Carol together. See [13, Appendix D] for a proof.

**Lemma 9.** $\beta \mapsto \alpha$ implies $\beta \mapsto \alpha \boxdot \gamma$

By combining independence and slavery, we obtain the notion of *conditional slavery*: Bob is a conditional slave of Alice iff Alice and Bob not being independent implies that Bob is a slave of Alice.

**Definition 10 (Conditional slave relation).** *The conditional slave relation, denoted by* $\rightarrowtail$, *is the relation on* $\mathbb{P}\textsc{a} \times \mathbb{P}\textsc{a}$ *defined as:*

$$\beta \rightarrowtail \alpha \text{ iff } \left[ \beta \asymp \alpha \text{ or } \beta \mapsto \alpha \right]$$

The next lemma states that if Bob is a conditional slave of Alice, they conditionally strongly agree (i.e., Alice and Bob are independent or Alice forces her will upon Bob). See [13, Appendix D] for a proof (which uses Lemmas 6, 8).

**Lemma 10.** $\beta \rightarrowtail \alpha$ **implies** $\beta \, \lozenge \, \alpha$

The combination of Lemma 10 and Theorem 1 implies that substituting $\boxtimes$ with $\boxdot$ is semantics-preserving, if the PA involved satisfy the conditional slave relation. Moreover, checking the conditional slave relation costs the same as checking the slave relation (i.e., less than checking whether PA conditionally strongly agree). The next lemma states another important property, namely that $\boxdot$ preserves conditional slavery: if Bob is a conditional slave of Alice and Carol individually, he is a conditional slave of Alice and Carol together. The corollary following this lemma generalizes this result from 2 to $k$ individuals. See [13, Appendix D] for a proof (which uses Lemmas 7, 9).

**Lemma 11.** $\left[ \beta \rightarrowtail \alpha \text{ and } \beta \rightarrowtail \gamma \right]$ **implies** $\beta \rightarrowtail \alpha \boxdot \gamma$

**Corollary 1.** $\left[ \beta \rightarrowtail \alpha_1 \text{ and } \cdots \text{ and } \beta \rightarrowtail \alpha_k \right]$ **implies** $\beta \rightarrowtail (\alpha_1 \boxdot \cdots \boxdot \alpha_k)$

With conditional slavery, in contrast to independence alone, one can characterize a sufficiently large class of PA that satisfies the premise of Theorem 1 (i.e., for which substituting $\boxtimes$ with $\boxdot$ is semantics-preserving), as follows. Suppose that we have a list of $k$ PA such that every $i$-th PA in the list is a conditional slave of all PA in a higher position. Then, the l-product of all PA in this list, starting from the ones with the highest positions and working our way down, is in the class. The following definition formalizes this (recall that $\boxdot$ is right-associative).

**Definition 11.** $\mathcal{A}$ *denotes the smallest set induced by the following rule:*

$$\frac{\left[ i \neq j \text{ implies } \alpha_i \rightarrowtail \alpha_j \right] \text{ for all } 1 \leq i < j \leq k}{\alpha_1 \boxdot \cdots \boxdot \alpha_k \in \mathcal{A}}$$

Strictly, $\mathcal{A}$ contains terms over $(\mathbb{P}\textsc{a}, \boxdot)$, which represent PA, rather than actual elements from $\mathbb{P}\textsc{a}$. Nevertheless, we often call the elements from $\mathcal{A}$ "PA" for simplicity. Also, instead of writing $\alpha_1 \boxdot \cdots \boxdot \alpha_k$, we sometimes write $\alpha_1 \cdots \alpha_k$.

The following theorem states that for every PA in $\mathcal{A}$, substituting $\boxtimes$ for $\boxdot$ is semantics-preserving. See [13, Appendix D] for a proof (which uses Lemma 10 and Corollary 1).

**Theorem 2.** $\alpha_1 \boxdot \cdots \boxdot \alpha_k \in \mathcal{A}$ **implies** $\alpha_1 \boxdot \cdots \boxdot \alpha_k = \alpha_1 \boxtimes \cdots \boxtimes \alpha_k$

Although $\alpha_1 \boxdot \cdots \boxdot \alpha_k = \alpha_1 \boxtimes \cdots \boxtimes \alpha_k$ generally does not imply $\alpha_1 \boxdot \cdots \boxdot \alpha_k \in \mathcal{A}$, it does for the examples considerd in this paper. For instance, Figures 3, 4 show that $\beta \boxdot \delta = \beta \boxtimes \delta$ (Figure 2 defines $\beta$ and $\delta$). By the commutativity of $\boxdot$ and $\boxtimes$, we have also $\delta \boxdot \beta = \delta \boxtimes \beta$. Now, because $\delta$ is a slave of $\beta$, we conclude that $\delta \boxdot \beta$ is an element of $\mathcal{A}$: indeed, if $\delta$ makes a transition involving ports common with $\beta$ (only B), it fires no other ports ($\beta$, in contrast, does fire another port in that case, namely C).

Previously, we claimed that the subclass of PA characterized in this section (i.e., $\mathcal{A}$ in Definition 11) does not restrict the applicability of $\boxdot$ for our purpose. We end this section by substantiating that claim. We start by introducing a further restricted class of PA with a more natural interpretation in our context.

**Definition 12.** $\mathcal{B}$ *denotes the smallest set induced by the following rule:*

$$\frac{\begin{bmatrix} i_1 \neq i_2 \text{ implies } \alpha_{i_1} \Bumpeq \alpha_{i_2} \end{bmatrix} \text{ for all } 1 \leq i_1, i_2 \leq k \end{bmatrix} \text{ and} \\ \begin{bmatrix} j_1 \neq j_2 \text{ implies } \beta_{j_1} \asymp \beta_{j_2} \end{bmatrix} \text{ for all } 1 \leq j_1, j_2 \leq l \end{bmatrix} \text{ and} \\ \begin{bmatrix} \alpha_i \Bumpeq \beta_j \text{ for all } 1 \leq i \leq k, 1 \leq j \leq l \end{bmatrix}}{\alpha_1 \boxdot \cdots \boxdot \alpha_k \boxdot \beta_1 \boxdot \cdots \boxdot \beta_l \in \mathcal{B}}$$

The following proposition follows directly from the previous definition.

**Proposition 2.** $\mathcal{B} \subseteq \mathcal{A}$

The combination of Proposition 2 and Theorem 2 implies that substituting $\boxtimes$ with $\boxdot$ is semantics-preserving for every PA in $\mathcal{B}$.

Informally, every PA in $\mathcal{B}$ is the l-product of (i) $k$ PA that are conditional slaves of *all* other PA in the term and (ii) $l$ pairwise independent PA that are "masters" of the $k$ conditional slaves. The masters, being pairwise independent, do not *directly* communicate with each other. However, when two or more masters share the same slave (the definition of $\mathcal{B}$ allows this), communication between those masters occurs *indirectly* through that slave. Such indirect communication is always asynchronous: if it were synchronous, the slave involved would fire ports of more than one of its masters in the same transition, which slavery forbids.

The previous interpretation of masters and slaves corresponds exactly to the notion of synchronous and asynchronous *regions* in the Reo literature [5,8]. Roughly, one can always split a connector into subconnectors—the regions—such that firings of ports in such a subconnector are either purely independent (i.e., always, only one port fires at a time) or require some synchronization (i.e., at least once, more than one port fires). Furthermore, the synchronous regions of a connector are maximal in the sense that no two synchronous regions have common ports: all synchronous regions are, by definition, pairwise independent. Consequently, the PA describing the $l$ synchronous regions of a connector can act as the $l$ masters in a PA term from $\mathcal{B}$.

To actually obtain those PA, for every synchronous region, a code generator during compilation computes the *existing* product of the PA describing the constituents of that particular region (finding the synchronous regions of a connector is trivial). At compile-time, this resembles the purely centralized approach, while at run-time, it ensures high throughput between interdependent "small" PA for constituents of the same synchronous region (i.e., no run-time computation of product operators within synchronous regions). The asynchronous regions then form the "glue" between the synchronous regions: the PA for every asynchronous region has the same shape as $\delta$ in Figure 2,[6] and consequently, they can act as the $k$ conditional slaves in a PA term from $\mathcal{B}$. Finally, at run-time, the automaton threads executing the generated code compute the 1-product operators.

In summary: a code generator can always process the set of PA describing a connector to a form that satisfies $\mathcal{B}$, by computing $\boxtimes$ between interdependent PA belonging to the same synchronous region at compile-time (for the sake of throughput), and by computing $\boxdot$ between the resulting "medium" PA plus the PA for the asynchronous regions at run-time (for the sake of parallelism). Proposition 2 and Theorem 2 ensure that this is semantics-preserving.

## 5   Note on Associativity

The associativity of $\boxtimes$ plays a role in the centralized approach and is even more important in the distributed approach. In the centralized approach, it guarantees that it does not matter in which particular order a code generator computes the product of the port automata (PA) for the constituents of a connector—all have the same semantics. In the distributed approach, it guarantees that it does not matter in which order PA threads communicate with each other: the PA term corresponding to a particular communication order is always bisimilar to the original (because one can freely move parentheses).

Now, recall from Section 3 that $\boxdot$ is generally *not* associative. The structure of the PA terms from $\mathcal{A}$ also reflects this (and the proof of Theorem 2 exploits this structure). This means that the PA constituting such terms must communicate in a particular order at run-time for the substitution of $\boxtimes$ with $\boxdot$ to be semantics-preserving. This can kill performance and seems a serious practical problem. For reasons of space, we postpone a full exposition of our solution to this problem to a future paper; interested readers may consult [13].

## 6   Related Work and Conclusion

*Related work.* Closest to ours is the work on splitting connectors into (a)synchronous regions for better performance. Proença developed the first implementation based on these ideas, demonstrated its merit through benchmarks, and invented an automaton model—*behavioral automata*—to reason about split connectors in his PhD thesis and associated publications [7,8,9]. Furthermore, Clarke and

---

[6]  Port automaton $\delta$ in Figure 2 describes the behavior of an asynchronous Reo primitive, called Fifo [1,2], with a buffer (of capacity 1) that accepts data on one port (i.e., B), buffers it, and at a later time dispenses that same data on another port (i.e. C). Of the currently common Reo primitives, only Fifo is asynchronous, and so, only Fifo instances induce asynchronous regions in the current practice. In general, a PA modeling an asynchronous region can have more than two states or ports but, crucially, each of its transitions has a singleton set of ports as label (as does $\delta$), which guarantees that that PA can act as a conditional slave in a $\mathcal{B}$-term.

Proença explored connector splitting in the context of the connector coloring semantics [3]. They discovered that the standard version of that semantics has undesirable properties in the context of splitting: some split connectors that intuitively *should* be equivalent to the original connector are not equivalent under the standard version. To address this problem, Clarke and Proença propose a new variant—*partial connector coloring*—which allows one to better model locality and independencies between different parts of a connector. Recently, Jongmans et al. studied a formal justification of connector splitting in a process algebraic setting [5]. Although, as shown in Section 4, one can use the notion of (a)synchronous regions to apply our results to code generation for connectors, our results go beyond that. (They can, for instance, also be applied to code generation for Web service proxies in Reo-based orchestrations [6].)

Also related to the work presented in this paper is the work of Kokash et al. on *action constraint automata* (ACA) [14]. Kokash et al. argue that ordinary port/constraint automata describe the behavior of Reo connectors too coarsely, which makes it impossible to express certain fine parallel behavior. In contrast, ACA have more flexible transition labels which, for instance, allow one to explicitly model the start and end of interaction on a particular port (one cannot make this distinction using port/constraint automata). Consequently, ACA better describe the behavior of existing connector implementations (under certain assumptions). However, the increased granularity of ACA comes at the price of substantially larger models. This makes them less suitable for code generation.

*Conclusion.* Existing approaches to implementing connectors force one to make a choice between high throughput (at the cost of parallelism) and maximal parallelism (at the cost of throughput). In this paper, we proposed a formal basis to support a solution for this problem. We found and formalized a middle ground between those approaches by defining a new product operator on port automata (PA) and by showing that in all practically relevant cases (with respect to code generation for connectors), one can use this new operator instead of the existing one to get both high throughput and maximal parallelism in a semantics-preserving way.

Although we developed our results for PA, they generalize straightforwardly to the more powerful constraint automata (CA) [10]. See [13] for more details.

While inspired by Reo, our results apply to every language whose programs can be described by automata satisfying the characterizations in Section 4. For instance, a possible application of our results outside Reo is *projection* in choreography languages [15,16,17,18,19,20]. See [13] for more details.

# References

1. Arbab, F.: Reo: a channel-based coordination model for component composition. MSCS 14(3), 329–366 (2004)
2. Arbab, F.: Puff, The Magic Protocol. In: Agha, G., Danvy, O., Meseguer, J. (eds.) Formal Modeling: Actors, Open Systems, Biological Systems. LNCS, vol. 7000, pp. 169–206. Springer, Heidelberg (2011)

3. Clarke, D., Proença, J.: Partial Connector Colouring. In: Sirjani, M. (ed.) COOR-DINATION 2012. LNCS, vol. 7274, pp. 59–73. Springer, Heidelberg (2012)
4. Jongmans, S.S., Arbab, F.: Modularizing and Specifying Protocols among Threads. In: Proceedings of PLACES 2012. EPTCS. CoRR, vol. 109, pp. 34–45 (2013)
5. Jongmans, S.S., Clarke, D., Proença, J.: A Procedure for Splitting Processes and its Application to Coordination. In: Proceedings of FOCLASA 2012. EPTCS. CoRR, vol. 91, pp. 79–96 (2012)
6. Jongmans, S.S., Santini, F., Sargolzaei, M., Arbab, F., Afsarmanesh, H.: Automatic Code Generation for the Orchestration of Web Services with Reo. In: De Paoli, F., Pimentel, E., Zavattaro, G. (eds.) ESOCC 2012. LNCS, vol. 7592, pp. 1–16. Springer, Heidelberg (2012)
7. Proença, J., Clarke, D., De Vink, E., Arbab, F.: Dreams: a framework for distributed synchronous coordination. In: Proceedings of SAC 2012, pp. 1510–1515. ACM (2012)
8. Proença, J.: Synchronous Coordination of Distributed Components. PhD thesis, Leiden University (2011)
9. Proença, J., Clarke, D., De Vink, E., Arbab, F.: Decoupled execution of synchronous coordination models via behavioural automata. In: Proceedings of FOCLASA 2011. EPTCS. CoRR, vol. 58, pp. 65–79 (2011)
10. Baier, C., Sirjani, M., Arbab, F., Rutten, J.: Modeling component connectors in Reo by constraint automata. SCP 61(2), 75–113 (2006)
11. Jongmans, S.S., Arbab, F.: Overview of Thirty Semantic Formalisms for Reo. SACS 22(1), 201–251 (2012)
12. Koehler, C., Clarke, D.: Decomposing Port Automata. In: Proceedings of SAC 2009, pp. 1369–1373. ACM (2009)
13. Jongmans, S.S., Arbab, F.: Global Consensus through Local Synchronization (Technical Report). Technical Report FM-1303, CWI (2013)
14. Kokash, N., Changizi, B., Arbab, F.: A Semantic Model for Service Composition with Coordination Time Delays. In: Dong, J.S., Zhu, H. (eds.) ICFEM 2010. LNCS, vol. 6447, pp. 106–121. Springer, Heidelberg (2010)
15. Bravetti, M., Zavattaro, G.: Towards a Unifying Theory for Choreography Conformance and Contract Compliance. In: Lumpe, M., Vanderperren, W. (eds.) SC 2007. LNCS, vol. 4829, pp. 34–50. Springer, Heidelberg (2007)
16. Bravetti, M., Zavattaro, G.: Contract Compliance and Choreography Conformance in the Presence of Message Queues. In: Bruni, R., Wolf, K. (eds.) WS-FM 2008. LNCS, vol. 5387, pp. 37–45. Springer, Heidelberg (2009)
17. Fu, X., Bultan, T., Su, J.: Conversation protocols: a formalism for specification and verification of reactive electronic services. TCS 328(1-2), 19–37 (2004)
18. Fu, X., Bultan, T., Su, J.: Realizability of Conversation Protocols with Message Contents. IJWSR 2(4), 68–93 (2005)
19. Carbone, M., Honda, K., Yoshida, N.: Structured Communication-Centered Programming for Web Services. TOPLAS 34(2), 8:1–8:78 (2012)
20. Honda, K., Yoshida, N., Carbone, M.: Multiparty Asynchronous Session Types. In: Proceedings of POPL 2008, pp. 273–284. ACM (2008)

# On Density in Coordination Languages

Jean-Marie Jacquet[1], Isabelle Linden[2], and Denis Darquennes[1]

[1] Faculty of Computer Science,
University of Namur, Belgium
{jean-marie.jacquet,denis.darquennes}@unamur.be
[2] Business Administration Department,
University of Namur, Belgium
isabelle.linden@unamur.be

**Abstract.** Coordination languages have been proved very suitable for modeling and programming service-oriented applications. In particular, those based on tuple spaces offer an elegant way of making different components of such applications interact smoothly through the deposit and retrieval of tuples in a shared space. However, in their basic form, these languages only allow one tuple to be put at a time and, when more than one tuple matches a required one, the selection is made non deterministically. This is obviously too weak to capture popularity or quality measures, which are nevertheless central in service oriented applications. To that end, we propose an extension of a Linda-like language aiming at promoting the notion of density and, based on De Boer and Palamidessi's notion of modular embedding, establish that it strictly increases the expressiveness of Linda. Following our previous work, we also study the hiearchy of the sublanguages induced by considering subsets of tuple primitives.

**Keywords:** coordination languages, service oriented applications, density, expressivity.

## 1 Introduction

Service-oriented applications have become more and more available on Internet. The rapid evolution of their demand induces a concurrency between them, requiring a huge adaptive capacity. Their ability to measure their popularity and quality of services are then crucial for their evolution, as well as their survival on Internet.

Besides, coordination languages have been proved very suitable for modeling and programming service-oriented applications (see eg [4,12,20]). Among them, those based on tuple spaces offer an elegant way of making different components of such applications interact smoothly through the deposit and retrieval of tuples in a shared space. However their basic form does only allow one tuple to be put at a time and, when more than one tuple matches a required one, the selection is made non-deterministically.

C. Canal and M. Villari (Eds.): ESOCC 2013, CCIS 393, pp. 189–203, 2013.

Previous pieces of work [5–7,16–18,21] have considered a global perception of the tuple space. They consider the multiset-based language Gamma or the non blocking bulk primitives collect or copy-collect developped for accessing globally the tuple space. In this paper, following the chemical model, we regard tuple spaces as chemical solutions mixing elements of possibly different nature, each being characterised by a certain density in the solution. Based on this metaphor, this paper enriches traditional data-based coordination languages by associating such a density to tuples.

In doing so, we believe that many applications may take advantage of densities associated to information. The intuition is that the more a tuple is present on the tuplespace, the more likely it will be discovered to provide an answer to an interest or quality request. Moreover, by requiring tuples with a minimum level of density, one may make sure that only those with a sufficient recognition will be selected. Within this context, for recommendation systems, like Amazon or the auction selling web site Ebay, it will be posible to measure the number of positive (or negative) advices on an auction selling web sites, or the measure of popularity of a service providers through the number of advertisements having effectively been read.

The aim of this work is to focus on theoretical issues by presenting an abstract language and establishing that it strictly enhances the expressiveness of Linda-like languages. More concretely, our extension is formulated in a dialect of Linda, developed at the University of Namur, and named Bach (see [11]). This language is based on four primitives accessing a tuplespace, also named subsequently store, as follows. A $tell(t)$ primitive puts an occurrence of the tuple $t$ on the store. An $ask(t)$ primitive checks the presence of the tuple $t$ on store while a $nask(t)$ primitive checks its absence. Finally a $get(t)$ primitive removes an occurrence of the tuple $t$ on the store. It is worth noting that the $tell$ primitive always succeeds whereas the last three primitives suspend as long as the presence/absence of the tuple $t$ is not met. Moreover, the store is seen as a multiset of tuples, which naturally leaves room for multiple occurrences and subsequently a notion of density relying on counting this multiplicity.

Since our purposes are of a theoretical nature and for the sake of simplicity, we shall actually consider a simplified version where tuples are taken in their simplest form of flat and unstructured tokens. Nevertheless, it is easy to observe that our results extend directly to more general tuples.

This paper complements work already done by some of the authors: [6,7,13–15]. We shall subsequently follow the same lines of research and employ De Boer and Palamidessi's modular embedding to test the expressiveness of languages. As a result, the rest of this paper is organized as follows. Section 2 presents our extended coordination language, called Dense Bach. Then, after having reminded the reader with the notion of modular embedding introduced in [10], we proceed in section 3 with an exhaustive comparison of the relative expressive power of the languages Bach and Dense Bach. Finally, section 4 compares our work with related work, draws our conclusions and presents the expectations for future work.

## 2   Dense Bach

### 2.1   Language Definition

As stated in the introduction, the language under study in this paper relies on tokens and attaches to them a density, seen as their multiplicity of occurrences. This is formally defined as follows.

**Definition 1.** *Let* Stoken *be an enumerable set, the elements of which are subsequently called tokens and are typically represented by the letters t and u. Define the association of a token t and a strictly positive number $n \in \mathbb{N}_0$ as a dense token. Such an association is typically denoted as $t(n)$. Define then the set of dense tokens as the set $SDtoken$. Note that since Stoken and $\mathbb{N}$ are both enumerable, the set $SDtoken$ is also enumerable.*

*Intuitively, a dense token $t(m)$ represents the simultaneous presence of $m$ occurrences of $t$. As a result, $\{t(m)\}$ is subsequently used to represent the multiset $\{t, \cdots, t\}$ composed of these $m$ occurrences. Moreover, given two multisets of tokens $\sigma$ and $\tau$, we shall use $\sigma \cup \tau$ to denote the multiset union of elements of $\sigma$ and $\tau$. As a particular case, by slightly abusing the syntax in writing $\{t(m), t(n)\}$, we have $\{t(m)\} \cup \{t(n)\} = \{t(m), t(n)\} = \{t(m+n)\}$. Finally, we shall use $\sigma \uplus \{t(m)\}$ to denote, on the one hand, the multiset union of $\sigma$ and $\{t(m)\}$, and, on the other hand, the fact that $t$ does not belong to $\sigma$.*

The primitives of the language under consideration extend to dense tokens the primitives of the Bach language recalled in section 1. As a result, $tell(t(m))$ atomically puts $m$ occurrences of $t$ on the store. Similarly, $ask(t(m))$ and $get(t(m))$ require the presence of at least $m$ occurrences of $t$ with the latter removing $m$ of them. Dually, $nask(t(m))$ verifies that there are less than $m$ occurrences of $t$. We subsequently formally defined these primitives as well as, for completion purposes, those of the Bach language.

**Definition 2.** *Define the set $\mathcal{T}$ of the token-based primitives as the set of primitives $T$ generated by the following grammar:*

$$T ::= tell(t) \mid ask(t) \mid get(t) \mid nask(t)$$

*where $t$ represents a token.*

**Definition 3.** *Define the set of dense token-based primitives $\mathcal{T}_d$ as the set of primitives $T_d$ generated by the following grammar:*

$$T_d ::= tell(t(m)) \mid ask(t(m)) \mid get(t(m)) \mid nask(t(m))$$

*where $t$ represents a token and $m$ a positive natural number.*

The statements of the languages, also called *agents*, are defined from these primitives by possibly combining them by the classical choice operator $+$, parallel operator (denoted by the $\parallel$ symbol) and the sequential operator (denoted by the ; symbol). The formal definition is as follows.

$$(\mathbf{T_d}) \quad \frac{m \in \mathbb{N}_0}{\langle\, tell(t(m)) \mid \sigma\,\rangle \longrightarrow \langle\, E \mid \sigma \cup \{t(m)\}\,\rangle}$$

$$(\mathbf{A_d}) \quad \frac{m \in \mathbb{N}_0}{\langle\, ask(t(m)) \mid \sigma \cup \{t(m)\}\,\rangle \longrightarrow \langle\, E \mid \sigma \cup \{t(m)\}\,\rangle}$$

$$(\mathbf{G_d}) \quad \frac{m \in \mathbb{N}_0}{\langle\, get(t(m)) \mid \sigma \cup \{t(m)\}\,\rangle \longrightarrow \langle\, E \mid \sigma\,\rangle}$$

$$(\mathbf{N_d}) \quad \frac{n < m}{\langle\, nask(t(m)) \mid \sigma \uplus \{t(n)\}\,\rangle \longrightarrow \langle\, E \mid \sigma \uplus \{t(n)\}\,\rangle}$$

**Fig. 1.** Transition rules for dense token-based primitives (Dense Bach)

**Definition 4.** *Define the Bach language $\mathcal{L}_B$ as the set of agents $A$ generated by the following grammar:*

$$A ::= T \mid A\,;\,A \mid A \parallel A \mid A\,+\,A$$

*where $T$ represents a token-based primitive. Define then the Dense Bach language $\mathcal{L}_{DB}$ similarly but by taking dense token-based primitives $T_d$:*

$$A ::= T_d \mid A\,;\,A \mid A \parallel A \mid A\,+\,A$$

*Subsequently, we shall consider sublanguages formed similarly but by considering only subsets of these primitives. In that case, if $\mathcal{H}$ denotes such a subset, then we shall write the induced sublanguages as $\mathcal{L}_B(\mathcal{H})$ and $\mathcal{L}_{DB}(\mathcal{H})$, respectively.*

## 2.2   Transition System

We are now in a position to define a transition system. Our configuration consists of agents (summarizing the current state of the processes running on the blackboard) and a multi-set of tokens (denoting the current state of the tuple space). In order to express the termination of the computation of an agent of $\mathcal{L}_{DB}$, we extend the set of agents by adding a special terminating symbol $E$ that can be seen as a completely computed agent. For uniformity purpose, we abuse the language by qualifying $E$ as an agent. To meet the intuition, we shall always rewrite agents of the form $(E; A)$, $(E \parallel A)$ and $(A \parallel E)$ as $A$. This is technically achieved by defining the extended set of agents as $\mathcal{L}_{DB} \cup \{E\}$ and by justifying the simplifications by imposing a bimonoid structure.

The rules of the transition systems are listed in Figures 1 to 2(b). Figure 1 provides the transitions for the dense token-based primitives. Rule $(T_d)$ states that for any store $\sigma$ and any token $t$ with density $m$, the effect of the tell primitive is to enrich the current set of tokens by $m$ occurrences of token $t$. Note that $\cup$ denotes multi-set union. Rules $(A_d)$ and $(G_d)$ specify the effect of ask and get primitives, both requiring the presence of at least $m$ occurrences of $t$, but the

(T)    $\langle\,tell(t)\mid\sigma\,\rangle\longrightarrow\langle\,E\mid\sigma\cup\{t\}\,\rangle$

(S)    $\dfrac{\langle A\mid\sigma\rangle\longrightarrow\langle A'\mid\sigma'\rangle}{\langle A\,;\,B\mid\sigma\rangle\longrightarrow\langle A'\,;\,B\mid\sigma'\rangle}$

(A)    $\langle\,ask(t)\mid\sigma\cup\{t\}\,\rangle\longrightarrow\langle\,E\mid\sigma\cup\{t\}\,\rangle$

(P)    $\dfrac{\langle A\mid\sigma\rangle\longrightarrow\langle A'\mid\sigma'\rangle}{\substack{\langle A\parallel B\mid\sigma\rangle\longrightarrow\langle A'\parallel B\mid\sigma'\rangle\\ \langle B\parallel A\mid\sigma\rangle\longrightarrow\langle B\parallel A'\mid\sigma'\rangle}}$

(G)    $\langle\,get(t)\mid\sigma\cup\{t\}\,\rangle\longrightarrow\langle\,E\mid\sigma\,\rangle$

(C)    $\dfrac{\langle A\mid\sigma\rangle\longrightarrow\langle A'\mid\sigma'\rangle}{\substack{\langle A+B\mid\sigma\rangle\longrightarrow\langle A'\mid\sigma'\rangle\\ \langle B+A\mid\sigma\rangle\longrightarrow\langle A'\mid\sigma'\rangle}}$

(N)    $\dfrac{t\notin\sigma}{\langle\,nask(t)\mid\sigma\,\rangle\longrightarrow\langle\,E\mid\sigma\,\rangle}$

(a) Token-based primitives (Bach)        (b) Operators

**Fig. 2.** Transition rules

latter also consuming them. Rule $(N_d)$ defines the nask primitive, which tests for the absence of $m$ occurrences of $t$.

For the sake of completeness, Figure 2(a) recalls the transition rules for the Bach language. As easily observed, they amount to the rules of Figure 1 where the density $m$ is taken to be 1, and union symbol interpreted on multi-sets. Figure 2(b) details the usual rules for sequential composition, parallel composition, interpreted in an interleaving fashion, and CCS-like choice.

### 2.3   Observables and Operational Semantics

We are now in a position to define what we want to observe from the computations. Following previous work by some of the authors (see eg [6, 7, 13–15]), we shall actually take an operational semantics recording the final state of the computations, this being understood as the final store coupled to a mark indicating whether the considered computation is successful or not. Such marks are respectively denoted as $\delta^+$ (for the successful computations) and $\delta^-$ (for failed computations).

**Definition 5.**

1. *Define the set of stores Sstore as the set of finite multisets with elements from Stoken.*
2. *Let $\delta^+$ and $\delta^-$ be two fresh symbols denoting respectively success and failure. Define the set of histories Shist as the cartesian product $Sstore \times \{\delta^+, \delta^-\}$.*
3. *Define the operational semantics $\mathcal{O} : \mathcal{L}_B \cup \mathcal{L}_{DB} \to \mathcal{P}(Shist)$ as the following function: for any agent $A \in \mathcal{L}_B \cup \mathcal{L}_{DB}$*

$$\mathcal{O}(A) = \{(\sigma, \delta^+) : \langle A|\emptyset\rangle \to^* \langle E|\sigma\rangle\}$$
$$\cup \{(\sigma, \delta^-) : \langle A|\emptyset\rangle \to^* \langle B|\sigma\rangle \nrightarrow, B \neq E\}$$

**Fig. 3.** Basic embedding

# 3  Comparisons of Bach and Dense Bach

## 3.1  Modular Embedding

A natural way to compare the expressive power of two languages is to determine whether all programs written in one language can be easily and equivalently translated into the other language, where equivalent is intended in the sense of conserving the same observable behaviors.

According to this intuition, Shapiro introduced in [19] a first notion of embedding as follows. Consider two languages $\mathcal{L}$ and $\mathcal{L}'$. Assume given the semantics mappings (*Observation criteria*) $\mathcal{S} : \mathcal{L} \to \mathcal{O}_s$ and $\mathcal{S}' : \mathcal{L}' \to \mathcal{O}'_s$, where $\mathcal{O}_s$ and $\mathcal{O}'_s$ are on some suitable domains. Then $\mathcal{L}$ can *embed* $\mathcal{L}'$ if there exists a mapping $\mathcal{C}$ (coder) from the statements of $\mathcal{L}'$ to the statements of $\mathcal{L}$, and a mapping $\mathcal{D}$ (decoder) from $\mathcal{O}_s$ to $\mathcal{O}'_s$, such that the diagram of Figure 3 commutes, namely such that for every statement $A \in \mathcal{L}' : \mathcal{D}(\mathcal{S}(\mathcal{C}(A))) = \mathcal{S}'(A)$.

This basic notion of embedding turns out however to be too weak since, for instance, the above equation is satisfied by any pair of Turing-complete languages. De Boer and Palamidessi hence proposed in [10] to add three constraints on the coder $\mathcal{C}$ and on the decoder $\mathcal{D}$ in order to obtain a notion of *modular* embedding usable for concurrent languages:

1. $\mathcal{D}$ should be defined in an element-wise way with respect to $\mathcal{O}_s$, namely for some appropriate mapping $\mathcal{D}_{el}$

$$\forall X \in \mathcal{O}_s : \ \mathcal{D}(X) = \{\mathcal{D}_{el}(x) \mid x \in X\} \qquad (P_1)$$

2. the coder $\mathcal{C}$ should be defined in a compositional way with respect to the sequential, parallel and choice operators:

$$\begin{aligned}
\mathcal{C}(A \ ; \ B) &= \mathcal{C}(A) \ ; \ \mathcal{C}(B) \\
\mathcal{C}(A \parallel B) &= \mathcal{C}(A) \parallel \mathcal{C}(B) \\
\mathcal{C}(A \ + \ B) &= \mathcal{C}(A) \ + \ \mathcal{C}(B)
\end{aligned} \qquad (P_2)$$

3. the embedding should preserve the behavior of the original processes with respect to deadlock, failure and success (*termination invariance*):

$$\forall X \in \mathcal{O}_s, \forall x \in X : \ tm'(\mathcal{D}_{el}(x)) = tm(x) \qquad (P_3)$$

where $tm$ and $tm'$ extract the termination information from the observables of $\mathcal{L}$ and $\mathcal{L}'$, respectively.

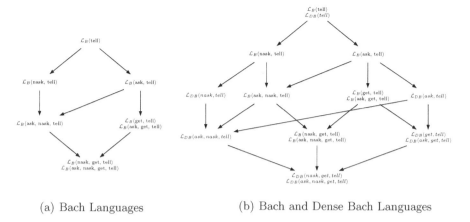

(a) Bach Languages          (b) Bach and Dense Bach Languages

**Fig. 4.** Embedding hierarchy

An embedding is then called *modular* if it satisfies properties $P_1$, $P_2$, and $P_3$. The existence of a modular embedding from $\mathcal{L}'$ into $\mathcal{L}$ is subsequently denoted by $\mathcal{L}' \leq \mathcal{L}$. It is easy to prove that $\leq$ is a pre-order relation. Moreover if $\mathcal{L}' \subseteq \mathcal{L}$ then $\mathcal{L}' \leq \mathcal{L}$ that is, any language embeds all its sublanguages. This property descends immediately from the definition of embedding, by setting $\mathcal{C}$ and $\mathcal{D}$ equal to the identity function.

### 3.2   Summary of Results

We now proceed to an exhaustive comparison of the relative expressive power of the languages Bach and Dense Bach. In both case, we focus on the non-trivial sublanguages, namely on those sublanguages containing the *tell* operation.

The expressive power of the different sublanguages of Bach has been studied in [5–7] from which the expressiveness hierarchy of Figure 4(a) can be established. Building upon these results, Figure 4(b) summarizes the embedding relations between the different sublanguages of Bach and Dense Bach, as well as those relations between the different sublanguages of Dense Bach alone. This figure results from a series of propositions, proved in the next subsection.

In both figures, an arrow from a language $\mathcal{L}_1$ to a language $\mathcal{L}_2$ means that $\mathcal{L}_2$ embeds $\mathcal{L}_1$, that is $\mathcal{L}_1 \leq \mathcal{L}_2$. When an arrow from $\mathcal{L}_1$ to $\mathcal{L}_2$ has no counterpart from $\mathcal{L}_2$ to $\mathcal{L}_1$, then $\mathcal{L}_1$ is strictly less expressive than $\mathcal{L}_2$, that is $\mathcal{L}_1 < \mathcal{L}_2$. If $\mathcal{L}_1 \leq \mathcal{L}_2$ and $\mathcal{L}_2 \leq \mathcal{L}_1$ then $\mathcal{L}_1$ and $\mathcal{L}_2$ are equivalent, that is $\mathcal{L}_1 = \mathcal{L}_2$. In that case, they are depicted together. If $\mathcal{L}_1 \nleq \mathcal{L}_2$ and $\mathcal{L}_2 \nleq \mathcal{L}_1$ then $\mathcal{L}_1$ and $\mathcal{L}_2$ are not comparable with each other. Thanks to the transitivity, both figures contain only a minimal amount of arrows. Apart from these induced relations, no other relation holds.

It is worth noting that the hierarchy relations presented in Figure 4(a) appear in the center of Figure 4(b). This reflects the fact that Bach is a special case of Dense Bach. Moreover, the hierarchy of the Dense Bach sublanguages resembles that of the Bach sublanguages. This intuitively results from the very nature of the ask, nask and get primitives, which are not altered by the density of tokens.

Nevertheless, except for the sublanguage reduced to a tell primitive, it is worth observing that the dense sublanguages are strictly more expressive than their Bach counterparts. This highlights the fact that Dense Bach is an extension of Bach bringing more expressiveness.

### 3.3   Formal Propositions and Proofs

Let us now turn to the formal proofs. Due to space limits, we shall only give sketches of the easiest ones. However, the complete ones can be obtained upon request to the authors. As a first result, thanks to the fact that any language contains its sublanguages, a number of modular embeddings are directly established. In subsequent proofs, this is referred to by *language inclusion*.

**Proposition 1.** $\mathcal{L}_{DB}(\psi) \leq \mathcal{L}_{DB}(\chi)$, for any subsets of $\psi, \chi$ of primitives such that $\psi \subseteq \chi$.

A second observation is that Bach primitives are deduced from the primitives of Dense Bach by taking single occurrences, namely a density of 1. As a result Bach sublanguages are embedded in the corresponding Dense Bach sublanguages.

**Proposition 2.** $\mathcal{L}_B(\chi) \leq \mathcal{L}_{DB}(\chi)$, for any subset of $\chi$ of primitives.

By coding any $tell(t(m))$ primitive as $m$ successive $tell(t)$ primitives, $\mathcal{L}_{DB}(\text{tell})$ and $\mathcal{L}_B(\text{tell})$ appear to be equivalent. Moreover, as a result of the expressiveness hierarchy [5] (see figure 4(a)), it also comes that both languages $\mathcal{L}_B(\text{ask,tell})$ and $\mathcal{L}_B(\text{nask,tell})$ are strictly more expressive than $\mathcal{L}_{DB}(\text{tell})$ since both have been established strictly more expressive than $\mathcal{L}_B(\text{tell})$. Let us now compare $\mathcal{L}_B(\text{ask,tell})$ with its dense counterpart.

**Proposition 3.** $\mathcal{L}_B(ask,tell) < \mathcal{L}_{DB}(ask,tell)$

*Proof.* On the one hand, $\mathcal{L}_B(\text{ask,tell}) \leq \mathcal{L}_{DB}(\text{ask,tell})$, by proposition 2. On the other hand, $\mathcal{L}_{DB}(\text{ask,tell}) \not\leq \mathcal{L}_B(\text{ask,tell})$ is established by contradiction by considering $A = tell(t(1)); ask(t(2))$. Indeed as $\mathcal{O}(A) = \{(\{t(1)\}, \delta^-)\}$, any computation of $\mathcal{C}(A)$ fails whereas it is possible to construct a successful computation. To that end, let us observe that as $\mathcal{O}(tell(t(1)) ; tell(t(1)) ; ask(t(2))) = \{(\{t(2)\}, \delta^+)\}$, any computation of $A = \mathcal{C}(tell(t(1)); tell(t(1)); ask(t(2)))$ starting on the empty store is successful, and hence so does any computation of $\mathcal{C}(tell(t(1)))$. Consider such a computation and let $\sigma$ denote the final store. Given that $\mathcal{C}(tell(t(1))$ is composed of ask and tell primitives, it is possible to repeat the computation in order to deliver a successful computation for $\mathcal{C}(tell(t(1)) ; tell(t(1)))$ ending in $\sigma \cup \sigma$ as final store. In view of agent $A$, this computation can be continued by a successful computation for $\mathcal{C}(ask(t(2)))$. However, as $\mathcal{C}(ask(t(2)))$ is composed of ask and tell primitives only, this continuation succeeds also starting on $\sigma$ (instead of $\sigma \cup \sigma$), which induces a successful computation for $\mathcal{C}(tell(t(1)); ask(t(2)))$. □

Symmetrically, $\mathcal{L}_B(\text{nask,tell})$ is strictly less expressive than $\mathcal{L}_{DB}(\text{nask,tell})$.

**Proposition 4.** $\mathcal{L}_B(nask,tell) < \mathcal{L}_{DB}(nask,tell)$.

*Proof.* On the one hand, $\mathcal{L}_B$(nask,tell) $\leq \mathcal{L}_{DB}$(nask,tell) holds by proposition 2. On the other hand, $\mathcal{L}_{DB}$(nask,tell) $\nleq \mathcal{L}_B$(nask,tell) is establisehd by contradiction by using the same reasoning as in the proof of proposition 3 but for $A = (\mathcal{C}(tell(t(1)))\ ;\ \mathcal{C}(nask(t(2))))$.

$\mathcal{L}_{DB}$(nask,tell) and $\mathcal{L}_B$(ask,tell) are not comparable with each other, as well as $\mathcal{L}_{DB}$(ask,tell) with regards to $\mathcal{L}_B$(nask,tell).

**Proposition 5.**

(i) $\mathcal{L}_{DB}(nask,tell) \nleq \mathcal{L}_B(ask,tell)$   (iii) $\mathcal{L}_{DB}(ask,tell) \nleq \mathcal{L}_B(nask,tell)$
(ii) $\mathcal{L}_B(ask,tell) \nleq \mathcal{L}_{DB}(nask,tell)$   (iv) $\mathcal{L}_B(nask,tell) \nleq \mathcal{L}_{DB}(ask,tell)$

*Proof.* **(i)** Otherwise we have $\mathcal{L}_B$(nask,tell) $\leq \mathcal{L}_B$(ask,tell) which has been proved impossible in [7]. **(ii)** By contradiction, by considering $A = tell(t)\ ;\ ask(t))$. **(iii)** Otherwise we would have $\mathcal{L}_B$(ask,tell) $\leq \mathcal{L}_B$(nask,tell) which has been proved impossible in [7]. **(iv)** By contradiction, by considering $A = tell(t)\ ;\ nask(t))$. ☐

$\mathcal{L}_{DB}$(nask,tell) and $\mathcal{L}_{DB}$(ask,tell) are not comparable with each other, as well as $\mathcal{L}_{DB}$(nask,tell) with regards to $\mathcal{L}_B$(ask,nask,tell).

**Proposition 6.**

(i) $\mathcal{L}_{DB}(nask,tell) \nleq \mathcal{L}_{DB}(ask,tell)$   (iii) $\mathcal{L}_B(ask,nask,tell) \nleq \mathcal{L}_{DB}(nask,tell)$
(ii) $\mathcal{L}_{DB}(ask,tell) \nleq \mathcal{L}_{DB}(nask,tell)$   (iv) $\mathcal{L}_{DB}(nask,tell) \nleq \mathcal{L}_B(ask,nask,tell)$

*Proof.* **(i)** Otherwise $\mathcal{L}_B$(nask,tell) $\leq \mathcal{L}_{DB}$(ask,tell), which contradicts proposition 5(iv). **(ii)** and **(iii)** Otherwise $\mathcal{L}_B$(ask,tell) $\leq \mathcal{L}_{DB}$(nask,tell), which contradicts proposition 5(ii). **(iv)** The proof proceeds as in proposition 4(ii). ☐

Symmetrically, $\mathcal{L}_B$(get,tell) and $\mathcal{L}_{DB}$(ask,tell) are not comparable with each other.

**Proposition 7.** *(i)* $\mathcal{L}_B(get,tell) \nleq \mathcal{L}_{DB}(ask,tell)$ *and*
*(ii)* $\mathcal{L}_{DB}(ask,tell) \nleq \mathcal{L}_B(get,tell)$

*Proof.* **(i)** By contradiction, by considering $tell(t)\ ;\ get(t)$ which induces successful computations for $\mathcal{C}(tell(t))\ ;\ \mathcal{C}(get(t))$ and consequently for $\mathcal{C}(tell(t))\ ;\ \mathcal{C}(get(t))\ ;\ \mathcal{C}(get(t))$, as $\mathcal{C}(get(t))$ is composed of ask and tell primitives only. **(ii)** Let first observe that $\mathcal{O}(tell(t(1))\ ;\ tell(t(1))\ ;\ ask(t(2)))$ succeeds. Therefore by $P_3$ any computation of $B = \mathcal{C}(tell(t(1))\ ;\ tell(t(1))\ ;\ ask(t(2)))$ starting on the empty store is successful, and so does any computation of $\mathcal{C}(tell(t(1)))$. Consider such a computation $C$ and let $\sigma$ denote the final store. Given that $\mathcal{C}(tell(t(1)))$ is composed of get and tell primitives, it is possible to repeat the computation in order to deliver a successful computation for $\mathcal{C}(tell(t(1))\ ;\ tell(t(1)))$ ending in $\sigma \cup \sigma$ as final store. In view of agent $B$

above, this computation can be continued by a successful computation $C'$ for $\mathcal{C}(ask(t(2)))$. The first step $s$ of $C'$ is either a (single) tell which always succeeds or a (single) get which also succeeds on $\sigma \cup \sigma$, and therefore on $\sigma$. This leads to a first successful step $s$ of $\mathcal{C}(ask(t(2)))$ after the computation $C$. As $(tell(t(1)) \, ; \, ask(t(2)))$ fails, this computation prefix $C.s$ has only failing computation. Nevertheless, $C.s$ is a computation prefix of $\mathcal{C}(tell(t(1)) \, ; \, (ask(t(2)) + tell(t(1))))$, which leads to a failure and to the contradiction. $\quad\square$

Let us now include the get primitive in the Dense Bach language. We first prove that $\mathcal{L}_{DB}(get,tell)$ and $\mathcal{L}_{DB}(ask,get,tell)$ are equivalent.

**Proposition 8.** $\mathcal{L}_{DB}(get,tell) = \mathcal{L}_{DB}(ask,get,tell)$

*Proof.* Direct by coding $ask(t(m))$ as $get(t(m)) \, ; \, tell(t(m))$. $\quad\square$.

**Proposition 9.** $\mathcal{L}_B(get,tell) < \mathcal{L}_{DB}(get,tell)$

*Proof.* On the one hand, $\mathcal{L}_B(get,tell) \leq \mathcal{L}_{DB}(get,tell)$ holds by proposition 2. On the other hand, $\mathcal{L}_{DB}(get,tell) \not\leq \mathcal{L}_B(get,tell)$ may be proved exactly as in proposition 7(ii), where we replace any occurrence of ask(t(2)) by get(t(2)). $\quad\square$

**Proposition 10.**

(i) $\mathcal{L}_{DB}(ask,tell) \leq \mathcal{L}_{DB}(get,tell)$   (iii) $\mathcal{L}_{DB}(ask,tell) \not\leq \mathcal{L}_B(nask,get,tell)$

(ii) $\mathcal{L}_{DB}(get,tell) \not\leq \mathcal{L}_{DB}(ask,tell)$   (iv) $\mathcal{L}_B(nask,get,tell) \not\leq \mathcal{L}_{DB}(ask,tell)$

*Proof.* **(i)** Immediate by coding $ask(t(1))$ as $get(t(1)) \, ; \, tell(t(1))$. **(ii)** The proof proceeds as in proposition 7(i), by considering $A = tell(t(1)) \, ; \, get(t(1))$.

We can now prove that $\mathcal{L}_{DB}(get,tell)$ is not comparable with respectively $\mathcal{L}_B(nask,tell)$, $\mathcal{L}_{DB}(nask,tell)$, $\mathcal{L}_B(nask,get,tell)$, $\mathcal{L}_B(ask,nask,tell)$ and $\mathcal{L}_{DB}(ask,nask,tell)$.

**Proposition 11.**

(i) $\mathcal{L}_{DB}(get,tell) \not\leq \mathcal{L}_B(nask,tell)$       (vi) $\mathcal{L}_B(nask,get,tell) \not\leq \mathcal{L}_{DB}(get,tell)$

(ii) $\mathcal{L}_B(nask,tell) \not\leq \mathcal{L}_{DB}(get,tell)$      (vii) $\mathcal{L}_{DB}(get,tell) \not\leq \mathcal{L}_{DB}(ask,nask,tell)$

(iii) $\mathcal{L}_{DB}(get,tell) \not\leq \mathcal{L}_{DB}(nask,tell)$    (viii) $\mathcal{L}_{DB}(ask,nask,tell) \not\leq \mathcal{L}_{DB}(get,tell)$

(iv) $\mathcal{L}_{DB}(nask,tell) \not\leq \mathcal{L}_{DB}(get,tell)$    (ix) $\mathcal{L}_{DB}(get,tell) \not\leq \mathcal{L}_B(ask,nask,tell)$

(v) $\mathcal{L}_{DB}(get,tell) \not\leq \mathcal{L}_B(nask,get,tell)$    (x) $\mathcal{L}_B(ask,nask,tell) \not\leq \mathcal{L}_{DB}(get,tell)$

*Proof.* **(i)** Indeed, otherwise we have $\mathcal{L}_{DB}(ask,tell) \leq \mathcal{L}_{DB}(nask,tell)$ which contradicts proposition 6(ii). **(ii)** The proof proceeds as in proposition 5(iv). **(iii)** Otherwise we have $\mathcal{L}_B(ask,tell) \leq \mathcal{L}_{DB}(nask,tell)$ which contradicts proposition 5(ii). **(iv)** Otherwise we have $\mathcal{L}_B(nask,tell) \leq \mathcal{L}_{DB}(get,tell)$ which contradicts (ii) above. **(v)** Otherwise by proposition 10(i) we have $\mathcal{L}_{DB}(ask,tell) \leq \mathcal{L}_B(nask,get,tell)$ which contradicts proposition 10(iii). **(vi)** Otherwise $\mathcal{L}_B(nask,tell) \leq \mathcal{L}_{DB}(get,tell)$ which contradicts (ii) above. **(vii)** The proof proceeds as in proposition 7(i), by considering $\mathcal{O}(tell(t(1)) \, ; \, get(t(1))) = \{(\emptyset, \delta^+)\}$ and by constructing $(\mathcal{C}(get(t(1))) \, || \, \mathcal{C}(get(t(1))))$. **(viii)** Otherwise $\mathcal{L}_{DB}(nask,tell) \leq \mathcal{L}_{DB}(get,tell)$ which contradicts proposition (iv) above. **(ix)** Otherwise $\mathcal{L}_{DB}(get,tell) \leq \mathcal{L}_{DB}(ask,nask,tell)$ which contradicts (vii) above. **(x)** Otherwise $\mathcal{L}_B(nask,tell) \leq \mathcal{L}_{DB}(get,tell)$ which contradicts (ii) above. $\quad\square$

Let us now establish that $\mathcal{L}_{DB}(\text{nask,tell})$ and $\mathcal{L}_B(\text{ask,nask,tell})$ are strictly less expressive than $\mathcal{L}_{DB}(\text{ask,nask,tell})$.

**Proposition 12.** *(i)* $\mathcal{L}_{DB}(nask,tell) < \mathcal{L}_{DB}(ask,nask,tell)$ *and* *(ii)* $\mathcal{L}_B(ask,nask,tell) < \mathcal{L}_{DB}(ask,nask,tell)$.

*Proof.* **(i)** By sublanguage inclusion and by proposition 6(ii). **(ii)** By proposition 2 and by using a reasoning similar to that of proposition 3(ii).

$\mathcal{L}_{DB}(\text{ask,tell})$ is strictly less expressive than $\mathcal{L}_{DB}(\text{ask,nask,tell})$.

**Proposition 13.** $\mathcal{L}_{DB}(ask,tell) < \mathcal{L}_{DB}(ask,nask,tell)$

*Proof.* By language inclusion and by proposition 6(i).  □

Symmetrically to proposition 10(iii) and 10(iv), $\mathcal{L}_B(\text{nask,get,tell})$ is not comparable with $\mathcal{L}_{DB}(\text{nask,tell})$.

**Proposition 14.** *(i)* $\mathcal{L}_B(nask,get,tell) \nleq \mathcal{L}_{DB}(nask,tell)$ *and* *(ii)* $\mathcal{L}_{DB}(nask,tell) \nleq \mathcal{L}_B(nask,get,tell)$

*Proof.* **(i)** Otherwise, $\mathcal{L}_B(\text{ask,tell}) \leq \mathcal{L}_{DB}(\text{nask,tell})$ which contradicts proposition 5(ii). **(ii)** By contradiction, consider $T2NoT = (tell(t(1)) \parallel tell(t(1)))$ ; $(nask(t(2)) + tell(t(1)))$, which has one successful computation and for which, we shall nevertheless construct a failing one for its coder. To that end, consider $T = \mathcal{C}(tell(t(1)))$. Given that $tell(t(1))$ succeeds, its coder $T$ has only successful computations starting on the empty store. Consider one of them, say $C$, ending in the store $\sigma$. By repeating in turn each of its steps, it is possible to construct a successful computation, say $CC$, for $\mathcal{C}(tell(t(1)) \parallel tell(t(1)))$ ending in the store $\sigma \cup \sigma$. Consider now

$$T2N = \mathcal{C}((tell(t(1)) \parallel tell(t(1)))\ ;\ nask(t(2)))$$
$$= (\mathcal{C}(tell(t(1))) \parallel \mathcal{C}(tell(t(1))))\ ;\ \mathcal{C}(nask(t(2)))$$

As $tell(t(1))$ ; $nask(t(2))$ succeeds, the computation $C$ of $\mathcal{C}(tell(t(1)))$ can be continued by a successful computation for $\mathcal{C}(nask(t(2)))$. Consider such a computation and let $s$ denote its first step. As $C$ ends in the store $\sigma$, step $s$ can also be successfully performed after $CC$, which ends in store $\sigma \cup \sigma$. However, $CC.s$ is a computation prefix for $T2N$, which, in view of the fact that $(tell(t(1)) \parallel tell(t(1)))$ ; $nask(t(2))$ fails, can only be continued by failing computations. However, these computations are also computations of $T2NoT$, which, thus provide the announced failing computation.  □

$\mathcal{L}_B(\text{nask,get,tell})$ is not comparable with $\mathcal{L}_{DB}(\text{ask,nask,tell})$.

**Proposition 15.**
*(i)* $\mathcal{L}_{DB}(ask,nask,tell) \nleq \mathcal{L}_B(nask,get,tell)$  *(iii)* $\mathcal{L}_B(ask,nask,tell) \nleq \mathcal{L}_{DB}(ask,tell)$
*(ii)* $\mathcal{L}_B(nask,get,tell) \nleq \mathcal{L}_{DB}(ask,nask,tell)$  *(iv)* $\mathcal{L}_{DB}(ask,tell) \nleq \mathcal{L}_B(ask,nask,tell)$

*Proof.* **(i)** Otherwise, $\mathcal{L}_{DB}(\text{ask,tell}) \leq \mathcal{L}_B(\text{nask,get,tell})$ which contradicts proposition 10(iii). **(ii)** The proof proceeds as in proposition 7(i), by considering $(\mathcal{C}(get(t(1))) \parallel \mathcal{C}(get(t(1)))))$. **(iii)** Otherwise, $\mathcal{L}_B(\text{nask,tell}) \leq \mathcal{L}_{DB}(\text{ask,tell})$ which contradicts proposition 5(iv). **(iv)** Otherwise, $\mathcal{L}_{DB}(\text{ask,tell}) \leq \mathcal{L}_B(\text{nask,get,tell})$ which contradicts (i) above. $\qquad\square$

$\mathcal{L}_{DB}(\text{nask,get,tell})$ and $\mathcal{L}_{DB}(\text{ask,nask,get,tell})$ are equivalent.

**Proposition 16.** $\mathcal{L}_{DB}(nask,get,tell) = \mathcal{L}_{DB}(ask,nask,get,tell)$

*Proof.* On the one hand, $\mathcal{L}_{DB}(\text{nask,get,tell}) \leq \mathcal{L}_{DB}(\text{ask,nask,get,tell})$ is established by language inclusion. On the other hand, to establish $\mathcal{L}_{DB}(\text{ask,nask,get,tell}) \leq \mathcal{L}_{DB}(\text{nask,get,tell})$ we shall provide a coder such that the coding of the primitives $ask(t(n))$ and $nask(t(n))$ manipulate different tokens. To that end, as the set of tokens is enumerable, it is possible to associate each of them, say t(n), to a pair $(t_1(n), t_2(n))$. Given such a coding of tokens, we define the compositional coder $\mathcal{C}$ as follows:

$$\mathcal{C}(ask(t(n))) = get(t_2(n)) ; tell(t_2(n)) \quad \mathcal{C}(get(t(n))) = get(t_2(n)) ; get(t_1(n))$$
$$\mathcal{C}(nask(t(n))) = nask(t_1(n)) \qquad\qquad \mathcal{C}(tell(t(n))) = tell(t_1(n)) ; tell(t_2(n))$$

The decoder $\mathcal{D}$ is defined as follows: $\mathcal{D}_{el}((\sigma,\delta)) = (\overline{\sigma},\delta)$, where $\overline{\sigma}$ is composed of the tokens $t(n)$ for which $t_1(n)$ and $t_2(n)$ are in $\sigma$, the multiplicity of $t(n)$ being that of pairs $(t_1(n), t_2(n))$ in $\sigma$. $\qquad\square$

$\mathcal{L}_{DB}(\text{ask,nask,tell})$ is strictly less expressive than $\mathcal{L}_{DB}(\text{ask,nask,get,tell})$, and then from $\mathcal{L}_{DB}(\text{nask,get,tell})$, by proposition 16.

**Proposition 17.** $\mathcal{L}_{DB}(ask,nask,tell) < \mathcal{L}_{DB}(ask,nask,get,tell)$

*Proof.* By language inclusion and proposition 11(*vii*). $\qquad\square$

$\mathcal{L}_{DB}(\text{get,tell})$ is strictly less expressive than $\mathcal{L}_{DB}(\text{nask,get,tell})$.

**Proposition 18.** $\mathcal{L}_{DB}(get,tell) < \mathcal{L}_{DB}(nask,get,tell)$

*Proof.* On the one hand, $\mathcal{L}_{DB}(\text{get,tell}) \leq \mathcal{L}_{DB}(\text{nask,get,tell})$ results from language inclusion. On the other hand, $\mathcal{L}_{DB}(\text{nask,get,tell}) \nleq \mathcal{L}_{DB}(\text{get,tell})$ is established as in proposition 5(iv), by considering $A = tell(t(1)) ; nask(t(1))$.

Finally, $\mathcal{L}_B(\text{ask,nask,get,tell})$ can be proved strictly less expressive than $\mathcal{L}_{DB}(\text{ask,nask,get,tell})$.

**Proposition 19.** $\mathcal{L}_B(ask,nask,get,tell) < \mathcal{L}_{DB}(ask,nask,get,tell)$

*Proof.* By propositions 2 and 11(v). $\qquad\square$

# 4   Conclusion

This paper has presented an extension aiming at introducing a notion of density to tuples with the intuition that the more a tuple appears on a tuple space, the more it is of interest and, dually, that tuples are of interest for the test of their presence or absence only if they appear in a sufficient number of occurrences. This is technically achieved by associating a number of occurrences to the arguments of the Bach primitives of [11], this resulting in a new language, named Dense Bach.

Our work builds upon previous work by some of the authors [6, 7, 13–15]. We have essentially followed the same lines and in particular have used De Boer and Palamidessi's notion of modular embedding to compare the families of sublanguages of Bach and Dense Bach. Accordingly, we have established a gain of expressivity, namely that Dense Bach is strictly more expressive than Bach. We have also shown that the very nature of the tell, ask, nask and get primitives of Bach is not altered by the introduced notion of density. In other terms, the expressiveness relations of the sublanguages of Dense Bach produce an hierarchy similar to that of the Bach sublanguages. Our main contribution with respect to [6, 7, 13–15] is to have demonstrated how the techniques used in these pieces of work can be adapted to Dense Bach.

Our work has similarities but also differences with several work on the expressiveness of Linda-like languages. Compared to [22] and [23], it is worth observing that a different comparison criteria is used to compare the expressiveness of languages. Indeed, in these pieces of work, the comparison is performed on (i) the compositionality of the encoding with respect to parallel composition, (ii) the preservation of divergence and deadlock, and (iii) a symmetry condition. Moreover, we have taken a more liberal view with respect to the preservation of termination marks in requiring these preservations on the store resulting from the execution from the empty store of the coded versions of the considered agents and not on the same store. In particular, these ending stores are not required to be of the form $\sigma \cup \sigma$ unions) if this is so for the stores resulting from the agents themselves.

In [1], nine variants of the $\mathcal{L}_B$(ask,nask,get,tell) language are studied. They are obtained by varying both the nature of the shared data space and its structure. Rephrased in the setting of [10], this amounts to considering different operational semantics. In contrast, in our work we fix an operational semantics and compare different languages on the basis of this semantics. In [9], a process algebraic treatment of a family of Linda-like concurrent languages is presented. Again, different semantics are considered whereas we have sticked to one semantics and have compared languages on this basis. In [8], a study of the absolute expressive power of different variants of Linda-like languages has been made, whereas we study the relative expressive power of different variants of such languages (using modular embedding as a yard-stick and the ordered interpretation of tell).

It is worth observing that [1, 8, 9, 22, 23] do not deal with a notion a density attached to tuples. In contrast, [2] and [3] decorate tuples with an extra field in order to investigate how probabilities and priorities can be introduced in the

Linda coordination model. Different expressiveness results are established in [2] but on an absolute level with respect to Turing expressiveness and the possibility to encode the Leader Election Problem. Our work contrast in several aspects. First, we have established relative expressiveness results by comparing the sublanguages of two families. Moreover, some of these sublanguages incorporate the *nask* primitives, which, as can be appreciated from Figure 4(b), strictly increases the expressiveness. Finally, the introduction of density resembles but is not identical to the association of weights to tuples. Indeed, in contrast with [2,3] we do not modify the tuples on the store and do not modify the matching function so as to retrieve the tuple with the highest weight. In contrast, we modify the tuple primitives so as to be able to atomically put several occurrences of a tuple on the store and check for the presence or absence of a number of occurrences. As can be appreciated by the reader through the comparison of Bach and Dense Bach, this facility of handling atomically several occurrences produces a real increase of expressiveness. One may however think of encoding the number of occurrences of a tuple as an additional weight-like parameter. It is nevertheless not clear how our primitives tackling at once several occurrences can be rephrased in Linda-like primitives and how the induced encoding would still fulfills the requirements of modularity. This will be the subject for future research.

In [21], Viroli and Casadei propose a stochastic extension of the Linda framework, with a notion of tuple concentration, similar to the weight of [2] and [3] and our notion of density. The syntax of this tuple space is modeled by means of a calculus, with an operational semantics given as an hybrid CTMC/DTMC model. This semantics does however not consider nask like primitives. Moreover, no expressiveness results are established.

These three last pieces of work tackle probabilistic extensions of Linda-like languages. As a further and natural step in our research, we aim at studying how our notion of density can be the basis of such probabilistic extensions. As our work also relies on the possibility to atomically put several occurrences of tokens and test for their presence or absence, we will also examine in future work how Dense Bach compares with the Gamma language.

# References

1. Bonsangue, M.M., Kok, J.N., Zavattaro, G.: Comparing coordination models based on shared distributed replicated data. In: ACM Symposium on Applied Computing (1999)
2. Bravetti, M., Gorrieri, R., Lucchi, R., Zavattaro, G.: Quantitative Information in the Tuple Space Coordination Model. TCS 346(1) (2005)
3. Bravetti, M., Gorrieri, R., Lucchi, R., Zavattaro, G.: Probabilistic and Prioritized Data Retrieval in the Linda Coordination Model. In: De Nicola, R., Ferrari, G.-L., Meredith, G. (eds.) COORDINATION 2004. LNCS, vol. 2949, pp. 55–70. Springer, Heidelberg (2004)
4. Bravetti, M., Zavattaro, G.: Service Oriented Computing from a Process Algebraic Perspective. Journal of Logic and Algebraic Programming 70(1) (2007)
5. Brogi, A., Jacquet, J.-M.: On the Expressiveness of Linda-like Concurrent Languages. ENTCS 16(2) (1998)

6. Brogi, A., Jacquet, J.-M.: On the Expressiveness of Coordination Models. In: Ciancarini, P., Wolf, A.L. (eds.) COORDINATION 1999. LNCS, vol. 1594, pp. 134–149. Springer, Heidelberg (1999)
7. Brogi, A., Jacquet, J.-M.: On the Expressiveness of Coordination via Shared Dataspaces. Science of Computer Programming 46(1-2) (2003)
8. Busi, N., Gorrieri, R., Zavattaro, G.: On the Turing equivalence of Linda coordination primitives. ENTCS 7 (1997)
9. Busi, N., Gorrieri, R., Zavattaro, G.: A Process Algebraic View of Linda Coordination Primitives. TCS 192 (1998)
10. de Boer, F., Palamidessi, C.: Embedding as a Tool for Language Comparison. Information and Computation 108(1), 128–157 (1994)
11. Jacquet, J.-M., Linden, I.: Coordinating Context-aware Applications in Mobile Adhoc Networks. In: Proceedings of the First ERCIM workshop on eMobility, The University of Bern (2007)
12. Jongmans, S.-S.T.Q., Santini, F., Sargolzaei, M., Arbab, F., Afsarmanesh, H.: Automatic Code Generation for the Orchestration of Web Services with Reo. In: De Paoli, F., Pimentel, E., Zavattaro, G. (eds.) ESOCC 2012. LNCS, vol. 7592, pp. 1–16. Springer, Heidelberg (2012)
13. Linden, I., Jacquet, J.-M.: On the Expressiveness of Absolute-Time Coordination Languages. In: De Nicola, R., Ferrari, G.-L., Meredith, G. (eds.) COORDINATION 2004. LNCS, vol. 2949, pp. 232–247. Springer, Heidelberg (2004)
14. Linden, I., Jacquet, J.-M.: On the Expressiveness of Timed Coordination via Shared Dataspaces. ENTCS 180(2) (2007)
15. Linden, I., Jacquet, J.-M., Bosschere, K.D., Brogi, A.: On the Expressiveness of Relative-Timed Coordination Models. ENTCS 97 (2004)
16. Butcher, P., Wood, A., Atkins, M.: Global Synchronisation in Linda. Concurrency: Practice and Experience 6(6), 505–516 (1994)
17. Rowstron, A., Wood, A.: Solving the Linda multiple rd problem. In: Hankin, C., Ciancarini, P. (eds.) COORDINATION 1996. LNCS, vol. 1061, pp. 357–367. Springer, Heidelberg (1996)
18. Rowstron, A., Wood, A.: Bonita: A Set of Tuple Space Primitives for Distributed Coordination. In: Proceedings of the 30th Hawaii International Conference on System Sciences, vol. 1. IEEE Computer Society Press. Springer (January 1997)
19. Shapiro, E.: Embeddings Among Concurrent Programming Languages. In: Cleaveland, W. (ed.) Proceedings of COORDINATION 1992. LNCS, Springer (1992)
20. Tolksdorf, R.: Laura - A Service-Based Coordination Language. Science of Computer Programming 31(2-3), 359–381 (1998)
21. Viroli, M., Casadei, M.: Biochemical Tuple Spaces for Self-organising Coordination. In: Field, J., Vasconcelos, V.T. (eds.) COORDINATION 2009. LNCS, vol. 5521, pp. 143–162. Springer, Heidelberg (2009)
22. Zavattaro, G.: On the incomparability of Gamma and Linda. In: Electronic Transactions on Numerical Analysis (1998)
23. Zavattaro, G.: Towards a Hierarchy of Negative Test Operators for Generative Communication. ENTCS 16 (1998)

# A Tag Contract Framework for Heterogeneous Systems

Thi Thieu Hoa Le[1], Roberto Passerone[1], Uli Fahrenberg[2], and Axel Legay[2]

[1] DISI, University of Trento, Italy
[2] INRIA/IRISA, Rennes, France

**Abstract.** In the distributed development of modern IT systems, contracts play a vital role in ensuring interoperability of components and adherence to specifications. The design of embedded systems, however, is made more complex by the heterogeneous nature of components, which are often described using different models and interaction mechanisms. Composing such components is generally not well-defined, making design and verification difficult. Several frameworks, both operational and denotational, have been proposed to handle heterogeneity using a variety of approaches. However, the application of heterogeneous operational models to contract-based design has not yet been investigated. In this work, we adopt the operational mechanism of tag machines to represent heterogeneous systems and construct a full contract model. We introduce heterogeneous composition, refinement and dominance between contracts, altogether enabling a formalized and rigorous design process for heterogeneous systems.

## 1 Introduction

Modern computing systems are increasingly being built by composing components which are developed concurrently by different design teams. In such a paradigm, the distinction between what is constrained on environments, and what must be guaranteed by a system given the constraint satisfaction, reflects the different roles and responsibilities in the system design procedure. Such distinction can be captured by a component model called *contract* [1]. Formally, a contract is a pair of *assumptions* and *guarantees*, which intuitively are properties that must be satisfied by all inputs and outputs of a design, respectively. The separation between assumptions and guarantees supports the distributed development of complex systems and allows subsystems to synchronize by relying on associated contracts.

In the particular context of embedded systems, *heterogeneity* is a typical characteristic since these systems are usually composed from parts developed using different methods, time models and interaction mechanisms. To deal with heterogeneity, several modeling frameworks have been proposed oriented towards the representation and simulation of heterogeneous systems, such as the Ptolemy framework [2], or towards the unification of their interaction paradigms, such as those based on *tagged events* [3]. The latter can capture different notions of time, e.g., physical time, logical time, and relate them by mapping tagged events over a common tag structure [4]. However, due to the significant inherent complexity of heterogeneity, there have been only very few attempts at addressing heterogeneity in the context of contract-based models. For instance, the HRC model from the SPEEDS project[1] was designed to deal with different viewpoints

---

[1] www.speeds.eu.com

C. Canal and M. Villari (Eds.): ESOCC 2013, CCIS 393, pp. 204–217, 2013.

(functional, time, safety, etc.) of a single component [5,6]. However, the notion of heterogeneity in general is much broader than that between multiple viewpoints, and must take into account diverse interaction paradigms. Meanwhile, heterogeneous modeling frameworks have not been related to contract-based design flows. This has motivated us to study a methodology which allows heterogeneous systems to be modeled and interconnected in a contract-based fashion.

Our long term objective is to develop a modeling and analysis framework for the specification and verification of both heterogeneous components and contracts. In order to support formal correctness proofs, the framework must employ an underlying (or intermediate) semantically sound model that can be used to represent different computation and interaction paradigms uniformly. Because simulation is an essential design activity, the model must also be executable. At the same time, the semantic model must be able to retain the individual features of each paradigm to avoid losing their specific properties. In particular, the framework must interact with the user through a front end that exposes familiar models that feel native and natural. In this paper we focus on the intermediate semantic model and defer the discussion on how specific front ends may be constructed to our future work. To this end, we advocate the use of heterogeneous Tag Machines (TMs) as a suitable semantic model for system specification. The expressive power of TMs has been demonstrated though various concurrency models such as asynchronous, synchronous reactive, causality [7] as well as in job-shop modeling and specification [8]. In our previous work we have proposed and studied the compositional properties of heterogeneous Tag Machines (TMs) for *component* specification [9]. Here, we instead discuss their extension to a *contract* model, and define a full set of operations and relations such as contract satisfaction, contract refinement and contract dominance. To do this, we rely on a generic meta-framework [10] that we extend with tags and mapping between tags to define model interactions. In this paper, we shall discuss extensively the technical difficulties in making such an extension.

The rest of the paper is organized as follows. In Sect. 3, we recall basic notions of tag behaviors and tag machines. Section 4 presents our tag contract methodology for heterogeneous systems built on top of TM operations such as composition, quotient, conjunction and refinement. In the same section, we discuss an application of our methodology to a simplified water control problem and model it using incrementing TMs. Finally we conclude in Sect. 5.

## 2   Related Work

The notion of contract was first introduced by Bertrand Meyer in his design-by-contract method [1], based on ideas by Dijkstra [11], Lamport [12], and others, where systems are viewed as abstract boxes achieving their common goal by verifying specified contracts. De Alfaro and Henzinger subsequently introduced interface automata [13] for documenting components and established a more general notion of contract, where pre-conditions and post-conditions, which originally appeared in the form of predicates, are generalized to behavioral interfaces. The differentiation between assumptions and guarantees, which is implicit in interface automata, is made explicit in the trace-based contract framework of the SPEEDS HRC model [5,14]. The relationship between specifications of component behaviors and contracts is further studied by Bauer et al. [10]

where a contract framework can be built on top of any *specification theory* equipped with a composition operator and a refinement relation which satisfy certain properties. The mentioned trace-based contract theories [5,14] are also demonstrated to be instances of such framework. We take advantage of this formalization in this work to construct our tag contract theory. Assume-guarantee reasoning has also been applied extensively in declarative compositional reasoning [15] to help prove properties by decomposing the process into simpler and more manageable steps. Our objective is conceptually different: assumptions specify a set of legal environments and are used to prove (or disprove) contract satisfaction. In contrast, classical assume-guarantee reasoning uses assumptions as hypotheses to establish whether a generic property holds. Naturally, this technique can be used in contract models, as well.

Heterogeneity theory has been evolving in parallel with contract theory, to assist designers in dealing with heterogeneous composition of components with various Models of Computation and Communication (MoCC). The idea behind these theories and frameworks is to be able to combine well-established specification formalisms to enable analysis and simulation across heterogeneous boundaries. This is usually accomplished by providing some sort of common mechanism in the form of an underlying rich semantic model or coordination protocol. In this paper we are mostly concerned with these lower level aspects. One such approach is the pioneering framework of Ptolemy II [2], where models, called *domains*, are combined hierarchically: each level of the hierarchy is homogeneous, while different interaction mechanisms are specified at different levels in the hierarchy. In the underlying model, intended for simulation, each domain is composed of a scheduler (the *director*) which exposes the same abstract interface to a global scheduler which coordinates the execution. This approach, which has clear advantages for simulation, has two limitations in our context. First, it does not provide access to the components themselves but only to their schedulers, limiting our ability to establish relations to only the models of computation, and not to the heterogeneous contracts of the components. Secondly, the heterogeneous interaction occurs implicitly as a consequence of the coordination mechanism, and can not be controlled by the user. The metroII framework [16] relaxes this limitation, and allows designers to build direct model adapters. However, metroII treats components mostly as black boxes using a wrapping mechanism to guarantee flexibility in the system integration, making the development of an underlying theory complex. These and other similar frameworks are mainly focused on handling heterogeneity at the level of simulation.

Another body of work is instead oriented towards the formal representation, verification and analysis of these system. The BIP framework uses the notion of connector, on top of a state based model, to implement both synchronous and asynchronous interaction patterns [17]. Their relationship, however, can not be easily altered, and the framework lacks a native notion of time. Benveniste et al. [4] propose a heterogeneous denotational semantics inspired by the Lee and Sangiovanni-Vincentelli formalism of tag signal models [3], which has been long advocated as a unified modeling framework capable of capturing heterogeneous MoCC. In both models, tags play an important role in capturing various notions of time, where each tag system has its own tag structure expressing an MoCC. Composing such system is thus done by applying mappings between different tag structures. TMs [7] are subsequently introduced as finite representations of homogeneous tag systems. We have chosen to use this formalism for our work, as it provides an operational representation based on rigorous and proven semantics, and extended their definition to encompass heterogeneous components [9]. TMs are quite expressive, and ways to map traditional interaction paradigms have been reported in the literature [7]. TMs have also been applied to model a job-shop specification [8] where any trace of the composite tag machine from the start to the final state results in a valid job-shop schedule. Alternatively, tag systems can be represented by functional actors forming a Kleene algebra [18]. The approach is similar to that of Ptolemy II in that both use actors to represent basic components.

## 3   Background

We consider a component to be a set of behaviors in terms of sets of events that take place at its interface, intended as a collection of visible ports. Tags, which are associated to every event, characterize the temporal evolution of the behaviors. By changing the structure of tags, one can choose among different notions of time. Formally, a *tag structure* $\mathcal{T}$ is a pair $(T, \leq)$ where $T$ is a set of *tags* and $\leq$ is a partial order on the tags. The tag ordering is used to resolve the ordering among events at the system interface.

### 3.1   Tag Behaviors

Events occur at the interface of a component. A component exposes a set $V$ of *variables* (or *ports*) which can take values from a set $D$. An *event* is a snapshot of a variable state, capturing the variable value at some point in time. Formally, an *event* $e$ on a variable $v \in V$ is a pair $(\tau, d)$ of a tag $\tau \in T$ and a value $d \in D$. The simplest way of characterizing a behavior is as a collection of events for each variable. To construct behaviors incrementally, the events of a variable are indexed into a sequence, with the understanding that events later in the sequence have larger tags [4]. A behavior for a variable $v$ is thus a function $\mathbb{N} \mapsto (T \times D)$. A behavior $\sigma$ for a component assigns a sequence of events to every variable in $V$, i.e. $\sigma \in V \mapsto (\mathbb{N} \mapsto (T \times D))$. Each event of behavior $\sigma$ is identified by a tuple $(v, n, \tau, d)$, capturing the $n$-th occurrence of variable $v$ as a pair of a tag $\tau$ and a value $d$. In the following, we denote with $\Sigma(V, \mathcal{T})$ the universe of all behaviors over a set of variables $V$ and tag structure $\mathcal{T}$.

Combining behaviors $\sigma_1$ and $\sigma_2$ on the same tag structure, or *homogeneous* behaviors, amounts to computing their intersection provided that they are consistent, or *unifiable*, written $\sigma_1 \bowtie \sigma_2$, with each other on the shared variables, i.e. $\sigma_1|_{V_1 \cap V_2} = \sigma_2|_{V_1 \cap V_2}$, where $\sigma|_W$ denotes the restriction of behavior $\sigma$ to the variables in set $W$. We may then construct a unified behavior $\sigma = \sigma_1 \sqcup \sigma_2$ on the set of variables $V_1 \cup V_2$ where $\sigma(v) = \sigma_1(v)$ for $v \in V_1$ and $\sigma(v) = \sigma_2(v)$ for $v \in V_2$. When behaviors are defined on different tag structures, before unifying them, the set of tags must be equalized by mapping them onto a third tag structure that functions as a common domain. The mappings are called *tag morphisms* and must preserve the order.

**Definition 1 ([4]).** *Let $\mathcal{T}$ and $\mathcal{T}'$ be two tag structures. A tag morphism from $\mathcal{T}$ to $\mathcal{T}'$ is a total map $\rho : \mathcal{T} \mapsto \mathcal{T}'$ such that $\forall \tau_1, \tau_2 \in \mathcal{T} : \tau_1 \leq \tau_2 \Rightarrow \rho(\tau_1) \leq \rho(\tau_2)$.*

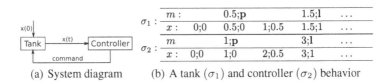

<table>
<tr><td rowspan="2">$\sigma_1$ :</td><td>$m$ :</td><td></td><td>0.5;p</td><td></td><td>1.5;1</td><td>...</td></tr>
<tr><td>$x$ :</td><td>0;0</td><td>0.5;0</td><td>1;0.5</td><td>1.5;1</td><td>...</td></tr>
<tr><td rowspan="2">$\sigma_2$ :</td><td>$m$</td><td></td><td>1;p</td><td></td><td>3;1</td><td>...</td></tr>
<tr><td>$x$ :</td><td>0;0</td><td>1;0</td><td>2;0.5</td><td>3;1</td><td>...</td></tr>
</table>

(a) System diagram     (b) A tank ($\sigma_1$) and controller ($\sigma_2$) behavior

**Fig. 1.** Water controlling system

Here, the tag orders must be taken on the respective domains. Using tag morphisms, we can turn a $T$-behavior $\sigma \in V \mapsto (\mathbb{N} \mapsto (T \times D))$ into a $T'$-behavior $\sigma \circ \rho \in V \mapsto (\mathbb{N} \mapsto (T' \times D))$ by simply replacing all tags $\tau$ in $\sigma$ with the image $\rho(\tau)$. Unification of heterogeneous behaviors can be done on the common tag structure. Let $\rho_1 : \mathcal{T}_1 \mapsto \mathcal{T}$ and $\rho_2 : \mathcal{T}_2 \mapsto \mathcal{T}$ be two tag morphisms into a tag structure $\mathcal{T}$. Two behaviors $\sigma_1$ and $\sigma_2$ defined on $\mathcal{T}_1$ and $\mathcal{T}_2$ respectively are *unifiable in the heterogeneous sense*, written $\sigma_1 \;_{\rho_1}\!\bowtie_{\rho_2} \sigma_2$, if and only if $(\sigma_1 \circ \rho_1) \bowtie (\sigma_2 \circ \rho_2)$. The unified behavior $\sigma$ over $\mathcal{T}$ is then $\sigma = (\sigma_1 \circ \rho_1) \sqcup (\sigma_2 \circ \rho_2)$. It is convenient, however, to retain some information of the original tag structures in the composition, since they are often referred to in the heterogeneous composition, as we will see in the sequel. To do so, we construct the behavior composition over the fibered product [4] $\mathcal{T}_1 \;_{\rho_1}\!\times_{\rho_2} \mathcal{T}_2 = (\mathcal{T}_1 \;_{\rho_1}\!\times_{\rho_2} \mathcal{T}_2, \leq)$ of the original tag structures, extending the order component-wise: $(\tau_1, \tau_2) \leq (\tau'_1, \tau'_2) \iff \tau_1 \leq \tau'_1 \wedge \tau_2 \leq \tau'_2$, where $\mathcal{T}_1 \;_{\rho_1}\!\times_{\rho_2} \mathcal{T}_2 = \{(\tau_1, \tau_2) \in \mathcal{T}_1 \times \mathcal{T}_2 : \rho_1(\tau_1) = \rho_2(\tau_2)\}$.

*Example 1.* We consider a simplified version of the water controlling system proposed by Benvenuti et al. [14]. It consists of two components: a water tank and a water level controller, connected in a closed-loop fashion, c.f. Fig. 1. We assume that the water level $x(t)$ is changed linearly as follows:

$$x(t) \stackrel{\text{def}}{=} \begin{cases} \Delta_t * (\mathbf{f_i} - \mathbf{f_o}) & \text{when command is Open} \\ \mathbf{h} - \Delta_t * \mathbf{f_o} & \text{when command is Close} \end{cases} \tag{1}$$

where $\mathbf{f_i}$ and $\mathbf{f_o}$ denote the constant inlet and outlet flow respectively, $\mathbf{h}$ denotes the height when the tank is full of water and $\Delta_t$ denotes the time elapsed since $t_0$ at which the tank reaches the maximum/minimum water level $\mathbf{H}$, i.e., $\Delta_t = t - t_0$. Let $\epsilon_1 = \epsilon_2 = -\infty$, the tank behaviors are naturally defined on tag structure $\mathcal{T}_1 = (\mathbb{R}_+ \cup \{\epsilon_1\}, \leq)$ and the controller behaviors on $\mathcal{T}_2 = (\mathbb{N} \cup \{\epsilon_2\}, \leq)$ representing continuous and discrete time respectively. In addition, both components contain behaviors for two system variables, namely the command variable $m$ and the water level $x$, thus $V_1 = V_2 = \{m, x\}$. The command values can be Open (**p**) or Close (**l**) and the water level is of positive real type and between 0 and $\mathbf{h}$, i.e., $D_m = \{\mathbf{p}, \mathbf{l}\}$ and $D_x = [0, \mathbf{h}]$.

Consider the tank behavior $\sigma_1$ and the controller behavior $\sigma_2$ described in Fig. 1(b), where $\sigma(v, n)$ is described when the parameter setting is $\mathbf{f_i} = 2, \mathbf{f_o} = 1, \mathbf{h} = 1$. These are different behaviors whose composition is only possible under the presence of morphisms such as $\rho_i : \mathcal{T}_i \mapsto \mathcal{T}_1$ given by $\rho_1(\tau_1) = \tau_1, \rho_2(\tau_2) = 0.5 * \tau_2$.

Our interest in this system is to construct the contracts of these components which will be provided later in this paper. Intuitively, the tank contract guarantees a linear evolution of the water level $x(t)$ upon the reception of in-time commands. Meanwhile, the controller contract only assumes the initial emptiness of the tank and guarantees to send proper commands upon detecting its emptiness or fullness.

### 3.2 Operational Tag Machines

TMs were first introduced to represent sets of homogeneous behaviors [7] and have been recently extended to encompass the heterogeneous context [9]. To construct behaviors, the TM transitions must be able to *increment* time, i.e., to update the tags of the events. An operation of *tag concatenation* on a tag structure is used to accomplish this.

**Definition 2 ([7]).** *An* algebraic tag structure *is a tag structure* $\mathcal{T} = (T, \leq, \cdot)$ *where* $\cdot$ *is a binary operator on* $T$ *called* concatenation, *such that:*

1. $(T, \cdot)$ *is a monoid with identity element* $\hat{\imath}_{\mathcal{T}}$
2. $\forall \tau_1, \tau_1', \tau_2, \tau_2' \in T : \tau_1 \leq \tau_1' \wedge \tau_2 \leq \tau_2' \Rightarrow \tau_1 \cdot \tau_2 \leq \tau_1' \cdot \tau_2'$
3. $\exists \epsilon_{\mathcal{T}} \in T : \forall \tau \in T : \epsilon_{\mathcal{T}} \leq \tau \wedge \epsilon_{\mathcal{T}} \cdot \tau = \tau \cdot \epsilon_{\mathcal{T}} = \epsilon_{\mathcal{T}}$

Tags can be organized as *tag vectors* $\boldsymbol{\tau} = (\tau^{v_1}, \dots, \tau^{v_n})$, where $n$ is the number of variables in $V$. During transition, tag vectors evolve according to a matrix $\mu : V \times V \mapsto T$ called a *tag piece* [7]. The new tag vector is $\boldsymbol{\tau}_\mu \stackrel{\text{def}}{=} \boldsymbol{\tau} \cdot \mu$ where $\tau_\mu^{v_i} \stackrel{\text{def}}{=} \max(\tau^u \cdot \mu(u, v_i))^{u \in V}$ and the maximum is taken with respect to the tag ordering. As the order is partial, the maximum may not exist, in which case the operation is not defined.

Intuitively, a tag piece $\mu$ represents increments in all variable tags over a transition and provides a way to operationally renew them. To represent also changes in variable values, $\mu$ can be labeled with a partial assignment $\nu : V \rightarrow D$, which assigns new values to the variables. A *labeled* tag piece $\mu$ thus specifies events for all variables for which $\nu$ is defined. In the following, we denote by $\mathfrak{dom}(\nu)$ the domain of $\nu$ and by $L(V, \mathcal{T})$ the universe of all labeled tag pieces, or simply labels, over a variable set $V$ and tag structure $\mathcal{T}$. By abuse of notation, we assume that every tag piece $\mu$ has an associated assignment $\nu$.

*Example 2.* The algebraic tag structure $(\mathbb{N} \cup \{-\infty\}, \leq, +)$, where $+$ is the concatenation operator, can be used to capture logical time by structuring tag pieces $\mu$ to represent an integer increment of 1. For instance, $\begin{bmatrix} 1 & 3 \end{bmatrix} \cdot \begin{bmatrix} 0 & 1 \\ -\infty & 1 \end{bmatrix} = \begin{bmatrix} 1 & 4 \end{bmatrix}$. The tag of the second variable is increased by 1 while that of the first variable remains the same since the least element $-\infty = \epsilon$ is used to cancel the contribution of an entry in the tag vector.

A tag machine $M$ is a finite automaton where transitions are marked by labels.

**Definition 3 ([9]).** *A* tag machine *is a tuple* $(V, \mathcal{T}, S, s_0, F, E)$ *where:*

- $V$ *is a set of variables,*
- $\mathcal{T}$ *is an algebraic tag structure,*
- $S$ *is a finite set of states and* $s_0 \in S$ *is the initial state,*
- $F \subseteq S$ *is a set of accepting states,*
- $E \subseteq S \times L(V, \mathcal{T}) \times S$ *is the transition relation.*

A TM run $r$ is a sequence of states and transitions $r : s_0 \xrightarrow{\mu_0} s_1 \xrightarrow{\mu_1} s_2 \dots s_{m-1} \xrightarrow{\mu_{m-1}} s_m$ such that $s_m \in F$ and for all $i$, $1 \leq i \leq m$, $(s_{i-1}, \mu_{i-1}, s_i) \in E$. Intuitively, a

TM is used to construct a behavior (as defined in Sect. 3.1) by following its labeled transitions over a run, and concatenating the tag pieces sequentially to the initial tag vector $\tau = (\hat{\imath}_T, \ldots, \hat{\imath}_T)$. A new event is added to the behavior whenever a new value is assigned by the label function $\nu_i$. Run $r$ is *valid* if the concatenation is always defined along the run and $s_m \in F$. The language $\mathcal{L}(M)$ of tag machine $M$ is given by the behaviors of all its valid runs.

### 3.3 Tag Machine Composition

As TMs are used to represent sets of behaviors, combining TMs amounts to considering only behaviors which are consistent with every TM. In particular, over every transition, the TMs involved in the composition must agree on the tag increment and the value of the shared variables, i.e., their labels are *unifiable*. While TMs defined on the same tag structure, or *homogeneous* TMs, can always be composed, TMs on different tag structures, or *heterogeneous* TMs, can be composed if there exists a pair of *algebraic* tag morphisms mapping the tag structures $T_1, T_2$ to a common tag structure $T$ and preserving the concatenation operator. The homogeneous composition can thus be regarded as a special case of the heterogeneous one when tag morphisms are identity functions mapping a tag to itself.

**Definition 4** ([9]). *A tag morphism $\rho : T \mapsto T'$ is algebraic if $\rho(\hat{\imath}_T) = \hat{\imath}_{T'}$ and $\rho(\epsilon_T) = \epsilon_{T'}$ and $\rho(\tau_1 \cdot \tau_2) = \rho(\tau_1) \cdot \rho(\tau_2)$ for all $\tau_1, \tau_2 \in T$.*

The newly-composed TM will be defined on a unified tag structure and a unified label set. Referring to the previous notation, two labels $\mu_1$ and $\mu_2$ are *unifiable* under morphisms $\rho_1$ and $\rho_2$, written $\mu_1 \; _{\rho_1}\bowtie_{\rho_2} \mu_2$, whenever a) $\rho_1(\mu_1(w, v)) = \rho_2(\mu_2(w, v))$, and b) $\nu_1(v) = \nu_2(v)$, for all pairs $(w, v) \in W \times W$ where $W = V_1 \cap V_2$. Their unification $\mu = \mu_1 \; _{\rho_1}\sqcup_{\rho_2} \mu_2$ is defined over $T_1 \; _{\rho_1}\times_{\rho_2} T_2$ and is any of the members of the unification set of pieces given by

$$\mu(w, v) = \begin{cases} (\mu_1(w, v), \mu_2(w, v)) & \text{if } (w, v) \in W \times W \\ (\mu_1(w, v), \tau_2) & \text{if } w \in V_1, v \in V_1 \setminus V_2 \\ (\mu_1(w, v), \tau_2) & \text{if } w \in V_1 \setminus V_2, v \in V_1 \\ (\tau_1, \mu_2(w, v)) & \text{if } w \in V_2 \setminus V_1, v \in V_2 \\ (\tau_1, \mu_2(w, v)) & \text{if } w \in V_2, v \in V_2 \setminus V_1 \\ (\epsilon_{T_1}, \epsilon_{T_2}) & \text{otherwise} \end{cases}$$

where $\tau_2 \in T_2$ is such that $\rho_2(\tau_2) = \rho_1(\mu_1(w, v))$, and similarly $\tau_1 \in T_1$ is such that $\rho_1(\tau_1) = \rho_2(\mu_2(w, v))$. The unified labeling function agrees with individual functions on the shared variables:

$$\nu(v) = \begin{cases} \nu_1(v) \text{ if } v \in V_1 \\ \nu_2(v) \text{ if } v \in V_2 \end{cases}$$

The composition $M = M_1 \; _{\rho_1}\|_{\rho_2} M_2$ of heterogeneous TMs can then be defined over the unification of heterogeneous tag structures and labels.

**Definition 5** ([9]). *The composition of $M_1$ and $M_2$ under algebraic tag morphisms $\rho_1$ and $\rho_2$ is the tag machine $M = M_1 \; _{\rho_1}\|_{\rho_2} M_2 = (V, T_1 \; _{\rho_1}\times_{\rho_2} T_2, S, s_0, F, E)$ such that*

- $V = V_1 \cup V_2$,
- $S = S_1 \times S_2$, $s_0 = (s_{01}, s_{02})$, $F = F_1 \times F_2$,
- $E = \{((s_1, s_2), \mu_1 \,_{\rho_1}\sqcup_{\rho_2} \mu_2, (s_1', s_2')) : \mu_1 \,_{\rho_1}\bowtie_{\rho_2} \mu_2 \wedge (s_i, \mu_i, s_i') \in E_i, i = 1, 2\}$
  where $\mu_1 \,_{\rho_1}\sqcup_{\rho_2} \mu_2$ extends to all the members of the unification set.

As homogeneous composition is a special case of the heterogeneous one with identity morphisms, we shall omit the morphisms in the homogeneous notations in the sequel.

## 4    A Contract Framework for Heterogeneous Systems

Our goal is to use TMs as an operational means for modeling heterogeneous systems in contract-based design flows. To this end, we equip TMs with essential binary operators such as composition to combine two TMs [9] and refinement, quotient and conjunction to relate their sets of behaviors (Sect. 4.1). Moreover, we limit TMs to their *deterministic* form where labeled tag pieces annotated on transitions going out of a state are all different. On top of these TM operators, we propose a heterogeneous contract theory for TM-based specifications with universal contract operators such as composition, refinement and dominance (Sect. 4.2).

### 4.1    Tag Machine Operators

Two TMs can be related in a refinement relation when the behavior set of one machine is included in that of the other under the morphisms. In the operational point of view, the refined TM can always take a transition unifiable with that taken by the refining TM. Let $M_i = (V_i, \mathcal{T}_i, S_i, s_{0i}, F_i, E_i)$ be TMs and $\rho_i : \mathcal{T}_i \mapsto \mathcal{T}$ be algebraic tag morphisms, where $i \in \{1, 2\}$. The TM refinement is defined as follows.

**Definition 6.** $M_1$ *refines* $M_2$, *written* $M_1 \,_{\rho_1}\preceq_{\rho_2} M_2$, *if there exists a binary relation* $R \subseteq S_1 \times S_2$ *such that* $(s_{01}, s_{02}) \in R$ *and for all* $(s_1, s_2) \in R$ *and* $(s_1, \mu_1, s_1') \in E_1$ :

$$\exists (s_2, \mu_2, s_2') \in E_2 : \mu_1 \,_{\rho_1}\bowtie_{\rho_2} \mu_2 \wedge (s_1', s_2') \in R \wedge (s_1' \in F_1 \Rightarrow s_2' \in F_2)$$

The following theorem shows that our TM theory supports (homogenous) *independent implementability*: refinement is preserved when composing components.

**Theorem 1.** *Let* $M_i'$ *be TMs defined on* $\mathcal{T}_i$ *and* $V_i$ :

$$(M_1 \preceq M_1') \wedge (M_2 \preceq M_2') \Rightarrow (M_1 \,_{\rho_1}\|_{\rho_2} M_2) \preceq (M_1' \,_{\rho_1}\|_{\rho_2} M_2').$$

We remark that Theorem 1 only holds for *homogenous* TM refinement, and note that heterogeneous refinement in general is *not* preserved even by homogeneous composition. The reason is that the morphisms involved in the former are generally many-to-one functions and can map two different tags into the same tag.

*Example 3.* We consider an example where:

- $\mathcal{T}_1 = \{\tau_1\}, \mathcal{T}_2 = \{\tau_2, \tau_2'\}$
- $V_1 = V_2 = \{z\}, D_z = \{\top\}$
- $\rho_1(\tau_1) = \rho_2(\tau_2) = \rho_2(\tau_2') = \tau$

Let $M_i$, $M_i'$ be defined on $\mathcal{T}_i$ and $V_i$ where $i \in \{1, 2\}$. For the sake of simplicity, assume all TMs have a single state which is both initial and accepting state. In addition, there is only one self-loop at this state annotated with $\mu_i$ for machine $M_i$ and $\mu_i'$ for machine $M_i'$ such that $\mu_1 = \mu_1' = [\tau_1], \mu_2 = [\tau_2], \mu_2' = [\tau_2'], \nu_1(z) = \nu_1'(z) = \nu_2(z) = \nu_2'(z) = \top$. It is easy to see that $M_1 \ _{\rho_1}\preceq_{\rho_2} M_2$ since $\mu_1 \ _{\rho_1}\bowtie_{\rho_2} \mu_2$ and $M_1' \ _{\rho_1}\preceq_{\rho_2} M_2'$ since $\mu_1' \ _{\rho_1}\bowtie_{\rho_2} \mu_2'$. However, $(M_1 \parallel M_1') \ _{\rho_1}\npreceq_{\rho_2} (M_2 \parallel M_2')$ since the right composition is empty while the left is not.

While the refinement operator enables us to compare two TMs in terms of sets of behaviors, the composition and quotient operators allow us to synthesize specifications. The TM composition computes the most general specification that retains all unifiable behaviors of two TMs. The dual operator to TM composition is TM quotient which computes the maximal specification as follows.

**Definition 7.** *The quotient* $M_1 \ _{\rho_1}/_{\rho_2} M_2$ *is a machine* $M = (V, \mathcal{T}_{12}, S, s_0, F, E)$, *where*

- $V = V_1 \cup V_2, \mathcal{T}_{12} \overset{\text{def}}{=} \mathcal{T}_1 \ _{\rho_1}\times_{\rho_2} \mathcal{T}_2, s_0 = (s_{01}, s_{02}),$
- $S = (S_1 \times S_2) \cup \{\mathfrak{u}\},$ *where* $\mathfrak{u}$ *is a new universal state,*
- $F = ((S_1 \times S_2) \setminus ((S_1 \setminus F_1) \times F_2)) \cup \{\mathfrak{u}\} = (F_1 \times F_2) \cup (S_1 \times (S_2 \setminus F_2)) \cup \{\mathfrak{u}\},$
  $E = \{((s_1, s_2), \mu_1 \ _{\rho_1}\sqcup_{\rho_2} \mu_2, (s_1', s_2')) \mid$
  $\qquad (\mu_1 \ _{\rho_1}\bowtie_{\rho_2} \mu_2) \wedge ((s_1, \mu_1, s_1') \in E_1) \wedge ((s_2, \mu_2, s_2') \in E_2)\}$
  $\cup\{((s_1, s_2), \mu_1 \ _{\rho_1}\sqcup_{\rho_2} \mu_2, \mathfrak{u}) \mid$
  $\qquad (\forall s_2' \in S_2 : (s_2, \mu_2, s_2') \notin E_2) \wedge (\exists \mu_1 \in L(V_1, \mathcal{T}_1) : \mu_1 \ _{\rho_1}\bowtie_{\rho_2} \mu_2)\}$
  $\cup\{(\mathfrak{u}, \mu, \mathfrak{u}) \mid \mu \in L(V, \mathcal{T}_{12})\}.$

We give an example of a quotient construction in Fig. 4. The dual relation between composition and quotient is presented in the next theorem.

**Theorem 2.** *The quotient* $M$ *satisfies refinement* $(M_2 \ _{\text{id}_2}\parallel_{\text{proj}_2} M) \ _{\text{proj}_1'}\preceq_{\text{id}_1} M_1$ *where:*

$$\forall i \in \{1, 2\}, \forall \tau_i \in \mathcal{T}_i : \text{id}_i(\tau_i) = \tau_i$$
$$\forall i \in \{1, 2\}, \forall (\tau_1, \tau_2) \in \mathcal{T}_{12} : \text{proj}_i((\tau_1, \tau_2)) = \tau_i$$
$$\forall (\tau_2, \tau_{12}) \in \mathcal{T}_2 \ _{\text{id}_2}\times_{\text{proj}_2} \mathcal{T}_{12} : \text{proj}_1'((\tau_2, \tau_{12})) = \text{proj}_1(\tau_{12})$$
$$\forall (\tau_1, \tau_{12}) \in \mathcal{T}_1 \ _{\text{id}_1}\times_{\text{proj}_1} \mathcal{T}_{12} : \text{proj}_2'((\tau_1, \tau_{12})) = \text{proj}_2(\tau_{12})$$

*Moreover, for* $M'$ *defined on* $\mathcal{T}_{12}$ *and* $V$: $(M_2 \ _{\text{id}_2}\parallel_{\text{proj}_2} M') \ _{\text{proj}_1'}\preceq_{\text{id}_1} M_1 \Rightarrow M' \preceq M$.

Thus, the quotient $M$ is the *greatest*, in the (homogeneous) refinement preorder, of all TMs $M'$ defined in Theorem 2. This universal property is generally expected of quotients [10], and it alone implies that the quotient is uniquely defined up to two-sided homogeneous refinement [19]. As an example, Fig. 3(c) shows a homogeneous quotient and Fig. 4(a) shows a heterogeneous quotient using the morphisms of Example 1.

Finally, the operator of *heterogeneous conjunction*, denoted $_{\rho_1}\wedge_{\rho_2}$, is defined as the greatest lower bound of the refinement order. Conjunction, thus, amounts to computing the intersection of the behavior sets, in order to find the largest common refinement. Thus, for tag machines, conjunction can be computed similarly to composition. The two operators, however, serve very different purposes, and must not therefore be confused.

## 4.2  Tag Contracts

We use the term *tag contract* to mean that in our framework each contract is coupled with an algebraic tag structure, thereby allowing the contract assumption and guarantee to be represented as TMs.

**Definition 8.** *A tag contract is a homogeneous pair of TMs* $(M_A, M_G)$ *where* $M_A$ - *the assumption and* $M_G$ - *the guarantee are TMs defined over the same tag structure* $\mathcal{T}$ *and variable set* $V$.

*Example 4.* We consider the simplified water controlling system in Example 1 and present a contract for each component. To simplify the behavioral construction, we rely on a special clock inc added to the variable set of both components. Tag pieces $\mu$ are then structured to represent an increment of $\delta$ by always assigning $\delta$ to $\mu(\text{inc}, \text{inc})$ and assigning $\delta$ to all entries $\mu(\text{inc}, v)$ where $v \in \mathfrak{Dom}(\mu)$, and the least element $-\infty$ to other entries. The tags of $x$ and $m$ are thus renewed to the tag of clock inc over every transition. To keep the figures readable we represent tag pieces as $[\delta]$. In addition, the clock value is always equal to its tag and thus is omitted from the labeling function.

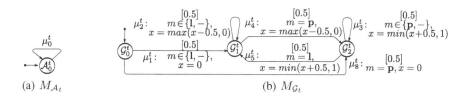

(a) $M_{A_t}$      (b) $M_{G_t}$

**Fig. 2.** The tank contract

Figure 2 depicts the tank contract $C_t = (M_{A_t}, M_{G_t})$ which guarantees a linear evolution of the water level $x(t)$ (Fig. 2(b)) given the assumption satisfaction (Fig. 2(a)). That is, the water level will evolve linearly as specified in Example 1, provided that the controlling command is received at the right time (i.e., open when the tank is empty and close when it is full). For the sake of simplicity, the events described by the tank contract are timestamped periodically every 0.5 time unit.

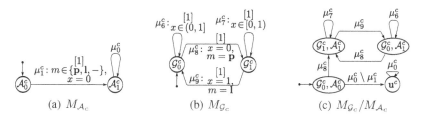

(a) $M_{A_c}$      (b) $M_{G_c}$      (c) $M_{G_c}/M_{A_c}$

**Fig. 3.** The controller contract

The controller contract is shown Fig. 3, where it assumes the tank to be empty initially (Fig. 3(a)), i.e., $x = 0$ and places no requirement on its output which is the command signal. As long as such assumption is satisfied, the controller guarantees (Fig. 3(b)) to send a proper command upon knowing of the tank emptiness or fullness. Intuitively, the controller behaviors ensure timely control over the water evolution while the tank behaviors accept untimely control and allow water spillages or shortages. While the tank system uses physical time to stamp its behaviors, the controller system instead timestamps its events logically, which can be described by the integer tag set $\mathbb{N}$. In both figures, the initial states are marked with short arrows arriving at them and all states are accepting states. For the sake of expressiveness, some of the labeled tag pieces can be represented symbolically. For example, to capture any event of variable $x$ happening at a specific time point within an interval, we label with the tag piece expressions such as $x \in (0, 1)$, meaning that in such an event $x$ can take any value between 0 and 1. Similarly, $m \in \{\mathbf{p}, \mathbf{l}, -\}$ means the command value can either be open, close or undefined. In addition, we use $\mu_0^t$ to denote the universe set of labels $L(V_1, \mathcal{T}_1)$ and $\mu_0^c$ the set of labels $L(V_2, \mathcal{T}_2)$.

The tag contract semantics is subsequently defined through the notions of contract environments and implementations. Let $M_{\mathcal{I}}$ and $M_{\mathcal{E}}$ be TMs defined over tag structure $\mathcal{T}$ and variable set $V$ in Def. 8. We call $M_{\mathcal{E}}$ an environment of contract $\mathcal{C}$ when $M_{\mathcal{E}}$ refines $M_{\mathcal{A}}$. Let $[\![\mathcal{C}]\!]_e$ be the set of all such environments, we call $M_{\mathcal{I}}$ an implementation of contract $\mathcal{C}$, if it holds that $\forall M_{\mathcal{E}} \in [\![\mathcal{C}]\!]_e : M_{\mathcal{I}} \parallel M_{\mathcal{E}} \preceq M_{\mathcal{G}} \parallel M_{\mathcal{E}}$. The set of implementations is similarly denoted by $[\![\mathcal{C}]\!]_p$. Hence, the implementation checking is done based on instantiating all possible environments of a contract. When the contract is *normalized*, such a check can be done independently of the assumption instantiation.

**Definition 9.** *A tag contract* $\mathcal{C} = (M_{\mathcal{A}}, M_{\mathcal{G}})$ *is in normalized form if and only if:*

$$\forall M_{\mathcal{I}} : M_{\mathcal{I}} \in [\![\mathcal{C}]\!]_p \Leftrightarrow M_{\mathcal{I}} \preceq M_{\mathcal{G}}.$$

The following theorem states the preservation of tag contract semantics under the normalization operation: whenever a tag contract is in a normalized form, checking contract satisfaction is reduced to finding a refinement relation between two TMs.

**Theorem 3.** *Tag contract* $(M_{\mathcal{A}}, M_{\mathcal{G}}/M_{\mathcal{A}})$ *is in normalized form and has the same semantics as* $\mathcal{C} = (M_{\mathcal{A}}, M_{\mathcal{G}})$ *does.*

*Example 5.* We use the tag contracts in Example 4 and perform the quotient between the guarantees and assumptions in order to normalize them. Since the tank assumption is the universe of all possible behaviors, i.e., $\Sigma(V_1, \mathcal{T}_1)$, normalizing the tank guarantee adds no more behaviors to the guarantee, i.e., $M_{\mathcal{G}_t}/M_{\mathcal{A}_t} = M_{\mathcal{G}_t}$. Figure 3(c), on the other hand, shows the normalized controller guarantee having more behaviors than the un-normalized one. It is easy to see that the behavior $\sigma_1$ in Example 1 is included in $M_{\mathcal{G}_t}$ and $\sigma_2$ is in $M_{\mathcal{G}_c}/M_{\mathcal{A}_c}$.

As we will see later, working with normalized tag contracts can simplify the formalization of contract operators (e.g. contract refinement and dominance) as well as provide a unique representation for equivalent contracts, thus we will often assume contracts to be in normalized form hereafter.

**Tag Contract Refinement.** The refinement relation between two tag contracts is subject to the tag morphisms and is determined by that between their sets of implementations and environments as follows. Let $C_i = (M_{A_i}, M_{G_i})$ be tag contracts defined on $T_i$ and $V_i$ and $\rho_i : T_i \mapsto T$ be algebraic tag morphisms where $i \in \{1, 2\}$

**Definition 10.** *Contract $C_1$ refines contract $C_2$ under morphisms $\rho_1$ and $\rho_2$, written $C_1 \;_{\rho_1}\preceq_{\rho_2} C_2$, if the following two conditions hold:*

1. $\forall M_{\mathcal{E}_2} \in [\![C_2]\!]_e : \exists M_{\mathcal{E}_1} \in [\![C_1]\!]_e : M_{\mathcal{E}_2} \;_{\rho_2}\preceq_{\rho_1} M_{\mathcal{E}_1}$
2. $\forall M_{\mathcal{I}_1} \in [\![C_1]\!]_p : \exists M_{\mathcal{I}_2} \in [\![C_2]\!]_p : M_{\mathcal{I}_1} \;_{\rho_1}\preceq_{\rho_2} M_{\mathcal{I}_2}$

The following theorem shows that for two normalized tag contracts, checking refinement can be done at the *syntactic* level, i.e., by finding a TM refinement relation between their assumptions and guarantees.

**Theorem 4.** $C_1 \;_{\rho_1}\preceq_{\rho_2} C_2 \Leftrightarrow (M_{A_2} \;_{\rho_2}\preceq_{\rho_1} M_{A_1}) \wedge (M_{G_1} \;_{\rho_1}\preceq_{\rho_2} M_{G_2})$

**Tag Contract Composition and Dominance.** In composing two heterogeneous tag contracts, it is essential to guarantee that composing implementations of each contract results in a new implementation of the composite contract. In addition, every environment of the composite contract should be able to work with any implementation of an individual contract in a way that their composition does not violate the other contract assumption. In fact, there exists a class of contracts, including the composite contract, able to provide such desirable consequences. We refer to them as *dominating* contracts [10].

**Definition 11.** *A contract $C = (M_A, M_G)$ is said to* dominate *the tag contract pair $(C_1, C_2)$ under morphisms $\rho_1$ and $\rho_2$ if :*

1. *$C$ is defined over tag structure $T_{12} \overset{\text{def}}{=} T_1 \;_{\rho_1}\times_{\rho_2} T_2$ and variable set $V = V_1 \cup V_2$*
2. $\forall M_{\mathcal{I}_1} \in [\![C_1]\!]_p, \forall M_{\mathcal{I}_2} \in [\![C_2]\!]_p : M_{\mathcal{I}_1} \;_{\rho_1}\|_{\rho_2} M_{\mathcal{I}_2} \in [\![C]\!]_p$
3. $\forall M_{\mathcal{E}} \in [\![C]\!]_e : \begin{cases} \forall M_{\mathcal{I}_1} \in [\![C_1]\!]_p : (M_{\mathcal{I}_1} \;_{\text{id}_1}\|_{\text{proj}_1} M_{\mathcal{E}}) \;_{\text{proj}_2'}\preceq_{\text{id}_2} M_{A_2} \wedge \\ \forall M_{\mathcal{I}_2} \in [\![C_2]\!]_p : (M_{\mathcal{I}_2} \;_{\text{id}_2}\|_{\text{proj}_2} M_{\mathcal{E}}) \;_{\text{proj}_1'}\preceq_{\text{id}_1} M_{A_1} \end{cases}$

*where the morphisms are defined as in Theorem 2.*

The composition of heterogeneous tag contracts can then be defined as follows.

**Definition 12.** *The composition of tag contracts $C_1$ and $C_2$, written $C_1 \;_{\rho_1}\|_{\rho_2} C_2$, is another tag contract $((M_{A_1 \rho_1}/_{\rho_2} M_{G_2}) \curlywedge (M_{A_2 \rho_2}/_{\rho_1} M_{G_1})_{\text{swap}}, M_{G_1} \;_{\rho_1}\|_{\rho_2} M_{G_2})$ where* swap $: T_2 \;_{\rho_2}\times_{\rho_1} T_1 \mapsto T_1 \;_{\rho_1}\times_{\rho_2} T_2$ *is such that* swap$((\tau_2, \tau_1)) = ((\tau_1, \tau_2))$ *and $M_{\text{swap}}$ is $M$ where all pieces $\mu$ are replaced with $\mu \circ$ swap.*

Let $C_i'$ be normalized tag contracts defined on $T_i$ and $V_i$ such that $C_i' \preceq C_i$ where $i \in \{1, 2\}$. The following theorem states important results: the composition of two normalized contracts dominates the individual contracts and is the *least*, in the homogeneous refinement order, of all contracts dominating them under the same morphisms.

**Theorem 5.** *Let* $C = C_1 \,_{\rho_1}\|_{\rho_2} C_2$, *then:*

1. $C$ *dominates the contract pair* $(C_1, C_2)$ *under morphisms* $\rho_1$ *and* $\rho_2$.
2. *If* $C'$ *dominates* $(C_1, C_2)$ *under morphisms* $\rho_1$ *and* $\rho_2$ *then* $C \preceq C'$.

The next theorem is another of *independent implementability*: homogeneous tag contract refinement is preserved under the heterogeneous contract composition.

**Theorem 6.** *Let* $C = C_1 \,_{\rho_1}\|_{\rho_2} C_2$, *then:*

1. *If* $C$ *dominates* $(C_1, C_2)$ *under morphisms* $\rho_1$ *and* $\rho_2$ *then it also dominates* $(C'_1, C'_2)$ *under the same morphisms*.
2. $(C'_1 \,_{\rho_1}\|_{\rho_2} C'_2) \preceq (C_1 \,_{\rho_1}\|_{\rho_2} C_2)$.

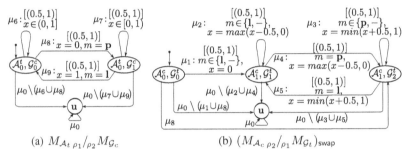

(a) $M_{\mathcal{A}_t \,\rho_1/\rho_2} M_{\mathcal{G}_c}$            (b) $(M_{\mathcal{A}_c \,\rho_2/\rho_1} M_{\mathcal{G}_t})_{\text{swap}}$

**Fig. 4.** Quotient components of the composite assumption of $C_1 \,_{\rho_1}\|_{\rho_2} C_2$

## 5 Conclusions

We have presented a modeling methodology based on contracts for designing heterogeneous distributed systems. Heterogeneous systems are usually characterized by their heterogeneity of components which can be of very different nature, e.g. real-time component or logical control component. Without a heterogeneous mechanism, modeling the interaction between components may not be feasible, thereby making it difficult to do verification and analysis based on the known properties of the components. This problem is further complicated for distributed systems where components are developed concurrently by different design teams and are synchronized by relying on their associated contracts. To deal with such problem, we adopt the TM formalism [7,9] for specifying components in terms of operational behaviors. We subsequently propose a contract methodology for synchronizing heterogeneous components based on a set of useful operations on TMs such as composition, quotient and refinement. Our next step is to demonstrate our methodology through a prototype tool and validate it through case studies. The development of such a tool is therefore included in our future work.

## References

1. Meyer, B.: Applying "Design by contract". Computer 25(10), 40–51 (1992)
2. Eker, J., Janneck, J.W., Lee, E.A., Liu, J., Liu, X., Ludvig, J., Neuendorffer, S., Sachs, S., Xiong, Y.: Taming heterogeneity - the ptolemy approach. In: Proceedings of the IEEE, pp. 127–144 (2003)

3. Lee, E., Sangiovanni-Vincentelli, A.: A framework for comparing models of computation. IEEE Trans. CAD of Integ. Circ. and Systems 17(12), 1217–1229 (1998)
4. Benveniste, A., Caillaud, B., Carloni, L.P., Caspi, P., Sangiovanni-Vincentelli, A.L.: Composing heterogeneous reactive systems. ACM Trans. Embed. Comput. Syst. 7(4), 43:1–43:36 (2008)
5. Benveniste, A., Caillaud, B., Ferrari, A., Mangeruca, L., Passerone, R., Sofronis, C.: Multiple viewpoint contract-based specification and design. In: de Boer, F.S., Bonsangue, M.M., Graf, S., de Roever, W.-P. (eds.) FMCO 2007. LNCS, vol. 5382, pp. 200–225. Springer, Heidelberg (2008)
6. Damm, W., Hungar, H., Josko, B., Peikenkamp, T., Stierand, I.: Using contract-based component specifications for virtual integration testing and architecture design. In: Proceedings of the Conference on Design, Automation and Test in Europe, Grenoble, France (2011)
7. Benveniste, A., Caillaud, B., Carloni, L.P., Sangiovanni-Vincentelli, A.: Tag machines. In: Proceedings of the International Conference on Embedded Software, pp. 255–263. ACM (2005)
8. Dey, S., Sarkar, D., Basu, A.: A tag machine based performance evaluation method for job-shop schedules. IEEE Trans. CAD of Integ. Circ. and Systems 29(7), 1028–1041 (2010)
9. Le, T.T.H., Passerone, R., Fahrenberg, U., Legay, A.: Tag machines for modeling heterogeneous systems. In: Proceedings of the 13th International Conference on Application of Concurrency to System Design, ACSD 2013, Barcelona, Spain, July 8-10 (2013)
10. Bauer, S.S., David, A., Hennicker, R., Guldstrand Larsen, K., Legay, A., Nyman, U., Wąsowski, A.: Moving from specifications to contracts in component-based design. In: de Lara, J., Zisman, A. (eds.) FASE 2012. LNCS, vol. 7212, pp. 43–58. Springer, Heidelberg (2012)
11. Dijkstra, E.W.: Guarded commands, non-determinancy and a calculus for the derivation of programs. In: Bauer, F.L., Samelson, K. (eds.) Language Hierarchies and Interfaces. LNCS, vol. 46, pp. 111–124. Springer, Heidelberg (1976)
12. Lamport, L.: win and sin: Predicate transformers for concurrency. ACM Trans. Program. Lang. Syst. 12(3), 396–428 (1990)
13. de Alfaro, L., Henzinger, T.A.: Interface automata. SIGSOFT Softw. Eng. Notes 26, 109–120 (2001)
14. Benvenuti, L., Ferrari, A., Mangeruca, L., Mazzi, E., Passerone, R., Sofronis, C.: A contract-based formalism for the specification of heterogeneous systems. In: Proceedings of the Forum on Specification, Verification and Design Languages, Stuttgart, pp. 142–147 (2008)
15. de Roever, W.P.: The quest for compositionality—a survey of assertion-based proof systems for concurrent programs, part i: Concurrency based on shared variables. In: Proc. of the IFIP Working Conference "The role of Abstract Models in Computer Science" (1985)
16. Davare, A., Densmore, D., Guo, L., Passerone, R., Sangiovanni-Vincentelli, A.L., Simalatsar, A., Zhu, Q.: metroII: A design environment for cyber-physical systems. ACM Transactions on Embedded Computing Systems 12(1s), 49:1–49:31 (2013)
17. Bliudze, S., Sifakis, J.: The algebra of connectors: Structuring interaction in BIP. IEEE Transactions on Computers 57(10), 1315–1330 (2008)
18. Dey, S., Sarkar, D., Basu, A.: A Kleene algebra of tagged system actors. IEEE Embedded Systems Letters 3(1), 28–31 (2011)
19. Fahrenberg, U., Legay, A., Wąsowski, A.: Vision paper: Make a difference (Semantically). In: Whittle, J., Clark, T., Kühne, T. (eds.) MODELS 2011. LNCS, vol. 6981, pp. 490–500. Springer, Heidelberg (2011)

# Matching Cloud Services with TOSCA*

Antonio Brogi and Jacopo Soldani

Department of Computer Science, University of Pisa, Italy

**Abstract.** The OASIS TOSCA specification aims at enhancing the portability of cloud-based applications by defining a language to describe and manage service orchestrations across heterogeneous clouds. A service template is defined as an orchestration of typed nodes, which can be instantiated by matching other service templates. In this paper, after defining the notion of *exact matching* between TOSCA service templates and node types, we define three other types of matching (*plug-in, flexible* and *white-box*), each permitting to ignore larger sets of non-relevant syntactic differences when type-checking service templates with respect to node types. We also describe how service templates that plug-in, flexibly or white-box match node types can be suitably adapted so as to exactly match them.

## 1 Introduction

How to deploy and manage, in an efficient and adaptive way, complex multi-service applications across heterogeneous cloud environments is one of the problems that have emerged with the cloud revolution. Currently, migrating (parts of) an application from one cloud to another is still a costly and error-prone process. As a result, cloud users tend to end up locked into the cloud platform they are using since it is practically infeasible for them to migrate (parts of) their application across different clouds platforms [16].

In this scenario, OASIS recently created a Technical Committee on *Topology and Orchestration Specification for Cloud Application* (TOSCA), whose goal is to ease the portability of cloud-based applications by defining a language to describe and manage service orchestrations across heterogeneous clouds. The first specification of TOSCA [14] defines a XML-based language that permits to specify —in a vendor-agnostic way— topology and behaviour of complex multi-cloud applications as service templates that orchestrate typed nodes.

As stated in the TOSCA primer ([15], page 35): *"node types can be made concrete by substituting them by a service template"*. However, while the matching between service templates and node types is mentioned with reference to an example (*"service template ST may substitute node type N because the boundary of ST matches all defining elements of N"*), no formal definition of *matching* is given either in [14] or in [15]. A definition of matching is employed in [17] to merge TOSCA services by matching entire portions of their topology templates.

---

* Work partly supported by EU-FP7-ICT-610531 SeaClouds project.

C. Canal and M. Villari (Eds.): ESOCC 2013, CCIS 393, pp. 218–232, 2013.

The definition of matching employed in [17] is however very strict, as two service components are considered to match only if they expose the same qualified name.

The objective of our work is to contribute to the TOSCA specification by first providing a formal definition of the notion of *exact matching* between TOSCA service templates and node types, and by then extending such definition in order to provide three other types of matching (*plug-in*, *flexible* and *white-box*), each permitting to ignore larger sets of non-relevant syntactic differences when type-checking service templates with respect to node types. To allow exploiting the new notions of matching not only during type-checking but also for node instantiation, we describe how a service template that plug-in, flexibly or white-box matches a typed node can be suitably adapted so as to exactly match it.

The results presented in this paper intend to contribute to the formal definition of TOSCA. The different types of matching defined in this paper can be fruitfully integrated in the TOSCA implementations that are currently under development in order to enhance their type-checking capabilities. More in general, the definitions of matching presented in this paper can be exploited to implement type-checking mechanisms over service descriptions by taking into account, beyond functional features, also requirements, capabilities, policies, and properties.

The rest of paper is organised as follows. The main notions of TOSCA are introduced in Sect. 2. The notion of *exact matching* between a service template and a node type is defined in Sect. 3, where three other notions of matching (*plug-in*, *flexible* and *white-box*) are introduced, along with the corresponding adaptation techniques. Related work is discussed in Sect. 4, while some concluding remarks are drawn in Sect. 5.

## 2   Background: TOSCA

In this section we briefly recall the main notions of the *Topology and Orchestration Specification for Cloud Application (TOSCA)* [14] which will be used in the rest of the paper[1].

The main aim of TOSCA is to enhance the portability of multi-cloud applications by enabling an interoperable description of application and infrastructure cloud services, of the relationships between service parts, and of the operational behaviour of services, independently of the supplier creating the service and of any particular cloud provider or hosting technology.

Syntactically speaking, TOSCA is an XML-based language for describing service templates. All definitions are contained in the XML *Definitions* element (the root of a TOSCA XML document). The *ServiceTemplate* element defines all the topological and management aspects of a service by means of *TopologyTemplate* and *Plans* elements (Fig. 1). A *TopologyTemplate* specifies the topological structure of a service as a directed graph, whose nodes are *NodeTemplates* and whose

---

[1] More information on TOSCA can be found in the TOSCA specification [14] as well as in the TOSCA primer [15].

arcs are *RelationshipTemplates*. *Plans* contains *Plan* elements that specify how to manage the associated service template during its whole lifetime. *Boundary-Definitions* can be used to specify which internal nodes, relationships and other features are externally exposed by a *ServiceTemplate*.

*NodeTemplates* are typed by means of *NodeTypes*, which define the structure of the service features whose values are specified in a *NodeTemplate*. Such features include properties, interfaces, requirements, capabilities, and policies. While properties and interfaces can be defined internally, requirements and capabilities must be typed by referring to external *RequirementTypes* and *CapabilityTypes*. Finally, *NodeTemplates* and *ServiceTemplates* can declare QoS information by exposing *Policy* elements, which must be typed by referring to *PolicyTypes*. A *PolicyType* defines the structure of policy, while a *Policy* assigns actual policy values.

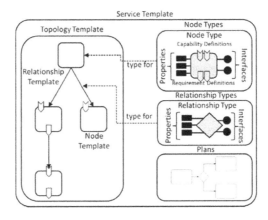

**Fig. 1.** TOSCA *ServiceTemplate*

## 3   Matching Service Templates with Node Types

As stated in the TOSCA primer ([15], page 35): *"node types can be made concrete by substituting them by a service template"*. While the matching between *ServiceTemplates* and *NodeTypes* is mentioned with reference to an example, no definition of *matching* is given either in [14] or in [15].

In this section we formally define four ways in which a *ServiceTemplate* can match a *NodeType*: *exact* ($\equiv$), *plug-in* ($\simeq$), *flexible* ($\sim$), and *white-box* ($\square$). Each definition of matching relaxes the previous one (viz., $\equiv \subset \simeq \subset \sim \subset \square$) in order to identify larger sets of *ServiceTemplates* that can be adapted so as to (exactly) match a *NodeType*.

### 3.1   Exact Matching

In this section we formalize the definition of exact matching between a *ServiceTemplate* and a *NodeType*, which mirrors the definition of exact matching between a *NodeTemplate* and a *NodeType* discussed in [14]. The following definition specifies when a *ServiceTemplate* $ST$ exactly matches a *NodeType* $N$ in terms of the requirements (Reqs), capabilities (Caps), policies (Pols), properties (Props) and interfaces (Ints) of $ST$ and $N$[2].

**Definition 1.** *A* ServiceTemplate $ST$ *exactly matches a* NodeType $N$ *($ST \equiv N$) if and only if:*

   (1) $\mathsf{Reqs}(ST) \equiv_R \mathsf{Reqs}(N)$ *and*
   (2) $\mathsf{Caps}(ST) \equiv_C \mathsf{Caps}(N)$ *and*
   (3) $\mathsf{Pols}(ST) \equiv_{PO} \mathsf{Pols}(N)$ *and*
   (4) $\mathsf{Props}(ST) \equiv_{PR} \mathsf{Props}(N)$ *and*
   (5) $\mathsf{Ints}(ST) \equiv_I \mathsf{Ints}(N)$.

Requirements must have the same name and type, and they must be in a one-to-one correspondence. The same holds for capabilities.

**Definition 2.** *Let $N$ be a* NodeType *and let $ST$ be a* ServiceTemplate. *Then:*
$\mathsf{Reqs}(ST) \equiv_R \mathsf{Reqs}(N)$ *iff*
   $\forall x \in \mathsf{Reqs}(ST)\ \exists! y \in \mathsf{Reqs}(N) : name(x) = name(y) \wedge type(x) = type(y)$, *and*
   $\forall y \in \mathsf{Reqs}(N)\ \exists! x \in \mathsf{Reqs}(ST) : name(x) = name(y) \wedge type(x) = type(y)$.
$\mathsf{Caps}(ST) \equiv_C \mathsf{Caps}(N)$ *iff*
   $\forall x \in \mathsf{Caps}(ST)\ \exists! y \in \mathsf{Caps}(N) : name(x) = name(y) \wedge type(x) = type(y)$, *and*
   $\forall y \in \mathsf{Caps}(N)\ \exists! x \in \mathsf{Caps}(ST) : name(x) = name(y) \wedge type(x) = type(y)$.

According to [14], a policy can be associated with a set of *NodeTypes* to which it is applicable[3]. The type of each policy of $ST$ must therefore be one of the policy types applicable to $N$. As far as properties are concerned, since a *NodeType* only specifies the XML schema of its observable properties (while *ServiceTemplates* specify actual values of properties), property matching reduces to comparing XML types.

**Definition 3.** *Let $N$ be a* NodeType *and let $ST$ be a* ServiceTemplate. *Then:*
$\mathsf{Pols}(ST) \equiv_{PO} \mathsf{Pols}(N)$ *iff* $\forall x \in \mathsf{Pols}(ST) : type(x) \in \mathsf{Pols}(N)$.
$\mathsf{Props}(ST) \equiv_{PR} \mathsf{Props}(N)$ *iff* $\mathsf{XMLtype}(\mathsf{Props}(ST)) = \mathsf{XMLtype}(\mathsf{Props}(N))$.

Finally, interfaces must have the same name and must be in a one-to-one correspondence. The same holds for interface operations and for operation parameters. Operation parameters must also have the same type.

**Definition 4.** *Let $N$ be a* NodeType *and let $ST$ be a* ServiceTemplate. *Then:*
$\mathsf{Ints}(ST) \equiv_I \mathsf{Ints}(N)$ *iff*
   $\forall x \in \mathsf{Ints}(ST)\ \exists! y \in \mathsf{Ints}(N) : name(x) = name(y)\ \wedge$

---

[2] Strictly speaking, the definition relates the *Requirements* of $ST$ with the *RequirementDefinitions* of $N$, the *Capabilities* of $ST$ with the *CapabilityDefinitions* of $N$, the policies exposed by $ST$ with the policy types applicable to $N$, and the *Properties* exposed by $ST$ with the *PropertyDefinitions* declared by $N$.

[3] We assume that a policy is applicable to all *NodeTypes* if not specified otherwise.

$$\forall o_x \in \mathsf{Ops}(x) \; \exists! o_y \in \mathsf{Ops}(y) : o_x \equiv_o o_y \; and$$
$$\forall y \in \mathsf{Ints}(N) \; \exists! x \in \mathsf{Ints}(ST) : name(x) = name(y) \; \wedge$$
$$\forall o_y \in \mathsf{Ops}(y) \; \exists! o_x \in \mathsf{Ops}(x) : o_x \equiv_o o_y$$

*where* $\mathsf{Ops}(.)$ *denotes the set of operations of an interface and where*
$o_x \equiv_o o_y$ *if and only if* $name(o_x) = name(o_y)$ *and*

$\forall a \in \mathsf{I}(o_x), \exists! b \in \mathsf{I}(o_y) : name(a) = name(b) \wedge type(a) = type(b)$, *and*
$\forall b \in \mathsf{I}(o_y), \exists! a \in \mathsf{I}(o_x) : name(a) = name(b) \wedge type(a) = type(b)$, *and*
$\forall a \in \mathsf{O}(o_x), \exists! b \in \mathsf{O}(o_y) : name(a) = name(b) \wedge type(a) = type(b)$, *and*
$\forall b \in \mathsf{O}(o_y), \exists! a \in \mathsf{O}(o_x) : name(a) = name(b) \wedge type(a) = type(b)$

*where* $\mathsf{I}(o)$ *and* $\mathsf{O}(o)$ *denote the input and output parameters of operation* $o$.

It is easy to observe that the notion of exact matching is quite strict, as illustrated by the following example.

*Example 1.* Consider *NodeTypes* $N1$ and $N2$ and *ServiceTemplate* $ST$ of Fig. 2, where $C$ and $Csup$ denote sets of capabilities, $R$ and $Rsub$ denote sets of requirements, $p_j$ a property, $i_j$ an interface, $o_j$ an operation, and where policies and operation parameters are omitted for readability. Suppose that $ST$ exactly matches $N1$ (viz., $ST \equiv N1$) and that $N2$ differs from $N1$ since it exposes "more" requirements than $N1$ and "less" capabilities, properties and operations than $N1$. While, according to Defs. 1—4, $ST$ cannot exactly match $N2$ (viz., $ST \not\equiv N2$), a less strict definition of matching should allow $ST$ to match also $N2$, as we are going to discuss in the next section. □

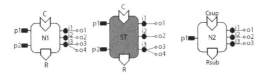

**Fig. 2.** Exact matching examples

### 3.2  Plug-in Matching

Intutively speaking, a *ServiceTemplate* plug-in matches a *NodeType* if the former "requires less" and "offers more" than the latter. As in Def. 1, the following definition specifies when a *ServiceTemplate* $ST$ plug-in matches a *NodeType* $N$ in terms of the requirements, capabilities, policies, properties and interfaces of $ST$ and $N$. As *NodeTypes* do not specify concrete policies (just applicable policies), the matching of policies ($\equiv_{PO}$) is unchanged.

**Definition 5.** *A ServiceTemplate $ST$ plug-in matches a NodeType $N$ ($ST \simeq N$) if and only if:*

   (1)  $\mathsf{Reqs}(ST) \simeq_R \mathsf{Reqs}(N)$ *and*
   (2)  $\mathsf{Caps}(ST) \simeq_C \mathsf{Caps}(N)$ *and*
   (3)  $\mathsf{Pols}(ST) \equiv_{PO} \mathsf{Pols}(N)$ *and*
   (4) $\mathsf{Props}(ST) \simeq_{PR} \mathsf{Props}(N)$ *and*
   (5)  $\mathsf{Ints}(ST) \simeq_I \mathsf{Ints}(N)$.

Intuitively speaking, a *ServiceTemplate* must expose "less" requirements than a *NodeType*. According to [14], names of requirements can be ignored, and types do not need to strictly coincide. In the following we write $t' \geq t$ when type $t'$ extends[4] or is equal to $t$.

**Definition 6.** *Let $N$ be a* NodeType *and let $ST$ be a* ServiceTemplate. *Then:*
$\mathsf{Reqs}(ST) \simeq_R \mathsf{Reqs}(N)$ *iff* $\forall x \in \mathsf{Reqs}(ST) \; \exists y \in \mathsf{Reqs}(N) : type(y) \geq type(x)$.

Dually, a *ServiceTemplate* must expose "more" capabilities and properties of a *NodeType*. According to [14], names of capabilities can be ignored, and types do not need to strictly coincide.

**Definition 7.** *Let $N$ be a* NodeType *and let $ST$ be a* ServiceTemplate. *Then:*
$\mathsf{Caps}(ST) \simeq_C \mathsf{Caps}(N)$ *iff* $\forall y \in \mathsf{Caps}(N) \; \exists x \in \mathsf{Caps}(ST) : type(x) \geq type(y)$.
$\mathsf{Props}(ST) \simeq_{PR} \mathsf{Props}(N)$ *iff* $\mathsf{XMLtype}(\mathsf{Props}(ST)) \geq \mathsf{XMLtype}(\mathsf{Props}(N))$.

Finally, a *ServiceTemplate* must expose all the operations exposed by a *Node-Type*. The matching can focus on operations and abstract from (names of) interfaces.

**Definition 8.** *Let $N$ be a* NodeType *and let $ST$ be a* ServiceTemplate. *Then:*
$\mathsf{Ints}(ST) \simeq_I \mathsf{Ints}(N)$ *iff* $\forall y, o_y : y \in \mathsf{Ints}(N) \wedge o_y \in \mathsf{Ops}(y)$
$$\exists x, o_x : x \in \mathsf{Ints}(ST) \wedge o_x \in \mathsf{Ops}(x) : \; o_x \equiv_o o_y.$$

It is worth noting that when a *ServiceTemplate* $ST$ plug-in matches a *NodeType* then $ST$ can be easily adapted into a new *ServiceTemplate* $ST'$ that exactly matches that *NodeType*. Such $ST'$ is built by creating a new *ServiceTemplate* having $ST$ as its only node, and by simply exposing (via the *BoundaryDefinitions*) the capabilities, policies, properties, and interfaces of the *NodeType* to be matched. If requirements plug-in match (but do not exactly match) then a dummy *echo* node is introduced to (artificially) extend the set of requirements of $ST$ so as to expose the same requirements of the *NodeType* to be matched.

*Example 2.* Example 1 illustrated a *ServiceTemplate* $ST$ that cannot exactly match a *NodeType* $N2$ since the latter exposes "more" requirements and "less" capabilities, properties and operations than the former. Since $ST$ exposes one property ($p2$) and one operation ($o4$) more than $N2$, we have that $\mathsf{Props}(ST) \simeq_{PR} \mathsf{Props}(N)$ and $\mathsf{Ints}(ST) \simeq_{PR} \mathsf{Ints}(N)$ by Defs. 7 and 8, respectively. Therefore, if $R \simeq_R Rsub$ and $C \simeq_R Csup$ hold too, then $ST$ plug-in matches $N2$ ($ST \simeq N2$). Figure 3 illustrates how *ServiceTemplate* $ST$ can be adapted so as to exactly match *NodeType* $N2$.

Consider now *NodeType* $N3$ of Fig. 3, which differs from $N2$ only since it exposes property $pA$ instead of property $p1$. While, according to Def. 7, $ST$ cannot plug-in match $N3$ ($ST \not\simeq N3$), if $p1$ and $pA$ were (syntactically) different names for the same property and if the type of $p$ were "compatible" with the type of $pA$, then a less strict definition of matching should allow $ST$ to match also $N3$, as we are going to discuss in the next section. □

---

[4] More precisely, if $t$ and $t'$ are TOSCA elements then $t'$ extends $t$ if $t'$ is (directly or undirectly) `DerivedFrom` $t$. If $t$ and $t'$ are instead XML types then the standard notion of XML extension applies.

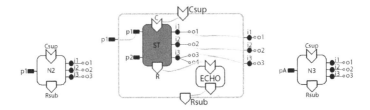

**Fig. 3.** Plug-in matching examples

### 3.3 Flexible Matching

We now further extend the definition of matching of a *ServiceTemplate* with a *NodeType* in order to ignore non-relevant syntactic differences between names of features. Since the semantics of requirements, capabilities and policies depends only on types, the following definition extends Def. 5 only on properties and interfaces.

**Definition 9.** *A* ServiceTemplate *ST flexibly matches a* NodeType *N* (*ST* ∼ *N* ) *if and only if:*

   (1)  $\mathsf{Reqs}(ST) \simeq_R \mathsf{Reqs}(N)$  *and*
   (2)  $\mathsf{Caps}(ST) \simeq_C \mathsf{Caps}(N)$  *and*
   (3)  $\mathsf{Pols}(ST) \equiv_{PO} \mathsf{Pols}(N)$  *and*
   (4) $\mathsf{Props}(ST) \sim_{PR} \mathsf{Props}(N)$ *and*
   (5)  $\mathsf{Ints}(ST) \sim_I \mathsf{Ints}(N)$.

We assume cloud services to be equipped with ontology-based descriptions of their functionalities [13]. In particular we assume *NodeTypes* and *ServiceTemplates* to include ontology-based annotations associated with the names of their properties and operations. We use the notation $n \bowtie n'$ to denote that a name $n$ is semantically equivalent[5] to a name $n'$.

A *ServiceTemplate* must expose all properties of a *NodeType*. Names of properties can be semantically equivalent, and types of properties do not need to stricly coincide.

**Definition 10.** *Let N be a* NodeType *and ST a* ServiceTemplate. *Then:*

$\mathsf{Props}(ST) \sim_{PR} \mathsf{Props}(N)$ *iff* $\forall y \in \mathsf{Props}(N)\ \exists x \in \mathsf{Props}(ST)$:
$$name(x) \bowtie name(y) \ \wedge \ type(x) \geq type(y).$$

A *ServiceTemplate* must also expose all the operations exposed by a *NodeType*. Names of operations can be ignored, while names of operation parameters can be semantically equivalent and their types do not need to strictly coincide.

---

[5] In this paper we abstract from a specific implementation of (cross) ontology match-making (like, e.g., [8] or [11]).

**Definition 11.** *Let $N$ be a* NodeType *and let $ST$ be a* ServiceTemplate. *Then:*
$\mathsf{Ints}(ST) \sim_I \mathsf{Ints}(N)$ *iff* $\forall y, o_y : y \in \mathsf{Ints}(N) \wedge o_y \in \mathsf{Ops}(y)$
$$\exists x, o_x : x \in \mathsf{Ints}(ST) \wedge o_x \in \mathsf{Ops}(x) : \ o_x \sim_o o_y.$$
*where $o_x \sim_o o_y$ if and only if*
$\quad |\mathsf{I}(o_x)| = |\mathsf{I}(o_y)|$ *and*
$\quad |\mathsf{O}(o_x)| = |\mathsf{O}(o_y)|$ *and*
$\quad \forall a \in \mathsf{I}(o_x), \exists! b \in \mathsf{I}(o_y) : name(a) \bowtie name(b) \wedge type(b) \geq type(a)$ *and*
$\quad \forall b \in \mathsf{O}(o_y), \exists! a \in \mathsf{O}(o_x) : name(a) \bowtie name(b) \wedge type(a) \geq type(b).$

In Sect.3.2 we illustrated how a *ServiceTemplate ST* that plug-in matches a *NodeType* can be easily adapted so as to exactly match that *NodeType*. The same holds for flexible matching, that is, a *ServiceTemplate ST* that fexibly matches a *NodeType* can be easily adapted into a new *ServiceTemplate ST′* that exactly matches that *NodeType*. As for the case of plug-in matching, *ST′* is built by creating a new *ServiceTemplate* having *ST* as its only node, and by simply exposing (via the *BoundaryDefinitions*) the capabilities, policies, properties, and interfaces of the *NodeType* to be matched. If requirements flexibly match (but do not exactly match) then a dummy *echo* node is introduced to (artificially) extend the set of requirements of *ST* so as to expose the same requirements of *NodeType* to be matched. Moreover, differently from plug-in adaptation, flexible adaptation may rename properties as well as interfaces, operations, and operation parameters.

*Example 3.* Example 2 illustrated a *ServiceTemplate ST* that cannot plug-in match a *NodeType N3* since *ST* exposes a property $p1$ different from property $pA$ exposed by *N3*. It is easy to see that Def. 10 permits *ST* to flexibly match *N3* (viz., $ST \sim N3$) if the type of $p1$ extends or is equal to the type of $pA$ and if $p1$ and $pA$ —even if syntactically different—refer to the same property (viz., $name(p1) \bowtie name(pA)$). Figure 4 illustrates how *ST* can be adapted so as to exactly match *N3*, by letting the new *ServiceTemplate ST′* expose also the renamed property $pA$. □

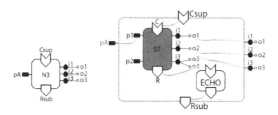

**Fig. 4.** Flexible matching example

*Example 4.* Suppose that a cloud application developer needs to emply a *WeatherAppType NodeType* (Fig. 5), whose interface *getTemp* exposes a homonym operation with *country* and *city* as input parameters, and *perceivedTemperature* as output parameter: *getTemp*: {*country,city*} → {*perceivedTemperature*}. Suppose also that a *ServiceTemplate ST* is available, and that it exhibits an interface *GetWeather* which exposes the operations:

- *TemperatureAndHumidity*: {*country,city*} → {*temperature, humidity*}
- *Wind*: {*country,city*} → {*windSpeed*}
- *Weather*: {*country,city*} → {*sky, temperature, humidity, windSpeed*}
- *ComputePerceived*: {*temperature, humidity, windSpeed*} → {*perceivedTemp*}

with *perceivedTemp* ⋈ *perceivedTemperature*[6].

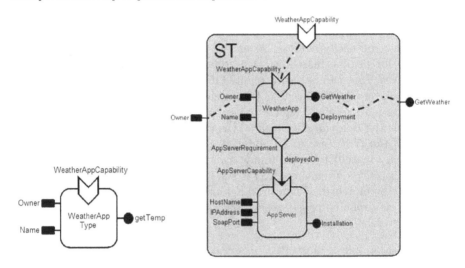

**Fig. 5.** *ServiceTemplate* that cannot flexibly match a *NodeType*

It is easy to see that while *ST* capabilities exactly match *WeatherAppType* ca-pabilties, *ST* properties and interfaces cannot flexibly match *WeatherAppType*'s ones since *WeatherAppType* is exposing one property more (*Name*) than *ST* and since *ST* does not offer operation *getTemp* exposed by *WeatherAppType*. Still, one may observe that property *Name* may correspond to one of the properties of an internal node of *ST* and that operation *getTemp* might be offered by *ST* by suitably combing (some of) its operations. This suggests that a "white-box" definition of matching could allow *ST* to match *WeatherAppType*, as we are go-ing to discuss in the next section.    □

### 3.4  White-Box Matching

When a *ServiceTemplate ST* cannot flexibly match a *NodeType* because of some missing requirement, capability, policy, or operation, *ST* may include such miss-ing elements internally, wihout exposing them on its boundaries.

As for the previous definitions of matching, the following definition specifies when a *ServiceTemplate ST* white-box matches a *NodeType N* in terms of the

---

[6] For the sake of simplicity in this example we assume that $name(x)$ ⋈ $name(y)$ implies $type(x) = type(y)$.

requirements, capabilities, policies, properties and interfaces of $ST$ and $N$. As we already observed in Sect.3.2, intuitively speaking, a *ServiceTemplate* $ST$ must expose "less" requirements than a *NodeType*. Moreover, *NodeTypes* do not specify concrete policies. For these reasons, the following definition extends Def. 9 only on capabilities, properties and interfaces.

**Definition 12.** *A* ServiceTemplate *$ST$ white-box matches a* NodeType *$N$ ($ST \square N$) if and only if:*

   (1)  $\mathsf{Reqs}(ST) \simeq_R \mathsf{Reqs}(N)$  *and*
   (2)  $\mathsf{Caps}(ST) \square_C \mathsf{Caps}(N)$  *and*
   (3)  $\mathsf{Pols}(ST) \equiv_{PO} \mathsf{Pols}(N)$  *and*
   (4) $\mathsf{Props}(ST) \square_{PR} \mathsf{Props}(N)$ *and*
   (5)  $\mathsf{Ints}(ST)\ \square_I\ \mathsf{Ints}(N)$.

The following definition extends the matching of capabilities and properties (Defs. 7 and 10) to consider also the internal nodes of a *ServiceTemplate*. We denote by $ST \to elem$ the fact that $elem$ is an internal element of $ST$.

**Definition 13.** *Let $N$ be a* NodeType *and let $ST$ be a* ServiceTemplate. *Then:*

$\mathsf{Caps}(ST)\square_C\mathsf{Caps}(N)$ *iff* $\forall y \in \mathsf{Caps}(N)\ \exists x :$
      $(x \in \mathsf{Caps}(ST)$
      $\vee$
      $(\exists E : ST \to E \wedge E\ is\ NodeTemplate \wedge x \in \mathsf{Caps}(E)))$
   $\wedge$
   $(type(x) \geq type(y))$.

$\mathsf{Props}(ST)\square_C\mathsf{Props}(N)$ *iff* $\forall y \in \mathsf{Props}(N)\ \exists x :$
      $(x \in \mathsf{Props}(ST)$
      $\vee$
      $(\exists E : ST \to E \wedge (E\ is\ NodeTemplate\ or\ RelationshipTemplate)$
               $\wedge\ x \in \mathsf{Props}(E)))$
   $\wedge$
   $(name(x) \bowtie name(y) \wedge type(x) \geq type(y))$.

The following definition extends the matching of operations (Def. 11) to consider also operations that a *ServiceTemplate* can feature by combining its operations in a suitable plan.

**Definition 14.** *Let $N$ be a* NodeType, *let $ST$ be a* ServiceTemplate, *and let $\Pi(ST)$ the set of all possible plans combining $ST$ operations. Then:*

$\mathsf{Ints}(ST)\square_I\mathsf{Ints}(N)$ *iff* $\forall y, o_y : y \in \mathsf{Ints}(N) \wedge o_y \in \mathsf{Ops}(y):$
   $(\exists x, o_x : x \in \mathsf{Ints}(ST) \wedge o_x \in \mathsf{Ops}(x) \wedge o_x \sim_o o_y)$
   $\vee$
   $(\exists p : p \in \Pi(ST) \wedge [p] \sim_o o_y)$

*where $[p]$ is the operation modelling the overall input-output behaviour of plan $p$.*

$FindOperations(Ops, op, selectedOperations, needed, available)$ {
1    $needed = \{x \mid x \in needed \land \nexists y \in available : y \triangleright x\}$;
2    **if** $needed = \emptyset$
3      **then return** $selectedOperations$;
4      **else** {
5        $c = \textbf{choose}(needed)$;
6        $needed = needed \setminus \{c\}$;
7        $opSet = \{o \in Ops \mid \exists d \in \mathsf{O}(o) : d \triangleright c\}$;
8        **if** $opSet = \emptyset$
9          **then fail**;
10          **else foreach** $o \in opSet$ **do** {
11            $selectedOperations = selectedOperations \cup \{o\}$;
12            **if** $nonMinimal(selectedOperations, op)$
13              **then fail**;
14              **else** {
15                $available = available \cup \mathsf{O}(o)$;
16                $needed = needed \cup \mathsf{I}(o)$;
17                $FindOperations(Ops, op, selectedOperations, needed, available)$
18              }
19          }
20      }
21 }

**Fig. 6.** Algorithm to discover sets of operations that can be composed into plans featuring the input-output behaviour of a given operation

The existence of a plan that suitably combines a set of operations into an input-output behaviour equivalent to a given operation can be determined by adapting the ontology-aware discovery algorithm of [3].

The $FindOperations$ algorithm (Fig. 6), given a set of available operations $Ops$, returns a set of $selectedOperations \subseteq Ops$ that can be composed into a plan featuring the input-output behaviour of a given operation $op$. The algorithm inputs a set of available operations $Ops$, the operation $op$ to be simulated, a (initially empty) set of $selectedOperations$, the set $needed$ of outputs to be generated (initially the outputs $\mathsf{O}(op)$ of $op$), and the set of $available$ outputs (initially the inputs $\mathsf{I}(op)$ of $op$). First, if the set of $available$ outputs includes an output "equal to or more general than" some $needed$ output $z$, then $z$ is removed from the set of $needed$ outputs (line 1). The notation $y \triangleright x$ stands for $name(y) \bowtie name(x)$ and $type(y) \geq type(x)$. Then, if there are no missing outputs to be generated the current set of $selectedOperations$ is returned (lines 2-3). Otherwise, a missing output $c$ is nondeterministically chosen[7] and removed from the set of missing outputs (lines 5 and 6). The algorithm then checks (lines 7 and 8) whether there is at least one operation in $Ops$ that produces an output equal to or more general than $c$. If there is no such operation then (the instance of) the algorithm fails

---

[7] Execution of **choose** forks a new instance of the algorithm for each possible choice.

(line 9). Otherwise for each operation $o$ in $Ops$ producing an output equal to or more general than $c$, $o$ is added to the current set of *selectedOperations* (line 11). If the obtained set of *selectedOperations* is not minimal[8] then (the instance of) the algorithm fails (lines 12 and 13). Otherwise the set of *available* outputs is extended with the outputs of $o$ (line 15), and the set of *needed* outputs is extended (line 16) with the inputs of $o$. Finally, the algorithm recurs (line 17) on the new set of *selectedOperations*, and of *needed* and *available* outputs.

It is worth noting that when a *ServiceTemplate* $ST$ white-box matches a *NodeType* $N$ then $ST$ can be adapted into a new *ServiceTemplate* $ST'$ that exactly matches that *NodeType*. Differently from the cases of plug-in and flexible matching, the *BoundaryDefinitions* of $ST$ are first extended in order to expose the capabilities, properties or plans internal to $ST$ that were detected by the white-box matching. The obtained *ServiceTemplate* $ST_{temp}$ flexibly matches *NodeType* $N$, and the adaptation described in Sect. 3.3 can be now applied to build a *ServiceTemplate* $ST'$ having $ST_{temp}$ as its only node, and by simply exposing (via the *BoundaryDefinitions*) the capabilities, policies, properties, and interfaces of the *NodeType* $N$ to be matched. If requirements plug-in match (but do not exactly match) then a dummy *echo* node is introduced to (artificially) extend the set of requirements of $ST$ so as to expose the same requirements of the *NodeType* to be matched.

*Example 5.* Example 4 illustrated a *ServiceTemplate* $ST$ that cannot flexibly match a *WeatherAppType NodeType* since the latter exposes one property more (*Name*) than the former, and since $ST$ does not offer operation *getTemp*. We observe that Def. 12 permits $ST$ to white-box match *WeatherAppType* (viz., $ST \square WeatherAppType$) if, for instance, property *HostName* of node *AppServer* of $ST$ is semantically equivalent to property *Name* of *WeatherAppType*, and if there exists a plan $p$ combining some $ST$ operations, whose input-output behaviour simulates operation *getTemp* (viz., $[p] \sim_o getTemp$). It is easy to observe that algorithm *findOperations* returns two minimal sets of operations of $ST$ that can simulate *getTemp*, namely {*TemperatureAndHumidity*, *Wind*, *ComputePerceived*} and {*Weather*, *ComputePerceived*}, which can be used to build three plans that simulate the input-output behaviour of operation *getTemp*:

$p_1 = TemperatureAndHumidity.Wind.ComputePerceived$
$p_2 = Wind.TemperatureAndHumidity.ComputePerceived$
$p_3 = Weather.ComputePerceived$

Figure 7 illustrates the adaptation of $ST$. The *BoundaryDefinitions* of $ST$ are first extended to expose property *HostName* of node *AppServer* as property *Name*, and to expose one of the plans $p_1$, $p_2$ or $p_3$ as operation *getTemp*. Then, the resulting *ServiceTemplate* $ST''$ is incapsulated into a new *ServiceTemplate* $ST'$

---

[8] Because of space limitations, we do not include here the definition of the *nonMinimal* function, which can be found in [3]. Following [3], a set $S$ of operations can simulate the input-output behaviour of an operation $op$ iff (1) $\forall x \in O(op) \exists y \in \bigcup_{o \in S} O(o) : y \triangleright x$, and (2) $\forall y \in \bigcup_{o \in S} I(o) \exists x \in (\bigcup_{o \in S} O(o) \cup I(op)) : x \triangleright y$. A set $S$ of operations that can emulate an operation $op$ is minimal iff $\nexists S' \subset S$ that can emulate $op$.

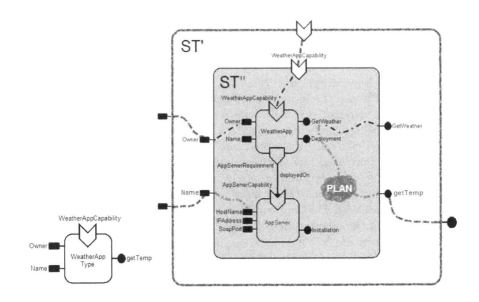

**Fig. 7.** White-box adaptation of a *Service Template*

so as to expose only the capabilities, properties, and interfaces of the *Weather-AppType NodeType* to be matched.                                      □

## 4   Related Work

As we mentioned at the beginning of Sect. 3, our work started from the observation that while the matching between *Service Templates* and *NodeTypes* is indicated in [15] as a way to instantiate abstract TOSCA *NodeTypes*, no definition of *matching* is given in either [14] or [15]. A concrete definition of matching for TOSCA is used [17] to define a way to merge TOSCA services by matching entire portions of their topology templates. The definition of matching of single service components employed in [17] is however very strict, as two service components are considered to match only if they expose the same qualified name. Our work aims to contribute to the TOSCA specification by proposing four definitions of matching between *Service Templates* and *NodeTypes*, each identifying larger sets of *Service Templates* that can be adapted so as to (exactly) match a *NodeType*.

The problem of how to match (Web) services has been extensively studied in recent years. Many approaches are ontology-aware [13], like for instance the ontology-aware matchmaker for OWL-S services described in [8]. Other approaches are behaviour-aware, like the (ontology-aware) trace-based matching of YAWL services defined in [4], the (ontology-aware) behavioural congruence for OWL-S services defined in [2], or the graph transformation based matching defined in [5] and the heuristic black-box matching described in [7] for WS-BPEL processes. The main difference between the aforementioned approaches and ours is the type of information considered when matching single nodes. The matching levels considered for instance in [8] and [7] are all defined in terms of input and output data, while we consider also technology requirements and capabilities, properties and policies.

On the other hand, many proposals of QoS-aware service matching have been developed, like for instance [10] or [12]. Generally speaking, the notion of matching defined in the present paper differs from most QoS-aware matching approaches since it compares *types* rather than actual *values* of extra-functional features like QoS. A type-based definition of matching is defined in [6] to type check "stream flows" for interactive distributed multimedia applications. While the context of [6] is different from ours, two of the matching conditions considered in [6] resemble our notions of exact and plug-in matching, even if for simpler service abstractions.

Summing up, to the best of our knowledge, our definition of matching is the first definition of (TOSCA) node matching to take into account both functional and extra-functional features, by relying both on types and on ontologies to overcome non-relevant syntactic information.

## 5   Concluding Remarks

In this paper, after defining the notion of *exact matching* between TOSCA *ServiceTemplate*s and *NodeType*s, we have defined three other types of matching (*plug-in*, *flexible* and *white-box*), each permitting to ignore larger sets of non-relevant syntactic differences when type-checking *ServiceTemplate*s with respect to NodeTypes. To allow exploiting the new notions of matching not only for type-checking but also for node instantiation, we have also described how a *ServiceTemplate* that *plug-in*, *flexibly* or *white-box* matches a NodeType can be suitably adapted so as to *exactly* match it.

As we already mentioned in Sect. 1, the results presented in this paper intend to contribute to the formal definition of TOSCA. We already developed a proof-of-concept implementation of exact and plug-in matching. Furthermore, the different types of matching defined in this paper can be fruitfully integrated in the TOSCA implementations that are currently under development — such as the Winery editor [9] and the OpenTOSCA IDE [1] — in order to enhance their type-checking capabilities.

The definitions of matching presented in this paper can be extended to take into account, besides *types*, also actual *values* of policies and properties, so as to allow verifying also the compliance of a *ServiceTemplate* with *NodeTemplate*s that instantiate a matching *NodeType*. This is actually the scope of our immediate future work.

## References

1. Binz, T., Breitenbücher, U., Haupt, F., Kopp, O., Leymann, F., Nowak, A., Wagner, S.: OpenTOSCA – A Runtime for TOSCA-based Cloud Applications. In: Proceedings of ISCOC 2013. Springer (2013)

2. Bonchi, F., Brogi, A., Corfini, S., Gadducci, F.: A Net-based Approach to Web Services Publication and Replaceability. Fundam. Informaticae 94(3-4), 205–309 (2009)
3. Brogi, A., Corfini, S.: Behaviour-aware discovery of Web service compositions. International Journal of Web Service Research 4(3), 1–25 (2007)
4. Brogi, A., Popescu, R.: Service Adaptation through Trace Inspection. International Journal of Business Process Integration and Management 2(1), 9–16 (2007)
5. Corrales, J.C., Grigori, D., Bouzeghoub, M.: BPEL processes matchmaking for service discovery. In: Meersman, R., Tari, Z. (eds.) OTM 2006. LNCS, vol. 4275, pp. 237–254. Springer, Heidelberg (2006)
6. Eliassen, F., Mehus, S.: Type Checking Stream Flow Endpoints. In: Middleware 1998, pp. 305–320 (1998)
7. Eshuis, R., Grefen, P.: Structural Matching of BPEL Processes. In: Proceedings of the Fifth European Conference on Web Services (ECOWS 2007), pp. 171–180 (2007)
8. Klusch, M., Fries, B., Sycara, K.: OWLS-MX: A hybrid Semantic Web service matchmaker for OWL-S services. Web Semantics: Science, Services and Agents on the World Wide Web archive 7(2), 121–133 (2009)
9. Kopp, O., Binz, T., Breitenbücher, U., Leymann, F.: Winery – Modeling Tool for TOSCA-based Cloudq Applications. In: Proceedings of ISCOC 2013. Springer (2013)
10. Mahdikhani, F., Hashemi, M.R., Sirjani, M.: QoS Aspects in Web Services Compositions. In: Proceedings of IEEE SOSE 2008, pp. 239–244 (2008)
11. Martinez-Gil, J., Navas-Delgado, I., Aldana-Montes, J.F.: MaF: An Ontology Matching Framework. Journal of Universal Computer Science 18(3), 194–217 (2012)
12. Mokhtar, S.B., Preuveneers, D., Georgantas, N., Issarny, V., Berbers, Y.: EASY: Efficient semAntic Service discoverY in pervasive computing environments with QoS and context support. Journal of Systems and Software 81(5), 785–808 (2008)
13. O'Sullivan, D., Lewis, D.: Semantically driven service interoperability for pervasive computing. In: Proceedings of ACM MobiDE 2003, pp. 17–24 (2003)
14. OASIS TOSCA TC. Topology and Orchestration Specification for Cloud Applications Version 1.0 (2013),
    http://docs.oasis-open.org/tosca/TOSCA/v1.0/TOSCA-v1.0.pdf
15. OASIS TOSCA TC. Topology and Orchestration Specification for Cloud Applications (TOSCA) Primer Version 1.0 (2013), http://docs.oasis-open.org/tosca/tosca-primer/v1.0/tosca-primer-v1.0.pdf
16. Petcu, D., Macariu, G., Panica, S., Craciun, C.: Portable Cloud Applications - From Theory to Practice. Future Generation Computer Systems 29(6), 1417–1430 (2012)
17. Weiss, A.: Merging of TOSCA Cloud Topology Templates. Master thesis, Institute of Architecture of Application Systems, University of Stuttgart (2012), http://elib.uni-stuttgart.de/opus/volltexte/2012/7932/pdf/MSTR_3341.pdf

# First Hand Developer Experiences of Social Devices

Niko Mäkitalo, Timo Aaltonen, and Tommi Mikkonen

Department of Pervasive Computing
Tampere University of Technology, Tampere, Finland
PL 553, 33101 Tampere, Finland
{niko.makitalo, timo.aaltonen, tommi.mikkonen}@tut.fi

**Abstract.** Contemporary Internet connected devices, such as tablets and mobile phones, have excellent computing power, which creates a possibility for complex, cooperative multi-device platforms. We have introduced a concept of Social Devices and its reference implementation Social Devices Platform. The system offers an intuitive way to build interactions between co-located people and their devices, and then trigger these when people meet face-to-face. In this paper we study how developers experience the concept and the platform. We hired a four-person team to design and implement a multiplayer game, and afterwards interviewed the team members about their experiences. Based on their feedback we evaluate the system. Moreover, we raise some open questions that require attention and more research in the future.

## 1 Introduction

Custom-built native apps have become one of the dominant ways people use software. In the mobile space, the time span of the users' actions is usually significantly shorter than in the desktop space; the users wish to perform rapid, focused actions instead of long-lasting sessions; actions must be simple yet focused, and they must be accomplished with ease, using only a minimal number of keystrokes or finger presses, often while the user is walking, driving a car or is somehow otherwise distracted by other activities. The different usage modalities and smaller screen sizes have a significant impact on application design; generic web pages geared towards laptop or desktop computer users are not usually ideal for mobile use.

While numerous apps for mobile devices are meant to be social – think about mobile Facebook and Twitter clients, Instagram, and Foursquare – the actual means for programming follow the traditional device centric development approach. For instance, in the context of iPhone, apps are defined as individual applications that are separately activated by the user, and communication patterns follow the practices that have been developed for conventional networking.

The benefits of using an already established application model are many. Users are accustomed to installing and activating applications, and appear to be willing to do so. From the developer perspective, development tools and the

C. Canal and M. Villari (Eds.): ESOCC 2013, CCIS 393, pp. 233–243, 2013.
© Springer-Verlag Berlin Heidelberg 2013

programming model are already familiar, and although at times some of the design details appear cumbersome and impractical, the fact that these issues are similar in most settings have taught us to circumvent them in designs.

However, smart devices have excellent computing power and connectivity and at the same time are used for various purposes. Moreover, we have learned to accept that mobile devices play more and more proactive role in daily activities. This creates the possibility for complex, cooperative multi-device programs, for which current programming paradigms are not well-suited. Hence, we have tackled the above problem by introducing a new paradigm: an action-oriented programming model for pervasive computing [1]. Actions are proactively initiated pieces of functionality, which synchronize and coordinate joint behavior of several devices. The action-oriented programming model is realized within the cloud-based Social Devices Platform. So far, the technical feasibility of the approach has been demonstrated in our earlier papers [3], together with the description of applications that have been developed using our platform. However, the developer perspective has not been addressed. At the same time, the developer experience is a key issue in obtaining a large number of applications that are available for end users.

In this paper, we present experiences gathered from outside developers who have been using the platform to develop an application during Spring 2013. The paper includes both the developers' opinion about the concept as well as experiences in programming using it. The application was developed in cooperation with Demola[1], an innovation instrument targeted for fostering innovation and experimenting with radical ideas.

The rest of this paper is structured as follows. In Section 2, we discuss the background of this work. In Section 3 we introduce the developer team and their application. In Section 4 we present the results regarding developer experience, and list claims regarding the way of developing applications with the Social Devices platform. In Section 5 we briefly address related work, and in Section 6 we pinpoint some open issues. In Section 7, we draw some final conclusions.

## 2    Background

The concept of *Social Devices* and its reference implementation *Social Devices Platform (SDP)* was first introduced in [3]. The aim of Social Devices is to increase, facilitate, and enrich social interactions between people in various kinds of co-located and face-to-face situations. For example, when people meet, the devices can greet each other aloud to help people to remember each others' names, or the devices can automatically chance contact information when a group of businessmen meets. Also device-to-device interaction can be enriched: Social Devices can make otherwise invisible device interaction explicit to users. For instance, a mobile phone can say aloud to a car navigator where to go in addition to setting the destination based on a calendar entry. Moreover, Social Devices can be used for suggesting and proactively initiating social multiuser

---

[1] http://www.demola.fi

applications when like-minded are nearby. For example, when friends meets in cafeteria Social Devices can proactively suggest them to view photos if one of the friends has added a new album to Flickr and enabled photo sharing feature on her phone. Another obvious example of social applications are games that can be suggested for co-located people, for instance when people are traveling by the same bus or are in the same bar.

The Social Devices Platform currently runs in Amazon cloud, consisting a number of cloud services, as can be seen in Figure 1. The client side currently consists of Android devices and Python capable devices, such as Linux laptops and MeeGo phones. As the system infrastructure is cloud based, it abstracts the differences of the devices. However, instead of hiding or ignoring the different resources of each device, Social Devices accents the differences by regarding them as capabilities, which describe what a device can do. For instance, the device may have a TalkingDevice capability meaning that the device is equipped with text to speech translator. In addition to the existing capabilities, the platform allows developers to create their own new types of capabilities, which other users can then install in their devices.

The interactions between devices are defined in terms of Actions, which is a novel modular unit for describing how several co-located devices operate together. The Actions are defined with classes of Python programming language, and they contain a precondition and a body methods. The precondition is used for defining when the Action can actually take place and what is required from the participating devices. The body part is used for defining the device coordination logic with the help of device capabilities. Naturally, the platform also offers an easy way for developers to define their own Actions.

## 3 Experiment

To get input from developers who have no previous experience regarding the concept of Social Devices, we hired a four-person developer team from Demola. The team had a project manager, a graphic designer, and two software developers. The project manager and the graphic designer had only limited knowledge about software development, and also the two developers had no previous experience of pervasive system or mobile cloud development. The team was given free hands to develop what they wanted, and they came up with an idea about a set of mini Olympic Games, where users' avatars are zombies. Each zombie comes from different country, and hence has its stereotypic characteristics. The game was named as *Apocalympics*. See demo[2].

An example setting for a gaming scenario could be as follows: Alice and Bob don't know each other, although they travel daily by the same bus. Bob is interested in playing games and also likes zombie splatter movies. Alice also likes to play some games every now and then. Now, when Alice gets bored in the bus, she can indicate this to Social Devices Platform: By pressing a ZombieGame icon on her phone, she can challenge someone nearby to play with her. The Social Devices

---

[2] http://youtu.be/ZzhUiwO-v14

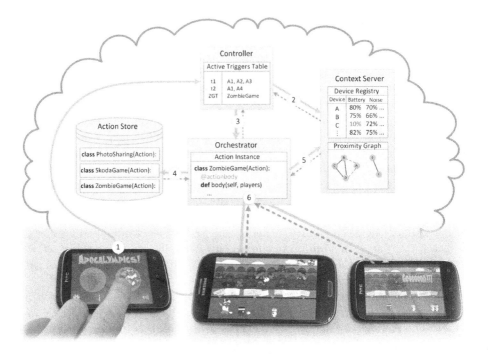

**Fig. 1.** The SDP architecture and work flow in Zombie game scenario

Client then sends a ZombieGameTrigger to Controller component (see phase #1, in Figure 1). The system knows what other Social Devices are near Alice as the clients gather proximity information that is based on Bluetooth signal strengths (RSSI), and periodically report this and other device state information to the Context Server.

The Controller component uses the proximity and state information, while it tries to find participants for the Action (see phase #2). As Bob happens to be in the same bus and has several likes of zombie movies in Facebook, the Controller chooses him as one of the players. Carol, who is also in the bus, is not selected to participate as her battery is almost dry. After collecting the players, the ZombieGameTrigger with the participants is send to the Orchestrator component (see phase #3). The Orchestrator fetches the Action body (see phase #4), and then allocates the devices for the ZombieGame action (see phase #5). Finally, it starts coordinating the devices (see phase 6). Now, if Bob wants he can of course decline from the gaming challenge.

Figure 2 shows how the team defined the game with the terms of Action. The total number of code lines was 240, but from Figure 2 some boilerplate code was omitted for brevity. The omitted parts mainly contained capability method calls that were related to the game initialization on the devices, such as selecting the country for the avatar. Also code for showing the winning screens and game selection were omitted, as well as three developer defined classes: Player, Game and Constant.

```
    class Apocalymbics(Action):
      # Player, Game and Constant class deifinitions omitted (11 rows)

      @actionprecondition
5     def precondition(self, players):
        return proximity(players, 15.0) and\
          haveFacebookLikes(players, ['Gaming', 'Zombies'])

      @actionbody
10    def body(self, players):
        # initializations, game and country selection omitted (66 rows)

        # Mainloop exists until less that 2 players
        while (len(players) > 1):
15        # Mini Game initializations omitted (14 rows)

          # GAME PLAY LOOP FOR EACH MINI GAME STARTS HERE
          if game == Game.gameSkullThrow:
            random.shuffle(players)
20
            for round in range(3):
              for player in players:
                player.device.zombieGame.startRound(round)

25            # Loop every player's turn of current round
              for currentPlayer in players:
                # Inform clients which player is in turn
                for player in players:
                  player.device.zombieGame.updateTurn(currentPlayer.number)
30
                # Get player's throw length
                currentPlayer.throwAngle = Constant.uninitialized
                while (currentPlayer.throwAngle == Constant.uninitialized):
                  currentPlayer.throwAngle = currentPlayer.device.\
35                zombieGame.getThrowAngle()

                # Inform everyone how far the player managed to throw
                for player in players:
                  player.device.zombieGame.showThrow(currentPlayer.number,\
40                currentPlayer.throwAngle)

                # Wait until every client has shown the throw
                for player in players:
                  ready = False
45                while not ready:
                    ready = player.device.zombieGame.isReady()

              # Winner Screen and next game choosing omitted (32 rows)

50      # Game ends
```

**Fig. 2.** The definition of the Apocalymics Action

The precondition (lines 5-7) shows that the Action can take place if the participating players are less than 15 meters apart from each other, and that they have
liked Gaming and Zombies on Facebook. The server side game and coordination
logic is defined in the body part of the Action (lines 9-50). For example, on lines
22-23 each player's device is commanded to start a new round on SkullThrow
mini game. On lines 32-35 the game waits until the player in turn has thrown the
skull, and on lines 39-40 this throw is then shown to other players. The communication behind the capability calls is taken care by the Orchestrator component,
and developers don't need to care about its dirty details.

# 4 Developer Experiences

In this section we review the experiences of the hired team, and evaluate the Social Devices concept and platform based on the team's feedback. The study was conducted by interviewing the team members after the project. The heterogeneous background of the members gave us an opportunity to get insight from different perspectives. With the project manager and the graphic designer we focused more on general and concept level questions. With the two software developers we focused more on the technical details, and tried to find out their understanding about Social Devices Platform development aspects.

## 4.1 Understandablity

The team was given a short five minute introduction of the Social Devices concept and platform in the first meeting. All members of the team agreed that the overall idea was easy to grasp. Everyone also agreed the the system was easy to explain for other people as well, for example in their networking pitch. However, the level of understanding seemed to vary between the members. On the one hand, it seems that the project manager and designer did not grasp all of the technical details of the system. On the other, it seems that this kind of technically detailed understanding was not even needed by them, as the concept seems to offer enough higher level abstractions. The developers, on the contrary, agreed that the system was also technically easy to grasp after we gave them a ten-minute presentation of the development aspects and technical details. One thing supports this claim is that the developers managed start implementing the game for Android phone almost immediately after the technical introduction, and on the following day had starting screen implemented. Moreover, the developers didn't have experience on Android development, and it follows that most of their time was spent on studying these things.

**Claim 1: Social Devices offers appropriate abstractions for developers.**

## 4.2 Acceptability

When asking from the team about the social acceptability of interactions that start proactively, the members agree that there might be some "shyness" among people, and add that probably people would start using proactive applications first with their family and friends. Based on their feedback, it seems that games would be an easily acceptable starting point for this type of proactive applications since they are not too serious, and many people also very willingly want to try out new types of games. They also say that applications that automatically and proactively help working in group (e.g. sharing schedules and notes) would be something that they would personally want to use.

The team had gotten enthusiastic feedback from other people while they had been introducing the system for third parties. People had generally liked the idea about using Bluetooth for detecting proximity of others, but some had also been a bit worried about their battery lives. According to the project manager some of his contacts want to hear about how the concept is handled in the future, and gave us contact information of a game studio that had gotten interested in our platform. The overall acceptability of the Social Devices concept is not in the scope of this paper, but instead will be reported separately based on our ongoing research[3].

**Claim 2: Social Devices is a socially inspiring concept.**

### 4.3   Coordination Aspects

According to the developers it was straight forwarded to coordinate the devices with the help of Social Devices platform and communication with the devices was made very easy. The developers also believe that the this kind of approach to coordinate the devices can be utilized in several other systems, in which a centralized communication point is needed to coordinate devices. However, they point out that a need for fast communication may limit the cases where the current implementation of the system can be utilized. In fact, the latency in communication was one of the reasons why the team chose to create turn–based game.

Currently the latency in device coordination is due to the cloud–based coordination paradigm. To reduce this lag we have considered complementing the system with Personal Network Area based coordination paradigm, which could be implemented on top of Bluetooth protocol for instance. In this paradigm one of the participating devices would be selected as a coordinator, which then would coordinate the other participants as well at itself. However, this would require support for Bluetooth or some other PAN protocol from the device, which all of the Social Devices don't necessarily have.

**Claim 3: Social Devices and Action–Oriented Programming Model offer appropriate means for coordinating functionalities in several devices.**

### 4.4   Programmability

Generally the developers liked the methods that Social Devices offers for implementing interactions. The concept of Action was described clear and the developers seemed to understand its purpose and features well. Constructing a similar application from scratch would have required concentrating on difficult connectivity and synchronization issues, whereas now, these are hidden by the concepts of the programming model.

The device capabilities also seemed to make sense as a unit of modularity. One of the developers describes them: *"The capabilities are pretty flexible and easy*

---

[3] http://www.cs.tut.fi/ihte/projects/CoSMo

*way for anyone to quickly enable games, applications, features etc. from available interfaces. It's like having a little library of things inside an application".*

Moreover, during their project the developers had couple of ideas how the concept of Action could be complemented. The first idea was that new devices could join in the Action during its execution. As we have had similar ideas, we would have wanted to implement this feature for the platform already during the project. Unfortunately, this wasn't possible due to timing reasons and thus remains as future work. The second idea was to complement the concept so that it would support concurrency inside Action processes: the body part of the Action could then contain multiple threads from which the devices could be coordinated parallel with other threads. The idea is intriguing but still requires further research. The downside of this kind of support for concurrency is that defining device coordination could become more complex.

**Claim 4: Social Devices' programming concept action is a clear unit of modularity.**

**Claim 5: Social Devices' programming concept capability is a "flexible and easy way for anyone to quickly enable games, applications, features".**

### 4.5 Reusability of Code

Based on our own experiences and also what can be seen from the team's approach to implement the game, it is hard to design generic capabilities that can be utilized in several different kinds of actions. For example the developed ZombieGame capability can only be utilized in different variants of the current game since so much of the game logic is implemented inside the capability, and not inside the Action. In future we try to research how the capabilities could be designed to be more generic.

### 4.6 Deployment Aspects

In the current implementation of the Social Devices Android client the capabilities can be dynamically loaded during the run time and enabled by the user's choices. The developers regarded the idea of loading the capabilities dynamically very good. However, they eventually encountered difficulties in using this feature which were mainly related to the limitations of Android platform: Android requires defining its Activities in Manifest-file before the application is compiled. This prevents defining and creating new interaction windows from capability code on runtime. Our own experiences are very similar to theirs, and hence this aspect requires also further research. This feature would also cause problems on other more closed platforms, like iOS and Windows Phone for instance.

The heterogeneity of devices also caused some problems. With cheap low–end devices the lack of memory caused their game to crash at times, but the developers were unanimous that this problem was not related to the Social Devices platform. They had also encountered problems with some 10" Android tablet which they were unable to solve. With other Android tablets and smart phones the game seems to work fine.

## 5   Related Work

Previously, the approaches to coordinate multiple devices have focused mainly on information presentation techniques (e.g., [2,4,5]), and multimedia synchronization (e.g., [6,5]). However, the approach in our work is different as we are not focusing on automating services in pre-defined locations, like in smart spaces for instance, but rather at coordinating devices wherever they are in near proximity of each other. We are also not focusing on generating user interfaces and coordinating them on devices as [2,4]. Instead, our focus is to make the devices interact and socialize independently, and to inform users about the ongoing operations.

## 6   Open Questions

In this section we raise some open questions of the Social Devices concept and current implementation of the system. The aspects raised here require more research and will remain as future work.

### Question 1: How Should Joint Behavior of Devices be Programmed?

Action has proven to be an excellent abstraction for coercing multi-party applications. However, still some aspects require more studying. How should the triggering condition be described; Is the current precondition decent or should there be a more easily computable function? What about body: Should there be threads? Is there a need for dynamic number of participants? How should the Action be modified to enable it? Does introducing a dynamic number of participants lead to a need for merging two running Actions to one (for example, two zombie games could be merged).

### Question 2: What Would be a Sufficient Set of Device Capabilities for Developers?

Capability describes a functionality that a device has. Our goal is to develop universal capabilities which can be utilized in many Actions. What would be a sufficient set of capabilities for developers? For example, the zombie game has been developed based on a single dedicated capability: ZombieGame. Which universal capabilities could it be based on?

### Question 3: How Should an Automatic Triggering of Apps be Carried Out?

Triggering is carried out half manually in the example. User simply pushes a button on her device, then the system uses proximity and state information to find possible participants for the Action. How much of this could be automated? What kind of strategies could be used for retrying to trigger the Action?

**Question 4: What are the Contexts Where the Apps can be Triggered?**

Social Devices applications are meant to be triggered in various kind of social contexts. How to define an appropriate one for each Action to take a place? What kind of different contexts there exists where the Actions could be triggered? How to deduce the context, and how to protect users' privacy?

**Question 5: How to Evaluate and Measure the Quality of Apps?**

The goal of the Social Devices Platform is to offer easy manner for developers to create new applications. On the other hand, the quality of application is very important thing to consider when proactively triggering applications for users. What aspects need to be considered when measuring the quality of the developed SDP applications?

Furthermore, we plan to test the system in a code camp with students, and hence need to set some kind of criteria for evaluating their applications. What aspects needs to be taken into account in this evaluation process? For example, is reusability of the capabilities relevant aspect? Should the amount of features (and the code) implemented on server side (in Action) versus the client side (in capabilities) be taken into account in the evaluation? Or should the applications be evaluated more like regular mobile applications, and try to conceal the distribution and platform specific aspects totally from the developers?

## 7    Conclusions

Instead of reflecting the interactive capabilities between different devices, the development of mobile apps follows the conventional development fashion. However, there are also different programming models that allow focusing on interactions, as we have demonstrated with our earlier work [3]. In this paper, we listed experiences from developers who were new to our platform to gather feedback on the feasibility of the model as well as the maturity of our platform.

In the future, we plan to execute a more excessive experiment in the form of a one-week code camp with students. The data reported in this paper will be used to improve the platform as well as the instructions that will be given to the participants. In addition, we plan to work on improving the methodology used for the evaluation process.

**Acknowledgements.** We thank the demola team: Trent Pancy, Mikko Järvelä, Teemu Avellan and Sonja-Maria Juslin. The research was funded by Academy of Finland[4] (264422).

---

[4] http://www.aka.fi/en-GB/A/

# References

1. Aaltonen, T., Myllärniemi, V., Raatikainen, M., Mäkitalo, N., Pääkkö, J.: An Action-Oriented Programming Model for Pervasive Computing in a Device Cloud. In: Asia-Pacific Software Engineering Conference (APSEC) (to appear, 2013)
2. Elting, C.: Orchestrating output devices: planning multimedia presentations for home entertainment with ambient intelligence. In: Proceedings of the 2005 Joint Conference on Smart Objects and Ambient Intelligence: Innovative Context-Aware Services: Usages and Technologies, sOc-EUSAI 2005, pp. 153–158. ACM, New York (2005)
3. Mäkitalo, N., Pääkkö, J., Raatikainen, M., Myllärniemi, V., Aaltonen, T., Leppänen, T., Männistö, T., Mikkonen, T.: Social Devices: Collaborative Co-Located Interactions in a Mobile Cloud. In: Proceedings of the 11th International Conference on Mobile and Ubiquitous Multimedia, MUM 2012, pp. 10:1–10:10. ACM, New York (2012)
4. Myers, B.A., Nichols, J., Wobbrock, J.O., Miller, R.C.: Taking handheld devices to the next level. Computer 37(12), 36–43 (2004)
5. Rekimoto, J.: Multiple-computer user interfaces: "beyond the desktop" direct manipulation environments. In: CHI 2000 Extended Abstracts on Human factors in Computing Systems, CHI EA 2000, pp. 6–7. ACM, New York (2000)
6. Xing, B., Seada, K., Venkatasubramanian, N.: Proximiter: Enabling mobile proximity-based content sharing on portable devices. In: Proceedings of the 2009 IEEE International Conference on Pervasive Computing and Communications, PERCOM 2009, pp. 1–3. IEEE Computer Society, Washington, DC (2009)

# Social Index: A Content Discovery Application for Ad Hoc Communicating Smart Phones

Janne Kulmala, Mikko Vataja, Saku Rautiainen,
Teemu Laukkarinen, and Marko Hännikäinen

Tampere University of Technology, Department of Pervasive Computing,
PO BOX 553, FI-33101 Tampere
janne.t.kulmala@iki.fi,
{mikko.vataja,saku.rautiainen,teemu.laukkarinen,marko.hannikainen}@tut.fi

**Abstract.** A modern smart phone contains detailed information about the owner through the phone book, music lists, and social media integration, which can be used to recommend new interesting content to the user. Combining this information with ad hoc peer-to-peer communication of the smart phones allows users to find new interesting content and persons in the proximity and exchange messages. Social Index allows users to anonymously find interesting new content in the proximity. The prototype Social Index application was tested with a simulator running anonymized Facebook profiles, and with real test users. All the test users found interesting people using the simulator.

**Keywords:** social application, smart phone, interest graph.

## 1 Introduction

A modern smart phone contains detailed personal information of the owner. Tight integration with Facebook, LinkedIn, Twitter and other social media allow mobile recommending applications that react depending on the context and the location of the owner. E.g., an application can recommend a nearby restaurant that concentrates on sea food and plays medieval music to a person, who prefers fish and is a medieval enthusiast. Also, ad hoc communication methods allow smart phones to discover each other and communicate directly from device to device without any centralized infrastructure [1]. When this communication scheme is combined with the available personal information, a new social media is formed: smart phone users can discover interesting new content and new people with the same interests in the proximity. Forming and mining an *interest graph* for the user allows application to hilight encountered content and persons that might be interesting ones.

This paper presents a novel Social Index concept for any ad hoc communicating smart phone. Social Index evaluates automatically an anonymized profile (called an *index*) for the smart phone user according to the interests, current context, and user feedback. Interests are mined from the globally unique social objects found from the mobile phone. The indexes are shared through the ad hoc

C. Canal and M. Villari (Eds.): ESOCC 2013, CCIS 393, pp. 244–253, 2013.
© Springer-Verlag Berlin Heidelberg 2013

communication and used to discover new interesting content from the physical world while preserving privacy. To name a few the content can be other people with same interests, a restaurant, an event, or an upcoming gig of the user's favorite band in a nearby event venue. The user provides feedback of the discoveries to the engine through the user interface, and the feedback is used to refine the index to provide more interesting discoveries. The user can interact with the new content via the Social Index user interface, e.g. share a contact card or chat with other users.

A prototype of Social Index was developed for the Nokia N9 mobile devices, and it uses an experimental WLAN mesh communication implemented by Nokia Research Center [2]. The prototype was tested with a social network simulator developed by the authors. 900 anonymous Facebook profiles were mined and used as an input for the simulations. Real persons were recruited for the user tests to use Social Index prototype in the simulations to find out user experiences and insights of using such application.

Social Index concept is a continuum to our previous work, where ad hoc communication software was tested with 250 Nokia N900 devices with real people [3]. The idea for the Social Index concept was realized from the results of this large user experience.

The paper is constructed as follows. Section 2 discusses the related work. Section 3 presents the design of Social Index. The simulator is presented in Section 4 and the user tests and their results are presented in following Section 5. Section 6 discusses the user privacy issues. Open issues are discussed in Section 7. Finally, Section 8 concludes the paper.

## 2   Related Work

Social Index differs from the related work in two major areas. First, Social Index concentrates on the interest, learning, and discovering new interesting content without constant harassment of the user or specifying to a single interest group. There are similar proposals, but they lack the automated mining and learning of the user. E.g. MobiSoft [7] requires that user teaches the system and gives privilege to newly encountered person to mine his profile in the beginning. Similarly, MobiClique [9] allows users to discover each other, friendify, and exchange messages, but it does not mine interesting content on the background.

Second, Social Index works without any central infrastructure. It ensures privacy by only disseminating interest hashes and it provides security using the interest hashes common between communication parties as encryption keys without any centralized public key database etc. Related proposals either use central server, omit the privacy/security, or use central trusted party. E.g. Serendipity [6], Hocman [5], WhozThat [8], and Musubi [10] all require either central server or connection to the Internet to retrieve social media/network data.

Compared to related work, Social Index is completely decentralized during use. All information is mined from the mobile phone and exchanged using the local wireless connection. We emphasize the privacy and security of the identities

**Fig. 1.** The Social Index concept

without any centralized trusted party which is missing from related work. Such party is a security and privacy risk for the user, since he/she cannot know, if the security of the party is compromised. Therefore, Internet connectionless function ensures that the user cannot be continuously and remotely monitored by a 3rd party or a central server attacker. There is no 3rd party accessible trace of the user locations except the data exchanged between Social Index devices.

## 3   Social Index Design

The Social Index design (Fig. 1) consists of an analysis engine, a database for storing interests of the user, inputs that feed interests, a discovery protocol, and an user interface. The user interface provides feedback to the Social Index engine based on user actions.

Input components extract interest information and store it in the database. Interests are distinct objects that identify the user's preferences and can be used to find matches between users. The presentation for the interests is independent from the source to make processing the information easier. Social media interests (likes, connections, groups etc.), phone numbers, music and other media files, email addresses, visited places, and bookmarked web pages are examples of the sources for the interests.

The interests are connected together with links to form social interest graph, which is needed in order to understand relations in the analysis engine. Each information source needs its own extraction component, such as titles of songs from the media player in the device or taking a list of friends from an online service (e.g. Facebook).

Social Index engine uses a patented discovery protocol to find connection between devices in the background. The protocol is designed to cause minimum amount of traffic and to be secure against passive and active attacks by malicious users. It allows establishing an encrypted channel between people that have not previously encountered by only using the common interests. Basically, a hash is calculated for each interest periodically with a changing salt. If two users share the same interest from the same source, the hashes match. E.g. a common friend in Facebook is a source and a hash pair, or "fb:1234567". The hash can be then used to encrypt the message transferred between the users. It should be emphasized that the origins of the interest hashes remain secret for those in the proximity, who do not have the same origin interest.

When Social Index engine finds another user or new shared content, it uses an evaluation algorithm to determine how interesting the event might be to the user (Fig. 2). The algorithm uses the current context and preferences learned from the user. Each interest has associated learned information, which is stored in the interest database and adjusted as the user gives feedback through the Social Index application. The context consists of the current location and what is currently present in the network. The location is important because, finding somebody from the same university is more interesting in Honolulu than on the university campus. The actual GPS position of the device is not needed, as locations are identified by visible WLAN access points and cell IDs.

The evaluation results in a numeric Social Index value, which can be also presented to the user. When the value gets above a defined threshold the device notifies the user by vibrating or making sound and displays a message (Fig. 2). The user reacts to the notifications by responding either 'Like', which is positive feedback, or 'Not Interesting', which is used as negative feedback for learning. A learning algorithm is used to adjust the learning information stored in the interest database. Clicking 'Like' also sends a notification to the other device, which provides a lower "barrier" communication with interesting person than sending a chat message. A curious user can choose to see everything in the network by using the radar view as shown in Fig. 2. The user can also go further and use chat or exchange contact details over the network. For example, users can add each other as Facebook friends and from there on, the radar can show that friend's name. Obviously, users in the proximity can try to find each other physically through traditional communication methods, such as waving hands or yelling.

As a result Social Index can create such connection as, "two person have been in the same place", "two persons have a common friend", "there is a friend from

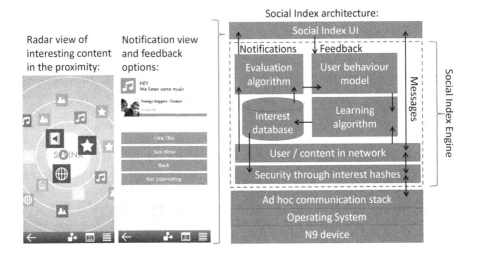

**Fig. 2.** The Social Index architecture consists of an engine and a user interface

Facebook in the proximity", "a nearby person is listening same kind of music", "two persons follow the same Twitter account", "a nearby person follows you in Twitter", "a nearby person knows same phone number than you", and "a nearby person is in your phone book".

## 4   Social Index Simulator

A network simulator was developed for testing Social Index concept so that the Nokia N9 Social Index prototype implementation can be connected to the simulator. The simulator models the network behavior and the movement of a large population in an urban environment, where each person has a daily schedule and a number of visits to different places. We use points of interests and road network from OpenStreetMap [11]. Fig. 3 shows the graphical user interface which displays a real time map view. The simulations can have tens of thousands of nodes and can be distributed to multiple processors and servers. We have used anonymized profiles from Facebook and Twitter as testing data.

## 5   User Tests with Social Index Simulator

Social Index was tested using the simulator with real test persons. The purpose of the tests was to find out if Social Index was an interesting concept to a real person. The simulator runs 900 anonymized random Tampere related Facebook profiles as simulated Social Index users on central area of Tampere. The test person imported his Facebook profile to one Social Index application that was run on the simulator in the simulated environment. One two hour test simulated five days and the test person interacted with the Social Index application

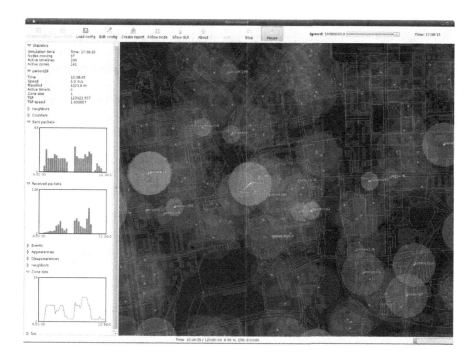

**Fig. 3.** The user interface of the Social Index network simulator

whenever there was an interesting encounter (e.g. person with similar likes). In addition to logging the simulation and the user inputs, the test persons answered to a questionnaire that concentrated on the features of the Social Index application, privacy issues, usability, and the Social Index concept. Nine test persons completed the questionnaire, and five test persons managed to complete the simulation. The test persons were recruited from the university and they represent typical young social media users.

Finding new people was found out to be the most interesting concept of the Social Index application by seven of the test persons. Only two persons were worried about privacy of the Social Index application. However, three persons thought "leaking personal information" was the worst case scenario when using the Social Index application. Nine of the test persons shared their Facebook data only with friends and certain groups. A few test persons reported that there was too much interesting content on the radar view at the same time. Thus, a precise threshold for presenting found content needs to be further explored.

Table 1 presents the logged data for those simulations that were completed in the reserved time. *Total Meetings* is the total number of encounters with simulated users. *Unique Users Seen* is a counter for meeting unique simulated Social Index users, and *Meaningful Users Seen* is a counter for meeting unique simulated user that share common interests with the test person. If the test person liked, chatted or shared a contact with some encountered simulated user, a score was added to the equivalent field. All the test persons had similar amount of meetings, but the different levels of likes etc. in Facebook resulted in varying amount of meaningful meetings. All the test persons found some interesting people and liked them. Chatting and sharing a contact was used rarely by A, B, and C, which may be due to the simulation of the test: it is not interesting to chat with a simulated person. However, the personality of the test persons was not considered. Therefore, it is difficult to analyze, if persons D and E were more social by nature or more interested to test this kind of technology.

**Table 1.** Data gathered from the user tests with completed five day simulation

| Test person | A | B | C | D | E |
|---|---|---|---|---|---|
| Total Meetings | 4431 | 3003 | 5052 | 5122 | 5175 |
| Unique Users Seen | 343 | 282 | 360 | 361 | 361 |
| Meaningful Users Seen | 55 | 101 | 79 | 103 | 122 |
| Liked | 10 | 39 | 34 | 35 | 61 |
| Chatted | 0 | 0 | 1 | 30 | 18 |
| Shared a contact | 0 | 4 | 1 | 26 | 30 |

Table 2 presents user actions after meaningful meetings. The same user might have been encountered several times, therefore, the total number of actions is higher than in Table 1. Overall, Social Index manages to discover and present interesting people to the user, since *See More* and *Later* actions were preferred over *Not Interesting*.

## 6    Privacy

Privacy, security and trust are wide research problem in Social Index and alike social ad hoc applications. Although test persons in our tests were not particularly concerned about the privacy, they did not share publicly anything on Facebook and the leaking of private information while using Social Index was concerning to some of the test persons. Therefore, we concentrate on describing how Social Index achieves privacy and what are the possible attacks on the presented privacy scheme.

Unlinkability means that it is not possible to distinguish whether two subjects are related. The prototype of Social Index uses WLAN with MAC addresses, which can be used to link different messages to the same user. Linking could be harder if the MAC address would be changed periodically, but the linkability remains during the same MAC address period. The same issue remains with all the ad hoc communication methods that utilize fixed device specific addresses at the medium access control layer. Social Index is usable with any ad hoc communication method that supports some underlying addressing, e.g. Bluetooth. Further, Social Index periodically rehashes interests with a new salt. This ensures that plain passive listening, recording of hashes, and comparing recorded

**Table 2.** User actions after meaningful meeting

| Test person | A | B | C | D | E |
|---|---|---|---|---|---|
| See More | 58 | 147 | 88 | 103 | 130 |
| Later | 90 | 226 | 207 | 290 | 228 |
| Not interesting | 62 | 103 | 28 | 133 | 39 |

hashes is not a sufficient attack to link user. Similar to dictionary attack against hashed passwords, the attacker would need a large database of possible interests for the comparison to link users. Still, this attack would require attacker to be in the proximity to listen the ad hoc communication.

Social Index itself provides anonymity, since only hashed interests are published. However, since the sender is in proximity, identity may be acquired with physical observation or another application using the same network might leak the identity. Pseudonymity is not interesting in the Social Index context since new encounters are with unknown users.

An attacker could detect that a query or a response message was sent in Social Index. The content is indistinguishable for the attacker, if the attacker does not know the set of shared interests between the Social Index users, since the content is decrypted using the hash of common interests as a decryption key. This also provides confidentiality, as long as the attacker does not know the interest.

# 7 Open Issues and Future Work

The usage of the interest graphs is a major research area in future social applications, where unknown people with same interests are attempted to be socialized. Determining the evaluation method for the strength between two persons is an open issue and currently there is not much research going on compared to the social graphs. Also, utilizing the feedback and learning are open for new proposals.

Another key question is the usage of Social Index like applications. Meeting new people is an obvious use case for Social Index, but more use cases would make Social Index like applications more appealing to the user. In our user tests, one person thought that he/she does not need new friends and therefore the application is useless. This kind of user attitude does not improve user experience for those, who might want to find similar people. Thus, some other intensive usage hook is needed for, so that even those who are not interested to seek new friends, would still be users and discoverable by others.

Social Index devices could exchange learned data and interest graphs could be expanded with correlated data. For example, if several persons like whip cream and strawberries, liking whip cream would also increase the weight of the connection to strawberries. However, finding such correlations and their true meaning is open for proposals.

The Social Index engine could be generalized as a platform to enable more advanced use in the mobile phone. E.g. when the index threshold is exceed for a multiplayer game that both persons play, the mobile phone could notify that there is a potential gamer available in the proximity. This would allow developing games that are based on the proximity of anonymous players.

The Social Index simulator could be improved by incorporating real public transportation routes and timetables to the movement model, since urban people often use public transportation. Incorporating social networks to the movement model would also improve the simulator. People often see their friends and hobby peers in certain locations. Mining these from crawled Facebook profiles is an interesting future task.

## 8  Conclusions

This paper presented Social Index, an architecture that allows mobile phone users to find new interesting content and people in their proximity. The communication happens automatically in an ad hoc manner without any centralized infrastructure. The user can exchange messages, contact cards, or endorse people in the application. A simulated use of the Social Index was used to examine real test person reactions to this kind of application. Generally, Social Index provided new interesting people to all of the test persons. Finally, the privacy of the Social Index was discussed.

**Acknowledgments.** The authors would like to thank Nokia Research Center for supporting this work.

## References

1. Ahtiainen, A., Kalliojarvi, K., Kasslin, M., Leppanen, K., Richter, A., Ruuska, P., Wijting, C.: Awareness networking in wireless environments. IEEE Vehicular Technology Magazine 4(3), 48–54 (2009)
2. Nokia Conversations, Nokia instant community gets you social (2013), http://conversations.nokia.com/2010/05/25/ nokia-instant-community-gets-you-social/
3. Väänänen-Vainio-Mattila, K., Saarinen, P., Wäljas, M., Hännikäinen, M., Orsila, H., Kiukkonen, N.: User experience of social ad hoc networking: Findings from a large-scale field trial of twin. In: Proceedings of the 9th International Conference on Mobile and Ubiquitous Multimedia, MUM 2010, pp. 10:1–10:10. ACM, New York (2010)
4. Terry, M., Mynatt, E.D., Ryall, K., Leigh, D.: Social net: using patterns of physical proximity over time to infer shared interests. In: CHI 2002 Extended Abstracts on Human Factors in Computing Systems, ser. CHI EA 2002, pp. 816–817. ACM, New York (2002)
5. Esbjörnsson, M., Juhlin, O., Östergren, M.: The hocman prototype: Fast motor bikers and ad hoc networks. In: Proceedings of MUM, Oulu, Finland, pp. 91–98 (2002)

6. Eagle, N., Pentland, A.: Social serendipity: Mobilizing social software. IEEE Pervasive Computing 4, 28–34 (2005)

7. Kern, S., Braun, P., Rossak, W.: MobiSoft: An agent-based middleware for social-mobile applications. In: Meersman, R., Tari, Z., Herrero, P. (eds.) OTM 2006 Workshops. LNCS, vol. 4277, pp. 984–993. Springer, Heidelberg (2006)

8. Beach, A., Gartrell, M., Akkala, S., Elston, J., Kelley, J., Nishimoto, K., Ray, B., Razgulin, S., Sundaresan, K., Surendar, B., Terada, M., Han, R.: WhozThat? evolving an ecosystem for context-aware mobile social networks. IEEE Network 22(4), 50–55 (2008)

9. Pietiläinen, A.-K., Oliver, E., LeBrun, J., Varghese, G., Diot, C.: Mobiclique: Middleware for mobile social networking. In: WOSN 2009: Proceedings of ACM SIGCOMM Workshop on Online Social Networks (August 2009)

10. Vo, I., Purtell, T.J., Dodson, B., Cannon, A., Lam, M.S.: Musubi: A mobile privacy-honoring social network (September 2011),
    http://mobisocial.stanford.edu/papers/musubi.pdf

11. OpenStreetMap contributors. OpenStreetMap (2012),
    http://www.openstreetmap.org/

# Mobile Web Service Infrastructure Supporting Successful Aging

Marc Jansen, Oliver Koch, and Michael Schellenbach

Computer Science Institute
University of Applied Sciences Ruhr West
Bottrop, Germany
{marc.jansen,oliver.koch,michael.schellenbach}@hs-ruhrwest.de

**Abstract.** One of the most stressing challenges in our culture is the demographic change. On the one hand, people become older and older, at the same time less young people are available in order to support the elderly. Currently, this fact already provides a number of social impacts that need to be solved in the near future. This paper concentrates on the integration of mobile devices in scenarios that allow elderly people to age successfully. Here, the term "aging successfully" refers to broad range of aspects from health to social life of elderly people. A special focus of this paper lies in the question whether services deployed to a mobile device provide advantages in the area of aging successfully. In order to answer this question, both technical challenges are explained and solved by example architectures, and scenarios that benefit from services deployed to mobile devices are explained.

**Keywords:** mobile devices, ageing, web services, sensing, mobile web service.

## 1    Introduction

Due to the demographic change that currently happens worldwide, the growing population of elderly people demands for stronger support for aging well. On the other hand the amount of younger people is decreasing due to decreasing birth rates, at least in industrial countries. In order to prevent the social systems to collapse, the next decades will have to find answers to this problem. Therefore, this paper describes a technology that allows to participate in a number of solutions, helping us to deal with the before mentioned problem of demographic change. The major idea that is described in this paper, is to make use of mobile devices like smart phones in order to actively participate elderly people in the society, and by this, allow what we call in this context successful aging. Here, successful aging on the one hand relates to health status of elderly people but also to their social integration. Both aspects could not be seen separately since they influence each other tremendously.

In order to support the goal of aging successfully we provide a technology that allows for a better integration of mobile devices into the everyday life of elderly people and support their needs in an improved way. Key to the presented ideas is a technology known as mobile Web Services that allows deploying standardized Web Services

C. Canal and M. Villari (Eds.): ESOCC 2013, CCIS 393, pp. 254–265, 2013.

to mobile devices. The provision of such services (in contrast to just consuming these kinds of services) provides, from an abstract point of view, the benefit of a much richer and more direct contextualization of a user of a mobile device, in our case, of the elderly. Furthermore, from a more technical point of view, this technology allows to provide a loose coupling between the provided service running on a mobile device and the service consumer that accesses the data provided by the mobile device and its user.

In order to achieve the description, this paper is organized as follows: the next section describes the state of the art in the context of this paper. Afterwards, the technical architecture is presented, both, with respect to a new perspective for mobile Web Services (in contrast to the traditional view of Web Services running in big data centers) and technical details of the implementation of mobile Web Services are presented. Followed by the architectural description, an example scenario in which mobile Web Services are utilized, is described in detail. Finally, this paper closes by a description of the outlook for this technology and the planned future work.

## 2    State of the Art

From a technical point of view, Web Services on mobile devices are nowadays usually limited to the consumption of Web Services deployed to large data centers. Nevertheless, the power of mobile devices as Web Service providers is not much focused so far. Furthermore, there is not much work done yet with respect to a change perspective for Web Services deployed to mobile devices.

On the other hand, from a scenario point of view, during all phases of life, human development unfolds within the range of opportunities and constraints that biological, psychological, and contextual characteristics provide. Such opportunities and constraints for development can be subsumed under the general notion of resources. Individuals differ in their access to resources. Moreover, within a given individual, quantity and quality of resources undergo fundamental changes throughout life. In contrast to earlier phases of life, development in late adulthood and old age is characterized by a shift in directions of less resource gains and more resource losses [1]. Individuals might continue to gain, e.g., in social status, material belongings, knowledge, and professional expertise. However, other resources such as physical fitness, health, sensory acuity, multi-tasking ability, and functional brain efficacy decrease throughout adulthood. Therefore one interesting approach to maintain abilities of elderly people is physical activity because it has the potential to improve cognitive performance as well [2], The advances can be generalized to untrained tasks and can also be retained for months after the training has concluded [3], suggesting that physical activity improves more general cognitive processes rather than specific stimulus-response associations [4]. Context-aware systems promoting physical activity are frequently used with obese patients, but not the elderly. Moreover, most research focuses on a representation of external context, disregarding the importance of a user's cognitive situation. According to Hong et al. [5], cognitive context information will be key to providing satisfying personalized services. By making use of such intelligent and assistive technology, individuals of all ages, and aging individuals in particular, can delegate control over certain aspects of their everyday lives to technology while continuing to exert direct control in others.

## 3     Architecture

This section describes challenges, and technical solutions to these challenges, that occur by deploying standardized Web Services to mobile devices. The section starts by defining a new perspective to Web Services deployed to mobile devices. Afterwards, technical challenges for the implementation of such an approach are outlined and, last but not least, a technical infrastructure is described that allows overcoming the outlined challenges.

**Different Perspective for Mobile Web Services**
The view on traditional Web Services, independent of ReST [6] or SOAP/WSDL [7] based Web Services, describes different scenarios in which such Web Services can be used. The major idea is always, that Web Services are utilized in order to extend limitations of a certain computational device with respect to the computational power of the device, e.g., the number of CPU's of the system or the performance of the single CPU's.

Furthermore, other limitations that could be extended either refer to the non-persistent random access memory (RAM) of the device or the persistent memory/storage.

Additionally, traditional Web Services can also be implemented in order to provide access to data that would otherwise not be available on the particular device.

Therefore, Web Services allow a broad range of possibilities for the extension of limitations of a local device, if the device itself is able to consume Web Services. Taking another step of abstraction, with all the before mentioned examples, any traditional Web Service could be understood as a mean for extending limitations of a usual computational device. This could be visualized as shown in Figure 1 together with some examples of prominent Web Services.

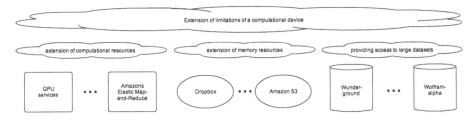

**Fig. 1.** Traditional perspectives to Web Services

Additionally, one major aspect that Web Services have in common is the fact that their implementations remain transparent for the service consumer.

Obviously, for a number of different reasons, the traditional view to Web Services does not work with respect to Web Services deployed to mobile devices. While mobile devices became more and more powerful in recent years, they are still not as powerful as a usual laptop or a stationary workstation, which are themselves not as powerful as modern server systems deployed in large data centers. Therefore, mobile devices could be seen as the least powerful computational devices we are currently using (beside very specialized systems usually running with microcontrollers). Therefore, using these kind of devices for the extension of limitations that exist with other devices, does not make sense. Nevertheless, mobile devices provide two major benefits in comparison to laptops, stationary workstations and large server systems: they are (by definition) mobile and they provide a large variety of sensors! Taking these two facts into account, a modified perspective to Web Services deployed to mobile devices could be developed, in which the provision of this kind of services makes perfect sense.

For example, having a look at the sensors of a mobile device, the sensors could of course be used in order to provide a certain assistance/source of information to the user of a mobile device, and by using mobile Web Services data and information provided by these different sensors could be made available to outside software components. Thus, with respect to the different abstraction layers presented previously, mobile Web Services could again be understood as a mean for providing data that would otherwise not be available: here, contextualized data of the user provided by the sensors of a mobile device.

Additionally, mobile Web Services also allow accessing these devices directly via a well-defined interface.

Therefore, with respect to the formerly described abstraction layers, it could be said that mobile Web Services extend the abstraction layer that allowed to access data that otherwise would not be available by providing access to the data provided by the sensors of a mobile device. Utilizing standardized Web Service protocols for these kinds of services on mobile devices, allows the easy integration of such services into any other software component. Furthermore, by allowing services that provide the possibility to directly access a mobile device mobile Web Services add a completely new abstraction layer. This change for the perspectives of mobile Web Services is shown in Figure 2, together with some examples of both scenarios in which this technology can be used and typical data provided by mobile devices.

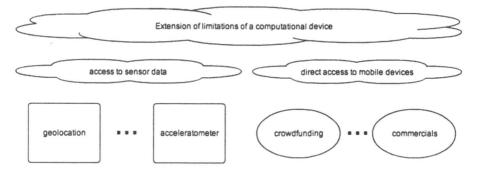

**Fig. 2.** Extension of traditional perspectives by mobile Web Services

Summing up, it could be said that also mobile Web Services extend limitations of current devices, and thus they support also the second level of abstraction described formerly. Also the characteristics of traditional Web Services providing a transparency about their implementation, holds for mobile Web Services.

### Technical Challenges

While trying to implement Web Services for mobile devices, a number of technical challenges occur [8]. These technical challenges become obvious by taking the mobility and the usual use-cases of mobile devices into consideration. The following three challenges provide a good starting point from which a further analysis of technical affordances for the support of mobile Web Services is possible:

— Since mobile devices are per definition mobile, one of the crucial facts for deploying any service, that should be reachable by someone else, is that mobile devices constantly change their IP address. For example, at home the user is usually connected to his local WiFi network. On his way to work, he/she gets connected to the Internet via the mobile network of his/her telecommunication company, and at work he might be connected to the local WiFi network of his/her employer. Therefore, the services deployed to his/her mobile device would not be available under a fixed network address, which makes it hard for a service consumer to (re-)find the service.

— Furthermore, the IP addresses used (in the formerly mentioned different networks) are usually not publicly available, but are IP addresses that are routed according to the rules of Network Address Translation (NAT). Therefore, a service deployed to a mobile device will usually not be available for a third party service consumer from outside the current network.

— Last but not least, mobile devices might not be connected at all to a network. This regularly happens in areas where the network connectivity of the mobile telecommunications company is so well established. Therefore, services deployed to a mobile device that is currently not connected to a network at all, would not be available for a potential service consumer. This is also the case if the mobile device is switched off at all.

These examples show that deploying Web Services to mobile devices provide a number of different challenges, which need to be faced in order to allow the provision of reliable Web Services on mobile devices. Here, especially with respect to the social impacts described later in this paper by the examples of aging successfully, a reliable availability of the services deployed to mobile devices is crucial.

### Architecture for Mobile Web Services

Since providing Web Services on mobile devices provides challenges, as described in the previous section, we implemented an architecture that allows solving them [9]. The major idea of the provided solution is to implement a central proxy infrastructure that acts as a façade (both according to the proxy and the façade design pattern [10]) to the Web Service running on a mobile device. A sequence diagram that shows the process for a service consumer to perform a request to a Web Service running on a mobile device is shown in Figure 3.

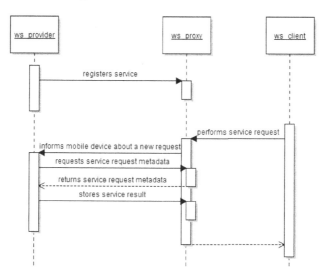

**Fig. 3.** Flow of method calls for a service consumer to perform a request to a mobile Web Service

First of all, the mobile Web Service provider, seen on the right hand side of Figure 3 needs to register the according Web Service with the Web Service proxy (in the middle of Figure 3). Afterwards, a consumer, as seen on the left hand side of Figure 3, of the mobile Web Service can perform a service request (technically, to the proxy of the Web Service). After the proxy has received the Web Service request, it can store certain metadata of the request in a database and inform the mobile Web Service about the new service request. This information to the mobile Web Service about a new service request could be implemented differently:

— First of all, techniques like GCM[1] (Google Cloud Messaging) or APNS[2] (Apple Push Notification Service) could be used in order to directly inform the mobile Web Service about a new service request. These techniques do not allow transferring a large payload of data (so that usually not all of the necessary information for the service request could be transferred, but only a notification about the new service request) and furthermore, they are limited to Android and iOS based mobile devices.

[1]  http://developer.android.com/google/gcm/index.html, last visited 05.06.2013

[2]  http://developer.apple.com/library/mac/#documentation/NetworkingInternet/Conceptual/RemoteNotificationsPG/ApplePushService/ApplePushService.html, last visited 05.06.2013

— For other mobile devices, the infrastructure allows to make use of a polling based approach in which the mobile device regularly contacts the Web Service proxy in order to check whether new service requests are available.

Storing information about the service request in a database, allows solving the problem mentioned in the previous section that a mobile device might not be available, either because of a bad network infrastructure or the device itself being switched off. At the same time, the proxy allows to overcome the challenges that occur because of the other challenges described in the previous section, like the constantly changing networks and the not publicly available IP addresses.

After the information about the service request is sent to the mobile Web Service, the mobile Web Service could be executed and the result could be transferred back to the centralized Web Service proxy, where it could also be stored in the database and transferred back to the Web Service consumer.

In order for the information about the service request to be transferred to the mobile Web Service, the mobile Web Service needs to explicitly ask for this information, either after receiving a notification about a new service request, or within the permanent polling intervals.

The reason for storing the result of the mobile Web Service beside the information about the service request in the database is, that this approach allows the proxy to perform usual tasks for a proxy, e.g., direct answers to similar service requests.

## 4     Scenario Description

Mobile Web Services are made available in aging well scenarios usually via smartphones. Smartphones are inferior to the current standard server systems and desktop pcs / laptops with respect the technical performance significantly. Their strength lies in the fact, that they have a number of built in sensor components (localization (GPS), acceleration, earth's magnetic field, sound, tactile sensors).

This offers the opportunity to characterize the smartphone user's context combined with times a good deal more precise than server systems or PCs could achieve. Furthermore a growing number of providers have specialized on pluggable sensor modules (e.g. vital parameters, RFID) to extend smartphone functionality towards telemedical Web Services.

Context information of elderly people such as location, time, persons nearby or the person's velocity facilitate an adequate selection of mobile Web Services designed to support people to grow old in an healthy and autonomous way.

The following scenario description aims to highlight the potential benefits of mobile Web Services for aging well: Ms. Miller, a 70-year-old widow, lives in her own apartment in a small town. Her family consists of two sons and their families. Ms. Miller is mentally fit and has no intention of giving up her apartment. A few years ago she developed hypertension and a few months ago she additionally suffered a stroke, she survived without sequelae. Her doctor suggested her to continuously monitor her blood sugar levels and weight and to adhere strictly to her drug therapy. In addition, Ms. Miller should incorporate as many physical activities into her daily routines as possible.

On last Christmas, she receives a smartphone from one of her sons. The device looks like a mobile phone and can be used as such. Ms. Miller has been using mobile phones for several years, and starts using the smartphone for this purpose, taking it with her on all errands. In addition to serving as a mobile phone, the new device also has other capabilities: it is equipped with all kinds of Sensors, e.g., GPS, a large and well-lit display and a movement sensor.

The day of Ms. Miller always starts with the same routine. Before breakfast, she measures her blood pressure and blood sugar as well as her weight via the pluggable vital parameter modules of her smart phone. The measured data is than available to the telemedical via the mobile Web Service running on her smart phone. The telemedical service reviews these values regularly by alert listener. If necessary, an alert is triggered and a doctor will contact her by video call. The telemedical web service doesn't only monitor short-term critical values, but also long-term processes, e.g. continuous increase in weight or blood pressure and blood sugar levels.

Beside the "objective" sensor data Ms. Miller additionally inputs subjective assessment information about her health status (smiley scale) that is also available via a mobile Web Service deployed to her smart phone.

Ms. Miller starts with breakfast. A balanced nutrition is very important for her health. She receives assistance from a Nutrition Manager service on her smart phone that gives her recommendations for healthy snacks as well as smaller and larger dishes depending on the time of day and her fridge contents. The nutrition manager automatically creates shopping lists and recommends alternative (healthier) products during her visit of a grocery store. The GPS-component is able to calculate her coordinates and based on this, whether she is located in a grocery store, all this data about her current context is made available, again, via the mobile Web Service running on her smart phone. Should a product she is looking for not be available, she gets a map-based recommendation for a shop nearby who have the product in stock.

After her healthy breakfast Ms. Miller is planning a museum visit. She needs to drive to the next town by her car. Her smart phone navigates her to the next park and ride parking in the neighboring town. Traffic jams and delays are automatically bypassed. Just before arriving at the Park & Ride she receives a voice message from her smart phone when the next bus to the city center departs.

Since Ms. Miller has moved only a little so far the Physical Activity monitor service coupled to the motion sensor of her smartphones recommends her to cover the distance from the bus stop to the Museum (1000 m) by foot.

Ms. Miller provides all the data about her physical activities via another mobile Web Service deployed to her mobile phone, in order to make it available to other external service. This data includes, e.g., calories burned and distance travelled.

In her stroke Ms. Miller has learned that every minute can matter. Therefore her smart phone has an "emergency" button. If Ms. Miller presses this button the nearest doctor or hospital gets an alert based on her GPS-coordinates. At that her current medical records and the latest data from the telemedicine are communicated automatically to the doctor in charge. Additionally, this doctor can also receive the latest information about the context of Ms. Miller from the mobile Web Services deployed to Ms. Millers' smart phone. As a result Ms. Miller feels save and is willing to walk long distances by foot. On her way to the museum, her smart phone logs on again.

Her Social Community Service has detected (with the help of other current context information) that a good friend of her is staying very close and offers to make a phone connection. Ms. Miller accepts this offer. Although her friend has no time for a leisurely visit to the museum, she suggests meeting for coffee with her after her museum visit. Ms. Miller agrees. This planned meeting is stored in Ms. Millers' context information and therefore made available through the mobile Web Service.

The smart phone automatically detects, that she has reached the museum. She pays the entrance fee by NFC-based micropayment. Her smart phone offers to take over a guided museum tour and to provide additional information about the artifacts.

About 10 minutes before the end of her 2 ½ hour guided tour her smart phone informs her friend and suggests a restaurant nearby, which fits to Ms. Millers and her friends preferences. The preferences are stored in her personal profile that she also made available through the mobile Web Service.

Arrived at the restaurant her nutrition organizer gives advice, which dishes are particularly recommendable. After eating Ms. Miller and her friend log in to a cloud service and view photos of the last visit of Ms. Miller's grandchildren on her smart phone. Afterwards, Ms. Miller says goodbye to her friend and makes his way back.

Before her way back to the Park & Ride her Physical Activity Monitor has found through communication with a weather service that a bad weather front is approaching. Instead suggesting walking the system shows the position of the next bus stop including departure times and navigates her to this position.

After this intense day Ms. Miller wishes to have a relaxing bath at home. She starts her Smart Living Service app and "orders" a relaxing bath via voice control of her smart phone. Based on her GPS-Position (provided by the mobile Web Service) the housing technology system detects that Ms. Miller will arrive at home in about 20 minutes and starts to let the water in tub.

Due to the described mobile Web Services nothing stands in Ms. Miller's way to age well.

## 5    Implementation

Based on the architecture for providing Web Services on mobile devices, the described scenario could be implemented with a set of mobile Web Services. The overall architecture of this implementation could be seen in Figure 4. This figure shows the mobile device of Ms. Miller and the services deployed to her device. Additionally, some external services are also shown that utilize the service deployed to Ms. Millers' mobile phone in order to provide higher level services that increase Ms. Millers' quality of life. Since Figure 4 only provides a first overview about the mobile Web Services along with the higher level services that utilize these mobile Web Services, not all of the higher level services described in the scenario above are shown and of course not all of the Web Services deployed to Ms. Millers' mobile phone are already used by the higher level services.

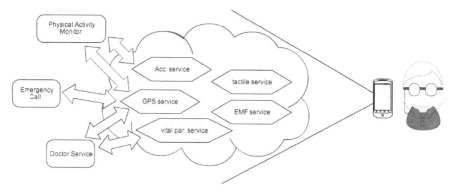

**Fig. 4.** Overview about an implementation that makes use of Web Service deployed to mobile devices

In detail the Web Services deployed to Ms. Millers' mobile phone provide the following functionality via standardized interfaces:

- Acc. service: provides access to the acceleration sensor of Ms. Millers' mobile phone, e.g., to receive information if Ms. Miller is currently moving
- GPS service: provides access to the geo location of Ms. Miller
- Vital par. service: provides access to some of Ms. Millers' vital parameters measured by additional sensors connected to her mobile device, e.g., blood pressure, pulse rate, …
- Tactile service: provides information from the tactile sensors of Ms. Millers' mobile device, e.g., for receiving information if Ms. Miller is currently working with the device
- EMF service: provides information from the earth magnetic field sensor, e.g., for a further contextualization of Ms. Millers' current position, along with the information provided by the GPS service

The higher level services provided in this example implementation are just examples and not to provide all the services mentioned in the scenario description above. Still, they show the basic idea of how the integration of Web Services deployed to mobile devices could be used in order to enrich the scenario described before.

## 6    Opportunities and Challenges

As described before a lot of supporting services for successful aging are possible. The mobile web service architecture provides new opportunities how information can be transmitted and where the personal data can be stored. Here the elderly have full control of their personal data e.g. by storing them on their personal device and just allow decentralized access without any third party infrastructure. So, in our view the mobile web services have potential to challenge open issues in the area of data security. In addition the concept of mobile web services also gives the opportunity to separate the user interface and the sensor and information layer and therefore allows for an easy and solid way to adapt the user interface during aging or to detach the user interface to additional devices if needed. So, based on this technical benefit the concept offers the chance to build an assistive service platform with a lifelong individual adapting user interface.

## 7    Future Work and Outlook

First of all, the described scenarios demonstrate the strength of mobile Web Services in order to support aging well. Furthermore, similar mobile Web Services to the ones mentioned above have the power to increase a number of other scenarios, too. These are partially already identified and include, e.g., voting systems, crowd sourcing, mobile learning and other scenarios in which the contextualization of a mobile user provides some benefit. Still there is not much work done with respect to data security and especially the question of who should have access to mobile Web Services (such as mentioned above) and how the necessary security restrictions could be handled, remains unanswered today. Therefore, one of the points for future work will be to concentrate on these security issues.

From a scenario point of view, an evaluation of the described scenario is one of the points on our to-do list. Additionally, new sensors will be integrated in the scenario and the integration of the mentioned services in a complete Service-Oriented Architecture (SOA) strategy is another goal for future work.

## References

1. Baltes, P.B.: Theoretical propositions of lifespan developmental psychology: on the dynamics between growth and decline. Developmental Psychology 23(5), 611–626 (1987)
2. Kramer, A.F., Willis, S.L.: Enhancing the cognitive vitality of older adults. Current Directions in Psychological Science 11(5), 173–177 (2002)
3. Ball, K., Berch, D., Helmers, K., Jobe, J., Leveck, M., Marsiske, M.: Effects of cognitive training interventions with older adults - a randomized controlled trial. JAMA 288(18), 2271–2281 (2002)
4. Erickson, K.I., Colcombe, S.J., Wadhwa, R., Bherer, L., Peterson, M.S., Scalf, P.E., Kim, J.S., Alvarado, M., Kramer, A.F.: Training-induced plasticity in older adults: Effects of training on hemispheric asymmetry. Neurobiology of Aging 28(2), 272–283 (2007)
5. Hong, J., Suh, E., Kim, S.: Context-aware systems: A literature review and classification. Expert Systems with Applications 36(4), 8509–8522 (2009)
6. Fielding, R.T., Taylor, R.N.: Architectural styles and the design of network-based software architectures, University of California, Irvine (2000)
7. Curbera, F., Duftler, M., Khalaf, R., Nagy, W., Mukhi, N., Weerawarana, S.: Unraveling the Web Services Web: An Introduction to SOAP, WSDL, and UDDI. IEEE Internet Computing 6(2), 86–93 (2002)

8. Svensson, D.: Assemblies of Pervasive Services. Dept. of Computer Science, Institutional Repository – Lund University (2009)
9. Jansen, M.: Evaluation of an Architecture for Providing Mobile Web Services. International Journal on Advances in Internet Technology 6(1&2), 32–41 (2013)
10. Gamma, E., Helm, R., Johnson, R., Vlissides, J.: Design Pattern – Elements of Reusable Object-Oriented Software. Addison-Wesley (1995)

# Cloud and Web Services Integration for mHealth Telerehabilitation Support

Angel Ruiz-Zafra[1], Manuel Noguera[1], Kawtar Benghazi[1], José Luis Garrido[1],
Gustavo Cuberos Urbano[2], and Alfonso Caracuel[3]

[1] Dpto. Lenguajes y Sistemas Informáticos, Granada, Spain
{angelr,mnoguera,benghazi,jgarrido}@ugr.es
[2] Dpto. Personalidad, Evaluación y Tratamiento Psicológico, Granada, Spain
gcuberos@ugr.es
[3] Dpto. Psicología Evolutiva y de la Educación, Granada, Spain
acaracuel@ugr.es

**Abstract.** Cloud Computing and mobile technology have become an integral part of society, changing how we interact with devices and each other. In this context, users are able to connect with other users/devices anywhere and anytime, taking advantage of endless possibilities in different areas. One of these areas is healthcare, where cloud features can cover important healthcare requirements such as information exchange, security, privacy and scalability of solutions to support users' needs. In this paper we introduce a Cloud-supported e-Rehabilitation platform for Brain-Injured patients and health professionals. The goal of the platform is the improvement of the quality of life of patients, providing asynchronous remote interaction between health professionals and patients.

**Keywords:** Brain-injured, cloud computing, remote interaction, e-Rehabilitation, mobile devices, telerehabilitation.

## 1    Introduction

The Cloud Computing is the convergence and evolution of several concepts like virtualization, distributed storage, grid and automation management with the goal of providing a flexible approach for deploying and scaling applications through a large group of interconnected computers [1].

The service delivery model of the cloud consists in three different layers: Infrastructure as a Service (IaaS), Platform as a Service (PaaS) and Software as a Service (SaaS) [2]. Cloud-based solutions present different attributes or characteristics such as: on-demand self service, broad network access, resource pooling, rapid elasticity and measured service [3].

These features provide a set of benefits as the delocalized access to resources through Internet anywhere and at any time, pay-per-use business models and simple data sharing. This makes cloud computing a very efficient paradigm to the deployment of applications. Another key advantage of cloud computing is that cloud

C. Canal and M. Villari (Eds.): ESOCC 2013, CCIS 393, pp. 266–276, 2013.
© Springer-Verlag Berlin Heidelberg 2013

services are updated by the provider, which means that users and devices that use these services are always working with the latest platform version and do not need to worry about upgrades.

Thanks to these features, new technologies with scarce resources, as mobile devices, have grown over the last years, especially by the delocalized use of services through the Internet and the possibility to run heavy tasks out of these devices (cloud servers).

Healthcare cloud-supported has many advantages. For health professionals, cloud computing can be a useful tool to exchange medical information between different medical centers and departments at any time and anywhere.

This collaborative information exchange improves the efficiency in the use of medical resources [4] in comparison to the classical methods, where two different organizations change patient's records or medical information using their own standards or infrastructures.

Health professionals also seek for the improvement of care and support to patients, with the aim of the improvement their quality of life. By using cloud technology, health professional and patients can have an asynchronous social and remote interaction unlike the classical face-to-face interaction. This social interaction through the cloud enables continuous monitoring of patients, being this information accessible to the health professionals anywhere and at any time, with low-cost by reducing displacement of patients. In this way, the health professional can have a better interaction or social relation with their patients, maximize the use of medical resources, the quality of life of the patients and their evolution.

This fact is particularly important in some rehabilitation contexts, like Brain Injury Rehabilitation processes, where the evolution of patient strongly depends on how they perform the exercises. In the rehabilitation programs health professionals usually supervise several patients at the same time so some details about the performance of the rehabilitation exercise can be unnoticed. The possibility to store the performance of the rehabilitation exercise and the asynchronous and delocalized access to this performance can ensure that professionals can review the rehabilitation exercise to check if the rehabilitation exercise was performed correctly, detect mistakes, etc.

Therefore, cloud features like interoperability or unlimited storage perfectly fit with the set of requirements of a rehabilitation system. In addition, other cloud features like scalability and robustness make the cloud paradigm a more efficient solution than classical client-server architectures.

In this paper, we introduce CloudRehab, a cloud-supported mobile Rehabilitation platform for brain-injured patients that shows how the rehabilitation through the cloud can improve the rehabilitation progress of the patients over the time, due to the full time asynchronous social interaction between health professionals and patients. The paper is organized as follows:.CloudRehab, is described in detail in the Section 2. Section 3 describes the related work, some cloud-supported systems/applications and Conclusions and future work are presented in Section 4.

# 2     CloudRehab

## 2.1     Approach

Brain-injured patients have to perform periodically rehabilitation exercises designed by health professionals to regain their motor, language, cognitive and/or daily living skills. This approach usually entails patients to move to the hospital to perform the exercise, which represents an important drawback for this kind of patients.

Likewise, health professionals have to supervise the rehabilitation sessions to ensure correct rehabilitation exercises performance. This social relation based on a face-to-face supervision implies that health professionals must be in the same place where the patient is.

Unlike these classic rehabilitation programs, home-based rehabilitation programs by remote supervision of exercises have proven to reduce the need for face-to-face rehabilitation sessions with health professionals and patients and keep or improve their relation using new technologies like cloud computing. This technology may reduce displacements of patients to the hospital, some premature discharges of patients and health-care costs. Likewise, some devices allow a proper monitoring of patient's performance of activities of daily living (ADL). Although home-based rehabilitation could reduce final rehabilitation costs, there is a requirement for effectiveness; it must be assured the correct performance of the rehabilitation exercises without a direct supervision, just using medical feedback.

## 2.2     Platform Overview

The proposal presented in this paper to keep and/or improve the social relations between patients and health professionals using cloud technology is called CloudRehab [17].

CloudRehab is a customizable home-based e-rehabilitation platform for brain-injured patients that makes use of mobile devices, commercial heart rate sensors, Web and Cloud Computing technologies, which has been validated with several patients.

One of the main aims of CloudRehab is to provide a remote supervision platform for health professionals (doctors, occupational therapists, physiologists) who can use the platform to train daily activities, increase independence and reduce patient displacements. To achieve this, professionals design training sessions and help patients to learn how to perform them, which is stored in a video file.

In each training session different information is stored: the performance of the exercise (video recorded by means of the frontal camera of the mobile device) together with the heart rate values obtained from a chest strap Bluetooth sensor [13]. This information is simultaneously stored in the mobile device and in a remote cloud. This way, the video sessions and the heart rate values recorded can be accessed anywhere and anytime. This is an important feature, since it enables asynchronous interaction and work with the platform of patients and health professionals, which in turn, permit that certain activities, such as eating, can be performed fitting the usual schedule of the patient.

This asynchronous interaction as requirement is the main reason for using cloud technology. The interaction is supported by different healthcare services implemented as web services and supported by cloud technology, ensuring the correct exchange of information, management of the patient information providing different disseminations, etc.

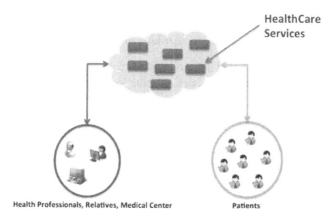

**Fig. 1.** CloudRehab Platform Overview

Only a mobile device with Bluetooth and a frontal camera, as well as Internet connection (for real-time monitoring and cloud storage of session information) is needed. Figure 1 provides an overview of the platform. Figure 1 shows an overview of CloudRehab.

## 2.3    Functionalities

CloudRehab platform uses a mobile based-component architecture called Zappa,[14]. The different components of the platform have been designed to manage the different concerns involved in the healthcare area such as the management of the information, allowing the easy management of patients, management of the different communication protocols like Bluetooth or Wifi enabling the easy connectivity with medical devices based on this kind of communication protocols like commercial heart rate sensors or even Arduino board.

In addition, and specifically for this project, a new component to work with cloud technology was developed. The component, which is integrated in the Zappa platform, allows work with cloud technology easily.

In this way, the component allows, among other features:

— The use of any service supported by cloud technology and the automatic transformation of cloud dissemination to custom objects (source code). This is possible defining and creating a custom bean object at execution time with the specific features of the result of the cloud service.

— The component has a internal petition stack allowing that cloud unprocessed petitions due to connectivity problems, server problem, etc. run when its possible.
— The possibility to upload and download any type of file to the cloud.
— The execution of cloud tasks, allowing that heavy tasks can be performed in the cloud instead of the mobile device.
— The component is able to launch a service (background process) to support the real-time cloud interaction even when the application is closed. This allows that patients can receive notifications or other kind of information anytime.

The use of a component-based solution ensures that changes in one component or add and remove new components do not alter the behavior and operation of the system.

In the cloud server context, specific services have been developed to manage all the information of the platform: get specific information of patient, register new patient, update information patient, create rehabilitation sessions, upload or download file, register into the system a new health professional, etc. Each action in the cloud server is supported by a service. These services are used, so far, by the mobile application and the web platform.

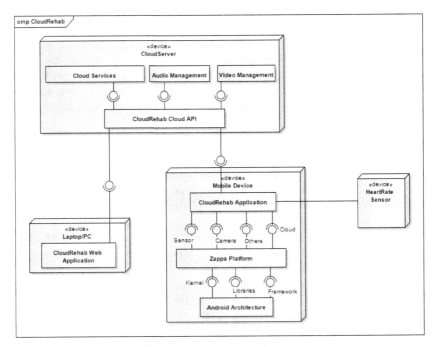

**Fig. 2.** CloudRehab Architecture

One of the main functionalities of the platform is the video and audio management. This is supported by complex processes for which two different cloud-supported tasks have been developed. When the patients upload, through the mobile device, the zip file that contains the video files recorded in the rehabilitation session one of the task decompress the zip file, convert the different video files (mp4) to WebM video files and merge all the different files into one. In the same way, when the health professionals upload a video or audio file in any file extension or video-audio codec, the task management this files to convert to WebM (video) and OGG (audio) using a open-source library [16]. In this way, audio and video files could be reproduced using the web player of HTML5, avoiding the use of Flash or other weight technologies that, usually, are not compatible with mobile devices. Fig.2 shows the architecture of the system.

## 2.4    Architecture

CloudRehab encompasses three main components:

*Mobile Application*
Based on Android OS (at least 2.2) and used by patients, the mobile application uses different services and task of the cloud, components of the Zappa platform and open-source libraries to provide different functionalities such as real-time data storage (cloud server and mobile device), medical device management (heart rate sensor), statistics charts and mobile device camera recording, among others.

*Web Application*
The administrative tool is a web application developed using different technologies such as: HTML5, JavaScript, Ajax, CSS3 and open-source frameworks. The web application, through AJAX, uses different services and tasks of the cloud to provide different functionalities as the data management and representation, video, audio and images management or real-time monitoring.

*Cloud Technology*
The Cloud Technology used to support CloudRehab is called *G*, a novel technology designed and developed by Gnubila [15].

   G is a cloud native platform based on open standards and composed by an applications server, databases, BPM and middleware technologies combined with a set of tools which enabling the development, deployment and running of applications and services. G could be deployed in publics or private servers, creating hybrids clouds.

   About the service delivery model, G is independent of the IaaS so can be used with Amazon EC2, VMWare, Windows Azure or FlexIT, among others. In the PaaS layer, G provides a custom PaaS platform called GPaaS.

   GPaaS is a platform for the development, deployment and running of applications which core is a multitenant applications and databases server. This platform provides functionalities such as management and data federation, management of multimedia contents, applications integration, metadata management, etc. Over this layer, the developers could deploy or create new applications with Multilanguage support (PHP, Ruby, Perl, Java, Python, etc) using a useful web development environment that provides services over the SaaS layer.

The data storage in G is supported by a NoSQL graph-oriented database. The information is stored as objects, which at the same time could be grouped into types. The structure of each object (attributes) could be different, enabling that G manage the information using different models as relational, hierarchical, analytical or network. Although the information is stored in a NoSQL database, the GPaaS layer allows to developers the use of SQL queries.

For this project, G has been deployed in a custom Linux installation (CentOS 6.0) and the GPaaS web development environment has been used to generate the application which provide the different services used by web and mobile application. The programming language used is Perl.

## 2.5    Platform Applications

The platform includes two end-user applications.

*CloudRehab Administrative Tool*
It consists of a web application that can be used by any user of the system (health professionals, patient's relatives and patients). Although all of them use the same web application, each type of user has its own interface and restricted access to different sets of functionalities. The different functionalities provided are:

— *Manage patient information*: A health professional can register into the system his/her owns patients and define the medical and personal information.
— *Manage session's patient*: One session is made up of a training video of a patient performing an activity in a training process, a set of audio and image files used when the heart rate value of the patient reach a certain value, the recorded video of the session, the heart rate values, and alerts to be triggered, among others. The professional can define new sessions with new training activities and, once the patient has completed them, review session information to evaluate patient progress.
— *Review information generated by the patient* such as completed sessions (recording video, recording audio, heart rate records) (Fig. 3), heart rate between two different dates or charts (sectors, bars) of the patient's progress over time.

**Fig. 3.** Information of Completed Rehabilitation Session

*CloudRehab Mobile Application*

A mobile application that allows the training session of an exercise to be played and recorded while obtaining heart rate using a chest strap sensor [13] to monitor patient's stress level.

The application divides the device screen into two different parts. The upper part shows the images captured by the frontal camera, while the bottom part of the screen displays the training video previously recorded with the supervision of a therapist (Fig. 4 – Left). This provides to the patient a useful real-time feedback about how to perform the exercise correctly and how he/she is approaching to the intended model.

If the application detects that the heart rate signal of the patient has reached the threshold defined by the professionals, the application plays an information sound and shows a pop-up dialog with different options (i.e., review the video session by steps, play custom help audio or view relaxing images) in order to aid the patient to reduce his/her stress level (Fig.4 – Center).

The mobile application also provides other functionalities such as real-time heart rate sensor detection, change screen mode (only video, camera and video or only camera mode) and statistical information display (Fig. 4 right), among others.

**Fig. 4.** CloudRehab Mobile Application

# 3    Related Work

Different cloud-supported systems and applications in different fields/areas have appeared over the last years. These systems, which in most cases make use mobile devices, are examples of how cloud computing paradigm has changed the way we interact.

There are many fields such as online gamming, e-Learning, social networks or data storage which has been supported by cloud technology. The most representative cloud-supported systems that show how the cloud changes our social relations are instant messaging systems (WhatsApp, LINE), the social networks (Facebook, Twitter) or data storage (Dropbox).

In other areas, cloud-supported systems that provide a new way of social communication have appeared with the main goal of the improvement of users experience, like CloudMov. CloudMov is a novel mobile social TV system, which can effectively utilize the cloud computing paradigm to offer a living-room experience of video watching to disparate mobile users with spontaneous social interactions [5].

The work presented in [6] shows a mobile application, which uses Facebook API, cloud computing and social networking services to help people to prepare for emergencies and obtain support from friends and relatives in the aftermath. The work presented in [7] that is related with educational field and show the Scholar-Oriented Social Network Cloud (SOSN) extract academic information from various web sources on the Internet and provides an application model for the social interaction through the cloud.

Other works, as the one presented in [8] are most focused in the security of architectures or environment supported by the cloud, such as e-Commerce, where the users execute e-transactions with real money and the security is absolutely essential.

In the field related with this paper, healthcare, have appeared many systems or applications, which are supported by cloud technology. Due to the dynamic and extensive healthcare systems nature, they fall into different categories such as: Emergency Medical Systems (EMS), Health Cloud Exchange, Digital Image and Communications in Medicine or HealthCloud [8].

In each category there are many cloud-supported systems/applications that shows how the cloud computing applied in healthcare field could improve the social relations, and therefore, the medical results. A good example is the work shown in [9], an emergency medical system that provides access to personal health records of patients and is used by different group of users (Ambulance Paramedics, Emergency Department of Physicians and Nurses).

The system presented in [10] is a distributed web interactive system that provides a private cloud-based data sharing service allowing information exchange between different Electronic Health Record systems. In this way, two different systems with different standards can share information due to the cloud computing paradigm, increasing and improving the social relations.

Other work, more related with the approach of the work presented in this paper, is the system presented in [11], called BioTrack Home. This system, which is part of the project TEREHA [12], is e-Rehabilitation system for brain-injured patients developed by the Polytechnic University of Valencia (LabHuman-I3BH), health professionals from the NeuroRehabilitation Deparments of Nisa del Mar and Sevilla Aljarafe Hospital and Bienetc company. BioTrack, which is based in virtual reality and cloud technology, allows patients to perform the rehabilitation session at home. The patients' record themselves performing the rehabilitation sessions using a camera like Kinect connected to TV, a motion-tracking platform as Wii Balance Board and a laptop or PC. When the patient finished the performance of the session, all the information generated is sent to a cloud server. In this way, this information is being accessible by health professionals, who can evaluate the results of sessions and improve the diagnoses.

Other works [18] based in the concept of mobile cloud computing (decentralized architecture – peer to peer) have appeared lately, making possible that each mobile device can work as service provider. This concept applied to the healthcare area or rehabilitation context could ensure the security and privacy of patient's information because professionals, who want to get information about a patient, have to consume the services of patients. However, if professionals can list different information about several patients have to consume services from each patient, which can be a heavy task, so the cloud-mobile as solution in this context is not efficient. Moreover, in some cases where patients have the mobile phone off or without Internet connection the services are not accessible, so this solution could be inadequate or useless for a healthcare system. The platform presented in this paper, called CloudRehab, not only provides access to personal health records/information of patients as other systems [9], it provides a useful rehabilitation performance based on video recording and the transparent cloud support to the user. This rehabilitation process using video files ensures that health professionals can review the rehabilitation exercise without losing any detail of the performance.

With this platform the health professionals and patients have a remote and asynchronous interaction during all the rehabilitation process thanks to cloud technology, where unlike other systems, and as far as we know, these systems only use the cloud technology to data storage but not as communication tool [11] [12]. In addition, CloudRehab allows to health professionals the management of the rehabilitation sessions, customizing each of them.

# 4    Conclusions and Future Work

This paper describes CloudRehab, a cloud-supported e-Rehabilitation platform for brain-injured patients. The aim of CloudRehab is to improve of the quality of life and the effectiveness of rehabilitation of patients, providing useful cloud-supported applications and healthcare cloud services by enabling remote, asynchronous, continuous and at home monitoring of rehabilitation exercises. Thanks to these services, patients can perform his/her rehabilitation sessions at home and health professionals can monitor the patient's outcomes asynchronously. This new way of interaction between patients and health professionals through the cloud has been tested with different patients and with satisfactory results.

As future work we are currently working in the design and development of new functionalities such as the use of face or shape recognition to automatically check the correct performance of the rehabilitation exercises, the integration of CloudRehab with information systems and processes of the public health service of our country.

In addition, new functionalities for Zappa Platform are currently under development, such as the automatic management (detection, synchronization and pairing) of any device with any communication protocol in order to enable to interoperate with any device (medical device, other mobile devices, etc.), as well as cloud PaaS platforms (GAE, Azure, EC2).

**Acknowledgments.** This research work has been funded by the CEI BioTIC Granada (20F12/36), Innovation Office from the Andalusian Government (TIN-6600) and the Spanish Ministry of Economy and Competitiveness (TIN2012-38600).

## References

[1]   Ullah, S., Xuefeng, Z.: Cloud Computing: a Prologue. International Journal of Advanced Research in Computer and Communication Engineering 1(1) (March 2012)

[2]   Scott, K.: The Basics of Cloud Computing. White Paper (November 2010)

[3]   Mell, P.: The NIST Definition of Cloud Computng. Special Publication 800-145 (2011)

[4]   Meglic, M., et al.: Feasibilty of and eHealth Service to Support Collabora-tive Depression Care: Results of a Pilot Study

[5]   Wu, Y., Zhang, Z., Wu, C., Li, Z., Lau, F.C.M.: CloudMoV: Cloud-Based Mobile Social TV. IEEE Transactions on Multimedia 15(4) (June 2013)

[6]   Greer Jr., M.B., Ngo, J.W.: Personal Emergency Preparedness Plan (PEPP) Facebook App: Using Cloud Computing, Mobile Technology, and Social Networking Services to Decompress Traditional Channels of Communication during Emergencies and Disasters. In: 2012 IEEE Ninth International Conference on Services Co., pp. 494–498 (2012)

[7]   Li, J., Zhao, G., Rong, C., Tang, Y.: Semantic description of scholar-oriented social network cloud. J. Supercomput., 410–425 (2013)

[8]   Wooten, R., Klink, R., Sinek, F., Bai, Y., Sharma, M.: Design and Implementation of a Secure Healthcare Social Cloud System. In: 12th IEEE/ACM International Symposium on Cluster, Cloud and Grid Computing (2012)

[9]   Koufi, V., et al.: Ubiquitous access to cloud emergency medical services. In: The Proceedings of 10th IEEE International Conference on Information Technol-ogy and Applications in Biomedicine (ITAB), Corfu, Greece, pp. 1–4 (November 2010)

[10]  Mohammed, S., et al.: HCX: A Distributed OSGi Based Web Interaction Sys-tem for Sharing Health Records in the Cloud. In: The Proceedings of 2010 IEEE/WIC/ACM International Conference on Web Intelligence and Intelligent Agent Technology (WI-IAT), Toronto, Canada, vol. 3, pp. 102–107 (September 2010)

[11]  http://www.biotracksuite.com

[12]  http://www.everis.com/global/en-US/press-room/news/
      Paginas/tereha-integrated-tele-rehabilitation.aspx

[13]  http://www.polar.com/en/products/accessories/Polar_WearLink
      _transmitter_with_Bluetooth

[14]  Ruiz-Zafra, Á., Benghazi, K., Noguera, M., Garrido, J.L.: Zap-pa: An Open Mobile Platform to Build Cloud-based m-Health Systems. In: Ambient Intelligence-Software and Applications, pp. 87–94. Springer International Publishing (2013)

[15]  http://www.gnubila.com

[16]  http://www.ffmpeg.org/

[17]  Ruiz-Zafra, A., Noguera, M., Benghazi, K., Garrido, J.L., Cuberos Urbano, G.-V., Caracuel, A.: A Mobile Cloud-Supported e-Rehabilitation Plaform for Brain-Injured Patients. In: PervasiveHealth 2013. Re-hab Workshop (2013)

[18]  Srirama, S.N., Paniagua, C., Flores, H.: Social group information with mobile cloud services. Service Oriented Computing and Applications 6(4), 351–362 (2012)

# Architecting Infrastructures for Cloud-Enabled Mobile Devices

Javier Miranda[1], Joaquín Guillén[1], Javier Berrocal[2], Jose Garcia-Alonso[2],
Juan Manuel Murillo[2], and Carlos Canal[3]

[1] Gloin, Calle de las Ocas 2, Cáceres, Spain
{jmiranda,jguillen}@gloin.es
[2] Department of Information Technology and Telematic Systems Engineering,
University of Extremadura, Spain
{jberolm,jgaralo,juanmamu}@unex.es
[3] Department of Computer Science, University of Málaga, Spain
canal@lcc.uma.es

**Abstract.** The slow adoption of cloud computing by the industry has collapsed the initial expectations of everything shifting rapidly to the cloud. Big and complex services are either postponing their migration to the cloud, or have simply not considered it as an option. The real success is coming from small services which exploit the elasticity and availability of cloud resources to become available to hundreds and millions of users, many of which are using mobile devices. However, little or no progress has been made in developing new architectures that exploit the capabilities offered by cloud and mobile computing. In this paper, the cloud-enabled mobile devices concept is defined, making an overview of the related fields. People-as-a-Service is proposed as a new service model based on that concept, describing a high level architecture to support it, and presenting a business application based on this technology. As a result, cloud-enabled mobile devices promote the emergence of new scenarios and mobile applications based on new architectures where devices can act both as clients and servers.

**Keywords:** mobile, cloud, social, software, applications.

## 1 Introduction

The cloud paradigm has meant a revolution in the way in which computational resources are offered and consumed. It has contributed in the development of new service models which offer a set of desirable features like elasticity in the provisioning of resources, energy efficiency improvements, and enhanced costs control by using pay-as-you-go billing models [15].

Although this provide a favourable scenario for the adoption of cloud by the industry, such expectations are not being met [13]. Its major success is not currently coming from the biggest and most complex software systems, but the massively consumption of basic services by millions of users.

C. Canal and M. Villari (Eds.): ESOCC 2013, CCIS 393, pp. 277–287, 2013.
© Springer-Verlag Berlin Heidelberg 2013

Additionally, the use of these services from mobile devices like smartphones and tablets is currently growing. This has led to the adoption of cloud computing as the perfect matching piece of the puzzle in order to support the heavy-load processes of those applications and services which have been designed to be consumed from mobile devices. Cloud-based servers are perfectly suited for deploying the back-end components of a mobile-oriented application, since cloud offers several mechanisms for scaling and adapting the computing resources which are dedicated to the application depending on the user's demand [10]. Additionally, the cloud-based model solves the data ubiquity problem providing almost-unlimited storage capacity and transparent syncing mechanisms for accessing to the same information anywhere, and from any device.

In contrast, mobile applications and services are currently based on very simple architectures where the role of mobile devices is always defined as client. However, the current improvements on mobile devices features and capabilities allows us to start thinking about more advanced architectures which could make a different use of mobile resources, enabling smartphones and tablets to act not only as service consumers but also providers, leading to P2P architectures between mobile devices. In such context, this paper firstly present and approximation of the cloud-enabled mobile devices concept, following with a review of it contribution from different related fields, and finishing with an specific implementation of the proposed service model as a real industrial application of it.

The paper is structured as follows. In section 2, we define the concept of cloud-enabled mobile devices as we understand it, and we also present a set of related fields where the application of such concept could make some contribution. Based on that concept, section 3 describes the PeaaS approach, introducing a definition of the term, presenting the proposed architecture of such model, and describing nimBees®, a business application that makes use of the PeaaS paradigm. Finally the conclusions and future lines of work are described in section 5.

## 2    Cloud-Enabled Mobile Devices

In this section, we introduce the definition of the cloud-enabled mobile devices concept.

Due to the mobile's increasingly level of incursion in society, it begins to be a daily life's element whose impact in several social-related aspects becomes to be an interesting fact to be considered. Because of the personal nature of mobile phones, they can be understood as the digital mirror of its owner identity, containing representative information about its relationships, preferences, activities and behavior. Also, from a more social perspective, every device contains a huge amount of information and resources which can be used, processed and shared with other people, making use of the proper services and available applications. Additionally, from a computational perspective, mobile devices conform a complex network of distributed nodes with high processing capabilities, where each of them can collect information from its sensors about the surrounding environment.

In this context, mobile devices as a whole could be considered as a big 'cloud' environment of computational and information resources. As result, the concept of *cloud-enabled mobile devices* emerges from those factors, and it can be summarized with the following ideas:

– **Mobile devices can act as service providers.** Far from considering mobile devices as fool terminals for consuming services, the cloud-enabled mobile devices concept implies the service provider role of such devices. Current state-of-art allows the development and deployment of service providing applications in mobile environments, using technologies based on the most common web-services protocols like SOAP or REST for providing standard-based service interfaces.
– **Services deployed in mobile devices consume available resources and information.** The deployment and execution of services in cloud-enabled mobile devices treat the information and available mobile resources as sources of data that could be consumed and conveniently served.
– **Resources, information and patterns of use of mobile devices can be understood as the digital identity of their owners.** The manner in which people use their mobile phones can define accurately their social profile. These devices are increasingly used for reading and answering e-mails, taking photos, messaging, interacting in social networks, or browsing the web. How, when, and where is all this activity done is logged in the device, and such information, that represents the virtual behavior of each owner, could be exploited by new social-oriented mobile applications and services.

Having all the above in mind, cloud-enabled mobile devices (CEMD) could be defined as a conceptual perspective of mobile computing that highlights smartphones as the digital extension of their owners, and as unique devices able to depict the social profiles of their users, capable enough to provide and consume services and resources between them in a not necessarily centralized way of connection.

Based on this concept, we have compiled an initial set of related fields in where the CEMD concept can bring new ideas for the opening of new researching lines.

In the following subsections, a briefly review of such related fields is conducted.

## 2.1 Service Deployment Technology on Mobile Devices: CMED as Servers

Since mobile devices are enough capable of running complex processes, the use cases of that devices started to be closer to those of desktop systems. Today's differences are not so related with performance but has to be with the accessibility peripherals constraints like screen and keyboard sizes, and the battery draining issues. Consequently, the idea of considering mobile devices as servers has been explored by literature for a long time.

In [5], the WSAMI middleware is presented as a solution for developing mobile computing components based on Web-services, taking into account the network environment requirements in the definition of the component model. This solution uses a SOAP-based core broker and the CSOAP container, a compact container for Web-services adapted for allowing service deployments in mobile environments. In [6], an approach that allows mobile devices to behave as cloud service providers is presented. An implementation based on the JavaScript language is chosen, which aims to execute tasks as mobile-based Web Services. A mobile-based hosting and serving architecture is proposed in [11] in order to eliminate the common cloud-based hosting of the content being shared. This work proposes a server-based architecture where the meta-information about the connected devices is managed, acting also as a proxy for bandwidth optimization and offline content delivering. There are also some related projects working on the development of mobile-based web servers, like i-Jetty[1] and kWS[2] for the Android platform, and CocoaHTTPServer[3] for iOS platform.

The idea of cloud-enabled mobile devices is completely aligned with the target of the cited works. Probably, current technologies are scattered solutions which solve the main problem individually focused on different application areas. Maybe the pooling of the common requirements and its abstraction in order to build a more generic platform or framework could help in the evolution of the current mechanisms towards an standardized technology for mobile services provisioning and deployment.

### 2.2  CEMD as an Alternative to Client/Server Mobile Architectures

As exposed in the previous section, the current capabilities of mobile devices allow scenarios where mobile applications are functionally self-sufficient, in contrast with traditional full back-ended (and still partially back-ended) mobile applications. Current mobile performance and energy management allows begin to develop applications which can dispense with the server part that makes the heavy-load work. This starts to open ideas about designing novel architectures which differ from traditional client/server approaches, motivating alternatives like Mobile P2P.

In such context, [2] proposes the architectural principles enabling Mobile P2P. [7] presents an adaptation of traditional Peer-to-Peer network architecture for mobile devices and mobile networks using an XML-based protocol. [8] proposes an intelligent agent mediated peer-to-peer service-oriented-architecture (SOA) based on a Hybrid P2P architecture. In [9] an efficient Mobile P2P architecture wireless-centered approach is described, presenting performance enhancements from existing Mobile P2P schemes based on a hierarchical classification using clustering mobile peers.

Mobile Peer-to-Peer architectures perfectly fit with the proposed support environment for the cloud-enabled mobile devices concept. Such architecture model

---

[1] i-Jetty - http://code.google.com/p/i-jetty/
[2] kWS for Android -http://play.google.com/store/apps/details?id=org.xeustechnologies.android.kws
[3] CocoaHTTPServer - http://github.com/robbiehanson/CocoaHTTPServer/wiki

and its communication protocols could be enriched in order to include extra properties or attributes in node descriptions related with the nature of the services which are exposed on each one.

### 2.3 CEMD Supporting the Distributed Processing of Individual Social Profiles

This field, more social-related than technical-based, includes techniques, works and mechanisms for the treatment of individual social profiles based on the mobile-resident information. In such multidisciplinary area we want to underscore works like [3], where a system for sensing complex social systems with data collected from mobile phones over a long time is described. Also, the work highlight mobile phones as wearable sensors and their particularly usefulness as measuring human behavior. We can also cite [12], where authors argue that the technological and social characteristics of this device make it a useful tool in social science for allowing automatic observations and studies.

The cloud-enabled mobile devices concept contributes posing the basis for the development of novel applications and services which could make use of an underlying platform for getting an snapshot of the collectivism and social trends.

### 2.4 CEMD Towards Privacy Awareness

Following the previous subsection, the social trends and behavior measurement must be done in a secure and trusted environment. The cloud-enabled mobile devices concept implies the privacy-friendly treatment of the personal information, encouraging a service model based on the distributed processing of the information, avoiding its centralized storage. This idea promote the development of applications oriented to query the available resources and information inside the mobile environment, extracting raw data but keeping the information source on it.

### 2.5 CEMD as the 'Digital Interface' of Users

The information gathered by the different social networks about their users trends to be unified by such users in a kind of unique profile by allowing each social network to access the information of the others through their integration APIs. This allows make use of a variety of services using, for example, Twitter or Facebook credentials to log-in in them.

Growth of social networks and social applications consumption from mobile devices turns them as the key and the visible face of their owners from the other user's perspective. Mobile devices gather enough information about their owners to become as the digital representation of them in the virtual society. Could novel applications and services emerge, based on the cloud-enabled mobile devices concept, for extending such representation from social network avatars to real fields of society like healthcare or e-governance?

As a summary, there are several fields where the proposed cloud-enabled mobile devices concept can be understood as an additional motivation, inspiration or questionable perspective for considering different approaches for developing novel social-oriented mobile-based applications and services. The following section introduces our particular implementation of a service model based on this concept, proposing a high-level conceptual architecture to support that model, and an industrial application based on it.

# 3  People-As-A-Service

PeaaS is a mobile service model based on a *cloud-enabled mobile devices* platform. This platform is built on a cloud-inspired technological infrastructure that considers each subscribing mobile device as a provider in which multiple services can be deployed, instantiated and executed.

## 3.1  Description

The People-as-a-Service model relies on four basic principles:

- **Growing capabilities of mobile devices.** The capabilities of current smartphones and tablets are more than sufficiently advanced for them to assume the role of service providers beyond mere service consumers.
- **Cloud-enabled mobile devices.** Understanding a mobile device as a service provider introduces smartphones and tablets as new potential players in the resource provision battleground. PeaaS shifts the concept of an application server and a service deployment to the mobile device scenario, in a similar way as it is done by the PaaS model in cloud computing.
- **Personal mobile devices.** Mobile devices are highly personal, and they can be considered more than a technological infrastructure where applications and services are executed. Some works, such as [14], have even defined them as a combination of person plus technology, such that neither of them can stand alone. The way in which people make use of their smartphones today commonly implies the storing their personal information, contacts, relationships and preferences inside the device. Therefore, mobile devices are a virtual representation of their owners, including their location, trends, leadership capabilities, and behaviour.
- **Privacy-friendly.** The PeaaS model must have a highly-secure set of mechanisms to ensure the privacy policies established by the owner of each device.

These four pillars summarize the fundamentals of the PeaaS model. In order to provide the basis for creating and deploying new mobile services based on the described features, the PeaaS model should have the following capabilities:

- **Execution environment for services.** The PeaaS-based mobile services are deployed and run in a common execution environment that is platform-independent. Such environment provides an homogeneous access to the mobile device's resources, including the network, thereby allowing deployed services to communicate with other services or even instances of itself distributed across other mobile devices.

- **Networks of mobile devices**. The PeaaS model provides mechanisms for implementing private or public networks of mobile devices that may require any of the devices to be authenticated prior to accessing services in certain networks.
- **Discovery service.** The PeaaS model has a mechanism for discovering other connected devices which are supplying PeaaS-based services.
- **Device permission control.** The service execution environment allows device owners to define access policies to the device's resources for each of the deployed services.
- **Device-to-device communications.** The PeaaS model allows peer-to-peer communication between services deployed in different mobile devices.
- **Crowd-oriented services.** People's responsiveness to stimuli like questions or surveys sent to them through their mobile device is another form of service, with a strong social connotation, that is also considered in the PeaaS model. The aggregation of results extracted from the execution of crowd-oriented services (e.g. public opinion research surveys) is one of the possibilities tackled by the PeaaS model.

## 3.2   Architecture

A high-level conceptual architecture is proposed in order to support the previously described features and capabilities of the PeaaS model. Such architecture, inspired by similar solutions which have been developed in other fields like distributed services[4] or multi-agent systems[1], is composed by two basic elements: a mobile service environment and a catalogue server.

The *catalogue server* is a non-mobile element with a fixed and well defined service entrypoint where every new mobile device added to the PeaaS network must be connected, in order to authenticate and provide information about itself, and to retrieve information about the rest of connected devices. The *mobile service environments* are basically mobile applications that must be installed on every mobile device that wants to be part of a PeaaS network, providing an execution platform in which PeaaS-designed services can be deployed and executed. The mobile service environment is divided in four layers of abstraction, as illustrated in the PeaaS Architecture side of Figure 1:

- **Service Manager.** The service manager layer constitutes the core of the mobile service environment. It provides the capabilities required for deploying, removing, running or stopping services in the service container, and a basic communication interface to establish a link with the catalogue server. It also provides an interface to the user of the device to configure the mobile service environment properly.
- **Service Container.** This layer provides the execution environment where the PeaaS-based services are allocated, similar to a virtualization engine. The lifecycle of the allocated services is managed by the service manager layer.

– **Permission Control Layer.** The access permissions to the resources and services provided by the mobile device are verified by this layer, thereby avoiding accesses to certain resources by unauthorized services.
– **Resources Access Layer.** This layer abstracts PeaaS-based services from platform-specific implementations of each resource and service offered by mobile devices, providing a standard interface to be used homogeneously by the services.

### 3.3    nimBees®

As a result of transferring the research carried out on the PeaaS model towards the industry, a new mobile advertising product based on this service model is currently being developed by Gloin, a Spanish start-up, in order to be exploited commercially. The product is being launched commercially under the name of **nimBees®**.

The nimBees® architecture, illustrated in Figure 1, is a specialization of the one defined for the PeaaS model. Hence, the server and mobile architectures are designed as follows:

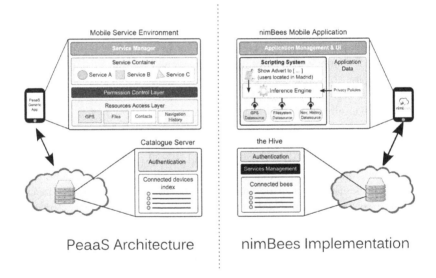

**Fig. 1.** nimBees® implementation of PeaaS architecture

– **Catalogue server.** Based on the concept of the catalogue server, the nimBees® platform is managed by a centralized server system that we call **the Hive**. Such server behaves as an index of connected devices, that carries out authentication processes, service participation monitoring, service launching and devices discovering tasks, amongst others.

– **Mobile service environment.** The mobile application of nimBees® is
based on the layered structure defined for the PeaaS model. According to
this structure, the application can be sliced into the following layers:

- **Service Manager.** This layer is represented by the core functions of
the application. Such functions include the notification management (for
messages, adverts or surveys), the user interface that allows users interact with the application, the communication and coordination functions
with the Hive, and the background processes in charge of managing the
deployment and the execution of services in the service container layer.
Additionally, the inference engine is also included in this level. It consists on a component that monitors user activity to extract behavioural
patterns that enrich the personal information profile. The information
generated by this component is used to determine whether the owner
matches the user profile required by the advertiser for a certain service
execution.
- **Service Container.** This layer has been implemented as a scripting
engine that provides an execution environment in which to run the
nimBees® services, which are written using our own scripting language.
- **Permission Control Layer.** The access to resources by the scripting
engine and, consequently, by the deployed services is subject to the privacy settings and access policies established by the user. Thus, users can
block the access to certain resources or information at every moment
and for any service.
- **Resources Access Layer.** Access to the device's resources is provided
to the deployed services in form of "sources of information". Such source
can be accessed by the scripting language with the proper syntax.

# 4  Discussion

In this paper we have introduced our definition of the cloud-enabled mobile
devices concept based on the increasing personal role that mobile devices are
taking in society and the new possibilities opened up by the growing processing capabilities of such devices for designing more complex applications and
architectures. Based on that concept, a new mobile service model have been
described as a reference model for depicting, serving and consuming personal
profiles within mobile devices, including a reference architecture of the model.
Finally, an industrial case based on the proposed architecture has been implemented and briefly described as a proof of concept. Notwithstanding, we have
identified some challenges and open issues that have not been addressed yet, but
for which we present some routes of possible solutions.

On one hand, there remains the search for scenarios in which the use of the architecture proposed in this paper is an indispensable requirement, and not an option. As a part of an initial set of such scenarios we point to environments where
the traditional workflow for downloading and installing mobile applications is
inverted, allowing trusted sources of software to install updates or components

in the mobile devices without user intervention. We also include scenarios in which the collective information processing cannot be done centrally, but only distributively. An additional candidate environment where those scenarios could be found is the development of applications for social-oriented interactions using device-to-device communications that are context-aware and proximity-aware. For instance, these applications may establish a kind of dialogue with surrounding devices automatically, accessing to the social profile of the device's owners in a peer-to-peer way, in order to find matches about likes (based on the privacy preferences of each user). In such scenarios, this approach may provide an efficient mechanism for offering and consuming context-aware personal profile information without storing it in third-party servers.

On the other hand, the role of the inference engine as a critical element for profiling the owners of mobile devices is another open issue to be considered. A deeper analysis of the heterogeneous sources of information from where the inference engine is fed and how could they be optimally used taking into account the limitations due to mobile environments are some the current open challenges in this line. In this sense, the resource-related efficiency of the approach is considered as an additional challenge to be addressed. We encouraged the use of battery friendly mechanisms like notifications-based protocols to bring alive the application execution process on demand instead of the traditional backgrounded polling-based protocols that could drain the device battery life.

## 5    Conclusions and Future Work

The increasing number of mobile devices and their growing performance capabilities provide a reasonable basis for designing and developing complex services which could be deployed over the proposed cloud-enabled mobile devices infrastructure.

This work attempts to make and advance in the opportunities that can be faced in the field of service provisioning in mobile devices, proposing a new service model that treats personal information, inherent to smartphones, as a new kind of content that can be served by mobile devices to other ones, conforming the PeaaS model.

nimBees® is a specific PeaaS implementation, that can be taken as an example of the potential capabilities of this model. Future lines of work include the application of the PeaaS model to other environments, the definition of collective intelligence services, and the inclusion of information from external sensors connected to the mobile phone, as well as the integration of the model into the Internet of Things paradigm.

**Acknowledgements.** This work has been partially funded by the former Spanish Ministry of Science and Innovation under Project TIN2012-34945 and the C.I.C.Y.T Project TIN2012-35669, and the current Spanish Ministry of Economy and Competitiveness. It has also been funded by the Government of Extremadura and FEDER funds.

# References

1. Athanasopoulos, D., Zarras, A.V., Issarny, V., Pitoura, E., Vassiliadis, P.: Cowsami: Interface-aware context gathering in ambient intelligence environments. Pervasive and Mobile Computing 4(3), 360–389 (2008)
2. Charas, P.: Peer-to-peer mobile network architecture. In: Proceedings First International Conference on Peer-to-Peer Computing, pp. 55–61 (2002)
3. Eagle, N., Pentland, A.(S.): Reality mining: sensing complex social systems. Personal and Ubiquitous Computing 10(4), 255–268 (2005)
4. Gu, T., Qian, H.C., Yao, J.K., Pung, H.: An architecture for flexible service discovery in octopus. In: ICCCN 2003, pp. 291–296 (2003)
5. Issarny, V., Tartanoglu, F., Liu, J., Sailhan, F.: Software Architecture for Mobile Distributed Computing. In: WICSA 2004, Oslo, Norvège, pp. 201–210 (2004)
6. Jansen, M.: About using mobile devices as cloud service providers. In: CLOSER 2012, pp. 147–152 (2012)
7. Kato, T., Ishikawa, N., Sumino, H., Hjelm, J.: A platform and applications for mobile peer-to-peer communications. Emerging Applications (2003)
8. Leong, P., Miao, C., Lim, B.: Agent mediated peer-to-peer mobile service-oriented architecture. In: DEST 2007, pp. 414–419 (2007)
9. Li, H., Bok, K., Park, Y., Yoo, J.: An efficient mobile peer to peer architecture in wireless ad hoc network. Convergence and Hybrid Information, 1–8 (2011)
10. Qi, A.H., Gani: Research on mobile cloud computing: Review, trend and perspectives. In: DICTAP 2012, pp. 195–202 (2012)
11. Raatikainen, M., Mikkonen, T., Myllarniemi, V., Makitalo, N., Mannisto, T., Savolainen, J.: Mobile content as a service a blueprint for a vendor-neutral cloud of mobile devices. IEEE Software 29(4), 28–32 (2012)
12. Raento, M., Oulasvirta, A., Eagle, N.: Smartphones: An Emerging Tool for Social Scientists. Sociological Methods & Research 37(3), 426–454 (2009)
13. RedShift research. Adoption, Approaches & Attitudes. The future of Cloud Computing in the Publicand Private Sectors. Technical report, AMD & RedShift research (2011),
http://www.amd.com/us/Documents/Cloud-Adoption-Approaches-and-Attitudes-Research-Report.pdf
14. Roure, D.D.: Research on the web - the rise of new digital scholarship. In: WEBIST 2012, p. 5 (2012)
15. Zhang, Q., Cheng, L., Boutaba, R.: Cloud computing: state-of-the-art and research challenges. Journal of Internet Services and Applications 1(1), 7–18 (2010)

# Improving Security Assurance of Services through Certificate Profiles

Marioli Montenegro, Antonio Maña, and Hristo Koshutanski

Escuela Técnica Superior de Ingeniería Informtica
Universidad de Málaga, Spain
{marioli,amg,hristo}@lcc.uma.es

**Abstract.** Cloud and Web Services technologies offer a powerful cost-effective and fast growing approach to the provision of infrastructure, platform and software as services. However, these technologies still raise significant concerns regarding security assurance and compliance of data and software services offered. A new trend of a service security certification has been recently proposed to overcome the limitations of existing security certificates by representing security certification in a structured, machine-processable manner that will enable automated reasoning for certified security features in security-critical domains. However, the richness and flexibility of the underlying certificate models and languages comes with the price of increased *complexity* in processing and comparing those certificates and related security claims in practice. In this paper, we propose the concept of *certificate profile* to provide a mechanism to address processability and interoperability of service security certificates. We present a conceptual model and a concrete realization of the model within the context of the European project ASSERT4SOA.

## 1 Introduction

Service Oriented Computing (SOC) has facilitated a paradigm shift in software provisioning models, such as Software as a Service (SaaS), Platform as a Service (PaaS), Infrastructure as a Service (IaaS), providing enormous benefits [1]. However, lack of security assurance of third-party services is hampering their wider adoption in business- and security-critical domains. In traditional software provisioning models, security certification of software by trusted third party entities is used to provide *security assurance* to consumers. Certification schemes such as Common Criteria [2] are well established and quite successful in providing the required security assurance to consumers. Thus, software *compliance* to established security certification criteria will provide certain guarantees on security assurance of that software.

However, applying security certification as is to SOC is infeasible. A key obstacle being the natural language representation of the certificates, that requires manual inspection, preventing their usage in typical SOC scenarios like service discovery, selection, and composition. To overcome the limitations of existing security certificates, and facilitate adoption of security certification in security-critical domains, the concept of *service security certification* has been proposed

C. Canal and M. Villari (Eds.): ESOCC 2013, CCIS 393, pp. 288–302, 2013.
© Springer-Verlag Berlin Heidelberg 2013

[3,4,5]. Consequently, an outcome of a service security certification is a security certificate of a service. A security certificate is realized by a language that enables the representation of a certificate in a structured, machine processable manner that would enable automated reasoning to be performed on them and thus make it feasible for certified security features to be part of any SOC scenario [6].

Given the complexity of the service provisioning models, the languages describing security certificates are expected to cover a rich set of fields and structures that enables the representation of processes and results of different services security certification activities. For example, representing certification artefact for cloud-based services would require complex and rich representation of underline security properties and evidences supporting those properties. Therefore, languages provide users with different representation alternatives and structural choices that are necessary to accommodate the heterogeneity of the processes and results of certification.

However, this flexibility and expressiveness comes with the price of an increased difficulty in determining the semantic soundness of a certificate with respect to the certification that is the origin of such certificate, and places higher complexity on the process of comparing certificates. As a side effect, security assurance of services provided by certification activities may not face expected adoption and success given the complexity in processing and comparing security certificates, thus making impractical any sort of automated reasoning to be performed on them, and consequently neglect an adequate scalability of any service selection based on certified security features.

For service consumers, the possibility to compare the certified security features of a service with their security requirements is an important aspect during service discovering, selection and composition process. The integration of non-functional security aspects of services with other non-functional properties (such as performance and scalability) can be well handled on the level of service query language and the corresponding service selection logic [7].

We propose the use of a concept of *certificate profile* to provide a mechanism to address processability and interoperability of service security certificates. There are three main use cases where the certificate profile plays a key role:

(i) *Facilitate comparison among security certificates.* Given the flexibility and richness of certificate languages and ability to express similar security assertions in a different way, a certification authority may wish to define a certificate profile (e.g., by defining various certificate structure and content mandatory) to enforce uniformity of content of certificates when issued by accredited entities.

(ii) *Facilitate production of security certificates compliant to specific certification criteria.* Given that a certificate language can support various certification schemes, a certification authority has to define its certification criteria in a certificate profile, so that all issued security certificates will conform to the criteria defined by the certificate profile.

(iii) *Enable consumers to specify their security requirements for the services.* Similarly to CC-PP [8], the consumers or consumer groups may wish to define a certificate profile with domain-specific security requirements (criteria). When services conform to such certificate profiles, it eases the decision making process for the consumers as the conformance to a profile implies that their requirements are met by the service.

The rest of the paper is organized as following. Section 2 presents related work on security certification of services. Section 3 introduces the concept of certificate profile and its structure. Section 4 presents the core of profile-based management of security certificates. Section 5 describes a proof-of-concept realization of certificate profile within a European project ASSERT4SOA. Section 6 concludes the paper and outlines future work.

## 2    Related Work

**Security Certification Schemes**: There are quite a few established and successful schemes such as Common Criteria for Information Security (CC), Commercial Product Assurance (CPA) and so on. Security certification schemes can be broadly classified based on the domains that they are applicable in, the recognition of the certification schemes, the descriptive or normative character of the issued certificates and so on. Among the existing schemes, CC is a widely recognized, used descriptive certification scheme. The CC scheme avoids an all or nothing benchmark, by providing security assurance at varying levels, called Evaluation Assurance Levels (EAL). This provides flexibility for product vendors to get their product certified at lower assurance levels and improve the EAL over time. The CC scheme is primarily "claims" based, where the vendor makes claims about the security functionalities in the product in a document called "Security Target" (CC-ST) [2]. However, consumers can specify their requirements in a document called "Protection Profile" (CC-PP), and vendors can build products that conform to a CC-PP (and claim conformance in the CC-ST).

However, in practice, the comparison of products having different "claims" can be very hard. This is due to the representation of the CC-related documents (CC-PP, CC-ST) in natural language, which is often filled with legalese and heavy security jargon making it rather complex to understand for non-security experts. Hence, it becomes quite difficult to determine if a particular product satisfies a consumer's security requirements and to compare different products against their requirements.

**Digital Security Certificates**: The resulting security certificates from current security certification schemes are not represented in a digital format. Though there are a few "digital security seals" such as the TRUSTe privacy seal [9], McAfee SECURE seal [10] and so on. These seals are normative statements regarding the security feature of an entity, which can be seen as a step towards digital security certificates, but cannot provide any meaningful assurance to consumers as they do not contain any information regarding the certified entity.

There are several digital certificate standards for identity and authorization management used in SOC, such as X.509 [11] and SAML [12]. Both standards support public-key (identity) certificates and attribute certificates for purposes of user authentication and authorization. These certificates are used as a means to gain a *security functionality* (such as authentication and authorization) and are quite different from the notion of digital security certificates used to provide *security assurance*.

**Security Certification of Web Services**: The wide spread adoption of Service-Oriented Architectures (SOAs) and Software-as-a-Service (SaaS) provisioning model enables large-scale heterogeneous ICT infrastructures be dynamically built from loosely coupled, well-separated services, where key non-functional properties like security, privacy, and reliability are of increased and critical importance. In such scenarios, certifying service's security properties will be crucial. Today's certification schemes do not provide, from an end-user perspective, a reliable way to assess the trustworthiness of composite services in the context where (and at the time when) these will be actually consumed.

ASSERT4SOA project [5] is filling this gap by producing novel techniques and tools  fully integrated within the SOA lifecycle  for expressing, assessing and certifying security properties for complex service-oriented applications. The purpose of ASSERT4SOA is to provide a framework for handling Advanced Security Service Certificates, called ASSERTs. The originality of these new ASSERT certificates resides in the embedded abstractions  security properties, targets of certification, evaluation-specific results (such as formal model-based, or test-based), validation algorithms, and service binding mechanisms.Therefore, when an ASSERT certificate is bound to a service, the service consumer will benefit from an insight on the security capabilities of the service, going well beyond the information conveyed by existing digital certificates (refer also to Section 5).

**Security Certification of Cloud Services**: Cloud technology offers a powerful and fast growing approach to the provision of infrastructure (IaaS), platform (PaaS) and software (SaaS) as services. However, despite its appeal, cloud technology still raises significant concerns regarding the security, privacy, governance and compliance of data and software services offered through it. Such concerns arise from the difficulty to verify security properties of the different types of services available through clouds and the uncertainty of the owners and users of such services about the security of their services once the services are uploaded and offered through a cloud. This difficulty stems from the fact that the provision and security of a cloud service is sensitive to potential interference between the features and behaviors of all the inter-dependent services in all layers of the cloud stack, as well as dynamic changes in them.

CUMULUS project [4] proposes a research program whose aim is to address these limitations by developing an integrated framework of models, processes and tools supporting the certification of security properties of infrastructure (IaaS), platform (PaaS) and software application layer (SaaS) services in cloud using multiple types of evidences regarding security, such as service testing, monitoring and trusted computing proofs, and based on models for hybrid, incremental and multi-layer security certification.

**Service Security Certification and SLAs**: The concept of Service Level Agreement (SLA) was introduced with an objective similar to the one of our proposal. SLAs provide means for service providers to declare explicitly claims about "quality" aspects of their services. SLAs can be used to inform users about different aspects of a service such as performance, limitations of use, security, etc. There are many scenario in which these provider-backed claims are enough for clients. However, there are also other scenarios in which clients need additional assurance provide by trusted external entities. In these cases, SLAs do not suffice and other mechanism are required in order to establish the necessary trust between elements and services. It is important to note that our proposal is not an alternative to SLAs, but much more a complement. In fact, an important application of security service certificate is their use in conjunction with SLAs. For example, by using WS-Agreement [13], a widely used SLA standard, a service provider can provide (claims) non-functional security properties to potential consumers described via an *agreement template* specifying the service and its guarantees including the security properties provider's services are certified for. Thus, service consumers will gain additional level of security assurance provided by the service security certificates to the trust in the claims stated by the service provider on the security aspects of his services. Other approaches define SLAs to enable specification of trust relationships used to derive service interactions enriched with security functionality such as authentication and non-repudiation [14]. These approaches focus on specifying security functionality of services but not on specifying security assurance of services.

## 3   Certificate Profile

The main goal of a certificate profile is to provide suitable means for creation of certificates by ensuring semantic uniformity of certificates for a specific (domain of) certification capturing any certification scheme of expertise, evaluation specific expertise, products certified, specific vocabulary of use for expressing security aspects of certified products, and other certification artefacts relevant to defining the semantics of certificates.

### 3.1   Profile Structure

A certificate profile is a mechanism to specify the contents and semantics of a class of security certificates. A certificate profile is composed of three parts: (i) *Certificate Template*: specification of the common structure and the values of specific fields mandatory for a given certificate class, (ii) *Semantic Rules*: specification of the semantics of the certificate class in the form of semantic rules, and (iii) *Vocabulary*: specification of vocabulary terms (ideally ontology-referenced terms) providing restrictions on use of vocabulary for language artefacts of security certificates of the given certificate class.

Figure 1 shows the abstract structure of the certificate profile. The three profile components provide certificates content uniformity in three different dimensions: certificate template ensures structural uniformity; semantic rules ensure

**Fig. 1.** Certificate Profile Structure

integrity of intended semantics of certification; while certificate vocabulary ensures common ontology-based ground of terms and ranges of possible values of certification (in a given domain).

**Certificate Template.** The certificate template is a partially filled certificate that establishes the common structure and content of all certificates created based on a certificate profile. Therefore, any certificate conformant to a profile must include the fields, structure and values defined in the template of the profile. A certificate template specifies an incomplete certificate structure with respect to a given certificate syntax (e.g., XML schema). It is used as baseline for creating new certificates.

Alternatively, a certificate template can be considered as a set of implicit (semantic/integrity) rules. These rules are simple and easy to understand. For this reason, it is not required to represent a template as a set of rules, but used as a certificate template - a more intuitive notion for expressing predefined structure and values of profile elements. We have defined some high-level interpretation rules for any certificate template structure:

(i) If a template defines a certificate artefact instance but with an empty content (value), the resulting certificate must have the identified artefact as part if its structure with possibly any (syntactically valid) structure or content inside.

(ii) If a template defines a certificate artefact instance but with certain content (value), the resulting certificate must have the identified artefact instance as part if its structure and the same value determined by the template.

(iii) If a template defines N number instances of a specific certificate artefact (if certificate syntax allows) where each instance with specific structure and content, the resulting certificate must have at least the same number of the certificate artefact instances each one with the same structure and content as defined in the template.

If we want to enforce the existence of a certificate artefact but with an empty structure one can achieve that by using rule (i) defining the artefact with empty content in a template, and by using a semantic rule that enforces, restricts or checks whether the given artefact has an empty content (value) in a resulting certificate structure.

The goal of rule (iii) is to allow a template to predefine multiple instances of a certificate artefact each one with specific structure and content. For example, a template may define two instances of a certificate artefact TypeSpecificEvaluation, the first one defining some specific structure and content of test-based service evaluation with mandatory test cases, while the second instance defining formal model based service evaluation under a specific formal model language.

**Semantic Rules.** The Semantic Rules define semantic constraints and dependencies between content of certificate artefacts within a given class of certificates. While the implicit rules defined by the certificate template are enough for structure-wise restrictions (requiring an optional element be mandatory, constraining specific structure or content of certificate artefacts, etc.), there are cases where more complex restrictions are needed. Some examples of more complex rules can be (but not limited to):

(i) Artefact dependencies: define presence or content of an artefact depending on the presence or content of another artefact.
(ii) Artefact content constraints: restrict an artefact content within a range of acceptable values, or restrict artefact content as a function of the content of other artefacts.

Semantic rules represent a solution, allowing to formulate rules to ensure integrity of an intended semantics of a given certificate class, i.e., preserving specific semantics of certification artefacts. Semantic rules can be formulated in rule based languages (such as Schematron [15] or variants of OCL [16]) or imperative languages (such as Java or Javascript) in function of the underlying certificate language and supported implementation. The choice of a language for expressing semantic rules has an important implication to achieve machine processability and reasoning of the rules. The language should allow rich fine-grained expression of *patterns* over certificates content and structure.

Some examples of rules are the following:

(i) The content of an artefact TargetOfCertification must be of type one of "Software-as-a-service" or "Platform-as-a-service";
(ii) A security property definition artefact and the property formal model definition artefact of model-based evaluation must use the same abstract security property category (e.g., "Confidentiality");
(iii) Restrict the certification of security mechanisms to a pre-defined set of mechanisms for a given application domain. For example, in the domain of eHealth a profile can define by semantic rules that all confidentiality properties on storage services must be certified based on the evaluation of the use of AES block cipher [17] with the approved modes of operation [18].

**Certificate Vocabulary** The certificate vocabulary part of the profile provides a means to define and restrict use of vocabularies on different certificate artefacts. One of the goals of the vocabulary part is to enable specific per profile (i.e., per a class of certificates) integration of the underlying certificate language with different ontology terms coming from different domains of knowledge. In that way, ontology integration will enhance the semantic robustness among all certificates conformant to a given profile and even among certificates conformant to different profiles, which have been diminished by flexibility and openness of security certificate languages (models). Ontologies provide not only a source of semantically defined terms but also provide means to define relations between terms, and equivalences between different terms. That gives us a powerful way to query ontologies for different aspects of certification and related semantics.

Restricting the range of values of certificate artefacts to terms defined in ontology will make all certificates conforming to the given profile processable and comparable on those artefacts, as their values are ontology terms with defined semantics and relations among them. For example, a vocabulary used for a certificate artefact named AbstractSecurityProperty can be restricted to one of "Confidentiality", "Integrity" or "Availability" (also known as CIA triad of core attributes of information security), and other properties could be ontology-modeled using meta-data or relationships between information. For example, non-repudiation can be viewed as a property related to integrity of relationship between information and information issuer.

Similarly to the certificate template and semantic rules, one can see the certificate vocabulary section of the profile as a set of implicit rules each one restricting use of vocabulary for certificate artefacts. However, by defining explicit vocabulary section we have, first a more intuitive notion for expressing vocabulary restrictions and, second enable the use of dynamic values based on queries over ontologies, which otherwise would be difficult to achieve as semantic rules.

The certificate vocabulary section enables the use of *static* or *dynamic* vocabularies. A static vocabulary defines actual terms inside a profile. It is suitable for offline processing, but could be out-dated by an ontology evolution/update. In contrast, a dynamic vocabulary defines actual terms by means of a query over ontology, which requires Internet connection for online processing. Ontology queries will be executed at the time of use of a given profile, i.e., the actual terms (values) will be dynamically retrieved from ontology when the profile is used. Static vocabulary provides a means to define ontology terms or just terms without any ontology context to be used statically without subject to further refinements/changes.

By the time being, we limit the use of either static or dynamic type vocabularies per certificate artefact, but not both types. Our main motivation is to provide a consistent vocabulary solution across all certificates during the lifetime of a certificate profile. If one specifies both types vocabulary per artefact, assuming dynamic vocabulary takes precedence over static vocabulary, there could be a case where ontology evolves (e.g., removing some terms or redefining those) in a way that makes the static part of the vocabulary inconsistent with respect to the actual values in ontology. Then, in the case of offline use of the profile, certificates will be created considering the static vocabulary, which will be inconsistent with those certificates created based on the dynamic vocabulary. This aspect may significantly decrease processability of certificates conformant to the profile given that the ontology of the dynamic vocabulary gives the semantics (interpretation/reasoning) of the vocabulary terms when used to process or compare the corresponding certificate artefacts.

It is the responsibility of the issuer of a certificate profile to ensure that any domain ontology used as part of the certificate profile is consistent with the overall vocabulary of the profile. We assume that certification authorities produce *well-formed* certificate profiles with consistent vocabulary definitions.

An issuer of a profile may decide to enforce or not the use of vocabularies. When a vocabulary specification is defined mandatory the referenced language artefact must have a value from the vocabulary. If a vocabulary is optional the referenced language artefact should have a value from the vocabulary.

## 4   Profile-Based Certificate Management

We will describe two core certificate management operations based on profiles: profile-based creation of certificates, and the opposite one, profile conformance verification of certificates. The former facilitates certification authorities, certificate issuers or even service providers/owners (in case of self-signed certificates) in creation of certificates conformant to a profile, while the latter operation will facilitate service consumers be that developers or system designers during a service-based system development lifecycle.

For example, during system design to discover relevant services a client can query a service repository for functional and non-functional security aspects for services of interests [7]. However, given the openness and flexibility of certificate language artefacts in expressing security properties and related evidences supporting those, the client would be much more interested in referring to a certificate profile along the query to the repository in order to restrict (not use the entire variety of) security assertions to a limited subset of those specified by a certificate profile. In that way, certificate profiles enable much more effective and practical comparison of security aspects of services during a service discovery phase, where matching and discovery of non-functional security aspects is reduced to matching within those services with security certificates conformant to a profile. Certificate profiles provide an important step towards a fully automated security assessment of non-functional security aspects of certified services.

There are also other relevant aspects of profile-based certificate management that can occur during a service composition phase and during runtime system adaptation, where service replacement is achieved not only based on functional service aspects but also if non-functional security properties are preserved by the new service [19]. In this case, certificate profiles can be well used to verify if the new replaced service is certified conforming to a given certificate profile specifying the required security assertions.

### 4.1   Profile-Based Creation of Certificates

Given that a certificate language can support various certification schemes, profile-based certificate creation process will facilitate production of security certificates compliant to specific certification criteria. Figure 2(a) shows the profile-based creation process. Prerequisite to the creation process is the discovery or selection of a certificate profile specifying domain specific security aspects relevant to the certification process a service has to undergone. Once the

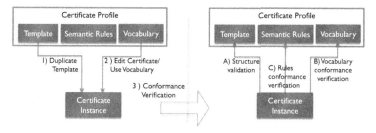

(a) Profile-based Certificate Creation (b) Profile Conformance Verification

**Fig. 2.** Profile-based Certificate Management

profile is selected and loaded, all dynamic vocabulary specifications (e.g., ontology queries) are processed. If some dynamic vocabulary specifications depend on other artefacts and values in order to be processed, these vocabularies should be processed at the time when the issuer creates the corresponding artefacts.

Once the profile is processed, first a duplicate of certificate template is done, and a certificate instance is created with an initial structure and content of the duplicated template data. Next step is the actual process of editing the certificate artefacts and creation of new artefacts as needed by the issuer. This step heavily relies on the use of certificate vocabulary defined in the profile. When an artefact's vocabulary is specified as mandatory, the process should enforce the choice of the vocabulary terms. Otherwise, if optional, the process should recommend, suggest a choice of terms but leaving the issuer to specify own terms when he finds necessary. Third step of certificate creation process, the final certificate instance is verified for conformance to the profile (presented in the next subsection). All non-properly used artefacts and corresponding vocabularies will be reported. Step 3 will give a feedback to redo step 2 of the creation process by repeating it until the certificate instance conforms to the profile.

### 4.2   Profile Conformance Verification of Certificates

The conformance verification process described can be generally used to verify a certificate for profile conformance, and not only as part of the certificate creation process. Figure 2(b) shows the three main steps of conformance verification process. There is always a validation step taking place before the conformance verification process, validating if the certificate instance conforms to the syntax of a given certificate model, that is, if the certificate instance is a syntactically valid certificate. Otherwise, the verifier should not proceed with the verification process. If the certificate instance is a valid certificate, the first step of conformance verification is a certificate structure validation against the template part of the given profile. The certificate structure is validated if it contains all the required artefacts and artefacts' content as defined in the template.

If structure validation succeeds, the second step is vocabulary conformance verification. Prerequisite to this step is to first process all dynamic vocabularies.

That is, retrieving all certificate artefacts' vocabulary terms from the corresponding ontologies by executing the queries. Once dynamic vocabularies are instantiated, all certificate artefacts' vocabulary terms within the vocabulary part are checked against the corresponding artefacts' content in the certificate instance. All certificate artefacts defined to have an optional (non-mandatory) vocabulary will not be verified for conformance.

If vocabulary conformance succeeds, the third step is the semantic rules conformance verification. All semantic rules are processed, checked if satisfied by the certificate structure and content. Since the semantic rules of the profile may depend on the actual content (vocabulary) of a certificate artefacts in order to determine the semantic integrity of the certificate content, it is important to verify vocabulary conformance first, and then the semantic rules conformance.

We note that the vocabulary section of the profile does not enforce mandatory use of certificate artefacts. An optional certificate artefact can be forced to be mandatory either by the template part of the profile or by the semantic rules.

## 5   Proof-of-Concept Realization

We will present a realization of the concept of security profile within the European project ASSERT4SOA. The project has developed a concept of a digital security certificate for services, called ASSERT. An ASSERT certificate is realised by an XML-based language which enables representation of a service security features in a structured, machine processable manner [6].

### 5.1   ASSERT Certificate

An ASSERT security certificate consists of the following main parts: *ASSERT-Core* and *ASSERTTypeSpecific*. An ASSERTCore artefact defines the common aspects of a certificate, which are evaluation independent, such as certification process-specific information, target of certification, security property, security problem definition, service binding information, ASSERT issuer, etc. A *TargetOfCertification* artefact, part of the ASSERTCore, provides details about the service and its underlying architecture. Services can be of different types, such as SaaS, PaaS, or IaaS. It is important to define the TOC type in order to analyse if the certified properties are sufficient for a particular service type. A *SecurityProperty* artefact, part of the ASSERTCore, provides consumers with information on what property is certified and how the security property is realized by the service. Defines varying levels of abstraction such as an abstract security property, property context, assets being protected, etc.

An ASSERTTypeSpecific artefact defines the representation of details and results of a service evaluation process supporting the certified security property. Three evaluation categories are defined: Evaluation through testing, called ASSERT-E [20], Evaluation through formal analysis, called ASSERT-M [21], and Evaluation through ontology-based analysis, called ASSERT-O [22]. A *Property*

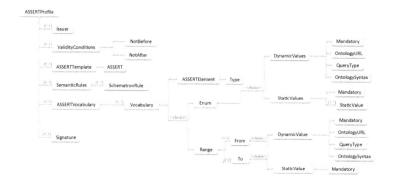

**Fig. 3.** ASSERT Profile Structure

artefact, part of the ASSERTTypeSpecific, defines type-specific property specification facilitating advanced reasoning such as comparison/ordering of security
properties among services of same type evaluation.

## 5.2   ASSERT Profile

We have defined the structure of a certificate profile as an XML scheme, shown
in Figure 3, and called the new structure an ASSERT Profile. For the sake of
presentation, we show the profile structure in a rather informal way abstracting
away some irrelevant XML schema details to better focus on the actual structure.

We will go through the main elements. The certificate template is called *AS-
SERTTemplate*. An ASSERTTemplate contains one element of type ASSERT
certificate. Thus, an ASSERTTemplate contains an incomplete XML instance of
an ASSERT certificate (according to the ASSERT XML schema). The semantic
rules are implemented in Schematron [15]. Thus, semantic rules contain a set of
*SchematronRule* elements. Schematron is an ISO standard rule-based validation
language expressed in XML. Using Schematron, it is possible to make assertions
about the presence or absence of patterns in XML trees.

The certificate vocabulary is called *ASSERTVocabulary*, which contains a set
of *Vocabulary* elements each defining a specific vocabulary per an artefact (or set
of artefacts) of ASSERT certificates. An *ASSERTElement*, part of the Vocabulary, identifies the ASSERT field(s) where specific vocabulary will be applied.
Currently, we support the use of XPath [23] as a query language to identify nodes
of ASSERT certificates where the vocabulary is to be applied. There is a choice
of *Enumeration* or *Range* type of a Vocabulary. The former defines an explicit
set of values, while the latter instead defines a range of values as *From* and *To*
boundaries, such as integer range, double range (e.g., percentage), date range,
etc. Each of the Enumeration and Range types are further defined as a choice
of *DynamicValues* or *StaticValues* with an attribute field Mandatory indicating
mandatory or optional use of the vocabulary data.

The *DynamicValues* artefact defines an OntologyURI of how to retrieve the
ontology; OntologySyntax specifies the ontology syntax; QueryType identifies

```
<ASSERTProfile>
 <ASSERTTemplate>
  <ASSERT>
   <ASSERTCore>
    <ASSERTIssuer>O=University of Malaga,OU=Computer Science Department,C=ES</ASSERTIssuer>
    <TargetOfCertification Type="http://assert4soa.eu/ontology/a4s-language#Platform-as-a-service"/>
   </ASSERTCore>
   <ASSERTTypeSpecific>
    <ASSERT-E/>
   </ASSERTTypeSpecific>
  </ASSERT>
 </ASSERTTemplate>
 <SemanticRules>
  <sch:schema queryBinding="xslt" xmlns:sch="http://purl.oclc.org/dsdl/schematron">
   <sch:pattern>
    <sch:rule context="ASSERT/ASSERTTypeSpecific/ASSERT-E/Property/PropertyName">
     <sch:assert test="//ASSERT/ASSERTCore/SecurityProperty[@PropertyAbstractCategory=current()]">
      [Property E and property Core integrity check] SecurityProperty.PropertyAbstractCategory
      has to match the same value of ASSERT.ASSERTTypeSpecific.ASSERT-E.Property.PropertyName
     </sch:assert>
    </sch:rule>
   </sch:pattern>
  </sch:schema>
 </SemanticRules>
 <ASSERTVocabulary>
  <Vocabulary>
   <ASSERTElement Type="XPATH">//ASSERT/ASSERTCore/SecurityProperty/@PropertyAbstractCategory</ASSERTElement>
   <Enum Mandatory="true">
    <DynamicValues OntologyURI="http://assert4soa.eu/ontology/security.owl" OntologySyntax="RDF/XML" QueryType="SPARQL">
     PREFIX rdfs: &lt;http://www.w3.org/2000/01/rdf-schema#&gt;
     SELECT ?subClass WHERE { ?subClass rdfs:subClassOf
                  &lt;http://assert4soa.eu/ontology/security#AbstractSecurityProperty&gt;. }
    </DynamicValues>
   </Enum>
  </Vocabulary>
  <Vocabulary>
   <ASSERTElement Type="XPATH">//ASSERT/ASSERTCore/SecurityProperty/@PropertyContext</ASSERTElement>
   <Enum Mandatory="false">
    <StaticValues>
     <StaticValue> http://assert4soa.eu/ontology/a4s-language#PersistentStorage</StaticValue>
     <StaticValue> http://assert4soa.eu/ontology/a4s-language#TemporalStorage</StaticValue>
     <StaticValue> http://assert4soa.eu/ontology/a4s-language#Transit</StaticValue>
     <StaticValue> http://assert4soa.eu/ontology/a4s-language#Usage</StaticValue>
    </StaticValues>
   </Enum>
  </Vocabulary>
 </ASSERTVocabulary>
</ASSERTProfile>
```

**Fig. 4.** ASSERT Profile Example

the query language used to encode the query; and the actual query value. We currently support the use of SPARQL [24] as an RDF query language to retrieve information and manipulate data store in RDF format. The *Static Values* artefact defines a set of vocabulary terms as a simple list of values, or in case of a Range type a single vocabulary term.

### 5.3   ASSERT Profile Example

An example of an ASSERT profile structure shown in Figure 4 defines the following class of ASSERT certificates. The ASSERTTemplate defines all AS-SERTs conformant to this profile must: *(i)* Be for software-as-a-service (SaaS) model services, i.e., all ASSERTs must have TargetOfCertification element with an attribute Type qualified as "http://assert4soa.eu/ontology/a4s-language# Platform-as-a-service"; *(ii)* Be issued by the University of Malaga as authority, i.e., all ASSERTs must have an ASSERTIssuer element with the defined value structure; *(iii)* Be produced by a test-based certification process, i.e. must contain ASSERT-E type-specific structure, but without defining any particular content for ASSERT-E. This means that ASSERTs conformant to the profile can contain any specific ASSERT-E content.

The SemanticRules define one Schematron rule which forces the security property abstract category value as defined in the SecurityProperty element in the ASSERTCore of the ASSERT be the same value with that of the Property-Name of Property definition of ASSERT-E. The ASSERTVocabulary defines two vocabularies one for the PropertyAbstractCategory attribute of the SecurityProperty element and another for the PropertyContext attribute again of the SecurityProperty element. The first vocabulary defines dynamic values encoded as a SPARQL query marking those as mandatory. These terms are defined as subClassOf of the ontology class "http://assert4soa.eu/ontology/security#AbstractSecurityProperty". The second vocabulary defines static values for the artefact PropertyContext as terms within an ontology-specific definition.

# 6    Conclusions and Future Work

We have presented the concept of certificate profile to provide a mechanism to address processability and interoperability of service security certificates. We have presented the conceptual model and a concrete realization of the model within the context of the European project ASSERT4SOA. Validation of the use of security certificates and certificate profiles under specific criteria have been conducted and results reported in [25].

A direction of future work will focus on using certificate profiles to express certificate issuer competence (accreditation). This is an important aspect for end-users when they receive a security certificate of a service but wishes to know if the issuer of the security certificate does have the competence, expertise for the certified security claims. Our initial idea is to use attribute certificates (e.g., X.509) to encapsulate so-called "competence" profiles so that a certificate issuer can attach or provide his accreditation along the issued security certificates. The verification of such issuer competence will follow the same lines of profile conformance verification, i.e., if a security certificate issued by a given issuer conforms to the issuer's competence profile then the security certificate is verified to be issued by an accredited issuer.

**Acknowledgments.** This work was supported by the European funded projects ASSERT4SOA (grant no. 257361) and CUMULUS (grant no. 318580) of Framework Programme 7.

# References

1. Gartner: Forecast overview: Public cloud services. report G00234817 (2012)
2. Common Criteria: Common criteria part 1: introduction and general model (2012), http://www.commoncriteriaportal.org/files/ccfiles/CCPART1V3.1R4.pdf
3. Sunyaev, A., Schneider, S.: Cloud services certification. Commun. ACM 56(2), 33–36 (2013)
4. Spanoudakis, G., Damiani, E., Maña, A.: Certifying services in cloud: The case for a hybrid, incremental and multi-layer approach. In: 14th IEEE International Symposium on High-Assurance Systems Engineering (HASE), pp. 175–176 (2012)

5. Anisetti, M., Ardagna, C.A., Guida, F., Gürgens, S., Lotz, V., Maña, A., Pandolfo, C., Pazzaglia, J.-C., Pujol, G., Spanoudakis, G.: ASSERT4SOA: Toward security certification of service-oriented applications. In: Meersman, R., Dillon, T., Herrero, P. (eds.) OTM 2010. LNCS, vol. 6428, pp. 38–40. Springer, Heidelberg (2010), http://dx.doi.org/10.1007/978-3-642-16961-8_11

6. Paul, S., Koshutanski, H., Cerbo, F.D., Kaluvuri, A.M.: Security assurance of services through digital security certificates. In: 20th IEEE International Conference on Web Services, ICWS 2013 (2013)

7. Mahbub, K., Pino, L., Foster, H., Spanoudakis, G., Maña, A., Pujol, G.: D2.1 - ASSERTs aware service query language and discovery engine. Technical report, ASSERT4SOA Project (2011), http://assert4soa.eu/deliverable/D2.1.pdf

8. Ramli, N.A.: Protection profile, a key concept in the common criteria. In: SANS Institute InfoSec Reading Room (2003)

9. Benassi, P.: TRUSTe: an online privacy seal program. Commun. ACM 42(2), 56–59 (1999)

10. McAfee: Mcafee secure (2007), http://www.mcafee.com/us/mcafeesecure/index.html

11. X.509: The directory: Public-key and attribute certificate frameworks, ITU-T Recommendation X.509:2005 | ISO/IEC 9594-8:2005 (2005)

12. SAML: SAML v2.0 (2005), http://saml.xml.org/saml-specifications

13. Andrieux, et al.: Web services agreement specification (ws-agreement), OGF - Grid Resource Allocation Agreement Protocol WG, v. gfd-r.192 (2011)

14. TAPAS Project: Trusted and QoS-Aware Provision of Application Services, http://tapas.sourceforge.net

15. Schematron: ISO/IEC 19757-3 (2006) http://www.schematron.com

16. Object Constraint Language: ISO/IEC 19507: 2012 (2012) http://www.omg.org/spec/OCL

17. FIPS-197: Advanced encryption standard (2001), http://csrc.nist.gov/publications/fips/fips197/fips-197.pdf

18. NIST-SP-800-38A: Recommendation for block cipher modes of operation (2001), http://csrc.nist.gov/publications/nistpubs/800-38a/sp800-38a.pdf

19. Pino, L., Spanoudakis, G.: Constructing secure service compositions with patterns. In: 8th IEEE World Congress on Services, SERVICES 2012 (2012)

20. ASSERT4SOA Project Consortium: D4.1 - Design and description of evidence-based certificates artifacts for services. Technical report, ASSERT4SOA Project (2011), http://www.assert4soa.eu/deliverable/D4.1.pdf

21. Fuchs, A., Gürgens, S.: D5.1 Formal models and model composition. Technical report, ASSERT4SOA Project (2011), http://www.assert4soa.eu/deliverable/D5.1.pdf

22. D'Agostini, S., Giacomo, V.D., Pandolfo, C., Presenza, D.: An Ontology for runtime Verification of Security Certificates for SOA. In: Proc. of the 1st International Workshop on Security Ontologies and Taxonomies, SecOnt 2012 (2012)

23. XPath: XML path language W3C, http://www.w3.org/TR/xpath/

24. SPARQL: SPARQL query language for RDF, W3C (2008), http://www.w3.org/TR/rdf-sparql-query/

25. ASSERT4SOA Project Consortium: D7.3 - Validation of the ASSERT4SOA framework based on the study case. Technical report, ASSERT4SOA Project (2013)

# A Domain-Specific Model for Data Quality Constraints in Service Process Adaptations

Claus Pahl[1], Neel Mani[1], and Ming-Xue Wang[2]

[1] CNGL, School of Computing, Dublin City University
Dublin 9, Ireland
[2] Network Management Lab, Ericsson Ireland
Ericsson Software Campus, Athlone, Ireland

**Abstract.** Service processes are often enacted across different boundaries such as organisations, countries or even languages. Specifically, looking at the quality and governance of data or content processed by services in this context is important to control different constraints in this cross-boundary processing. In order to provide a context-aware solution that takes into account data and data processing requirements, a rule-based constraints specification and adapation of processes shall be proposed. A domain ontology shall capture the key data/content data types, activities and constraints, which forms the basis of a rule-based policy monitoring solution. A provenance model is at the core of this ontology solution. The key contribution is a domain-specific model and specification template for constraint policy definition, which can be applied to adapt service processes to domain-specific needs.

**Keywords:** Service Process, Process Adaptation, Content Services, Constraint Monitoring, Quality and Governance, Domain-Specific Model, Provenance.

## 1 Introduction

Digital content and data is increasingly processing in distributed settings by different agents - human and/or software. As a consequence, maintaining quality across a boundary-crossing service process is a challenge. The focus of this paper is content and data quality in domain-adapted content processes. While work on quality in service processes has been covered widely, our focus is on domain-specific processes and here specifically those centering on content and data processing. We take on board approaches for constraints specification through rule and policy languages

We aim to, firstly, enable domain-specific service processes for content manipulation and change based on a formalised content model, which requires a layered content model. This layered model consists of the bottom layer with core content (in a formal representation), the states and stages of processing on top of that, and a provenance layer linking content and processing to their origins and dates as the third layer. The provenance model [18] will turn out the solution

C. Canal and M. Villari (Eds.): ESOCC 2013, CCIS 393, pp. 303–317, 2013.

to the need to link content/data into the process. An activities and operations framework that defines the processing and manipulation activities on content in the context of provenance data. The W3C provenance model [18] plays again a pivotal role here for logging process activities, but also as a metadata framework for constraints and rules.

The second aim is to translate this into a dynamic environment. We aim to define a content and data-centric quality assurance and adaptation framework that allows quality requirements to be defined as constraints to be monitored and managed dynamically. This results in the definition of an inclusive framework for the definition, adaptation, monitoring and handling of quality concerns as dynamic constraints. Particular problems are, firstly, the domain-specific categorisation of constraints into policies and, secondly, a rule-based policy definition and process adaptation based on constraints. While constraints monitoring in service processes has been widely covered [3,13,20,24], our solution provides novel contributions in the form of an ontology-driven policy constraints configuration framework.

Our contribution is a domain-specific model for content modelling, covering content, operators and constraints. Our exploration of quality management for content processes, i.e., to define, monitor and analyse, focuses on model aspects here, with the aim of addressing integration and interoperability problems at description level. In a wider sense, this is a governance concern. Our solution specifically extends process adaptation and customisation techniques [1,7], e.g., generic policy adaptation for service processes [21,20], by a domain-specific configuration solution.

We first provide some background on text content processing in service processes in Section 2 and outline challenges and analyse a use case in detail in order to elicit specific requirements. Section 3 defines the domain-specific model for content quality constraints. The rule language we used for quality constraints is then introduced and explained in terms of its utilisation here in Section 4. We describe our implementation in Section 5 where we show how this domain constraints definition approach can be implemented using an existing, generic service policy customisation solution. We end with a discussion of related work in Section 6 and some conclusions in Section 7.

## 2    Scenario – Service-Based Content Processing

### 2.1    Scenario Introduction

Service-base content processing is a distributed problem. Content is created, searched, manipulated (translated, localised, adapted and personalised) and integrated across different processing agents, exposed as services. We refer to this as intelligent content (IC), if the quality is automatically maintained. A process model for this content path is modelled in Fig. 1. This iterative process consists of a number of content processing activities, such as creation, search, translation or adaptation. This process is specific to text-based content and data as an application domain. Management and quality assurance concerns are specific to

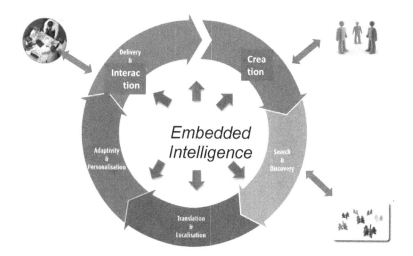

**Fig. 1.** Application Domain: Intelligent Content Processing for Text-based Content

this context. For instance, translatable text is capture in specific formats (e.g. XLIFF) and quality concerns are subject specific.

This challenges quality assurance across the lifecycle of content in distributed service processes. The starting point for the implementation of content quality assurance is an integrated content service process enabled by a content service bus, into which the different processing, integration and management applications are plugged into, see Fig. 2. This scenario defines our wider objective and context beyond this paper. Our aim here is to configure the quality component of this bus by a domain-specific constraints policy language [19]. The provenance model PROV [18] forms the abstract constraints layer. PCPL, the Process Customisation Policy Language [21], is part of the process platform and controls the process adaptation through its policy engine.

In order to facilitate an interoperable content and constraints notation, we assume a core RDF content metadata model (basis of a domain ontology). The data manipulation services and notification trigger functions for constrained processing activities and governance can be defined based on SPARQL query templates over the content and meta-data entities. A possible implementation through synchronous, functional granularity patterns of WSDL/BPEL needs to take this into account, i.e., a mapping to query and data model profiles would need to be considered rather than solely mappings to operations and parameters.

## 2.2   Challenges and Scenario Analysis

This context description allows us to extract the following research challenges:

- Process model: firstly, to define standard activities and process composition constructs; secondly, to select a host process language to realise the content quality constraints description and monitoring; and, thirdly, to define integration of constraints into processes through a weaving technique [21].

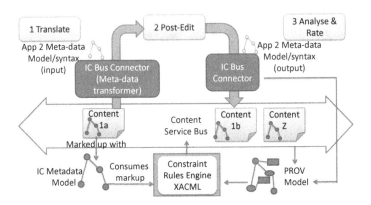

**Fig. 2.** Content Process Interoperability Infrastructure - Service Bus Architecture

- Content model: the definition of a content model consisting of content structure (in terms of standard format such as XML or RDF, but also more specific formats such as XLIFF [15] for content subject to translation) and its link to provenance data [18] that enables tracking and analysis.
- Quality constraints model: a rule language that allows individual constraints (conditions and processing) to be combined into policies and enforced on processes, thus requiring an adaptation and extension of normally service-centric policy languages to deal with quality concerns in a process context.

Obviously, the three individual elements are interlinked. The first step is an empirical determination of detailed requirements for quality management DSL.

A use case shall allow the elicitation of detailed requirements in order to further define the research solution. This documented requirements elicitation process is part of the DSL definition process. This elicitation results in a domain ontology, which will then form the basis of the constraints policy definition.

A sample text localisation process describes the translation of text content through a sequence of services, Fig. 3, where the corresponding provenance model gives context. The provenance model accompanies a localisation process model, consisting of the following steps:

1. Translate(SRV-TR): Text being machine translated (node 15601)
2. PostEdit(CS-PE): The machine-translated text now being posted-edited (crowd-sourced) resulting in a revised string (node 15709)
3. QA-Rate(CS-ANT): Further crowd-sourced effort is then utilised the annotate the translated string with a translation rating (node 15771)
4. Translate(EXP-TR): Given that the crowd-sourced post-editing of the machine translation produced poor results, it is decided to opt for a professional human translation (node 16723)
5. TextAnalytics(SRV-ANL): A text analytics service is then used to compare the style of the translation to a corpora in the desired style (node 16727)
6. QA-Rate(EXP-ANL): Due to poor ratings, execute human QA (node 16734).

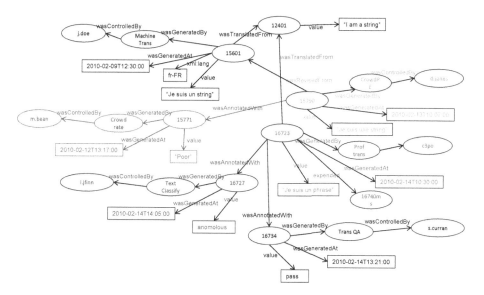

**Fig. 3.** Provenance Model  Localisation/Translation of Text Content

In an abstracted form, this is content life-cycle change or evolution that is enabled through the service process and recorded using PROV [11]. In the process description, we have added two domain-specific categorisations. Activities are the first – we distinguish standard activities in a specific domain, here text translation. Translation, post-editing, or analysis are sample core activities. Roles are the second – we distinguish three service roles in this example: software services (SRV), individual human experts (EXP) and crowds (CS).

The node references in the process refer to the provenance model, Fig. 3. This RDF graph may be build up using the provenance model as the text passes through the process to create an abstract process activity log. Some core activities have been singled out, like translate or post-edit. The process can be formalised by identifying a range of standard content processing operations: extraction, segmentation, curation, text analysis, terminology extraction, translation, post-editing, translation QA and reassembly. In addition to the operation, we can distinguish a core set of actors like EXP - human expert, CS - crowds for crowd-sourced activities and SRV - automated services. The roles can be annotated by activities, e.g. SRV-TR, if translation is the concern, or SRV-ANL for automated text analytics. These annotations are part of the domain model.

A remaining question concerns the quality aspects. We can identify the following concerns for process and content quality and process governance. The quality aspects shall be distinguished into four high-level constraint categories, which we try to motivate here through specific concerns:

- Authorisation/access control:
    - Restricting access to content, following classical access control specifications (subject, access operation, object)

- Managing resource assignment as a mapping between content and agents
- Location-dependent storage and content access in distributed processing

  − Accountability/audit/tracing:
    - Storage/Backup/Secrecy: decide and control where are data is kept
  − Workflow governance:
    - Workflow status (untranslated, postedited, etc.) ensuring that required stages of the content process are reached
    - Containment as a subprocess, e.g. audit tracking to be included
  − Quality for content/process:
    - Rating of content quality (poor, sufficient)
    - Performance as a rating of process quality (slow, satisfactory, etc.)
    - Responsibility assignment and tracking as an accountability concern

The constraint format needs to take into account the PROV structure: (i) single element type, e.g., PROV Timestamps (start/end or interval constraints) or Rating (liveness constraints: should always be 'satisfactory' or better; safety constraints: should never be 'poor') and (ii) multi-element type, e.g., access control in terms of PROV (agent, activity, entity), status (entity, 'generatedBy', activity) or governance (entity, 'controlledBy', agent).

## 3   Domain-Specific Model for Quality Constraints

The different formats involved, based on the research concerns, are:

− Content: RDF as the canonical meta-format, which facilitates controlled access to RDF stores as the targeted storage infrastructure and modelling of different content types, such as terminology, translation memory, text (to be translated), including XLIFF where required.
− Process: For process modelling, BPEL could be assumed as a textual notation or a graphical format such as BPMN, which if complemented by jBPM and Java process engines for execution, could also be considered). Providing a runtime process execution environment is essential here.
− Constraints: PCPL [21], a process customisation policy language adapted from [14], provides a generic policy notion, extended to a process framework (similar to XACML policy language extension for service processes [20,21]). Here, an integration with BPMN shall be implemented, following similar work on BPMN constraint extensions [2,22].

What is needed is a domain-specific model that can be captured as a domain-specific constraints ontology with the following main concepts. Content is of specific types, based on RDF/XML, but often specifically XLIFF for translatable material. Processing activities are content processing oriented. The categorisation of constraints is specific to the different types of quality and governance constraints for content processing.

## 3.1    Content

The content notations involved are XLIFF to capture text and its translation with associated meta-data [15] and PROV to capture objects with origins (actors) and operations (creation and manipulation) [18]. RDF is the core format in which all data is stored and processed. Content formats are assumed to be given for this research.

A layered domain model based on content, process and provenance ontology data to support constraints shall be proposed. Some questions in relation to this model organisation have to be considered, in particular since the solution serves as the basis of a wider analytics framework for a content processing implementation. The objective here should be modularity and separation of concerns.

## 3.2    Provenance

A provenance model can be maintained with the processing of content. In the provenance model (RDF linked data), the following is reflected (Fig. 3).

Firstly, change operators are activities, such as GeneratedBy, TranslatedFrom, AnnotatedWith. These can be aligned to the standard content processing operations defined earlier.

Secondly, actors/participants are agent, such as m.bean, j.doe. These are named service providers that can be classified by our role categorisation scheme, e.g., the next expression j.doe:EXP→Translate links a service to an agent in charge of its execution.

Thirdly, objects are entities, such as text being translated (in XLIFF in this case, as a reflection of a specific content type).

## 3.3    Process

The provenance model can be presented as a process of change operations [11]. This results in a 3-layered architecture (Fig. 4). The upper layer (based on W3C PROV) is made up by the provenance model (extended state-by-state for changes). The middle layer (based on BPMN/BPEL service process descritpions) is a process model based on PROV activities (the changes themselves). Finally, the bottom layer (based on formats such as XLIFF or RDF captures the content aspect. (processed by change operations). BPMN is used here for the modelling of business processes. This can include production processes such as the content process across different participants.

Our aim is to allow a process to be adapted to domain-specific constraints. Two principle solutions to deal with policy constraints can be distinguished. A minimal invasive one weaves quality constraints into a process, where all constraints are monitored and managed by external services. An explicit extension of BPMN models constraints within the language itself and to map quality constraints into this BPMN extension [22,2]. Regarding the second option, BPMN

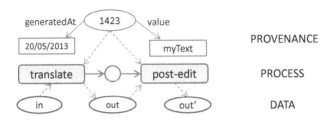

**Fig. 4.** Sample 3-Layered Service Process Model

constraints have been proposed as a BPMN extension. Three types of constraints are distinguished: containment, authorisation and resource assignment. Containment means, for instance, that the activity of managing a shopping cart is a subprocess which contains an activity of removing products from the cart. While we adopt their constraints classification to some extent, our implementation will favour the less invasive solution [21] in order to achieve interoperability.

## 4   Constraints and Rules

Quality constraints and their formulation as policy rules are at the core.

### 4.1   Requirements and Examples

The first problem to be addressed is the identification of all relevant constraint types. We have already provided a classification of several quality and governance concerns: authorisation, accountability, workflow governance and quality, which takes the BPMN constraints extension into account. The objectives of rule-based process quality constraints for domain-specific process adaptation and monitoring are twofold: firstly, optimisation, i.e., to improve quality of content and the process (by looking at ratings or performance measures) and, secondly, governance, i.e., to enforce access control and privacy rules (user defined policies or legal requirements).

Constraints are technically conditions on concerns. A rule associates an action related to a condition in the Event-Condition-Action (ECA) format, that checks on an event the correctness of a condition and triggers the execution of an action, if required by the condition. Thus, based on the four constraint types, we define four rules types to link conditions and actions (illustrated by some examples):

- Authorisation/access control – example: to restrict content in data stores
- Accountability/audit/tracing – example: where are records/copies kept
- Workflow governance – example: *status = untranslated → translate(..)* or *status = translated → crowdsource-PostEdit(..)*

- Quality for content/process – example content rating: $automatedQA = poor$ $\rightarrow humanQA()$; or for process performance: $time(translation) > t \rightarrow alert$

## 4.2  Formalisation

A number of rule and policy and rule languages exist that would allow constraints to be specified. Examples are XACML, which allows security policies to be defined, or rule languages such as RuleML or SWRL. While these generic language are in prinicpal suitable, we need a platform, not only a language. This platform needs to allow remote constraints definition, coordination and weaving betweem service clients and providers. We follow [21] and use the PCPL policy language and its supporting platform for process customisation [19,14] to implement PROV-based constraint policies based on individual rules. PCPL serves as a policy engine for PROV constraints. The generic PCPL is utilised here for a specific context. It controls content process adaptation. Process constrains are defined in the process adaption policy. Provenance constrains can be integrated in the process constrains as parts of conditions (XPath or SPARQL queries). PCPL policies consist of the following notational elements:

- Objects: here content defined in terms of XLIFF and XML text, processed by activities like translate or post-edit
- Activity states: capturing processing state and quality assurance state based on the domain activities
- Conditions covering the content context (owner, format etc.), the activity context (service price, failure rate etc.) or provenance/log data (authorisation, state etc.):
  - Performance/Time for processing, includes manual effort (asynchronous) and execution time of service (synchronous)
  - Authorisation: who can process/access content including the location of objects (e.g. no externalisation/outsourcing allowed as a condition)
  - Existence of entity/object in a state: e.g. translated (in XLIFF) as a workflow stage
- Actions: process adaptation decisions, which cover the constraint violation handing strategies
- Fault handlers: adaption policy execution fault handler
- Algorithms: configurations of the policy execution behaviours, such as policy conflicts

The policy model is designed for a generic process. The PCPL example below illustrates this policy definition: a document must be post-edited before sent for QA-Rating:

```
<p1:Policy policyId="QA-Rate-policy1" priority="0">
  <p1:Objects>
    <p1:ObjectsAnyOf>
      <p1:ObjectsAllOf>
        <p1:Activity>
          <Name>QA-Rate crowd-sourced</Name>
```

```
      </p1:Activity>
    </p1:ObjectsAllOf>
  </p1:ObjectsAnyOf>
</p1:Objects>

<p1:ActivityStates>
  <p1:ActivityState>Validating-Pre</p1:ActivityState>
</p1:ActivityStates>

<p1:Rule priority="0" ruleId="constraintRule-QA-Rate">
  <p1:Conditions>
    <p1:ConditionExpression type="Provenance-Context">
        <p1:Para>//Document/ID</p1:Para>
          <p1:Expr>constraintRule-QA-Rate_query.sparql</p1:Expr>
    </p1:ConditionExpression>
  </p1:Conditions>

  <p1:Actions>
    <p1:Pa-Violate>
      <p1:Violation>
        <Type>Functional:Protocol</Type>
      </p1:Violation>
    </p1:Pa-Violate>
  </p1:Actions>

  <p1:FaultHandler>
    <p1:Ca-Log level="5"> </p1:Ca-Log>
  </p1:FaultHandler>
</p1:Rule>

<p1:ConstraintCombiningAlgorithm type="Pa-Validate-Unless-Pa-Violate-TA"/>
<p1:RemedyCombiningAlgorithm type="Pa-Cancel-Unless-Defined-Sequence-TA">
  <DefinedSequenceElement>Pa-Cancel</DefinedSequenceElement>
  <!-- more DefinedSequenceElement ... -->
</p1:RemedyCombiningAlgorithm>
<p1:SequencingAlgorithm type="Ordered"/>
</p1:Policy>
```

The policy has one constrain rule and a fault rule (the fault rule is skipped in the code). The policy targets the "QA-Rate crowd-sourced" activity before its be excuted. The constraint rule has a condition on the provenance context or the document history. A parameterized SPARQL query checks if the current document (using the document ID as parameter) has NOT been post-edited. If the condition is true, the rule results in a functional:Protocol violation, see [21,20] where protocol violation refers to faults related to the consistent exchange of messages between services involved in a service composition to achieve their goals. A fault rule can be defined for handling the violation. The policy will cancel the current process based the defined RemedyCombiningAlgorithm, if no remedy action was found in the fault rule for violation handling.

At a pre post-editing stage (i.e., before post-editing starts for a document translation), a request must be made for post-editing to take place, in this case through crowd-sourcing (CS). A quality rating condition could be violated, resulting in different handling actions to take place (Cancel and Skip, in Sequence). We assume respective handling algorithms to be defined.

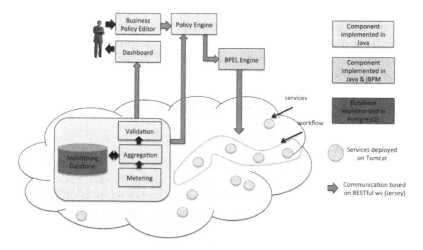

**Fig. 5.** Constraints Implementation architecture

# 5  Implementation – Policy Definition and Adaptation

In this section, we outline a suitable architecture for constraints definition and process adaptation, see Fig. 5. The main components are a policy definition editor, a process engine, a monitoring system and a policy engine. The diagram details the interaction between the rule engine and the process from Fig. 2. The rule engine from Fig. 2 is here decomposed into policy definition, monitoring and policy validation engine. The implementation platform is here assumed to be a BPEL engine. This engine needs to be combined with constraint weaving to allow the quality constraints to be automatically added to a business or technical process as a adaptation.

Enhanced, flexible adaptivity is a key concern, which is addressed by the architecture. This architecture allows the policies to be defined locally at the client side and then the process adapted to client domain needs and enacted by a central process engine. Thus, it allows easy adaptation to specific domains and user needs. More details about the generic architecture without the domain extension are provided in [21], which presents the two major components. This is firstly the policy language to define the constraints and secondly a coordination framework based on WS-COORDINATION, which allows the client-side specified constraints to be communicated and woven into the server-side process.

The following components for service processing describe the currently implemented service process customisation and adaptation prototype illustrated in Fig. 5: Jersey, Tomcat, PostgreSQL, jBPM and Eclipse. This prototype is a generic processes adaptation infrastructure, described in detail in [21]. It support the generic PCPL language.

Here, we utilise this generic infrastructure for service processes to configure user-specific domain constraints following the domain model approach above.

Thus, the solution here is an extension of the generic policy management infrastructure for domain-specific customisation. Consequently, in this paper, the focus has been on notational rather than infrastructure aspects. Future work in the implementation context will concentrate on domain-specific implementations. For instance, a focus will be on the translation activity, where content is marked up in the XML-based XLIFF format and respective processing and quality constraints (such as *isPostEdited*) are implemented.

## 6   Related Work

Current open research concerns for service computing include customisation of governance and quality policies and the non-intrusive adaptation of processes with policies [19,20,14,7,17,25]. Service management and monitoring techniques are combinations of rule or policy-based modelling languages that can be enforced at runtime. Today, one-size-fits-all service monitoring techniques exist and provide support for software systems in classical sectors such as finance and telecommunications [3]. However, their inherent structural inflexibility makes constraints difficult to manage, resulting in significant efforts and costs to adapt to individual domains needs.

We discuss related work in the field of constraints and policy definition and adaptive BPEL processes. While we have also refered to BPMN, there is more work on WS-BPEL in our context, which we discuss here. These approaches can be classified into two categories.

– In the first category are BPEL process extensions that are designed to realize platform-independence. [23] and [24] allow BPEL specifications to be extended with fault policies. Exception handling policies are bound into process schemas as a BPEL extension. The SRRF approach [13] generates BPEL processes based on the defined policies. However, binding domain-specific policies into business processes directly are not an option for our objective, as it is difficult to support user/domain-specific adaptation needs adequately.
– In a second category, BPEL engines can also be modified, but the solution is platform-dependent. The limitation of the Dynamo project [3] is that BPEL event handlers must be statically embedded into the process prior to deployment, i.e. the recovery logic is fixed and can only be customised through the event handler itself [3]. This approach does neither support dynamic policies nor a customisation and adaptation environment. The PAWS framework [1] extends ActiveBPEL to provide a flexible process that can change its behaviour dynamically, according to variable execution contexts and constraints.

Furthermore, process-centricity is a concern. Recently, business-processes-as-a-service is discussed. While not addressed here, this perspective needs to be further complemented by an architectural style for its implementation [21].

We now address specific constraints and provenance aspects. We have proposed a classification of several quality and governance concerns: authorisation, accountability, workflow governance and quality. This takes the BPMN constraints extensions [22,2] that suggest containment, authorisation and resource assignment as categories into account, but realises these in a less intrusive, less invasive process adaptation solution.

Some provenance-enabled workflow systems have been developed [8,6]. These workflow systems monitor workflow or process executions and record task names, execution durations or parameters as provenance information. Other work has focused on data [10,9], recording owner or creation and modification time for provenance. Various query mechanisms such as SQL, SPARQL, and proprietary APIs are supported for different provenance data storage solutions. However, for a document or content-centric service process system where the activities of processes are responsible for content manipulations and changes, a domain-specific should be defined in a content-centric way to capture provenance information at process level and, thus, to support provenance-based process adaptation. Work in [12] focuses on using PROV to collect and analyse data in change processes. Our system is a hybrid approach, which supports both data-oriented and process-oriented provenance requirements, such as content and process activity access control. Moreover, the provenance query is integrated into a process customization policy model to enable provenance-based process adaptation.

## 7   Conclusions

We have proposed a notation for the description of quality and governance constraints for adaptive content processes. This is a domain-specific data/content constraints model, here applied to translatable text content. The content is of specific types, based on RDF/XML, but often specifically XLIFF for translatable material. Processing activities are content processing and translation oriented. The categorisation of constraints is specific to the different types of quality and governance constraints for content processing. A layered, modular information model covering content, processes and constraints facilitates its implementation in a wider interoperable content integration system. Interoperability is a critical driver in the application context. PROV has played a critical role, for the monitoring and recording as well as supporting the adaptivity for domains (here localisation workflow processes). Mappings between solution technologies and interoperable platforms need to be considered. This application serves as a template for domain-specific constraints and policy definition. Together with the user-based customisation architecture, service processes can be adapted to meet domain-specific needs (e.g., for the translation industry).

As part of our future work, an exploration of RDF-based SWRL rules and SPARQL queries as more RDF-interoperable notations shall be conducted that extent the PCPL approach taken so far. Also, PROV can possibly play a more central role as the process analytics model. For the exploration of the concept in this paper, the domain ontology has not been fully formalised. This would need to be done for a comprehensive evaluation. An implementation within PROV/XLIFF-based workflow system can be considered as a more targeted domain system. We have already mentioned the translation focus in the implementation section.

**Acknowledgements.** This material is based upon works supported by the Science Foundation Ireland under Grant No. 07/CE/I1142 as part of the Centre for Next Generation Localisation (www.cngl.ie) at Dublin City University (DCU).

# References

1. Ardagna, D., Comuzzi, M., Mussi, E., Pernici, B., Plebani, P.: Paws: a framework for executing adaptive web-service processes. IEEE Software 24(6), 39–46 (2007)
2. Awad, A., Grosskopf, A., Meyer, A., Weske, M.: Enabling resource assignment constraints in BPMN. Technical report, Business Process Tech. HPI (2009)
3. Baresi, L., Guinea, S.: Self-supervising bpel processes. IEEE Transactions on Software Engineering 37(2), 247–263 (2011)
4. Baresi, L., Guinea, S., Plebani, P.: Policies and aspects for the supervision of bpel processes. In: Intern. Conf. on Adv. Information Systems Engineering (2007)
5. Barrett, R., Patcas, L.M., Murphy, J., Pahl, C.: Model Driven Distribution Pattern Design for Dynamic Web Service Compositions. In: International Conference on Web Engineering ICWE 2006, pp. 129–136. ACM Press, Palo Alto (2006)
6. Davidson, S.B., Freire, J.: Provenance and Scientific Workflows: Challenges and Opportunities. In: ACM SIGMOD Intl. Conference on Management of Data (2008)
7. Erradi. A.: Policy-Driven Framework for Manageable and Adaptive Service-Oriented Processes. PhD thesis. The University of New South Wales (2008)
8. Freire, J., Koop, D., Santos, E., Silva, C.T.: Provenance for Computational Tasks: A Survey. Computing in Science and Engineering 10(3), 11–21 (2008)
9. Glavic, B., Dittrich, K.R.: Data Provenance: A Categorization of Existing Approaches. In: 12th GI Conference on Database Systems in Business (2007)
10. Hartig, O.: Provenance Information in the Web of Data. In: Workshop on Linked Data on the Web (2009)
11. Javed, M., Abgaz, Y.M., Pahl, C.: A pattern-based framework of change operators for ontology evolution. In: Meersman, R., Herrero, P., Dillon, T. (eds.) OTM 2009 Workshops. LNCS, vol. 5872, pp. 544–553. Springer, Heidelberg (2009)
12. Javed, M.: Operational Change Management and Change Pattern Identification for Ontology Evolution. Ph.D. Thesis. Dublin City University (2013)
13. Kareliotis, C., Vassilakis, C., Panayiotis, G.: Enhancing bpel scenarios with dynamic relevance-based exception handling. In: Intl. Conf. on Web Services (2007)
14. OASIS: Extensible access control markup language (xacml) 3.0 (2010), http://docs.oasis-open.org/xacml/3.0/xacml-3.0-core-spec-cs-01-en.html
15. OASIS: XLIFF (XML Localisation Interchange File Format) (2013), http://docs.oasis-open.org/xliff/xliff-core/xliff-core.html
16. Pahl, C., Giesecke, S., Hasselbring, W.: An Ontology-Based Approach for Modelling Architectural Styles. In: Oquendo, F. (ed.) ECSA 2007. LNCS, vol. 4758, pp. 60–75. Springer, Heidelberg (2007)
17. Riegen, M., von, H.M., Fink, S., Ritter, N.: Rule-based coordination of distributed web service transactions. IEEE Trans. on Serv. Comp. 3(1), 60–70 (2010)
18. W3C: PROV-O: The PROV Ontology (2013), http://www.w3.org/TR/prov-o/
19. W3C web services policy 1.2 - framework (ws-policy), http://www.w3.org/Submission/WS-Policy

20. Wang, M.X., Bandara, K.Y., Pahl, C.: Process as a Service - Distributed Multitenant Policy-based Process Runtime Governance. In: IEEE International Conference on Services Computing SCC 2010. IEEE Press (2010)
21. Wang, M.X.: A Policy-based Governance Framework for Cloud Service Process Architectures. Ph.D. Thesis. Dublin City University (2012)
22. Wolter, C., Schaad, A.: Modeling of task-based authorization constraints in BPMN. In: Alonso, G., Dadam, P., Rosemann, M. (eds.) BPM 2007. LNCS, vol. 4714, pp. 64–79. Springer, Heidelberg (2007)
23. Wu, Y., Doshi, P.: Making bpel flexible and adapting in the context of coordination constraints using ws-bpel. In: Intl. Conf. on Services Computing (2008)
24. Zeng, L., Lei, H., Jeng, J.J., Chung, J.Y., Benatallah, B.: Policy-driven exception-management for composite web services. In: IEEE Intl. Conf. on E-Commerce Tech. (2005)
25. Zhou, Y.C., Liu, X.P., Wang, X.N., Xue, L., Tian, C., Liang, X.X.: Context model based soa policy framework. In: IEEE Intern. Conf. on Web Services (2010)

# Run-Time Verification of Behaviour-Aware Mashups in the Internet of Things

Laura González[1], Javier Cubo[2], Antonio Brogi[3], Ernesto Pimentel[2], and Raúl Ruggia[1]

[1] Instituto de Computación, Facultad de Ingeniería, Universidad de la República, Uruguay
{lauragon,ruggia}@fing.edu.uy
[2] Department of Computer Science, University of Málaga, Spain
{cubo,ernesto}@lcc.uma.es
[3] Department of Computer Science, University of Pisa, Italy
brogi@di.unipi.it

**Abstract.** With the new vision of the Internet of Things, physical world entities are integrated into virtual world things. Then, the Internet of Things could benefit from the Web Service architecture like today's Web does; so Future service-oriented Internet things will offer their functionality via service-enabled interfaces. As demonstrated in previous work, there is a need of considering the behaviour of things to develop applications in a more rigorous way. We proposed a lightweight model for representing such behaviour based on the service-oriented paradigm and extending the standard DPWS profile to specify the order with which things can receive messages. To check whether a mashup of things respects the behaviour, specified at design-time, we proposed a static verification. However, at run-time a thing may change its behaviour or receive requests from instances of different mashups. Then, it is required to check and detect dynamically possible invalid invocations provoked by changes of behaviour. Here, we extend our static verification with an approach based on mediation techniques and complex event processing to detect and inhibit invalid invocations. The solution automatically generates the required elements to perform run-time validation of invocations. It may be extended to validate other issues.

**Keywords:** Composition, Mashup, Run-Time Verification, Mediation Patterns, Complex Event Processing, Behaviour, Thing as a Service, Internet of Things.

## 1    Introduction

With the new vision of the Internet of Things (IoT), physical world entities are integrated into virtual world things. Future service-oriented Internet devices will offer their functionality via service-enabled interfaces adopting the vision of the Web of Things (WoT) (inspired from the IoT), via SOAP-based Web Services or RESTful APIs [1,2]. The IoT, including the mass of resource-constrained devices, could benefit from the Web Service architecture. Recent work [3,4] has focused on applying the paradigm of Service-Oriented Architecture (SOA) [5], in particular Web Services standards, directly on devices. In general, applying SOA to networked systems is a crucial solution to achieve reusability and interoperability of heterogeneous and

C. Canal and M. Villari (Eds.): ESOCC 2013, CCIS 393, pp. 318–330, 2013.
© Springer-Verlag Berlin Heidelberg 2013

distributed things. The goal is to provide the functionality of each thing as a Web Service in an interoperable way that can be used by other entities such as enterprise applications or even other devices. However, adapting a given device to SOA is not a trivial problem. It is required to implement efficiently the things, and efforts are still needed to handle composition and interaction of things from diverse sources. Several SOA initiatives (OSGi, UPnP, Jini) have evolved to interconnect heterogeneous devices and services. Not all of them can equally adapt to the others using the same hood. And the lack of standardization makes programming for devices an arduous task.

The emergent OASIS standard Devices Profile for Web Services (DPWS)[1] has been designed as a set of guidelines based on WS-* specifications to provide interoperability among different devices and services in a networked environment: a printer, a smartphone, a sensor or other new devices can detect DPWS-enabled devices on a network. Some convincing points in favor of DPWS are that it is an OASIS standard, it employs a Web Service mode being built on the standard W3C Web Service architecture, and it is natively integrated into from Windows Vista. In DPWS, every device is abstracted as a service where features of the device are exhibited as hosted services. The comparison between the important properties of reuse and research challenges of Web Services shows a gap in the use of DPWS in the future focused on reusability [6]. DPWS shows, for example, those topics like business processes, context dependencies or quality factors have to get more focus in order to increase the reuse of DPWS devices and use this standard more easily in the area of software engineering.

In [7], we detected the need to explicitly represent the (implicit) behaviours of things to develop applications in a more rigorous way. We promoted the usage of WS-* technologies to specify service interfaces of things by extending the standard DPWS with behavioural descriptions, in order to facilitate to developers the implementation of DPWS-compliant things (or devices) that host services by considering their behaviour in terms of the (partial) order in which the actions visible at the interface level are performed. We proposed a static verification technique to check whether or not a mashup of things respects the behaviour of the composed things specified at design-time. However, at run-time a thing may change its behaviour or receive requests from instances of different mashups. Then, it is required to check and detect dynamically possible invalid invocations provoked by the behaviour's changes.

In this work, taking as starting point our first attempt presented in [8], we extend our static verification with an approach based on mediation techniques and Complex Event Processing (CEP) [9] to detect and inhibit invalid invocations, checking that things only receive requests compatible with their behaviour. Our proposal consists in processing invocations of services hosted in devices through a mediation platform, in order to detect and block the invalid ones using CEP techniques. As main contribution, the solution automatically generates the required elements to perform the run-time validation of invocations, and it may be easily extended to validate other issues. Here, we have also dealt with quality of service (QoS) and temporal restrictions.

This paper is organized as follows. In Section 2, we motivate and list the contributions of our proposal. Section 3 describes our proposal to perform run-time verification of mashups of things, and we discuss advantages, deployment alternatives and

---

[1] http://docs.oasis-open.org/ws-dd/ns/dpws/2009/01

comparison of this solution with our previous one. In Section 4, we compare our approach to related work. Section 5 draws conclusions and outlines future work.

## 2     Motivating Our Approach

This section motivates our proposal, describing the problem statement as regards the model we have proposed in our previous work based on extending DPWS to support the behavior of things. Then, we introduce CEP, mediation patterns and discovery proxy, which we use to tackle the run-time verification of the behaviour-aware composition of things. Finally, we give an overview of our approach to detect and manage invalid invocations at run-time during the composition of things.

### 2.1     Problem Statement: Static Verification of Behaviour-Aware Mashups

DPWS uses the primitives of the Web Services Architecture to create a framework for interoperable and standardized communication between embedded devices. In DPWS, every device is abstracted as a service where features of the device are exhibited as Web Services. Some of the specifications in which DPWS is based are: (i) WSDL for describing messages each hosted service may send and receive, (ii) SOAP for transporting the messages, (iii) WS-Discovery and SOAP-over-UDP for device discovery, or (iv) WS-Transfer / WS-MetadataExchange for device and service description. In [7] we motivated the necessity of extending DPWS to facilitate the implementation of a device (or thing) as a full-service considering that its WSDL description should specify not only signature, but also the behaviour with the order in which input and output actions are performed while the networked system interacts with its environment. Input actions model methods that can be called, or the end of receiving messages from communication channels, as well as the return values from such calls. Output actions model method calls, message transmission via communication channels, or exceptions that may occur during methods execution. In order to include this extension in the DPWS profile, in our previous proposal we applied rigorous and lightweight methodologies to develop things by promoting WS-* technologies, to specify interfaces of things, and adding the behaviour of things to the DPWS profile. This extended DPWS specification will facilitate to the developers the implementation of DPWS-compliant things (or devices) that host services by taking into account their behaviour (using *constraints* or *finite state machines*) in terms of the order in which actions, visible at the interface level, are performed while things are composed.

- **Constraints**. When only a partial order of the behavior of things is required, we propose to use three types of behavioural constraints to be added to the guidelines (statements) exposed by DPWS:

$$\{b_i\}\texttt{afterAll}\{a_i\}, \{b_i\}\texttt{afterSome}\{a_i\}, \texttt{onlyOneOf}\{a_i\}$$

where $\{b_i\}$ and $\{a_i\}$ are actions of a service hosted in a device. The `afterAll` constraint is used to specify that any action $\{b_i\}$ only can be executed if all the actions $\{a_i\}$ have been previously executed. The `afterSome` constraint is less restrictive than `afterAll`, since any action $\{b_i\}$ can be executed whether some action $\{a_i\}$ have been already executed. The `onlyOneOf` constraint means that only one of the sets of actions $\{a_i\}$ can be executed in an interaction session.

- **Finite State Machines**. In those cases where it is required to specify not only the partial order, but also the ordered full-sequence among operations with the corresponding states changes according to the messages execution, we propose to use Finite State Machines (FSMs) [10] as a simple and user-friendly graphic solution to represent the complex relationships between messages.

***Running Example.*** To illustrate this model, we considered in [7] a complex real-world example: *an airport surveillance system* composed by heterogeneous devices hosting services (a motion detector, and a surveillance camera – hosting a record control service – located in a specific area in the airport, and a video device – hosting a video streaming service and a media ejection service – located in a control center – and people (using other devices), everything interconnected.

We focus on a scenario where a security guard connects, by means of an application installed within a mobile device to a new motion sensor and a new camera, both installed in a specific area of the airport. The behaviour of the system is the following: once Bob finds the new devices, when a non-expected motion is detected, Bob is notified with the exact position of the movement detected. He logins to access the camera, and after he can perform three actions: (i) move the camera to the desired position, (ii) start to record, and/or (iii) make a zoom. If Bob considers there is an emergency situation, then he sends a command to warn the control center to start the streaming at real-time of the video being recorded by the camera. After this, the control center staff may reproduce and analyze the video, while it is recorded concurrently, and act accordingly. When monitoring and surveillance of the concrete situation is complete, then Bob can finish recording.

In this scenario it is required the handling of the behaviour of the hosted services into the heterogeneous and distributed devices, not only to achieve a correct, but also to get appropriate specifications of every behaviour-aware service and application.

- **Constraints**. The behaviour of the service record control hosted in the device camera, with actions such as *auth*, *move*, *record*, or *halt*, can be specified by means of the following constraints:

    $C1$: {*move, record*} `afterAll` {*auth*}; $C2$: {*halt*} `afterSome` {*move, record*}

- **Finite State Machines**. The behaviour of the service video streaming, hosted in the device video, requires a considerable number of exchanged messages (*on, play, pause, stop, rewind, fast-forward*, and *off*) in a concrete order (as detailed in [7]), so its handling may require of a more complicated model as provided by the FSMs. Fig. 1 depicts the control of the message full-sequence of this service using FSM representation.

The explicit specification of the behaviour of things by means of constraints or full-sequences with FSMs is the foundation to develop behaviour-aware compositions of

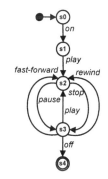

**Fig. 1.** FSM for Complex Behaviour

things. These compositions will create applications generated in form of mashups with new functionalities to be remotely accessed (e.g., as Software-as-a-Service - SaaS, or Mashups-as-a-Service). But it is required to check whether a composition of things fulfills or violates their behaviour, so we proposed a simple and efficient verification technique at design-time. Therefore, we defined a checker function in order to perform the static verification, analysing traces and actions executed of the orchestration specified by the user, according to a sets of constraints and/or finite state machines, both determining the behaviour of the things.

However, as aforementioned, a thing may change its behaviour at run-time. Then, a change in the behaviour of a thing may cause that various compositions do not fulfill its behaviour anymore. Although compositions could be redesigned to comply with the new behavior, it would be appropriate to design run-time verifications techniques to react when this situation occurs. Moreover, given that a thing can receive at run-time requests from instances of different mashups, these requests could violate the behaviour of that thing, even though each mashup fulfills such behaviour, because of the state's change of the thing. This kind of situations cannot be detected at design-time, so run-time mechanisms are required to become aware of it and act accordingly.

## 2.2    Background

Here we present background information on the technologies used: (i) complex event processing, (ii) integration and mediation patterns, and (iii) WS-Discovery.

**Complex Event Processing (CEP).** CEP refers to methods, techniques, and tools for processing events while they occur. It allows deriving relevant higher-level events (i.e. complex events) from a combination of lower-level events, in a timely fashion and permanently [11]. To this end, event queries are continuously monitoring incoming streams of simple events. These queries are used to specify situations as a combination of simple events occurring, or not occurring, over time.Various products (e.g. Drools Fusion) rely on the production rules approach to implement event queries [11]. In this case, whenever an event occurs a corresponding fact must be created in the so-called working memory and rules specify actions to be executed when certain states are entered. These states are detected through event queries expressed as conditions over these facts. CEP platforms provide support for various types of event patterns, which allow specifying combinations of events. Some of those types are logical operator patterns, subset selection patterns, temporal patterns and spatial patterns [12].

**Integration and Mediation Patterns**. Integration and mediation solutions are usually based on probed and well-known patterns, which have also been documented in the literature [13,14,15]. This section reviews the relevant patterns for our proposal.

Service virtualization patterns take an existing service and deploy a new virtual service in a mediation platform. These patterns introduce a point of mediation which can be used to validate, route, transform or normalize requests, among others [13].

The VETO pattern [14], which consists in applying a sequence of mediation mechanisms: validate, enrich, transform and operate, is a frequently applied mediation pattern that can be used in conjunction with the previous one. The validate mechanism checks incoming requests and blocks invalid ones. The enrich mechanism adds additional data to a request. The transform mechanism converts the request to the required target format. The operate mechanism invokes the target service.

Event-driven integration patterns deal with distribution of events in real time and integration with CEP engines. The event extractor pattern monitors interactions across a mediation platform and passes relevant events to a CEP engine. The event reactor pattern extends the previous one by supporting a synchronous interaction with a CEP engine to check if the latest event has triggered a complex event [13].

**WS-Discovery.** DPWS leverages WS-Discovery for discovering devices [16]. WS-Discovery supports both an ad-hoc discovery and a managed discovery mechanism. Using the ad-hoc mechanism the client sends multicast Probe messages to discover devices on the local network. This mechanism has some limitations: the network range of multicast messages is limited and multicast messages increase network traffic [16]. To deal with these limitations, WS-Discovery also supports a managed discovery mechanism where a specialized component, a discovery proxy, is used. This proxy usually stores the network address of services that are present on the local subnet and on a wider network. In such a way, clients may directly communicate with the discovery proxy to discover devices avoiding the generation of multicast traffic [16].

### 2.3 Approach and Contribution

The main idea of our proposal is to process, through a mediation platform, the interactions between clients (e.g. mashups) and devices in order to validate the requests that are sent to hosted services. Our platform handles the invocations of services hosted in devices to detect and block the invalid invocations using CEP techniques. In this way, devices only receive requests which are compatible with their behaviour.

The platform can be placed as a specialized device within the same network where devices are located. Fig. 2 presents the high level architecture of the proposal and the interactions that take place between the different components.

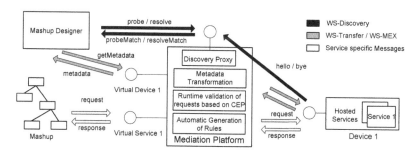

**Fig. 2.** High Level Architecture of the Proposal

Following the Virtual Services mediation pattern, devices and hosted services are exposed through the mediation platform via Virtual Devices and Virtual Services, respectively. These virtual elements are automatically configured when devices advertise themselves in the platform (via WS-Discovery) or when the platform receives the metadata of hosted services (via WS-MetadataExchange).

In order to intercept the interactions that take place during the discovery process (WS-Discovery interactions), the platform includes a Discovery Proxy. This component sends to clients the proper information (i.e. network addresses) so that the subsequent WS-Transfer/WS- MetadataExchange interactions, between clients and devices, are processed through the platform via Virtual Devices. This allows that the metadata obtained from the devices can be modified in a way that clients receive the network's addresses of Virtual Services instead of the ones of Hosted Services. Thus, service requests are processed by the platform and they can be validated, and even blocked, before reaching the services. Run-time validation of invocations is performed leveraging CEP: production rules are automatically generated and deployed in the platform, according to the behaviour of the devices, so that the requests can be validated against them. The main contributions of the platform we propose are the following:

1. Detecting and blocking invalid invocation at run-time.
2. Validating behaviour with automatically generated rules.
3. Dealing with temporal constraints and quality of service.

## 3     Run-Time Verification of Mashups of Things

### 3.1     Detecting and Blocking Invalid Invocations at Run-Time

To detect and block invalid invocations, the platform uses a combination of mediation and CEP techniques. Fig. 3 shows how a service invocation is processed by the platform and the components that allow the runtime verification of the invocations.

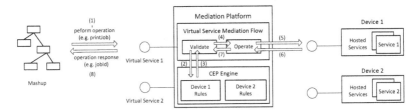

**Fig. 3.** Detecting and Blocking Invalid Invocations

As stated before, hosted services are invoked through virtual services deployed in the platform, tag (1) in Fig. 3, following the Virtual Services pattern. Virtual services consist of a mediation flow, which is a simplification of the VETO pattern, and comprises two mediation steps: validate and operate. The validate step synchronously interacts with a CEP Engine (2), following the event reactor pattern, to check if the invoked operation is invalid. If so, a complex event is triggered (3) and the invocation is blocked. Otherwise, the operate step is executed (4) which invokes the target operation in hosted service (5). Lastly, the response is returned to the client (6), (7) and (8).

In order to specify when a given invocation is invalid for a device, a set of production rules has to be deployed on the CEP Engine. These rules can be automatically generated based on the specified behaviour of each device, which is obtained by the platform from the metadata of the hosted services (see details in Section 3.2).

Also, when the platform receives an invocation a new event is generated and sent to the engine. These events and the deployed rules constitute the basic elements to trigger a complex event when an invalid invocation for a service is received, allowing the platform to detect this situation and act accordingly (e.g. block the invocation).

### 3.2    Validating Behaviour with Automatically Generated Rules

In order to validate the interactions between clients and devices, the platform includes a set of modules which automatically generate rules based on the specified behaviour of devices. For example, the platform includes modules which automatically generate rules based on constraints and FSM. Also, the platform can be extended with other modules to generate rules based on other information (e.g. regarding QoS).

This section describes how production rules can be used to detect invalid invocations according to the behaviour of devices and how these rules can be automatically generated based on those behaviours, which can be specified through constraints or FSMs. Drools Rule Language (DRL)[2] is used to exemplify our proposal over the running example (though this kind of rules can be specified in other languages like Jess).

**Behaviour specified with Constraints.** When the behaviour of a device is specified with constraints, one or more rules are required to perform the run-time validation. Giving the temporal support that CEP technologies provide, in most of the cases rules can be specified in a very intuitive way. For instance, the rule depicted in Fig. 4 detects invalid invocations for the constraint C1 presented in Section 2.1. More precisely, it detects when a *"move"* or *"record"* operation is received and an *"auth"* operation was not received before, in the context of the same mashup's instance.

```
rule "check-c1" // {move, record} afterAll {auth}
    when
        $op: ServiceOperation(operationName=="move" ||
                              operationName=="record")
        not (ServiceOperation(this before $op,
                              instanceId==$op.instanceId,
                              operationName=="auth"))
    then
        insert (new InvalidInvocation("Constraint C1 violated"));
end
```

**Fig. 4.** A DRL Rule to Check the Constraint C1

Each `afterAll` constraint leads to a rule with the overall structure of the previous one. Indeed, given a specific constraint, the corresponding rules can be automatically generated with the Freemarker[3] template engine.

---

[2] http://www.jboss.org/drools/
[3] http://freemarker.org/

**Behaviour specified with FSMs.** When the behaviour of a device is specified by means of FSMs, the run-time interactions can also be validated with rules. In this sense, our approach builds rules which handle the state of a device and detect when invalid operations are invoked for the current state. Concretely, for each operation of a hosted service two rules have to be created. One of them detects when the operation is received in an invalid state and trigger a complex event to inform this situation. The other one detects when the operation is received in a valid state and, if needed, updates the current state of the device. Fig. 5 presents the first one of these rules, specified with DRL, for the operation *"on"* of the example presented in Section 2.1.

```
rule "ON-1"
    when
        // detects when an "on" operation is received for service SRV1
        $op: ServiceOperation(operationName=="on", srvId=="SRV1")

        // the current state of the service SRV1 is not S0
        $curState: ServiceState (srvId==$op.srvId, state!="S0")
    then
        insert (new InvalidInvocation("The operation ON cannot be
                                      invoked in the current State"));
end
```

**Fig. 5.** A DRL Rule for the "on" Operation

As with constraints, the overall structure of the rules is the same for any behaviour specified using FSMs, so they can be automatically generated given a specific FSM.

### 3.3    Dealing with Temporal Constraints and Quality of Service

Considering the proposal is based on mediation and CEP techniques, it provides a suitable infrastructure to deal with QoS issues and to handle temporal constraints. For example, regarding QoS, if a hosted service specifies the maximum number of invocations it can handle in a specific period of time, a rule can detect when this maximum is reached. On the other side, given the built-in support of temporal patterns in CEP solutions, the platform is able to handle temporal constraints. For instance, if the behaviour of a device allows specifying a maximum period of time between operations in the same session, a rule can be created so that if an operation is not received within this period of time the device returns to the initial state.

### 3.4    Further Discussion

We envision three main deployment alternatives for the platform: intra-organization, gateway and "as a service". The intra-organization alternative can be used to validate the interactions between devices and clients located within an organization. The gateway approach can be used to deliver the functionalities of the devices to other organizations. In these cases, the platform is a specialized hardware/software infrastructure located in the same network where the other devices are. Finally, the "as a service" alternative can be used to deliver the functionalities of the devices to other organizations but delegating the validation of invocations to an external entity which, for example, can be located within a cloud infrastructure. One of the advantages of the proposed solution is the agility to respond to changes in the behaviour of things (i.e. rules are automatically generated and deployed when the behaviour of a thing changes). Also, given that the solution verifies invocations before reaching the devices, it presents several other advantages: it prevents devices from being saturated with invalid invocations, it reduces network traffic arriving to devices and, when invalid invocations are received, it provides a suitable place to perform compensation actions. On the other side, the main disadvantage of the proposed solution is the time overhead in the invocations: they have to pass through the mediation platform where there is always a synchronous interaction with the CEP engine. Thus, although CEP engines are well known by supporting high throughputs per second with low latency [17], the proposed solution has an impact in performance. As well, the main limitation of the proposed solution is that it detects invalid invocations when mashups are already being executed, not before. Also, the solution still does not provide mechanisms to handled invalid invocations according to different situations (e.g. an incompatible change in a thing while a mashup, which uses that thing, is being executed). Compared with the static verification approach presented in our previous work, the proposed run-time verification solution provides complementary mechanisms. These mechanisms are required to be able to deal with changes at run-time in the behaviour of the devices once mashups have already been designed and deployed. There are also different situations that cannot be detected with static verification techniques like temporal related issues, QoS aspects and the concurrent execution of mashups. On the other side, the run-time verification solution detects problems as they occur, while the static verification mechanisms allow detecting that a mashup does not comply with the behaviour of devices at design time. Thus, we believe that both approaches have to be used in conjunction to provide an integral verification solution for the behaviour-aware mashups in the Web of Things paradigm.

## 4    Related Work

In this section, we analyze different approaches focused on the run-time verification of things in the context of service-oriented and event-based solutions. Mainly, we compare our proposal to works using CEP and mediation techniques for the WoT.

With the rise of the Future Internet as a reality, there exists the necessity of considering contents, devices, sensors, and things included in the new challenges of the service-oriented computing. Thus, some works have proposed service-oriented solutions for Home Network System [18] or Smart Home [19]. The former presents a sensor mashup platform which allows the dynamic composition of the existing sensor services. They mainly focus on helping non-expert developers to create context-aware services within the home network system, but their framework does not offer a guide to control the behaviour of the system, only messages are exchanged by using WSDL and REST/SOAP. The latter is closer to our approach. Authors propose an application logic distribution where devices in a smart home incorporate a set of rules than can govern their behaviour, following ECA (Event-Condition-Action) rules: they listen to external messages (notifications coming from other services) and, according to some conditions defined in these rules, they decide to perform their own actions. In comparison to our approach, this mechanism is not lightweight and rules may be not enough to determine the correct order among operations of a service. Therefore, we propose not only to define rules from the scratch, but to generate them to check the invocations at run-time, based on the specified behavior of each device.

CEP and mediation techniques are being increasingly used for run-time monitoring, verification and adaptation in service-oriented and event-based solutions. In [17] the authors describe an approach to deal with differences between Web Services protocols, by using CEP to adapt their interactions and resolve conflicts. Compared to our approach, message consumption and transmission are modeled as events, and adaptation is specified using automata and deployed as CEP adapters. In [20] an event-based approach to verify the compliance of the overall sequence of inter-organizational choreography operations is presented. Each message received or sent by an organization is associated to an event and CEP is used to verify whether the participating parties have performed their tasks according to the choreography. In [21] the authors propose an integrated solution for run-time compliance governance in SOA, focusing on QoS, security and licensing issues. In a similar way to our proposal, this solution uses CEP to monitor the compliance of business processes during their execution. However, although these proposals leverage CEP and mediation techniques for run-time verification, none of them focus neither in the field of the WoT nor in verifying the compliance of invocations according services' behaviour.

Nevertheless, recently, CEP techniques and mediation solutions have been applied and considered relevant in the field of the WoT in a separate way. On the one hand, as regards CEP applied to the things world, in [22] the authors propose a solution to deal with imprecise timestamps and events order in this highly distributed context. Also, in [23] a solution to solve the integration of heterogeneous event information resources is proposed. However, none of these solutions uses CEP techniques for the run-time verification of invocations. On the other hand, mediation solutions have been also proposed in the field of the Web of Things. In [3] a middleware infrastructure focused on enabling an efficient collaboration between device-level services and enterprise applications is presented. To this end, the infrastructure includes mediation capabilities to provide connectivity with non-DPWS enabled devices. In turn, DPWS enabled devices can directly interact with enterprise applications or they can be accessed through the infrastructure to get more advanced features (e.g. asynchronous invocations). In [24] the authors propose the concept of Gateway as a Service: a cloud computing framework for the WoT, focused on integrating devices into service compositions and business processes. Also, in [25] an integrated development and run-time environment for the future Internet is proposed, which include a Light Service Bus to address the access to things considering their resource constraints and leveraging DPWS. All these proposals focus on using mediation capabilities to enable the connectivity to heterogeneous things; but unlike our proposal, they do not provide mechanisms to detect invalid invocations to things according their behaviour.

Therefore, to the best of our knowledge there is not any effort in the field of the Web of Things that uses both CEP and mediation techniques jointly to address the run-time verification of the behaviour of things.

# 5    Concluding Remarks

In this paper, we have presented an approach to detect and inhibit invalid invocations at run-time while things are composed, by using mediation techniques and CEP, as well as a discovery proxy. We complement our previous static verification mechanism by automatically generating required elements to perform run-time validation of invocations of things, in order to check things only receive requests compatible with their behavior. Our approach may be easily extended to validate other issues, such as QoS and temporal restrictions. We have illustrated it applying and generating production rules for a service-based (airport surveillance) system with both behavioural constraints and FSMs, and deploying them in a particular CEP engine. We plan to extend the general architecture with an IDE as Mashup Editor to specify the orchestration corresponding to mashups and a Mashups Execution Environment to deploy the generated mashups. In addition, we are considering studying the inclusion of some recovery strategy in case an invalid invocation occurs. We are also planning to perform the evaluation of potential performance issues in scenarios with a big number of things.

**Acknowledgements.** Work supported by projects TIN2008-05932, TIN2012-35669, CSD2007-0004 funded by Spanish Ministry MINECO & FEDER; P11-TIC-7659 by Andalusian Gov; Univ. Málaga, Campus Exc. Int. Andalucía Tech.

# References

1. Guinard, D., Ion, I., Mayer, S.: In Search of an Internet of Things Service Architecture: REST or WS-*? A Developers' Perspective. In: Puiatti, A., Gu, T. (eds.) MobiQuitous 2011. LNICST, vol. 104, pp. 326–337. Springer, Heidelberg (2012)
2. Pautasso, C., et al.: RESTful Web Services vs. "big" Web Services: Making the Right Architectural Decision. In: Proc. of WWW 2008, pp. 805–814. ACM (2008)
3. de Souza, L.M.S., Spiess, P., Guinard, D., Köhler, M., Karnouskos, S., Savio, D.: SOCRADES: A Web Service Based Shop Floor Integration Infrastructure. In: Floerkemeier, C., Langheinrich, M., Fleisch, E., Mattern, F., Sarma, S.E. (eds.) IOT 2008. LNCS, vol. 4952, pp. 50–67. Springer, Heidelberg (2008)
4. Jammes, F., Smit, H.: Service-Oriented Paradigms in Industrial Automation. IEEE Trans. Ind. Informatics 1(1), 62–70 (2005)
5. Erl, T.: Service-Oriented Architecture: Concepts, Technology, and Design. Prent Hall (2005)
6. Zinn, M., et al.: Device Services as Reusable Units of Modelling in a Service-Oriented Environment-An Analysis Case Study. In: Proc. of ISIE 2010, pp. 1728–1735. IEEE CS (2010)
7. Cubo, J., Brogi, A., Pimentel, E.: Behaviour-Aware Compositions of Things. In: Proc. of iThings 2012 in conjunction with GreenCom 2012, pp. 1–8. IEEE CS (2012)
8. Cubo, J., González, L., Brogi, A., Pimentel, E., Ruggia, R.: Towards Run-Time Verification of Compositions in the Web of Things using Complex Event Processing. In: Proc. of JCIS 2013 in Conjunction with CEDI 2013, pp. 147–154 (2013)
9. Luckham, D.: The Power of Events: An Introduction to Complex Event Processing in Distributed Enterprise Systems. Addison-Wesley (2002)

10. Brand, D., et al.: On Communicating Finite-State Machines. J. ACM 30(2), 323–342 (1983)
11. Eckert, M., Bry, F., Brodt, S., Poppe, O., Hausmann, S.: A CEP Babelfish: Languages for Complex Event Processing and Querying Surveyed. In: Helmer, S., Poulovassilis, A., Xhafa, F., et al. (eds.) Reasoning in Event-Based Distributed Systems. SCI, vol. 347, pp. 47–70. Springer, Heidelberg (2011)
12. Etzion, O., Niblett, P.: Event Processing in Action. Manning Publications (2010)
13. Wylie, H., Lambros, P.: Enterprise Connectivity Patterns: Implementing integration solutions with IBM's Enterprise Service Bus products. Accessible at IBM website
14. Chappell, D.: Enterprise Service Bus: Theory in Practice. O'Reilly Media (2004)
15. Hohpe, G., Woolf, B.: Enterprise Integration Patterns: Designing, Building, and Deploying Messaging Solutions. Addison-Wesley Professional (2003)
16. Jeyaraman, R., Modi, V., Driscoll, D., Bullen, G., Nixon, T.: Understanding Devices Profile for Web Services, WS-Discovery, and SOAP-over-UDP. Microsoft (2008)
17. Taher, Y., Parkin, M., Papazoglou, M.P., van den Heuvel, W.-J.: Adaptation of Web Service Interactions Using Complex Event Processing Patterns. In: Kappel, G., Maamar, Z., Motahari-Nezhad, H.R. (eds.) Service Oriented Computing. LNCS, vol. 7084, pp. 601–609. Springer, Heidelberg (2011)
18. Nakamura, M., et al.: Application Framework for Efficient Development of Sensor as a Service for Home Network System. In: Proc. of SCC 2011, pp. 576–583. IEEE CS (2011)
19. Parra, J., et al.: Flexible Smart Home Architecture using Device Profile for Web Services: A Peer-to-Peer Approach. International Journal of Smart Home 3, 39–55 (2009)
20. Baouab, A., et al.: An Event-Driven Approach for Runtime Verification of Inter-Organizational Choreographies. In: Proc. of SCC 2011, pp. 640–647. IEEE CS (2011)
21. Birukou, A., D'Andrea, V., Leymann, F., Serafinski, J., Silveira, P., Strauch, S., Tluczek, M.: An Integrated Solution for Runtime Compliance Governance in SOA. In: Maglio, P.P., Weske, M., Yang, J., Fantinato, M., et al. (eds.) ICSOC 2010. LNCS, vol. 6470, pp. 122–136. Springer, Heidelberg (2010)
22. Fengjuan, W., Xiaoming, Z., Yongheng, W., Kening, C.: The Research on Complex Event Processing Method of Internet of Things. In: Proc. ICMTMA 2013, pp. 1219–1222 (2013)
23. Wang, W., Guo, D.: Towards Unified Heterogeneous Event Processing for the Internet of Things. In: Proc. of IOT 2012, pp. 84–91 (2012)
24. Wu, Z., et al.: Gateway as a Service: A Cloud Computing Framework for Web of Things. In: Proc. of ICT 2012, pp. 1–6 (2012)
25. Ben Hamida, A., Kon, F., Ansaldi Oliva, G., Dos Santos, C.E.M., Lorré, J.-P., Autili, M., De Angelis, G., Zarras, A., Georgantas, N., Issarny, V., Bertolino, A.: An Integrated Development and Runtime Environment for the Future Internet. In: Álvarez, F., et al. (eds.) FIA 2012. LNCS, vol. 7281, pp. 81–92. Springer, Heidelberg (2012)

# Designing a Service Platform for Sharing Internet Resources in MANETs

Gabriel Guerrero-Contreras, José Luis Garrido,
Carlos Rodríguez-Domínguez, Manuel Noguera, and Kawtar Benghazi

Software Engineering Department
University of Granada
Avenida del Hospicio S/N
18071 Granada, España
zahara@correo.ugr.es,
{benghazi,jgarrido,carlosrodriguez,mnoguera}@ugr.es

**Abstract.** Nowadays, there is great interest to develop future Internet applications supporting resource sharing in mobile networks. This usually entails maintaining the consistency of those shared resources, that is, between different replicas of the resources. Moreover, mobile networks are characterized by varying capacity, in part, caused by their mobility, which also derives in frequent networking disconnections and network partitions. Therefore, to ensure the consistency of replicated resources being shared in a mobile network is more complicated that in networks with infrastructure support, as it requires to process events associated with the use of the resources themselves as well as those related with the state of the network. In response, in this paper an event-driven platform consisting of two services (monitoring and synchronization) and an underlying middleware has been designed in order to address the consistency of shared Internet resources in mobile networks in a simple way. The synchronization service only needs to be specialized to adapt the resource, depending on its type, to the required use in a particular system. The proposal is illustrated through the example of a collaborative document editor.

**Keywords:** Service Oriented Architecture, Event-driven Architecture, MANET, Future Internet, Resource Consistency.

## 1 Introduction

Nowadays, there is great interest to develop future Internet applications supporting human collaboration in mobile networks. These networks are characterized by features such as *localized scalability* and *uneven conditioning* [1]. Localized scalability is defined as "*a good system design has to achieve scalability by severely reducing interactions between distant entities*" [1]. It avoids network congestion. Uneven conditioning is the difference between devices capacities or the difference between different environments (e.g. GPS is not available indoors) [1]. These features have a

C. Canal and M. Villari (Eds.): ESOCC 2013, CCIS 393, pp. 331–345, 2013.

direct relation with the quality properties associated to the network, like performance. More recently, in highly dynamic environments Mobile ad-hoc Networks (MANET) [2] are being imposed. One key aspect of these networks is that they self-configure their infrastructure, according to the nearby, available devices at a given time. That is, MANETs do not have a static communication scheme and, therefore, the management of shared data becomes more complicated. Furthermore, more and more services are offered in the "cloud" [3]. Since the term was coined by George Gilder [4] the cloud has expanded enormously, in particular software as a service model (e.g. Google or Amazon) [5].

In this networks type, replication is a useful design technique to achieve some objectives, such as localized scalability. Data replication is recommendable in order to obtain high-availability and good performance in a system. As the number of replicas increases, the probability of being able to reach at least a replica of a resource increases. However, to obtain these benefits it is necessary maintain the correctness of the data. In replicated data, one key aspect of correctness is mutual consistency, that is, that "all copies of the same logical data item must agree on exactly one current value for the data item" [6].

Maintaining the correctness of the shared data is not a simple task, particularly in environments where network disconnections are frequent. To overcome this issue, there are different solutions which can be classified in two dimensions: *pessimistic strategies*, which consist in preventing inconsistencies; and *optimistic strategies*, which do not prevent inconsistencies, but allow them to happen, and when they are detected, they are resolved.

Nowadays, some research initiatives proposed solutions based on a peer-to-peer (p2p) architecture [7, 8, 9]. Nevertheless, these initiatives are focused in resource location and utilization and don't pay attention to the consistent management of resources when accessed concurrently under frequent disconnections. In this paper an event-driven, SOA-based (*Service Oriented Architecture*) [10] platform consisting of two services (monitoring and synchronization), and an underlying middleware, is presented. This platform has been designed to facilitate the consistent management of shared resources in mobile systems. The developer will only need to specialize the synchronization service to be adapted to each resource, depending on its type and the required use in a particular system. The aim is to be able to integrate advanced applications and heterogeneous systems using standard protocols in the business field (business processes) and notably in the Web (web services) [11, 12].

The rest of this paper is organized as follows. Section 2 presents related works for the management of shared data in mobile networks; Section 3 describes the proposed service platform intended to support resource sharing in future Internet applications taking into consideration the use of mobile networks; Section 4 presents the real example of a collaborative document editor to illustrate the proposal; Section 5 discusses the proposal; and finally, conclusions and future work are summarized.

## 2    Related Work

MANETs networks have proved its usefulness in fields such as automobile (*Vehicular Ad-Hoc Network*) [13, 14, 15]; disaster management, when the communication network is not available [16, 17, 18]; and sensors networks [19]. However, MANETs networks present a series of challenges such as [20]: *knowledge representation*, is a key issue in MANETs networks due to heterogeneous nature of these networks; *knowledge discovery*, MANETs networks are highly dynamics, thus find resources available in other hosts effectively is a fundamental task; *caching*, the use of cache data allows offline operations, but it complicates the task of maintain the shared resources consistent; *replication*, is another strategy to optimize the data management process and it allows brings closer the data to user; *query processing*, this issue is important because the applications that run in MANETs networks are context aware ;and *security*, with regard this, security is an important and complicated task due to are the device themselves the network infrastructure, and it changes constantly with a high numbers of connections and disconnections. In response, in recent years some research initiatives proposed solutions to shared resources management in MANETs, like DRIVE [7], MoGATU [8] and CHaMeLeoN [9].

DRIVE (*Dissemination of Resource Information in Vehicular Environments*) is a software platform designed to deploy in vehicles, PDAs, sensors or any device with wireless capabilities. The platform uses a p2p approach to data sharing and it is based in a layered model. The model is made up of three layers (from bottom to top): data layer, support layer and utility layer. The data layer implements the data model; the support layer defines how queries are processed and how the data is disseminated; and finally, the utility layer contains the modules to access at the different resources. Some aspects of the platform can be highlighted, such as its economic model to guarantee the dissemination of the information to the largest possible audience. With this model a node of the network will transmit the information even if it is not interested in the particular data.

MoGATU proposes a model to share data in MANETs trough p2p approach. Like DRIVE, it proposes a layered model with three layers and two intermediate sublayers. MoGATU uses a main storage system out of MANET network, however, if a device lost connection or a network partition occurs, MoGATU uses caching and replication. Besides, it defines its own transaction model, called NC-Transaction. With this model, MoGATU increases the number of successful transactions, however, this model not guarantee the global consistency of the shared data.

The main purpose of CHaMeLeoN is exchange multimedia data in a MANET network, including in streaming. CHaMeLeoN's philosophy is adapting the application to user and the user's context. Moreover, CHaMeLeoN implements motion prediction algorithms, in order to anticipate possible disconnections. This allows to place resource's replicas within the network efficiently.

The exposed software platforms are complete platforms to address resource management in MANET networks. However, these platforms are focused in resource location and utilization and don't pay attention to the consistent management of resources.

The work presented in [21] is based on a SOA approach to manage the data consistency in heterogeneous systems. In that context, there are several applications with different local data models. The models are different but they refer to the same data. The main objective of the work is that the modifications in a local model automatically disseminate to the remainder local models. The proposed architecture is based on a synchronization service and a directory service. The directory service linking local models between them and the synchronization service solves possible inconsistencies. This solution presents two main limitations: first, it does not cover the possibility of disconnections or network partitions; and second, it is an ad-hoc solution.

With reference to collaborative systems in mobile environments, these are being greatly accepted in areas such as health [22, 23] and education [24, 25]. Environments such as hospitals and schools have the advantage of a static infrastructure that can facilitate the shared data management, e.g. servers and storage systems, and therefore facilitate collaborative applications develop.

## 3    Service Platform Design

This section presents an event-driven, SOA-based proposal in order to address the consistent management of shared Internet resources in mobile networks in a simpler way. On the one hand, the SOA approach is used as it provides some benefits such as reuse, interoperability, scalability and ease of maintenance. On the other hand, event-driven architecture provides benefits such as broadcast communications, asynchrony and timeliness. Besides, both of these approaches reduce the coupling between the different system's components and platforms. Furthermore, this proposal is intended to be a generic solution that can be adapted to any resource type, as discussed below.

Figure 1 shows a general architecture of the service platform. The main component is the synchronization service. This service maintains the consistency of shared resources. The shared resources can be modified by several users concurrently. The synchronization service is a high-level service based on monitoring service. The latter is a basic service which stores all kind of information about changes on shared data. Both services can be replicated in order to improve the availability, e.g. when the network becomes partitioned.

Moreover in order to provide a complete development platform, these services have been deployed on a communication middleware for ubiquitous systems: BlueRose [26, 27]. The middleware notifies events occurring in the system under a publish/subscribe paradigm. This feature is interesting in mobile systems, with a heterogeneous communication environment, due to it reduces coupling between interfaces. The presented services are exposed through WSDL interfaces and are accessed remotely using SOAP. However, due to event-driven approach, they also can generate or receive events. In the next subsections the platform components are described in more detail.

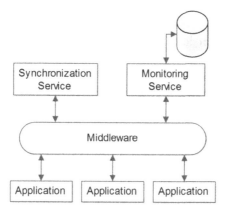

**Fig. 1.** General scheme of the platform to synchronizing shared resources in mobile networks.

### 3.1    Monitoring Service

Monitoring is a basic service which stores all kind of information about changes on shared data. This information can fulfill several purposes, e.g. version control, security control or system debug. In the synchronization service case, this information will be required when it will be needed to apply synchronization algorithms. In a device disconnection case, this information is fundamental to allow offline operations in the system.

Monitoring service supports different configurations in the system. It can be accessed from other system component to store some event, for example from the Synchronization service; or it can work as a subscriber too. With this last, the monitoring service can have different replicas which are subscribed to different events. This allows an efficient monitoring, due to the monitoring work can be divided between different replicas.

As has been mentioned, this solution expects to be a generic solution, not an ad-hoc solution. Therefore the monitoring service is designed to monitor any resource type. This is possible because in the platform all actions performed on shared resources are represented by events. The middleware BlueRose allows represent any information through resources and the monitoring service can monitor any event. Consequently the monitoring service is completely reusable and no need to modify its code.

Furthermore, the monitoring service uses a storage service as Figure 1 shows. This storage service can be replicated and/or distributed. Besides, the storage service can be in the cloud, with all the benefits that this entails. Also, if more control over data is desired monitoring service can uses a local storage service. Concerning the DBMS, a NoSQL system has been chosen in order to provide an efficient and flexible system to store events. Flexibility is needed owing to the structure of the events is unknown a priori.

## 3.2    Synchronization Service

The main service of the proposed platform is the synchronization service. This service is based on the monitoring service. Thus, with the information that monitoring service provides, the synchronization service can overcome the challenges of mobile networks (disconnections and network partitions) and it allows users working without connection.

In the case of a user disconnection (Figure 2), the user can continues working with cache data. While the connection is lost the generated events must be stored locally. When it recovers the connection, the first step is synchronizing the changes with the rest of the system through the synchronization service. For this, the synchronization service requires: local events of the device, disconnection interval and generated events in the system in this interval. Hence, the monitoring service is fundamental for the synchronization. Otherwise, if the synchronization service has not the generated events in the system in the interval disconnection, it cannot compare local events of the user and it cannot detect the possible conflicting changes with the remainder users. As mentioned above, cache is necessary to allow offline operations. Consequently, the client application must store the necessary data for user to continue working in disconnection case.

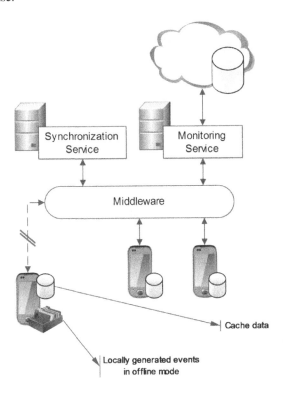

**Fig. 2.** A device working offline

The monitoring service is a general service, however, this is not possible for the synchronization service as the synchronization algorithms are dependent of the resource type. That is, synchronize images is not the same as synchronize text, because how to solve possible inconsistencies is distinct for each case. For this reason and with the goal of providing a reusable service, the synchronization service is a general service that must be specialized according to resource to synchronize. In this way, the common part related to manage the resource synchronization is identified and solved in the service, and the issues related with particular requirements of resources are addressed in service specialization. In this way, the proposal is intended to be applicable to any type of shared resource.

Another important issue is how the synchronization service can obtain the correct sequence of events. This is an important issue because the service is working in a distributed system where the clock values may differ. To resolve it, first is necessary adding a timestamp to event definition and use a time server to provide the same clock value to all devices of the network. Owing to different networks can interoperate (thought service replicas) Lamport's algorithm [28] to determine the order of events in a distributed computer system has been implemented.

It is especially necessary to take into account that offline operations are permitted and network partitions can occur. For these cases, when the time server is inaccessible, it will acts as follow. When the device lost connection and it starts to generate local events, it uses its clock value to generate a relative timestamp for local events. When this device recovers connection, before to connect with the synchronization service, it gets clock value from time server. With this value, it calculates the difference between its clock and the clock of time server and it recalculates the timestamp of local events. In this way, the correct sequence of events to the synchronization service is guaranteed and therefore it can apply synchronization algorithms correctly.

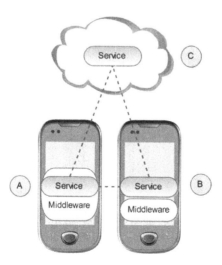

**Fig. 3.** Possible services deployments within platform architecture

### 3.3    Deployment

Regarding the deployment of services, they support different configurations, thus the platform can be adapted to requirement of a specific application. The possible configurations are:

- *Services within the communication middleware* (Figure 3, point A). They are disposed inside of middleware in order to obtain efficiency, regardless middleware overload is increased with each service added to it.
- *Services disposed over the middleware* (Figure 3, point B). This configuration matches when exists a high computational performance device in the network working as a server. Other devices benefits of decreased computational load offered by the dedicated server device.
- *Services on cloud infrastructure* [3] (Figure 3, point C). Cloud benefits are accessibility and scalability. The information or service are available wherever an Internet connection exists and resources could be increased or decreased as needed.

A possible system deployment is depicted in Figure 4. Figure 4 shows three MANET networks, these networks are not directly connected, however, they interoperate through services proposed above. To make this possible some replication protocol [29, 30] must be used to keep the service replicas updated and consistent. Replicating not only improves service availability, moreover, it helps to achieve localized scalability due to it reduces network traffic. This is possible owing to replicating allows devices use the nearest replica, as Figure 4 shows.

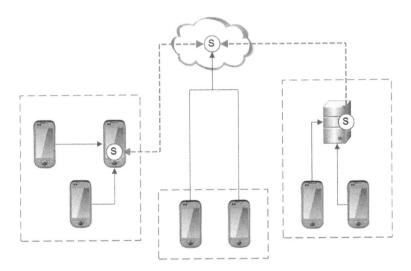

**Fig. 4.** A possible configuration of services in several MANET networks

## 4    Example: Collaborative Document Editor

As mentioned above, the synchronization service is a generic service that must be specialized with concrete synchronization algorithms of the shared resource to manage. To test the validity of the service platform proposed, the synchronization service has been specialized into a document repository service. In this case, shared resources are text documents.

The system displays the following behavior (see Figure 5). The repository service keeps the full set of documents in the system. While users are online they are working with the documents of repository service. Users make changes to documents, these changes can be modified created or deleted a document. Moreover, these changes can be done concurrently and users who are working with same document can see these changes in real time.

The repository service, it is a specialization of the synchronization service, is responsible to integrate these changes consistently in documents set. Besides, the client application must have a cache copy of documents with which user is working, since it is not possible to foresee a disconnection. The number of files in cache is determined by several factors, such as disconnection frequency. To solve this, there are different approaches to caching in mobile environments [31].

Meanwhile, the monitoring service stores all generated events in the system. These events contain information about changes over documents and they are notified under a publish/subscribe paradigm.

When a client device disconnection occurs (User 1 in Figure 5), the client application starts working with cache documents copy. Besides, the client application starts storing generated events by user locally (Figure 5, step 1). These local events will be necessary to synchronize when connection is re-established. The client application can continue working offline with the unique limitation about the memory capacity of the device to store all the events that can be generated.

When connection is re-established, the client application first re-adjusts the events' timestamps generated offline (see section 3.2). Then it requests be synchronized with the system through the synchronization service (Figure 5, step 2). With this purpose, the application provides to synchronization service the disconnection interval and the generated events locally. This is the client application notifies to the synchronization service the changes that user has made on shared documents while the device was offline.

The repository service receives this request and it requests to monitoring service the modifications made by system users on shared documents during disconnection interval. The monitoring service queries the storage service for events set generated within the disconnection interval (Figure 5, step 3). When the monitoring service gets response, it sends the events set to the synchronization service (Figure 5, step 4). When the synchronization service has the generated events in the system and the generated events of the disconnected user, it can apply the synchronization algorithms and it can apply the resulting changes on documents repository (Figure 5, step 5). In this case (shared document), when the synchronization algorithm is appliqued the following cases can occur:

- *The document that has been modified by offline user has not been modified by another user in the system.* In this case, the changes can be applied directly.

- *The document that has been modified by offline user also has been modified by other user. But there are not conflicting changes.* In this case, the repository service automatically integrates both changes in the document. We have deemed that a conflictive change is when two or more users modify the same position of the document (the same *byte*). There are other options, such as consider conflictive modify the same word or phrase. Due to if two users modify the same phrase unknowingly the resulting phrase would be probably inconsistent.
- *The document that has been modified by offline user also has been modified by other user. There are conflicting changes.* In this situation, the repository service creates a parallel version of the document with the changes of the disconnected user. Thus, two or more versions of the documents are maintaining. The users themselves are responsible to resolve the conflict. The repository service only has the responsibility to ensure that do not miss a single user's change.

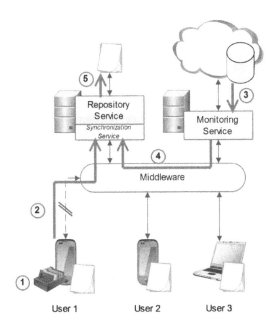

**Fig. 5.** Behavior of repository service when a reconnection occurs

This way, the consistency can be guaranteed, due to if there are conflicting modifications, these are saved in different versions of the document and none modification is lost. There are other strategies to maintain the consistency of shared documents when there are multiple writers [32]. For example, lock a document when there is a writer. This approach is simpler to implement, however, a tool that implements this approach really is not a collaborative tool, because users cannot write collaboratively in real time. Other derived approaches are interesting. For example, only some parts of a document can be locked. A weakness of this approach is that a disconnected user cannot lock the document, but even so it could uses this approach combined with others.

With regard to the repository service, we must note that the implemented synchronization algorithms are independent of client editor application. Consequently, the repository service can be used in any text editor conforming to the adopted event model. For last, underscore that it has not been necessary modify the monitoring service (see section 3.1), this service is sufficiently flexible to adapt to any shared resource. On the contrary, the synchronization service has been extended, through inheritance, to adapt to the shared resources of the case, text documents.

## 5    Discussion

With the objective of obtaining a higher acceptance in the use of advanced applications in MANET networks, the service platform presented in this paper intends to address the following requirements:

- Interoperability. As shows Figure 3, though the networks are not directly connected however, they can interoperate through services proposed due to service replicas.
- Adaptability. The designed services are not an ad-hoc solutions, the proposal is a generic solution that can be adapted to any shared resource type. On one hand, for the monitoring service this is possible due to event-driven approach (see section 3.1). On the other hand, for the synchronization service this is not possible. In this case, the synchronization service is designed as a generic service that can be extended through inheritance to adapt it to any shared resource type (see section 3.2).
- Platform-independent. Owing to use a SOA-based approach and to standards of publications, communications and access, the services implemented are platform-independent.
- Offline operations. As it has been explained above, this proposal is specially oriented to allow offline operations. This is particularly interesting in environments with problems maintaining connections, where disconnection of devices and network partitions are frequent. This feature is achieved owing to replication techniques, caching and the designed protocols to obtain ordered events.

However, some problems could be found such as network congestion, for instance, in collaborative document editing (see section 4). In this case, due to the synchronization is at low level (character/byte), each time that a character is introduced or deleted an event is generated and published. In a case with many users and many modifications, would be possible generate and transmit too many events. To solve this problem, would be possible synchronize at word level or study other possibilities such as partly block the documents when a writer is present in a particular document area. This will reduce the events generated in the system.

Moreover, use a SOA-based approach entails some issues to consider [33], particularly in large systems. Amongst other issues, it should be taken into consideration that when a service is integrated and working in a large system, before to modify it an impact study is necessary. This may limit system evolution, besides, as the system grows could be more complicated conforming to all standards of SOA approach.

# 6    Conclusions and Future Work

The service platform presented in this paper is a combination of a distributed computation techniques and event-driven and service-based architectures. The platform is composed of an underlying event-driven communication middleware which provides a publish/subscribe service to propagate the events. Over this middleware two services are disposed: the monitoring service, a basic service, which monitors and stores any event of the system and the synchronization service which process these events (provided them by monitoring service) in order to synchronize the replicas of shared resources. Besides, these services have been developed with the aim of being generic services. The monitoring service is reusable and it can be used with any resource type and no need to modify its code. However, the synchronization service needs to be adapted to the resource, depending on its type and the required use in a particular system. This is due to the synchronization algorithms are dependent of the resource type. Therefore, the common part related to manage the resource synchronization is identified and solved in the service, and the issues related with particular requirements of resources are addressed in service specialization.

The proposal presented especially addresses the case of systems that exhibit discontinuous operation. For this reason, the platform has been designed to make sure that synchronization service always gets the right events sequence. Even with the possibility of some devices are working offline or with network partitions. This is achieved, in particular, using a time server, adding timestamps to events and using Lamport's algorithm [28] to determine the order of events in the distributed computer system.

Besides, replication and caching techniques have been used in order to achieve localized scalability and high availability of the proposed services. Additionally, to get a better fulfillment of the applications requirements, the services have been designed for they can be deployed within the middleware, in order to obtain efficiency, regardless middleware overload is increased; on the middleware, when exists device in the network working as a server; or in a cloud infrastructure, in order to provide benefits such as accessibility and scalability. This way, flexibility of the platform is increased and it can provide greater adaptation of the system to the requirements of a particular application.

Moreover, for validity purposes of the proposal, the synchronization service has been specialized into a document repository service. The repository service implements application-independent algorithms to synchronize consistently text documents in collaborative environments. Consequently, the repository service can be used in any text editor conforming to the adopted event model. Besides, there are no restrictions about maximum disconnection time, while the user device has space to store local events, the user can continue working. With the use of the resulting repository service, users can edit document collaboratively in real time when they have connection with the system, and also they can edit the documents when they are offline. These documents will be synchronized when the connection recovers.

For last, the proposal platform seeks for benefits such as reusability, scalability, availability, interoperability, low coupling with platforms and its design facilitates offline operations.

Regarding future work, a depth study of the specific synchronization requirements of certain applications will be carried out, in order to provide synchronizations algorithms and assess adaptability and performance of the proposed platform. Additionally, a performance study of system is foreseen.

Moreover, the proposed platform will applied in ambits such as context information management; and semantic annotation tools for web, under which a high level of collaborative capabilities is desirable. Finally, the platform will integrate other high levels services, such as a location service [34], in a largest platform for context-aware and ubiquitous systems.

**Acknowledgments.** This research work has been funded by the Ministry of Economy and Competitiveness of the Spanish Government under the Research Project TIN2012-38600 and by the Vice-Rector's for Scientific Policy and Research of the University of Granada.

# References

1. Satyanarayanan, M.: Pervasive computing: Vision and challenges. IEEE Personal Communications 8(4), 10–17 (2001)
2. Bansal, M., Rajput, R., Gupta, G.: Mobile ad hoc networking (MANET): Routing protocol performance issues and evaluation considerations (1999)
3. Armbrust, M., Fox, A., Griffith, R., Joseph, A.D., Katz, R., Konwinski, A., Zaharia, M.: A view of cloud computing. Communications of the ACM 53(4), 50–58 (2010)
4. Gilder, G.: The information factories. Wired 14(10) (2006)
5. Cusumano, M.: Cloud computing and SaaS as new computing platforms. Communications of the ACM 53(4), 27–29 (2010)
6. Davidson, S.B., Garcia-Molina, H., Skeen, D.: Consistency in a partitioned network: a survey. ACM Computing Surveys (CSUR) 17(3), 341–370 (1985)
7. Xu, B., Wolfson, O.: Data management in mobile peer-to-peer networks. In: Ng, W.S., Ooi, B.-C., Ouksel, A.M., Sartori, C. (eds.) DBISP2P 2004. LNCS, vol. 3367, pp. 1–15. Springer, Heidelberg (2005)
8. Perich, F., Joshi, A., Chirkova, R.: Data Management for Mobile Ad-Hoc Networks. In: Enabling Technologies for Wireless E-Business, pp. 132–176. Springer, Heidelberg (2006)
9. Ghandeharizadeh, S., Helmy, A., Krishnamachari, B., Bar, F., Richmond, T.: Data Management Techniques for Continuous Media in Ad-Hoc Networks of Wireless Devices. In: Furht, B. (ed.) Encyclopedia of Multimedia. Springer, Heidelberg (2008)
10. MacKenzie, C.M., Laskey, K., McCabe, F., Brown, P.F., Metz, R., Hamilton, B.A.: Reference model for service oriented architecture 1.0.OASIS Standard, 12 (2006)
11. Pasley, J.: How BPEL and SOA are changing Web services development. IEEE Internet Computing 9(3), 60–67 (2005)
12. Schroth, C., Janner, T.: Web 2.0 and SOA: Converging concepts enabling the internet of services. IT Professional 9(3), 36–41 (2007)

13. Zeadally, S., Hunt, R., Chen, Y.S., Irwin, A., Hassan, A.: Vehicular ad hoc networks (VANETs): status, results, and challenges. Telecommunication Systems 50(4), 217–241 (2012)
14. Studer, A., Shi, E., Bai, F., Perrig, A.: TACKing together efficient authentication, revocation, and privacy in VANETs. In: 6th Annual IEEE Communications Society Conference on Sensor, Mesh and Ad Hoc Communications and Networks, SECON 2009, pp. 1–9. IEEE (2009)
15. Godbole, V.: Intelligent Driver Mobility Model and Traffic Pattern Generation based Optimization of Reactive Protocols for Vehicular Ad-hoc Networks. International Journal of Information and Network Security (IJINS) 2(3), 207–215 (2013)
16. Reina, D.G., Toral, S.L., Barrero, F., Bessis, N., Asimakopoulou, E.: Evaluation of ad hoc networks in disaster scenarios. In: 2011 Third International Conference on Intelligent Networking and Collaborative Systems (INCoS), pp. 759–764. IEEE (November 2011)
17. Reina, D.G., MaríN, S.L., Bessis, N., Barrero, F., Asimakopoulou, E.: An evolutionary computation approach for optimizing connectivity in disaster response scenarios. Applied Soft Computing (2012)
18. Reina, D.G., Toral, S.L., Barrero, F., Bessis, N., Asimakopoulou, E.: Modelling and assessing ad hoc networks in disaster scenarios. Journal of Ambient Intelligence and Humanized Computing, 1–9 (2012)
19. Cordeiro, C.D.M., Agrawal, D.P.: Ad hoc and sensor networks: theory and applications. World Scientific (2011)
20. Islam, N., Shaikh, Z.: A survey of data management issues & frameworks for mobile ad hoc networks. In: 2011 International Conference on Information and Communication Technologies (ICICT), pp. 1–5. IEEE (July 2011)
21. Svensson, E., Vetter, C., Werner, T.: Data consistency in a heterogeneous IT landscape: a service oriented architecture approach. In: Proceedings of the Eighth IEEE International Enterprise Distributed Object Computing Conference, EDOC 2004, pp. 3–8. IEEE (September 2004)
22. Selanikio, J.D., Kemmer, T.M., Bovill, M., Geisler, K.: Mobile computing in the humanitarian assistance setting: an introduction and some first steps. Journal of Medical Systems 26(2), 113–125 (2002)
23. Rahbar, A.: An E-Ambulatory Healthcare System Using Mobile Network. In: 2010 Seventh International Conference on the Information Technology: New Generations (ITNG), pp. 1269–1273. IEEE (April 2010)
24. Sancristobal, E., Martin, S., Gil, R., Orduna, P., Tawfik, M., Pesquera, A., Castro, M.: State of art, Initiatives and New challenges for Virtual and Remote Labs. In: 2012 IEEE 12th International Conference on Advanced Learning Technologies (ICALT), pp. 714–715. IEEE (July 2012)
25. Kahiigi, E., Ekenberg, L., Hansson, M.: Exploring the e-Learning State of art. In: Conference on E-Learning, Academic Conferences Limited, pp. 349–368 (2007)
26. Rodríguez-Domínguez, C., Benghazi, K., Garrido, J.L., Valenzuela, A.: A platform supporting the development of applications in ubiquitous systems: the collaborative application example of mobile forensics. In: Proceedings of the 13th International Conference on Interacción Persona-Ordenador, p. 41. ACM (2012)
27. Rodríguez-Domínguez, C., Benghazi, K., Noguera, M., Garrido, J.L., Rodríguez, M.L., Ruiz-López, T.: A Communication Model to Integrate the Request-Response and the Publish-Subscribe Paradigms into Ubiquitous Systems. Sensors 12(6), 7648–7668 (2012)
28. Lamport, L.: Time, clocks, and the ordering of events in a distributed system. Communications of the ACM 21(7), 558–565 (1978)

29. Hara, T.: Effective replica allocation in ad hoc networks for improving data accessibility. In: Proceedings of the IEEE Twentieth Annual Joint Conference of the IEEE Computer and Communications Societies, INFOCOM 2001, vol. 3, pp. 1568–1576. IEEE (2001)
30. Karumanchi, G., Muralidharan, S., Prakash, R.: Information dissemination in partitionable mobile ad hoc networks. In: Proceedings of the 18th IEEE Symposium on Reliable Distributed Systems, pp. 4–13. IEEE (1999)
31. Barbará, D., Imieliński, T.: Sleepers and workaholics: caching strategies in mobile environments. ACM Sigmod Record 23(2), 1–12 (1994)
32. Posner, I.R., Baecker, R.M.: How people write together [groupware]. In: Proceedings of the Twenty-Fifth Hawaii International Conference on System Sciences, vol. 4, pp. 127–138. IEEE (1992)
33. Lewis, G.A., Morris, E., Simanta, S., Wrage, L.: Common misconceptions about service-oriented architecture. In: Sixth International IEEE Conference on Commercial-off-the-Shelf (COTS)-Based Software Systems, ICCBSS 2007, pp. 123–130. IEEE (February 2007)
34. Ruiz-López, T., Rodríguez-Domínguez, C., Noguera, M., Garrido, J.L.: Towards a Reusable Design of a Positioning System for AAL Environments. In: Chessa, S., Knauth, S. (eds.) EvAAL 2011. CCIS, vol. 309, pp. 65–79. Springer, Heidelberg (2012)

# A Model-Driven Approach for Web Service Adaptation Using Complex Event Processing

Yéhia Taher[1], Juan Boubeta-Puig[2], Willem-Jan van den Heuvel[1],
Guadalupe Ortiz[2], and Inmaculada Medina-Bulo[2]

[1] European Research Institute for Service Science,
Tilburg University, The Netherlands
{y.taher,wjheuvel}@uvt.nl

[2] Department of Computer Science and Engineering, University of Cádiz,
C/ Chile 1, 11002 Cádiz, Spain
{juan.boubeta,guadalupe.ortiz,inmaculada.medina}@uca.es

**Abstract.** Web Services are often developed independently and follow different standards or approaches in constructing their interfaces. Therefore, it is likely that most Web Services will be incompatible since many services will not support the same interface. In order to solve it, a model-driven approach is defined in this paper to automatically generate adapters between incompatible web service interfaces. In concrete, a graphical modeling editor is developed to detect such incompatibilities, create the adapters between the modeled interfaces and transform these adapters into code. This code will be deployed into a complex event processing engine, the software which will perform the web service adaptation. We illustrate this approach through a case study for two web services with incompatible interfaces. Results confirm that this approach provides a suitable solution for web service adaptation using complex event processing.

**Keywords:** Web Service adaptation, model-driven development, complex event processing.

## 1 Introduction

Web Services (WS) provide a solution to the integration of distributed software through the standardization of data format, interface definition language, transport mechanism and other interoperability aspects such as security and quality of service. The Web Service Description Language (WSDL) defines a WS interface as a document in XML format, and a service as a set of endpoints which operate on messages containing either document-oriented or procedure-oriented information. The interface document provides a contract between the provider of a service and its users, and allows some flexibility for the service provider as it hides the implementation details.

WS interfaces define the messages and protocol which should be used to communicate with the service [15]. However, if two services wish to interact successfully, they must both support the same messages and protocol through the

C. Canal and M. Villari (Eds.): ESOCC 2013, CCIS 393, pp. 346–359, 2013.
© Springer-Verlag Berlin Heidelberg 2013

implementation of compatible WSDL documents. Unfortunately, this is difficult to achieve in practice: WS are often developed independently and follow different standards or approaches in constructing their interfaces. Furthermore, WS compositions will often use services in ways that were not foreseen in their original design and construction [9,11]. Therefore, it is likely that most WS will be incompatible since many services will not support the same interface.

In order to solve such problems, adapters can be created between WS interfaces. It is important to mention that the process for building these adapters will require incompatibility identification, adaptation rules encoding and execute code generation. However, if this process was manual then it would be extensive, expensive and error-prone.

For that reason, Taher et al. [18] propose an approach to automate this adapter generation process. Firstly, they define an algorithm for detecting WS incompatibilities. In concrete, it compares two different WS interfaces represented as automatons, and determines what are the existing incompatibilities by means of specific "incompatibility patterns", defined by Li et al. [11] for detecting protocol mismatches. Afterwards, the authors propose an algorithm for constructing such adapters which transforms every recognized incompatibility pattern into one of their proposed operators ("resolution patterns") to solve both signature and protocol incompatibilities. Notice that these operators can be applied individually or in combination to incoming messages to achieve a transformation in both the structure, type and number of messages sent to the destination. Finally, they describe a method to run these adapters into a Complex Event Processing (CEP) engine to execute the resolution operations.

Basically, CEP [12] is a technology that can process and analyze large amounts of events and correlate them to detect and respond to relevant situations in real time, making possible the creation of new events, known as "complex events" (relevant situations), which summarize other events. In the context of WS, events occur when SOAP messages are sent and received.

To our knowledge, there are not user-friendly enough modeling editors that help end users to take an active part in the process of the adaptation of Web Service using CEP. In this paper, we propose a model-driven approach which enables end users a user-friendly visualization of the provider and client service interfaces, the incompatibility patterns and the adapters automatically generated by such Taher's algorithms. These patterns and adapters will be represented as models in our approach.

Some of the main advantages of using a model-driven approach is that these incompatibility patterns and adapters models can be validated conforming to our defined metamodel as well as transformed into Continuous Computational Queries (CCQ), making use of model-to-code transformations. Then, these CCQs, written in a Continuous Computation Language (CCL), will be deployed into a CEP engine in runtime to execute the resolution operations which will make the WS adaptation. Furthermore, experts on WS adaptations will be able to modify such models, from their experience, later on causing the generation of new CCQs according to the changes introduced by these experts. Therefore, the code of adaptation rules will be automatically created.

The rest of this paper is organized as follows. Section 2 describes the types of incompatibilities that may exist between WS interfaces and the operators to resolve these incompatibilities; in addition, a definition of complex event processing is given. Section 3 describes a metamodel for defining the provider and client service interfaces, the incompatibility patterns and the adapters. Afterwards, Section 4 presents a model-driven approach for WS adaptation using CEP. Section 6 compares related work. Finally, conclusion and future work are described in Section 7.

## 2    Background

The types of incompatibilities that may exist between WS interfaces and the operators to resolve these incompatibilities are described in this section. Furthermore, the CEP technology is explained.

### 2.1    Web Service Incompatibilities

Incompatibilities between WS protocols can be classified as either [9,11]:

**Signature Incompatibilities** arise due to the differences between services in expected message structure, content and semantics. In WS, XML schema provides a set of "built-in" types to allow the construction of complex input and output message types from these primitives. This flexibility in constructing message types in XML often means that a message from one WS will not be recognized by another. Therefore, there is a requirement to provide some function that maps the schema of one message to another [13].

**Protocol Incompatibilities** are found when WS wish to interact but are incompatible because they support different message exchange sequences. For example, if two services perform the same function, e.g., accept purchase orders, but *Service A* requires a single order containing one or more items while *Service B* expects an order message for each item, there is a mismatch in their communication protocols that must be resolved in order for them to interoperate. To solve these incompatibilities, there are two approaches: a) to force one of the parts to support the other's interface, or b) to build an adapter that receives messages, converts them to the correct sequence and/or maps them into a desired format and sends them to their destination.

### 2.2    Adaptation Operators

Li et al. [11] describe five basic transformation patterns that can reconcile protocol mismatches. In our previous work [19], we have developed an operator for each of these patterns that can be applied individually or in combination to incoming messages to achieve a transformation in both the structure, type and number of messages sent to the destination —i.e., to resolve both signature and protocol incompatibilities.

The operators developed for each of the transformation patterns are:

- *Match-Make*: it translates one message type to another, solving the *One-To-One* transformation.
- *Split*: a solution for the *One-To-Many* pattern, which separates one message sent by the source into two or more messages to be received separately.
- *Merge*: the opposite of the *Split* operator —i.e., it performs a *Many-To-One* transformation. It combines two or more messages into a single message.
- *Aggregation*: it is used when two or more of the same message from the source service interface correspond to one message at the target service and it is a solution for the *One\*-To-One* transformation.
- *Disaggregation*: it performs the opposite function to *Aggregation* operator.

### 2.3   Complex Event Processing

CEP is a technology which can discover relationships between events through the analysis and correlation of multiple events, and trigger and take actions (e.g., generate new events) from these observations. CEP platforms allow streams of data to run through them to detect conditions that match CCQs —written in a CCL— as they occur. As a result, CEP has an advantage in performance and capacity compared to traditional approaches [8].

As was mentioned before, in the context of WS, events occur when SOAP messages are sent and received. Therefore, CEP adaptation requires the platform to consume incoming messages, process them and send the result to its destination. To offer a universal solution and a scalable method for WS protocol adaptation, we automate the generation and deployment of CCQs to transform incoming message(s) into the required output message format(s) using the adaptation operators previously described.

## 3   Adaptation Metamodel

In this section, we propose and define a metamodel which has as main objective the modeling of the provider and client service interfaces, the incompatibility patterns and the adapters generated automatically by such Taher's algorithms for solving both signature and protocol incompatibility problems that may exist between WS protocols. Furthermore, experts on WS adaptations will be able to modify from their experience the models conformed to this metamodel and obtained from these algorithms.

This metamodel, represented using UML class diagram, is sketched in Figure 1, where class attributes are not shown for clarity reason. These attributes are described below:

- *Service* → *s* := *(name : String, type : ServiceType)*, where *ServiceType* ∈ *{Consumer, Provider}*.

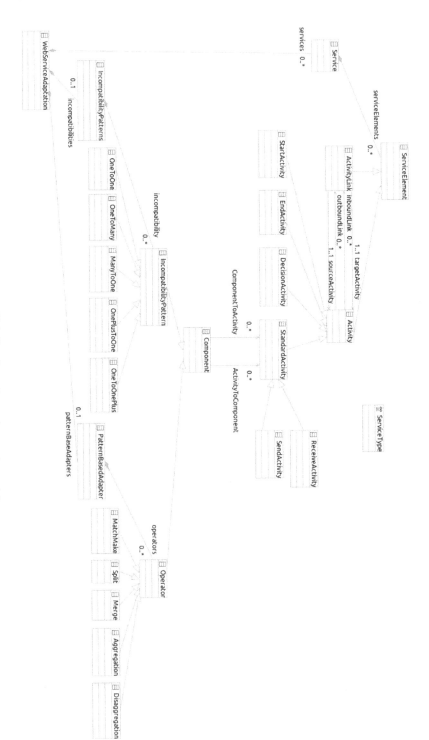

**Fig. 1.** Web Service adaptation metamodel

- *ServiceElement* → *(name : String)*
- *Component* → *(name : String)*
- *IncompatibilityPatterns* → *i := (name : String)*
- *PatternBasedAdapter* → *p := (name : String)*

Notice that *ServiceElement, StandardActivity, Component, IncompatibilityPattern* and *Operator* are abstract classes.

The *WebServiceAdaptation* class is the core element of this metamodel which is composed of some provider or consumer services (*0..\* Service*) and can have one incompatibility patterns (*0..1 IncompatibilityPatterns*) and one pattern based adapter (*0..1 PatternBasedAdapter*). In the following subsections, these elements will be described in detail.

### 3.1    Service

The *Service* class represents a provider or consumer service which may interact with another service. It has two attributes: *name*, a string that defines service's name, and *type*, an enum type that allows to specify if the service is a consumer or provider.

This class is composed of some service elements (*0..\* ServiceElement*). The abstract *ServiceElement* class has a string attribute to specify the name of this element and is specialized into two classes: *Activity* and *ActivityLink*. These classes will be used for defining the service interfaces by means of simplified UML activity diagrams.

We have adopted activity diagram instead of automata diagram because we consider the former is a better user-friendly representation to define service interfaces. Activity diagrams are graphical representations of actions and activities. In our context, activities represent different phases a service may go through during its interaction with clients. Each interaction is considered as an action. When a message is sent or received, the corresponding action is fired.

The *ActivityLink* class represents the link between two activities: the source activity (*1..1 sourceActivity*) and the target activity (*1..1 targetActivity*). Each of these activities may have some inbound links (*0..\* inboundLink*) and outbound links (*0..\* outboundLink*).

The *Activity* class is the generalization of the following four classes: *StartActivity, EndActivity, DecisionActivity* and *StandardActivity*. *StartActivity* represents the initial state to begin the definition of the service interface. *EndActivity* specifies the final state of the definition of the service interface. *DecisionActivity* presents alternatives between activities. Finally, *StandardActivity* is an abstract class which is sub-divided into two activity sub-classes: *SendActivity* and *ReceiveActivity*. *SendActivity* specifies a message which will be sent to another service while *ReceiveActivity* defines the message which will be received from another service.

Moreover, the *StandardActivity* class can link to some *Component* class (*0..\* ActivityToComponent*) and vice versa, the *StandardActivity* can be linked by none or more *Component* class (*0..\* ComponentToActivity*). *Component* is an abstract class which has a *name* attribute and is the generalization of *IncompatibilityPattern* and *Operator* classes. These classes will be discussed in detail in the subsequent subsections.

## 3.2   Incompatibility Patterns

*IncompatibilityPatterns* class is composed of the patterns which are used for representing the incompatibilities between messages of different services (*0..\** *IncompatibilityPattern*). This abstract class is sub-divided into the following sub-classes, namely *OneToOne*, *OneToMany*, *ManyToOne*, *OnePlusToOne* and *OneToOnePlus*. The meaning of these sub-classes is described in Section 2.2.

Notice that *IncompatibilityPattern* is a specialized class of the *Component* class, so it can be linked to *StandardActivity* class.

## 3.3   Pattern-Based Adapter

*PatternBasedAdapter* class is composed of the operators which are used for resolving both signature and protocol incompatibilities (*0..\* Operator*). This abstract class is sub-divided into the following sub-classes, namely *MatchMake*, *Split*, *Merge*, *Aggregation* and *Disaggregation* (see Section 2.2 for further information about the definition of these sub-classes and their relationships with incompatibility patterns).

*Operator* is a specialized class of the *Component* class. It can also be linked to *StandardActivity* class in order to establish such incompatibilities.

## 4   Model-Driven Approach for Web Service Adaptation

In this section, we propose a model-driven approach for adaptation of WS using CEP. As a result, a graphical modeling editor for WS adaptation has been implemented using Epsilon [1], a family of interoperable task-specific programming languages which allows to perform common Model-Driven Development (MDD) [16] tasks such as model validation, model-to-model transformation and code generation, among others. The use of a graphical modeling editor provides some advantages like domain-specific graphical elements in the modeling palette and domain-specific modeling constraints for preventing semantically incorrect models.

### 4.1   Overview

This approach comprises the following main functionalities (see Figure 2): service interface modeling, compatibility test and incompatibility detection, adapter generation and CCL code generation and deployment.

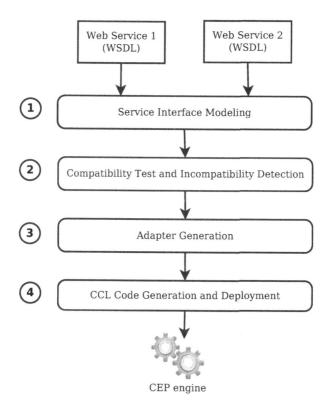

**Fig. 2.** Model-Driven Approach for Web Service Adaptation

**Service Interface Modeling.** This functionality aims to model the structural interfaces described in WSDL of both the services which interact with each other. To this end, we have created a module which will transform the WSDL code into the XML code (model) corresponding to the activity diagrams representing such WS interfaces in a user-friendly way. It has been possible making use of XSLT (Extensible Stylesheet Language Transformations).

One of the advantages of our approach is that end users will be able to modify the model of these interfaces which is conformed to our metamodel described in Section 3. If they introduce any changes, then the constraints defined on the metamodel using Epsilon Validation Language (EVL) will be checked. These constraints will allow to validate if the updated models continue to be conformed to the metamodel.

**Compatibility Test and Incompatibility Detection.** Once the service interfaces have been modeled as activity diagrams, making them more understandable for end users, the obtained model will be transformed into automatons which will received by the Taher's algorithm to check if there are any incompatibilities between them. If so, the model of service interfaces will be transformed into another model containing the incompatibility patterns returned by this algorithm. The model-to-model transformation is done by using Epsilon Transformation Language (ETL).

Notice that the detection of incompatibilities is formalized by specifying the set of incompatibility patterns described in Section 2.2 —*One-To-One*, *One-To-Many*, *Many-To-One*, *One\*-To-One* and *One-To-One\**.

**Adapter Generation.** As previously mentioned, adapters are the components which solve sets of incompatibilites found between two services. Furthermore, these adapters are aggregations of predefined operators whose purpose is to solve individual and specific incompatibilities.

Once the incompatibility patterns have been modeled, then they will be used by the another Taher's algorithm for constructing such adapters, transforming every recognized incompatibility pattern into one of the adaptation operators (see Section 2.2) to solve both signature and protocol incompatibilities. Afterwards, the model containing incompatibility patterns will be transformed into another model with the adaptation operators returned by this algorithm.

Notice that the adapter generation relies on the configuration and composition of the set of adaptation patterns described in Section 2.2 —*Match-Make*, *Split*, *Merge*, *Aggregation* and *Disaggregation*.

**CCL Code Generation and Deployment.** Finally the model, which contains the adapter automatically generated to solve the adaptation between WS, will be transformed into CCL code. Then, this code will be deployed into the CEP engine in runtime. This model-to-code transformation is done by using Epsilon Generation Language (EGL).

As previously described, if end users introduce some changes into such model, then the editor will be able to obtain a new CCL code corresponding the updated model, deploying it into the CEP engine again. Further information about how the CEP engine will work and manage this CCL code can be found in [19].

### 4.2   Graphical Modeling Editor

Figure 3 illustrates a screen view of the implemented graphical modeling editor. As can be seen, there are three relevant elements in the editor: menu bar, palette and canvas.

The menu bar has been extended with a new menu called "Canvas tools", which has the following functionalities:

- Importing provider and client service interfaces from WSDL files.
- Running the algorithm which compares services and detecting if there are some incompatibilities between them.
- Exporting the results of incompatibility detection in XML format.
- Constructing adapters from the modeled services.
- Exporting the generated adapter in XML format.
- Deploying the generated CCL code into the CEP engine.

The palette has also been customized, its elements have been classified into the following five categories. *Connections* category contains elements for linking activity to activity, activity to component (i.e., incompatibility pattern, or operator), and component to activity. *Pattern elements* groups the main compartments: service, incompatibility patterns and pattern-based adapter (see Section 3 for further information about these elements). *Activities* category integrates all activities which allow to define services by means of activity diagrams. Finally, *Incompatibility Patterns* and *Operators* categories present the patterns and operators described in Section 2.2, respectively.

The canvas is the editor area where palette's elements can be inserted in a drag-and-drop fashion to modify models which conform to the metamodel described in Section 3. These elements' attributes may be set from the application's properties view.

# 5  Case Study

In this section, the model-driven approach defined for WS adaptation using CEP in Section 4 is demonstrated making use of the implemented graphical editor.

## 5.1  Description

This case study consists of two web services. Basically, one service (the provider) is intended to offer goods for sale and the other service (the consumer) is meant to place orders against the provider. This provider obtains the consumer's details, the delivery address and returns the total price. Finally, the consumer proceeds the online payment with his credit card.

Concretely, the provider service starts waiting that the consumer places an order. To do this, the consumer has to send as many messages as items to be ordered. To end an order, the consumer sends a specific message. Then, the provider is able to calculate the total price. If the consumer agrees, it is now required to get the consumer's details, as well as the delivery address. The "conversation" is completed when the payment with credit card has been proceeded.

## 5.2  Evaluation

In this case study, the interfaces of both consumer and provider services are not compatible. Particularly, the provider service starts waiting an item order list with consumer's complete order, instead of a message by item to be ordered. On the other hand, the provider is waiting for a unique message that contains delivery address and credit card number, while the consumer is sending this information splitted into two messages. For this reason, interactions between these services will fail.

First of all, our graphical editor will be used to automatically detect if the interfaces of such imported two services are compatible. As a result, Figure 3

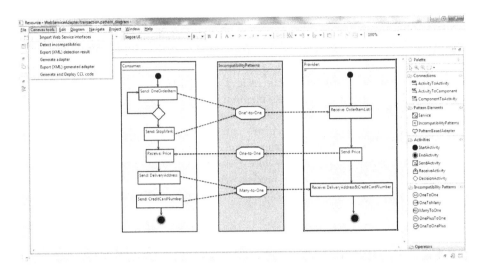

**Fig. 3.** Incompatibility detection

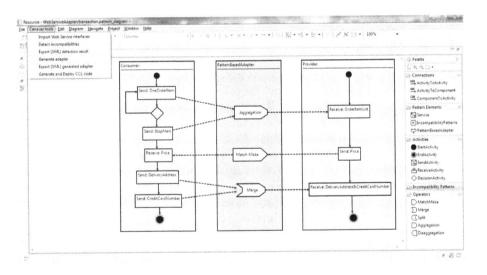

**Fig. 4.** Adapter generation

shows a set of incompatibility patterns detected between these service interfaces, which are modeled as activity diagrams.

Next, the editor will generate the adapter for these interfaces. Figure 4 shows the pattern-based adapter which sketches out the adapter behaviour which should sit between the two services to solve their detected incompatibilities at runtime. In particular, *One*-To-One* pattern has beed replaced by *Aggregation*, *One-To-One* has been replaced by *Match-Make* and *Many-To-One* has been replaced by *Merge*.

Finally, the editor will be able to generate the CCL code from the model which contains the pattern-based adapter. Then, this code will be deployed into the Sybase engine [17], thanks to its API which allows to create, compile and deploy CCQs in runtime.

## 6  Related Work

In this section, we position our work with respect to other papers about WS incompatibilities and existing tools for WS adaptation. These tools are classified into commercial and academic categories.

Academic research exists in resolving signature incompatibilities through the use of semantic web technology (i.e., OWL), such as that described in [14] which presents a context-based mediation approach to the semantic heterogeneities between composed WS. Besides, Web Service Modeling Ontology (WSMO) specification [5] provides a foundation for common descriptions of WS behavior and operations. However, this research does not attempt to resolve the associated problem of protocol incompatibility.

On the other hand, active research is also being performed into the adaptation of WS protocols, although all work we have surveyed does not tackle both problems of signature and protocol incompatibility, and uses different approaches to our CEP-based technique. For example, although [11] presents mediation patterns together with corresponding BPEL templates, a technique and engineering approach for semi-automatically identifying and resolving identifying protocol mismatches and a prototype implementation (the Service Mediation Toolkit), it does not solve the signature adaptation problem. Moreover, Brogi and Popescu [7] propose a methodology for the automated generation of adapters allowing to solve behavioral mismatches between BPEL processes; however, their approach fails with signature mismatches. Similarly, [9] discusses the notion of *protocol compatibility* between WS and [5] again only focusses on the protocol mismatches, leaving data mismatches apart. Therefore, all these authors present solutions to protocol mismatches but do not tackle the associated problem of signature incompatibility, while our chosen approach solves both signature and protocol incompatibilities.

According to Li et al. [11], there are many commercial tools to achieve WS *signature mediation* and solve signature incompatibilities, including: Microsoft's Biztalk mapper [2], Altova's MapForce [3] and Stylus Studio's XML Mapping [4].

Regarding the existing academic tools, Aumueller et al. [6] implement a schema matching tool called COMA++, which assists the developer to adapt new version of existing WS; however, the generation of the mismatch tree to solve protocol incompatibilities is not automatic. There are other tools for WS adaptation, such as [10] and [13]. Nevertheless, in our opinion, our graphical modeling editor improves such tools, regarding its user-friendly and usability features.

## 7    Conclusion and Future Work

In this paper we have proposed a model-driven approach which makes possible the automatic generation of adapters which can be created between WS interfaces to solve their both signature and protocol incompatibility problems. Particularly, this approach tackles four main functionalities: service interface modeling using activity diagrams, compatibility test and incompatibility detection, adapter generation, and CCL code generation and deployment into CEP engines.

We have used model-driven development because it hides the complexity of languages, libraries and frameworks, and offers some degree of platform-independence, among others. In particular, Epsilon family languages have been used to develop this approach.

In order to show its usefulness, the implemented editor has been applied to a case study about two web services which have incompatible interfaces. In concrete, a service provider offering goods for sale and a client placing orders against the provider. We can confirm that our editor, and thereby our approach, allow the adaptation of WS using CEP in a user-friendly manner.

In our future work, we plan to apply and validate our editor on various empirical experiments and real-world case studies. This will allow us to measure the performance of adapter generation CEP-based approach as compared to other WS adaptation approaches.

**Acknowledgments.** This work was partially funded by the Spanish Ministry of Science and Innovation under the National Program for Research, Development and Innovation, project MoD-SOA (TIN2011-27242). Juan Boubeta-Puig thanks the hospitality received at the European Research Institute for Service Science at Tilburg University when visiting them, where part of this work was developed.

## References

1. Epsilon (2013),
   http://www.eclipse.org/epsilon/
2. Microsoft BizTalk Server (2013),
   http://www.microsoft.com/biztalk/en/us/default.aspx
3. Web Services Mapping (2013),
   http://www.altova.com/mapforce/web-services-mapping.html
4. XML Mapping (2013),
   http://www.stylusstudio.com/xml_mapper.html
5. Ardissono, L., Furnari, R., Petrone, G., Segnan, M.: Interaction Protocol Mediation in Web Service Composition. International Journal of Web Engineering and Technology 6(1), 4–32 (2010)
6. Aumueller, D., Do, H., Massmann, S., Rahm, E.: Schema and Ontology Matching with COMA++. In: Proceedings of the International Conference on Management of Data, pp. 906–908. ACM, New York (2005)
7. Brogi, A., Popescu, R.: Automated Generation of BPEL Adapters. In: Dan, A., Lamersdorf, W. (eds.) ICSOC 2006. LNCS, vol. 4294, pp. 27–39. Springer, Heidelberg (2006)

8. Chandy, K.M., Schulte, W.R.: Event Processing: Designing IT Systems for Agile Companies. McGraw-Hill, USA (2010)
9. Dumas, M., Benatallah, B., Nezhad, H.: Web Service Protocols: Compatibility and Adaptation. IEEE Data Engineering Bulletin 31, 40–44 (2008)
10. Kongdenfha, W., Motahari-Nezhad, H., Benatallah, B., Casati, F., Saint-Paul, R.: Mismatch Patterns and Adaptation Aspects: A Foundation for Rapid Development of Web Service Adapters. IEEE Transactions on Services Computing 2(2), 94–107 (2009)
11. Li, X., Fan, Y., Madnick, S., Sheng, Q.Z.: A Pattern-Based Approach to Protocol Mediation for Web Services Composition. Information and Software Technology 52(3), 304–323 (2010)
12. Luckham, D.C.: The Power of Events: An Introduction to Complex Event Processing in Distributed Enterprise Systems. Addison-Wesley, USA (2001)
13. Motahari Nezhad, H.R., Benatallah, B., Martens, A., Curbera, F., Casati, F.: Semi-Automated Adaptation of Service Interactions. In: Proceedings of the 16th International Conference on World Wide Web, pp. 993–1002. ACM, New York (2007)
14. Mrissa, M., Ghedira, C., Benslimane, D., Maamar, Z., Rosenberg, F., Dustdar, S.: A Context-Based Mediation Approach to Compose Semantic Web Services. ACM Transactions on Internet Technology 8(1) (November 2007)
15. Papazoglou, M.: Web Services: Principles and Technology. Pearson Education (2008)
16. Stahl, T., Voelter, M.: Model-Driven Software Development: Technology, Engineering, Management, 1st edn. Wiley (May 2006)
17. Sybase: SAP Sybase Event Stream Processor (2013),
    http://www.sybase.com/products/financialservicessolutions/
    complex-event-processing
18. Taher, Y., Ait-Bachir, A., Fauvet, M., Benslimane, D.: Diagnosing Incompatibilities in Web Service Interactions for Automatic Generation of Adapters. In: International Conference on Advanced Information Networking and Applications, pp. 652–659 (May 2009)
19. Taher, Y., Parkin, M., Papazoglou, M.P., van den Heuvel, W.-J.: Adaptation of Web Service Interactions Using Complex Event Processing Patterns. In: Kappel, G., Maamar, Z., Motahari-Nezhad, H.R. (eds.) Service Oriented Computing. LNCS, vol. 7084, pp. 601–609. Springer, Heidelberg (2011)

# An ESB-Based Infrastructure for Event-Driven Context-Aware Web Services

Laura González[1] and Guadalupe Ortiz[2]

[1] Instituto de Computación, Facultad de Ingeniería,
Universidad de la República, Uruguay
`lauragon@fing.edu.uy`
[2] UCASE Software Engineering Group,
University of Cádiz, C/ Chile, 1.11002 Cádiz, Spain
`guadalupe.ortiz@uca.es`

**Abstract.** Web services are nowadays one of the preferred technologies to implement service-oriented architectures and to communicate distributed applications. On the other hand, context-awareness is highly demanded for distributed applications. However, even though there are excellent tools and frameworks for service development, getting services to be context-aware is still under investigation. In turn, an Enterprise Service Bus (ESB) is a standards-based integration platform, which provides mediation capabilities (e.g. routing, transformation). ESBs are being increasingly used in conjunction with Complex Event Processing (CEP) engines to support event-driven architectures scenarios. In this regard, this paper proposes an ESB-based infrastructure which, leveraging its mediation capabilities and a CEP engine, allows the construction of context-aware web services. Concretely, CEP techniques are used to detect the complex situations that may affect services and mediation mechanisms are used to adapt service requests and responses to make them context-aware.

**Keywords:** web services, context-awareness, complex event processing, enterprise service bus.

## 1    Introduction

Thanks to the use of XML-based protocols for interface description –WSDL- and message exchange –SOAP-, among other facts, web services provide us with a loosely-coupled and platform-independent communication among distributed systems. This is why they have become an efficient solution for the implementation of distributed systems in which modularity and communication among third parties are key factors.

On the other hand, context-aware software solutions have hugely increased in popularity and are highly demanded, especially by mobile users. The great amount of devices and their continuous use clearly illustrate the importance of access not only to desktop services but also to mobile ones. It is important to mention that, even though context awareness seems to be strongly associated with mobile applications, many users start to demand desktop context-aware applications, therefore both markets are relevant for software developers.

C. Canal and M. Villari (Eds.): ESOCC 2013, CCIS 393, pp. 360–369, 2013.
© Springer-Verlag Berlin Heidelberg 2013

Even though there are excellent tools and frameworks for service development, their adaptation to context has not been properly focused on to date. This is an emerging field in which many industry and scientific community are starting to provide their proposals. However there are not clear solutions in the scope of web services. In the past, we proposed a method for adapting services to the invoking device [1] as well as to adapt them to the client-specific context [2]; in this paper, we will go one step further setting the basis in order to tackle their adaptation also to the external context making use of an *Enterprise Service Bus* (ESB) and *Complex Event Processing* (CEP) according to the envisaged architecture presented in [3]. In this regard, first of all, the proposed solution leverages well-known ESB mediation patterns (e.g. transformation) in order to adapt services to context transparently, not only for the final user but also for the service developer. Secondly, complex event processing has been used to analyze the events received from external sources to detect relevant situations for the context of the service in question. Finally, a context reasoner which provides the transformations to be done depending on the context events has been provided.

The rest of the paper is organized as follows: Section 2 provides background on context-awareness, complex event processing, ESB patterns and an adaptive ESB infrastructure. Then, Section 3 explains the proposed infrastructure which makes use of the ESB and the CEP engine. Afterwards, Section 4 outlines main related work. Finally, conclusions and future work are provided in Section 5.

## 2    Background

This section provides background on context-awareness, CEP, ESB patterns and on an Adaptive ESB. These concepts and solutions are the basis for our proposal.

### 2.1    Context-Awareness

Abowd et al.'s context definition in [4] is specially well-known –page 3, section 2.2: *"Context is any information that can be used to characterize the situation of an entity. An entity is a person, place, or object that is considered relevant to the interaction between a user and an application, including the user and applications themselves"*.

In this regard, a system is context-aware if it uses the context to provide relevant information or services to the user, adapting the system behavior to the particular needs of a specific user.

A context-classification can be found at [5]; in this paper we will focus on the environmental context, which describes the environmental conditions of both user and services. Sensors or specific services are normally used in order to provide such kind of information as location, weather, noise, social events, etcetera. This type of context will imply adapting the information sent to the client; for instance, if the user is in a location where it is raining when searching for cultural activities, outdoors ones will be avoided.

## 2.2    Complex Event Processing

CEP [6] is a technology that provides a set of techniques to help discover complex events by analyzing and correlating other basic and complex events. Therefore, CEP allows the detection of complex and meaningful events, known as situations, and inferring valuable knowledge for end users.

In order to detect complex events, event queries have to continuously monitor incoming streams of simple events [7]. These queries specify situations as a combination of simple events occurring, or not occurring, over time. One approach to implement event queries is by using production rules. This approach is followed by various well-known products like Drools Fusion[1], which is the component of the Drools platform providing CEP support.

These events will help make decisions when necessary and will ensure that services do not only exchange messages between them, but also publish events and receive event notifications from others. For this purpose, an Enterprise Service Bus (ESB) will be necessary to process, enrich and route messages between services of different applications. Further information on the integration of CEP with SOA in other scenarios can be found at [9].

## 2.3    ESB Patterns

ESB behavior has been characterized through different patterns. This section reviews the relevant connectivity and mediation patterns for this work.

**Connectivity patterns** specify high level integration styles for ESB-based solutions [10]. For example, service virtualization patterns take an existing service and deploy a new virtual service in the ESB. These patterns introduce a point of mediation in the ESB, between the client and target service, which can be used to route and transform messages, among others. Gateway patterns are used to apply a common set of mediations to all incoming and/or outgoing messages (e.g. security related mediations). Event-driven integration patterns deals with distribution of events through the ESB and the integration with CEP engines. In particular, the event distributor pattern allows the distribution of events to multiple interested parties, the event extractor pattern monitors interactions across the ESB and passes relevant events to a CEP engine, and the event reactor pattern extends the previous one by synchronically interacting with a CEP engine to be informed if the latest event has triggered a complex event.

**Mediation patterns** specify families of mediation operations that can be performed over messages passing through the ESB [11][12]. Two commonly supported types of mediation operations are routing and transformation. Routing patterns dynamically determines the message path according to different factors. For example, the content-based routing pattern determines the message path based on its content

---

[1] http://www.jboss.org/drools/drools-fusion.html

and the itinerary-based routing determines the message destination based on an itinerary included in the message itself [13]. Transformation patterns deal with the runtime transformation of messages [14]. In particular, the content transformation pattern deal with data transformation (e.g. data model transformation, data format transformation [15]), the content enrichment pattern consists of complementing the message content with data obtained from other sources and the content filter patterns consist of removing unimportant data items from messages.

### 2.4    Adaptive ESB Infrastructure

This section describes the Adaptive ESB Infrastructure proposed in [16], which has the goal of dynamically and automatically dealing with adaptation requirements in service based systems at runtime.

The proposed adaptive solution assumes that services communicate by sending messages through the ESB, applying service virtualization patterns. The approach to achieve adaptation at runtime is to intercept all incoming ESB messages and, if an adaptation is required for the invoked service, drive them through adaptation flows. These flows include all the mediations steps (e.g. transformations, routings) required to carry out a specific adaptation strategy (e.g. invoke an equivalent service). In order to know if an adaptation is required for a specific service, the infrastructure maintains a table with adaptation directives for each service. These directives are generated based on monitored service properties and service level requirements.

In order to show the general operation of the infrastructure, Fig. 1 presents an example of an adaptation flow which consists of applying a transformation before invoking the target service.

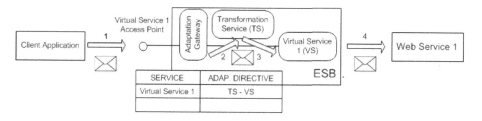

**Fig. 1.** Adaptive ESB Infrastructure

First, the client sends a message through the ESB (1) to invoke the target service. The message is intercepted by an adaptation gateway following the gateway pattern. Given that there is an adaptation directive for the invoked service, the adaptation gateway attaches an adaptation flow to the message and routes it to the first step in the flow (2), following the itinerary-based routing pattern. After the required transformation (also specified in the message) is performed, the message is routed to the next step in the flow (3) which finally invokes the target web service (4).

# 3     The Proposed ESB-Based Infrastructure

This section presents the proposed solution which, leveraging ESB and CEP capabilities, allows the construction of context-aware web services. The examples in this section are an adaptation of the ones presented in [17].

## 3.1     General Description

The approach consists of applying service virtualization patterns to build and expose context-aware services through the ESB, based on services which are not necessarily context-aware. The context-aware adaptation logic is executed within the ESB, using its mediation capabilities, and it is automatically generated according to the situations in which the invoking users are. These situations are detected, thanks to their previous definition in the CEP engine, as complex events that are triggered based on the contextual data arriving to the ESB from different sources. Fig. 2 presents a high level view of the proposed architecture.

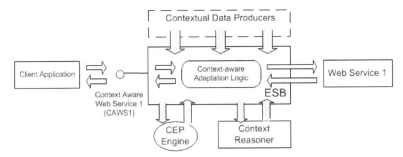

**Fig. 2.** General Architecture

Contextual data producers provide different type of contextual data to the ESB in the form of events. The CEP Engine receives contextual data through the ESB (event distributor pattern) and, based on rules deployed in the engine, detects the complex situations in which users are. The Context Reasoner receives these situations and automatically generates the required adaptations for each configured service. Finally, the ESB receives these adaptations for each pair (user, service) and, when an invocation arrives, applies these adaptations leveraging the ESB mediation capabilities.

## 3.2     Receiving Contextual Data

Contextual data are obtained from the providers as events, configuring the built-in connectivity capabilities that ESBs offer. The received events are then passed to the CEP Engine. Table 1 presents different examples for types of contextual data.

**Table 1.** Examples of Contextual Data

| Contextual Data | Description | Structure | Example |
|---|---|---|---|
| Weather in City | It specifies the weather conditions in a city. | [city, temp, rain?] | (Madrid, 17°C, true) |
| User Location | It specifies the current geographic coordinates of a user. | [userId, lat, long] | (jsmith, 40.41, -3.71) |

## 3.3    Detecting Situations

Situations are detected as complex events by the CEP Engine. In order to specify when a user is in a particular situation, a set of rules have to be deployed within the engine for each situation. These rules can be based on: the received contextual data, other detected situations and utility functions. Table 2 shows some situations that can be detected using the examples of contextual data presented in section 3.2 and the required elements in order to detect them.

**Table 2.** Examples of Situations

| Situation | Description | Elements to Detect the Situation |
|---|---|---|
| InCity | The user is in a specific city. | Contextual Data: User Location |
|  |  | Utility Function: getCityFromCoords (lat, long) |
| InCityRaining | The user is in a city where it is raining. | Contextual Data: Weather in City |
|  |  | Situations: InCity |

In order to specify the rules to detect these situations, many languages can be used. In the following examples, the Drools Rule Language (DRL) is used to exemplify. Fig. 3 presents a DRL Rule to trigger the InCity situation. Concretely, whenever user location data are received, the utility function getCityFromCoords is used to get the current city of the user and trigger an InCity event with this information.

```
rule "User in City"
    when
        $usrLoc : UserLocation()
    then
        InCity usrCity = new InCity();
        usrCity.setCity(getCityFromCoords($usrLoc.getLat(), $usrLoc.getLon()));
        usrCity.setUserId($usrLoc.getUserId());
        usrCity.setTimestamp($usrLoc.getTimestamp());
        // trigger the situation InCity
        insert (usrCity);
end
```

**Fig. 3.** DRL Rule to Trigger the InCity Situation

## 3.4    Configuring Context-Aware Adaptations

In order to adapt services according to the situations in which the invoking users are, the following data have to be configured in the Context Reasoner: i) the situations which affect each service; ii) the adaptations to be applied in each case; iii) the moment to apply these adaptations (i.e. in the service request or response).

As an example, consider an Attractions service with an operation named getAttractions which optionally receives the name of a city and returns a list of attractions. For each attraction the following data is returned: name, short description, long description and a Boolean value indicating if the attraction involves outdoor activities. Table 3 presents some adaptations that can be configured for this service, according to the situations presented in Section 3.3, and the required mediation patterns to implement these adaptations.

**Table 3.** Configuration of Adaptations

| Situation | Adaptation / Moment | Pattern |
| --- | --- | --- |
| InCity | Add to the request the optional parameter to specify the city. | Content Enrichment |
| InCityRaining | Remove from the response the attractions involving outdoor activities. | Content Filter |

In order to implement the adaptations, the mediation patterns which are used in each one of them have to be configured with all the required information. For instance, in the first adaptation of Table 3, an XSLT transformation can be specified for the content enrichment pattern so that SOAP request messages can be transformed by adding the city parameter. Note that these adaptations are not going to be completely specified until a specific situation is detected for a user, i.e., in the aforesaid XSLT transformation the concrete city is not specified at this time.

An ESB can provide different implementations for a given mediation pattern. For instance, the content transformation pattern is usually implemented through XSLT transformations or template engines. Also, ESBs are designed to be easily extended, for example, with new mediation patterns and new implementations for them. In this way, if a complex transformation logic is required (e.g. language translation) the proper implementation (e.g. using an external translation service) can be set up in the ESB using its extensibility mechanisms.

Finally, the adaptations for each service have to be prioritized so that the ESB knows which one applies first, in case more than one has to be performed.

## 3.5    Adapting Services within the ESB

After configuring the adaptations for each service, when the Context Reasoner receives information regarding the situation of a user, it can automatically generate the required adaptation logic to be performed for the pair (user, service) and communicate it to the ESB. For example, assuming that the Context Reasoner was informed that the users "jsmith" and "awright" are in Madrid and London, respectively, Table 4 presents two different concrete adaptations, to be sent to the ESB, resulting from the first adaptation of Table 3.

**Table 4.** Adaptations to be Applied in the ESB

| Service / Operation | User | Adaptation |
|---|---|---|
| AttractionsService / getAttractions | jsmith | XSLT transformation adding the Madrid value, for the city parameter, in the SOAP request. |
| AttractionsService / getAttractions | awright | XSLT transformation adding the London value, for the city parameter, in the SOAP request. |

This way, users receive different results from the Attractions service according to their specific situation, in this case, the city where they currently are.

In order to dynamically apply these adaptations within the ESB, the Adaptive ESB Infrastructure presented in Section 2.4 is used. Concretely, the information which is sent to the ESB is treated as adaptation directives to be applied to the invocations to the Attractions service coming from the specified users. To this end, the Adaptive ESB Infrastructure was enhanced to consider users information in the requests.

# 4    Related Work

This section highlights the main research on the use of complex-event processing for context-awareness and approaches for context-aware service implementation.

Most of the work found in the context adaptation area specially focuses on client side adaptation. We can mention, for instance, the paper from Laakko and Hiltunen [18] where content adaptation is done through a proxy. They focus on adapting XHTML (Extensible Hypertext Markup Language) with XHTML MP (XHTML mobile profile) and WML (Wireless Markup Language). Another example is URICA [19]: a technique for automatic content adaptation for mobile devices presented by Mohomed et al. The system can learn through interaction with the user, identifying the most relevant context for the latter. It is very interesting work, but it overheads the client computation.

The paper from Gilman et al [20] also deserves special mention. They provide a framework for adapting services to context through a complex architecture composed of several components, among them a context-reasoner, context discoverer and observers, handlers and managers. There are also systems based on multi-agents, such as the one presented by Fraile et al [21], which uses them for implementing context-aware computing for home care. Sheng et al [22] proposes ContextUML: a modeling language for context-aware model-driven web services. Several years later they improved their proposal supplying [23] a platform for developing context-aware web services. This platform, named ContextServ, is based on ContextUML and provides an integrated environment where developers can specify and deploy context-aware services as well as generating BPEL code. The main drawback of this proposal is the rather complex way in which context has to be modeled; it requires a high learning curve and it does not seem to be intuitive for a software developer. Follow-ups on the project are more focused on BPEL compositions [24], or user personalization [25]. In any case, none of these works takes advantage of the use of the ESB and CEP, which leverages the context-aware system usability and maintenance. A thorough analysis of context-awareness related work can be found in [5].

To sum up, our proposal mainly differs from others in benefiting from the advantages of the use of CEP and an ESB to adapt services to context information in a decoupled way, where the context can be automatically detected through real time events.

## 5    Conclusions

Even though context-awareness is an important capability in current distributed systems, solutions to provide context-aware web services are still under investigation. This paper addresses this issue by proposing an ESB-based infrastructure which, leveraging its mediation capabilities and a CEP engine, allows the construction of context-aware web services. CEP techniques are used to detect complex situations that may affect services and mediation mechanisms are used to adapt services requests and responses to make them context-aware. The proposal benefits from a transparent adaptation of services and from the ability of processing several context sources information thanks to the use of CEP.

**Acknowledgments .** G. Ortiz acknowledges the support from Ministerio de Ciencia e Innovación (TIN2011-27242)

## References

1. Ortiz, G., Garcia de Prado, A.: Improving Device-Aware Web Services and their Mobile Clients through an Aspect-Oriented, Model-Driven Approach. Information and Software Technology Journal 52(10), 1080–1093 (2010)
2. Ortiz, G., Garcia de Prado, A.: Web Service Adaptation: A unified approach versus multiple methodologies for different scenarios. In: 5th International Conference on Internet and Web Applications and Services, pp. 569–572. IEEE CS Press, California (2010)
3. Ortiz, G., Boubeta-Puig, J., García de Prado, A., Medina-Bulo, I.: Towards Event-Driven Context-Aware Web Services. In: Adaptive Web Services for Modular and Reusable Software Development: Tactics and Solutions, pp. 148–159. IGI Global (2012)
4. Abowd, G.D., Dey, A.K.: Towards a Better Understanding of Context and Context-Awareness. In: Gellersen, H.-W. (ed.) HUC 1999. LNCS, vol. 1707, pp. 304–307. Springer, Heidelberg (1999)
5. García de Prado, A., Ortiz, G.: Context-Aware Services: A Survey on Current Proposals. In: 3rd International Conferences on Advanced Service Computing, pp. 104–109. Xpert Publishing Services, Italy (2011)

6. Luckham, D.: The Power of Events: An Introduction to Complex Event Processing in Distributed Enterprise Systems. Addison-Wesley, MA (2002)
7. Eckert, M., Bry, F., Brodt, S., Poppe, O., Hausmann, S.: A CEP Babelfish: Languages for Complex Event Processing and Querying Surveyed. In: Helmer, S., Poulovassilis, A., Xhafa, F., et al. (eds.) Reasoning in Event-Based Distributed Systems. SCI, vol. 347, pp. 47–70. Springer, Heidelberg (2011)
8. Sosinsky, B.: Cloud Computing Bible. Wiley, Indiana (2011)
9. Boubeta, J., Ortiz, G., Medina, I.: An Approach of Early Disease Detection using CEP and SOA. In: 3rd International Conferences on Advanced Service Computing, pp. 143–148. Xpert Publishing Services, Italy (2011)
10. Wylie, H., Lambros, P.: Enterprise Connectivity Patterns: Implementing integration solutions with IBM's Enterprise Service Bus products,
    http://www.ibm.com/developerworks/library/
    ws-enterpriseconnectivitypatterns/index.html
11. Hérault, C., Thomas, G., Fourier, U.J.: Mediation and Enterprise Service Bus: A position paper. In: Proceedings of the First International Workshop on Mediation in Semantic Web Services, MEDIATE (2005)
12. Schmidt, M.-T., Hutchison, B., Lambros, P., Phippen, R.: The enterprise service bus: making service-oriented architecture real. IBM Syst. J. 44, 781–797 (2005)
13. Chappell, D.: Enterprise Service Bus: Theory in Practice. O'Reilly Media (2004)
14. Hohpe, G., Woolf, B.: Enterprise Integration Patterns: Designing, Building, and Deploying Messaging Solutions. Addison-Wesley Professional (2003)
15. Erl, T.: SOA Design Patterns. Prentice Hall PTR (2009)
16. González, L., Ruggia, R.: Adaptive ESB Infrastructure for Service Based Systems. In: Ortiz, G., Cubo, J. (eds.) Adaptive Web Services for Modular and Reusable Software Development: Tactics and Solutions, pp. 1–32 (2013)
17. Kapitsaki, G.M., Prezerakos, G.N., Tselikas, N.D., Venieris, I.S.: Context-aware service engineering: A survey. Journal of Systems and Software 82, 1285–1297 (2009)
18. Laakko, T., Hiltunen, T.: Adapting Web Content to Mobile User Agents. IEEE Internet Computing 9(2), 46–53 (2005)
19. Mohomed, I., Cai, J.C., Chavoshi, S., de Lara, E.: Context-aware interactive content adaptation. In: Proceedings of the 4th International Conference on Mobile Systems, Applications and Services, New York, NY, USA, pp. 42–55 (2006)
20. Gilman, E., Su, X., Davidyuk, O., Zhou, J., Riekki, J.: Perception framework for supporting development of context-aware web services. International Journal of Pervasive Computing and Communications 7(4), 339–364 (2011)
21. Fraile, J.A., Paz, Y., Bajo, J., Paz, J.F., Pérez-Lancho, B.: Context-aware multiagent system: Planning home care tasks. Knowledge and Information Systems (May 2013)
22. Sheng, Q.Z., Benatallah, B.: ContextUML: a UML-based modeling language for model-driven development of context-aware web services. In: International Conference on Mobile Business, ICMB 2005, pp. 206–212 (2005)
23. Sheng, Q.Z., Pohlenz, S., Yu, J., Wong, H.S., Ngu, A.H., Maamar, Z.: ContextServ: A platform for rapid and flexible development of context-aware Web services. In: IEEE 31st International Conference on Software Engineering, ICSE 2009, pp. 619–622 (2009)
24. Yahyaoui, H., Mourad, A., Almulla, M., Yao, L., Sheng, Q.Z.: A synergy between context-aware policies and AOP to achieve highly adaptable Web services. Service Oriented Computing and Applications 6, 379–392 (2012)
25. Yu, J., Han, J., Sheng, Q.Z., Gunarso, S.O.: PerCAS: An Approach to Enabling Dynamic and Personalized Adaptation for Context-Aware Services. In: Liu, C., Ludwig, H., Toumani, F., Yu, Q. (eds.) Service Oriented Computing. LNCS, vol. 7636, pp. 173–190. Springer, Heidelberg (2012)

# Author Index